*Nathanael Greene by Rembrandt Peale
after the original by C. W. Peale*

(Courtesy of Mrs. Thomas Casey Greene
and Thomas Casey Greene, Jr.
On loan to the Rhode Island Historical Society)

THE PAPERS OF
General Nathanael Greene

VOLUME II
1 January 1777–16 October 1778

Richard K. Showman
EDITOR

Robert E. McCarthy
ASSOCIATE EDITOR

Margaret Cobb
ASSISTANT EDITOR

Assisted by Nathaniel N. Shipton, Mary MacKechnie Showman,
and John Ifkovic

THE UNIVERSITY OF NORTH CAROLINA PRESS
Chapel Hill

Published for the
RHODE ISLAND HISTORICAL SOCIETY

© 1980 The University of North Carolina Press
All rights reserved
Manufactured in the United States of America
ISBN 0-8078-1384-2
Library of Congress Catalog Card Number 76-20441

Library of Congress Cataloging in Publication Data

Greene, Nathanael, 1742–1786.
    The papers of General Nathanael Greene.

    Includes bibliographical references and indexes.
    CONTENTS: v. 1. December 1766–December 1776—
v. 2. 1 January 1777–16 October 1778.
    1. Greene, Nathanael, 1742–1786.   2. United States—
History—Revolution, 1775–1783—Sources.   I. Showman,
Richard K.   II. Rhode Island Historical Society.
E203.G73   1976   973.3'3'0924   76-20441
ISBN 0-8078-1285-4 (v. 1)
ISBN 0-8078-1384-2 (v. 2)

TABLE OF CONTENTS

ILLUSTRATIONS

MAPS

FOREWORD

Volume I of *The Papers of General Nathanael Greene* took him through 1776 and the triumph at Trenton, in which he played a significant part. This volume brings him to the autumn of 1778, an extremely busy period. Except for a week he spent with his family in Rhode Island in September 1778, he was with Washington's army virtually day and night. He fought in the battles of Brandywine and Germantown in the fall of 1777, and in March 1778 he reluctantly agreed to accept the thankless post of quartermaster general. He took part in the battle of Monmouth in June 1778 while still serving in the post, but when he returned to Rhode Island a month later to participate in the attack on Newport, he turned over his quartermaster duties to Charles Pettit, an assistant, for two months. When he bade farewell to his brothers in Rhode Island in mid-October to rejoin Washington at Fredericksburg, N.Y., it would be five years before he again set foot in his native state.

With his acceptance of the quartermaster post, his correspondence became increasingly heavy. Coincidentally, a larger proportion of his letters from this period have survived, for, as noted in Volume I (pp. xxx), the papers he accumulated from May 1775 to April 1778 have disappeared. (The history of his papers can be found on pp. xxvii–xxxiii.) Volume II contains almost twice as many letters as Volume I, although this is due in part to the greater number of general orders in the first volume: 130 out of slightly more than 400 documents compared with 20 out of 530 in this volume. As a major general he issued few orders; as quartermaster general, none.

As the series enters a period of heavier correspondence, it has been necessary to calendar and abstract a greater proportion of the documents, more than 170 of the 530 in this volume being so treated. In future volumes well over half will be calendared. Fortunately, many are routine documents that lend themselves to being abstracted, while others are duplicates. But the selection process is no simpler, for there remain hundreds and hundreds of letters and documents that are not only revealing of Greene and the War for Independence but also of the economic, social, and political history of the era.

As the war years come and go, Nathanael Greene not only takes an increasingly active role, but, as his letters reveal, he becomes a keen observer and a more eloquent writer.

Providence, R.I.   RICHARD K. SHOWMAN
22 February 1979   *Editor*

ACKNOWLEDGMENTS

As with volume one of *The Papers of General Nathanael Greene*, the title page contains but a fraction of the names of persons who have made this volume possible. High on the list of contributors are members of the staff of our Rhode Island Historical Society, most particularly one who has too infrequently received credit for his contributions—the director, Albert T. Klyberg. He initiated the project in 1972 and has been responsible for its continued funding. As a historian he has helped solve a variety of editorial problems, despite innumerable other demands on his time. Two former staff members who worked part time for the Greene Papers until early 1978 are Noel Conlon and Joyce Boulind, both of whom have the editor's thanks. We are grateful to Frances Howles for her typing of annotations and Carolyn Brown, who filled in as emergency typist and translator of French. Elizabeth Stevens, a newcomer to the staff of the Greene Papers, assisted in the final stages. We also wish to thank Nancy Chudacoff and the library staff for their help.

We continue to be grateful to those persons and institutions that are acknowledged in volume one for having made copies of Greene documents available. Although we cannot do so by name, we appreciate the help that newer staff members of those repositories have given us.

Since the publication of volume one, we have acquired documents from a number of additional institutions. For these new accessions we thank Kenneth H. MacFarland, Albany Institute of History and Art; Estelle Davis, Copley Library, La Jolla, Calif.; Robert G. Wheeler and Edward R. Kukla, Greenfield Village and Henry Ford Museum; Martin I. Yoelson and Robert L. Giannini III, Independence National Historical Park, Philadelphia; The Mary Buie Museum, Oxford, Miss.; R. Nicholas Olsberg and Fred Smith, Massachusetts Archives; John R. McCravy and Mrs. C. H. Goudelock, Pickens County Historical Society, Pickens, S.C.; Roland M. Baumann, Pennsylvania Historical and Museum Commission, Harrisburg, Pa.; Stephen Caldwell Millett, The Society of the Cincinnati; Jeffrey L. Sturchio, Edgar F. Smith Memorial Collection, University of Pennsylvania; The James Mitchell Varnum House, East Greenwich, R.I.; and Randolph K. Tibbits, Washington University Libraries, St. Louis, Mo.

The Library of Congress has made documents available from the

Archives Nationales, Paris; the Public Record Office, London; and the Kungliga Biblioteket, Stockholm.

Individual collectors who have furnished letters for this volume include Francis F. Brooks, East Weymouth, Mass.; David H. Coblentz, Chase City, Va.; Richard Maass, White Plains, N.Y.; Bernard N. Nightingale, Brunswick, Ga.; and John F. Reed, Valley Forge, Pa. Peter Agnew of Port Washington, N. Y., and S. Howard Goldman of New York City have provided copies from their collections for future volumes.

We are also grateful to George Lowry of Swann Galleries, New York City; Irwin Weinberg of the Miner Stamp Company, Wilkes Barre, Pa.; and George Rinsland, Allentown, Pa., for providing copies of documents. Thomas Clark of Sotheby Parke Bernet has been generous in steering us to individuals who have since made copies of letters available.

Staff members of a number of libraries have aided the Greene Papers in other ways. We are especially indebted to Fred Bauer, American Antiquarian Society; Madeline F. Gross, Shelley Hurdis, and Stuart C. Sherman of John D. Rockefeller, Jr., Library, Brown University; John Broderick, Paul T. Heffron, Paul Sifton, and Charles Lahood of the Library of Congress; Jo Ann Reeser, Lutheran Theological Seminary, Philadelphia; Cynthia H. Requardt, Maryland Historical Society; the staff of Providence Public Library; Phyllis Silva, Rhode Island State Archives; Helen Kelly, University of Rhode Island Extension Library, Providence; and Susan Riggs, Virginia Historical Society.

We have continued to gain from a mutual exchange with editors and staffs working in the same period. In addition to those listed in volume one, we should mention Robert J. Taylor and Gregg L. Lint of the Adams Papers; Harold C. Syrett of the Hamilton Papers; Stanley Idzerda, Linda J. Pike, and Peggy John of the Lafayette Papers; Carl E. Prince of the William Livingston Papers; and Edith von Zemenszky and Robert J. Schulmann of the Steuben Papers.

Members of the staff of the National Historical Publications and Records Commission frequently came to our aid. Director Frank G. Burke, Roger Bruns, and George L. Vogt have not only provided administrative help but have furthered our work, as they have of others, by bringing the many editorial projects together through conferences and newsletters. Especially helpful on numerous occasions have been NHPRC staff members Richard N. Sheldon, Joyce E. Eberly, Sara Dunlap Jackson, Mary A. Giunta, and Dianne M. Buncombe.

In addition to the groups of persons named above, we should like to thank a number of individuals: Professor Don Higginbotham of The University of North Carolina at Chapel Hill for again sharing his expertise and judgment with us; Mrs. Thomas Casey Greene and

Thomas Casey Greene, Jr., who not only have provided the frontispiece portrait of Nathanael Greene but have permitted us to hang the original by Rembrandt Peale in our office and have shared with us their knowledge of NG's family; John Dann, director of our co-sponsor, the William L. Clements Library, who has provided most of the facsimile illustrations of letters for this volume and has shared with us copies of recent additions to the library's superb collection; Wendell Garrett, member of our publications committee and editor and publisher of *The Magazine Antiques* for his help in promoting our first volume; Robert Schnare, librarian of the U.S. Military Academy at West Point for his vigilance in watching out for Greene documents in dealers' catalogs; Chester M. Destler of West Hartford, Conn., for permitting us to quote from the manuscript of his biography of Jeremiah Wadsworth; Erna Risch for the use of pertinent chapters of her manuscript on the supply services for Washington's army and to Robert W. Coakley, Deputy Chief Historian, Department of the Army, for providing authorization and copies of those chapters; Tracy G. Thurber of Providence, Eric Newman of St. Louis, and Professor William G. Anderson of Suffolk County College, Selden, N.Y., for information on quartermaster department certificates; Laurence E. Tilley for his photography; and Phillips D. Booth for his maps.

EDITORIAL METHOD

Arrangement of Material

Letters and documents are arranged chronologically. If two or more related items are dated the same day they are arranged in sequence; if unrelated to each other, they are arranged as follows:

1. Military orders and documents (as opposed to letters)
2. Letters from NG, alphabetically by recipient
3. Letters to NG, alphabetically by sender

Undated Items

If a date omitted by the writer can be determined, it is printed in brackets, and the item takes its place chronologically. A doubtful conjecture is followed by a question mark.

If a precise day cannot be established, the shortest conjecturable time span is placed in brackets and the item arranged as follows:

Conjectured Time Span	Chronological Arrangement
[10–18] September 1776	Placed at 10 September 1776
[April] 1776	Placed at end of April 1776
[November 1775–February 1776]	Placed at end of November 1775
[1775]	Placed at end of 1775
[1776–78]	Placed at end of 1776
[before 12 December 1776]	Placed at end of 11 December documents

All such conjectures are explained in footnotes. If no time period can be conjectured, the item will be placed at the end of the last volume of the series.

Misdated Items

If a correct date can be determined for a misdated item, it follows the incorrect date in brackets; if a date is suspected of being incorrect, a question mark in brackets follows.

Form of a Letter

The form of a letter is rendered as follows, regardless of the original:

1. Place and date is at top right.

2. Complimentary close is set continuously with the body.

3. Paragraphs are indented, and paragraphing is sometimes introduced to relieve long, unbroken segments.

4. Author's interlineations or brief additions in the margin are incorporated into the text silently unless of unusual significance, when they are explained in a footnote.

5. Scored-out or erased passages are ignored unless mentioned in a footnote.

6. Address sheet and docketing are normally omitted.

Calendared Items

Many less important items are calendared, with an abstract of the contents set within brackets. The item is arranged according to date. If the writer's original wording is included, it is set off by quote marks, or if in a lengthy passage, by indentation.

MANUSCRIPT TEXTUAL POLICY

Following the practice established by Julian Boyd, Leonard Labaree, and other modern editors, manuscripts are rendered in such a way as to be intelligible to the present-day reader while retaining as much as possible the essential form and spirit of the writer. The following guidelines reflect this compromise.

Spelling

Spelling is retained as written. If a misspelled word or name is not readily recognizable, the correct spelling follows in brackets. Names are correctly spelled in notes and index.

Obvious slips of the pen and inadvertent repetition of words are corrected silently.

Capitalization

The only instance in which an author's capitalization is always followed is the eighteenth-century practice of capitalizing words within sentences—usually, but not confined to, nouns. In other cases an author's capitalization is changed where necessary to conform to the following rules:

1. All sentences begin with initial capitals.

2. Personal names and titles used with them, honorifics (such as "His Excellency"), geographical names, and days of the week and months are capitalized.

Abbreviations and Contractions

1. Shortened word forms still in use or those that can easily be understood (as "t'was" or "twixt") are rendered as written.

2. Those no longer readily understood are expanded silently, as in "dn" to "deacon."

3. Abbreviations of names or places—forms known only to the correspondents or their contemporaries—are expanded in brackets, as in S[amuel] A[dams] or Chsn [Charleston].

Symbols Representing Letters and Words

When any of the following symbols are expanded they are done so silently.

1. The ampersand is expanded to "and" except in "&c," "&ca.," and "& Co." in business firms.

2. The thorn, which by 1750 had been debased to "y" as in "ye," is expanded to "th." Such abbreviations as "ye" "yᵗ" or "yᵐ" are rendered as "the," "that" or "them."

3. The tilde is replaced by the letter(s) it represents—as in com̄ission.

4. The ℔ sign is expanded to the appropriate letters it represents (e.g., per, pre, or pro).

5. Superscript letters are brought down to the line as in 9ᵗʰ to 9th or Regᵗ to Regt.

Punctuation

Where necessary, punctuation is changed to conform to the following rules:

1. A period or question mark is placed at the end of every sentence.

2. Within a sentence, punctuation is sparingly added or deleted in order to clarify a confusing or misleading passage.

3. Dashes used in place of commas, semicolons, periods, or question marks are replaced with appropriate punctuation; dashes are retained when used to mark a suspension of the sense or to set off a change of thought.

4. No punctuation is used after a salutation.

Missing or Indecipherable Passages

If such passages cannot be conjectured, they are indicated by italicized editorial comments in brackets, such as [*mutilated*], [*indecipherable*], [*remainder of paragraph (or letter) missing*].

If missing or indecipherable portions can be conjectured they are treated in one of the following ways:

1. If no more than four letters are missing they are supplied silently.
2. If more than four letters are conjectured they are inserted in brackets. If there is some doubt about the conjecture, it is followed by a question mark: Ch[arleston?].
3. If such portions can be supplied from a variant version of the manuscript they are set in angle brackets: ⟨Washington⟩.
4. A blank left by the author is so depicted and the fact mentioned in a footnote.

PRINTED MATERIAL

In reprinting documents from printed sources the capitalization, spelling, punctuation, and paragraphing have been faithfully followed—except for obvious printer's errors.

The earlier practice of italicizing names, however, is dropped, as are the italicization of passages by the former editor.

SOURCE NOTE

An unnumbered source note directly follows each document. For manuscript material it consists of a symbol describing the type of manuscript, followed by the symbol or name of the repository that owns the document, or the name of an individual owner. Pertinent facts or conjectures concerning the manuscript are added when required. A list of manuscript symbols and a list of the Library of Congress repository symbols follow the section on annotation below.

ANNOTATION

A few points need emphasis:

1. Identification of persons is usually made at the first appearance of their names and is not repeated. References to these biographical notes are found in the index. Identifications are omitted for such leading figures as Washington or Franklin, as well as for obscure persons who played an insignificant role in NG's career.

2. Cross-references in the notes are to documents rather than to page numbers, as in "See below, NG to Washington, 9 November 1776." If a cross-reference is to a document within the same year, the year is often omitted: "See above, 13 September." Cross references may refer to dates found in a later volume. Cross references to an earlier volume are designated, for example, as: "See above, vol. 1: 352n."

3. When a page number does not appear in a citation, the reader can assume the work is in dictionary form.

DESCRIPTIVE SYMBOLS FOR MANUSCRIPTS

Following are the symbols employed in source notes to describe the kinds of manuscripts used in the texts.

AD	Autograph document
ADS	Autograph document signed
ADf	Autograph draft
ADfS	Autograph draft signed
AL	Autograph letter
ALS	Autograph letter signed
D	Document
DDf	Document draft
DS	Document signed
Df	Draft
DfS	Draft signed
LS	Letter signed
LB	Letter book copy
FC	File copy
Cy	Copy (made contemporaneously with original)
ACy	Autograph copy
ACyS	Autograph copy signed
Tr	Transcript (later copy made for historical record)

[A]   Indicates some uncertainty about the autograph
[S]   Indicates signature has been cropped or obliterated
(No symbol is given to printed letters or documents)

LIBRARY OF CONGRESS SYMBOLS OF REPOSITORIES

The following institutions have provided copies of manuscripts which are printed or calendared in volume two:

CSmH	Henry E. Huntington Library, San Marino, Calif.
Ct	Connecticut State Library, Hartford, Conn.
CtHi	Connecticut Historical Society, Hartford, Conn.
CtY	Yale University, New Haven, Conn.
DLC	U.S. Library of Congress, Washington, D.C.
DNA	U.S. National Archives, Washington, D.C.
ICU	University of Chicago, Chicago, Ill.
M-Ar	Massachusetts Archives, Boston, Mass.
MB	Boston Public Library, Boston, Mass.
MH	Harvard College Library, Cambridge, Mass.
MHi	Massachusetts Historical Society, Boston, Mass.
MMeT	Tufts University, Medford, Mass.
MWA	American Antiquarian Society, Worcester, Mass.
MiDbF	Greenfield Village and Henry Ford Museum, Dearborn, Mich.
MiU-C	William L. Clements Library, University of Michigan, Ann Arbor, Mich.
MnHi	Minnesota Historical Society, St. Paul, Minn.
N	New York State Library, Albany, N.Y.
NHi	New-York Historical Society, New York, N.Y.
NN	New York Public Library, New York, N.Y.
NNC	Columbia University, New York, N.Y.
NNS	New York Society Library, New York, N.Y.
NSchU	Union College, Schenectady, N.Y.
NcD-MC	Duke University Medical Center, Durham, N.C.
NhHi	New Hampshire Historical Society, Concord, N.H.
Nj	New Jersey State Library, Trenton, N.J.
NjHi	New Jersey Historical Society, Newark, N.J.
NjMoW	Morristown National Historical Park, Morristown, N.J.
NjP	Princeton University, Princeton, N.J.
OClWHi	Western Reserve Historical Society, Cleveland, Ohio
OMC	Marietta College, Marietta, Ohio
PHC	Haverford College, Haverford, Pa.

PHarH   Pennsylvania Historical and Museum Commission,
Harrisburg, Pa.
PHi   Historical Society of Pennsylvania, Philadelphia, Pa.
PPAmP   American Philosophical Society, Philadelphia, Pa.
PPIn   Independence Hall National Park, Philadelphia, Pa.
PPL   Library Company of Philadelphia, Philadelphia, Pa.
PU   University of Pennsylvania, Philadelphia, Pa.
PWcHi   Chester County Historical Society, West Chester, Pa.
R-Ar   Rhode Island State Archives, Providence, R.I.
RHi   Rhode Island Historical Society, Providence, R.I.
RNHi   Newport Historical Society, Newport, R.I.
RPJCB   John Carter Brown Library, Providence, R.I.
ScHi   South Carolina Historical Society, Charleston, S.C.
Vi   Virginia State Library, Richmond, Va.
WHi   State Historical Society of Wisconsin, Madison, Wis.

SHORT TITLES FOR WORKS FREQUENTLY CITED

Alden, *Lee*

Alden, John Richard. *General Charles Lee: Traitor or Patriot?* Baton Rouge: Louisiana State University Press, 1951.

Arnold, *R.I.*

Arnold, Samuel Greene. *History of the State of Rhode Island and Providence Plantations.* 3rd ed. 2 vols. New York and London, 1878.

Baker, "Camp"

Baker, William S. "The Camp by Schuylkill Falls," *PMHB* 16 (1892): 28–41.

Balch, *French*

Balch, Thomas. *The French in America During the War of Independence of the United States, 1777–83.* Translated by Edwin Swift Balch and Elise Willing Balch. Philadelphia, 1895.

Balch, *Maryland Line*

Balch, Thomas, ed. *Papers Relating Chiefly to the Maryland Line during the Revolution.* Philadelphia, 1857.

Bartlett, *Records*

Bartlett, John Russell, ed. *Records of the State of Rhode Island and Providence Plantations in New England.* 10 vols. Providence, 1856–65.

Baurmeister, *Revolution*   Baurmeister, Carl Leopold. *Revolution in America: Confidential Letters and Journals 1776–1784 of Adjutant General Major Baurmeister of the Hessian Forces.* Translated and edited by Bernhard A. Uhlendorf. New Brunswick, N.J.: Rutgers University Press, 1957.

Bell, *Morgan*   Bell, Whitfield J., Jr. *John Morgan: Continental Doctor.* Philadelphia: University of Pennsylvania Press, 1965.

Bezanson, *Prices*   Bezanson, Anne. *Prices and Inflation during the American Revolution: Philadelphia, 1770–1790.* Philadelphia: University of Pennsylvania Press, 1951.

Boatner, *Encyc.*   Boatner, Mark Mayo, III. *Encyclopedia of the American Revolution.* New York: David McKay Co., 1974.

Bowman, *Captive Americans*   Bowman, Larry G. *Captive Americans: Prisoners during the American Revolution.* Athens, Ohio: Ohio University Press, 1976.

Burnett, *Letters*   Burnett, Edmund C., ed. *Letters of Members of the Continental Congress.* 8 vols. Washington: Carnegie Institution of Washington, 1921–36.

Butterfield, *Adams Family*   Butterfield, L. H., et al., eds. *Adams Family Correspondence.* Cambridge, Mass.: Belknap Press of Harvard University Press, 1963–.

Butterfield, *Rush*   Rush, Benjamin. *Letters of Benjamin Rush.* Edited by Lyman H. Butterfield. 2 vols. Princeton: Princeton University Press, 1951.

Callahan, *Knox*   Callahan, North. *Henry Knox: General Washington's General.* South Brunswick, Me., and New York: A. S. Barnes and Co., 1958.

Clinton, *Papers*   Clinton, George. *Public Papers of George Clinton, First Governor of New York.*

Edited by Hugh Hastings. 10 vols. Albany, 1899–1914.

Coleman, *McKean*
Coleman, John M. *Thomas McKean: Forgotten Leader of the Revolution*. Rockaway, N.J.: American Faculty Press, 1975.

Commager and Morris, *Spirit of '76*
Commager, Henry Steele, and Morris, Richard B., eds. *The Spirit of 'Seventy-Six: The Story of the American Revolution as Told by Participants*. 2 vols. Indianapolis and New York: Bobbs-Merrill Co., 1958.

Conn. Men in Rev.
Record of Service of Connecticut Men in the War of the Revolution. Hartford, 1889.

DAB
Johnson, Allen, and Malone, Dumas, eds. *Dictionary of American Biography*. 21 vols. New York: Charles Scribner's Sons, 1928–36. 5 supplements, 1944, 1958, 1973, 1974, and 1977.

Dearden, "R.I. Campaign"
Dearden, Paul F. "The Rhode Island Campaign of 1778: Inauspicious Dawn of Alliance." Master's Thesis, Providence College, 1972.

DNB
Stephen, Leslie and Lee, Sidney, eds. *Dictionary of National Biography*. 21 vols. New York and London: Oxford University Press, 1885–1901.

Doniol, *France*
Doniol, Henri. *Histoire de la Participation de la France à l'Établissement des États-Unis d'Amérique*. 5 vols. Paris, 1886–92.

Dupuy and Hammerman, *People*
Dupuy, Trevor N., and Hammerman, Gay M., eds. *People & Events of the American Revolution*. New York and London: R. R. Bowker Co., 1974; Dunn Loring, Va.: T. N. Dupuy Associates, 1974.

Ferguson, *Power of Purse*
Ferguson, E. James. *The Power of the Purse: A History of American Public Finance, 1776–90*. Chapel Hill: University of North Carolina Press, 1961.

Fitzpatrick, *GW*

Washington, George. *The Writings of George Washington, from the Original Manuscript Sources, 1745–1799.* Edited by John C. Fitzpatrick. 39 vols. Washington: United States Government Printing Office, 1931–44.

Flexner, *GW*

Flexner, James Thomas. *George Washington in the American Revolution (1775–1783).* Boston and Toronto: Little, Brown and Co., 1967.

Force, *Archives*

Force, Peter, ed. *American Archives.* Fourth and Fifth Series. 6 vols. and 3 vols. Washington: 1837–53.

Fortescue, *British Army*

Fortescue, J. W. *A History of the British Army.* 2nd ed. 13 vols. London: Macmillan and Co., 1910–30.

Freeman, *GW*

Freeman, Douglas Southall. *George Washington.* 7 vols. The last volume by John C. Alexander and Mary W. Ashworth. New York: Charles Scribner's Sons, 1948–57.

Furman, *Letters*

Furman, Moore. *The Letters of Moore Furman.* Compiled and edited with genealogical notes by the New Jersey Society of the Colonial Dames of America. New York: Frederick H. Hitchcock, 1912.

Gordon, *History*

Gordon, William. *History of the Rise, Progress and Establishment of the Independence of the United States of America.* 4 vols. London, 1788.

Gottschalk, *Lafayette*

Gottschalk, Louis. *Lafayette Joins the American Army.* Chicago: University of Chicago Press, 1937.

Gottschalk, *Letters of Lafayette*

Lafayette, Marquis de. *The Letters of Lafayette to Washington, 1777–1779.* Edited by Louis Gottschalk. New York: Helen Fahnestock Hubbard, 1944.

Graydon, *Memoirs*

Graydon, Alexander. *Memoirs of His Own Time, with Reminiscences of the Men and Events of the Revolution*. Philadelphia, 1846.

Greene, *Greene*

Greene, George Washington. *The Life of Nathanael Greene, Major-General in the Army of the Revolution*. 3 vols. 1871. Reprint. Boston and New York: Houghton Mifflin and Co., 1897–1900.

Gruber, *Howe Brothers*

Gruber, Ira D. *The Howe Brothers and the American Revolution*. New York: Atheneum, 1972.

GWG Transcript

Greene, George Washington

Hammond, *Sullivan*

Sullivan, John. *Letters and Papers of Major-General Sullivan, Continental Army*. Edited by Otis G. Hammond. 3 vols. Concord: New Hampshire Historical Society, 1930–39.

Hawke, *Rush*

Hawke, David F. *Benjamin Rush: Revolutionary Gadfly*. Indianapolis: Bobbs-Merrill Co., 1971.

Heitman, *Register*

Heitman, Francis B., comp. *Historical Register of Officers of the Continental Army during the War of the Revolution*. 1914. Reprint. With addenda by Robert H. Kelby. Baltimore: Genealogical Publishing Co., 1967.

Heusser, *Erskine*

Heusser, Albert H. *George Washington's Map Maker: A Biography of Robert Erskine*. Edited with an introduction by Hubert G. Schmidt. New Brunswick, N.J.: Rutgers University Press, 1966.

Higginbotham, *Morgan*

Higginbotham, Don. *Daniel Morgan: Revolutionary Rifleman*. Chapel Hill: University of North Carolina Press, 1961.

Higginbotham, *War*

Higginbotham, Don. *The War of American Independence: Military Attitudes, Policies, and Practice, 1763–1789*. New York: The Macmillan Co., 1971.

Hoadly, *Records*

Hoadly, C. J., and others eds. *Public Records of the Colony of Connecticut, 1636–1776*. 15 vols. Hartford, 1850–90. *Public Records of the State of Connecticut, 1776–1803*. 11 vols. Hartford, 1894–1922.

Idzerda, *Lafayette Papers*

Lafayette, Marquis de. *Lafayette in the Age of the American Revolution: Selected Letters and Papers, 1776–1790*. Edited by Stanley J. Idzerda and others. Ithaca, N.Y.: Cornell University Press, 1977–.

JCC

Ford, Worthington C., and others, eds. *Journals of the Continental Congress, 1774–1789*. 34 vols. Washington: Government Printing Office, 1904–37.

Johnson, *Dictionary*

Johnson, Samuel. *A Dictionary of the English Language*. 2 vols. 1755. Reprint. New York: AMS Press, 1967.

Johnson, *Greene*

Johnson, William. *Life and Correspondence of Nathanael Greene, Major General of the Armies of the United States*. 2 vols. Charleston, S.C., 1822.

Kemble, *Journal*

Kemble, Stephen. "Journal." In *Kemble Papers*, New-York Historical Society, *Collections*. 2 vols. New York, 1884.

Kemble Papers

Kemble, Stephen. "Order Books." In *Kemble Papers*, New-York Historical Society, *Collections*. 2 vols. New York, 1884.

Knollenberg, *GW*

Knollenberg, Bernhard. *Washington and the Revolution: A Reappraisal*. New York: Macmillan Co., 1940.

Laurens, *Letters*

Laurens, John. *The Army Correspondence of John Laurens in the Years 1777–78*. Edited with a memoir by William Gilmore Simms. New York, 1867.

Lee Papers

Lee, Charles. *The Lee Papers*. New-York Historical Society, *Collections*. 4 vols. New York: 1872–75.

Leiby, *Hackensack*

Leiby, Adrian C. *The Revolutionary War in the Hackensack Valley: The Jersey Dutch*

	and the Neutral Ground, 1775–1783. New Brunswick, N.J.: Rutgers University Press, 1962.
Lesser, *Sinews*	Lesser, Charles H., ed. *The Sinews of Independence: Monthly Strength Reports of the Continental Army.* Chicago: University of Chicago Press, 1976.
Ludlum, *Winters*	Ludlum, David McWilliams. *Early American Winters.* Boston: American Meteorological Society, 1966.
Lundin, *Cockpit*	Lundin, Leonard. *Cockpit of the Revolution: The War for Independence in New Jersey.* 1941. Reprint. New York: Octagon Books, 1972.
McMichael, "Diary"	McMichael, James. "Diary of Lieutenant James McMichael, of the Pennsylvania Line, 1776–78." *PMHB* 16 (1892): 129–59.
MacKenzie, *Diary*	MacKenzie, Frederick. *The Diary of Frederick MacKenzie.* 2 vols. Cambridge, Mass.: Harvard University Press, 1930.
Mackesy, *War*	Mackesy, Piers. *The War for America, 1775–1783.* Cambridge, Mass.: Harvard University Press, 1964.
MHS, *Coll.*	Massachusetts Historical Society, *Collections.*
MHS, *Proc.*	Massachusetts Historical Society, *Proceedings.*
Mintz, *Morris*	Mintz, Max M. *Gouverneur Morris and the American Revolution.* Norman: University of Oklahoma Press, 1970.
Montresor, *Journals*	Montresor, John. "The Journals of Capt. John Montresor," New-York Historical Society, *Collections.* Edited by G. D. Scull. New York: 1881, pp. 115–542.
Murray, *Life*	Murray, John. *The Life of the Rev. John Murray.* 7th edition, with notes by L. S. Everett. Utica, N.Y., 1840.

Nelson, *Gates*

Nelson, Paul David. *General Horatio Gates: A Biography*. Baton Rouge: Louisiana State University Press, 1966.

N.J. Archives

New Jersey Archives. Documents Relating to the Revolutionary History of the State of New Jersey. 2nd series. 5 vols. Trenton, N.J.: State of New Jersey, 1901–17.

NJHS, *Coll.*

New Jersey Historical Society, *Collections*.

NJHS, *Proc.*

New Jersey Historical Society, *Proceedings*.

N.J. Rev. Correspondence

Selections from the Correspondence of the Executive of New Jersey from 1776 to 1786. Newark, N.J., 1848.

Nickerson, *Turning Point*

Nickerson, Hoffman. *The Turning Point of the Revolution, or Burgoyne in America*. Boston and New York: Houghton Mifflin Co., 1928.

N-YHS, *Coll.*

New-York Historical Society, *Collections*.

Pa. Archives

Pennsylvania Archives. Selected and Arranged from Original Documents in the Office of the Secretary of the Commonwealth. 119 vols. Philadelphia and Harrisburg, 1852–1935.

Pa. Col. Records

The *Pennsylvania Colonial Records* constitute the first sixteen volumes of the *Pennsylvania Archives*. See above, *Pa. Archives*.

PCC

Papers of the Continental Congress.

Peckham, *Toll*

Peckham, Howard H. *The Toll of Independence: Engagements & Battle Casualties of the American Revolution*. Chicago and London: University of Chicago Press, 1974.

Pickering, *Pickering*

Pickering, Octavius. *The Life of Timothy Pickering*. 4 vols. Boston, 1867–73.

PMHB

Pennsylvania Magazine of History and Biography.

Pratt, *Eleven Generals*

Pratt, Fletcher. *Eleven Generals: Studies in American Command*. New York: W. Sloane Associates, 1949.

Reed, *Campaign*

Reed, John F. *Campaign to Valley Forge, July 1, 1777–December 19, 1777*. Philadelphia: University of Pennsylvania Press, 1965.

Reed, *Valley Forge*

Reed, John F. *Valley Forge: Crucible of Victory*. Monmouth Beach, N.J.: Philip Freneau Press, 1969.

Reed, *Reed*

Reed, William B. *Life and Correspondence of Joseph Reed*. 2 vols. Philadelphia, 1847.

R.I. Biog. Cycl.

Biographical Cyclopedia of Representative Men of Rhode Island. Providence, 1881.

R.I. Acts

Rhode Island Acts and Resolves, 1747–1800. 31 vols. Providence: State of Rhode Island, 1908–25.

RIHS, *Coll.*

Collections of the Rhode Island Historical Society (1827–1902). Rhode Island Historical Society, *Collections* (quarterly 1918–41).

Robertson, *Diaries*

Robertson, Archibald. *His Diaries and Sketches in America, 1762–1780*. Edited by Harry Miller Lydenberg. New York: The New York Public Library, 1930.

Roche, *Reed*

Roche, John F. *Joseph Reed: A Moderate in the American Revolution*. New York: Columbia University Press, 1957.

Rossman, *Mifflin*

Rossman, Kenneth R. *Thomas Mifflin and the Politics of the American Revolution*. Chapel Hill: University of North Carolina Press, 1952.

Smith, *Brandywine*

Smith, Samuel S. *The Battle of Brandywine*. Monmouth Beach, N.J.: Philip Freneau Press, 1976.

Smith, *Monmouth*

Smith, Samuel S. *The Battle of Monmouth*. Monmouth Beach, N.J.: Philip Freneau Press, 1964.

Smith, *The Delaware*

Smith, Samuel S. *Fight for the Delaware 1777*. Monmouth Beach, N.J.: Philip Freneau Press, 1970.

Sosin, *Frontier*

Sosin, Jack M. *The Revolutionary Frontier, 1763–1783*. New York, Chicago, San Francisco, Toronto, London: Holt, Rinehart and Winston, 1967.

Sparks, *Morris*

Sparks, Jared. *The Life of Gouverneur Morris: With Selections from his Correspondence and Miscellaneous Papers*. 3 vols. Boston, 1832.

Staples, *R.I.*

Staples, William R. *Rhode Island in the Continental Congress, with the Journal of the Convention that Adopted the Constitution, 1765–1790*. Edited by Reuben A. Guild. Providence, 1870.

Syrett, *Hamilton*

Hamilton, Alexander. *The Papers of Alexander Hamilton*. Edited by Harold C. Syrett and others. New York: Columbia University Press, 1961–.

Thayer, *Monmouth*

Thayer, Theodore. *Washington and Lee at Monmouth: The Making of a Scapegoat*. Port Washington, N.Y., and London: Kennikat Press, 1976.

Trussell, *Valley Forge*

Trussell, John B. B., Jr. *Birthplace of an Army: A Study of the Valley Forge Encampment*. Harrisburg, Pa.: Pennsylvania Historical and Museum Commission, 1976.

Wallace, *Traitorous Hero*

Wallace, Willard M. *Traitorous Hero: The Life and Fortunes of Benedict Arnold*. New York: Harper and Row, 1954.

Ward, *Delaware*

Ward, Christopher L. *The Delaware Continentals, 1776–1783*. Wilmington: Historical Society of Delaware, 1941.

Ward, *War*

Ward, Christopher L. *The War of the Revolution*. 2 vols. Edited by John Richard Alden. New York: Macmillan Co., 1952.

Weedon Orderly Book	Weedon, George. *Valley Forge Orderly Book*. New York: Dodd, Mead & Company, 1902.
Whittemore, *Sullivan*	Whittemore, Charles P. *A General of the Revolution: John Sullivan of New Hampshire*. New York and London: Columbia University Press, 1961.
Wildes, *Wayne*	Wildes, Harry Emerson. *Anthony Wayne: Trouble Shooter of the American Revolution*. Westport, Conn.: Greenwood Press, 1970.
Willcox, *Clinton*	Willcox, William B. *Portrait of a General: Sir Henry Clinton in the War of Independence*. New York: Alfred A. Knopf, 1964.
WMQ	*William and Mary Quarterly*
WRMS	War Department Collection of Revolutionary War Records

A GLOSSARY OF MILITARY TERMS

ABATIS
A barrier of felled trees, with limbs pointing toward the enemy; usually temporary.

ARTILLERY PARK
An encampment for artillery.

ARTILLERY TRAIN
An army's collection of cannon and the materiel for firing them.

BARBETTE
A platform or mound of earth for artillery, usually separated from a main fortification.

BASTION
An outward projection of a fort enabling gunners to fire along the wall of the fort at an enemy.

BATTALION
See Regiment.

BOMB, BOOMBE
A powder-filled iron sphere that is fired from a mortar and fused to explode after falling.

BREASTWORK
An improvised fortification, usually consisting of a trench and earthen barrier.

BRIGADE
A formation of two or more regiments.

BROADSIDE
The firing of all artillery on one side of a warship.

CANISTER
A tin cylinder containing metal balls that scattered when fired from a cannon.

CARCASS
An incendiary device fired from a cannon at wooden structures or ships.

CARTOUCHE
Cartridge made of a paper cylinder, containing powder and lead ball.

CHANDELIER
Wooden frame filled with fascines, for protection where earth could not be dug.

CHEVAL-DE-FRISE
Used usually in the plural; a portable defense barrier bristling with long, iron-tipped wooden spikes. An underwater version consisted of a rock-filled wooden frame, on which sharpened timbers were set at an angle to rip the hull of a vessel.

COULOURMAN
Soldier responsible for the more disagreeable cleaning and sanitation tasks.

DIVISION
A unit of two or more brigades.

DRAGOON
Once a mounted infantryman, by 1775 term was used interchangeably with cavalryman.

DURHAM BOAT
A shallow-drafted boat developed to transport iron ore. Varying in length from forty to sixty feet

and around eight feet in width, it could carry a company of troops and was usually poled.

EMBRASURE   An opening through which cannon were fired.

ENFILADE   To sweep with gunfire along a line of works or troops from end to end.

FASCINE   A firmly tied bundle of wooden sticks or small limbs.

FATIGUE   Manual and menial duty performed by troops.

FIREBOAT   A vessel filled with a variety of combustibles for burning enemy vessels.

FLECHE   An outwork of a fort, shaped like an arrow, the point toward the enemy.

FRIGATE   A two-decked warship built for swift sailing, mounting twenty to thirty-eight guns on the upper deck.

GLACIS   A bank sloping away from a fortification.

GRENADE   A hand-thrown metal device that exploded when the lighted fuse reached the powder inside.

GRENADIERS   Once hurlers of grenades, by 1775 an elite corps.

GUN   Although technically used to describe a cannon, the term was also regularly used in the colonies for a musket or rifle.

INVALIDS   Disabled soldiers who were assigned to limited duties.

JÄGER   German light infantry chosen for their marksmanship with the German rifle (not the German-American long-barreled rifle).

LIGHT INFANTRY   Lightly equipped, highly mobile troops.

MARQUEE   A canvas tent designed especially for officers; also, a cover for another tent.

MATROSS   Assistant to an artillery gunner.

MORTAR   A short-barreled cannon used for lobbing shells, bombs, etc., over an obstacle.

MUSQUETEER   Soldier armed with a musket.

ORDNANCE   Military equipment and supplies.

OUTWORK   A defensive work outside a fort.

PALISADE   Timbers set in the ground, close together and sharpened at the top.

PAROLE   A prisoner's oath on being freed that he will not bear arms until exchanged.

PETTY AUGER   An open, flat-bottomed boat, generally two-masted, carrying some thirty tons.

PICKET, PICQUET   An outguard to warn of an enemy approach.

PIKE — Wooden spear of varying length, with a steel point.

PIONEERS — Men responsible for digging trenches, repairing roads, preparing fortifications, etc.

PLATFORM — A wooden bed upon which a cannon was placed.

PRIVATEER — A privately owned armed vessel commissioned to take enemy merchantmen as prizes.

REGIMENT — During this period, regiment and battalion were used interchangeably. Usually composed of eight companies and at full strength numbering from 520 to 780.

REVETMENT — A wall to retain an earthen rampart or side of a ditch.

ROW GALLEY — A low, flat vessel with one deck, varying in length up to 130 feet; manned by oarsmen and carrying several small cannon.

SCHOONER — A small fore-and-aft-rigged vessel with two masts.

SHIP — A large vessel with three masts, each composed of a lower mast, top mast, and top gallant mast.

SLOOP — Small, one-masted vessel.

SUBALTERN — Commissioned officer below the rank of lieutenant.

SUTLER — A provisioner for an army camp who operates for profit.

TRANSPORT — A vessel for carrying troops.

XEBEQUE — A three-masted ship with long overhanging bow and stern which originated in the Mediterranean.

1777	2–3 January	Battle of Princeton.
	Mid-March	Birth of Martha Washington Greene.
	June	Catharine comes to live for a year with the Abraham Lotts at Beverwyck, N.J.
	12 June	Howe's army moves from Amboy, N.J., in hopes of luring Americans into battle.
	15–25 July	Army camped at Smith's Clove, N.Y.
	25 August	Howe's army lands at Head of Elk, Md.
	11 September	Battle of Brandywine.
	26 September	British occupy Philadelphia.
	4 October	Battle of Germantown.
	20–29 November	NG in New Jersey in vain attempt to protect fort at Red Bank.
	5–8 December	Howe confronts American forces at Whitemarsh, Pa.
	19 December	American army arrives at Valley Forge.
1778	2 March	NG appointed quartermaster general.
	18 June	British evacuate Philadelphia.
	28 June	Battle of Monmouth.
	11 July	Count d'Estaing's fleet arrives at New York.
	28 July	Washington sends NG to Rhode Island.
	9–20 August	Sullivan's army, under Lafayette and Greene, prepares for attack on Newport, R.I.
	29 August	Battle of Rhode Island and American retreat from Aquidneck Island.
	23 September	Cornelia Lott Greene is born.
	13 October	NG rejoins Washington's army at Fredericksburg, N.Y.

THE PAPERS OF
General Nathanael Greene

To General John Cadwalader

Dear Sir   Trenton [N.J.] January 1, 1776[1777]
    From some circumstances we have great reason to Apprehend
the Enemy are in motion, and I apprehend they are meditating an
Attack, and upon you. Youl hold yourself in readiness, and send out
scouts and parties and get what intelligence you can and send us the
same.[1] Yours Sincerely

                                                           N GREENE

Send out Horse Padroles

ALS (PHi).
    1. Washington's army had recrossed the Delaware to Trenton on 30 December
1776, where they were very nearly caught by the advance of Cornwallis's forces the
night before the battle of Princeton. Cadwalader was at Crosswicks (the address sheet
has it as Crossix), eight miles southeast of Trenton and not far from Hessian forces. On
the battle of Princeton, see above, vol. 1: 379–80n and below, NG to Governor Cooke,
10 January.

To Thomas Paine[1]

                                            [Morristown, N.J.] 9 January 1777
    Not a line have I received from you since you left us at New-
town.[2] I am much obliged to you for the attention. Were I not fully
persuaded that you are anxious to know the success of our late
manoeuvres, I would not have wrote you a syllable this fortnight. I
almost think the author of the Crisis a prophet where he says the
Tories will curse the day that Howe arrived upon the Delaware. I
verily believe the observation is coming true. The two late actions at
Trenton and Princeton have put a very different face upon affairs.
Within a fortnight past we have taken and killed of Howe's army
between two and three thousand men. Our loss is trifling. We are
daily picking up their parties. Yesterday we took seventy prisoners
and thirty loads of baggage.[3]
    Great credit is due to the Philadelphia militia; their behaviour at
Trenton in the cannonade, and at Princeton was brave, firm and
manly; they were broken at first in the action at Princeton, but soon
formed in the face of grapeshot, and pushed on with a spirit that
would do honor to veterans, besides which they have borne a winter's
campaign with a soldier like patience.[4] General Cadwallader is a
brave and gallant officer.

Excerpt reprinted from *N.J. Archives* (2), 1: 256–57; attributed to *The Pennsylvania Evening Post*, 14 January 1777, which listed the writer as "Major
General G_____."

1. The recipient was not given in the *Evening Post*, but despite the reference to the author of the *Crisis* in the third person, the contents point to Paine. This is corroborated by a short excerpt in the George Bancroft transcripts (NN). On Paine's writing of the *Crisis* while serving as NG's aide, see above, vol. 1: 324 n and 364n.

2. In Bucks County, Pa., about ten miles west of Trenton. After the battle of Trenton, the Hessian prisoners were brought to Newtown before being sent to Philadelphia (Ward, *War*, 1: 304).

3. On the same day, Washington reported this skirmish to Congress as being carried out by General Maxwell's militia at Elizabethtown, N.J. (Fitzpatrick, *GW*, 6: 487) His figure agrees with NG's, but Peckham lists only forty prisoners taken (*Toll*, p. 29). NG's estimate of total British losses in the fortnight is double the actual figures.

4. This generous appraisal of the militia contrasts with his more frequent swipes at their behavior. See above, NG to Cooke, 4 December 1776, vol. 1: 362, and below, NG to Jacob Greene, 20 April 1777, and to John Adams, 2 May 1777.

To Governor Nicholas Cooke of Rhode Island

Dear sir   Morristown [N.J.] Jan. 10, 1777

Long before this will reach you the surprize of Trenton will come to hand. We crosssed the Delaware on the 25 of December at night 8 miles above the town in one of the severest Hails and rain storms I ever saw. We reached the town the next morning about 8 oclock and surprized it. We attacked it by storm and soon carried the garrison. The number of the killed and wounded and prisoners amounts to upwards of 1200. We crossed the Delaware again that night. I was out 30 hours in all the storm without the least refreshment. Our loss was inconsiderable in carrying the place. The Troops behaved incomparably well. We took 6 field pieces and a large number of small arms and a considerable quantity of stores.[1]

On 30 of Dec we crossed the Delaware again. The day following all the N England troops were free. His Excellency gave them a bounty to engage for only 6 weeks anew.[2] God Almighty inclnd [inclined] their hearts to listen to the proposal and they engaged anew, happy for America. This is the greatest evidence of N E virtue I ever saw. Let it be remembered to their Eternal honor.

We crossed the river in two places and drew our forces together at Trenton. On the 3d of this instant the enemy advanced from Princeton towards Trenton 12 miles distant. There is a little river called the Mill Creek that runs through Trenton. We drew up on one side of it and the enemy on the other. Some skirmishing and a severe cannonade ensued, and lasted untill night. We stole a march that night and attacked Princeton next morning. We left all our sentries standing and moved off as silently as possible. The guards had orders to decamp in three hours after our march began. No person knew where we were going except the Genl Officers. There was about 1200 men at Princeton. They made an obstinate resistance. The killed, wounded and prisoners of the enemy amounted to upwards of 600.[3]

We immediately quitted Princeton. Our loss was not great. Genl Mercer was badly wounded and two field officers killed.[4] We brought off a large number of arms and 2 field pieces and a great quantity of ammunition. We made a move towards Brunswick. The enemy marched from Trenton to Brunswick in the greatest confusion imaginable. Had we had a 1000 fresh troops that night we could have destroyed all their baggage at that place but our troops were so fatigued that it was impossible to attempt any thing further. Every day since the Princeton action we have been engaged in small parties; several hundred prisoners have been taken. We are now in possession again of Fort Lee, Hackensack, Newark, Elizabeth Town and Princeton. The enemy has nothing but Brunswick and Amboy.

Great credit is due to the Philadelphia Militia who were in the Princeton action and who behaved exceeding well considering they were never in action before. Great bodies of militia of this State and Pennsylvania are coming on to join us. We have most sanguin hopes of being in possession of all the Jerseys in a few days. My heart overflows with Gratitude to divine Providence who hath smote our enemies with very great pannick and worked wonders in our favor. The enemies whole collective loss in the several engagements amounts to between 2 and 3000.

The enemies ravages in the Jerseys exceeds all description. Many hundred women ravished. Those that were high tories when the enemy entered the Jerseys are now warm whigs. The country are in high spirits and breath nothing but revenge.[5]

I hope the N England governments will exert themselves to fill up the new Regiments. Nothing but spirit and resolution is wanting to free the Country from this accursed race of more than savage oppressors.

I should be exceeding happy to hear the History of the times with you. My best respects to all friends particularly Mr. Ward. I have only time to add that I am sincerely your friend, and very humble servant.

NATHL GREENE

Tr (Sparks Transcripts: MH).

1. On the battle of Trenton, see above, NG to Catharine, 30 December 1776, vol. 1: 377–80.

2. Washington's action was sanctioned by Congress on 27 December 1776 (JCC, 6: 1043).

3. The British had 28 killed, 58 wounded, and 129 captured. (Peckham, Toll, p. 29)

4. Hugh Mercer died of his wounds two days later. See below, NG to Catharine, 20 January 1777.

5. He did not greatly exaggerate the enemy "ravages." (See above, vol. 1: 362, 365, 368, and 375). Despite Howe's strict orders and the harsh punishment handed offenders, British officers testified to constant plundering and atrocities by both British and Hessians. (Gruber, Howe Brothers, pp. 194–95; Kemble, Journal, 96–102 passim; Commager and Morris, Spirit of '76, 1: 524–29). Under British protection, moreover,

New Jersey loyalists frequently shared in plundering their patriot neighbors. (For example, see Leiby, *Hackensack*, pp. 84–90). The loyalists were themselves often the victims of Hessian soldiers, who, in their ignorance of the language, could not distinguish loyalist from patriot. Such acts did, indeed, turn "high tories" into "warm whigs."

Patriots were by no means innocent of plundering their "tory" neighbors after the British withdrew. American soldiers, especially militiamen, were even more ruthless. (Lundin, *Cockpit*, pp. 235–36, 246–47, and Commager and Morris, *Spirit of '76*, 1: 529). Washington may have inadvertently encouraged the practice by his orders permitting scouting parties to divide up "enemy" property "as a reward for the extraordinary fatigues, hardship, and danger they were exposed to." He acknowledged this order (probably of early January, but not since found) in an order of 21 January 1777, which admonished troops against "plundering the Inhabitants, under the specious pretence of their being Tories" (Fitzpatrick, *GW*, 7: 46–47).

From Major William S. Livingston[1]

[Morris County, N.J., 15 January 1777. A fulsome letter thanking NG for his kindness and praising his numerous virtues as a model that he had "resolved to coppy." Tr (MiU-C; typescript furnished to William L. Clements in 1930; location of original unknown) 2 pp.]

1. William Smith Livingston, an aide to NG from August 1776, had resigned to become a lieutenant colonel of one of the newly formed "additional regiments" under Col. Samuel B. Webb. A well-connected young man, he was the son of Gov. William Livingston of New Jersey, nephew of Lord Stirling, and brother-in-law of John Jay. He married Catherine, daugher of the Abraham Lotts, who were to become close friends of NG. (Heitman, *Register*; *PMHB*, 70 [1946]: 296n)

To [   ]

[Morristown, N.J., 17 January 1777. He is "miserably off for want of a horse." Asks the unidentified recipient to help him acquire one. Tr (G. W. Greene Transcripts; CSmH) 1 p.]

To Catharine Greene

My Dear   Morristown [N.J.] January 20, 1777

You see by the ⟨constant run⟩ of Letters pouring in upon you that I employ almost every leisure hour to give you an account of my situation.[1] This is the only consolation I can offer you to make amends for the injury you sustain by my absences. Letters, like repeated assureances of affection, are always welcome altho they contain nothing new. I am unhappy in not hearing from you, not a line has come to hand for months past. Surely my friends have not forgot me. If all the World forsake me in you my beloved I am sure of a boosom friend. But the much greater part of ones friends hang upon the stem of success, and drop off in the first storm of adversity. The disagreeable situation that our affairs were in of late has fully evinced this truth. The smiles of heaven has changd the face of affairs. Respect and courtesy flows in upon us from all quarters. This is a picture of human life: I see the difference betwixt moveing on with the Tide of success—or sinking under a load of misfortunes. I should be glad to know the current conversation among you. I am exceeding happy in the full confidence of his Excellency General Washington, and I found ⟨that confidence⟩ to increase every hour, the more ⟨difficult⟩ and distressing our affairs grew. But thanks be to God they now are in a much better train but by no means so agreeable as I could wish. I want to get the Enemy out of the Jerseys that I may get *Liberty to come Home*.

I hope you are as happy as the state of the Times will admit. Pray dont neglect to apply to my brothers for every thing you need. If you are not fully supplied or there appears the least reluctance among the brothers let me know it and I assure you not a syllable shall ever be mentiond and I will take care that you are supplied through other channels. Heaven preserve you until my return. How is your health, how is my Son, how are my friends? Where is Nancy Vernon? Is the Doctor and she like to form a connection? I think not. Pray inform me. How is brother Bill? Where is Elihue? My best respects to him and his Wife. Pray is there harmony amongst you? Where is Griffin and his wife? Not a word have I heard from him since he left Camp—out of Sight out of mind.[2] Where do you live? Does [the] Innoculation business go on? I hope our oppera⟨tion⟩ here will soon free you from the British pirates at Rhode Island. God grant it may. The alarms they are perpetually giveing you must render life distressing. I forgot to mention in my last the death of poor Colo Hitchcock[3] who dyed of the Pleuresy at this place. He was buryed with all the honnors of War as the last mark of respect we could show him. Poor General Mercer is also dead of the wounds he receivd in the Princetown action. He was a fine companion, a sincere friend, a true patriot and a brave General. May Heaven bless his spirit with Eternal peace. Several more brave officers fell that day. Particularly one Capt Neale of the Artillery.[4] The Enemy refusd him ⟨quarter⟩ after he was wounded. He has left a poor Widow ⟨overwhelmed⟩ with grief. She is as fine a woman as ever ⟨I saw;⟩ her distress melts the hearts of all around her. [damaged] steal'd with fortitude. Such instances paints all the horror of war—beyound description.

The Tories are melting away very fast in this Country. The different treatment they meet with from the Enemy from what they expect works great reformations. This will be handed you by Capt Gouch[5] who can give you a full History of the times here. God bless you my dear Angel. Adieu

N GREENE

Billy is here and is well and hearty.[6]

ALS (NjP); damaged. Words in angle brackets from Greene, *Greene*, 1: 308–9.
  1. No "constant run" of letters has been found; the last was 30 December.
  2. The references in this paragraph are to NG's year-old son, George Washington Greene, whom he had not seen since the boy was a few months old; Nancy Vernon, a Newport friend who apparently had come to East Greenwich when the British occupied Newport; the doctor is unidentified. Elihue was a younger brother; his wife of one month was the former Jane (Jenny) Flagg. Griffin Greene was his cousin.
  3. See battle of Princeton above, vol. 1: 379n.
  4. Daniel Neil was a captain-lieutenant in the N.J. artillery.
  5. John Gooch, a Rhode Island friend, had served as a captain in the Ninth Continental Regiment throughout 1776, distinguishing himself during the battle of Mt. Washington (see above, vol. 1: 359n). In July 1777 he was appointed an assistant deputy quartermaster general for Massachusetts and later served under NG in that capacity.
  6. William Littlefield, brother of Catharine Greene. A recent good biography of Catharine is one by John F. Stegeman and Janet A. Stegeman, *Caty: A Biography of Catharine Littlefield Greene* (Providence: Rhode Island Bicentennial Foundation, 1977).

To Christopher Greene[1]

Dear Sir   Morristown [N.J.] January 20, 1777

This moment receivd your favor of the 30th of November. It has been to Philadelphia and come up from thence this morning.[2] I am much obligd to you for the account you give of family matters. Not a word have I heard from home since you left me. Great changes has taken place here. The distress and difficulties you can have no Idea off. After the loss of Fort Washington and the Enemy crost over [into the] Jerseys, everything wore the face of abject submision. The Inhabitants of New Jersey and those of Pensylvania lost all spirit. The time for which the old Troops stood engag'd expird as we were retreating through the Jerseys. Brigade after Brigade left us when the Enemy were within an hours March of us at Brunswick. Had the Enemy push't us hard they would have ruin'd us for we had not three thousand men. With this small force we made good a retreat over the Delaware where we baffled all their attempts to follow us. General Lee['s] slow motions distrest us amazeingly and to compleat our misfortune the General was taken prisoner.[3] But from that hour Providence has seem'd to smile upon us as if he meant the freedom of America should be established by Americans only. The loss of the General was great and the more so as the hearts and confidence of the People were much bound up in him. He undoubtedly is a great General but all the military knowledge is not confind to him.

His Excellency General Washington never appeard to so much advantage as in the hour of distress. With the few Troops we had and the small reenforcement we receivd of General Lees division after he was made Prisoner we made an attack on Trenton. Fortune favord us.

That and the Princeton action has put our affairs upon quite a respectable footing, but History must inform you how small the force was that this change was wrought with. I have been in three sucessful Battles this Campaign, and soon expect to be in a fourth.[4] God grant it may be victorious. I have servd my Country with as much fidelity and attention as any mortal breathing yet I am informd it is insufficient to screen me from the attacks of calumny and reproach, but conscious of virtuous intentions I despise the Shafts.[5] Happy I am in the full confidence of the General whose approbation I dayly experience. If the Army gets recruited we have nothing to fear. Our forces are equal to the Enemies in point of bravery and activity and we shall out number them by far.

The Hessians and British Troops are geting into a fine quarrel. Deserters are dayly come in. The Enemy are decreast within a month past near three thousand men, and the rest begins to get uneasy and dissatisfied. I pray God Almighty to multiply their discontent.

The Congress have given General Washington full powers to do and act as he thinks proper, to make such establishments and take such measures as the safety and interest of the States may require. Had this been done some months ago, the American Affairs would have been upon a very different footing.[6]

I thank you for your friendly offers of waiting upon Mrs Greene here. I thank my stars you did not set out as her comeing must have added to my distresses. I hope youl take care of her and render her situation as comfortable at home as possible. God only knows whether I shall ever see you or her again, but let your friendship for me be extended to her and her offspring during my absence. The Quakers have taken a very dishonorable part in Pensylvania and I fear will smart for their folly. I have never heard from Capt Garsia.[7] Pray write me a full History of family matters. The Enemy have taken possession of Newport, I learn, but you may expect to be rid of them soon if not already as I [am] well inform'd they are recald. God grant it may be true. If you or any of the brothers can find time or have curiosity enough to lead you this way your faces will meet a hearty welcome. We are well assurd a French War is inevetable—in a few months[?]. I hope to see the American Affairs upon a far more respectable footing than they ever were upon.

My love to all freinds, to your Wife and all my brothers.

This will be handed you by Capt Gouch [Gooch] who can give you a History of all the affairs of the Army from the defeat of Fort Washington to this hour, haveing been a spectator to most of the movements and in several skirmishes. I am with kind wishes for the health and happiness of you and family. Your sincere and Affectionate brother

N GREENE

NB I enclose you a Crisis[8] and some papers from Virginia. See their spirit.

ALS (MWA).
    1. Addressee not given, but brother Christopher was the only family member to have visited him—in New York in September 1776.
    2. Letter not found.
    3. On Gen. Lee's "slow motions" and capture, see above, vol. 1: 367n and 369n.
    4. He refers to Harlem Heights, Trenton, and Princeton (vol. 1: 300–302 and 377–80). The expected fourth battle—an attack against the British outpost at Brunswick—did not come about. Although Washington was unwilling to call an end to the campaign of 1776–77 "unless the Enemy quits the Jerseys," the departure of large numbers of his troops ruled out such an offensive. (Fitzpatrick, GW, 7: 43)
    5. He had come under severe criticism for the loss of Fts. Washington and Lee. See above, vol. 1: 352n and 363n.
    6. Washington had been empowered to offer bounties and to change the system of promotion in hopes of luring more troops to stay. He was also authorized by Congress to raise sixteen additional regiments for the Continental service (JCC, 6: 1043–46).
    7. John Garzia was a captain-lieutenant in the R.I. Artillery. (Heitman, Register)
    8. This would have been a copy of Paine's Crisis Number One. See above, NG to Paine, 9 January.

To Governor Nicholas Cooke of Rhode Island

Dear sir   Morris Town [N.J.] January the 23d 1777
    I am exceeding unhappy to hear of your resolution of raising Troops at the expence of the State before your proportion of the Continental Regiments are completed.[1] Forming of new Regiments only serve to burthen the State with expence without giving it any additional strength. There is not a State upon the Continent whose interest and happiness depends so much on a union with the others as yours. You are the most exposed and the least capable of making a seperate defence, consequently 'tis your interest to cultivate every measure that may tend to form the union of strength, and it must be considered bad policy to give an example to others from which you can derive little or no advantage and that may prove so ruinous in its consequences. Suppose for instance every State was to neglect the completion of the Continental Regiments and prepare for their own internal security. Where is the State that's able to withstand the Enemies collective force? If the Continent had Troops enough on foot to baffle all the Enemies attempts and were located to particular States, they must inevitably fall a sacrafice for want of a power of drawing the whole collective force together. You have no reason to hope if you neglect the general interest and take measures for your own particular safety but that others will do the same, and it is a folly to expect that Troops rais'd for the defence of any particular State will enter into the service of the States in general. It is in vain to expect more of Soldiers than they are bound by Contract to execute. The resource [source] of all our evils has been by taking measures from

speculative Principles rather than from real life. The policy of the States have been pregnant with many evils by rateing our Patriotism too high. This kind of policy have distressed the army beyond description, and if I mistake not this measure of yours has a direct tendency to continue things in the same Channel; it may afford you a temporary relief, but never can remove the principal evil.

Divine Providence has given a very favorable turn to affairs and at an Hour when People least expected it. *Now* is the happy Hour to complete the Continental establishment. Every State to the Southward are exerting themselves to fill up their proportion. Not a moment shou'd be lost; if the Regiments dont fill by voluntary inlistments they must be drafted. I hope the powers of Government are strong enough to do it. I have not the least shadow of doubt upon my mind of the success of the War if the different States raise their men, but on that the whole depends. I hope the Cause is not less righteous nor opposition less necessary than it was at the commencement of this dispute. It was a folly to embark in the Cause, and sink under the weight of a few misfortunes. He that goes to War and always expects a flowing Tide is a novice in the Art and ignorant of human affairs. Our sufferings, tho' great, bear no proportion to our expectations at first.

Our resources are daily increasing. We have now a fine nursery of officers whose Judgments are daily ripening by experience and observation. A systematical Plan is form'd for the exertion of our whole strength. Magazines and Military Stores of every kind are forming and form'd to supply the wants of the Army. If it was prudent to engage in this War without any of those advantages, how foolish must our Conduct appear to despair at an Hour when we have much to hope and little to fear. I must confess I did not expect to find the Americans such Slaves to contingencies, but more especially New England, and in particular Rhode Island. Such a depression of Spirit under misfortunes and elevation upon successes betrays a want of Principle fortitude that I wou'd fain flatter myself were the foundation of our opposition. Let any Man examine the history of any War in Europe and compare ours with theirs and see if there has anything happened different from the common course of events that attend every War. Nay, I think we have abundant cause to bless God that our sufferings have not been greater than they have. A General Officer is in a very disagreeable situation, subject to the censure and reproach of every little dirty Politician ignorant of every circumstance necessary to form a right Judgment; but such is the disposition of Mankind that success only marks the man of wisdom while the unfortunate are execrated without any allowances for Providential interpositions or human accidents.

I am very sorry to hear of the distraction and confusion that prevails in your Councils and Public measures. The liberality with which you confer Favors on some and fix Stigmas on others must make Men of real merit somewhat cautious how they put themselves in a situation where they may be reduced from the highest pitch of Glory to the Lowest state of contempt. It was ever the policy of the Romans to be cautious whom they trusted and how they disgraced those they had once honored.

I saw a Letter from one Malmedy, a French Gentleman, to his Excellency General Washington whom you have appointed a Brigadier General, and a copy of a Letter from General Lee to your State recommending him for chief Colonels Commission.[2] General Lees Letter contains some infamous and very illiberal reflections upon the Genius of all the New England States. However just the observations with respect to particular appointments tis certainly very unjust when applied to the whole body of the People. There are as many men of Spirit, activity, and understanding in New England as in any part of the World, according to their numbers. The novelty of things of foreign growth often makes us rate them above those of more solid worth of [our] own production. ⟨The gentleman that General Lee recommended, may be deserving, and possess every quality ascribed to him; but I must con⟩fess I have not the highest veneration for the Generals recommendation. His temper scarce admits of a proper medium to form a just estimate of People and things. His approbation and execration depend often upon trifles; besides, the General dont know the Power he has over the Americans and consequently is not cautious enough in his recommendations not to abuse it.

Some amongst you, I am told, are uncharitable enough to charge the Army with a design of protracting the War for their own private advantage. The Bosom that can harbour such a thought must be very ill principled and ignorant of our sufferings. For my own part, Heaven knows there is not a man in America that woud more sincerely rejoice at the close of this unhappy dispute than myself, neither have I a single wish to continue in service a moment longer than the interest and happiness of my Country require it. I wou'd freely give place to any man that shou'd be found more deserving. I am conscious of having faithfully discharged my duty to the utmost of my power, and altho' I have not been able to command success I have religiously endeavoured to deserve it. I am happy in the confidence of the General whose merit and worth cannot be too high rated; yet I am told there are some ungodly tongues among you (whose greatest Virtues dont equal the Generals very Vices) give themselves a latitude of censure.

Ever since the Trenton affair we have had a continual train of successes. The Lord seems to have smote the Enemy with a Panic. I wish our strength wou'd admit a proper improvement but our delicate situation requires the utmost ⟨caution⟩ and prudence. The Enemy ⟨are near⟩ three thousand ⟨weaker than they were⟩ a month ago. ⟨Our parties⟩ Have daily Skirmishes in which we have been allways successful. His Excellency has Ordered General Heath to advance on New York to cooperate with us, the result of which I have not learnt, but we have a rumour it is attended with success.³ General Spencer and Arnold⁴ are with you e'er this. I long to hear your situation. I expect General Knox will pass through Providence. I beg leave to recommend him to your warmest Friendship as a most deserving man. His spirit, military knowledge, and ripeness of Judgment is inferior to very few if any in America. I shall close this long Letter with strongly recommending the filling the Continental Regiments immediately. I am with the greatest sincerity and truth Your most obedt And very hble sert

NATH GREENE

LS (R-Ar). Words in angle brackets from Bartlett, *Records,* 8: 115–17.

1. In a resolution of 16 September 1776, Congress had called for the recruitment of eighty-eight battalions (regiments) to serve in the Continental army "during the present war," of which Rhode Island was to furnish two regiments. (*JCC,* 5: 762–63)

This precipitate letter was based on misinformation, but it was a faithful expression of his nationalistic convictions. Since Washington had written Cooke a few days earlier in the same vein (although less caustically), it is possible that NG wrote at the urging of Washington. (Fitzpatrick, *GW,* 7: 42–44). NG addressed the subject in more muted tones in a letter to Cooke, 1 February, below. The misunderstanding was resolved with Cooke's letter to NG of 7 February and NG's response of 6 March, below.

2. Francois Lellorquis de Malmedy, a French volunteer, had been brevetted a major in the Continental army in September 1776. In December 1776 he was appointed chief engineer and director of defense in the R.I. militia, with the rank of brigadier general. After holding the posts for only a few months, he sought unsuccessfully to reenter the Continental service with his Rhode Island rank but finally settled for a colonelcy. (Bartlett, *Records,* 8: 64; Balch, *French,* p. 174; Washington to Malmedy, 16 May 1777, Fitzpatrick, *GW,* 8: 68–70. Lee's letter to Cooke of 7 December 1776 is in Bartlett, *Records,* 8: 111–12.)

3. It was, instead, a fiasco. Gen. William Heath, left to guard the Hudson Highlands with some 3,300 men, was ordered by Washington in early January to create a diversion toward New York City in order to draw some of Howe's troops from New Jersey. With three brigades assembled before Ft. Independence, he demanded the garrison's surrender under dire threats—threats that proved to be empty. After a week the greatly outnumbered British garrison came out and drove the Americans back. Washington, embarrassed and indignant, was never again to trust Heath with a field command. On this affair see Freeman, *GW,* 4: 384, and Washington to Heath, 4 February 1777, Fitzpatrick, *GW,* 7: 99–100.

4. Benedict Arnold (1741–1801), the Connecticut-born great-grandson of an early Rhode Island governor of the same name, is of course best known for his vast ambitions and eventual treason. It should be kept in mind, however, that he was also one of the most capable field commanders in the Continental army. His actions in Canada and in the Danbury raid demonstrated both his courage and his ability, qualities that were to help overcome Burgoyne at Saratoga later in the year. For a scholarly study of Arnold, see Willard Wallace, *Traitorous Hero: The Life and Fortunes of Benedict Arnold* (New York: Harper and Row, 1954).

The British had occupied Newport in force on 8 December 1776. In response to Gov. Cooke's appeal for reinforcements to prevent the takeover of the whole of Narragansett Bay, Washington sent Spencer and Arnold to organize the defenses, but he did not send the troops that Cooke requested. (Cooke to Washington, 8 December 1776, and Washington to Cooke, 21 December 1776, Bartlett, *Records*, 8: 112–13; see also Freeman, *GW*, 4: 285.)

To Governor Nicholas Cooke of Rhode Island

Morristown [N.J.]

Dear sir   January 28, 1777

By a Letter from Col Lamb of the Artillery I am informed that all the New England States have come to into a resolution to give an additional *Bounty of ten Pounds* to every private that engages in the Continental service during the War.[1] The plan is charitable but I fear not political as it will affect the raising the Troops in other States. Every State in taking any public measure shou'd pay some regard to the affect it will have upon others least the measure should be more prejudicial than beneficial to the Community. If the powers of Government had been strong enough to draft the Men it would have been much the more eligible, the Regiments would have been soon compleated, and every man left at Liberty to come himself or procure one in his stead. For my own part I can see no injustice or impropriety in drafting men where it is general. I am glad there is no augmentation of pay as well as Bounty. Troops upon different pay will never serve harmoniously together. I am not a little afraid that the Soldiery will think they may as well have a hundred as fifty Dollars and refuse to engage accordingly. Shou'd that be the case you will be under the necessity of drafting the Men at last as the service requires the Regiments to be compleated as soon as possible.

Col Hitchcocks death leaves a vacancy in that Regiment that will be necessary to fill up. Col. Angel stands in the Line of Promotion. Captn Olney will make either a good Lt. Col. or Major.[2] There is Thayer, Ward and Tappan, all old Captains and deserving Characters.[3] These are all exchanged and at liberty to engage again. Major Sherburne is appointed Col of a Regiment in the last Voted sixteen Battalions ordered to be raised in addition to the eighty eight. Wm Bradford is appointed Major of Sherburnes Regt. Lt. Col. Greene is not yet exchanged.[4] Whether he is desirous of serving again I am not able to say. His merit and intentions are too well known in the State to make it necessary to say anything upon the Subject. I shou'd recommend the Vacancies below Field Officers to be fill'd by the Field Officers of the Regt. They have the most at stake and consequently will be careful to have none but deserving Characters appointed. I hope the Assembly will take some Vigorous measures to compleat the Battalion.

I am well informed by Col Cox, a Gentleman of Philadelphia, that the Enemy left [at] their evacuation of Elizabeth Town a large number of Leases[5] wherein every Man that took Protection within sixty Days, agreeable to the Proclamation issued the 30th November last by Lord and General Howe, were to hold their Lands under the Crown, And to give his Farmers (by him appointed) the refusal of all the Grain and other produce at certain prices to be fixd by him, and every Man that sold his Estate in any State to pay one fourth part of the Sale for the benefit of the Crown. Every man that did not submit within the sixty Days, his Estate to be confiscated and the Proprietors to hold them immediately under the Crown during his pleasure. A strict search is making after the Leases but as the information did not come to the General for some Days after the Enemy left the Town I fear the Tories remaining there have destroyed [them?]. This seems to resemble the ancient Feudal tenures. From Col Cox's Character I have no doubt of the truth of the information altho' we may not be able to prove it by the Leases which I am hoping will still come to light.

The Enemy remain much in the same situation as when I wrote last. I inspected our Posts at Bound Brook yesterday. Just as I arrived an Express came from the advanced Guard that the Enemy were advancing but from a more strict inquiry it appeared false. Some People who came out of Brunswick say the Enemy were going on to Staten Island. I wish it may be true or that we had more Men to drive them away which would be far more agreeable.

The Southern States are filling up their Regiments as fast as possible. I hope N. E[ngland] will be among the foremost. I've nothing more to ad but am with the greatest Respect Yours &c

NATH GREENE

LS (David Coblentz, Chase City, Va., 1978)

1. A committee of New England delegates meeting in Providence in late December 1776 recommended to their state governments a "bounty of £10, and a blanket, each year, while in service" (Bartlett, *Records*, 8: 103–4). Rhode Island, accordingly, raised its existing bounty of £6 to conform to the recommendations.

2. Israel Angell (1740–1832), a cooper from Providence, was a major in the R.I. Army of Observation when NG took command in May 1775. He had already been appointed to succeed Hitchcock as commanding colonel of the regiment before NG wrote this letter. Angell distinguished himself, as did the regiment, for heroic action at Brandywine, Red Bank, and Springfield, N.J. (*DAB*) Jeremiah Olney is identified above, vol. 1: 153.

3. Simeon Thayer, Samuel Ward, Jr., and John Topham had marched with Arnold to Quebec in 1775, where they were captured and held as prisoners for months. Thayer (1737–1800), a Providence wigmaker who had fought in the French and Indian War, kept a journal that was to become an important source for the history of Arnold's expedition. He was named major in Angell's regiment in February 1777, but he was not exchanged until July 1777. Thayer is especially remembered for his desperate defense of Ft. Mifflin later in 1777, but he took part also in several other major engagements—including Monmouth, where he lost an eye. Thayer's journal of the

Canadian expedition was printed in RIHS, *Coll.* 6 (1867): 1–45. A biographical sketch is on pp. 70–80.

John Topham, chosen captain of the First R.I. Regiment in February 1777, eventually rose to colonel of the regiment. After the war he served in the R.I. Assembly. Samuel Ward, Jr., was NG's long-time friend.

4. William Bradford, son of the deputy governor and formerly an aide of Gen. Charles Lee, had been made major of Sherburne's regiment just before NG wrote. NG's third cousin, Christopher, was not exchanged until the summer of 1777.

5. No such leases have come to light. The Howe brothers' proclamation of 30 November to which NG refers made no threats of confiscating estates. Positive and conciliatory in tone, the proclamation in essence simply extended to all Americans who may have been guilty of treason a "full and free pardon" if they would only declare before a suitable British officer that they would "remain in a peaceable obedience to his Majesty." The pardon, moreover, covered "all forfeitures, attainders, and penalties for the same." (The proclamation is printed in Force, *Archives*, [5], 3: 927–28) Most of the five thousand odd people who took advantage of the proclamation did so in December before the battle of Trenton—at a time when British victory seemed assured. Their loyalist neighbors were bitterly critical of the proclamation—not only because it dealt no punishment to such treasonable offenders, but in a sense rewarded them by returning any land they might have forfeited. Some of the forfeited land had in the meantime come under loyalist ownership in one fashion or another. What, the loyalists might have asked, were the rewards for loyalty? With British withdrawal to the eastern part of New Jersey (following the battle of Princeton), many of those in the rest of the state who had declared their loyalty to the king in December were equally receptive to Washington's proclamation of 25 January. (See note, NG to Elisha Boudinot, 17 February 1777, below.) If leases such as Col. Cox described to NG had actually existed, they did not have the blessing of Gen. Howe. Reaction to the Howes' proclamation is covered in Gruber, *Howe Brothers*, pp. 146–47, 149, 156.

Col. John Cox was later to serve under NG as one of his two assistant quartermasters. See below, NG to Joseph Reed, 9 March 1778.

To Governor Nicholas Cooke of Rhode Island

[Morristown, N.J., 1 February 1777. Repeats in more moderate language the criticism he made to Cooke, 23 January above, on Rhode Island recruiting practices.[1] "What will Congress think? What will the General [Washington] say?" To deputy Gov. Bradford's[2] criticism of his recommendations on R.I. officers, he declares with two exceptions he followed recommendations of R.I. colonels. He has not "one relation to serve"; only the "honor and interest of the State." From RIHS, *Coll*, 6 (1867): 183–85.]

1. His criticism was still based on misinformation; see below, NG to Cooke, 7 February.

2. William Bradford (1729–1808), a descendant of the first governor of Plymouth Colony, left medicine for the law. Prominent in the R.I. Committee of Correspondence, he was made deputy governor under Cooke. He was speaker of the R.I. Assembly for some years, later a U.S. senator. His quarrel with NG is obscure. Perhaps he was annoyed that his son was not advanced beyond the rank of major at this time. (See below, NG to Jacob Greene, 2 February.)

To Catharine Greene

[Morristown, N.J., 1 February 1777. The enemy has prevented his coming home. Wishes her a "safe and happy time" during her confinement.[1] No need to fear enemy in Newport since they will be called to defend New Jersey.[2] Excerpt from Parke-Bernet *Catalog* No. 1756, (1957)]

1. Martha Washington Greene was born mid-March.
2. He was overly optimistic; Newport was not evacuated until October 1779.

To Jacob Greene[1]

Dear Sir   Morristown [N.J.] Feb 2, 1777
    I have wrote you and wrote you again but to very little purpose, for I can hear nothing from you in return.[2] To what cause am I to attribute it, to want of opportunity or inclination? The former I can hardly suppose, the latter I am unwilling to beleive. Not a letter of yours if any you have wrote has come to hand for above three months past.
    I can get but an unintelligible account from Rhode Island of your Proceedings either Legislative or military. However I hear too much of the former to be satisfied. I am well informd you are raising Troops for the defence of the State and neglecting the Continental Regiments. I must confess I am ignorant of the Reasons that could induce you to take such a measure. I wish you may not have reason to repent it. The General is greatly dissatisfied with the plan and thinks it an indirect breach of the Union. The measure is calculated to burthen the State with a great expence without affording it any additional security. You and every other man in the State that has the least acquaintance with the number of Inhabitants in the Government must be sensible that the four Regiments cannot be fild. Your propotion of the Eighty Eight Battallions will be demanded in the most peremtory manner by the Congress and the General, and if they are not furnisht cannot you expect the other States will send their forces for your protection when you neglect to raise your quota for the reciprocal defence of the whole States. I know not who was the author of this premature plan, but be he who he may he is a short sighted Politician who views things only for a day.[3]
    I am told Govenor Bradford found great fault with the Officers that were Recommended. The extent of his plan is the promotion of his own family; gratify him in that and all things will go smoothly on, but disappoint him there and he would defeat the measure if the Salvation of America depended on it. Such contracted spirits and selfish Souls are fit for nothing but the purposes of gain. I am sure if I

know my own heart I have not a single wish in the appointment of the Officers different from the honnor and interest of the State.[4]

I am told the Govenor threw out some reflections in the House, that it was adeem'd partial recommendation, that it was not General Washington[s] but mine. I wish to know the Particulars; if it please God to return me safe home again I will call him to an account. I will not be the subject of his reflection undeservedly. I am sure no man breathing could take more pains to fix upon the best officers than I did. There was no particulars that I wanted to gratify. General [James M.] Varnum, Col [Daniel] Hitchcock, Col [Christopher] Lippitt and Col Comstok[5] recommended out of their respective Regiments; such as they reccommended, such I recommended and never named in no instance except [Silas] Talbot and [Elijah] Lewis, unless Major [William] Blodget commited any blunders in copying from the original Papers.

There was a small action yesterday near the Enemies lines between a forageing Party of theirs and a Reconnoitering Party of ours. The particulars I have not learnt, but our People drove them off the ground notwithstanding the Enemy had superior numbers and several Field Pieces and we none.

The People of Providence I am told were most horidly frighted, few in the Town but that flew out into the Country and went to purchaseing farms, crying all the way *Save us, Save us*, from the fear of the Lord and the Terrors of How[e]. Those great Politicians that march and meet on the Bridge I am told had formd a resolution to dismiss the Congress and the Continental Army—excellent Policy, wonderful councellors.[6] You have raisd the Interest of money I hear in Providence. I wish you may be more careful in varying from the general plan. I fear the absurd and ridiculous plans pursueing throughout N E[ngland] will render them ridiculous throughout America.[7] Pray be particular in your next Letter. All things goes on smoothly; the Southern States are raising their men very fast. The Enemy are in great distress. I have no doubt of freeing America in Six months of the British Pestilence if the respective States furnishes their men. I must beg your care of my family. God knows what will become of Mrs Green in her situation. My love to all freinds, to your wife and Children. Give me a history of the Navigation matters.[8] Yours affec

N GREEN

ALS (MWA).

1. The contents of this unaddressed letter point unmistakably to brother Jacob.
2. His last known letter to Jacob was February 1776.
3. For background see above, NG to Cooke, 23 January and 1 February.
4. The Bradford matter is also discussed above, NG to Cooke, 1 February.
5. Adam Comstock was lieutenant colonel of the First R.I. Regiment from August 1776 to April 1778 (Heitman, *Register*).

6. The sarcasm is directed toward the reaction to British occupation of Newport.

7. The "plans" were either for bounties (see above, NG to Cooke, 28 January, and below, Cooke to NG, 7–9 February) or price regulations.

8. The reference is to privateers owned by NG and brothers. (For the extent of their joint ventures, see below, Griffin to NG, 28 November 1779.) Many army officers invested money in privateers, not excepting Washington. (See, for example, Fitzpatrick, GW, 10: 61.)

From Governor Nicholas Cooke of Rhode Island

Sir   [Providence, R.I.], Feb. 7 [9][1] 1777

Yours of the 23rd ult. has been recd and laid before the General Assembly, and they regret their not advising General Washington at the time they did the Genl Congress, of the reasons and motives which urged them to a Measure which (we hope thro' wrong information) his excellency holds in an unfavorable light, and which has drawn upon them your severest censure.[2] However, as they are conscious of the Rectitude of their intentions, they are prepared to sustain the weight of hasty and unmerited reproofs, and able notwithstanding the perplexed state of Affairs to give sufficient reasons for the Measures they have adopted.

And in order that you may yet be undeceived They will state the Motives of their conduct, and from which they think it justified.

You are not unacquainted with the Powerful Armament that invaded this little State: (not less than 7,000 Land forces and a Number of Ships of Force and many Transports);[3] you know the Extensive Coast which at such a time it was necessary should be defended, and on many parts of which they could have thrown their whole force in a very few hours. Unprovided as we were, we did every thing in our power for defence. Every man able to bear Arms was called out to duty, and every precaution taken which the Nature and circumstances of things would permit. They were sensible of the impracticablility of keeping Militia (drawn suddenly from their homes at so rigid a season and for such a length of time as Necessity might require) Embodied, and in the Field; the distressed Situation of the Continental Army and the Impossibillity of obtaining relief from them; these were considerations not a little embarrassing to those who had all the Horrors of War, and the prospect of Instant destruction before them, and will account for the subsequent proceedings, without recurring to a regular Systematic design of introducing innovations or making a separate defence.

⟨In this situation, when it was impracticable to fill the Continental battalions, the Assembly set on foot two regiments of seven hundred and fifty men, each; and one regiment of artillery, of three hundred men, to serve for fifteen months. The following is the form of the enlistment of the non-commissioned officers and privates:

"I, the subscriber, do hereby solemnly engage and enlist myself as a soldier in the pay of the state of Rhode Island and Providence Plantations, for the preservation of the liberties of America, and the defence of the United States in general, and of this state in particular, from the day of my enlistment, for and during the term of fifteen months, unless sooner discharged by the General Assembly; and I hereby promise to submit myself to all the orders and regulations of the army; and faithfully to observe and obey all such orders as I shall receive from time to time, from my officers."

And the following is the clause in the commission issued to the officers:

"And in case of an invasion or assault of a common enemy to infest or disturb this, or any other of the said states, you are to alarm and gather together the———under your command, or any part, thereof, as you shall deem sufficient; and therewith to the utmost of your skill and ability, you are to resist, expel, kill and destroy them, in order to preserve the lives, liberties and properties of the good people of this, and the other United States."

Consequently, those regiments are as much held and designed to do duty in every part of the United States as the Continental battalions; and to render them effectually so, they are by act of government put under the command of General Spencer, and the other generals of the Continental army. And when Congress shall have ordered them into their service, there will be no other difference between them, than that the former are enlisted for fifteen months, and the latter for three years, or during the war.

Early information of the footing upon which these troops are raised, was given to our delegate in Congress, who tells us in a letter of the 7th ultimo, that he had laid the same before the Congress, and that the measures we had taken gave him great satisfaction; and I am extremely sorry it had not been also immediately transmitted to Your Excellency, as I am persuaded, in that case, you would have entertained a very different opinion of this measure, and been convinced that it was adopted from necessity alone; and not with the most distant idea of our making a local or separate defence, or of obstructing the enlistments into the Continental battalions.[4]

It is true, that it hath had a tendency in some degree, to cause such obstruction, which was very early obviated by an order permitting enlistments from those troops into the Continental battalions. In consequence of which, Captain Thayer has, in a short time, enlisted forty men out of one of those regiments.

I will now inform Your Excellency of the measures taken by this state to fill up the two Continental battalions assigned by Congress as our quota of the eighty-eight battalions first ordered to be raised.

We have filled up the greater part of the vacancies in them, and enclose you a list of the officers appointed, who are directed to exert themselves in recruiting. We have also given a bounty of £16, in addition to the encouragement given by Congress; and engaged to furnish each man, in behalf of the Continent, with arms, accoutrements, a blanket and knapsack.[5]

The Assembly will make a short adjournment to try the effect of this great encouragement; and in case these measures fail of the hoped-for success, will make still greater efforts to fill those battalions.⟩

You may be assured that the Subjects of this State have the highest veneration for the inestimable General Washington, and a becoming respect for the Brave and worthy Generals and Commanders under him, and cannot concieve on what the suggestions contained in your Letter concerning him are founded; and request you will give us the Authors of such infamous insinuations that a proper enquiry may be had, and condign punishment inflicted upon such base Calumniators.

Hoping that time, Patience and a dispassionate enquiry will set things in their true light, they Congratulate and rejoice with you on the late, almost unhoped successes of the American Arms in which the interpositions of Divine Providence very legibly appear. They fervently wish the same to continue until the Enemies of America are confounded and exterminated from her Shores, her Inhabitants restored to Peace in Liberty and Safety, and her brave and worthy Generals returned to their Families and friends, crowned with Glory and surrounded with the Blessings of Heaven and of Freemen. In a becoming confidence that their wishes will be granted in due time, they will continue chearfully to contribute everything in their Power in support of every Measure calculated to effect that desirable issue.

Dr (R-Ar). Draft drawn up on 7 February by a committee of the R.I. Assembly, which instructed Cooke to send a copy over his signature to NG and to include a portion of his 9 February letter to Washington. That portion, shown in angle brackets, is reprinted from Bartlett, *Records*, 8: 140–41.

1. See source note above.

2. See above, NG to Cooke, 23 January and 1 February for background.

3. British troops landed at Newport on 8 December 1776. Cooke's figures were too high.

4. Delegate William Ellery's letter of 7 January (Staples, *R.I.*, 115–16) undoubtedly referred to Cooke's letter of 22 December, in which he stated that the legislature had ordered two regiments of 750 each to be raised. (Ibid., 108–10) There is no record of Ellery's having laid it before Congress, however. If the letter had been misplaced, it could account for some misunderstanding about recruiting on the part of Washington and Greene.

5. The R.I. bounty was £10, not £16. See note, NG to Cooke, 28 January.

To the Rev. Mr. James Caldwell[1]

Dear Sir   Morris Town [N.J.], Febuary 11, 1777

Your favor of the 8 and 10 are before me.[2] In answer to your first, respecting the conditions upon which the light Horse are to be raised, I can only say the Continental Congress have not fixt upon any certain conditions. They have the matter now under consideration. Whatever rank, pay or provision is fixt upon for the Horse in general, such will be the pay of the Company the Doctor is to raise. His Excellency desires that he would not get any but good men and Horses, the Horses to be valued and the men properly accoutered, an account of the Cost and charges to be kept, a warrant for the payment of which will be given.

The General is not inclind to raise a company of light Horse upon the plan you propose but is willing to make satisfaction for the services of those that have been employd in that way, providing a proper account with sufficient Vouchers are produced.[3]

With respect to exempting the militia from service to thrash their Grain, General Maxwell can better Judge of the propriety and Utillity of the measure.[4] His Excellency therefore refers you to him, but at the same time would observe as this is a critical period it may be dangerous to open a door for the Militia falling off. His Excellency thinks we had better suffer the loss of [a] little Grain than reduce our strength.

I observe your remarks upon the Army on the other side of the North River.[5] I am at a loss whether you mean to impeach the troops or the General through the Troops. If the charge is against the former, they can be off no use to us here, for if they will not fight there, neither will they here; but if the charge is against the General I would only observe that under the cloud of misfortunes the same reproaches lay against the commander in chief as now lies against that army. But you see that time has proved the wisdom and prudence of the Generals delays. I would not be understood to mean to draw a paralel between the men. I would further observe for your satisfaction that a considerable part of the Troops on the other side are ordered over here, and now on their march to join us: *but all this under the Rose*.

My dear Sir, You may rest assured the routing the Troops from the Jerseys is a most desirable object with the General; but who can form so good a Judgment of the practibillity as he who knows the strength on both sides? This is a critical area. The New Army in its infancy, we unable to support misfortunes, great caution is necessary to preserve our standing. Did you but know the real situation of things you would applaud the General's prudence. I shall only add that nothing but the fullest conviction of your prudence and Zeal would have induced me to unboosom myself with so much freedom. I am, with the sincerest regard, your friend and very humble Servant.

N GREENE

ALS (NjP).

1. Caldwell (1734–81), a Princeton graduate and militant clergyman, had used his pulpit in Elizabeth, N.J., before the war for patriotic sermons. As chaplain of Dayton's N.J. brigade, he was known as the "Soldier Parson." At this time he was an assistant deputy quartermaster general. He met his death at the hands of an American sentry at Elizabethtown in 1781. (DAB)

2. Letters not found.

3. It is not clear why NG, instead of an aide, should speak for Washington in this letter. In May 1777 Congress reimbursed Caldwell for "4,873 54/90 dollars" for "horse hire and expenses" of an Essex County company of light horse. (JCC, 8: 393; Caldwell's petition is in PCC, Item 136.)

4. William Maxwell (1733–96), born in Ireland of Scottish descent, came to America at age fourteen. He was a member of the N.J. Provincial Congress in May 1775. As a brigadier general, he had just taken command of four N.J. regiments. Later in the year, he would see action at Brandywine and Germantown. (DAB)

5. The reference is to Heath's proposed attack on Ft. Independence. See note, NG to Cooke, 23 January, above.

To Elisha Boudinot[1]

Baskenridge [N.J.] Head Quarters[2]
Dear Sir
Feby 17th 1777

Yours of this Day I rec'd, the contents whereof I shall strictly observe.[3] The indulgence granted to Jonathan Sears is now cancelled and you will please to treat him as you may think proper.[4] His Excellency does not mean to deviate from the plain words of the Proclamation. Whether he is acquainted with the Law of the State or not is a matter I am ignorant off. Any Orders from His Excellency General Washington must be particularly attended to.[5] If he has Ordered any Person to carry their Furniture with them who intend to withdraw themselves within the Enemies Lines they must be allowed; otherwise no more than their wearing Apparell. Pray keep a *Strict watch* on the Tories and treat the Scoundrels as they deserve. I am affectionately Yours

NATH GREENE

Cy (RPJCB).

1. Elisha Boudinot (1749–1819) is often confused with his older brother, Elias. During the war he held several civil posts in New Jersey and served in the militia. It is not clear in what capacity he had written NG; he was clerk of the Circuit Courts (N.J. Archives, 2: 34), but he also provided the army with intelligence as seen in his letter of 23 May below. See references to him in George Adams Boyd, Elias Boudinot: Patriot and Statesman, 1740–1821 (Princeton: Princeton University Press, 1952).

2. On NG's move to Basking Ridge, see below, NG to Washington, 20 February.

3. Letter not found.

4. Jonathan Sayre was an active loyalist in New Jersey at this time. (E. Alfred Jones, "The Loyalists of New Jersey in the Revolution," NJHS, *Proc.* 11 (1926): 488.

5. On 25 January, Washington countered the Howes' 30 November proclamation with one calling on all men (except those "conscientiously scrupulous against bearing arms") to defend their country, while giving those who had sworn loyalty to the king thirty days in which to choose between allegiance to the United States or withdrawing "themselves and families within the enemy's lines" (Fitzpatrick, *GW*, 7: 61–62. On the Howes' proclamation, see above, NG to Cooke, 28 January.)

Some fears were expressed that the proclamation usurped the legislative and executive powers of the states. Abraham Clark of New Jersey, a hard-nosed foe of military rule, offered a motion in Congress that would have prevented the proclamation from interfering with the "punishment of Traitors" under state laws. After considering the motion, a committee announced through its spokesman, John Adams, that the proclamation did not interfere with civil laws but "considering the situation of the Army was prudent and necessary." (*JCC*, 7: 95, 165–66; Fitzpatrick, *GW*, 7: 61n)

To George Washington

Dear Sir   Baskenridge [N.J.] Feb 20, 1777[1]

Your favor of the 18th came to hand last Evening.[2] I shall pay due attention to its contents, but I fear my situation is too remote to carry on a communication of intelligence to advantage. Ever since I have been here I have been revolving the matter over and over in my mind respecting the subject of intelligence. Nothing more elligible has occurd than the plan your Excellency suggests, but I hope the old channel of intelligence is not yet shut up.[3] Day before yesterday I was at Bounbrook and Qu'bbletown: there I met with Mr Lowrey the Commisary[4] who inform'd me the same Person that was employd by Col [Joseph] Read [Reed] and Col [John] Cox was expected out that day with intelligence, the purport of which he promisd to forward to you immediately.

I transmited a Return by Major [John] Clarke yesterday to Head Quarters with the strength of the Brigades and the places they are posted at. Lord Sterling has but few Troops in his Brigade except MacCoys[5] Regt and they are all at Quibbletown.

Lord Sterling, General Johnson[6] and myself will endeavor to fix upon the best places to collect the troops at. Little more can be done than agree upon proper alarm posts and make the Troops and ourselves acquainted with the ground. In order to make the Troops acquainted with the Ground, I propose to send down Scouting parties dayly, not so much for the annoyance of the Enemy, as to get them acquainted with the Ground, and to keep them employed.

Should the Enemy advance my plan would be to attack them with light Troops on the Rear and upon the flanks Avoiding a General Engagement unless we can attack them on some advantageous ground, where they cant bring but part of their Troops to act.

I am unacquainted with General Putnams strength but if he has any considerable force, Brunswick should be his object by all means.

But I must confess I think General Putnam is in much more danger than we. I cannot help still apprehending Philadelphia to be their object, the consequence to them and injury to us is infinitely greater than beating up our Quarters here and fighting us on such disadvantageous Ground.

If the Enemy have no expectation of crossing the Delaware I should think they would move toward Trentown to draw our forces on the flat Country; there they may give us a cappital blow, here they cannot. In the flat Country their artillery is off great importance; here it is not. There Regular Troops can act to advantage; here they cannot; at least they have not that superiority here as they would have there. Our Troops are almost all irregular and they know it. If they consult their own interest they will avoid fighting us upon our Ground that we are acquainted with and they ignorant off. Upon the whole, I think General How will find it difficult to move any way; but if he moves at all I am confident it will be towards Philadelphia. But notwithstanding I will make the best preparation our situation will admit.[7] Lord Sterling is going below tomorrow to endeavor to fix upon some plan to get intelligence. I will meet General Sullivan at the same time and form a plan for the purpose of supporting each other.

We sent down forty Waggons after forage Yesterday. Their success I have not heard but they are mostly returnd. This moment the Quartermaster came in and reports they all got full loads and have returnd safe. They were within a mile of the Enemies Quarters.

The Small Pox prevails amongst the Troops here.[8] I am with great respect your Excellencies most obedient and very humble Servt

N GREENE

ALS (Washington Papers: DLC).

1. NG's division (plus some of Lord Stirling's) had just moved to Basking Ridge, ten miles south of Morristown. Washington had determined to encamp his army at several locations nearer the British posts as the "best mode of distressing the Enemy and rendering their Situation still more disagreeable," keeping one division with him at Morristown. (Fitzpatrick, GW, 7: 96–97.) "Distressing the Enemy" involved stripping the countryside of food and forage and attacking enemy foraging parties in hit and run skirmishes. (See NG to Weedon, 24 February, below.) It also served, as Washington said, to retard the British in any early offensive operation. At Basking Ridge, NG had his headquarters on the estate of his friend Lord Stirling, who was stationed with a small force at an outpost at Elizabethtown.

2. Letter not found.

3. Washington's plan of intelligence suggested in the missing letter was probably the same as he had outlined to Stirling in early February of "engaging some of those People who have obtaind Protections, to go in [to British areas] under pretence of asking advice" (Fitzpatrick, GW, 7: 101).

4. Thomas Lowrey (1737–1806) was assistant to Commissary Joseph Trumbull.

5. Eneas McKay (often misspelled McCoy) was colonel of the Eighth Pennsylvania Regiment.

6. Thomas Johnson, Jr. (1732–1819), a brigadier general of the Maryland Militia, had marched some 1,800 militiamen to Morristown in January. He resigned in March to become Maryland's first governor.

7. The winter, spring, and early summer of 1777 were taken up with such speculation as to Howe's intentions.
   8. Washington did not exaggerate when he said in April that smallpox had been
more destructive than "the Enemy's Sword" (Fitzpatrick, *GW*, 7: 409). Mass inoculation
—long advocated by NG and Washington—had just been ordered for the entire army
as well as for incoming recruits. By mid-June, Washington could report knowing of but
a single case in the army (Fitzpatrick, *GW*, 8: 259).

To General George Weedon[1]

Baskenridge [N.J.]
Feb. 24, 1777

Dear Sir

Your favor of yesterday came to hand this morning.[2] I am ignorant who gave Col Guyger orders to come to this department.[3] The
first I knew of their comeing I met them coming to their Quarters near
the second ridge of the Mountains. I shall arm them agreeable to the
Generals order.

Col Pipers detachment here shall march and Join General Putnam.[4] From what you say he must be in more want of men than we.
Our ground is strong if the people [i.e., soldiers] will do their duty, ile
be sacraficed if they [i.e., the enemy] get *to Morris Town* this way
without blooddy *Noses*.

A large forrageing party of the Enemies came out yesterday
from Amboy and so consisting of about 4000, our People attackt
them with various successes. Col Striker says our parties kild and
wounded three Waggon Loads. Eleven was seen dead in one place.
The Enemies Cannon gave them a great superiority over our People.
The forrageing party continued out until Night and our Parties followd them towards Amboy till quite dark. Our party lost about Eight
or ten men; whether kild, wounded or taken Prisoners is uncertain.
This party took seven Prisoners, the Party that made this attack
was from General [William] Maxwells Brigade, [Edward] Hands and
Strikers Regiment and part of Col McKays. The Attack began about
Eleven in the forenoon. I was out from Home at Turkey viewing the
Bridges or else I should sent an express last night.[5]

Col [Thomas] Johnson was down with a party of Maryland Militia, made an attack upon Pascataway [Piscataway]. He kild three, and
if his men had stood their ground they would have taken forty men.
He formd an Ambushcade and sent out a flying party to draw them
into it. It succeeded according to his expectation, but his party cow-
ardly Deserted him just as the Enemy was in his power. General
Warner sent out a party last Night to bring off their Piquet at the
Bridge.[6] The guide was deceivd in the ground, and led the party
between the out centries and the Guard. They took two Prisoners and
drove the Guard [?] in, but what execution was done is unknown.

The Prisoners are coming up. As soon as they arrive they shall be sent on to Morris Town. Youl please to acquaint the General [Washington] with such parts of this Letter as may be agreeable and necessary for him to know. Yours sincerely

N GREENE

NB The Enemy kild two of the Inhabitants yesterday because they did not assist them with their Waggons to carry off their dead. One they shot through the Head, the other they kild with a Bayonet.

ALS (PPAmP).

1. George Weedon (ca. 1734–93), a veteran of the French and Indian War, was the colorful owner of a tavern in Fredericksburg, Va., where his friend George Washington was often a guest. Here in the 1770s, Weedon discussed politics with most of Virginia's future revolutionary leaders between sessions of card playing and horse racing. (He was secretary of the Jockey Club.) In February 1776 he became lieutenant colonel of the Third Virginia Regiment under the command of his brother-in-law Hugh Mercer, who died of wounds received at Princeton and whose children the Weedons raised. At the time NG wrote, Weedon was serving briefly as Washington's adjutant general and had just been made brigadier general. (On his quarrel with the other Virginia brigadiers, see below, NG to Weedon, 27 April 1778.) Serving under NG in the autumn of 1777, Weedon played a key role at the battles of Brandywine and Germantown. See notes, NG's orders, 13 September and 7 October 1777, below. As is evident from the surviving correspondence, Weedon and Greene took great delight in each other's company. For a sketch, see George H. S. King, "General George Weedon," *WMQ*, 2 Ser., 20 (1940): 237–53.

2. Letter not found.

3. Probably Henry Geiger, a German-born Pennsylvania farmer, who was colonel of a Pennsylvania regiment. (*PMHB*, 12 [1888]: 398, and 29 [1905]: 417)

4. John Piper was a colonel in the Pennsylvania militia (Heitman, *Register*). Putnam was then stationed at Princeton. (Fitzpatrick, *GW*, 7: 187–88)

5. This action occurred near Spanktown (Rahway), N.J. (Peckham, *Toll*, p. 31) George Stricker was lieutenant colonel of the Maryland "German Regiment" from July 1776 until his resignation in April 1777. (Heitman, *Register*) Turkey is about fourteen miles northwest of Elizabethtown, N.J.

6. Gen. Nathaniel Warner had arrived at Morristown in mid-January with some seven hundred Massachusetts militiamen that were engaged for two months. (Fitzpatrick, *GW*, 7: 29)

General Greene's Orders

[Headquarters, Basking Ridge, N.J., 26 February 1777. Troop returns to be made. Guyger's (Geiger's) regiment to join Stirling's brigade. Wagons not involved in daily troop provisioning to be used in foraging. Cy (MiU-C) 1 p.]

To The Reverend John Murray

[Basking Ridge, N.J., before 1 March 1777.[1] Describes distress of New Jersey people. Longs for a "few hours uninterrupted conversation with our dear Murray." Beseeches him to visit Mrs. Greene in Coventry. Excerpt from Murray, *Life*, p. 255]

1. The date is conjectured from Mrs. Greene's leaving Coventry in late February. For NG's relations with Murray, the founder of Universalism in America, see above, vol. 1: 81. On his defense of Murray, see "To Whom It May Concern," 27 May, below.

To Christopher Greene

Dear Sir   Baskenridge [N.J.] March 2, 1777
    I am to acknowledge the receipt of your letter by brother Jacob.[1] I have not time to answer it in full. I can only acknowledge your politeness, nay more, kindness to Mrs Greene. I am happy you have got her at Potowomut. There has happend several skirmishes of late here, nothing considerable or decisive has taken place, only a few hundreds of the Enemy disabled or so. My love to your partner. I shall write you more fully in a day or two. Yours

N GREEN

Please to deliver the inclosd Letters.

ALS (MWA).
    1. Letter not found.

To John Adams

Dear Sir   Baskenridge [N.J.] March 3d 1777
    It is a long time since I wrote to you or you to me; who stands in debt upon the schore of Letters I cannot tell, therefore I shall begin anew.[1] If you have time and inclination you will give it an answer, if not I shall consider it as the Ladies do their Visits after Marriage, if theres no return the acquaintance drops.
    I believe you are pretty well convinced of the truth of the observation I made to you last summer, which was that you were playing a desperate game. I fancy your Ideas and mine differd very widely at that time respecting the state of things. You consulted your own feelings rather than the History of mankind in general.
    I am sensible you have not the most exalted oppinion of your *Generals*.[2] Who is in fault? Every one would wish to be an *Epaminondas*, *Sertorius* or *Turenne* if they could, but if Nature has refusd to crown the sons of America with such choice Gifts, who is to blame, either she or we?[3] We cannot be blameable only as we stand in the way of better men. I can speak for myself, altho I have no wish to leave the service. Yet I value the freedom and happiness of America

so much higher than I do my own personal glory, that I am ready at all times to give place to a better man.

I am sensible from a review of the last Campaign there appears some considerable defects in the councils and conducts of its opperations, but give me leave to tell you Sir that our difficulties were inconcieveable to those who were not Eye witnesses to them.[4] To expect that bravery, firmness and good conduct from undiciplind Troops that is only to be found among Veteran Soldiers. General How had, the last Campaign, a large and well appointed Army, this Army strongly supported in all its opperations with a very formidable Naval force. Our forces were hastily drawn together, no time to dicipline or form them, very few that had ever been in Action. We had the Enimies intentions to collect, a large extent of Country on the Bays and Rivers to guard. It is true we have met with some misfortunes and great ones too, but not more so than might have been expected considering their strength and our situation. Perhaps the Generals may be thought blameable for not fighting more. I must confess I advisd to the bringing on an action at the White Plains and then thought it right, as our Army was dayly wasting away and the grounds being very strong on which the Army lay, but the dicipline of the British Troops and the superiority of their Artillery might have given us a general defeat. In that case the consequences would have been terrible. The alternative was disagreeable; if we did not defeat the Enemy the dissolution of our Army was soon to take place, and they left at liberty to range at large.

General How has invariably pursued the Maxims of an invader this Campaign, by indeavoring to bring us to a General Action, and avoid skirmishing. General Washington as every defender ought has followed directly the contrary conduct, by indeavoring to skirmish with the Enemy at all times, and avoid a general engagement. The short term of enlistments and the still shorter aid of the Militia has lost us almost all the benefit of those skirmishes. America abounds with Materials to form as good an army as the World can produce, but it requires time, for nothing but habit makes the Soldier, and Pride the Officer. I am in hopes if the new Army fills agreeable to the Resolution of Congress that America will display in some future Campaign as much heroism and bravery as Europe can boast off. With those advantages, if the reputation of the American Arms is not supported, let censure fall on the Heads of the guilty. I know that success marks the men of Wisdom while the unfortunate are execrated without any allowances for Providential accidents or misfortunes. Let us bury our past errors in the Cabinet and Field and join Heart and hand in concerting and executing the most effectual measures to free America from her cruel oppressors.

I beg leave to make some enquiry into the Policy of some late resolutions of Congress that respects General Lee.[5] Why is he denied his request of haveing some Persons appointed to confer with him? Can any injury arise? Will it reflect any dishonor upon your body to gratify the request of one of your Generals? Suppose any misfortune should attend him immediately, will not all his friends say, he was made a sacrifice off, that you had it in your power to save him, but refusd your Aid? He said in his Letter he has something of the last importance to propose with respect to himself and adds perhaps not less so as to the Publick. You cannot suppose the General would hold out a Proposition to bring us into disgrace or servitude; if he would it is certainly our interest to know it seasonably, that we may not make a sacrifice for a man that is undeserving of it. If he would not tis certainly a piece of Justice due to his merit to give him a hearing; to hear what he has to propose cannot injure us. Forces shall be at liberty to improve or reject his proposition.

But let us consider it in another point of view. Will not our Enemies, the disaffected, improve this report to our prejudice? They will naturally say that General How had a mind to offer some terms of Peace and that you refusd to lend an ear or give him a hearing and that you were obstinately bent in pursueing the War altho evidently to the ruin of the People. Had you not consented to hear General and Lord How last spring the Publick never would have been satisfied but that there might have been an accomodation upon safe and honorable conditions. For my own part I could wish you to give General Lee a hearing, but whether you give him a hearing or not, I cannot help thinking the sacrifice you are makeing for General Lee is impolitick as it respects the Hessians, and unjust as it respects our Prisoners with General How.[6] The Cartel that was settled between General Washington and General How was an exchange of Officers for Officers of equal Rank, Soldier for Soldier, and Citizen for Citizen. General How has never refusd this mode of exchange and is now pressing of us to comply with it. Had we a General Officer of equal Rank with General Lee we might demand him with some propriety, or had we an equal or superior number of Officers Prisoners with us the doctrine of retalliation would be reasonable and Just, but to retalliate for the injury offerd to one is bringing distress on many for no valuable purpose. General How has upwards of three hundred of our Officers in his hands and we only about fifty of his. If we put six field Officers in confinement because General Lee is kept confind, General How will immediately order an equal number of ours under the same confinement. The Officers themselves will have cause of complaint and all their friends will clamour loudly. If General How should not retalliate upon our officers, but call them together, show them they are in his power, by us devoted to destruction, and then enlarge [i.e, free] them, it will totally detach them and their connexions from our cause. If we make a sacrifice of the Enemy we dont hear the Groans and see the tears of their mourning friends, but if any of our Officers falls a sacrifice these multiplied distresses are amongst us, continually sounding in our Ears.

But the worst consequences and the most to be dreaded is the effect it will have upon the *Hessians*. The mild and gentle treatment the Hessian Prisoners have receivd since they have been in our possession has produced a great alteration in their disposition. Desertion prevails among them. One whole Brigade refusd to fight or do duty and were sent Prisoners to New York. Rancour and hatred prevails between them and the British Soldiery. It should be our policy to increase this hatred, not take a measure that may heal the difference. General How has been spreading papers among the Hessians with accounts of our haveing sold the Hessians Prisoners for slaves. This severity to their Officers will but too strongly confirm them in the account. If we can allienate the foreign Troops from the British service we inevitably ruin Great Britain, for her own Natural strenth is totally insufficient to conquer and hold in subjection these States. If the foreign Troops that are here can be debaucht, Great Britain must be discouragd from employing any more, as so little reliance is to be placed upon them. For these and many other reasons that will readily occur to you I would wish the resolution respecting Retalliation might be suspended for a time at least especially as General Lees confinment is not strict. The situation of our Army forbids our doing anything that may alarm the fears of the People anew. We have but the shadow of force, and are more indebted to the weather for security than to our own strength.

I fear your late Promotions will give great disgust to many, but what ever promotions you intend to make, pray let them be compleated as soon as possible that those difficulties of reconcileing discontented Persons may not be at a time when Harmony and concord is necessary.[7] Youl excuse the freedom I have taken and Pardon whats amiss. Yours Sincerely

N GREEN

LS (MHi).

1. The last known letter was from Adams, 4 August 1776. If it ever reached NG, he undoubtedly lost track of it during his critical illness and the ensuing British capture of Long Island and New York City.

2. How NG became "sensible" of Adams's opinions is not known. In his letter of 9 March below, Adams suspected a "busy Body" of doing "Mischief by Misrepresentation."

3. NG's knowledge of the Greek and Roman generals Epaminondas and Sertorius was probably gleaned from Plutarch. He was even more familiar with Marshal Turenne,

the great seventeenth-century French commander noted for his patient calculation and his emphasis on mobility and surprise. For his influence on NG, see Fletcher Pratt, "Nathanael Greene: The Quaker Turenne," in his *Eleven Generals: Studies in American Command* (New York: W. Sloane Associates, 1949).

4. NG reflected to some extent his sensitivity on the loss of Fts. Washington and Lee in these passages (vol. 1: 351–64), but beyond that he made as convincing a defense of Washington's strategy during the previous six months as Adams was likely to encounter.

5. NG's comments in this letter and Adams's response of 9 March, below, barely suggest the complex negotiations that were going on for the exchange of Charles Lee, a British prisoner for two months. (See above, vol. 1: 369n.) The resolutions to which NG refers were passed on 20 and 21 February in response to a letter of 10 February from Lee to Congress. (*JCC*, 7: 135, 140–41) Howe had refused to parole Lee and would have courtmartialed him at once for desertion had Lee not voluntarily given up his British pension before joining the American army. While waiting for instructions from London, Howe decided to use his prisoner to arrange for a congressional delegation to discuss a reconciliation between the warring sides. Lee proved a willing go-between, seeing an opportunity of winning his freedom and at the same time a possibility of bringing about a reconciliation that to him was the only alternative to a long and bloody stalemate. He wrote Congress (through Washington) with the enigmatic request that a delegation visit him so that he might "communicate what so deeply interests myself & in my opinion The Community." (*Lee Papers*, 2: 358; Gruber, *Howe Brothers*, p. 195, says Howe persuaded Lee to write the letter. Lee's imprisonment up to this point is covered in Alden, *Lee*, pp. 158–73.)

Congress quickly surmised Lee's two objectives. As Adams explained in his letter of 9 March below, Congress was unanimously opposed to sending a delegation (for reasons Adams enumerates) but favored doing everything possible to win Lee's freedom. (See note 6 below.)

In urging that a delegation visit Lee, NG was reflecting Washington's opinion. (Fitzpatrick, *GW*, 7: 224) Their insistence on the point is puzzling. Neither was so naive as not to share Congress's suspicions of a ruse on Howe's part to bring about a discussion on reconciliation—to which both Washington and Greene were unalterably opposed. John Alden sees their disagreement with Congress on sending a delegation as part of their "seeming unconcern about Lee's fate" and suggests it may be explained by their dislike of Lee (*Lee*, p. 173). No doubt some explanation exists, but their dislike of Lee is scarcely a logical reason for urging a delegation to visit him. While it could be a cause, as Alden believes, for their opposition to retaliation, which NG discusses later in the letter, their differences with Congress on that issue had a sounder basis, as is pointed out in note 6.

6. Whatever dislike Washington might have borne Lee, he had shown as much concern for Lee's safety as had Congress when rumors reached the Americans that Lee was suffering great hardship in confinement and might be courtmartialed as a deserter. Shortly after Washington received instructions from Congress in early January on dealing with Howe about Lee's imprisonment, he wrote to Howe in even stronger terms than suggested by Congress. (The resolution is in *JCC*, 7: 16; instructions to Washington are in Fitzpatrick, *GW*, 6: 501n.) The proposal was to exchange five Hessian field officers for Lee, but were this denied, Washington demanded that Lee as an American officer be paroled, and he warned that any violence committed on Lee would be "severely retaliated upon the Lives or Liberties of the British Officers, or those of their Foreign Allies at present in our hands." (Fitzpatrick, *GW*, 7: 2)

While waiting three weeks for Howe's unsatisfactory answer, Washington learned that, far from suffering, Lee had been given spacious quarters in New York, furnished good food and wine, and even permitted to entertain guests. (Alden, *Lee*, p. 167; see also Washington to Congress, 1 March, Fitzpatrick, *GW*, 7: 211.) As a consequence, Washington favored dropping threats of retaliation.

But on 20 February, when Congress received Lee's request for a delegation to visit him, it first resolved (perhaps to compensate for denying his request) to order five Hessian officers confined. Copies of the resolution were sent to them, intimating they should write Gen. Howe, because he was responsible for their confinement. Congress also asked the Massachusetts Council to lock up Col. Archibald Campbell, a former member of Parliament who had been on parole in Boston since July 1776. The overzealous Council ordered the hapless Campbell put in a dungeon in the Concord jail. (Washington's strong protest to the Council is in Fitzpatrick, *GW*, 7: 207–9.) In a letter of 1 March, Washington warned Congress in the same terms NG used in this letter that the Americans had far more to lose than the British in the game of retaliation, and he wrote privately to Robert Morris asking him to use his influence. (Ibid., 7: 211–13, 221–26) Congress, however, ignored all such warnings.

It was fortunate that their gamble did not lead to a chain of retaliations. By summer, Howe and Germain agreed to treat Lee as a prisoner of war. But it is questionable whether Lee actually benefited by the retaliation. It would appear that Howe never had a case for trying Lee as a deserter. And as far as the retaliation improving his confinement, Campbell's continued imprisonment in the Concord jail caused Howe in June to move Lee from his comfortable rooms to cramped quarters aboard the *Centurion* in New York Bay, considered by Lee as worse than a jail. Even when the Americans offered the captured Gen. Richard Prescott in exchange for Lee in July 1777, Howe stalled until April 1778 before agreeing on an exchange, although he did finally parole him in New York City in December 1777. (On Lee's exchange, see below, Meade to NG, 4 April 1778.)

7. Congress had just elevated five brigadier generals to major generals and had appointed ten additional brigadiers. (*JCC*, 7: 133, 141)

To Levi Hollingsworth[1]

Dear Sir   Baskenridge [N.J.] March 4, 1777

This will be handed you by my brother from Rhode Island, Jacob Greene, one of our Company in Trade. I beg leave to introduce him to your acquaintance. He is a stranger in the City of Philadelphia and doubtless will be glad to see its curiosities.

We have now and then a slap at the Enimy in the Skirmishing way, nothing very important has taken place since you left us. My best respects to Mrs Hollingsworth, and the Gentlemen of my acquaintance in the City, Particularly those belonging to the Light Horse. Believe me to be with sincere wishes for your family happiness and Publick security. Your most obedient and very humble Servant

NATH GREENE

ALS (PHi).

1. The letter appears to have been intended for Levi Hollingsworth, originally from Maryland, but known to NG since at least 1773 as a successful Philadelphia merchant who handled the Greenes' bar iron. (Advertisement in *Pennsylvania Gazette*, 12 May 1773, offers the "best bar iron made by N. Greene, & Co. at Warwick, R-I.") Hollingsworth had been a colonel in the militia. His brother, Henry, was deputy quartermaster for Maryland under Gen. Mifflin. Levi appears to have aided his brother when Gen. Howe landed on Elk River. (See below, Levi to NG, 2 September 1777, and note, which discusses the name of "Hollingsworth" as an alternate for "Elktown." When NG became quartermaster general, he kept Henry as deputy quartermaster for Maryland. (NG to Henry Hollingsworth, 7 April 1778, below)

To Governor Nicholas Cooke of Rhode Island

Baskenridge [N.J.] Head Quarters
Dear sir   6th March 1777

I am honored with your Favor of the 9th of Feby last, by which I find my Letter of the 23d of Jany had been laid before the House of Assembly.[1] I did not write it for public inspection. I wrote in the stile and freedom of one Friend to another. Had I conceived the production was for public inspection I shou'd have been more discriminate in my observations; I wrote to you sir as a Majistrate of the State of Rhode Island, and as an Inhabitant of the Town of Providence; my Letter being considered under those two Characters will speak my intentions and sentiments.

I am exceeding happy on the receipt of yours to find my information erroneous, and my apprehensions and fears in a great degree groundless respecting your departure from the Union and general plan. At the time I wrote, upwards of two Months had elapsed without receiving a single line from any Person in the State. Various reports were circulating here to the prejudice of the policy of New England. The enormous Bounty that was given, the effect it would have upon the other States, the resolutions of your Government to raise Men for its own internal defence, neglecting the Continental Regiments, were circumstances not a little alarming to His Excellency. These reports were confirmed by Lieutenant Allen of Providence, who arrived from that place much about the same time.[2] He must have been totally ignorant of the conditions upon which the Troops were raising, for I conceived them to be for the safety of the State only, and never knew but that they were located until the receipt of your Letter. I hope the House will pardon the freedom with which I delivered my Sentiments when I assure them that it was from a full persuasion that the reports were true and that the measure was calculated to fix a lasting disgrace upon the Legislators. I have felt no small share of unhappiness in remaining so long ignorant of the true history of your proceedings, for notwithstanding I am not accountable for any misconduct in legislation, yet I cannot help Feeling myself wounded when anything transpires to the prejudice of the State; and you may rest assured Sir, the language of my Letter was a true transcript of Peoples sentiments and opinions respecting your political transactions. If the love for my native place and zeal for the cause hath led me to a too hasty animadversion upon Administration, it hath arose from a strong desire to correct the Evil before it was rendered incurable.

I can assure you Sir, there are few Persons that feel more sensibly for your State than myself, and none that will go further to serve it;

but if you consider the critical situation of the American affairs, the importance of adhering to the general plan, the short time we had to prepare for the ensueing Campaign, the fatal consequences that might result from an unseasonable delay, to myself, the Army and to the Cause in general, you cannot be surprised to find my fears and apprehensions alarmed at the disagreeable situation things were reported to be in. I was sensible sir of your distress. I felt for the Inhabitants; the Calamities the People suffered here was a lively picture of what you had to expect there. Had I known the Governmental Regiments differed from the Continental only in point of time, I should have been silent upon the occasion, notwithstanding the policy does not correspond with my Sentiments. If the Enemy had intended to penetrate into the Country immediately on their arrival, no new Levies could have been raised seasonably; if they did not, then the Continental Regiments might have been as easily compleated as any others.

I feel a singular pleasure in hearing his Excellency General Washington continues in such high estimation among you. The strictures that were made on the Generals conduct by some of the Inhabitants of Providence gave me great uneasiness. If a Character so important, so truly worthy, is not shielded from calumny and reproach, what has lesser ones to expect?

Lieutenant Allen is the author, and from the Character he bears I make no doubt of its truth; but had I conceived my Letter was for the inspection of the General Assembly, I should not have troubled the House with such out of door politics.

I receive with peculiar attention your congratulation and hearty wishes for the success of the American Arms. I hope, if heaven continues to smile upon us and the respective States furnish their proportion of men, to exterminate from this land of Liberty those hostile invaders of human happiness and the rights of mankind. Believe me to be sir, with Sentiments of regard your most obedient and very humble servt

N GREENE

CY (R-Ar).

1. For both letters, see above.

2. William Allen was a lieutenant in the R.I. Militia until March 1777. The misinformation he gave NG doubtless had a bearing on his leaving the service.

To Governor William Livingston of New Jersey[1]

Dear Sir   Baskenridge [N.J.] March 8, 1777

I am sorry to acquaint you that his Excellency General Washington is very unwell. I receivd your Speech to the Assembly of this State. I think you are very severe upon our *Neighbours*.[2] It is reported they are makeing every preparation possible for a movement soon.

Pray how goes on the Militia Law. If there is not some spirited measures taken to get out the Militia until the Continental Troops can be drawn together, the Enemy will be left in a great degree at liberty to range at large without controul. In the State of Rhode Island every man is obligd to send his man or pay four dollars a day. The one half of your Militia ought to be out for a month or six weeks at least. It will be impossible to keep the Enemy from penetrateing the Country without some measure of this sort take place. I will not say how short our strength is off what it should be. Believe me to be with Sentiments of regard your most obedient and very humble Servt

N GREENE

ALS (MHi).
1. William Livingston (1723–90), born into a New York patrician family and educated at Yale, devoted much of his time and talents to writing essays and political satire. In 1772 he retired from the law to an elegant country estate (Liberty Hall) in Elizabethtown, N.J., to devote himself to literary pursuits; but he was soon caught up in revolutionary New Jersey politics. After serving in Congress, he was elected governor in 1776. With New Jersey often a battleground, the office was an exceedingly trying one. His reelection over a period of fourteen years attests both to his ability and to his humane concern for his constituents. Carl E. Prince, who is editing the papers of Livingston, has written a brief but informative booklet, *William Livingston: New Jersey's First Governor* (New Jersey Historical Commission, 1975), in the series "New Jersey's Revolutionary Experience," Larry R. Gerlach, editor. On the governor's son, who had been NG's aide, see letter from William Smith Livingston, 15 January, above.
2. The "Neighbours" were the British in eastern New Jersey, whom Livingston had excoriated in a lengthy speech on 25 February, wherein he spoke of "the disgust they have given to many of their own confederates amongst us, by their more than Gothic ravages." (His speech is reprinted in *N.J. Archives*, 1: 301–5, and credited to the *Pennsylvania Packet*, 4 March 1777.)

From John Adams[1]

Dear Sir   Philadelphia March 9, 1777

I had last Evening the Pleasure of yours of March 3 by your Brother, to whom in his Business to this Place I shall give all the Assistance in my Power. In whose favour the Ballance of Letters lies I cant Say: but if I am in debt, in Point of Numbers it must be because Some of my Remittances have miscarried.

I am not yet intirely convinced that We are playing a desperate Game, tho I must confess that my feelings are somewhat less Sanguine than they were last June. This diminution of Confidence is owing to Disappointment. I then expected that the Enemy would have Seen two or three Bunker Hills between the Point of Long Island and the Banks of the Delaware River. Two or three Such actions would have answered my Purpose, perhaps one alone.

I have derived Consolation however, from these Disappointments; because the People have discovered a Patience under them, greater than might have been expected. It was not very surprising to me that our Troops Should fly in certain situations, and abandon Lines of such extent, at the sudden Appearance of a formidable Enemy in unexpected Places, because I had learn'd from Marshall Saxe, and from others that Such Behaviour was not only common but almost constant among the best regular Troops. But there was Reason to apprehend that the People would be Seized with Such a Panick upon Such a Series of ill success that in the fright and Confusion whole States would have revolted instead of a few paltry Individuals. Whereas every State has stood firm, and even the most confused and wavering of them, have gained Strength and improved in order under all this Adversity. I therefore do not yet despair.

You Say you "are sensible I have not the most exalted Opinion of our Generals." From this Expression I Suspect that Some busy Body has been endeavouring to do Mischief by Misrepresentation. Be this as it may, I am generally So well Satisfied in my own Opinions, as to avow them.

I dont expect to see Characters, either among the Statesmen or the Soldiers of a young and tender State like ours, equal to Some who were bred to the Contemplation of great Objects from their Childhood in older and more powerfull Nations. Our Education, our Travel, our Experience has not been equal to the Production of such Characters, whatever our Genius may be, which I have no Reason to Suspect to be less than that of any Nation under the sun.

I dont expect to see an Epaminondas, to be sure, because in the opinion of Dr. [Jonathan] Swift all the Ages of the World have produced but Six such Characters, which makes the Chances much against our seeing any such. When such shall appear I shall certainly have an exalted opinion. *Untill then I believe my Opinion of our Generals will continue not very exalted.* [Italicized portion deleted in LB.]

Notwithstanding this I have a sincere Esteem of our General Officers taken together as a Body, and believe them upon the whole the best Men for the Purpose that America affords. I think them Gentlemen of as good Sense, Education, Morals, Taste and Spirit as any we can find, and if this Opinion of them is not exalted enough I am Sorry for it but cannot help it. I hope however that my Opinion as well as that of the World in general will be Somewhat more sublimated before next Winter. I do assure you that two or three Bunker

Hill Battles, altho, they might be as unsuccessfull as that was, would do it. I lament the Inexperience of all of them and I am sure they have all Reason to lament mine. But not to disguise my sentiments at all, there are Some of them, particularly from New England, that I begin to think quite unequal to the high Command they hold.[2]

It is very true that Success generally marks the Man of Wisdom, and in Some Instances Injustice is done to unsuccessfull Merit: But still it is generally true that Success is a Mark of Wisdom, and that Misfortunes are owing to Misconduct. The sense of Mankind has uniformly Supported this Opinion and therefore I cannot but think it just. The Same Sense has uniformly attributed the ill success of Armies to the Incapacity or other Imperfections of the General Officers, a Truth which I have Sometimes presumed to Hint to some of our General Officers with whom I could make So free. There Seems to be Justice in this because the Glory of Successfull Wars is as uniformly attributed to them.

I shall join with you, very chearfully, in burying past Errors and in wishing to concert and execute the most effectual Measures to free America from her cruel oppressors.

You ask why Gen. Lee is denied his Request?[3] You ask, can any Injury arise? Will it reflect any Dishonour upon Congress? I dont know that it would reflect any dishonour, nor was it refused upon that Principle. But Congress was of Opinion that great Injuries would arise. It would take up too much Time to recapitulate all the Arguments which were used upon occassion of his Letter. But Congress was never more unanimous than upon that Question. Nobody I believe would have objected against a Conference concerning his private affairs or his particular Case. But it was inconceivable that a Conference should be necessary upon Such Subjects. Any Thing relative to these might have been conveyed by Letter. But it appears to be an Artfull Stratagem of the two gratefull Brothers to hold up to the public View the Phantom of a Negotiation, in order to give Spirits and Courage to the Tories, to distract and divide the Whiggs, at a critical Moment when the Utmost Exertions are necessary to draw together an Army. They meant farther to amuse Opposition in England, and to amuse foreign Nations by this Maneuver, as well as the Whiggs in America, and I confess it is not without indignation, that I See Such a Man as Lee Suffer himself to be duped by their Policy So far as to become the Instrument of it, as Sullivan was upon a former occasion.

The Words of the Count La Tour [Turenne] upon a similar Occasion, ought to be adopted by Us. "Remember that now there is room neither for Repentence, nor for Pardon. We must no longer reason nor deliberate. We only want Concord and Steadiness. The Lot is cast. If we prove victorious, We shall be a just, free and Sovereign People; if We are conquered We shall be Traitors, perjured Persons, and Rebels."

"The Princes of the Union were not diligent enough in preparing for War: They Sufferd themselves to be amused with Proposals of Accomodation, they gave the League time to bring together great Forces, and after that, they could no longer brave it. They committed the fault which is very common in civil Wars, viz that People endeavour to Save Appearances. If a Party would Save Appearances, they must lie quiet, but if they will not lie quiet, they must push Things to an Extremity, without keeping any Measures. It rarely happens, but that otherwise they are at once both criminal and unfortunate." Bailes [Bayle?] *Life of Gustavus Adolphus*

But further. We see what use G[overnment] and the two Houses make of the former Conference with Lord How. What a Storm in England they are endeavouring to raise against Us from that Circumstance.

But another Thing. We have undoubted Intelligence from Europe, that the Embassadors and other Instruments of the B[ritish] Ministry at foreign Courts made the worst Use of the former Conference. That Conference did Us a great and essential Injury at the French Court you may depend upon it. Ld How knows it, and wishes to repeat it.

Congress is under no concern about any Use that the dissaffected can make of this Refusal. They would have made the worst Use of a Conference. As to any Terms of Peace, look into the Speech to both Houses, the answers of both Houses, look into the Proclamations. It is needless to enumerate Particulars which prove that the Howes have no Power but to murder or disgrace us.

The Retaliation that is to be practiced on Lees account, was determined on when I was absent, So that I can give no Account of the Reasons for that Measure. Yet I have no doubt of the Right, and as to the disagreeable Consequences you mention, these I hope and presume will not take Place. If they do, they will be wholly chargeable on the Enemy. The End of Retaliation is to prevent a Repetition of the Injury. A Threat of Retaliation is to prevent an Injury, and it seldom fails of its design. In Lees Case, I am confident it will Secure him good Treatment. If Lees Confinement is not Strict, that of Campbell and the Hessians ought not to be. The Intention was that they should be treated exactly as Lee is.

Our late Promotions may possibly give Disgust: But that cannot be avoided. This delicate Point of Honour, which is really one of the most putrid Corruptions of absolute Monarchy, I mean the Honour of maintaining a Rank Superior to abler Men, I mean the Honour of prefering a single Step of Promotion to the Service of the Public, must be bridled. It is incompatible with republican Principles. I hope for my own Part that Congress will elect annually all the general officers. If in Consequence of this Some great Men should be obliged at the Years End to go home and serve their Country in some other Capacity, not less necessary and better adapted to their Genius *I dont think the public would be ruined.* Perhaps it would be no harm.

The officers of the Army ought to consider that the Rank, the Dignity, and the Rights of whole States are of more Importance than this Point of Honour, more indeed than the Solid Glory of any particular officer. The States insist with great Justice and Sound Policy, on having a Share of the General Officers, in Some Proportion to the Quotas of Troops they are to raise. This Principle has occasioned many of our late Promotions, and it ought to Satisfy Gentlemen.[4] But if it does not, they as well as the Public must abide the Consequences of their Discontent. I shall at all Times think myself happy to hear from you, my dear sir, and to give the Utmost Attention to whatever you may suggest. I hope I shall not often trouble you to read So long a Lurry of small Talk.

LB (MHi). The additions made by Adams in his letterbook have been inserted at what appeared the most appropriate places.

1. This letter is almost a point-by-point response to NG's letter of 3 March, above.

2. In a letter to his wife Abigail on 21 February, he said that few people thought Gens. Schuyler, Putnam, Spencer, and Heath "capable of the great Commands they hold." And he added, "I wish they would all resign." All but Schuyler were New Englanders. (Butterfield et al., *Adams Family*, 2: 165)

3. On the Lee affair, see above, note, NG to Adams, 3 March.

4. One of the "Gentlemen" who was far from satisfied was Benedict Arnold, an able, ambitious man who made known his fierce resentment at seeing five brigadiers with less ability and less seniority advanced above him. Congress ostensibly based its discrimination on the "Baltimore resolution" of 19 February: that since Connecticut already had two major generals, three would be disproportionate to the number of troops raised. But the ill-will between Massachusetts and Connecticut over the Ticonderoga controversy of 1775 was also a factor. Washington, who thought it an injustice, asked Arnold not to "take any hasty steps." (Fitzpatrick, *GW*, 7: 234) In April, Congress reversed its decision and back-dated his appointment as major general to 17 February, but Arnold never recovered from that blow. (Wallace, *Traitorous Hero*, pp. 124–27)

Arnold's eventual treachery has obscured the fact, as Wallace has pointed out, that "Arnold was easily the outstanding battlefield officer of the Revolution." (Ibid., p. 314) Few modern historians would disagree. NG and Arnold were good friends until Arnold's dealings with André were discovered, at which time, ironically, NG was temporarily in command of Washington's army and later served as president of the court that ordered André's execution.

From General Benedict Arnold

Dear General   Providence [R.I.]
                                                March 10, 1777
I must rely on your good nature to Pardon my negligence In not
Answering your favour of the 7th Ult. before.[1] The day I receivd it I
set out for Boston with design to raise a few Continental Battallions
for our Intended Attacks, where I was detained a Fortnight. On my
Return I was Ordered by Genl Spencer to Point Judah [Judith] from
where I have but Just returned.[2]

I beg you will tho' late accept my Sincere thanks for the same
which I Esteem as a mark of your Friendship. I am never more happy
than when my Friends will favour me with there Sentiments and
advice, especially those who are so capable of giveing it on Matters of
such Importance to my Country, whose Safety and happiness every
honest man must have more at Heart than his own Personal Glory
and by no means can be Justified in risqueing the former for the
Latter.

I perfectly agree in Sentiments with You that Prudence forbids
our runing any unnecessary Risque untill our new levies are Compleated, the Army in a Condition to bear a Check. I am sensible that a
defeat at this Critical Juncture would be attended with most fatal
Consequences. The mode of Attack I mentioned to his Excellency
General Washington was not fully Determined on. It was what we
then had in Contemplation. It was thought most Prudent to attempt
Surpriseing the Posts Opposite Howlands and Bristol Ferrys, while
the main body landed below, the whole to form a Junction As soon as
Possible, by which means our retreat to Howlands Ferry would have
been secured. I doubt which would have been the best Plan—this or
Yours.[3] Had the whole Body been thrown Over at Howlands Ferry,
the Enemy would have retreated and join'd their whole force: Tho we
should have run less risque in retreating in case of a Repulse. I am
Sensible It is with the greatest difficulty the best Troops can be
embarked and Disembarked at any Time without Confusion. I beleave
it never was done when retreatg from and In View of the Enemy,
which was fully Considered and expected to be remedied by a Frigate
and one Gondulow lying on each Side the neck leadg to Howlands
Ferry, to Cover the retreat of the Troops which I make no Doubt they
would have effectually done, and prevented that Confusion which
otherwise must have undoubtedly happened. I never Suposed the
Enemy so blind to their own Security as to expect to Surprise them.
My Only hopes were (that from the extent of Ground the Enemy had
to defend, without Barracks to Cover their men who were of Course
oblidged to be Quarter'd In New Port) we should be able to land,

surprise their Posts at Howlands and Bristol Ferrys, and form a Junction before their Main Body could Attack us. I have calmly view'd the matters in every Point of Light. I am sensible of the Weight of Your Arguments against an attack which must evidently be made under every disadvantage on our Side. Indeed I am greatly at a loss wheather it would be prudent to drive the Enemy from their present quarters if in our Power, as they would undoubtedly Joyn the Army in the Jerseys which I am fearfull you are not In a Condition to Oppose.[4] If the Southern States are as Tardy In raising their new Levies as those of New England You can have but few Troops except Militia. Indeed I Tremble for You.

His Excellency General Washingtons orders for the Troops of Massachusets State to march Emmediately for Tyondroga [Ticonderoga] and those of Connecticut to be Innoculated for the Small Pox, renders an Attack on Newport Impracticable with any probability of Success, as we have only four Thousand raw Militia to guard a Sea Coast of one Hundred miles in extent.[5] Notwithstanding the Wise Assembly of This State have Passed a Vote Declareing it disgracefull to the States of New England (and to this State in Particular and of Course to the General Officers of the Army, that the Enemy on Rhode Island have remained so long unmolested, and have requested and directed Genl Spencer to attack them immediately. As he would avoid the Anathamas of the Great and General Assembly of the State of Rhode Island, which being fearfull of Incurring, he has In Conjunction with Governor Cooke given Orders for Collecting the Militia &c for the above purpose. Included is a Coppy of the Votes of Assembly.[6] I sent it you as a Curiosity.

By two deserters from a Transport at N'port, we are Informed that Two Thousand Troops have lately Arrived at N. Port from New York and as many Sailed for Marthas Vineyard. This day week nine or Ten Large Transports who appeared full of men Passed Point Judah to the Westward. We find It dificult to reconcile the Various Accounts we) receive on all hands. It is agreed that there is at Rhode Island at Least four Thousand Troops. I wish there was as many more there of them you have in the Jerseys. As we are both embarked in the Same Cause and must rise or fall with our Country, I shall ever Esteem it a Favour when you are Pleased to Communicate your Sentiments without reserve. I am with great Respect and Esteem Dear General Your most Obedit Humble Servt

BT ARNOLD

Cy (Greene Papers: DLC); damaged; enclosure missing. Portion in angle brackets from GWG Transcripts (CSmH).
1. Letter not found.
2. Gen. Joseph Spencer was in overall command in Rhode Island.

3. NG's plan is lost with his 7 February letter. The usually impetuous Arnold was undoubtedly restrained by Washington's paradoxical admonition of 3 March not to attack unless "you can reasonably promise yourself a *moral certainty* of succeeding," the same advice he had given Spencer. (Fitzpatrick, *GW*, 7: 233–34)

4. The English historian George Trevelyan thought it to the patriots' advantage that British troops remain in Newport. (See above, vol. 1: 366n)

5. Washington to Spencer, 3 March 1777 (Fitzpatrick, *GW*, 7: 232–33).

6. The R.I. Assembly, considering it a disgrace that no attempt "hath, as yet, been made against the enemy," urged Spencer to attack. It voted to raise volunteers to help, promising them $1,000 for taking a British general, $200 for a colonel, down to $20 for a private. (Bartlett, *Records*, 8: 154–56) The lure was insufficient at the time, however. By October, Spencer did have the men to attack but was thwarted by a severe storm. (See note, NG to Christopher, 5 January 1778, below.) It was August 1778 before the Americans again attempted to dislodge the British from Rhode Island. NG's response to Arnold's letter is printed below, 30 March.

To Governor Jonathan Trumbull of Connecticut[1]

Sir

Head Quarters Baskenridge [N.J.]
11th March 1777

Yours of the 7th Feby I received and am happy to find your Sentiments with respect to the conduct of the British Officers concur with my own.[2] At the time I wrote you on the subject of Building Barracks for the reception of such unfortunate wretches as had and might hereafter fall into our hands, I communicated the purport of it to His Excellency General Washington to whom you have referred the matter. I make no doubt he will give such directions as will prove satisfactory to the State. The precautions you have taken will in a great measure tend to prevent any correspondence being carried on by the Officers and privates, but as we have so many Villains among our own People I fear the Evil will still continue tho' in a less degree.[3] I am with real regard Your most Obedt and very hble Servt

N GREENE

LS (Ct Hi).

1. Jonathan Trumbull (1710–85) was trained for the ministry at Harvard but entered his father's business on the death of his brother. Until bankruptcy overtook him in 1766, he was one of Connecticut's most successful merchants. He was a member of the Assembly and Council as well as a judge before he was elected governor in 1769. A supporter of colonial rights, Trumbull was the only colonial governor to retain his post after statehood, serving until 1784. During the war his chief contribution lay in making Connecticut a principle source of supply for the army. His son Joseph was commissary general, son John was the noted painter, and Jonathan, Jr., was governor from 1797 to 1809. A recent biography is David M. Roth, *Connecticut's War Governor: Jonathan Trumbull* (Chester, Conn.: Pequot Press, 1974)

2. Letter not found.

3. The care of British prisoners was an acute problem. NG had written Trumbull in January (undoubtedly at Washington's request) about housing the prisoners in barracks. The letter is lost, but Trumbull enclosed it in a letter to Washington of 7 February with the comment that he had placed the prisoners with families in several towns because there were no barracks. He asked Washington's advice for the "most proper mode of treating them." (MHS, *Coll.*, 5 ser., vol. 10: 37–38)

Washington recommended that privates be "Cantoned in the Country" and that willing tradesmen among them be employed. He favored exchanging British officers, however, to prevent them from becoming familiar with American affairs and from spreading a "very pernicious influence among the People." (Fitzpatrick, *GW*, 7: 173) On the difficulties in working out an exchange of prisoners, see below, Washington to NG, 22 March.

From George Washington

Head Quarters Morris Town [N.J.]

Sir   Mar 18th 1777

The necessity of having the Congress well inform'd of many matters essential to the well being of this army, and the Impracticability of doing this fully by Letter, have induced me to request you (who intimately know our Circumstances) to repair immediately to Philadelphia for this purpose; at the same time to know how we are to be supplied with arms and many other articles of wch we are exceedingly deficient.[1]

To enumerate the several matters of information necessary to be given, and the enquiries proper to be made, would be as needless, as endless; your own good Sense assisted by such hints as you have recd will be abund'ly Suff't.

Two or three things, however, I must in a more particular manner, recom'd to your attention: the one is, the embarrassment I am laid under with respect to carrying the Exchange of Prisoners into Execution (agreeable to the Cartel settled with Genl Howe by order of Congress) on acct of the confinement of Lt Colo Campbell, and the Hessian Field officers.[2]

But I would have you enquire of the Quarter Master Genl how he stands provided with Tents, ammunition Carts or Waggons, Waggons for Intrenching Tools and Hatchets, or Tomahawks. Also of the Com[missar]y of stores, how he goes on in his Castings of Cannon, making Cartridges (of which numbers should be in readiness) and in general what forwardness the business of the Elaboratory is in, and urge him to the most diligent discharge of the duties thereof.[3]

One thing in particular I beg of you to Impress strongly upon Congress, and that is the necessity of keeping the Paymaster regularly supplied with the article of Cash; without it, every thing moves slowly on, and many and great disadvantages flow from the want of it, as we have most wofully experienced of late in numberless Instances.

As the Establishment of the horse with respect to the Pay seems to be upon an unstable footing and it is indispensably necessary that both officers and men should know what they have to depend upon, I should be glad if the pay could be settled upon such a just and liberal footing as to give satisfaction to the Parties.⁴ Given at head Quarters at Morris Town this 18th day of Mar 1777.

GO: WASHINGTON

ACyS (Washington Papers: DLC).
1. He informed Congress the same day that NG was being sent to confer because "This gentleman is so much in my Confidence, so intimately acquainted with my ideas, with our strength and our weaknesses, with every thing respecting the Army." (Fitzpatrick, *GW*, 7: 299)
2. The cartel approved by Howe and Washington in 1776 provided that prisoners would be exchanged for those of equal rank. (*JCC*, 5: 598–99; Washington to Howe, 30 July 1776, Fitzpatrick, *GW*, 5: 356–57) On the difficulties over Campbell and the Hessians, see note, NG to Adams, 3 March, above.
3. NG answers these queries in his letter to Washington of 25 March, below.
4. Congress had approved a pay schedule for the cavalry on 14 March. (*JCC*, 7: 178)

From George Washington

[Morristown, N.J., 21 March 1777. Unsure whether Congress intends to hold Hessian officers and Col. Campbell until Gen. Lee is exchanged or only until he is considered as a prisoner of war. Asks NG to transmit "sense of Congress" on the subject along with any resolutions on cartel for exchanging prisoners.¹ Cy (Washington Papers, DLC) 1 p.]

1. On the exchange of Gen. Lee, see note, NG to Adams, 3 March, above; on cartel, see note, Washington to NG, 22 March, below. NG's answer is below, 25 March.

From George Washington

Dr sir   Head Qrs Morristown [N.J.] March 22d, 1777
I am again called upon for another meeting between Colo Walcott and Mr Harrison to negotiate the Cartel,¹ so long the Subject of correspondence between Genl Howe and myself and those two Gentn. Without incurring a further charge of delay, I could not defer their interview longer than next Friday morning; I therefore request that you will transmit me by Express, who may arrive here early enough on Thursday for Mr Harrison to set out, such Resolution as Congress shall have or may form on your Application for their vesting me with powers for settling This Business; also their sense in direct and explicit terms on the Subject of my last Letter to you² Viz whether they mean to release and Exchange Colo Campbell and the Hessian Field officers, supposing Genl Howe should declare Genl Lee on the footing of other prisoners and liable to be exchanged on the principles of the Agreement now subsisting, or whether they are determined to detain them tho he should. I wish much to be satisfied in those points,

a knowledge of them may prevent further embarrassments and more unnecessary meetings upon the Subject of a Cartel.[3]

I have nothing material to advise you of unless it is that it was reported last night that five deserters came to Colo Hands Regmt yesterday morning, and seven the Eveng before. They are not arrived here yet, but I believe the Account is true. I am &c

G W

FC (Washington Papers: DLC).
1. Washington and Howe could not agree on interpreting the arrangement for prisoner exchange made in July 1776. In mid-February, Washington had sent Col. Robert H. Harrison, an aide, to hear Howe's proposals from Lieut. Col. William Walcott. On 4 March he empowered Harrison to work out an agreement on all matters concerning prisoners on the "principles of Justice and humanity." (Fitzpatrick, GW, 7: 155, 246–47)
2. See above, Washington to NG, 21 March 1777.
3. Congress resolved at once that only if the British acknowledged Gen. Lee as a prisoner of war could Washington proceed on the exchange of prisoners. (JCC, 7: 197) Harrison and Walcott met for the third time on 2 April, but their talks broke down because of the American position on Lee and American insistence on arranging a permanent cartel. (Bowman, Captive Americans, pp. 106–7.) British recognition of Lee's status as a prisoner of war in September 1777 met only half of the American demands; thus in March 1778 Harrison (with others) was again negotiating fruitlessly with Howe's representative. See note, NG to Weedon, 7 March 1778, below.

To George Washington

Dear Sir   Philadelphia March [25], 1777

I receivd your letter of the 21st. I was with a Committee of Congress who had the business of the Cartel and other matters under consideration when your Excellencies letter was deliverd me. I had explaind the matter fully to the Congress and Committee. I was two hours before the former and two Evenings with the latter. I believe the business of the Cartel will be settled agreeable to your wishes, that is, General How acknowledgeing General Lee a prisoner of War and holding him subject to exchange when ever we have an Equivalent to offer, the full execution of the old Cartel to take place as your Excellency and General How can agree, with full powers to annex such farther conditions as may be thought necessary to promote the comfort and happiness of the unfortunate.[1]

I explaind fully the State of the Army to the Congress, but I fear they can do but little more than has been done. There has gone from this City about 700 men within a Week past, a thousand more will be ready in eight or ten days. The Congress have wrote to Govenor Johnson to forward the Maryland Troops and to the Govenor of the three lower Counties. The Maryland Delegates which arrivd in town last night say their Regmts are above half full upon an Average. It is reported with some degree of confidence that the nine North Carolina

Regiments are on their march this side of Virginia, but I have no sufficient foundation for the Report to give full credit to it.

I believe the Congress thinks the alterations of the rout of the Massachusets Troops exceeding judicious. I explaind to the House your Excellencies Ideas of the next Campaign. It appeard to be new to them. However they readily admited the probability from the reasons offerd.[2]

I yesterday went to View the forts and fortification before the City. I think them quite insufficient for the purpose without a very strong opposition. I have road round the City and up the Scuylkill and give it as my oppinion that it cannot be fortified to advantage. The approaches may be made so many ways that it would take a greater number of Troops to defend the Works than would be prudent to have shut up in the City. However, I think an advantageous line may be drawn from the Schuylkill to the Delaware, begining at Morris Seat on the Schuylkill and runing from thence to Shippens, Hubleys and Dickinsons Country Seat, over to the Delaware. Those posts would be elligible upon the Enimies geting possession of the City.[3]

Inclosd is a return of the situation of the Quarter Master Generals department, the Waggons, spare Carriages and so not mentiond in the return, are in great forwardness, General Mifflin informs.

Col Flowers returnd yesterday from Carlille [Carlisle], the place for the Laboratory.[4] He has contracted for the Ground, provided materials and orderd the necessary buildings to be erected as soon as possible. There is cast at this place one 12 lb [pounder], two Sixes and Two five inch Howitsers that are good. They will continue to cast about two a Week. Col Flowers is makeing out a return of the State of his department; if he compleats it before this letter goes I shall inclose it. I am told by the Congress the pay and establishment for the light Horse is compleated and forward'd.

I have impressed upon the Congress in the strongest manner I was capable the necessity of keeping the paymaster fully supplied with Cash. The House requested the estimates. I told them I could not furnish any, but the demand would be great at the opening the Campaign to pay off the old reareages and satisfy the new demands.

There is so much deliberation and waste of time in the execution of business before this assembly that my patience is almost exhausted. I cannot get the resolve respecting the Cartel past so soon as I want it. I know your delicate situation and the Anxiety you must be under.

I think it is uncertain yet whether General Gates will serve as Adjutant General. I have directed General Fermoy to repair to Camp.[5] What measures the Congress will take respecting the rank of General officers appointed by the States I cannot pretend to say. The subject has been fully explaind to them and the injury that may arise from things continueing in their present situation.

Colonel Cox is gone out of town; whether he will accept the appointment of Commisary of Prisoners or not I cannot tell. I shall write him upon the subject.[6]

A Brigg arrivd this day from Nantz [Nantes]. Her Cargo consists of 272 Chests of arms containing Six thousand Eight hundred muskets, Sixty Chests of which, not being proved, the Capt sais he cannot so fully engage for their goodness, but the remaining 212 Chests are very fine provd Arms. Also 1500 excellent double bridled Gun Locks. When this Vessel left France there were great preparations in that Kingdom and Spain for war, which was expected to be general throughout Europe.

Another Vessel has Just past up the River from Hispanolia, deep laded, her Cargo unknown.

Major Conner, by land from Charles Town S Carolina, advises of a Ship belonging to that State arriving there 8 Days before he left that place with a number of arms, Ammunition and 12 brass Cannon from France.

Nothing could have happend more seasonable than these Arms as the Congress have none in Store. Colo Flowers has about four thousand out of repair and about 400 that are fit for use. The secret Committee have given me to understand that a large quantity of Arms, Ammunition and brass Cannon are dayly expected.

I shall stay today and tomorrow in Town and then set off for Camp unless I am detaind by the Congress. I am with the greatest respect your Excellencies most Obedient and very Humble Servant

NATH GREENE

ALS (Washington Papers: DLC). Enclosure missing.

1. For background on prisoner exchange, see above, NG to Adams, 3 March; Washington to NG, 21 and 22 March.

2. Washington had earlier ordered Massachusetts troops to Ticonderoga to meet an expected attack from Canada over the frozen waterways. He now diverted half of them to Peekskill on the lower Hudson to help hold the enemy in New York because he foresaw, among other possibilities, a probable British move from Canada down the St. Lawrence and thence by sea in a "formidable push towards Philadelphia" (Fitzpatrick, GW, 7: 125, 282–83). Massachusetts troops did not arrive in Peekskill until after the British raid of 23 March (see below, note 2, NG to Adams, 5 April).

3. The line of defense NG described would run east and west between the two streams, a mile north of Philadelphia.

4. Col. Benjamin Flower (1748–81), who had been commissary of military stores of the Flying Camp, was directed by Washington on 16 January 1777 to raise the regiment of artillery artificers.

Washington had preferred Yorktown, Pa., as the location of the laboratory, but Congress chose Carlisle. (Fitzpatrick, GW, 7: 23; JCC, 6: 1044)

5. Timothy Pickering, not Gates, was to become adjutant general. Matthias Alexis Roche de Fermoy, who had served under NG at Trenton, was shortly ordered to

Ticonderoga, where he disgraced himself in a series of blunders in the battle of 2–5 July 1777 (Balch, *French*, p. 216).

6. Elias Boudinot (1740–1821), became commissary of prisoners in June 1777, a difficult and thankless job in which he spent a great deal of his own money. He served until elected to Congress in May 1778. As president of Congress from November 1782 to November 1783, he and NG would carry on an extensive correspondence. In 1783 he was secretary of foreign affairs. (DAB; George Adams Boyd, *Elias Boudinot: Patriot and Statesman, 1740–1821* [Princeton: Princeton University Press, 1952])

To General Benedict Arnold

Dear sir   Morris Town [N.J.] March 30th 1777
I am favord with yours of March 10th covering several resolutions of the Assembly of the State of Rhode Island. I fear those were hasty measures, the product of disappointment and vexation, taken without adverting to consequences. I am very sure their hearts a right, and their zeal warm, but I fear they do not give themselves time to deliberate properly. I am sure the House of Assembly never meant the resolutions as a reflection upon the General officers; neither did they think their neighbouring States might take umbrage at the severity of the reproach. The State of Rhode Island may think it a great misfortune that the Troops on Rhode [i.e., Aquidneck] Island have not been attacked; but I am far from thinking so, and ever shall be, unless I can be first convinced of the certainty of the success of the attack. People that are unacquainted with military matters and the force of discipline think that numbers are sufficient to insure success; four thousand Troops well posted, with a good train of Artillery, may bid defiance to three times their numbers, especially when there is but little order, method or discipline among the assailants. I wish General Spencer may not hazard an Attack with such Troops as you describe; it is the opinion of the best military Judges we have in the Army, that the chance of an attack is against us.[1] It signifies nothing for a few spirited officers to rush upon danger, when they have little or no hope of being well supported. Spirit is essential in an Officer, but prudence is more so. If you make the attack, God grant you success! but I hope General Spencer will have more prudence than to run any unnecessary risque to gratify Popular clamor.

I am exceeding sorry to hear that the N E [New England] States are so tardy in furnishing their proportion of Men; the southern States are little Better. This army wants a large reinforcement to open the Campaign to advantage; fortune favors us with a very seasonable supply of Arms. I hear there is 12000 stand arrived to the Eastward at Portsmouth, and 1000 Bls Powder; there is also 6800 stand of Arms arrived at Philadelphia, and 660 Bls Powder arrived in Maryland. Several valuable prizes have been brought into Baltimore within a few Days past, two of the Enemies store Ships loaded with Provisions bound for N York.

General Gates goes again to Ticonderoga. It is uncertain who commands the North side of Hudsons River, but I think its probable General Putnam will.[2] I am with great sincerity and truth your most obedient and very hble Servt

N GREENE

FC (MiU-C).
1. The attack that the R.I. Assembly urged on Spencer (as noted in Arnold's letter of 10 March) was delayed until October, and then aborted. See note, NG to Christopher, 5 January 1778, below.
2. Washington had hoped that Gates would again accept the post of adjutant general, which he had held in 1775, but on 25 March, Congress ordered him to take command at Ticonderoga. (*JCC*, 7: 202). Putnam did indeed get the command on the "North" (i.e., the east) side of the Hudson River.

To Catharine Greene

Morris Town [N.J.] March 30, 1777

The great distance there is between us and the few opportunities I have to hear from [you] leaves me in a very disagreeable suspence. Eight long months have past amidst fatigue and toil since I have tasted the pleasures of domestick felicity.[1] I have been endeavering to collect a few tender sentiments and to call home my wandering thoughts, but General Knox and a few others put them all to the rout, and in vain do I endeaver to rally my Ideas. I am just returned from Philadelphia. Brother Jacob is gone to Maryland but is expected back in a day or two. The young ladies of Philadelphia appeared angelick. A few months Seperation more will put my virtue to a new tryal. If you dont wish to put my resolution to the torture, bless me with your company; that is, providing your health and other circumstances favors my wishes.[2] Pray how are you? A line from you will be most agreeable. Give my kind love to all friends. Your[s] sincerely

N GREENE

Tr (Nightingale Transcripts; furnished in 1973 by Bernard Nightingale, Brunswick, Ga. The transcripts were apparently made by a family member in the late nineteenth century before NG's letters to Catharine were sold to Joseph Sabin. Where a comparison can be made with the original manuscript, the transcripts are reasonably accurate.)
1. He had not been home, but Catharine had visited him in New York during the summer of 1776.
2. NG had yet to learn that two weeks earlier Catharine had given birth to a daughter, Martha Washington. In the summer she came to New Jersey to be near him, leaving the baby with NG's brother and wife. She remained in the vicinity for almost a year.

To John Adams

Morris Town [N.J.]

April the 5th 1777

Dear Sir

I have neither seen nor heard of any Resolution of Congress approving or disproving of the Laboratory being fixed at Springfield. If the Congress approves thereof it will be necessary for them to say so, there being now an Order for it's being fixed at Brookfield and the Council of the Massachusetts State commissioned to provide the materials for the erection of the necessary Buildings at that place. Please to enquire into the matter and write General Knox upon the Subject; it will forward the business if the Council has the same powers with respect to providing materials only at Springfield instead of Brookfield.[1]

Since my return to Camp, I am more at a loss to guess the Enemies intentions than ever. They are fortifying Brunswic. Two Spies who left that place a few Days since say the greater part of the Troops are gone to Staten Island; drafts have been made from the several Corps. There is a General Order of General Howes commanding all the Officers that are absent from Posts to join the 10th of this Instant. It is generally suggested some expedition is on foot. If 'tis up the North River, General Howe is the greatest blunderer of the age to put us on our Guard by such an ill tim'd Expedition as they made the other Day.[2] If his Expedition is to the Southward his delay has lost him the happy moment; a Fortnights delay longer will put it out of his power to do any great things. If the States furnish their Men and we have a good Train of Artillery provided seasonably, and General Howe dont shut himself up in some inaccessible Post, ten to one but ruin awaits him before Fall. But if every State is at liberty to furnish only a part of their men and those at their pleasure we shall have another crippled Campaign, indecisive and perhaps disgraceful.

General Schuyler is going to Congress armed with the imperial Cohorts of N York to support the assertion that the Northern operations depend entirely upon his being continued in the command. A dispassionate enquiry perhaps may convince you of his usefulness. If not it will afford you an opportunity to convince the State of N York that the Salvation of America dont Depend on the political sentiments of Albany County. General Schuyler thinks with me that it will be exceeding difficult if not to say impossible for the Enemy to penetrate the Country by the way of Ticonderoga. He also thinks if the Enemy push up the North River it will afford us the fairest opportunity to ruin them we can wish, notwithstanding it may prove distressing to that State.[3]

I am more and more alarmed every day of my life at the local preparations making in the several States for their own defence, in such a situation as we are in, surrounded with immaginary and real grievances, claims made by one State and refused by another. Men at the head of affairs full of caprice and humours, poisoned with little prejudices and conceited of their own importance, can easily throw the whole Empire into a convulsion unless there is some seasonable check provided to silence those little differences in their infancy. Human nature is capable of those ebullitions of folly, and prudence dictates the necessity of proceeding against them. It is my opinion there ought not to be any standing Troops but what are on the Continental establishment.[4] Believe me to be with sentiments of regard your most obedt And very huble servt

N GREENE

LS (MHi).
1. Congress had ordered a magazine and "elaboratory" built at Brookfield, Mass., the magazine capable of storing ten thousand stand of arms and two hundred tons of powder. (*JCC*, 6: 1044) At the urging of Gen. Knox, Washington, counting on congressional approval, ordered the works built at Springfield, Mass. (Fitzpatrick, *GW*, 7: 139, 146–47) In a letter of 13 April that he never sent, Adams backed the relocation, and Congress went along. (Adams Papers, MHi; *JCC*, 7: 266) Thus began the famed Springfield Arsenal. Progress was slow, however. It was June 1778 before the town of Springfield made land available, and as late as October 1778, the "elaboratory" was nothing but a barn. See below, William Smith to NG, 21 June and 1 October 1778.
2. On 23 March, 500 water-borne British troops destroyed most of the town of Peekskill, the barracks, and many valuable stores—including 150 wagons and several sloops. (Ward, *War*, 1: 323; *Kemble Papers*, 1: 112) As NG surmised, however, the raid was not preparatory to a major British offensive up the Hudson.
3. At the instance of Adams and other New England members, Congress had just reprimanded Schuyler for writing what was described as a "derogatory" letter. One consequence was that Congress gave Gates an independent command at Ft. Ticonderoga, with Schuyler still in overall command of the Northern Department. (*JCC*, 7: 180, 202) As a delegate to Congress a few weeks later, Schuyler pleaded his case so effectively that Gates was again made subordinate to him. With the fall of Ft. Ticonderoga in July 1777, however, Gates replaced him as commander of the entire northern army. The controversy is covered in Nelson, *Gates*, pp. 80–107; see also *JCC*, 7: 230, 364; 8: 375, 604.
4. See above, NG to Cooke, 23 January and 1 February 1777.

To Christopher Greene

Dear Sir   Morris Town [N.J.] April 5, 1777

Your letter of the 13th and 15th giving an account of family matters and Mrs Greens safe and happy delivery were most heartily welcome.[1] Nothing could have given me greater pleasure as some supersticious fears began to prey upon my immaginations. I beg leave to return you my warmest thanks for your polite, kind and friendly offices to Mrs Green. Gratitude shall record it in her books ever to be rememberd with acknowledgements of obligation. It gives me a singular pleasure to find health a reigning blessing among you.

May God in his Providence shower it down more abundantly upon you all. This is a happiness amidst every calamity and some alleviation of the worst of miseries. Brother Jacob is gone to Baltimore in Maryland. He expected to have been back long before this. The cause of his detention I am a stranger too but I suppose he cannot get the money he went after so soon as he expected.[2] Misfortune seems to give close shocks to your navigation, loss after loss in a successive train. It is by no means so difficult a task to learn to support ourselves with moderation and prudence under misfortunes, as it is in a flowing tide of prosperity. Never let a few obstacles discourage you; prosecute your business with the same Zeal as if the smiles of fortune invited you to share the profits and pleasures of the Eastern commerce. A steady perseverence generally gets the better of such partial Evils and is commonly crownd with a plentiful harvest as a reward for suffering patiently under misfortunes.[3]

You ask my Oppinion about erecting a slit[t]ing mill. I am ignorant of its advantages. The cost is considerable. If you have a prospect of feeding it with bar Iron the profits may be great, but without Bar Iron the slit[t]ing mill will be useless. With respect to the repairs of the Works at Potowomut I should go on with business the same as if no Enemy were near you. You need be under no apprehensions about the Enemies comeg [coming] up to burn them. I expect they will soon evacuate Rhode Island. If they should not it is by no means probable they will ever make an excursion into the Country at your place. I despise Doctor Bradford and his little dirty mallice. His resentment is without injury and his abuse unmerited. I hope to see this mighty Son of Mars in some future day when I shall have an opportunity to see whether his deeds are as bold as his language is scervy and clamarous.[4] [half a page missing] Enemy advance towards Philadelphia the 10th of this instant but I dont expect it so soon, but by the 20th I am sure they will be in motion if at all before a reenforcement comes. Many deserters come off who inform us they are very sickly at this time. I dont expect to see home this summer as the General will not suffer me to be absent an hour from Camp unless it be on some extraordinary business. I should be glad to see Mrs Greene to the westward if some of you could accompany her but not without, as life is uncertain in the Army and our situation unknown. I am perfectly easy and happy in her present condition, and submit her accomodation to your direction [half a page missing] it may be true. Give my kind love to your beloved, to my brothers at home and the Sisters of the family and to all my friends in general. Remember me kindly to Mother. Capt Collins past here a few days since on his way to Philadelphia.[5] I am with Sentiments of regard Your Affectionate brother

N GREENE

ALS (MWA). Incomplete. The letter is unaddressed, but in his letter to Catharine the next day, he refers to a letter from brother "Kitt."

1. Letters not found. Martha Washington Greene, their second child, was born about 14 March. During this period Catharine was living with Christopher and his family in Potowomut.

2. See Jacob to NG, 7 May, below.

3. On the current state of the family business, including shares in privateers, see below, Jacob to NG, 7 May.

4. The reference to Lt. Gov. William Bradford of Rhode Island is examined in NG to Cooke, 1 February, above.

5. Joshua Collins had been an officer in Varnum's regiment in the R.I. Army of Observation.

To Catharine Greene

My dear   Baskenridge [N.J.] April 8th 1777

I was most agreeably surprisd by a letter from brother Kitt with an account of your being in Bed. Thank God for your safe delivery.[1] I read the letter with a trembling hand. Some supersticious fears had been hovering round me for some time that something would happen to you. What gave rise to this troublesome train of visitants I cannot tell unless it was the extream anxiety I felt for you in your critical situation. Heaven be praisd for this second pledge of conjugal affection. When I shall see the poor little [beggar?] God only knows. I am exceeding happy at your being at Potowomut and rejoice [to] find the brothers so kind and attentive to your wants. How shall you or I repay their kindness? We must leave that to some after day. Nothing delights me more than to hear you all live in good fellowship.

I am now at Lord Sterlings Seat in a most agreeable family of Govenor Livingstons. There are three young ladies of distinguished merit: Sensible, Polite, and easy.[2] Their manners are soft and engageing. They wish much to see you here, and I wish so too but I expect long before that happy moment to be upon the march towards Philadelphia. The Enemy I expect will advance that way before ten days or a fortnight at most. If you have an inclination to come to the westward, bring somebody with you that can take care of you as it is uncertain whether I shall have an opportunity to see you at all. I never wisht more ardently to see you in my life than now. The hours grow tedious and the heart impatient. Fortune is rather unfriendly to afford but a few months enjoyment for several Years Marriage. However, I hope fortune has something better in Store—if not, we must learn contentment. Pray is Nancy Vernon and the Doctor become one? I saw doctor Young when I was in Philadelphia. his wife and Susa his daughter, Mrs Washington and Mrs Bland from Virginia are at Camp, happy with their better halves.[3] Mrs Washington is excessive fond of the General and he of her. They are very happy in each other.

General Knox informs me he and his Lucy had agreed to Visit you at Coventry. The morning was fixt to set out but the orders of the General pointed out a different rout. Pray my dear are you determind to Suckle your baby or not? On that depends your liberty. I wish you a speedy recovery and us a happy meeting. In the meantime believe me to be your most affectionate

N GREENE

ALS (MiU-C).
1. Martha Washington Greene was born about 14 March.
2. Stirling's elegant country seat at Basking Ridge was ten miles southwest of Morristown. The young ladies were daughters of Stirling and Governor Livingston, his brother-in-law.
3. NG had probably known Dr. Thomas Young, an army surgeon, during the siege at Boston. Active in politics, he had helped to frame the Pennsylvania constitution of 1776 (Lewis H. Meader, "The Council of Censors," *PMHB*, 22 [1898]: 282.) Martha Bland was the wife of Col. Theodorick Bland of Virginia.

To John Adams

Dear Sir   Bound Brook [N.J.] April 13, 1777

The Enemy made an attempt to surprise General Lincoln this morning. They advanceed by three divisions; one crossed the Raritan about a mile above Head Quarters, the second division came up in front of the Town, the third to the left of the Town and crossed the River cald Boundbrook. Besides these three divisions there was a Corps of reserve commanded by General Mathews.[1] The Padroles and Guards posted by General Lincoln were negligent or else the Tories who are perfectly acquainted with the ground brought the Columns in between the Padroles and Guards. Which of the two was the cause of the surprise or whether they both concurd to produce it I cant tell. The General had but Just time to draw off the Troops from between the heads of their two flank Columns which kept up a warm fire as our people past between them. Our Artillery consisting of three three-pounders and the Ammunition belonging to them fell into the Enemies hands and most of the men were made Prisoners belonging to the Artillery and two of the officers. There was about 20 Artillery men made Prisoners and about forty Battalion men kild, wounded and missing. General Lincoln had one aid de camp made Prisoner and lost almost all his Papers; this is a great misfortune as it will inform the Enemy of many disagreeable circumstances. The Enemy were supposd to be between four and five thousand strong at least. General Lincoln had about five hundred Continental and Militia Troops. The Action began about five oClock. The Enemies loss must be considerable. Col Butler with about three hundred excellent marksmen had a good fire upon one of the Heads of their Columns for a considerable time.² I am posted at Baskenridge about 12 miles from this place. The Enemy had Evacuateed the Town before I got here. They held it about an hour. I have not time to add anything further only that I am with great respect your obedient Servant

N GREENE

N B This opportunity presented to write and as its uncertain where [whether?] the Generals express will reach the City as soon as this Gentleman I thought proper to write you.

ALS (MHi).
    1. Edward Mathew (1729–1805), often spelled Mathews (Boatner, *Encyc.*).
    2. Gen. Cornwallis led the attack in apparent retaliation for American forays. NG's account here and in his letter to Jacob of 20 April, below, constitute the fullest accounts available. Except for the number of British involved, his facts appear accurate. Peckham lists two Americans killed, twenty captured (*Toll*, p. 33). In his letter to Catharine of 19 April, below, he tells of dining where Cornwallis had breakfasted. (Freeman has a summary of the skirmish and a note on sources in *GW*, 4: 408–9.) The vulnerability of Lincoln's post led Washington to move it into the hills to the west. Richard Butler (1745–91) was in temporary command of the Eighth Pennsylvania Foot. (Boatner, *Encyc.*)

From Governor Nicholas Cooke of Rhode Island¹

[Providence, R.I., 15 April 1777. Regrets that idle talk and rumors have burdened NG; "upon the whole I beg you rest assured that General Washington and yourself are at present very high in the Estimation of all the respectable People in this State." Cy (R-Ar.) 1 p.]

    1. This letter concludes a series of exchanges on raising R.I. troops for the Continental army and on the opinions held by some Rhode Islanders about the ability of the officers of the army. See above, NG to Cooke, 23 and 28 January, 1 February, and 6 March; and Cooke to NG, 7 [9] February.

To Catharine Greene

My dear   Morris Town [N.J.] April 19, 1777
    I had the pleasure to hear from you today by letters from brother Kitt and Sister Caty.¹ They write me you are cleaverly and in a fair way of geting well soon. God grant you may. The Child also they say is in a fair way. Heaven be praisd for its goodness. I most ardently wish to see you but when or where the lord alone knows. I dont expect to Visit Rhode Island till the close of this Campaign if fortune should preserve me through it. I could wish to see you here but how you will get here or who will come to take charge of you, God only knows. Our stay and condition at any one place is so uncertain that you must not expect any assistance or attendance from me; was I in private life nothing would be more agreeable.

By intelligence this moment receivd from a Spy, I learn the Enemy are [accoming?] to Philadelphia and that in a few days. I hear the Troops have all left Rhode Island. If true, it will free you from many disagreeable apprehensions.[2]

Remember me to all freinds and thank the brothers for their kindness to you, Particularly brother Kitt who is with you. I am in tollerable good health.

The Enemy made an attempt to surprise General Lincoln. They took three pieces of Cannon from him and about thirty men. The Enemy lost about that number kild and wounded. The next night we surprised one of their Piquets. We kild seven and took Sixteen. The British Generals breakfasted and I dind at the same house the same day—this is the State of War.[3]

By letters from Congress today I am assurd in the strongest terms a French War is inevitable. Yours sincerely

N GREENE

ALS (MiU-C; photocopy deposited at Clements Library from collection of Theodore Sheldon.)
1. Letters not found.
2. NG's intelligence was incorrect. It was several months before the British headed for Philadelphia, and although some troops were removed from Rhode Island to New Jersey, their number was not substantial. (NG to Lincoln, 19 April 1777, below)
3. The skirmish is described at greater length in NG to Adams, 13 April, above. They dined at the home of Col. Van Horne, a retired New York merchant. It made little apparent difference to the Van Hornes and their five daughters which side controlled their area, for they were equally hospitable to British and American officers. (Lundin, Cockpit, pp. 251–54)

To General Benjamin Lincoln

Dear General   Morris Town [N.J.] April 19, 1777
I returned to this place last night. Upon examining the condition of our outposts and those of the Enemys, from the intelligence of the Enemies strength and situation and the weak State our advance Posts were in, I find it impossible to make an attack upon the Enemy with any probabillity of success. General Maxwell and General Stevens [Stephen] are of the same oppinion. The latter wrote to General Washington this morning that he had intelligence of the Enemies makeing some new disposition. "The Regiment of Guards are orderd up from the Landing to Bonum Town, when the Enemy will have their principal force assembled thereabouts: Viz the 33d, 2d battallion of the 71, the light infantry from Rhode Island and the 42d and, I believe, the Grenadiers who came from Rhode Island."[1] This is an extract from General Stevens letter who is of oppinion that there will not be left above 1600 men at Brunswick and the landing. How well this oppinion is founded I leave you to Judge. General Stevens'

oppinion is the Enemy have some Stroke in contemplation. His Excellency wishes you to keep a good lookout. He thinks that the Cannon with you are in a dangerous situation and will in a great degree be useless if the Enemy make an attempt to surprise You. He therefore wishes you to send them to Morris Town immediately and only consider Boundbrook as an advance Piquet. The General thinks you had better order all the Stores back between the first and second Mountain,[2] and draw your dayly supplies from thence.

General Lees Servant and Dog is sent down to the Lines to be sent in to the General. You will please to give the necessary pasport accordingly.[3] I am dear Sir your most obedient and very humble Servt

                                                        N GREENE

ALS (NjP).
    1. Gen. Stephen's reports were sometimes far from accurate. See note at Council of War, 2 May, below.
    2. The Watchung Mountains.
    3. While a British prisoner, Charles Lee had asked Washington to send his much-loved dogs from Virginia. (*Lee Papers*, 2: 357–58: Fitzpatrick, *GW*, 7: 154–55)

To Christopher Greene[1]

Dear Sir   Morris Town [N.J.] April 20, 1777
    Yours of March the 31st came to hand yesterday.[2] I am much oblige to you for the intelligence. Nothing could be more agreeable to my own private feelings. I can assure you your resentment for my negligence produces a very agreeable punnishment, that of a repetition of your letters, go on and punnish me in this way continually. Was I ungenerous enough to lay aside the respect and civility due to your politeness, and was certain that was the most effectual way of continueing your Letters, I would not answer them at all, but duty on one hand and fear on the other compels me (altho with a trembling hand) to exercise my pen. I wrote an answer to your former letter by the Post before Jacob set out for Home. Pray has he got safe there, or is the Letter come to hand?[3] I commonly write amidst noise and confusion, with my thoughts very often absent from the subject I am writing upon (a sure mark of a little mind Lord Chesterfield says). If I make blunders you must excuse them.

    I am happy to find by Sister Caty['s] Letter that harmony and concord and good agreement subsists among you.[4] The little prejudices and disagreeaments that creeps into families often robs them of all the more substantial pleasures of life. Like the dispute subsisting between Great Britain and America, productive of nothing but misery and distress to both parties. A family is a little Government and its happiness depends upon the agreements of the constituent parts.

General How is preparing to take the field. I refer you to Jacobs letter per Post for further particulars.[5] Remember me to all friends. I would write your Wife but Capt Collins who will hand you this is waiting. Yours Affect

N GREEN

ALS (MWA).
1. Letter is unaddressed, but contents point unmistakably to Christopher.
2. Letter not found.
3. His letter of 5 April, above.
4. The letter from Christopher's wife, Caty, not found.
5. See the following letter.

To Jacob [?] Greene[1]

Morristown [N.J.] April 20th 1777

On Sunday last, Lord Cornwallis from Brunswick, made an attempt to surprize General Lincoln at Bounbrook. They in part effected it, owing to the valorous conduct of the militia, who were posted at a fording place on the Rariton. They deserted their post, without giving the general the least notice. The enemy were at the general's quarters before he had any knowledge of their approach. We lost three pieces of cannon, and about thirty men; they had about as many killed and wounded. The enemy had five generals, and four thousand troops; our General Lincoln had but about four hundred. Lord Cornwallis and General [James] Grant breakfasted at the house at which I dined. The enemy halted but an hour and a half. I marched from Baskenridge upon the first intelligence, but the distance was twelve miles, and the enemy had retreated before I got down. The next night we surprized one of their pickets, killed one officer and seven privates, and took sixteen prisoners.[2] Pray how goes on recruiting with you? *I am sure the continent must come to drafting at last, the sooner the better.* Very late news from Europe mentions that a French and Spanish war is inevitable, and that but few recruits can be got for the reinforcement of the British army in America. Our strength now is trifling. It is to be regretted, that the cause of freedom rests upon the shoulders of so few. General Howe is preparing with all imaginable diligence to take the field. His bridge to cross the Delaware, so much talked of, is arrived at Brunswick, as I am informed by a spy who left that place last night.[3] I would thank the British myrmidons[4] to protract the opening of the campaign for about three weeks, but that is not to be expected. Our army will appear like Gideon and his pitchers. God grant us the same success; the cause is equally righteous, and claims his heavenly protection.

Excerpt reprinted from Johnson, *Greene*, 1: 96–97.

1. The recipient is unidentified by Johnson, but the excerpt is printed in a series of letters to Jacob, all but this one identified as such by their contents.

2. An earlier account is in NG to Adams, 13 April, above.

3. It was not over a bridge across the Delaware by which the British finally reached Philadelphia in September, but by ship to Chesapeake Bay and an overland march.

4. Samuel Johnson's *Dictionary* defines as "Any rude ruffian; so named from the soldiers of Achilles."

To Catharine Greene

My dear Girl   Baskenridge [N.J.] April 27, 1777

I impatiently waited for the Post day in hopes of a letter but to my great mortification not a line. Yesterday Capt [Ebenezer] Flagg (who arrivd here a day or two past with the Rhode Island detachment) informd me he left you unwell with a fever. I hope before this it is removd or gone off. Pray write me. I long to hear from you but wish more to see you. That happy period I fear is at a great distance. I was in hopes to have seen you earlier than this. The Campaign I expect will open in a few days. Perhaps we may not see one another for some months.

By intelligence from N York and Brunswick yesterday we learn the Enemy are to take the field the first of June. Their delay is uncountable [unaccountable] already. What has kept them in their Quarters we cant immagin. We have got together a small force altho by no means equal to our expectations. The small Pox has provd a great hindrance to the Troops coming in.[1] However, if General How attempts to pass through the Jerseys we determin to play furry [fury] with him. There is little or no reinforcement expected from England. O that the Americans were but Spirited and resolute! How easy the attempt to rout those miscreants, but their foolish delays and Infernal disputes I fear will protract the War to a much greater length than is necessary to compleat the work. I am sure America will be Victorious finally, but her sufferings for want of Union and publick Spirit may be great first. There is no People on Earth that ever had so fair an opportunity to establish their freedom at so easy a rate if the opportunity had been properly improvd. God grant a happy issue to the War and [*one or more pages missing*].

ALS (NjP). Incomplete.

1. For the first five months of 1777, no official returns of troop strength have been found. The constant coming and going of men on short enlistments makes it virtually impossible to estimate the number at this time. There may have been no more than 3,000 effective troops by mid-April, but by 21 May, Washington reported a total of 10,000 men—7,363 of whom were listed as "PRESENT FIT FOR DUTY & ON DUTY." (Lesser, *Sinews*, p. 46)

On the successful efforts to stop the spread of small pox, see note, NG to Washington, 20 February, above.

To General Benjamin Lincoln

Dear Sir   Baskenridge [N.J.] April 27th 1777

I am directed by His Excellency General Washington to acquaint you the tents are arrived from Philadelphia and that he purposes encamping the troops in a few days. His Excellency desires you to give the necessary orders for each regiment to send the Quartermaster or some other proper officer to draw the necessary tents for the respective regiments: one tent for five men. His Excellency also desires you to give it out in orders that no parties go out of the lines except such as are authorized by the daily orders, unless the officer has permission. Gen. Maxwell had a party of about twenty surprised a few nights past that went out of their own accord without the necessary directions.[1]

I purpose to call and see you this afternoon or tomorrow. Inclosed you have a piece of intelligence from Brunswick yesterday. I had intelligence from N. York night before last. The intelligence gives an account of the enemy's being in great preparation cutting down a large ship to make a floating battery. Eleven sail of transport with troops are gone up the North River, as many with troops are gone down the Eastern [Long Island] Sound said to be bound for New Haven.[2] These movements are to divert our attention from their principal object and to keep the Eastern troops from coming on. The bridge at New York is complete and part of it is said to be at Brunswick.[3] Yours sincerely

N G

Tr (G. W. Greene Transcripts: CSmH). See note 3 on enclosure.

1. In an action near Amboy on 25 April, four Americans were killed and twenty-six taken prisoner (Peckham, *Toll*, p. 33).

2. They were bound for Westport and thence overland to Danbury. See below, NG to John Adams, 2 May.

3. An enclosure from an informer said the British would leave New Brunswick in ten days, leaving no garrison behind. The informer had probably been deliberately misled.

To George Washington

[Basking Ridge N.J.] [April, 1777][1]

General Maxwell to make a fient		
at Amboy	300	
at Bonum Town [Bonhamtown]	200	General Maxwell
at Pascataway [Piscataway]	300	
Landing	600	Stevens [Stephen]
	1500[2]	

General Putnam	1000
General Greene	1000
General Lincoln	1000
	3000
	1500

The whole Troops to be formd
including divisions agreeable   4500
to the above plan

General Maxwell to have the command of the Troops that attack Amboy and Bonum Town. General Stevens to command the Troops to attack at the landing and Pascataway. These are all meant as feints but the Troops to make such severe attacks as to make the Enemy think them real.

The principal attack to be made on Brunswick. This will be the more likely to succeed as it is the less expected. General Greene to command one division, General Lincoln another from Boundbrook, General Putnam to command the Princetown divisions the whole to make an attack at the same time. The Redoubts to be avoided if possible as they can contain but small propotion of the Troops. If the main body can be routed, those in the Redoubts will evacuate when the Troops are put in motion to form their respective divisions. The Boats in and about Newark and Elizabeth Town to be got in readiness as if our attack was to be on Staten Island to mislead the Enemies attention, the Troops to be put [in] motion tomorrow Morning; orders to be dispached this Evening and the attack to be made next day after tomorrow morning.

> Two pieces of Cannon for the Landing
> 2 ditto at Bonum Town and Amboy, none at Pascataway Camp
> Six pieces of Cannon with each of the Boundbrook
>   divisions and four with General Putnam

To make the attack upon the present Plan the chance is equal; had we a reserve Corps of 2000 I think it would be certainly attended with success. The Troops are more young and want to be better diciplind to attack to advantage. If the first onset is successful the Victory will be easy. If we defeat the Enemy it will ruin their measures for the Campaign. If they defeat us, it being the grand division of the Army, it will greatly discourage the opperations. Our loss upon a defeat cannot be great as the Troops may be safely drawn off into the Country and such as are scatterd will get off without any great loss. Upon the whole I am willing to lead a division to the attack and to risque my own Reputation upon the consequences, but I am not willing to recommend it very warmly if it be contradicted by the voices of the other Generals.³ Those are my Sentiments which are submited to your Excellency's further consideration.

N GREENE

ADS (Washington Papers: DLC).
    1. Washington dated the plan "Apl 1777." It was probably drawn up a few days before the meeting of 2 May below.
    2. The correct figure is 1,400; the total, 4,400.
    3. NG's plan was undoubtedly a response to a request by Washington. It was discussed at the Council of War of 2 May, below.

Proceedings of a Council of General Officers

At a Council of General Officers held at Baskenridge the 2d day of May 1777.
    Present His Excellency General Washington.

M.Generals		B.Generals	
	Greene		Maxwell
	Lord Stirling		Knox
	Stephen		
	Lincoln		

His Excellency the Commander in Chief stated to the Council the situation and strength of the Army under his immediate command at the several Posts in Jersey, laying before them returns of the whole, and propounded the following Questions.

Q. Will a general attack upon the Enemy in Brunswick and at the neighbouring Posts be advisable?

A. Unanimously, that the situation of our force, either in point of number or discipline, will not justify the measure.

Q. Will it be advisable to make a partial attack?

A. It will upon Bergen, if it can be attempted with a prospect of success. As to the other out Posts, though an attack upon them might succeed so far as to force the Enemy from them, yet it would be with certain loss on our side, as they could always retreat from the Works to the Main body of their Army when it should be necessary, and could dispossess us again of the Posts, whenever they should think proper.¹

Genl Stephen. Bonam Town or Piscataway may be attacked with a prospect of success without any great loss. The measure was held inexpedient by the rest of the Council for the reasons above.²

R.H. HARRISON

FC (Washington Papers: DLC).
    1. The proposals Washington put before the council were essentially those that NG outlined in his letter to Washington immediately above. NG nevertheless voted with the rest of the generals on both queries.

2. Although Gen. Stephen held out for attacking Bonhamtown or Piscataway, NG had seen Stephen's role at Piscataway only in concert with other brigades. The next week, however, Stephen attacked the town without authorization or without support from other brigades. He claimed a "considerable advantage" over the enemy, but Washington learned that the enemy, on the contrary, had routed Stephen's force. Washington's reprimand was the severest he ever made to a general officer. (Freeman, GW, 4: 417) Stephen was an incompetent braggart who was eventually dismissed for unofficerlike behavior and drunkenness. (Ibid., 4: 513n, 535–36; for the action at Germantown that led to his courtmartial, see Court of Inquiry, 1 November 1777, below.)

To John Adams

Dear Sir   Morris Town [N.J.] May 2d 1777

Your favor of April 22d came to hand a few days since.[1] General Lincoln is deservedly acquited from any blame. It is as you observe impossible to guard against the intrigues of the Tories and the negligence of the militia. However I hope with you that few such surprises will take place.[2]

I most sincerely lament the great inattention and indifference that appears among the People in general about the recruiting the Army. I live in hopes that a better spirit will prevail soon. If not I hope the drafting from the Militia and exempting all those from the militia service that procures a recruit will go near to fill the Army. If not we must supply the defect by more vigilance activity and Spirit.

The Monuments you are erecting to the Memory of the great Heroes Montgomery, Warren and Mercer will be a pleaseing circumstance to the Army in general and at the same time a piece of Justice due to the bravery of the unfortunate Generals.[3] These things are attended with but little expence and have great influence. I would beg leave to propose another Species of honnors to Animate the living to great and worthy actions. Patriotism is a glorious Principle, but never refuse her the necessary Aids. Let a number of Medals be Struck of different figures emblematical of great actions with a motto expressive of the same. These medals to be presented by the Congress to such of the Officers as shall perform some great and noble act, Specified by some previous Resolution of Congress for that purpose. The Officer that claims it to wear it as a mark of distinction due to his merit. These will be a species of honnors attended with no expence and at the same time have great influence. They will also serve to fix the honnors of the Army dependant upon the dignity of Congress and I conceive it an object of great importance to Unite the wishes of the Army with the vieus of Congress.

Doctor Lennard [Abiel Leonard] of Conecticut who was Chaplain to the Artillery last Campaign offers his service again in the Artillery department. There will be several Regiments this Year. They are commonly detacht to different Brigades and divisions of the Army. The Doctor thinks he can serve the whole. But he cannot think of engageing in the service unless there is a more Ample provision made than at present. If the Doctor would answer for the Three Regiments he would Merit some extraordinary allowance. He thinks his services will deserve the pay of a Lt Col of the Train. If any Man deserves it the Doctor does. He engagd early in the Army and has been indefattigable in the duties of his Station. In a word he has done everything in his power both in and out of his line of duty to promote the good of the service. The Clergy are most certainly useful and necessary in the Army and ought to be decently provided for. It is General Knoxes opinion and wish that the Doctor may be appointed to the office of Chaplain for the whole Artillery of this division of the Army. You will please to consider of the propriety of the measure.[4]

I concur with you in Sentiment as to the propriety and necessity of taxation. Had this measure been adopted in N E[ngland] instead of attempting to regulate the prices of things it would have had a much better effect. You may rely upon the Army in general and me in particular doing every[thing] in our power to aid and assist the Congress in carrying into execution every necessary resolve as far as our influence extends.[5]

The Enemy have destroyed our Stores at Danbury in Conecticut. For once give them credit for a bold Manoeuvre. I think they have paid dear for the attempt. It is supposd their loss in Kill'd, wounded and Prisoners cannot be less than 600.[6]

I observe by Doctor Lees letter to his brother that Burgoyne is to attack Boston. The Troops remaining so long at Newport seems to favor the opinion. Time only can unfold their further intentions. I observe by some late Resolves of Congress they are in fear for Ticonderoga. If Carlton comes over the Lakes with a vieu of penetrating into the Country, General How must be bound up the North River notwithstanding all his threats and preparations for Philadelphia.[7] Pray have a little patience with us here. I know you are tird of enquireing after News from this Army. I hope soon to be in a condition to make some movement. Yours sincerely

N GREENE

ALS (MHi).
    1. Letter not found.
    2. He refers to the action at Bound Brook (see above, NG to Adams, 13 April).
    3. A year earlier, Congress had authorized a monument to Gen. Richard Montgomery, who was killed in Quebec. (JCC, 4: 89–90) In April 1777 it voted to erect monuments also to honor Gens. Joseph Warren, hero of Bunker Hill, and Hugh Mercer, mortally wounded at the battle of Princeton. Congress also resolved to educate the sons of Warren and Mercer at government expense (JCC, 7: 79–80, 242–43, 258).

4. There is no evidence that Congress ever acted on the appointment of Dr. Leonard. See Adams on chaplains, 9 May, below.

5. In August 1777 Adams wrote his wife Abigail, "Taxation, as deep as possible, is the only radical Cure. I hope you will pay every Tax that is brought you, if you sell my Books, or Cloaths, or oxen or your Cows to pay it" (Butterfield et al., *Adams Family*, 2: 320).

6. Some 2,000 troops from New York under loyalist Gov. William Tryon landed from transports at Westport, Conn., on 25 March and marched to Danbury. After destroying much of the town and many military stores—including 1,700 tents—they were returning to their ships when they met fierce opposition from militia units under Gens. Benedict Arnold and David Wooster. Wooster was mortally wounded. (Ward, *War*, 2: 492–95; Peckham lists 171 British casualties and 95 American, *Toll*, p. 33.)

7. In late April, Congress voted to increase the garrison at Ticonderoga, to improve communications with the fort, and to hasten the completion of vessels on Lake Champlain. It also authorized Gates to concentrate on the defenses of Lake George and Ft. Independence if he deemed them more important than Ticonderoga in stopping the enemy. (*JCC*, 7: 304, 306–7) Sir Guy Carleton (1724–1808) was a British general and long-time governor of Canada. For Adams's views on the subject, see below, Adams to NG, 9 May.

To Catharine Greene

Morris Town [N.J.] May 3, 1777

I was almost thunderstruck at the recept of your letter.[1] How different its contents from my wishes: a lingering disorder of five Weeks continuance and from the present symtoms a confinement of two months longer. Heaven preserve you and bless you with patience and fortitude to support yourself under the cruel misfortune. Long had I pleasd myself with the pleasures of a happy meeting. But fortune seems to delight to sport with human happiness. Doubtless tis a necessary sacrafice to teach us the instability of human Happiness and to learn us the folly of indulging fond hope and pleasing expectation in the enjoyment of distant bliss.

I sincerely sympathise with you in your distress. How unfortunate to catch cold, the cause of such a train of misfortunes—cruel to you and distressing to me. O that I had but wings to fly to your relief. The healing balm should not be wanting to mitigate your pains. I have a slight disorder that has been hanging about me for several days past. I hope its duration will be short as I have neither time or inclination to be absent from duty. You must threaten the Doctors, if they dont cure you in a few days, with instant destruction. If Doctor Joslin attends you, let him know if he dont make a Radical cure in a fortnight at most he shall have more holes in his Hide to fill with tore wads.[2] Capt Flagg mentiond to me that you had a slight fever upon you when he left Greenwich, but he was in hopes it would not be lasting or of many days continuance. I wish he had not been mistaken.

My dear creature, my Heart mourns the Absence of its counterpart. Before the opening of this Campaign I flatterd myself with the pleasure of seeing you here. I dare not write very urgent for you to come on for fear you might venture abroad too soon. The pleasures of meeting would be great after so long an Absence. I have hithertoo stifled the anxiety and wish of my Heart to see you for fear it should make your situation more disagreeable.

The Ladies of Baskenridge, Govenor Livingstons daughters, Lord Sterlings youngest daughter, Lady Kitty, who is one of the sweetest Girls I ever saw, and Miss Nancy Brown, a very fine young Lady, form our Society—you never was among a more agreeable set of young Ladies in your life. They all most heartily wish you to come. This Sweet circle only serves to enliven my disquietude by bringing to remembrance past pleasures, too distant for enjoyment.

I am happy to hear you have such a fine daughter. As to her name I must beg to be excused from giveing her any name: that falls more immediately under your province. Mrs Washingtons Christian name is Martha.[3] I shall have no objection to that or any other name you think proper to give her.

Before this reaches you the account of the loss of the Stores at Danbury will come to hand. Our loss is considerable, in Stores; the Enemies in Men. This was a bold Manoeuver and does the Enemy great credit notwithstanding it is at our expence. It is supposed the Enemies loss amounted to upwards of Six hundred Men kild, wounded and taken Prisoners. Had not General Woster [Wooster] been wounded, ten to one but the whole party had been cut off. Before he was wounded the Enemy broke and run like fury, but after he was wounded there was nobody [to] lead the Troops on, which gave the Enemy time to rally again.[4]

By some late Accounts from England we learn that Boston is to be attackt. The Troops continueing so long at Rhode Island seems to favor the oppinion. General How still threatens Philadelphia. If he attempts it, it will be a bloody march. It is said Carlton is crossing the Lakes. If that be true General How must be bound up the North River, notwithstanding all his Parade for the Southward. Nothing remarkable has happend here since I wrote last. I write you by Every Post and every private opportunity. General Knox sends his Compliments to you. Mrs Knox is in the small Pox [innoculation] and has it very lightly. My love to all friends. Your affectionate

N GREENE

ALS (NjP).
1. Letter not found. On her illness, see below, Jacob to NG, 7 May.
2. His friend, Dr. Joseph Joslyn, is identified above, vol. 1: 56n.
3. Catharine chose the name Martha Washington.
4. The Danbury raid is described above in note, NG to Adams, 2 May.

To Benjamin Rush[1]

Dear Sir   Head Quarters Morris Town [N.J.] 3rd of May 1777

This Day your favor of the 26th of last Ult came to hand,[2] as also your observation on the best method of preserving the health of an Army; which very deservedly merit my approbation. In order that they may circulate more freely thro' the Army, I wou'd recommend to have a few Pamphlets printed, as many as you may think proper, and send them forward. Every assistance in my power to render them of that real utility for which they are intended, shall not be wanting.[3]

I rejoice to hear of a Gentleman of your abilities having entered in the Medical department and wish you all the honor and success that can be derived from so exalted a station. Doctor Cochran I make no doubt will, if necessity requires, call you to assist him.[4]

I hope you will soon complete the System you have began. The business of the Hospital I am ignorant of. I am happy to find Congress have been so liberal; it could not be expected they should have acquired a sufficient knowledge in Medicine on the formation of Hospitals. As a public body, necessity has bid them to point out a mode of proceeding, and prudence must regulate it.[5]

I shall be happy at all times to hear from you and am with the greatest regard and best wishes for your happiness and progress in useful knowledge Your most Obedt And very hble sert

N GREENE

FC (NcD-MC).
    1. Benjamin Rush (1745–1813), educated at the College of New Jersey (Princeton) and Edinburgh, was probably the best-known physician of his day. He had served in the Pennsylvania Provincial Conference and was a signer of the Declaration of Independence. When NG wrote he had just been made surgeon general of the Middle Department, advancing in July 1777 to physician general under Dr. William Shippen, Jr., director general of hospitals. The pamphlet described below was the first of many treatises he wrote. Although he espoused various reform movements, unhappily for his associates, he was often contentious and sometimes vindictive. "His complex personality," writes a recent biographer, "defied a single assessment." (Hawke, *Rush*, p. 392; this excellent work, subtitled *Revolutionary Gadfly*, does not deal with the last twenty-five years of his life.) On Rush's relations with NG and with Dr. Shippen, see his letters below, 2 December 1777 and 1 February 1778. He was one of Washington's severest critics in the so-called Conway Cabal, see note, NG to Jacob, 7 February 1778, below.
    2. Letter not found.
    3. Rush's "Directions for Preserving the Health of Soldiers" had been printed in the *Pennsylvania Packet* of 22 April, and it was probably this version he sent to NG. In September, the Board of War ordered it printed as a pamphlet as NG suggests, but it was not issued until 1778. (Butterfield, *Rush*, 1: 140–47) Rush undoubtedly knew of NG's concern for the health of his troops; see above, for example, vol. 1: 108, 251, 283, 311–12.
    4. Dr. John Cochran (1730–1807), who had seen extensive service during the French and Indian War, had just been appointed chief physician to the Middle Department. In January 1781 he succeeded Shippen as director general of hospitals, his tenure highlighted by improvements he brought about in hospitals. A recent biog-

raphy is Morris H. Saffron, *Surgeon to Washington: John Cochran* (New York: Columbia University Press, 1977).

5. Rush's medical committee had submitted a reorganization plan in February, which Congress passed 7 April 1777. (Hawke, *Rush*, 191–92; JCC, 7: 231–37).

To John Adams

Dear Sir   Bound Brook [N.J.] May 7th 1777

Yours of the 27th of April I am to acknowledge.[1] I cannot concur with you in Sentiment because the Enemy did not go to Philadelphia last December, that they had no intention then or since of going there. I am of opinion if the Enemy could have got over the Delaware immediately after our army crossd it, it would have been agreeable to their wishes. Had they effected it before the Junction of our forces under General Lee and General Gates, the consequences might have been disagreeable. The attempt was dangerous, the chain of communication from Brunswick being very extensive for the Number of their Troops to maintain, and yet I cannot think at that time they had much to fear either from Pensylvania or New Jersey.

General How has lost the most favorable opportunity this Spring of distressing us perhaps that he ever will have. Had he march'd for Philadelphia as soon as the season opend he might have performd it with less than one half the force necessary to accomplish it now. Such a stroke before the formation of our Army might have given us a deadly wound by retarding our preparations for some months,[2] increasing the Tory faction and depriving us of many valuable Stores.

You say your opinion is of no consequence to the Continent and you are happy that it is not. You add had you conceivd the conduct of our Army or the defence against the opperations of the Enemy depended in any degree upon you, you should not have contented your self with such vague conjectures. I am at a loss to conceive your meaning. Are not the Military opperations entirely under the direction of Congress? Have you not all the information that we have respecting the Enemies force and ours? Are you not acquainted with the Enemies motions and of ours also as early as possible? Are you not as deeply interested in the consequences of this dispute as any one man in America? Have not your Constituents a right to expect youl give your council in every instance where it may be useful? Would you perswade me you are insensible of the weight and influence your opinion hath in all Publick measures? Under all these considerations how am I to conceive your opinion is of no consequence and that you are happy it is not?

I readily agree with you in Sentiment that there is no one man either in the Civil or military line that is of such mighty consequence that the liberties of America are dependant upon his will or existence.

Yet there are several in both departments that America might sensibly feel the loss off at this time. If I could perswade myself that Ambition was the leading Principle either in the Cabinet or Field and not the common good of Mankind, I would have no farther connexion with the dispute, for I feel the principle of humanity too forcibly to think myself Justifiable to sacrafice the happiness of thousands only for the purpose of rearing up a few important Characters.

I note your observations upon a certain General [Washington?] that he might be of more importance to the Continent if he thought himself of less. Your opinion in this instance is very different (if I remember right) from what it was last Summer upon a similar ocasion. Then you said it was necessary to think more of ourselves and things less impracticable—this was the way to surmount difficulties. Altho I wish the Congress to support their dignity in every instance, yet I hope they will carefully avoid sporting with the finer feelings of the Gentleman [Gentlemen] of the Army unless it is necessary for the good of the publick or to preserve their own dignity.[3]

You observe that Prejudice, Caprice and Vanity are the common of[f]spring of all Revolutions and that I have less to fear from them than I immagin. These evils will rather in[crease] than decrease with the confusion of the times and they will rage in propotion as the dispute grows more or less doubtful. If you wish to establish your own authority; If you wish to give a proper tone to every State; If you wish to silence all the little factions that wrestless Spirits may produce; If you wish to be feard abroad and lovd and respected at Home, establish your Army in its full force. Nothing can give you so much Authority, weight and dignity as an Army at your command superior to all your foreign and domestick Enemies. The prospect of safety will be a pleasing circumstance to the People, and conciliate and reconcile them fully to your administration. An Army thus organized, Government fully established in the respective States, the authority of Congress fully acknowledged by each cannot fail of makeing America both easy and contented and happy at home and lovd and feard abroad. Nothing can be more mortifying and distressing to the feelings of humanity than a long continuance of the present calamities and more especially when we consider that by a proper exertion we may exterminate those hostile invadears of human happiness and the rights of mankind. Remember the long War with the United States, and the blood and treasure spent in that dispute for want of a proper exertion at first.[4]

I have no wish to see such a large propotion of important offices in the Military department in the hands of foreigners. I cannot help considering them as so many Spies in our Camp ready to take their measure as their Interest may direct.[5] If foreigners are introduceed their command should not be very extensive, then the injury cannot be great. But even in this case it is an injury to America, for the multiplying foreign officers gives us no internal strength. A good nursery of officers taught by experience firmly attacht to the interest of the Country is a great security against foreign invaders. The only tye that we have upon foreigners is the Sentiment of honnor too slender for the happiness of a Country to depend upon, while officers created from among the People are bound not only by the tyes of honnor but by that of Interest and family connexion. We in many instances see the force of British Gold. Let us not neglect to guard against its influence. I have no narrow prejudices upon this subject, neither have I any private difference with any of those Gentlemen. My opinion is founded upon the general conduct of mankind.

By a Spy out of Brunswick this day I am informed the Enemy are makeing preparations to leave that place. The disaffected Inhabitants are endeavoring to get Houses in N York. The Spy sais our friends in Brunswick have receivd letters from their friends at N York giveing an account of the Danbury affair. They write the Enemy lost nine hundred kild, wounded and missing. This account if true may console us in some degree for the loss of our Stores. The Enemy gives General Arnold the character of a devilish fighting fellow. Yours sincerely

N GREENE

ALS (MHi).
1. Letter not found. In his letterbook for that date, Adams noted that he was too fatigued to make a copy (Adams Papers, MHi). The highlights of the letter are mirrored in NG's responses.
2. On the increase in number of troops, see note, NG to Catharine, 27 April, above.
3. Adams's lost letter of 27 April was undoubtedly toned down considerably from a letter he recorded in his letter book on 13 April, which ended with the notation: "Intended for G. Green but not sent, being too impolite." (Adams Papers, MHi). In that letter he had harsh things to say of the officers who would not take the offensive when their men—"New England Men especially"—would follow a spirited enterprising officer anywhere. "If our officers will not lead their Men," he wrote, in one hyperbolic burst, "I am for shooting all who will not and getting a new lot." Although his comments in that letter were not intended as oblique references to NG, it was just as well that he did not send it.
4. Spain's war with the "United States" of the Netherlands.
5. NG was moved to his harsh judgment by the du Coudray appointment. (See below, note, NG to Adams, 28 May.) Washington expressed a similar criticism to Richard Henry Lee ten days later (Fitzpatrick, GW, 8: 74–76), as did Adams in his letter of 28 May, below. Congress was so besieged by requests from foreigners—especially French —that in mid-March it had asked its foreign agents to discourage applicants "unless they are masters of our language, and have the best recommendations" (JCC, 7: 174).

NG's sentiments of the moment were later forgotten in the warm friendships that developed between him and a number of foreign officers, especially Lafayette, Steuben, and Kosciuszko.

From Jacob Greene

Dear Sir   Potowomut [R.I.] May the 7, 1777

I Received your Kind Letter of the Twentieth of April Wherein you Express Great Concern For My Safe Arrival Which Was on the Ninth Day After I left you And A Very Tedious Journey It Was. I often Had To Stand Sentry over the Money While Howel Was Partaking of Something to Keep Him from Fainting. He Would Eat as Much as Two Men. He is A Poor Whineing Companion on the Road. I Dare Say We Shall Never Travel Together Again.[1]

When Arrived I Had the Pleasure To Find My own Family Well But Was Much Mortified To Find Caty Poorly With A Soar Brest. If thiss Misfourtune Had Not Befell Her She Would Have Been out in four Weaks. She Was A Little Two Much In A Hury in Drying away Her Milk, Did Not Have Her Breast Sufficiently Drawn, which Occasioned the Milk to Cake In Her Breast But Happily She is Likely to Get Well Soon Without Her Breast Breaking Which is Contarary To All the old Womens Expectations And of Her own Likewise. This Misfourtune Will Protract Her Intended Journey To the Camp A Considerable Time. But She Intends To Come as Soon as Her Health Will Permit Her. We Shall Take Care that Sum Person To Her Likeing Waits upon Her To Camp to Take Care of Her While their.[2]

Brother Cit [Christopher] Has Purchased the Westerly Farm or He And Griffin first Purchased it Together; But Grifin Could Not Sell What He Had In Coventry. He proposed the Companys Takeing the Whole of the Westerly Farm And Selling Him the Pettingil House And the Land Bought of uncle John Which they Have Done; this Will Hurt the Coventry Interust Much as it Layes So Near the Forge. The Westerly Farm is Much Better Land than that is At Coventry, But the Selling of this Peice of Land is A Great Disadvantage To the Whole of the Coventry Interust. How you Will Like these Alterations In the Interust Without Conssulting you I Cannot Tell, But the Brothers Have Almost Come To A Resolution Not To Venture To Sea Any More: as they Have Met With So Many Looses they think they Had Better Stop Before All is Gone. A General Division of the Interust Seems To Be the Plan Which Would Take Place If you Was At Home, But I tell them this Cannot Be Done Without Consulting you.[3]

But Divisions of Estates or Any Interust Will Not Be Left With us Without We Can Protect our Stoers Better. The Stoers Lost At Danbery Is Really Alarming, the Medisin And Tents Ireparable. This Must Be Laid To the Charge of Govener [Jonathan] Trumbull. If He Had Placed Four Hundred Militia At Danbery they Never Would Have Attempted the Destruction of the Stoers. What you Will Do For Tents for the opening of the Campaighn I Cannot Tell.[4]

Their is A Report Here that Burgoine Has Arrived At Halifax With Ten thousand Men And His Desighn is Against Boston. They Have ordered Seven Battalions To Be Raised for the use of that State. The filling of Continental Battallions is over for this Season in that State. Ours Are About Half Full And Are All Inoculated With Great Success. We Shall Never Fill our Batilions Without Comeing To Draught Which I Hope Will Be Done Immediately. The People that Intends To Inlist Are Waiting To Get More Money. If A Draught is fixed upon these People['s] Expectations Will Be over. I Would Have the Assembly Passed An Act When they Sat Last Against Giveing Any More Bounty. They Raised To Fifty Pounds, Proportioned the Men To the Towns, and Laid A fine on the Towns if they Did Not Raise their Men. All Will Not Answer. Drafting Must Be the Plan or they Will Not Be Raised. I must Refer you To Major [Samuel] Ward for News Who is the Barer of this. The People Are Much Dissatisfied At the Troops Leaveing the State When the Enemy is in the Body of it. Believe [me] To Be Sincearly yours

J GREENE

Sir

I Write From Coventry. I forgot To Mention to you that If you Did Not Approve of the Division Mentioned In My Last, Grifin Expects To Take Charge of your Interust And that by A Former Direction from you.[5] I Have Not your Last Here, Cannot Remember What your Directions were But you Need Not give yourself Any Trouble As He or I will Take Care for you. If you Send my Letters as Mentioned In My Last Let Mrs Greene Bring them. Brother Elihu Writes you By this opertunity.[6] He Has Lost His Child by Fits.

J G

ALS (NjP).

1. He and David Howell had been sent to Congress to collect money due Rhode Island. (Bartlett, *Records*, 8: 211)

2. For NG's reaction to her illness, see his letter of 3 May, above.

3. At the death of NG's father in 1770, the six sons had jointly inherited his estate, consisting of land and several houses, the forge and mill at Potowomut in Warwick, and part interest (with cousin Griffin) in the forge and mill complex in Coventry which NG had managed before the war. The brothers had continued to hold the estate "in company," had, in fact, added to it somewhat during the first few years, and supported their stepmother from the estate. NG's share of the joint profits had supplemented his meager army pay, although the family income had decreased as the anchor business fell into depression during the war. Despite their losses at sea, the brothers in Rhode Island continued privateering, sharing their profits, or losses with NG. A division of the estate was not made until 1779.

4. The Danbury raid is described above, NG to Adams, 2 May, and to Catharine, 3 May.

5. On NG's granting power of attorney to cousin Griffin, see document of 7 April 1778, below.

6. Letter not found.

From John Adams

Dear Sir   Philadelphia [Pa.] May 9, 1777

Yours of the 2d Instant came duly to hand. The Indifference of the People about recruiting the Army is a Circumstance which ought to make Us consider what are the Causes of it. It is not merely the Melancholly arising from the unfortunate Events of the last Campaign, but the unhappy [blurred] Small Pox, and above all the unhappy State of our Finances, which occasion this Evil. There are other Circumstances which are little attended to, which contribute much more than is imagined to this unfavourable Temper in the People. The Prevalence of Dissipation, Debauchery, Gaming, Prophaneness, and Blasphemy, terrifies the best people upon the Continent from trusting their Sons and other Relations among so many dangerous snares and Temptations. Multitudes of People who would with chearfull Resignation Submit their Families to the Dangers of the sword shudder at the Thought of exposing them to what appears to them, the more destructive Effects of Vice and Impiety. These Ideas would be received by many with Scorn. But there is not the less Solidity in them for that. It is Discipline alone that can Stem the Torrent. Chaplains are of great use, I believe, and I wish Mr Leonard might be in the Army, upon such Terms as would be agreeable to him, for there is no Man of whom I have a better Opinion. But there is So much difficulty in accomplishing any Thing of the Kind, that I wish G. Washington would either appoint him or recommend him to Congress.[1]

The Utility of Medals, has ever been impressed Strongly upon my Mind. Pride, Ambition, and indeed what a Philosopher would call Vanity, is the Strongest Passion in human Nature, and next to Religion, the most operative Motive to great Actions. Religion, or if the fine Gentlemen please, Superstition and Enthusiasm, is the greatest Incentive, and wherever it has prevailed, has never failed to produce Heroism. If our N. England men were alone, and could have their own Way, a great deal of this would appear. But in their present Situation, I fear We have little to expect from this Principle more than the Perseverance of the People in the cause. We ought to avail ourselves then of even the Vanity of Men. For my own Part I wish We could make a Beginning, by striking a Medal, with a Platoon firing at General Arnold, on Horseback, His Horse falling dead under him and He deliberately disentangling his Feet from the Stirrups and taking his Pistolls out of his Holsters before his Retreat. On the Reverse, He should be mounted on a Fresh Horse, receiving another Discharge of Musquetry, with a Wound in the Neck of his Horse. This Picture alone, which as I am informed is true History, if Arnold did not unfortunately belong to Connecticutt, would be sufficient to make his Fortune for Life. I believe there have been few such scenes in the World.[2]

We have not Artists at present for such Works, and many other Difficulties would attend an Attempt to introduce Medals.

Taxation is begun in N.E. The Mass.[3] raises 100,000 this year. The Regulation of Prices and the Embargo are measures of which I could never See the Justice or Policy.[4]

The Intimation in your Letter that the Enemy lost in kill'd, wounded and Prisoners 600 Men surprizes me much, mainly, because it exceeds, by at least two Thirds the largest Amount that has come from any other Authority.[5] I wish our N. England Men would practice a little honest Policy for their own Interest and Honour, by transmitting to Congress and publishing in the Newspapers, true States of the Actions in which they are concerned. The Truth alone would be sufficient for them, and surely they may be allowed to avail themselves of this Shield of Defence when So many Arts of dishonest Policy are practised against them.

Congress were too anxious for Ti[conderoga]. I wish our Army was encamped upon some Hill, twenty Miles from the Waters of the Lake, or at least Ten.

We are alarmed here with frequent Accounts of numerous Desertions from our Army. Is there no Remedy for this Evil? Howe is trying his Hand at Bribery. He is sending his Emmissaries all about and scattering ministerial Gold. They despair of the effects of Force and are now attempting Bribery and Insinuation which are more provoking than all their Cruelties. What Effect would these have in N. England!

Strechy the Secretary is an old Partisan at Electioneering, long hackneyed in the Ways of Corruption, long a ministerial Agent in that dirty Work and the greatest Master of it in the Nation, selected for that very Purpose to be sent here.[6] Pray dont you Generals sometimes practice Methods of holding up Such Characters among your Enemies, to the Contempt and Hatred of the Soldiery?

I find I have written a long Story. Excuse me, and believe me to be, with great Truth and Regard, your most obedient Servant.

LB (MHi).

1. For NG's recommendation of Leonard, see above, NG to Adams, 2 May. On 27 May, Congress authorized one chaplain to a brigade, to be named by the brigadier and appointed by Congress. None was to be recommended but "such as are clergymen of experience, and established public character for piety, virtue and learning." They were to receive the same pay, rations, and forage as a colonel. (JCC, 8: 390–91)

2. On Arnold's exploit see above, note, NG to Adams, 2 May. Being a Connecticut man temporarily cost Arnold a promotion to major general. (See above, note, Adams to NG, 9 March.)

3. Adams's native state was often called "The Massachusetts."

4. The New England Convention had recommended price regulation in December 1776. (Bartlett, *Records*, 8: 85–91; see also, above, vol. 1: 121n.) The delegates repeated their ineffectual recommendations in January 1778 as noted at William Greene to NG, 6 March 1778, below.

5. Peckham lists 171 British casualties (*Toll*, p. 33).

6. Henry Strachey was secretary to Gen. Howe as well as secretary of the British Peace Commission that had met with representatives of Congress in September 1776.

From John Adams

Philadelphia May 10, 1777

Yours of the 7th was brought me this Morning. My Meaning was that if the Conduct of our Army had depended on me, I should have taken more Pains to have obtained exact Information of the Enemies Numbers and our own, and should have considered every Indication of the Enemies Intentions of coming to Philadelphia more particularly. Altho there is no doubt that Congress have Authority to direct the military operations, yet I think they would be unwise to attempt it. This must be left to the General officers.

We have not the Information that you have respecting our own Force. There is not a Man in Congress who knows what Force you now have in N. Jersy. We have had no Returns a long time and the opinions of [the] Gentn who come from Camp are very various.[1] My Constituents have a Right to expect that I give my Council whenever it may be usefull: and my Constituents shall not be disappointed. If you knew how many dozens of my opinions are rejected where one is adopted, you would not think they had much Weight. But enough of this.

My opinion last Summer was very consistent I believe, with that in my last Letter. A Man may be humble before the Enemy, and proud before a Friend. Some who think too little of their Powers and Forces against the Enemy think too highly of their own Importance among their Friends, and treat the latter with less Delicacy than they would the former. For my own Part I care not how haughty Men are to the Enemies of their Country provided they have Regard to Truth and Justice, nor how humble they are among its Friends.

If by the finer Feelings of the Gentlemen of the Army are meant their Moral Feelings, no Man detests more than myself, the Idea of hurting them. But if Vanity and Pleasure is meant, I think no Harm would be done by mortifying it. I am much mistaken and much misinformed, if the nice Feelings the Pride, the Vanity, the Foppery, the Knavery and Gambling among too many of the Officers do not end in direct Endeavours to set up a Tyrant sooner or later, unless early Endeavours are used to controul them. I dont mean by this any General Reflection upon the officers, most of whom I believe to be good Citizens at present, but by the Representations We hear there are so many of an opposite Character, that there is danger that the Contagion will Spread.

The Necessity of establishing an Army Superiour to all our Enemies is obvious, and, for my own Part, I dont See any Thing in the Power of Congress to do to accomplish this great Purpose but what has been done. If you think of any Thing more that is proper to be done, I should thank you for the Hint. I have Reason to believe upon very good Authority, that foreign Troops might be hired, both Germans, Swiss and French. What think you of the Policy of hiring them?[2] The Waste of the Natives of the Country, in the Army, is a melancholly and an alarming Consideration. We want People for Agriculture, Manufactures, Commerce and War, both by Sea and Land.

AL (Adams Papers: MHi). This letter is not in Adams's letter book but among "letters received." It may never have been posted. In NG's next letter (of 28 May, below), he does not refer to a letter from Adams by date, but his comments are in response to Adams's letter of 9 May above.

1. On the long gap in returns, see above, note, NG to Catharine, 27 April.

2. For NG's view of the policy, see below, NG to Adams, 28 May. For suggestions by others on the use of mercenaries, see Burnett, *Letters*, 2: 451n.

From Samuel Adams[1]

My dear Sir   Philad'l May 12, 1777

Amidst your Hurry of Business and my own, I cannot help withdrawing myself for a moment to throw on paper a single Sentiment for your Consideration. Europe and America seem to be applauding our Introduction of the Fabian Method[2] of carrying on this war without considering as I conceive the widely different Circumstances of the Carthaginian and the British Generals. It will recur to your memory that the Faction of Hanno in Carthage prevented Hannibals receiving the Supplys from them which he had a Right to expect and his necessities required.[3] This left him to the Resources of his own mind, and obligd him to depend upon such Supplys as he could procure from the Italians. Under such a Circumstance, it was the Wisdom of Fabius to put himself in the State of Defence but by no means of inactivity by keeping a watchful Eye upon Hannibal and cuting of[f] his forraging and other Parties. By frequent Skirmishes he had the strongest Reason to promise himself the ruin of his Army without any necessity of risqueing his own by a general Engagement. But General Howe (whom, by the way, I am not about to compare to Hannibal as a Soldier) has at all times the best Assurances of supplies from Britain. There is no Faction there to disappoint him, and the

British Navy is resourceful enough to protect Transports and provision Vessels coming to him. Hannibal dispaird of Reinforcements from Carthage, but Howe has the fullest Assurances of early reinforcements from Britain and cannot fail of receiving them unless a general War has taken place which I think is at least problematical. They are expected any Day. Would Fabius, if he were his Enemy, pursue the Method he took with the Carthaginian General? Would he not rather attend to the [present?] Circumstances, and by Destroying the Army in Brunswick prevent as much as possible the Enemy increasing in Strength even if reinforcements should arrive, or putting a total end to the Campaign if they should not. I am sensible our own Circumstances have been such, thro' the Winter past, as to make it impracticable to attempt anything, but I hope we are or shall be very soon in a Condition to take a decisive part, and I do not entertain any Doubt but we shall see such an enterprising Spirit as will confound our Enemies and give assurances to the Friends of Liberty and Mankind that we still retain a just Sense of our own Dignity and the Dignity of our Cause, and are resolvd by Gods assistance to support it at all Hazzards.[4] I am &c.

ADf (NN). Since some of Adams's writing is virtually illegible, the editors have been aided by the transcription of the man most familiar with his hand—Harry A. Cushing, who edited the *Writings of Samuel Adams*, 4 vols. (New York: G. P. Putnam's Sons, 1904–8); see 3: 370–72.

1. Samuel Adams, the Massachusetts radical leader, who was then a member of Congress and its Board of War. (*JCC*, 7: 32) This letter and NG's answer of 28 May constitute the only correspondence between them that has been found.

2. Many American leaders equated Washington's delaying tactics with those used by the Roman Fabius against Hannibal. Although not a Latin scholar, NG indicates in his answer that he was familiar with the Roman wars.

3. Hanno, the leader of the land-owning party of Carthage, helped to bring about Hannibal's final failure in Italy by his unwillingness to send him supplies.

4. NG replied 28 May, below.

From George Washington

Dear Sir   Morris Town [N.J.] May 12, 1777

In your ride to and from Peeks Kill, I would have you make the best observations that time and Circumstances will admit, upon the Country, and point out, at your return, such places for Posts of Communication, as you shall conceive necessary.[1]

Determine upon the propriety of having a Post at Pompton, examine the Works throwing up at that place, and give such directions to General [Nathaniel] Heard or Officer Commanding the Militia there respecting them, as shall appear to you proper.[2]

After examining the State and Condition of the Forts in the Highlands (especially Fort Montgomery) the probability of an Attack by Water, and the practicability of approaching them by Land, After seeing, where, and how this is to be effected, viewing the Eminences, from whence these Forts can be annoyed and hearing the sentiments of the General Officers present, you will give such Orders for further defence, as shall appear to you necessary for the greater security of the Passes (by Land and Water) through the Highlands; and moreover, dispose of the Troops in such a Manner, as you shall judge most likely to answer the end in View.

The Pass through the Highlands on the West side of the North River should also be attended to, lest the Enemy by a Coup de Main should possess themselves of it, before a sufficient force could be assembled to oppose them. This however, may be the work of Militia, if to be had; if not, the Detachments of Eastern Troops under Colonels [Zebulon] Butler and [Jeremiah] Olney (upon giving me notice) shall be sent thither.

Turn your attention also to the Boats and direct them to be removed to the place or places of greatest safety and where they can be had for the transportation of our Troops over the North River, if occasion should require it. Examine into the State of Military Stores and Stock of Provisions at the Forts, and direct a Sufficiency, having an Eye to Circumstances; For if the Works are not tenable, or the passage of the River defensible, a large Stock of either wou'd only add to our losses; if they are, Supplies can easily (if the Enemy can be kept below the Highlands, and Carleton from our Backs) be brought to them.

Inquire what has been, or can be done towards removing the Stores from Derby,[3] and other places, to the West side of the North River, and learn, if possible, how the Country on this side is stored with Provisions and Forage for the Support of Troops, if any should be marched thither.

Keep the precise time of your return secret, lest the disaffected should avail themselves of the Knowledge to offer you an insult. I am Dear Sir Your Most [Humble] and Affecte. Servt.

G WASHINGTON

Tr (Varick Transcripts, Washington Papers: DLC).

1. To Washington, the British raids on Peekskill and Danbury portended a full-scale offensive up the Hudson River which would threaten the vital communications link between New England and the other states. After the British gained control of the lower Hudson in November 1776, the Americans opened several routes through the rugged Hudson Highlands west of the Hudson River. Washington had sent Greene and Knox to Peekskill to advise Gen. McDougall on improving the defenses of the area, with apparent authority to initiate any alterations NG saw fit. (Fitzpatrick, *GW*, 8: 45) The report to Washington of 17 May by NG and other general officers is printed below.

2. Pompton, N.J., was on a branch of the Passaic River, some twenty miles northwest of New York City.

3. Derby, Conn., was at the confluence of the Housatonic and Naugatuck Rivers, near New Haven.

To General George Clinton[1]

[Ft. Montgomery, N.Y., 14 May 1777. Greene, Knox, and McDougall,[2] having arrived at Ft. Montgomery after Clinton had left, wish to see him two days hence to discuss alterations in the fort as well as other defenses of the area. ALS (NjHi) 2 pp.]

1. George Clinton (1739–1812), recently named brigadier general in the Continental army, had been put in charge of Ft. Montgomery, a few miles north of Peekskill on the west bluffs of the Hudson River. After his failure to halt British Gen. Henry Clinton in the fall of 1777, he began an extraordinary career in politics, serving as governor of New York 1777–95 and 1800–1804 and as vice president under Jefferson and Madison. (E. W. Spaulding, *His Excellency George Clinton: Critic of the Constitution* [New York: MacMillan Co., 1938]).

2. Scottish-born Alexander McDougall (1732–86) had been a successful N.Y. merchant and early advocate of American rights, spending a year in prison in 1771 for his views. Before entering the army, he served in the N.Y. Provincial Congress. As a major general after October 1777, he proved an effective defender of the Hudson Highlands, where he was stationed for most of the war. He and NG had a long and amicable relationship. In the 1780s he represented New York in the Continental Congress. (*DAB*; a recent study is Roger Champagne, *Alexander McDougall and the American Revolution in New York* (Schenectady, N.Y.: Union College Press, 1975).

To the Continental Agents of New York

[New Windsor, N.Y., 17 May 1777. Cites Council's decision below on building frigates and galleys. "You will please therefore to give all the assistance in your power to get the Ships compleated as soon as possible." Men and guns for ships will be found. N.Y. Council of Safety will doubtless help. ALS (Washington Papers: DLC) 2 pp.]

To Captain John Grinnel[1]

[Peekskill, N.Y., 17 May 1777. Grinnel is to report immediately to commanding officer at Peekskill for instructions on quickest method of "haveing the Ships and Gallies fixt" for securing North River.[2] ACyS (Washington Papers: DLC) 1 p.]

1. Letter was addressed to Grinnel as commander of the "ship *Congress*."
2. For Washington's instruction on use of ships, see his letter to NG, 12 May, above.

To George Washington

Dear Sir   Peeks Kill [N.Y.] May 17, 1777

Inclosed is the opinion of the General Officers at this Post and General Wayne[1] who has had a very good opportunity to view the River and the fortifications upon the same. Agreeable to your Excellencies instructions I have given the necessary orders to carry the further obstructions in the River into execution.[2] I am going this day up to New Windsor to view the obstructions there and the passes through the High Lands to the Clove,[3] after which I shall be able to give your Excellency a very good history of the state of things here, which I shall do at my return. It will be impossible to be at Home under two days. I am with great respect your Excellency['s] obedient Sert

N GREENE

ALS (Washington Papers: DLC). Enclosure printed below.

1. Anthony Wayne (1745–96), in command of the Pennsylvania Line, had recently been made brigadier general, having earlier distinguished himself in the Canadian campaign of 1776. NG may have met him briefly on Long Island in 1776, but their meeting this time began a close friendship. After fighting courageously at Brandywine in September 1777, Wayne suffered a bloody defeat at Paoli the following week, although he was later exonerated of any blame. His resounding victory two years later at Stony Point (July 1779) helped to wipe out the memory of Paoli and earned him a congressional medal. Dashing in appearance, and impetuous at times, Wayne was far from deserving the sobriquet "Mad," which was given him by a disgruntled soldier and which stuck to him forever after. He served under NG in the South, driving the British from Georgia, and at the end of the war, Georgia gave Wayne and Greene adjoining plantations. Wayne was at Greene's bedside when he died in June 1786. Despite Wayne's contributions to the War for Independence, he is remembered primarily for his victory over the Indians at Fallen Timbers in Ohio Territory, 1794. See Harry Emerson Wildes, *Anthony Wayne: Trouble Shooter of the American Revolution* (New York: Harcourt Brace, 1941).

2. See letters this day, NG to John Grinnel, to Continental Agents of New York, and to unidentified person.

3. On Smith's Clove, see note, NG's orders, 15 July, below.

General Officers to George Washington

Peekskill [N.Y.]
May it please your Excellency   May 17th 1777

We have examined the Obstructions in the North River, and beg leave to observe that the object is too important to be trusted to its present security. If those obstructions in the River can be rendered effectual, and the Passes into the Highlands be properly guarded, which can be done with about four or five thousand Troops, the rest of the Army will be at liberty to operate elsewhere.

To render the obstruction at Fort Montgomery compleat it will be necessary to have a Boom across the River, and one or two cables in front of the chain to break the force of the ship[p]ing before they come up to it. The two Continental Ships should be immediately man'd and fix'd; and the Two Row-Gallies, to be stationed just above the obstructions, which will form a front fire equal to what the Enemy can bring against them. The fire from the Ships and Gallies in front, and the Batteries upon the flank, will render it impossible for the Shipping to operate there, if the obstructions in the River bring them up [i.e., stop them]; which, with the additional strength proposed, we have great reason to expect.

The communication between the Eastern and Western States is so essential to the Continent, and the advantages we shall have over the Enemy by the communication, and the great expence that will be saved in transportation of Stores by having the command of the River, warrants every expence to secure an object of such great magnitude. We are very confident if the obstructions in the River can be rendered effectual, the Enemy will not attempt to opperate by Land, the passes through the Highlands are so exceeding difficult.[1] We are with the greatest respect and esteem Your Excellency's most obed servts

NATH GREENE	ANTHY WAYNE
ALEX MCDOUGALL	GEO CLINTON
H KNOX	

DS (Washington Papers: DLC). Enclosed with NG to Washington, 17 May, above.

1. Although the cables and chain proved formidable barriers, NG and his fellow officers underestimated the enemy. In October, Gen. Henry Clinton landed troops several miles below Ft. Montgomery on the west side of the river and marched them up the "exceeding difficult" passes, capturing the undermanned Fts. Montgomery and Clinton (recently built) from the west. (Willcox, *Clinton*, pp. 180–81) For a description of the principal pass through the Highlands, see note, NG's orders, 15 July, below.

To [   ]

[From New Windsor, N. Y., 17 May 1777. Recipient to apply to Gen. George Clinton on manning and equipping vessels requested in the orders above. ALS (Washington Papers: DLC) 1 p.]

To Colonel Hugh Hughes[1]

Sir   New Windsor [N.Y.] May 18th 1777

His Excellency General Washington sent me and General Knox to this division of the Army, to examin the Forts, Fortifications and obstructions across the River; also the State of the Provision at each Post and the condition of the Quarter Master Generals department in this division of the Army.

I am sorry to find a general complaint at all the Posts of a want of Forage. You must be sensible by this [time] that a considerable part of the Continental forces are drawing together at Peeks Kills and its environs. You also must be sensible that no opperations can take place if the motions of the Enemy render it ever so necessary without the article of Forage.

The season is fast approaching when we may expect the Enemy

will be in motion, and to be unprepard to counteract them for want of Forage will be a great misfortune. I am told by some of your deputies the Evil originates through the neglect of the Agents of Mr Duer; if that is the case you must not trust to them for a supply any longer. Receive all that they send in, but immediately take such measures to establish proper Magizines as will afford a sufficent supply to all parts of the Army. If the Inhabitants will not furnish it voluntarily, you must apply to the commanding officer at Peeks Kill for a proper Guard to take it, paying or giving certificates for everything so taken.

Waggons and Horses to transport the Regimental baggage, artillery Horses and covered Waggons for Military Stores, should be provided as soon as possible. Your utmost Exertions will be necessary to provide these things seasonably.

Let the Provision be got over the North River agreeable to the resolve of Congress and order of General Washington, and lodgd at such places as General George Clinton shall direct.

I must intreat you to use all possible diligence to get everything in your department in the greatest forwardness. Your own industry is unexceptionable, but you will please to have an Eye to those that acts under you as few are faithful enough to discharge their duty without such attention. I am Sir, your obedt Servant

N. GREENE

ACyS (Washington Papers: DLC).
1. Hughes, deputy quartermaster for New York, is identified below at NG's letter to him of 31 March 1778.

To Catharine Greene

My dear   Morris Town [N.J.] May 20th 1777
I returnd last Night from Peeks Kill after a long tedious and hard Jorney. To crown all I fell from my Horse upon the Top of an exceeding high Mountain, cut my lip through and otherwise bruised myself exceedingly. Never did I undergo more fatigue in less time. Last night at Mr Lotts within about nine miles of this place, I heard you was gone on before me. O how my Heart leapt for Joy nothwithstanding I was sure it was impossible:[1] yet the thought was so pleasing I could not help indulging the sweet delusion. My dear, it is now a month and upwards since I receivd a line from one of the family. I think it exceeding unkind; if you are unwell and incapable of writing surely some of the brothers might do me that friendly office. However disagreeable consequences may be it is some consolation to know them. Nothing is more painful than a state of Suspense. Pray my love

let me know the worst that I may accomodate my mind to the evil. The last accounts I had from you was you was exceeding unwell, takeing four grains of Mercury every day. Think how you would feel if I had been in an engagement and left your mind under the torture of Suspense for upwards of a month. O how cruel!

I most ardently wish to see you but the great distance between us, the poor accomodacion on the roads, the uncertainty of the motions of the Enemy and your weak state of health are obstacles that prevent my pressing you to come agreeable to my wishes. Prudence restrains what my heart most inclines to. I cannot express the secret pleasure I felt at hearing you was come, altho I knew it must be false. Yet so strong were my wishes that reason was oblige to give place to my deluded hopes.

How are all the family? How are our little Progeny? Let me hear by the next Post. Remember me to all friends.

If you are in want of any new cloaths purchase them. Dont come on without being properly furnished with everything necessary. I will furnish you with such forms as may be necessary to discharge all your Bills. If you are in want of anything from Boston, write to Mrs. Knox. She will furnish you and Ill pay the General here. But remember when you write to Mrs Knox you write to a good scholar; therefore mind and spell well. You are defective in this matter, my love, a little attention will soon correct it. Bad writing is nothing if the spelling is but good. People are often laught at for not spelling well but never for not writeing well. It is said it is ungenteel for Gentlemen to make observations upon Ladies writeing. I hope you wont think it unkind in me. Nothing but the affection and regard I feel for you makes me wish to have you appear an accomplished Lady in every point of view. [2]

The Enemy remains at Brunswick in a frighted condition. Our Army are encamping near Boundbrook. Nothing material has happened since I left this place. By some late Arrivals from France a fresh supply of arms and cloathing is recievd, and it is said the British Ministry are not likely to get any Reinforcements from Germany. If so, poor General Howe is still at an humble distance from the great and important business of conquering America.

My hand trembles so prodigiously that I can scarcely write. Pray excuse me, and believe me to be most sincerely your affectionate

N GREENE

This is the last letter Ill write until I receive one. Tell your brother Bill to bring in the bald Horse if he is in good Order. How are Sister Sara and Nancy? [3]

ALS (MiU-C).

1. She did not arrive until June.

2. Catharine's spelling was no worse than that of many young women, including those brought up in better financial circumstances. It may have bothered the aristocratic Lucy Flucker Knox (who was never to care for her anyway), but Catharine's natural charm would win the admiration of countless of NG's fellow officers, including Washington, LaFayette, and Lucy's husband. NG's criticism undoubtedly embarrassed her and may have caused her, after his death, to destroy her letters to him. (See above, vol. 1: xxx.) Her surviving letters to Washington, Hamilton, Knox, Edward Rutledge, and Eli Whitney display no great improvement in spelling, but they are well written and often entertaining.

3. Sarah Greene, wife of NG's cousin Griffin, and Nancy Vernon. The somewhat petulant tone of this letter gave way to relief and joy over the receipt of a letter from his "dear Angel," as his reply of 20 May below reveals.

To Catharine Greene

My dear Angel   Morris Town [N.J.] May the 20, 1777

Since I wrote you this morning I receivd your letter of the 29th of April.[1] The contents has wrung drops of blood from my heart. Gracious God how much I wish to come to you. How unfortunate you are. How can that tyrant General delight in exercising cruelties towards the distressed,[2] to rob you of the society of your brother amidst your distress. He is as unfeeling as he is unpolite. That Gentleman has the least gratitude of any Person I ever saw that claims so much. Thank God the Liberties of America are not in his power. He may gratify his little resentment against you in my absence, but dare not do it if I was present to afford you the protection which I owe and wish to give. Bear with patience my beloved those little impositions. It will not be long in his power to tyrannise. I would have scornd to have treated his Lady in so ungenteel a manner.

I was exceeding unhappy at not hearing from you. I thought myself neglected and felt the force of the misfortune that no friendly hand would give me a History of domestic matters.

You dear Angel, how my Heart feels for you. I Pray Almighty God may restore your health and comfort again. Nothing would give me greater pleasure than to come and see you, but before this I Hope you are well enough to set out to see me as it is near three Weeks since you wrote; besides this the General will not permit me to go. I have had exceeding hard duty this spring. The General keeps me constantly upon the go. The love and friendship he has for me and the respect and kindness he shows me goes a great way to alleviate my pains. I am as well ⟨loved⟩ and respected in the Army as I can wish; but notwithstanding the honnors of War and the love and respect of ⟨men⟩ I feel a blank in my Heart which nothing but your presence can fill up. There is not a day or night, nay not an hour, but I wish to fold you to my Heart. If you think your Health and strength will endure the Jorney, my heart will leap for joy to meet you. If you are in want of any Cloaths write to Mrs Knox: she will get you what ever you want. The General has wrote to her for that purpose, and I am to pay the General here.

Mr Lotts family have engaged you to spend the Summer there.[3] It is about Nine Miles from this place and about twenty two or three miles from the place where we are going to encamp. They are one of the finest families you ever saw. The old Gentleman and his Lady are as merry as boys of fourteen. There are four or five fine young ladies of delicate Sentiments and polite Education. They are all anxious to see you and cultivate your acquaintance. They long to see you and impatiently wait your coming. Heaven grant it may be speedy. Mrs Hoffman and the Ladies of this place wish to see you as does Lady Sterling and Lady Kitty, one of the finest [ms damaged] Ladies I ever saw.[4] But Mr Lott claims the preference to your society. His Son in Law, Mr [William S.] Livingston, was one of my aid de camps last year which introduced me into the family. You may learn musick and French, too, there. Adieu my second self. Heaven grant you speady health is the prayer of your ever Affectionate

N GREENE

My love to all friends. Kiss the dear little Pledges of conjugal affection.

ALS (NjP); slightly damaged: words in angle brackets from Nightingale Transcripts (furnished in 1973 by Mr. Bernard Nightingale, Brunswick, Ga.).
  1. Letter not found.
  2. The "tyrant General" was NG's long-time friend, James M. Varnum, who commanded the newly formed R.I. brigade in which Catharine's brother William Littlefield was a captain. Since the brigade was in Rhode Island during Catharine's illness, NG saw no reason for her brother not to get leave. His exaggerated reaction in this letter was undoubtedly for her sake. The formal tone of Greene's and Varnum's later correspondence indicates that their relationship was not quite as amicable as it had been, although this incident was probably more a symptom than a cause of any rift. In fact, William Littlefield was anything but a conscientious officer; as revealed in several letters over the next few years, he was absent without apparent leave on more than one occasion.
  3. Abraham Lott (1714–94) was a wealthy merchant and active patriot who had fled New York City with his wife and daughters in 1776 to Beverwyck, an elegant country house ten miles northeast of Morristown. The gracious hospitality extended to NG and staff by the Lotts engendered a close friendship between the two families. Catharine, who was to be a long-time guest, named her second daughter Cornelia Lott Greene after one of the daughters. (A. V. Phillips, *The Lott Family in America* [Trenton, N.J., 1942]; *PMHB*, 70 [1946]: 294) Lott was not beyond using his friendship with his influential guests to further his own interests. See, for example, NG to Jeremiah Wadsworth, 19 May 1778, and William S. Livingston to NG, 20 June 1779, below.
  4. Lady Stirling was the wife of NG's friend, Lord Stirling (William Alexander); Lady Kitty was their daughter, who married William Duer the next year. NG had been an occasional guest at the Stirlings' imposing estate (which later bankrupted the family) at Basking Ridge, south of Morristown.

To [   ]¹

Dear Sir

Morris Town [N.J.] May 20, 1777

I embrace this opportunity by Capt [John] Gooch to write you. I have little or nothing to write about, but as there is no Postage to pay it will be the less exceptionable.

Sometime since I heard Henry Merchant Esqr was appointed Member of the Continental Congress to represent the State of Rhode Island. I am told he hesitates about the acceptance; should he refuse I wish some good, plain, honest man may be elected in his stead that is well acquainted with business.² The Congress have so many of those talking Gentlemen among them that they tire themselves and every body else with their long, labourd speeching that is calculated more to display their own talents than promote the publick Interest. One man of business that executes what he proposes and proposes nothing but what he means to execute will promote the Publick service more in one hour than a Captious, disputeing fellow will in a month. I have no objection to Mr Merchant, neither do I think these remarks characteristical of him but to warn you against an evil that now prevails in Congress and to prevent your increasing of it by an injudicious appointment. The reputation of the State is at stake in appointing a member. He ought to be a man of good sound Judgment, and a good English Education at least; so far is essential, further will be still more Ornamental, and consequently respectable. Mr. William Ellery is greatly respected in Congress. I wish whoever may be sent may be as much so.

I am sorry to hear of the little factions that still prevail in the State. However, this evil is inevitable. In a relaxation of Government the distresses of the People, multiplied by the calamities of the times, the natural ofsprings of every War, convulsions and changes of administration is to be expected. These are the times when the most worthless and contemptable can get into place by feeding the Jealousies and discontent of the People. It is a great Misfortune when such Novices gets into the Councils of the State. They have neither Wisdom, Virtue or experience to execute the business commited to their charge. This is an evil much to be lamented but how to remedy it I know not as the People will not be convinceed until it is at their cost. The credulity of the common People affords a fair opportunity to these miscreants to practice a temporary imposition. But the Virtue and wisdom of an Angel is insufficient to preserve the confidence of a People long who are struggling with distress. Like a drownding man they catch at everything however unsubstantial that promises the least relief. I could wish the Legislators of every State to avoid multiplying Penal Laws. Nothing gives the Populace such a contempt for the Authority of Government as the passing laws that are never carried into execution. The divisions among you between the Country and City is a great misfortune.

The Regulations of trade and halting Merchandise will only increase your difficulties. They will produce artificial scarcities now and real ones by and by. The Policy of these proceedings ever appeard to me to be grounded upon false maxims in commerce.[3] The prohibitary Laws against sending West India Goods out of the State to the Neighbouring States has given ⟨great⟩ disgust to the Neighbouring States, Particularly ⟨New York⟩ and New Jersey. The Sea Ports of those two States ⟨being⟩ Shut up and the Inhabitants deprivd of any means ⟨of getting⟩ supplies from the Neighbouring States is thought to be a great hardship. I wish that more Liberal and generous Principles pervaded your councils and the councils of all the States that there might be a Reigning harmony among the whole. I wish to see the several States consider themselves as one great body, and the different States as so many Limbs of the same body, each essential to the happiness of the whole, that they may cultivate a good understanding among one another.[4]

The Eastern [i.e., New England] Troops come in very slow. The innoculation detains them a long while but it is a necessary detention, yet it is much to be lamented. General How is very complasant: he has delayed his operations a long while to give us an opportunity to draw our forces together. We shall soon be strong enough here to bid him defiance. I hope the Peeks Kill and Ticonderoga divisions will soon be able to say the same. There are some very pleasing accounts from Europe. Fear not, the American cause is secure.

My love to all your family. I am with sincerity and truth your sincere friend

N GREENE

ALS (RHi). Words in angle brackets from a nineteenth-century transcript (MWA).

1. The recipient has not been identified but was obviously well known to NG and was knowledgeable about R.I. politics.

2. Henry Marchant (1741–96) had been chosen as a delegate to Congress in February, but, having been unable to attend, was reappointed in May and served until 1779. A Newport lawyer and ardent patriot, Marchant had been an agent for the colony of Rhode Island in England during 1771–72 and attorney general for colony and state, 1772–79. At the outbreak of war, he moved from Newport to South Kingstown. (*DAB*; his papers were recently given to the R.I. Historical Society.) Any criticism NG had of Marchant was a result of not knowing him. He came to respect and like him, although they were never close.

3. In December 1776, at the suggestion of a convention of New England delegates meeting in Providence, the state of Rhode Island fixed prices on virtually all "labor, goods, wares, merchandize and manufactures" and on such services as a shave, a night's lodging, and horseshoeing. Wages were modified in March and May 1777. (Bartlett, *Records* 8: 85–91, 183) Other New England states passed similar legislation,

but in the face of wartime scarcities and the overprinting of money, price controls were virtually unenforceable. This did not prevent the New England convention from recommending more stringent controls in January 1778. (See note, William Greene to NG, 6 March 1778, below. On the embargo against goods leaving a state, see below, NG to Cooke, 10/11 July 1777.)

NG too had once thought it possible to control prices. (For example, see his order of 19 September 1775, above, vol. 1: 120–21.) After becoming quartermaster general, he still favored controls on a single item—forage for the army. (NG to William Greene, 11 September 1778, and to Jonathan Trumbull, 14 September 1778). For a table on currency depreciation, see Appendix I at the end of this volume. A thorough study of the problems of wage and price controls is chapter two of Richard B. Morris, *Government and Labor in Early America* (New York: Columbia University Press, 1946.)

4. NG's continental view of the United States had been evident months before there was a United States. (See above, vol. 1: 122 and 135.) This viewpoint, shared by other general officers, was in marked contrast to the particularistic attitudes of state officials who imposed embargoes against goods leaving their borders (unless purchased by the army), making a mockery of the very term "United States." Embargoes were a response to wartime scarcities—scarcities that denied basic necessities to the poor and worked hardships on many others. Within a state the embargo was a companion of price regulation in having as its objective the sharing of available goods by all its citizens, but from the point of view of other states, or of a continentalist like NG, it was the very antithesis of sharing. Unfortunately, for the sake of unity among diverse states, it was far easier for an official to spot a boat being loaded with embargoed goods or a wagon rumbling toward a neighboring state than it was to detect money being passed under the table for price-controlled goods. Embargoes, therefore, were relatively successful; price regulations were an abysmal failure.

A secondary motive for levying embargoes was to prevent goods from falling into British hands or into American hands willing to sell to the British. This, for example, was especially applicable in Connecticut after August 1776 when the British controlled Long Island. But Connecticut passed its first embargo in May 1775 when no such reason existed (Hoadly, *Records*, 14: 415–16), adding to it until its repeal in 1781. That embargo was aimed primarily against neighboring Rhode Island and New York, both of which were partially dependent on Connecticut foodstuffs.

It was not until May 1777 that Rhode Island levied its first embargo on goods to other states—on goods normally imported and transshipped, such as rum, sugar, molasses, coffee, leather, sheep, and wool. The justification, according to the preamble, was that the British blockade made it "impossible to procure further supplies." (*R.I. Acts*, May 1777, pp. 13–14) In reality, substantial amounts of such goods regularly slipped in; the essential purpose of the act, it would appear, was to induce Connecticut to lift its embargo. Unfortunately, since Connecticut seamen were equally adept at slipping through the blockade, Rhode Island's embargo did not have the desired effect on Connecticut. As NG points out above, it did hurt New Jersey and New York, although New York had already embargoed certain goods, as noted, NG to Gov. Clinton, 14 September 1778, below.

Connecticut relented somewhat in the winter of 1778–79, when the desperate entreaties of Gov. William Greene for food finally moved officials to ease the embargo, but only temporarily. A year later, Rhode Island imposed another embargo on all the imported goods enumerated in the act of May 1777, adding a host of others. The legislators made no effort this time to hide their motives, declaring that the state had been greatly "injured and impoverished" by the embargoes of their "Sister States of *Connecticut*, for a long Time since, and of *Massachusetts-Bay* of late." (*R.I. Acts*, October 1779, p. 9) Retaliation, however, was no more effective than it had been in 1777. Connecticut maintained its embargo until 1781.

In NG's letter to Gov. Cooke of 10/11 July, below, he is even stronger in his denunciation of price controls and Rhode Island's retaliatory embargo.

From Elisha Boudinot

[Newark, N.J., 23 May 1777. An unnamed informer known to NG reports that fifty British sail are on the coast with ten thousand men; that the British are to march on Philadelphia when reinforcements arrive; and that a fifty-gun (British) ship had blown up at Newport.[1] ALS (CSmH) 2 pp.]

1. This is not untypical of the rumors, some planted by the enemy, that informers passed on to the army as intelligence. There were not fifty vessels off the coast, and during the entire summer, Howe received only six thousand reinforcements; Howe himself, moreover, had not decided what he would do in New Jersey (Gruber, *Howe Brothers*, pp. 197–205; Mackesy, *War*, pp. 118–19). And finally, no such explosion occurred at Newport.

To General John Sullivan

[Bound Brook, N.J., 24 May 1777. Has not the "least objection" to allowing Hazen's regiment to remain with Sullivan in place of German regiment. LS (NhHi) 1 p.]

To George Washington

Dear General   Bound Brook [N.J.] [May 24, 1777]
    Your Excellencies favor of yesterday this moment came to hand.[1] I am perfectly satisfied with the exchange of Hazens Regiment for the Barron Arends [Arendt].[2] I am by no means attacht to any particular Regiment. Nearly an equal distribution of the forces will be entirely satisfactory to me. I only wish to stand upon an equal footing with other Officers; then if I don't execute my duty as well, I am willing to be subject to censure.
    General Sullivans reasons for the exchange are very substantial and perfectly satisfactory. I ever wish to make the good of the service my principal object; when I deviate from that line I wish to be corrected.[3]
    I arrivd at this place yesterday about Noon and immediately issueed the necessary orders for collecting the Troops together from the out Posts.
    I fear without great exertion in the Commisaries department there will be a want of Provision. I shall endeavor to learn the design of the Enemies collection of Waggons.
    We shall begin to lay off the encampment this morning.[4] Colo [Clement] Biddle arrivd too late last Night to do anything more than

to ride round the ground. I am with the greatest Respect Your Excellencies Obedient Servt

N GREENE

ALS (Washington Papers: DLC).

1. Letter not found.

2. Moses Hazen (1733–1803), a Massachusetts-born Canadian, was colonel of the Second Canadian Regiment. He had served under Montgomery in 1775 and later fought at Brandywine, Germantown, and Yorktown. In 1781 he was made brigadier general. (DAB)

Henry (or Henri?) Leonard Philip, Baron d'Arendt, one of the earliest French volunteers to the American cause, was colonel of the so-called German regiment from Maryland and Pennsylvania. In August 1778 he returned to France because of ill health. (Balch, French, p. 41; Fitzpatrick, GW, 8: 301–2 and n)

3. For more on this exchange, see letters of same date, Arendt to NG, NG to Sullivan, and Sullivan to NG.

4. With British troops assembling at Brunswick, Washington concluded that at last Gen. Howe was preparing to march on Philadelphia. Aware that his main army at Morristown was too far off the invasion route to impede Howe, Washington decided to move the troops twenty miles to the south. He sent NG to lay out a camp at Middlebrook (near Boundbrook), eight miles up the Raritan River from Brunswick, behind the first range of Watchung Mountains. This strong defensive position allowed the Americans to keep watch on any British movement along the Brunswick-Trenton road, yet so positioned as to make a hasty retreat further into the mountains if necessary. (Ward, War, 1: 325). NG's brigades were the first to arrive from Basking Ridge.

From John Adams

[Philadelphia, 24 May 1777. In a lengthy discourse, Adams describes the bribes and false peace hopes by which the Roman General Sulla (whom he calls Sylla) defeated his enemies. He sees Howe as no Sulla but thinks many troops in the Continental army lack sufficient ties and loyalties to the cause.[1] LB (MHi) 3 pp.]

1. In February 1777 Gen. Howe had offered £3 to any "rebel" who would desert to the British, £4 if he brought his weapon. In April a large plot of land was added to the inducement if a man would serve the British for two years. Howe's biographer estimates thirty to forty American deserters a day joined the British during March and April—especially from among the Irish- and British-born soldiers in Washington's army. (Gruber, Howe Brothers, pp. 197–98, 205) Washington thought a principal cause of desertion was American officers withholding soldiers' pay, with another being American recruitment by purchasing "Convict Servants" from their masters. (Washington to Congress 12 and 13 May, Fitzpatrick, GW, 8: 45–46 and 56–57) Desertion, of course, was not a one-way street. Congress countered Howe's enticements by empowering Washington to "offer such rewards as he shall judge proper" to encourage British deserters. (4 June 1777, JCC, 8: 417)

From Baron d'Arendt

[Quibbletown, N.J., 24 May 1777. Acknowledges NG's letter[1] conveying Washington's orders to report to Princeton. Hopes to get tents for his regiment at Bound Brook and, on arriving at Princeton, to have ten days leave for important business in Philadelphia. ALS (NjHi) Original in French. 1 p.]

1. Letter not found. On Arendt's transfer, see above, NG to Washington, same day.

From General John Sullivan

[Princeton, N.J., 24 May 1777. Thanks NG for allowing Hazen's regiment to remain under his command. ALS (OClWHi) 1 p.]

To George Washington

Dear Sir   Bound Brook [N.J.] May 25th 1777

I find a great want of Tents in several Brigades. General [William] Maxwell sais he has none, neither has he had it in his power to get any. I shall endeavor to get a more particular state today and will notify your Excellency upon the subject. A small detachment of Col Lewis Regiment came in last Evening without Blankets or Tents and sais there were none to be had at Philadelphia. If that be true we shall be miserably off.[1]

Upon enquiry I find the Camp feever begins to prevail among some of the Troops. Nothing will correct this evil like the free use of Vinegar. The men feed principally upon animal food [meat] which produces a strong inclination to putrefaction. Vegetables or any other kind of food cannot be had in such plenty as to alter the state of the habit. Vinegar is the only sovereign remedy. Cost what it may, I would have it in such plenty as to allow the men a Gill if not a half Pinte a day. If cyder Vinegar cannot be had in such plenty as the State of the Army requires, Vinegar can be made with Molasses, Water and a little flour to produce a fermentation. One Hogshead of Molasses and one Barrel of Rum will make Ten hogshead of Vinegar.[2]

Vinegar can be made from the simple state of the materials fit for use in a fortnights time. I think it my dear General an object of great importance to preserve the health of the Troops. What can a sickly army do; they are a burden to themselves and the State that employs them. All the accumulated expence of raising and supporting an Army is totally lost unless you can find means to preserve the health of the Troops. No General, however active himself or whatever may be his knowledge or experience in the Art of War, can execute anything important while the Hospitals are crowded with the Sick. Besides such a spectacle as we beheld last Campaign is shocking to the feelings of humanity, distressing to the whole army to accomodate the Sick, but above all the Country is robd of many useful Inhabitants and the Army of many brave Soldiers.

Your own reputation, the protection of the Country and the success of the Campaign are dependant upon the health of the Army. Objects so important in their consequences demands your Excellencies serious attention.

Inclosd is an account of the state of things in Brunswick yesterday. Col [Daniel] Broadheads Piquet was attackt yesterday.[3] The Enemy took one foot centry and one Vidett [Vedette], the latter was lost by attempting too rashly to recover the foot Soldier which however was recoverd but wounded in a most shocking manner. The Troops are encamping as fast as possible. With love and esteem believe me to be your Excellencies obedient Servt

N GREENE

ALS (Washington Papers: DLC); enclosure missing.

1. Despite shortages elsewhere, the quartermaster general delivered 2,306 tents to Middlebrook two days later—more, said Washington, than the camp could use (Fitzpatrick, GW, 8: 145).

2. A few days later, Washington ordered the commissary general to "adopt every means in his power, to provide Vinegar" (Fitzpatrick, GW, 8: 142). NG had been an advocate of vinegar since reading Marshall Saxe's Memoirs. Saxe pointed out the universal use of vinegar in the Roman army, proving to his satisfaction that vinegar, added to the drinking water, helped French troops to maintain their health and vigor. NG had drawn the same conclusions from his experience the previous year. Dr. Benjamin Rush was an equally strong advocate in his "Directions for Preserving the Health of Soldiers." (Butterfield, Rush, 1: 140–47; see also above, note, NG to Rush, 3 May.)

3. Daniel Brodhead (1736–1809), formerly a lieutenant colonel of a Pennsylvania Rifle Regiment, had just been made colonel of the Eighth Pennsylvania Regiment. In January 1779 he replaced Lachlan McIntosh as commander at Ft. Pitt and was cited by Congress for his successful expedition against the Indians that year. He was brevetted a brigadier general in 1783. (DAB)

General Orders[1]

[Headquarters, Middlebrook, N.J., 26 May 1777. Appointment of deputy adjutant general; brigade returns and orders; instructions on guards and officers at grand parade each morning. "Muhlenberg Orderly Book," PMHB, 33 (1909): 258–59]

1. Washington had put NG in command of the newly established Camp Middlebrook until he (Washington) could move his headquarters from Morristown. See also general orders of 27 and 28 May below.

To General William Maxwell[1]

Head Quarters [Middlebrook, N.J.]
Dear Sir   May 26, 1777
You will order a Piquet at Vanvacten Bridge[2] consisting of one Capt, one Subaltern, two Sergeants, drum &so and forty privates. This Piquet to be relievd dayly during your stay where you are. But as a large number of Tents are come in perhaps you may get a full supply. Make out a return of your Numbers. This Piquet must remain until tomorrow morning at all events. The sooner you can encamp the better.

The Enemy were out this morning but were drove in as usual. We kild three of their light Horse. General Wayne commanded the party. They were coming to look for another General at Bound Brook.[3] Yours sincerely

N GREENE

ALS (MiU-C).
    1. The address sheet reads "To Brigadier-General Maxwell and to the commanding Officers of that Brigade up the Raritan."
    2. Van Veghtens Bridge crossed the Raritan a few miles west of the Middlebrook Headquarters.
    3. A reference to Gen. Charles Lee, who had been captured only a few miles north of Bound Brook on 13 December 1776. On his exchange, see below, Meade to NG, 4 April 1778.

General Greene's Orders

[Camp Middlebrook, N.J., 27 May 1777. Gen. Lincoln and officer of the day to determine where to post picket guards for "security of the Camp"; remaining orders concern instructions to guards, posting of sentries, and directing patrols. Lincoln and officers of the day to dine with NG. From "Muhlenberg's Orderly Book" PMHB, 33 (1909): 259]

To George Washington[1]

Dear Sir   Camp Middle Brook [N.J.] May 27, 1777
This moment the Commisary reports to me that the Provisions and supplies fall short and that its out of his power with his utmost exertion to procure a sufficient supply.

I wish your Excellency would order the Commisary at Morris Town down here as soon as possible to the assistance of this.

We must take [i.e., impress] Sheep and Cattle about the Country to supply the present deficiency. I think [Commissary Joseph] Trumbull should pay immediate attention to this matter.

A deserter of the 71 [Highlanders Regiment] this moment came

Head Quarters May. 26. 1777

Dear Sir

You will order a Piquet
at Vanvacten Bridge consisting of one Capt
one Sub Two Sergeants down do. and forty five
vates. this Piquet to be relievd dayly during
your stay where you are - But as a large
number of Torts are come in perhaps
you may get a full supply - Make out
a return of your Numbers. this Piquet
must remain until tomorrow morning
at all events: The sooner you can
en camp the better -

The Enemy were out
this morning but were drove in
as usual - we held three of their light
Horse - General Wayne commanded
the party - they were coming black
for another General at Bouns Brook,

Yours sincerely.

NGreene

Nathanael Greene letter to William Maxwell, 26 May 1777
(Courtesy of William L. Clements Library at the University of Michigan)

in from Bonum Town, sais very little. He sais it is the common talk in the British Army they are going to Philadelphia by Water and that Transports are prepard and preparing to go round to Philadelphia and that the Troops are all to embark. Believe me to be with the greatest Respect Your Excellencies obedient Sert

N GREENE

ALS (Washington Papers: DLC).
1. Washington, although twenty miles away at Morristown, replied to this letter the same day (see below).

To Whom It May Concern

Camp at Middle Brook [N.J.] May 27, 1777
These may Certify that Mr John Murry[1] was appointed Chaplain to Colonel Varnum's Regiment by his Excellency General Washington during the Army's lying before Boston; and during his officiating in that capacity his Conduct was regulated by the Laws of virtue and propriety. His actions were such as to make him respected as an honest man and a good Christian. He liv'd belov'd and left the Army esteemed by all his connection and Patrons.

NATHANAEL GREENE

DS (MMeT).
1. The Universalist Murray was a friend and former chaplain in NG's brigade (see above, vol. 1: 81). Citizens of Gloucester, Mass., resentful of his sermons on universal salvation, solicited letters from Ezra Stiles and others purporting to reveal his transgressions and excesses, some even proclaiming him a British spy. The tumult subsided somewhat when NG's letter appeared, with the attacks centering thenceforth on his religious views. (Richard Eddy, *Universalism in Gloucester* [Gloucester: 1892], pp. 11–18)

From George Washington

Dear Sir   Morris Town [N.J.] May 27th 1777
I have ordered the assistant Commissary at this place, to repair immediately to Camp. It is the peculiar misfortune of this Army to have generally speaking, the heads of the different departments always absent when they are most wanted. Two months was I labouring, as hard as a man could to get the Comy Genl to this place and had scarce accomplished it before Congress ordered him to Philadelphia; from whence I have used my utmost endeavours to bring him back but am answered that he is detained by order. In the mean while the Army may starve. I will again send to him by Express and for present supplies, advise the adoption of the mode [i.e., impressment] pointed out by you, beginning about Elizabeth Town, Newark and Milestone &c. because two ends will be answerd by it.[1]

On the Road today, I met a Person who told me that he left New York on Saturday abt noon, that he was desired by P——n S——tt——r to H——ds Reg² to let me know that a successful attack might be made upon the Troops in Brunswick, that there were, at this time a Captn, Lieut, and two Sergeants among us from New York, as spies, in the habit of Country men, that 70 Sail of Transports were ready by this time, he supposes, for sailing, that seven of them were fitted [for] Horses, and had got Forage on board, the rest design'd for Troops, Stores and Provisions, Philadelphia the destination talked of, that he understood some Transports from Newport arrivd at New York on Sunday last with Troops; but that no other Reinforcements had got in, nor any Vessels from Europe except the 17 Provision ships we have already heard of.³

I hope Colo Dayton reported to you the suspicious Person he met with at Bullions Tavern, and that you have had him under examination before this.⁴ I am Dr Sir yr most Affect

GO: WASHINGTON

PS Herewith you will receive a Blank Warrant for Major Parker [Samuel F.], as Commandant of a Corps of Rangers, and his Officers, as also a circular Letter to the Brigadiers for their Instructions which please to have delivered.

ALS (Greene Papers: DLC).
1. See above, NG's letter same day. Washington ordered Commissary Joseph Trumbull to Middlebrook the next day (Fitzpatrick, GW, 8: 135–36).
2. P——n was apparently "suttler" to Hand's or Heard's regiment.
3. The intelligence was accurate. Adml. Howe, at Gen. Howe's request, had spent weeks victualing transports in N.Y. harbor and outfitting small craft for horses, strongly suggesting an amphibious landing—perhaps at Philadelphia. But, at the same time, engineers were building a bridge across the Raritan at New Brunswick (where British troops were concentrating) and mounting flatboats on wheels, as if preparing for an overland thrust and a crossing of the Delaware River. Howe's intentions were as confusing to his staff (and perhaps to himself) as they were to the Americans. Washington could only bide his time at Middlebrook until Howe acted. (See Gruber, Howe Brothers, pp. 224–28; Lundin, Cockpit, pp. 312–13.)
4. Col. Elias Dayton (1737–1807), a former N.J. mechanic and storekeeper and a veteran of the French and Indian War, was colonel of the Third N.J. Regiment. Although he provided intelligence for Washington (reportedly he even headed a spy network), he nevertheless commanded his regiment at Brandywine in 1777 and at Yorktown in 1781. In 1783 he was promoted to brigadier general. (DAB; Dupuy and Hammerman, People, pp. 310–11)

General Greene's Orders¹

[Headquarters, Middlebrook, N.J., 28 May 1777. Troops, with twenty-four cartridges each, to be ready "to march to Action at a moments warning." Three cannon to be fired as an alarm. "Muhlenberg's Orderly Book," *PMHB*, 33 (1909): 259–60]

1. See note, Order of 26 May, above.

To John Adams

Dear Sir   Camp Middlebrook [N.J.] May 28, 1777
I receiv'd a letter from you some days since.[1] I have it not with me and therefore cannot be very particular in the answer. I remember you lament the general corruption of manners and the increase of vicious habits that prevail in the Army. It is a serious truth and much to be lamented. I know of nothing that a people can receive in exchange for the loss of their morals that is an equivelent. I am sensible of the force and Justness of your remarks, that the vices of the Army prevents many from engageing in the service more than the hardships and dangers attending it.

I am not one of those fine Gentlemen who dispises all moral rectitude and Religious duties. Altho I am no enthusiast, I nevertheless most devoutly believe in the observance of Religious duties.

I have had it hinted to me that General Schuyler was about to be created President of the Congress, and to hold his milatary command in the Army. I take this early opportunaty of expressing my abhorrence of such a measure. No free people ought to admit a junction of the Civil and Military; and no men of good Principles, with virtuous intentions, would ask it or ever accept of an appointment which may be improv'd by corruption to the prejudice and injury of the Rights of a free people. The best way to guard against evil is to avoid temptation. If General Schuyler is a mind to be in Congress let him resign his Commission and not hold two offices so incompatible one with the other. I have no objections to General Schuyler as a General, neither have I to his being President of the Congress if he is thought to be the most suitable person for that important trust. But he must cease to be a General before he commences a member of Congress. I will not hold a Commission under that State who blends those two Characters togather. I think them incompatable with the Safety of a free people, and I can assure you I am not fighting for a change of Masters, but to have none but the Law.[2]

I must again repeat the impropriety of creating so many foreign Officers.[3] A very considerable part of our force will get into their hands. What method can Great Britain take to defeat us more effectually than to introduce a great number of Foraigners into the Army and bind them to their interest by some very interesting considerations. That this is practacable nobody will doubt! That we ought to guard against it every body must allow. British Gold may reason forcible with those whose hopes and future expectations are not connected with the people they betray.

I am told by Capt Moduit[4], a French Gentleman lately created a Captain in the Train of Artillery, that one De Cudre[5] is engaged by Mr Dean as Major General of the Train.[6] The impropriety of putting a foraigner at the head of such a Department must be obvious to every body. Besides the Impropriety, you will deprive the Army of a most valuable Officer, universally acknowledged as such.[7] The exchange will be much against you, besides the injustice you will do to a man who has serv'd you with Fidelity and Reputation. I beg you will take it under consideration seasonably. I know not the powers of Mr Dean, but I think such powers are Dangerous and unfit to trust with any man. If this Gentleman is to be appointed a Major General I wish it may be of the foot instead of the Artillery.[8]

Our Army is now Encamped, and I hope will be very soon compleatly organnized, fit for some important purposes. Believe me to be Affectionately yr Friend and Hble Servt

N GREENE

LS (MHi).

1. He apparently refers to the letter of 9 May, above.

2. Schuyler retained his commission but was not elected president of Congress. Adams's views are in his letter of 2 June, below.

3. See NG to Adams, 7 May, above.

4. Thomas-Antoine, Chevalier Mauduit de Plessis (1753–91) had studied artillery from an early age in his native France. In April 1777 Washington made him captain of artillery, a post in which he performed outstandingly. On Washington's recommendation Congress in January 1778 brevetted him lieutenant colonel for his "gallant Conduct" at Brandywine, Germantown, and Fort Mercer. He returned to France at the end of 1778 with further plaudits from Congress and a large cash award. (Fitzpatrick, GW, 10: 303; JCC, 10: 64 and 12: 1104–5; Balch, French, pp. 176–78, has a biographical note.)

5. Philippe Tronson du Coudray (1738–77), an able French army engineer with good connections, had been most helpful to Deane in obtaining supplies. The lengthy agreement called for him to direct the artillery and engineers as "General of the Artillery and Ordnance," with the rank of major general in the Continental army. Deane far exceeded his instructions in his agreement with du Coudray. (Balch, French, pp. 106–7; the contract with Deane is printed in Force, Archives [5] 2: 283–85) For the end of the du Coudray affair, see references in note 8 below.

6. Silas Deane (1737–89), a Connecticut merchant and delegate to Congress, was sent to France in 1776 to procure supplies and was later made political commissioner to the French court. Although less villainous than portrayed by his fellow agent, the overly suspicious Arthur Lee, a modern study characterizes his career in Paris as filled with intrigue and self-serving business deals (Julian Boyd, "Silas Deane: Death by a Kindly Teacher of Treason?" WMQ, 3 ser., 16 (1959): 165–87, 319–42, 515–50; see also DAB).

7. He refers to Gen. Henry Knox, chief of artillery. In a letter to the president of Congress, Washington argued forcefully against replacing Knox (Fitzpatrick, GW, 8: 148–49). Adams, in his letter of 2 June below, agreed on the impropriety of Deane's agreement and stated his opposition to replacing Knox.

8. At this time NG saw du Coudray only as a threat to his friend Henry Knox. In approving the Frenchman as a major general "of the foot," he had yet to learn that

Deane had promised du Coudray his commission would date from 1 August 1776, thus outranking NG, whose commission was dated one week later. For NG's shocked reaction upon learning *this*, see his letter below to the President of Congress, 1 July, and its sequel, Adams to NG, 7 July.

To Samuel Adams

Dear Sir   Middle Brook [N.J.] May 28, 1777
    I was honourd with a letter from you some days since.[1] I have not the letter here, it is with my Papers back in the Country. I observe your remarks respecting Hannibals situation; and the comparison you draw between Hannibal and General Howe, the State of Carthage and that of Great Britain, the state of Fabius and that of General Washington. I am sensible the difference betwixt the State of Hannibal and General How is very great. The faction of Hanno distrest Hannibal, but General How receives all the aid and support that Great Britain can give, but the difference is not so great as to warrant the Generals [Washington] takeing a resolution to attack the Troops at Brunswick, fortified with an inferior number and those undeciplind. I agree with you it is the business of the army to fight, the temper and disposition of the people at large require it, the unsettled state of the Empire, the powers of government not being fully acknowledged and many wishing to give a stop to the powers of Congress and the present modes of Government in the different States. The unsettled State that Government is in throughout the Continent is the strongest argument for fighting that can be given as the hands of administration will be strengthened in propotion to the success of the Army. Altho I am not fond of fighting, I am ever ready when commanded. I hope soon to give the Enemy an opportunity to fight if they please. We insult them dayly, but they keep close within their lines. I still think the Enemy will operate to the Southward. Philadelphia seems to be their principal Object. It is said by a Person out of Brunswick last Night that the Baggage of General How is puting on board a Transport. Seventy Sail of Transports are fixed to receive Troops.[2] A few days will further explain the mystical proceedings of General How, but give me leave to tell you he never will have another opportunity to injure America as he had this Spring.
    Mr Merchant [Marchant] one of the Delagates for the State of Rhode Island will deliver you this. I hope he will be agreeable to Congress. He is a man of good understanding and activity. He has a great Zeal for the cause and I hope will be useful in Congress. With love and esteem I am dear Sir your obedient servt[3]

                                                                NATH GREENE

ALS (NN).
  1. See above, 12 May.
  2. See above, Washington to NG, 27 May.
  3. By the tone of NG's complimentary close, he seems undisturbed at Adams's armchair generalship.

To General Benjamin Lincoln

[Headquarters, Middlebrook, N.J., 28 May 1777. Wants to reconnoiter before placing men at Somerset; agrees there should be some light horse with the pickets; desires Lincoln to have thorough knowledge of the First Watchung Mountain to insure good communication with outposts. LS (MHi) 1 p.]

To Colonel Joseph Trumbull

[Middlebrook, N.J., 28 May 1777. Washington is anxious for supply of vinegar as "fever begins to Rage." Commissary Trumbull should turn his attention immediately to the matter. Repeats one mode of making vinegar from his letter to Washington of 25 May. Provisions at camp in poor state; need minimum of ten days supply. Now safe to provide magazines in the rear. LS (CtHi) 2 pp.]

From General Benjamin Lincoln

[Bound Brook, N.J., 29 May 1777. If NG approves, will move German corps to Quibbletown to support pickets and scout enemy movements. FC (MHi) 2 pp.]

To General John Sullivan[1]

Dear Sir   Camp Middle Brook [N.J.] May 31, 1777
    Inclos'd are two Letters for your Brigadiers. You will please to deliver them.[2]
    The Phylistines are upon thee, Samson. Take care of thyself. The Enemy are destroying their Works at Amboy, and reinforcing Brunswick. They threaten to attack us here: they are welcome if they please. If they are bound to Philadelphia, I think they will indeavor to Steal a march upon us, and either leave you to the right or make an attack upon you and give you a royal rout. I am going to view Millstone this afternoon to establish a Guard there of Horse and foot.[3] God bless you adieu

                                                      N GREENE

ALS (NhHi).
    1. Sullivan was stationed at Princeton, which presumably would be on or near Howe's route if he marched for Philadelphia.
    2. Letters not found.
    3. To guard against an encircling movement, the following day a troop of horse was stationed at Millstone (Somerset), five miles southwest of Middlebrook. (Fitzpatrick, *GW*, 8: 163.)

To General Benjamin Lincoln

Dear General   Camp Middle Brook [N.J.] June 1, 1777
    His Excellency thinks it advisable to fortify with a small Redoubt the pass's through the Mountains not stopt or hedg'd up. The bigness of the redoubts should be propotion'd to the strength of the Piquet. If it is made defenceable against small Arms it will be sufficient as no Cannon can be brought to play against them. Such works will render the pass's much more formidable and the Piquets quite secure. The very Name will have its weight upon the minds of the Enemy.[1] It will take but little time or labour to construct such Works. I purpose to fortify the Gap at Steels Tavern and I think a couple of small Redoubts is necessary upon my right to secure that flank. I would have but two passes leading into the Camp either in front or rear. Should be glad of your opinion upon the Subject. I am this morning going to Somerset to Post a Guard there. I shall be back again about Noon; should be glad to see you at my Quarters. Please to come and dine with me and the Young Gentlemen of your family. Col Parker sent in a Prisoner from Westfield last night. I think he is an American recruit. He gives much the same account about the Enemy as you heard before. Believe me to be with the sincerest regards yours

                                        N GREENE

ALS (MHi).
    1. It is not clear whether he refers to Steels Gap.

From John Adams

Dear Sir   Philadelphia June 2, 1777
    Yours of 28 Ult is before me. It is certain that Religion and Morality have no less obligation upon Armies than upon Cities and contribute no less to the Happiness of Soldiers than of Citizens. There is one Principle of Religion which has contributed vastly to the Excellence of Armies, who had very little else of Religion or Morality, the Principle I mean is the Sacred obligation of oaths, which among both Romans and Britons who seem to have placed the whole of Religion and Morality in the punctual observance of them, have done Wonders. It is this alone which prevents Desertions from your Ene-

mies. I think our Chaplains ought to make the Solemn Nature and the sacred obligation of oaths the favourite Subject of their Sermons to the Soldiery. Odd as it may seem, I cannot help considering a Serious Sense of the solemnity of an oath as the Corner Stone of Discipline, and that it might be made to contribute more, to the order of the Army, than any or all of the Instruments of Punishment.

The Information you rec'd, that General Schuyler was about to be created President, and to hold his Command in the Army, was a Mistake. No Gentleman would have been willing for that, as I know. I am pretty sure at least that a vast Majority would have detested the Thought. G. Schuyler is reserved for another Fate What that will be Time must discover.[1]

It is, in my humble opinion, utterly improper that this Gent. should hold a seat in Congress, and a Command in the Army, and I took the first opportunity to express my opinion of the Inconsistency and Danger of it. I think his Constituents much to blame for the late Choice of him. I shall think him much to blame if he does not immediately resign his seat. If he does not, I hope some Gentleman [will] bring in a Motion to destroy the Precedent, by obliging him to quit his seat or his Command. What the success of such a Motion will be, I know not, but I believe such a Motion will be made.

I agree entirely in your sentiments concerning the Danger of entrusting so many important Commands to foreigners. Mr Deane I fear has exceeded his Powers. Mr Du Coudray shall never have my Consent to be at the Head of the Artillery, and I believe he will have few advocates for placing him there. I hope, none. Pray what is your opinion of General Conway. He acquired a good Reputation here.[2]

It gives me great Joy, Sir, to find by your Letter, that you begin to feel your Army to be respectable. We are anxious to hear from Peeks Kill what Numbers are collected there.[3]

LB (MHi). Since the LB copy does not carry the notation "sent" that Adams generally, but not always, appended to the letters he posted, and since NG's response to the letter has not been found, it is possible that Adams never sent it.

1. On Gen. Schuyler's election to Congress see above, NG to Adams, 5 April and 28 May.

2. Thomas Conway (1735–1800), born in Ireland and raised in France, had risen to the rank of colonel in the French army before coming to America in 1777. His credentials so impressed Congress that it commissioned him a brigadier general in May of that year. He served well at Brandywine and Germantown in the autumn of 1777, but his involvement in the so-called Conway Cabal cut short his military career. On his role in Lafayette's Canadian venture, see below, note, NG to McDougall, 5 February 1778. On the "Conway Cabal," see note, NG to Jacob, 7 February 1778, below. Conway returned to France in 1779 (See sketch in DAB).

3. Washington had ordered New England troops to assemble at Peekskill near the east bank of the Hudson until Howe's intentions emerged, but he had been continually exasperated during May over the slow rate at which they appeared. (Fitzpatrick, GW, 8: 81, 124, 146, 164, 196)

To Jacob Greene

Camp at Middlebrook [N.J.], June 4th, 1777.

I have only time to acknowledge the receipt of a letter[1] from you, delivered me by Lieutenant Littlefield. I suppose you are a little out of temper at the ingratitude of the people in turning you out of your political chair.[2] The state of Rhode Island is too democratic for the happiness of the people; there is very little or no executive force in its government. Passion and prejudice have too much influence in administration to preserve the best and happiest line of conduct.

I think you mention a division of our interests. If you think it best I am content. Set me off such parts of the estate as you may judge equal; let it be valued, and I will either give or take. I had no thought of a division of our interests at present, but if it is necessary, I am content; every thing for the good of the whole.[3]

God knows how long this war may last—the want of union and virtue among the Americans may protract it for some time. We have now a very respectable force in the field from the southward, though not large. The eastern troops are very backward in coming on. The state of Pennsylvania is in great confusion. The Quakers are poisoning everybody; foolish people![4]

The congress and I do not agree in politics; they are introducing a great many foreigners. I think it dangerous to trust so large a part of the American army to the command of strangers. British gold is of a poisonous quality, and the human heart treacherous to the last degree. There are no less than four general officers of the [French] nation now in the American service. There is a French gentleman sent over by Mr. Dean to have the command of all the artillery in America.[5] If his appointment is confirmed, it will rob us of one of the best, or at least, as good an officer as we have in the service—General Knox. I tremble for the consequences, as I fear it will ruin the whole corps, and it is now upon a very respectable footing and increasing in perfection daily. Wisdom and prudence sometimes forsake the wisest bodies. I am exceedingly distressed at the state of things in the great national council.

Excerpt reprinted from Johnson, *Greene*, 1: 97. The contents unmistakably point to Jacob as the unnamed recipient.

1. Letter not found.
2. Jacob was not reelected to the R.I. Assembly in May 1777.
3. See letter from Jacob of 7 May, above.
4. Quaker resistance to numerous military measures and especially to joining the militia is described in Lundin, *Cockpit*, pp. 240–41. NG's personal disaffection is evidenced by his request of 5 April 1777 (as stated by the clerk) to be "Put from under the care of Friends . . . for the Futur" (Ms record of Monthly Meeting of East Greenwich [R.I.] Friends, 1751–1806, p. 67, RHi).
5. See note, NG to John Adams, 28 May, above, on du Coudray.

General Greene's Orders

[Headquarters, Middlebrook, N.J., 7 June 1777. Concerns drawing provisions from the division commissary and providing guards for same. From "Muhlenberg Orderly Book," *PMHB*, 33 (1909): 457]

General Greene's After Orders

[Headquarters, Middlebrook, N.J., 7 June 1777. Three men from each brigade to guard the commissary's cattle daily "till further orders." From "Muhlenberg Orderly Book," *PMHB*, 33 (1909): 457]

To General Benjamin Lincoln

Camp at Middle Brook [N.J.]
Dear General   June 9, 1777

Is there a Guard posted at the cross roads, upon your left? I think our front is very secure and our flanks tolerably well guarded, but a small Guard appears necessary to me at the cross roads on the left, and another advanced to the right towards Pluckemin.[1] The lat[t]er I shall pay particular attention too, the former I trust you will.

Pray what can these Gentry be about? I never was more perplext to unravel and adjust the contradictory intelligence.[2] I cannot think General How will attempt to Garrison Brunswick and divide his force. To march by land to Philadelphia with a divided force is not a little dangerous. The Militia may retard him more than he is aware off, and the Continental Troops will compleat his ruin. If he gives up the Jerseys and goes altogether by Water it will be a strong proof of his weakness and cannot fail to ruin their interest in the Country. The People will be afraid to be connected with those who can only afford them a temporary and water security. I cannot fix a Judgment satisfactory to myself, much less to anybody else. I am dear Sir your obedient Servt

NATH GREENE

ALS (NjHi).

1. Washington had ordered Lincoln's division to furnish guards for Quibbletown (modern New Market) and Lincoln's Pass (Mt. Pleasant). See Fitzpatrick, *GW*, 8: 185–86.

2. Many modern historians are no less "perplext" by Howe's indecision. Gruber thinks the many explanations that have been offered suggest that "Sir William was unwilling—perhaps unable—to describe the reasons for his delays and indecision" but that the memory of Trenton seems to have "immobilized him." (*Howe Brothers*, p. 227) By the time NG wrote, however, Howe had moved off dead center. See note, Council of War, 12 June, below.

To General Benjamin Lincoln

[Camp at Middlebrook, N.J., 12 June 1777. Washington, NG reports, regrets Lincoln's troops were mistakenly ordered to be on guard without adequate shelter and orders a gill of rum for each man. ALS (OMC) 1 p.]

Proceedings of a Council of General Officers

At a Council of General Officers held at Head Quarters at Middle Brook the 12th day of June 1777

Present His Excellency, General Washington

M. Generals	Greene	B. Generals	Wayne
	Lord Stirling		Muhlenberg
	Stephen		Weedon
	Lincoln		Woodford
B. Generals	Maxwell		Scott
	Knox		Conway
	Varnum		

His Excellency, the Commander in Chief, informed the Council, that from various intelligence and many concurring circumstances, it was evident, General Howe had collected nearly the whole of his Force at Brunswic in Jersey.[1] That it appeared to him, beyond doubt, that General Howe had one of two objects in view, either the defeat of the Army under his immediate Command, or to possess himself of Philadelphia. He stated the importance of the Highland passes and of the fortifications on the North River, in and contiguous to the Highlands and then proposed the following Questions.

Q. Will it be expedient in the present conjuncture of things, and from the information received, to draw any and what part of the Troops stationed at Peekskill near the Highlands, to reinforce this Army?

A. All the Troops should be drawn from Peekskill to reinforce the Army in Jersey, except *one* thousand effectives of the Continental Regiments. This number, with the Convalescents and such Militia as are there and can be occasionally drawn in, is esteemed sufficient to defend the posts there under the present appearences of affairs.

Q. Will it not be necessary to post Troops at Morris Town to preserve it, as a post of Communication? If it will, what number of men should be stationed there?

A. It will be necessary to maintain that post. The Detachment of Connecticut Troops under Lieut Colonel Butler and the two Wyoming Independent Companies should be employed in that Service.

Q. What will be the best mode of promotion of Field and other (inferior) Officers in the Army?

A. All Officers below the rank of a Major, should rise regimentally. Officers of that rank and superior should be promoted on a larger Scale, Viz on the line of their State. These Rules however, though they should be observed in general cases, where there lies no objection, should not be established as conclusive, or prevent promotion for particular merit. Original Minutes.[2]

ROBT H. HARRISON

FC (Washington Papers: DLC).

1. Howe had, indeed, assembled his entire army of some eighteen thousand men at Brunswick. On 13 June two columns under Cornwallis and Vaughan, accompanied by Howe, moved up the Raritan River to within a few miles of the American camp. There they began to construct redoubts. When Washington learned that they had left without the batteaus and bridge sections they had built for crossing the Delaware, he realized that Howe's objective was not to attack Philadelphia but to lure the Americans into battle. Despite a flow of recent recruits, the Continental army still numbered less than 8,000. (Lesser, Sinews, pp. 46–47, lists 7,363 effective troops.) Faced with such disparity, Washington was content to wait behind the range of hills at Middlebrook, a position Howe dared not attack.

After suffering five days of American sniper fire, Howe returned abruptly to Brunswick, his frustrated troops burning houses and barns along the way. Washington was too surprised to order an effective attack on the British rear. He did send three brigades under NG to pursue the enemy through Brunswick, but they were too far behind to inflict much damage. When Howe began to embark troops for Staten Island, Washington ordered Stirling to the Metuchen area, and he himself led the remaining troops from Middlebrook to Quibbletown, ten miles northwest of Amboy. Howe's embarkation was a ruse. In the middle of the night of 26 June, he disembarked and mounted a two-pronged attack against Stirling and Washington. The latter, half suspecting such a stratagem, was able to get his troops back to Middlebrook intact; Stirling's brigade, however, suffered an estimated thirty killed and fifty captured. (Peckham, Toll, p. 36)

Howe had let two months of prime campaign weather slip by with nothing to show for it. He was no closer to Philadelphia than he had been in January, while the American army was far stronger. When a few days later British troops next embarked from Amboy for Staten Island, it was no ruse. New Jersey had seen the last of Sir William Howe, although not the last of the British army. The British incursion into New Jersey of June 1777 is covered in Ward, War, 1: 325–28; Lundin, Cockpit, pp. 313–26; and Gruber, Howe Brothers, pp. 228–29.

As noted before, Howe's stategy for 1777 was as puzzling to his subordinates as it was to Washington and his general officers. Anyone with a claim to military expertise could only assume that Howe's next move would be to cooperate in some manner with Burgoyne's army, which was headed down from Canada toward Ticonderoga and Albany. It was unthinkable that he would soon be putting his army on vessels in New York Harbor for a sea voyage to Philadelphia, and yet that was precisely his intent. (See note, NG to Unknown Person, 9–10 July, below.)

Howe had submitted four plans to the cabinet for the 1777 campaign between 30 November 1776 and early April. His first plan, dependent on large reinforcements, envisioned one army of 10,000 pushing northward along the Hudson to cooperate with an army under Carleton from Canada and a similar-sized one attacking Boston overland from Rhode Island. When large reinforcements looked less likely, his second plan on 20 December called for attacking Philadelphia by land across New Jersey. The American victory at Trenton changed his mind, and in his final plan of early April (which did not reach England until late May) he outlined an attack on Philadelphia by sea with a garrison left in New York City. By this time he had learned that Burgoyne was to lead the Canadian army toward Albany, but preoccupied as Howe was with Philadelphia, he gave little or no thought to cooperating with Burgoyne.

For his part, Burgoyne scarcely considered Howe as part of his strategy, which called for an army of 1800 (half Indian) to attack Albany along the Mohawk Valley from Oswego, while he and the main army pushed down Lake Champlain, Lake George, and the Hudson. What he would do on reaching Albany he scarcely considered. As Willcox has pointed out, Howe and Burgoyne were "as far apart in their thinking as they were in distance." (*Clinton*, p. 143) The only person that could have unified the two separate armies was Germain, the cabinet secretary who was conducting the war. Germain apparently expected by some miracle that Howe would wrap up his Philadelphia campaign in a hurry and get back to the Hudson to cooperate with Burgoyne. But if this was what he expected, he gave no orders to insure it. In eight letters written to Howe in March and April he made no mention of cooperating with Burgoyne. Germaine's "unexacting and incorrigible optimism," Willcox has written, "was a gift without price to the American cause." (*Clinton*, p. 146) Before Clinton left England for America in April, he tried to cure Germain of such foolish optimism, but to no avail. By the time Clinton arrived in New York in early July, it was too late. Howe was ready for Philadelphia, while Burgoyne, on the eve of capturing Ticonderoga, was blissfully unaware of what lay before him.

In addition to Willcox, *Clinton*, pp. 130–68, see Gruber, *Howe Brothers*, pp. 189–210.

2. Promotion was a subject of never-ending concern and interest among officers. Even the threat of Howe's army, poised for an offensive to begin within hours, was not enough to postpone the discussion.

To General John Sullivan

Camp at Middle Brook [N.J.]
Dear Sir   June 24, 1777

Inclosd is a charge exhibited against Major Stewart of the 2d Maryland Regiment.[1] I know nothing of the young Gentleman. Col Palfrey came to me and complaind he had been greatly abusd by the Major and that the Major was abuseing and insulting the Inhabitants and encouraging his Soldiers to Plunder the People indiscriminately.[2] I was under the necessity of attending to the Colonels complaint and sent my aid de camp to execute the order which he did in the politest manner but the Major insulted him and abusd all the General officers of the Army. The Young Gentleman from the heat and confusion of the day may have acted very indiscreetly which he may condemn in a sober hour. He wrote me a letter demanding an explanation of his crime, Publishing himself as a man of fortune and a Gentleman of Liberal Education and insisting upon an immediate tryal. If the Young Gentleman thinks his being a man of fortune or haveing a liberal education authorises him to insult and abuse People with impunity, he will find himself mistaken. The more liberal a Gentlemans education the more polished his manners should be. He that dont behave with decency and propriety must take the consequences upon himself. For my part, I know nothing of the matter. You know Col Palfrey and that he is a very civil Gentleman. The Major must make satisfaction to the injured or risque the consequences of a tryal. I am very sorry when anything of this sort happens in the army because it is always productive of some bad consequences and never no good ones. I am with sincerity and truth your Most obedient and very humble Servant

NATH GREENE

ALS (NhHi). Enclosure missing.
1. There is no evidence that Maj. John Stewart of the Second Maryland Regiment was found guilty of the charges. He went on to distinguish himself at Stony Point in July 1779, for which he received a silver medal from Congress. (Heitman, *Register*)
2. Col. William Palfrey of Massachusetts, former aide to Gens. Lee and Washington, was lost at sea in 1780 en route to his post as consul in France. His grandson was the noted historian and editor, William Gorham Palfrey. (Heitman, *Register*)

Generals John Sullivan, Nathanael Greene, and Adam Stephen to Washington

[Camp at Middlebrook, N.J., 28 June 1777. In response to Washington's request they are of opinion that Col. Moylan outranks Col. Bland.[1] LS (Washington Papers: DLC) 1 p.]

1. The two men commanded newly formed cavalry units. Stephen Moylan (1737–1811), born in Ireland and educated in Paris, had served as muster master general and, briefly in 1776, as quartermaster general. The colorful Irishman commanded the Fourth Continental Dragoons until war's end. (*DAB*)
Theodorick Bland (1742–90), a leading Virginia patriot educated in England and Scotland, was colonel of the First Continental Dragoons. He was well meaning but not notably capable: his faulty reconnaissance at Brandywine very nearly brought disaster to the American army. (See note, NG's orders, 13 September 1777.) Bland later served in the Continental Congress and the first House of Representatives. (*DAB*)

To John Hancock, President of the Continental Congress

Camp at Middle Brook [N.J.]
Sir   July 1st 1777
A report is circulating here at Camp that Monsieur de Coudray a French Gentleman is appointed a Major General in the service of the United States, his rank to commence from the first of last August.[1] If the report be true it will lay me under the necessity of resigning my Commision as his appointment supercedes me in command. I beg youl acquaint me with respect to the truth of the report, and if true inclose me a permit to retire.[2] I am with respect Your most obedient humble Servant

NATH GREENE

ALS (PCC, Item 155: DNA).
1. For background on the appointment, see above, NG to Adams, 28 May, and Adams to NG, 2 June.
2. Gens. John Sullivan and Henry Knox wrote similar letters to Congress the same

day—after joint consultation. John Adams dealt at length in his letter of 7 July (below) on the violent reaction to the letters in Congress. It is pertinent here to examine one aspect of that reaction: why the letters were interpreted as attempts to influence Congress.

Congress obviously saw more in the letters than met the eye. Ostensibly the resignations were elicited by reports that du Coudray had already been appointed. The fact was that Congress had taken no such action, and most members were convinced that Sullivan, Greene, and Knox were well aware of this. Massachusetts's James Lovell, though no advocate of du Coudray, thought it "certain they knew we had not settled the matter or General Washington would have rec'd the Resolves." (Burnett, *Letters*, 2: 403)

A stronger assumption by Congress might have gone like this: since Congress had resolved on 28 June to take up the appointment the following week, and since news from Philadelphia—especially news concerning military careers—normally reached Camp Middlebrook in less than two days, the generals must, therefore, have known at the time they wrote that the matter was still to come up. If so, the letters in essence would have read: "We have learned you are soon to consider the du Coudray appointment. We warn you that if you make the appointment we shall resign." Whether the delegates reasoned precisely in this way or not, there was scarcely one that did not so interpret the letters. Eliphalet Dyer, one of the more moderate critics, was conscious of no other interpretation when he wrote that "these Gentn. before the matter was so much as debated in Congress have thrown in their threats to them as a body that if they do this etc. they will immediately leave the Army." (Burnett, *Letters*, 2: 406)

Sullivan, Greene, and Knox dared not be so forthright of course. They presumably resorted, therefore, to the transparent device of citing reports of an accomplished fact that were "circulating here at Camp" or attributed to an anonymous informant (Sullivan began his letter "I am Informed That" [Hammond, *Sullivan*, 1: 403.]) In his letter to Hancock of 19 July below, NG went so far as to say the reason he believed the appointment had been "ratified" was that a letter from a member (unnamed) "seem'd to stamp it with infallible certainty." It is doubtful, however, if he convinced any members that a fellow delegate had reported an action that had never taken place.

In their defense it can be said that the men acted in haste. Had they taken time to discuss the matter with Washington, they would never have written the letters, for although Washington was in complete sympathy with their attitude toward du Coudray, he would not have countenanced that approach. Ironically, as Adams pointed out in his letter of 7 July, below, Congress was almost as opposed to the appointment as were Sullivan, Greene, and Knox. As to why the three men did not simply write personal letters to their friends in Congress (to which, as Adams wrote on 7 July, he had no objection), it is possible that they purposely threw down the gauntlet to Congress, with which they were increasingly disenchanted. Many officers would have agreed with Gen. Samuel Holden Parsons when he wrote Adams on 28 July that the "fluctuating unstable State of your Councils are enough to disgust the whole World, and ruine the most flourishing Empire" (Adams Papers, MHi).

To General Thomas Mifflin

[Troy, N.J., 4 July 1777.[1] Recommends Maj. James Abeel as deputy quartermaster general of NG's division.[2] ALS (NHi) 1 p.]

1. NG had left Middlebrook on 3 July when the army shifted to Morristown. Troy was ten miles northeast of Morristown, near Beverwyck, the home of NG's friend Abraham Lott, where Catharine Greene was staying.
2. In June, Congress had authorized Gen. Mifflin to appoint a deputy quartermaster for each division, on the recommendation of the major general and the approval of the commander in chief. (See Washington's order of 2 July 1777, *PMHB*, 34 [1910]: 30.) When NG became quartermaster general, Abeel was his choice for deputy in charge of camp equipage. See below, NG to Abeel, 11 March 1778.

From John Adams

My dear Sir   Philadelphia July 7, 1777
   I never before took hold of a Pen to write to my Friend General
Green without Pleasure, but I think myself obliged to do it now upon
a Subject that gives me a great deal of Pain.[1]
   The Three Letters from the Generals Sullivan, Green and Knox
have interrupted the Deliberations of Congress, and given many
of the Members of it much Uneasiness.[2] They thought themselves
bound in Honour and Justice to the great Body of People whom they
represent, to pass the Resolution which, before this Letter reaches
you, will be communicated to you by General Washington.
   The Contract between Mr Deane and Monsr. Du Coudray is not
yet decided upon. It is in itself one of the most delicate and perplexing
Transactions that has ever fallen in our Way: but those three Letters
instead of relieving Us has only encreased our Mortification.
   Many great Questions arise upon that Contract. Such as these,
whether Mr Deane had Authority to make it? If he had not, how far it
is consistent with Sound Policy to confirm it? What Merit Monsr.
Du Coudray has in procuring Cannon, Arms, Ammunition and other
Things for our Use? What Interest the French Court may take in our
Complyance with the Contract? What Monsr. Du Coudray's Abilities
to Serve Us really are? How far we may comply consistently with Justice to our own Officers? And how far Such a Trust may be confided
to a foreign officer, with Safety to the public Interest? &c &c &c. In the
midst of these Deliberations, the Three Letters are received, threaten-
ing that if We fullfill the Contract, Three Officers, on whom We have
depended, will resign in the Midst of the Campaign when the Attention of every officer ought to be wholly taken up in penetrating the
Designs of the Enemy, and in Efforts to defeat them.
   If We dissagree to that Contract, what will our Constituents say?
What will foreign Nations say? Our Journals, upon which the Three
Letters must appear, will be read by both.
   Will not foreign Nations Say that the Ambition and Turbulence of
three of our best officers necessitated us to violate our public Faith?
   What Confidence will any Nation have in our Promises, if they
think that our Authority is so feeble among our own People and even
among our own officers, that We cannot perform our Covenants for
fear of disobliging them?
   What will our Constituents say? You have lost the Friendship of
foreign Powers, you have broken a Covenant with one of the best
Officers in Europe, and why? because your own officers would not
permit you to preserve your own Honour.
   It is impossible now for Congress even to determine that Deane

had no Authority to make the Bargain, without exposing themselves to the Reflections that their own Officers intimidated them into it.

I must be excused my Friend in Saying that if you or the other Generals Sullivan and Knox, had seriously considered the Nature of a free Constitution and the Necessity of preserving the Authority of the Civil Powers above the military, you never would have written such Letters.

The Right of an Officer to resign I shall not dispute, and he must judge for himself what Causes will justify him: but surely you ought to have waited till Monser. Du Coudray had appeared in Camp and assumed the command before you resigned, or at least untill you had Seen an attested Copy of our Journal in which he was appointed to supersede you.

I must needs surely Say, that there is more of Rashness, Passion and even Wantonness in this Proceeding than I ever expected to see in my Friends Green and Knox in whose Judgment and Discretion I had the Utmost Confidence. If the Letters had been written to individual Members of Congress, in private Confidence, desiring to be informed what Congress had done, and conveying the Same Sentiments, it would have been attended with no evil Consequences, but Letters addressed to Congress, which must be recorded in the Journals and published for the Inspection of all the World, are exposed to the Reflections of all the World, and one Instance of the Kind passing with Impunity establishes a Precedent for all future Officers, and one Stride after another will be taken, one Breach of the Priviledges of Congress after another will be made, and one Contempt of its Authority after another will be offered untill the Officers of the Army will do as most others have done, wrist all Authority out of civil Hands and set up a Tyrant of their own.

I hope these Letters will have no Influence upon Congress in determining Du Coudray's Pretensions, but of this I am sure, they will not induce them to grant him less Rank and Emoluments than they would otherwise have allowed him.

Nothing in this Affair gives me more Pain than the Necessity you have laid Us under of passing a Resolution, which will lessen your Characters and diminish the Confidence which the good People of America have in your Judgment and Attachment to the Principles of Liberty. But there was not one Member of Congress who dared to justify the Letters, very few who could say a World [Word] in Mitigation or Excuse. It was universally considered as betraying the Liberties of the People, to pass them by uncensured. Some were even for dismissing all three of you instantly from the service, others for ordering you to Philadelphia under Arrest to answer for this Offence.

The Resolution expresses an Expectation that some Acknowledgment or Apology will be made. I sincerely hope it will, for I think that in a cool Reconsideration of those Letters, the Impropriety and Danger of them must be manifest.

I would be far from dictating to you, or giving Advice unasked, but I really think that a Declaration that you had no Intention to influence Congress, to contemn its Authority or infringe the Liberties of the People or the Priviledges of Congress, a Declaration that you have the fullest Confidence in the Justice of Congress and their Deliberations for the public Good, is the least that you can do. Provided you can do this with Truth and Sincerity, if not I think you ought to leave the service ⟨with such a Declaration as this.⟩[3]

LB (MHi). Like the 2 June letter above, the LB copy does not carry the notation "sent" that Adams generally, but not always, appended to the letters he posted. Since (as noted below) their correspondence and friendship ended at this time, however, it is a reasonable assumption that Adams sent and that NG received this letter.

1. For background, see especially NG to Hancock, 1 July; also, NG to Adams, 28 May, and Adams to NG, 2 June.

2. On receipt of Sullivan's almost identical letter to Congress on 3 July, an indignant member had proposed informing Sullivan that "Congress have not been accustomed to be controled by their officers," that they "mean not to be controled by his letter," and that his resignation would be accepted whenever he transmitted it. Cooler heads prevailed, however, and the resolution was scrapped. (*JCC*, 8: 528)

When Greene's and Knox's letters were read a few days later, a somewhat more moderate resolution passed without dissent. It ordered the letters sent to Washington, who, in turn, was to inform the generals that Congress considered the letters as "an attempt to influence their decisions, and an invasion of the liberties of the people, and indicating a want of confidence in the justice of Congress"; the resolution stated further that Congress expected them to "make proper acknowledgements for an interference of so dangerous a tendency; but if any of those officers are unwilling to serve their country under the authority of Congress, they shall be at liberty to resign their commissions and retire." (*JCC*, 8: 537)

The resolution appeared to ask for their resignations unless they made "proper acknowledgments" (defined by Dr. Samuel Johnson as "confession of a fault"). Adams spoke of its requiring an "Acknowledgment or Apology." Whatever degree of humility was expected of the errant generals, the resolution turned out to be largely bluster. Sullivan and Knox ignored it with impunity, while NG wrote only a long justification for his original letter, not an apology or "acknowledgment." (See below, 19 July) Thus far the contest between military and civil government was a draw, but NG never again attempted to influence Congress by the use of such a device.

On the record, Washington's role was nothing more than delivering the resolution. Embarrassed as he may have been by the incident, there is no hint that he upbraided the men or that they had lowered themselves in his esteem. To Washington, however, in his anxiety over Gen. Howe's next move, the controversy must have seemed more and more like a tempest in a teapot.

The saddest consequence of the incident was that it terminated the friendship between Adams and Greene. NG later remembered the correspondence as having been dropped at Adams's "disinclination and not mine," but there is no other evidence that he answered Adams's scolding letter. NG's letter to Congress of 19 July must have further annoyed Adams.

Almost three years later, Adams wrote from Paris via the Viscount de Noailles that he was "reviving a Correspondence, which . . . was one of the most pleasing I ever had." NG did not receive the letter for months—possibly not until he was embroiled in the Southern Campaign—and he did not answer it until January 1782. His answer, a draft of which was later found among his papers, was apparently never received by Adams. Each man probably believed that the other had ended the renewed correspondence. (Adams's letter of 18 March 1780 from Paris and NG's of 28 January 1782 are printed in later volumes.)

During the following month, Congress struggled to place du Coudray where it would least displease him, his government, or the army generals. On 11 August it made him "inspector general of ordnance and military manufactories, with the rank of a major general." His commission was not back-dated nor was he made a line officer. (*JCC*, 8: 630) The ill-starred Frenchman was not to enjoy his status for long: he was drowned two months later while attempting to ride his horse onto the Schuylkill Ferry. (Boatner, *Encyc.*, on good authority gives his name as Tronson de Coudray, but in contemporary American records he is invariably du Coudray or Du Coudray.)

3. The phrase in angle brackets was crossed out by Adams in his letter book.

Council of General Officers

[Headquarters, Morristown, N.J., 9 July 1777. Present: "His Excellency"; Maj. Gens. Greene, Stirling, Mifflin, Stephen; Brig. Gens. Maxwell, Knox, Wayne, Muhlenberg, Weedon, Woodford, Scott, Conway. Agreed that Continental commissions of Virginia officers were to date from their colonial commissions and the men to rank accordingly; that in cases of promotions, Continental commissions should be dated when vacancies occur; that "Natives, deserters from the Enemy, may enlist in any Regiments in Continental Service." Signed Rob. H. Harrison. FC (Washington Papers: DLC) 1 p.]

To [   ]

[Morristown, N.J., 9–10 July 1777[1]]

We are still lying at Morristown, in a position easy to go to the North River, or to Philadelphia, as future intelligence may turn up.[2] How long we shall remain here is uncertain. By all our intelligence from the enemy below, from prisoners escaping, and deserters, &c., &c., they are a full remove from New York. Their prisoners who came in yesterday, and escaped the night before from New York, say, that the foreign troops are all embarked, and the British are embarking: that the troops are encamped on the same ground they first landed on, and it is remarkable that they returned to that spot the day twelve months from that they first took possession of it,[3] and the ships lie as then; that the transports are mostly large ships; they are fully wooded and watered; the merchants and others in New York are packing up their goods and furniture, and that everything looks like a general remove from that place. Indeed, these facts being true, it looks like a leaving the country. Supposing them embarking the troops only, and in large ships, and wooding and watering, that is against going up the North River, or along shore, except into large and deep harbours.

The size of the ships, and wooding and watering, sea-faring men can hardly be deceived in. They are our own people,[4] and we can't have so great distrust of their fidelity as of foreigners. In the whole, I conceive they are going off to leave us, removing wholly to Boston or Newport, I apprehend the latter, of the two. I can see an object for them there of importance, and which they may carry, probably before our army can get up. That is the fleet at Providence and the town, and they may think it easy to march across the country from thence to Boston. If they had ever done a wise thing, we might expect this movement from them. Then their leaving a garrison at Newport, and being in possession there, they can land their troops on that island at leisure, and securely, and there is room and depth of water enough for their fleet, large as it may be. I hope if they go that way that New England may not fall short of this and the other States in this way. In their exertions to save their country, they may depend on the greatest dispatch in the army's coming up to their assistance. I think, at any rate, it is best for the people to hasten their haying and harvest, to be in readiness. If they should come, it must take them some time, yet they can't embark and disembark such number, and fit out so large a fleet without expense of time.

I hope, from the size of the ships, they will not venture through the Sound, and that the coast of Connecticut may be free from their ravages. It will, doubtless be best, however, to have a good look-out kept to guard against sudden [   ][5] with small parties. I am sometime apprehensive of their turning their measures from the pursuit of conquest, to a war of plunder, revenge and destruction. Their behavior at quitting here carries strong marks of such a plan being adopted.[6]

Excerpt reprinted from RIHS, *Coll.*, 6 (1867): 197–98.

1. The undated letter was written shortly after British troops began embarking but before the army left Morristown on 11 July. There is a great deal of confusion among British sources on dates of embarkation: from Montresor, *Journals*, p. 427; Kemble, *Journal*, p. 124; and Cornwallis's orders in *Kemble Papers*, 1: 462, it appears they began 8 July and finished 11 July.

2. When word reached Morristown on 7 July that Howe was loading transports with a month's provisions and fitting horse stalls on some vessels, Washington began to question his latest assumption that Howe was planning to cooperate with Burgoyne on the Hudson. Hours after NG wrote, however, word of the American evacuation of Ft. Ticonderoga caused Washington to order the army north. (See NG to Cooke, 10/11 July, below) On Howe's preparations for the drive on Philadelphia, see note, Council of War, 12 June, above.

3. The first British troops had encamped on Staten Island at the beginning of July 1776. (See above, vol. 1: 254)

4. That is, American prisoners who had escaped.

5. The empty brackets are in the printed source.

6. They had burned houses and barns on abandoning New Jersey.

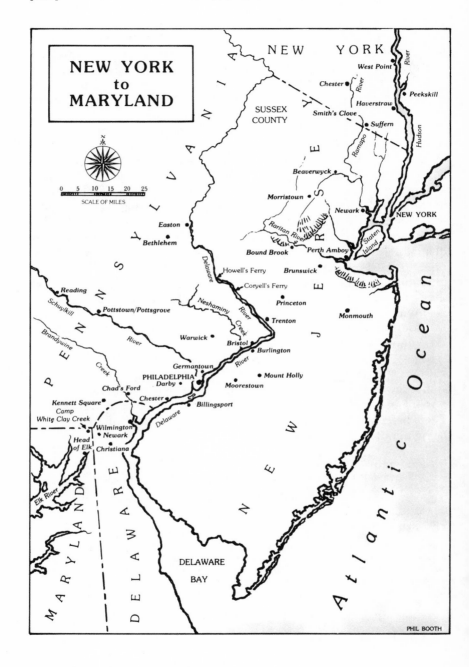

NEW YORK
to
MARYLAND

SCALE OF MILES

0 5 10 15 20 25

PHIL BOOTH

To Governor Nicholas Cooke of Rhode Island

Dear Sir,   Camp at Morristown [N.J.] July [10/11] 1777[1]
    I am favoured with yours of June 16th. Your letter of March was duly answered.[2] The reason of its not coming to hand I cannot imagine, unless the impertinent curiosity of some scoundrel broke the seal to examine the contents, and then the fear of detection made him add a second crime to the first, that of destroying the letter. However, it contained little more than an acknowledgment of the receipt of yours. You are much mistaken if you think me offended at my letter's being laid before the Assembly.[3] I did not wish it, but I had no conception that it was done with a view of injuring me, and therefore could have but little reason to resent it. It was not then, neither is it now, my opinion that you were under the least obligations to lay any letters before the House of Assembly, that are not official. It is true I was not pleased with the conduct of administration, as it was represented to me, and I wrote you with perfect freedom upon the subject. I don't wish to offend any public body, but I have no favours to ask of any. If I am not useful and necessary for the common good, in public employments, I shall cheerfully retire. The pleasures of domestic life have sufficient charms to compensate for the loss of public favors.
    I am still unhappy enough to dislike the policy of your State, and not only yours but that of all the New England States. I cannot see the utility of stating prices, neither can I see the wisdom and policy of prohibitory laws restraining a free commerce amongst the different States.[4] The stating the prices of articles will first produce an artificial scarcity, and then a real one. In the first instance, the people will conceal their goods, and in the second place, adventurers will cease to prosecute trade, when they are not at liberty to dispose of their effects. This policy will bring upon the people the very evils they are calculated to remedy. Every man that has studied the principles of commerce must be fully convinced of the absurdity of any attempts to regulate trade. It is a policy peculiar to itself. Deprive it of freedom and you destroy its existence. The mutual wants of the buyer and seller must be the governing medium to regulate the exchange in barter, for the prices of articles for sale. Legislators should prohibit monopolizing and the consumption of articles unnecessary for the happiness of the people. If they interpose farther than this, they injure society instead of benefiting it. Those kind of regulating laws are founded in public covetousness, a desire to have the property of a few at a less value, than the demand will warrant to the owners. The prices of things will always be in proportion to the consumption or demand of the thing offered for sale, and the quantity of circulating

cash. How far it may be necessary, and how far necessity may sanctify the seizing and stating the value of private property for public purposes, I shall not pretend to say, but the fewer instances the better, as it militates with the first principles of civil government, by destroying that security and confidence in the public faith plighted to every individual, to protect him in the enjoyment of personal liberty, and the free disposal of his property.

The prohibitory laws restraining a free commerce amongst the neighboring States, is founded in a little narrow policy, and if adhered to will be productive of the worst of evils. Nothing will sour the inhabitants of the different States against each other so effectually. Has this the appe[a]rance of sharing in common the unavoidable evils that attends every war, or does it look like relieving the distresses of places or people that have suffered by the accidental ravages of a merciless enemy? Where is the generous spirit that so liberally relieved the unhappy sufferers at Boston? The sea ports of the State of New York, and the State of New Jersey are now blocked up, and the inhabitants deprived of the opportunity of drawing their supplies through the usual channels. Has it not the appearance of cruelty to multiply their distress by refusing them the little alleviation that may be had by a free commerce with the neighboring States? Nothing will preserve a harmony like a free intercourse among the people. The want of it in these States will soon produce the same evils that existed amongst the Grecian States. They were always at war, one with another, for want of a generous and liberal intercourse. The New England States will be at war with each other before twelve months is at an end, if those prohibitory laws are continued, and the calamities of the people increase. History shows that human nature is capable of producing such evils, and therefore necessary to be guarded against.

May God in his mercy avert such terrible evils, and preside in the councils of his people, is the prayer of him who is, with great truth and sincerity, Your most obedient humble servant,

NATHANAEL GREENE

P. S. General Howe has evacuated the Jerseys, and is now on board his ships with all his troops. His destination is unknown. I think Providence not out of danger. General St. Clair has evacuated Ticonderoga.[5] His reasons for it are a mystery. What has become of the garrison we cannot learn. We are on our march to cross the North River, to join the eastern army. I will give you a fuller history hereafter. I something expect to be sent to Albany.

N. G.

Reprinted from RIHS, *Coll.*, 6 (1867): 193–95.

1. The letter itself was written 10 July, the postscript, 11 July. The date is determined by news in the postscript of Ticonderoga, which did not reach Morristown until the tenth—the last day the army was encamped there. (Fitzpatrick, *GW*, 8: 376) The postscript was added ("on our march") after the army left Morristown early on the eleventh.

2. None of the letters mentioned has been found.

3. See above, Cooke to NG, 7[9] February 1777.

4. On the background to the price regulation bill and embargoes, see NG to Unknown Person and notes, 20 May, above.

5. On the evacuation of Ft. Ticonderoga, see following letter to Jacob.

To Jacob Greene

Dear Sir   Pompton Plains N Jersey[1] July 13, 1777

General St Clair who commanded at Ticonderoga has evacuated that Important Post.[2] His Garrison, consisting of between Four and Five Thousand Men in good Health and high Spirits, with such a Garrison strongly intrenched and well armed, fully supplied with Provisions and Ammunition and the works Defended with 170 Pieces of Cannon, is evacuated without firing a Gun. General Schyler had 2000 Men with him at Fort Edward. General Nixon was on the March from Albany with upwards of a 1000 Troops Continental. The Militia of the Country coming in from all Quarters to the Aid of the Garrison and the Commanding officer of the Garrison fully acquainted with all these circumstances has deserted the Post. What could induce an officer to take such a Measure God only knows. Burgoynes whole Force did not consist of above 5500 Men.

The whole is a Mystery to all the Army. General Schyler is also at a loss to account for the conduct of the Garrison. Charity obliges me to suspend any ill natured Reflexions. But I fear there has been some grave Villainy or grave Cowardice. Our Affairs were never in so prosperous Train as they were before this. This Event will give a [desperate?] Wound. But by the Blessing of God I [we?] hope to recov[er] the Shock. What has become of the Garrison, whether they are prisoners or gone down to No 4 [Fort Stephen, N.H.] I cant learn. I think its probable I shall be sent to the Northwa[r]d.[3]

Mrs Greene arrived safe at Camp whom I was exceeding happy to see. She acknowledges with the warmest signs of Gratitude your Kindness to her since [our separation?]. Pray provide Molly that has the care of the children with such things as she may want for their comfort. Mrs Greene [is at?] Mr Lotts. Brother Kitt is gone to Philadelphia. If I go to the Northward Mrs Green returns home.

General Howe and all his Troops are embarkd, their Destination unknown. I have had some fears for Providence But Philadelphia or the North River are objects of much greater Importance. We are on our March for the Nor[t]h River to join General Putnam. God Bless you. Adieu

N GREENE

Tr (Theodore Foster Transcripts: RHi). On Foster transcripts, see source note, NG to Jacob, 2 July 1778, below.

1. Pompton Plains, eighteen miles northeast of Morristown, was the first encampment after the army left Morristown on 11 July. Rain had prevented the continuation northward for two days.

2. Not surprisingly those in the main army in New Jersey were largely ignorant of the situation at far-off Ticonderoga, the fort on Lake Champlain that guarded Burgoyne's invasion route from Canada. (See above, Burgoyne's plan, note, Council of War, 12 June.) NG, for example, was incorrect in virtually every assertion he made. Arthur St. Clair, the Scottish-born general who had taken command as recently as June, had no more than 2,500 troops—far too few to man the extensive defenses of the fort and of nearby Mt. Independence; many of the men, moreover, were neither in good health nor high spirits, and the garrison was anything but well supplied; Gen. Schuyler had 1,200, not 2,000, men; while Gen. John Nixon's brigade did not even arrive in Albany (still a week's march from Ticonderoga) until two days after the evacuation. Gen. Burgoyne, on the other hand, had over 9,000 well-equipped troops—some 7,000 of them British and German regulars—supported by a vast array of artillery. (Fortescue, British Army, p. 224)

Faced with such odds, St. Clair decided on 6 July to evacuate the fort when the British succeeded in dragging cannon to the top of Mt. Defiance, a mile to the southwest, overlooking Ticonderoga. Under the cover of darkness and the noise of a contrived artillery barrage, most of the American garrison managed to escape without detection. Despite numerous blunders by St. Clair's subordinates, invalid troops escaped by boat to the south, while St. Clair and the rest of the garrison made their way in a long, roundabout march to the east that brought them back a week later to the Hudson Valley some forty miles to the south, with the British at times in hot pursuit.

Although St. Clair was widely criticized—some even accusing him of disloyalty—he was exonerated by a courtmartial the next year, as he has since been by modern historians. (The courtmartial is printed in NYHS, Coll., [1880], pp. 1–72.) NG later revised his opinion on learning the facts.

Granted that St. Clair acted wisely, the loss of Ticonderoga nevertheless sent shock waves across the country, especially through New England and New York. The specter again arose of British control of the Hudson, isolating New England from the rest of the nation. Even more frightening to New Englanders was the fear that Burgoyne's army might cut across to Boston or Providence, a fear not without some basis. The shock soon diminished, however, as Burgoyne's progress southward was slowed.

The fall of Ticonderoga and St. Clair's retreat is covered in Ward, War, 1: 405–16, but the fullest account is the classic work, Nickerson, Turning Point, pp. 129–92. Despite Nickerson's antipathy to scholarly apparatus, his book is carefully researched.

3. On the possibility of his going northward, see note, NG to Catharine, 17 July, below.

General Greene's Orders

[Ramapo Clove,[1] N.Y., 15 July 1777. Each brigade to furnish guard for general baggage. Stewart Orderly Book (Typescript: NjP) 1 p.]

1. Also "The Clove" or "Smith's Clove," where the army had just arrived and where Washington established headquarters at Sufferns Tavern. The Clove was formed

by the Ramapo River, which cut a broad, steep-sided valley through the southern flank of the rugged New York Highlands. After the British got control of the lower Hudson River in the fall of 1776, the chief communication route between New Jersey and New England entered the Highlands at the Clove, ran north and east to the Hudson, thence by ferry to Peekskill and beyond to Connecticut.

To Catharine Greene

My dear   Ramapough Clove [N. Y.] July 17th 1777

Col Livingston past this place yesterday in the afternoon on his way to see his beloved—happy couple—last night.[1] I immagin we shall continue at this place for some days. However that is entirely dependant upon the motions of the Enemy. There is nothing new from Ticonderoga since I left you. Col Livingston has doubtless informd you of Lt Col Bartons noble exploit in captivating Major General Prescot, one of the boldest attempts of the War.[2]

General How remains at Statten Island and in York Bay. His Troops are all embarkt, their destination unknown. It is most probable Philadelphia is the object.[3]

It is not determind who goes to Ticonderoga. I can plainly see the General wants me to go but is unwilling to part with me. He has set several persons to sound my inclinations. I will go if the General gives the order and the good of the service requires it, but I feel a reluctance and the more so as it is so disagreeable to you. If I am left at liberty to consult my own inclination I shall not go, but if my honour and reputation becomes interested I must consent, and I am sure your love and affection is such if my character is at stake to give your consent also.[4]

Major Blodget is detaind on account of Major Clarkes absence who I expect this day. I wish you to go to Bethlehem. It will be a pretty Jorney. The Major will bring you a hundred dollars. Furnish yourself with every thing you want.[5]

How are the family, in good health? Mr and Mrs Lott are laying us under an obligation never to be canceld. Their politeness, kindness, hospitallity and friendship to you and me impresses my heart with a weight of gratitude that almost makes me unhappy from the little prospect I have of makeing suitable returns for their goodness. Never did I see a finer family in all my life. I am sure you will love and respect them. Major Blodget shall return to you the moment Major Clarke comes up. I long to be with you again. The soft delights, the sweet pleasures of social endearments I felt at our meeting still dances round my heart, makes me anxiously wish their continuance, but fate, cruel fate, cuts the thread and leave but the remembrance of past pleasures to console us for solid enjoyments. Heaven grant you protection, my dear Angel, through all the slippery paths of life, give you prudence, patience and health to enjoy your friends and make every body love you as I do—only in a less degree. Make my respectful complements to Mr and Mrs Lott and all the young Ladies. Tell Col Livingston and his Lady to exercise moderation. I am with love and affection yours sincerely

N GREENE

ALS (NjP).

1. William S. Livingston, former aide of NG, had married Catherine Lott, daughter of the Abraham Lotts, with whom Mrs. Greene was staying (*PMHB*, 70 [1945]: 296n). NG had spent a short time with her at the Lotts. Her arrival is not recorded, but on 4 June, NG's brother Jacob in Rhode Island had listed expenses of "£5 6S for your wifes Expenses to the Camp." (Jacob Greene Account Book, RHi)

2. William Barton, who had just been made lieutenant colonel of a R.I. Militia unit (Bartlett, *Records*, 8: 263), became a legendary hero on the night of 9 July 1777 with the capture of Gen. Richard Prescott, the arrogant commander of British forces in Rhode Island. Barton and forty-one volunteers made their way in whale boats across Narragansett Bay in the dark to the west side of Aquidneck Island, went inland a mile to capture the sleeping Prescott and his aide, and returned without detection. The R.I. Assembly rewarded Barton and his men with $1,120, and Congress voted him a sword (although the impecunious Barton preferred cash; NG to Robert Morris, 4 December 1777, below). Prescott had been captured before and exchanged for Gen. Sullivan; in the spring of 1778 he was exchanged for Gen. Charles Lee. (See note at Meade to NG, 4 April 1778.) He returned to fight in the battle of Rhode Island in August 1778 under Gen. Pigot and in 1779 again took command in Rhode Island. (On Barton's exploit, see *DAB*; Arnold, *R.I.*, 2: 402–3; and Bartlett, *Records*, 8: 290.)

3. Washington thought Howe's operations "not yet perfectly understood" (Fitzpatrick, *GW*, 8: 416), but two days later he rushed the army north to meet a reported push by Howe up the Hudson. See below, note, NG to Cooke, 29 July. On Howe's plans, see above, Council of War, 12 June.

4. Washington made no mention of this in his correspondence, but there is no reason to doubt NG's account. (He said the same thing to Jacob, 13 July, above.) With sentiment rising in Congress for removing Schuyler as commander of the Northern Army after Ticonderoga fell, it is very likely that Washington did consider NG as a replacement for Schuyler. Nevertheless, when Congress asked him on 3 August to name a replacement, he declined to do so. (*JCC*, 8: 600) Why? Ostensibly because the Northern Army had been a separate department with which, Washington said, he had never interfered and which he had advised only "on the requisitions" of the officers there. (Fitzpatrick, *GW*, 9: 8–9) But, in truth, he had never hesitated to give Schuyler strong advice—whether "requisitioned" or not. Just a week before the above letter, he not only volunteered to suggest Benedict Arnold as a commander of the militia opposing Burgoyne (ibid., 8: 377), but when Congress complied and asked Arnold to follow Washington's orders, he did not hesitate to direct Arnold. On 21 August, moreover, when it appeared that his army might join the Northern Army, he asked Congress to "place the Matter upon such a footing, as to remove all scruples or difficulties about the Command that could possibly arise on my arrival there." (Ibid., 9: 109) He was clearly asserting his right to be in command of the combined armies.

If Washington did favor NG for the northern post, it is doubtful that he refused to submit Greene's name because it amounted to interference in a separate command. Far more likely was the realization, after some reflection, that Congress would probably not approve NG since he had alienated most of that body by his letter of 1 July on the du Coudray affair and had smoothed no ruffled feathers with a second letter, 19 July. (See both letters and Adams to NG of 7 July, above.) New England delegates had been especially annoyed; even when NG was still high in their favor, they had been advocates of Gates for the northern command. On the same day that Congress asked

Washington to name Schuyler's replacement (2 August), a group of New England delegates—including John and Samuel Adams and Rhode Island's Henry Marchant—asked Washington to support Gates. (Washington Papers, DLC) Since Washington did not favor Gates (their friendship had cooled), he apparently thought it wise to name no one. With Howe's army somewhere in the offing it was no time to wrangle with Congress.

There is a curious parallel with the situation exactly three years later. In July 1780 Congress named Gates to command the Southern Army, although it was known that Washington preferred Greene. Only after Gates's defeat at Camden was NG given the southern command. Had he resisted writing Congress in July 1777 about the du Coudray appointment (thereby keeping John Adams's friendship), with Washington's backing, Greene—not Gates—could have been the victor of Saratoga in October 1777.

5. William Blodget and John Clark were aides. Bethlehem, Pa., was a Moravian community where the Greenes' daughters later attended school.

To John Hancock, President of the Continental Congress

Sir

Camp at Ramapough Cloves [N.Y.]
19th July 1777

His Excellency has communicated to me a resolution of Congress of the 7th Instant founded upon three Letters from the Generals Sullivan, Knox, and myself relative to Mr Du Coudrays supposed appointment agreeable to the contract between him and Mr Dean.[1]

I confess it was [a] matter of infinite surprise to me that an interpretation of so deep a complexion should be put upon a meaning so innocent and inoffensive as that contained in those letters, nor can I be persuaded but that Congress on a dispassionate review of the matter will readily perceive that they have embraced ideas by no means deducible from any thing we have done, and will in justice recall a censure equally severe, unmerited, and injurious. It is a fact well known that Mr Dean, a public envoy from these States, did make a contract with Mr Du Coudray investing him with the chief command of the Artillery and the rank of Major General from the first of August last. This contract I verily believed the Congress had confirmed and ratified: It is unnecessary to mention the reasons that induced that belief, but what seem'd to stamp it with infallible certainty was a letter from a member of Congress to that import who might be supposed to speak the sense of that body.

We could not possibly divine the secret intentions of Congress, and could only judge from appearances and circumstances of common notoriety, which concurred to establish the idea that prevailed. On the supposition that I was superseded by Mr Coudray could my feelings and determination be any other than what they there appear? And can it be said that I had not competent ground for making that supposition? It's not having at once been openly announced by Congress is no objection to it, for this was ascribed to, and might have proceeded from, motives of delicacy; for, altho reasons of policy might demand the sacrafice and necessity urge the measure, yet that delicacy would dictate the propriety that the knowledge of it should come to me through a different and more indirect channel.

I see not how similar applications to Congress from three officers equally interested in the same event and consequently speaking the same language, on a principle so natural and as well supported as that which actuated us, could be deemed a combination [i.e., a conspiracy] or construed into an attempt to "influence their decisions, an invasion of the liberties of the people, and indicating a want of confidence in the justice of Congress." Did I not know it to be the case, I could never immagine that these Expressions had no other foundation than merely a request (from Officers who had reason to believe themselves supersceded) to be permitted to retire. On condition it should be so, how could this be considered as an attempt to influence their decisions? For my own part I shall retire from the service without a single murmur when the interest or happiness of my Country demands so necessary a sacrafice. I trust the Congress in all their determinations have an eye to the common good, and never do violence to the feelings of individuals but where necessity sanctifies the measure; to refuse a person liberty to retire in this situation would be cruel and unjust. I do not hold my character as an officer in such high estimation as to think that declaring my intentions to resign could have any effect upon the determinations of Congress, especially in a matter in which tis to be supposed they act either from national views of policy or from a preference to superior merit. Neither am I disposed to enter into any unlawful combinations to do myself private justice, however great my injuries either real or immaginary. In the present case, my situation was rendered inelligible; my feelings as a Soldier forbids my holding a command that was mark'd with evident signs of personal degradation; I had no conception that an application, founded upon a supposed event, could either be affrontive to the delicacy or dignity of the Governors of a free people and therefore Am persuaded my meaning and intentions must have been wholy mistaken.

Whatever influence I could have must be in proportion to the importance of my Military character; take this away, and I stand upon the footing of a common Citizen, and it seems to me somewhat extraordinary that an offer to lay that aside should be deemed to import such dangerous consequences as are imputed to it. I did not complain of any injustice, or demand reperation for any injury, but simply stated the information I received and ask'd permission to retire if it was true. The question of right is entirely untouched.

There are often weighty motives for supersceding officers of whatever rank, and this might possibly have been the case in what I thought had happened so that the supposition did not by any necessary implication impeach the justice of Congress. But as I was not acquainted with those reasons and perhaps could hardly be brought to feel their force if I was, I only declared my wish to conform to those maxims universally established among civilized nations and necessary to be upheld in the military line, and to relinquish a station which I could no longer fill with satisfaction or honor to myself. I might ad[d] much to shew that my letter does not warrant the construction put upon it but tis a subject of a delicate nature and will not admit of a free discussion.

With respect to that part of the resolution which declared "that if any of those officers are unwilling to serve Their Country under the authority of Congress he shall have liberty to retire," I answer that I have all the respect for Congress a free Citizen ought to have for the representatives of himself and the collective body of the People, and that it is my glory and happiness to serve my Country under the authority of those delegated by her to direct her councils and support her interests. I have not a single thought or wish inconsistent with this. But at the same time I as freely answer that I esteem it my duty to do it in the manner most compatible with the dignity of the Man—the Citizen—and that of the Soldier while I sustain the character, and will immediately renounce any station in which I cannot act with honor and have recourse to that in which I can, As I flatter myself I shall always be ambitious of the character of an useful and good member of Society. In my military capacity I have and will serve my Country to the utmost of my ability while I hold it, but I am determined to hold it not a moment longer than I can do it unsullied and unviolated. With great respect and esteem Sir I have the honor to be Your most Obedt

NATH GREENE

LS (PCC, Item 155: DNA).
1. For background, see above, NG to Hancock, 1 July, and Adams to NG, 7 July. NG's letter was read in Congress 23 July and ordered to lie on the table, from which it was never taken up. (*JCC*, 8: 575)

To Catharine Greene

My dear   Ramapough [N.Y.] July 23, 1777
We are this moment returnd to our old Quarters at this place.[1] Our future motions will depend entirely upon General Hows motions. If he goes into N England we shall follow him. If he goes to Philadelphia we shall go there. Our march will [be] rappid if the fleet moves to the Westward. I hope however not so rappid but that I shall have an opportunity to call and see you.[2] If our accomodations

were better and your health and strength capable of enduring the fatigue, I could wish to see you here tomorrow, and some of the young ladies with you. Our accomodations are not good but you shall sleep in a room with only myself, and I hope you have no objection to that. However I believe our stay will be short here, perhaps we may march in the morning. If you should set out to come on if we march I shall send forward an aid de camp to notify you thereof. This I shall do whether you come or not if we march to Philadelphia or to the Eastward.

You will consult your health and pleasure and take your resolution accordingly. I receivd your letter by Lt Col Conner. I am sorry to find you in an ill state of health. I hope your fears are groundless respecting the Camp distemper. My heart pants to see you. God bless and preserve you is the prayer of your ever affectionate

                                                        N GREENE

My kind love to Mr and Mrs Lott and all the sweet young ladies. Tell the major he must soon leave that sweet place for [*words inde-cipherable*]

ALS (MiU-C).
    1. On the army's movements since mid-July, see below, note, NG to Cooke, 29 July.
    2. His march was not so "rappid" that he did not stop to see Catharine at the Lotts when the army marched back through Morristown.

General Greene's Orders

[Ramapo, N.Y., 24 July 1777. Horses destroying inhabitants' meadows; grass to be cut for cattle; vaults to be dug. Stewart Orderly Book (Typescript: NjP) 1 p.]

To General Alexander McDougall

Dear Sir   Coryells Ferry [N.J.] July 29th 1777
    Your favor of the 26th of this instant this moment came to hand.[1] I note your observations upon General Howes letter and future opperations.[2] The letter I believe was design'd to fall into our hands; the deception would be the most effectual in the manner you mention. I made the same observation to his Excellency upon the subject on the first sight of the letter, but I think notwithstanding, the ballance of evidence was in favor of their going to the Southward. But admiting the evidence was equal, we cannot with our force take any position to cover Boston, the North River and Philadelphia; therefore we must leave something to chance. The North River is the first object upon

the continent. Philadelphia, the next, considering the temper and disposition of the people. The Political principles of the Inhabitants of Pensylvenia, the lower Counties on the Delaware [as State of Delaware was called] and part of Maryland is a strong motive for General How to operate in that quarter. Philadelphia will influence allmost all the Southern States, and the solicitude for its preservation in the army is beyound your conception. If the British Ministry have conquest still in view, considering General Burgoynes situation, I should think General How should have opperateed up the North River. If they could have effected a Junction of their forces and then pushed down through the Country to *Boston* it would have had the appearance of a conquest. There are two reasons that induce me to believe General How will opperate against N E. There can be only part of the Continental forces to oppose him aided by the N E militia but if he opperate to the Southward he will have all the Continental forces against him and Burgoyne, aided by the militia of both Countries [i.e., regions]. This is one reason; the other is keeping such a body of Troops inactive at Rhode Island. The importance of that place cannot be propotionable to the injury it does his army in detaching such a body of men. Therefore it appears to me they are stationd there for some future design. But nevertheless I am still of opinion General How goes Southward or Returns to the North River. He will receive great aid in attacking Philadelphia from his Shiping and great assistance from the Inhabitants of all the lower counties. I think the Idea of conquest is given up and that Burgoyne and How will fix upon those objects that will appear the most splendid. Philadelphia will make the most noise in Europe and here, too. Burgoyne has made noise enough already.[3]

We are now upon the Delaware and dont propose to advance any farther until General Howes destination is reduced to a certainty. There is intelligence from Egg Harbour that part of the fleet were seen off there, beating to windward, but I leave you to Judge of the probabillity from your knowledge of the coast.[4]

If you can read what I have wrote I shall be glad, being in great haste, Col Brewer waiting with impatience. I am with sincere regard your most obedient and very humble Servt

NATH GREENE

ALS (NSchU).
1. Not found.
2. A reference to a letter that Gen. Howe had written as a ruse, purportedly intended for Burgoyne, saying that the expedition to Boston would replace one up the North River. Howe directed the letter to be planted on an "escaped American prisoner," who for the sum of ten guineas would appear at an American post, where he would be caught. The ruse did no credit to Howe's judgment of the Americans; as William Willcox has said, such a letter "would have been suspect to a moron." (*Clinton*, p. 166)

3. See note, Council of War, 12 June 1777, above.
4. Just after he wrote this letter, he received later news; see his letter to Gov. Cooke, below.

To Governor Nicholas Cooke of Rhode Island

Dear Sir   Coryells Ferry [N.J.][1] July 29th 1777
   General Howe is now at Sea. His destination is unknown, the ballance of evidence is generally thought to be in favor of Philadelphia. I most sincerely wish the fleet may be going to the westward for many reasons but the greatest is we shall be able to opperate against the British forces with all the continental Troops aided by the militia of the Eastern and Western States. If General How goes to the Eastward there will be only part of the continental forces aided only by the N England militia.
   General Burgoynes rappid progress to the Northward [i.e., from Canada southward] and General Howes continueing such a large detachment at Rhode Island makes me suspect the Enemy have some designs against New England, for I cannot see how General How can Justify himself in keeping such a considerable detachment of his forces to hold such an inconsiderable Island. The importance of the place bears no propotion to the injury it does the service in the demunition [diminution] of their force.
   It is reported the fleet is off the Capes of the Delaware. I dont credit the report.[2] We are encamped at this place about thirty miles from Philadelphia where we shall wait until better intelligence can be obtaind. General Howes avoiding our army dont look like conquering the country. I am with respect your most obedient and very humble Servant

                                                          N GREENE

ALS (MiU-C).
   1. Since 24 July, when word reached Washington at Sufferns Tavern in Smith's Clove that Howe had put out to sea, the army had been marching most of the time. From July 15 the main army had rested several days at the camp at Sufferns, near the entrance to Smith's Clove, while Howe's loaded transports lay at anchor in New York Harbor. (See note, Council of War, 12 June, above.) Washington had kept three divisions—Greene's, Stephen's, and Lincoln's—at Sufferns, ready to march toward the Hudson if Howe's transports headed that way or to turn back to the south if the British fleet should appear headed for Philadelphia. With Ft. Ticonderoga now occupied by the British and Burgoyne advancing toward Albany, it was inconceivable to Washington that Howe would not make some effort to form a junction with Burgoyne. Against that possibility he ordered Stirling's and Sullivan's divisions to join Putnam on the east side of the Hudson.
   On 19 July information reached Washington that some of Howe's vessels were sighted both in Long Island Sound and going up the Hudson. Early next morning the army marched eleven miles northward into the Clove toward the Hudson before learning the report was "premature." On 23 July he ordered NG's division and the artillery back to Sufferns and sent Stephen's and Lincoln's divisions further north to

Chester, N.Y., where they could march east toward the Hudson, or westward along the back route through Sussex County, N.J., to Philadelphia. On 24 July reliable intelligence reached Washington that the British armada had at last sailed from Sandy Hook the previous day and had taken on southern pilots before weighing anchor.

To the baffled commander in chief, it seemed at last that Howe must be leaving Burgoyne to his own devices and was pointing the fleet toward Philadelphia. Washington lost no time in meeting the new threat. He ordered Lincoln to join Schuyler at Albany in order to take command of the militia; Stephen was directed to lead his own and Lincoln's division by the back route from Chester through Sussex, N.J., toward Philadelphia; while Sullivan and Stirling were both directed to cross back to the west side of the Hudson ready to march south. Word went to Anthony Wayne in Pennsylvania to leave his brigade and proceed to rendezvous with the militia at Chester, Pa., and to Daniel Morgan's riflemen in New Jersey to head for Philadelphia. Other special units in New Jersey were similarly ordered to the Delaware. Washington rode back with NG's division to Sufferns, from which the following morning, 25 July, they set out for Pompton, where they had camped two weeks earlier. By noon on 26 July, the army was near enough to Beverwyck, the home of Abraham Lott, for Washington and Greene to stop for lunch and for NG to be reunited briefly with his wife. NG's division then spent the night near Morristown, and by evening of 28 July, they were on the New Jersey side of Coryell's Ferry. Half of NG's division (Muhlenberg's brigade) crossed that evening; Weedon's the next day. (See Biddle to James Wilson, 29 July 1777, *PMHB*, 32 [1908]: 165) By this time Stephen had reached Howell's Ferry, four miles north, with his own and Lincoln's divisions.

The march to Coryells and Howells in three days was a remarkable achievement for the poorly shod army. One day they slogged along muddy roads in a steady rain. Clement Biddle said that despite the men's fatigue they were "in fine spirit." (Biddle to James Wilson, ibid.) It must have been the apparent end of uncertainty that enspirited the men. Washington halted at Coryells until further word from Howe was received. He did not have long to wait. (See note 2.) Washington's moves and countermoves are covered in Fitzpatrick, *GW*, 8: 387–500, and Freeman, *GW*, 4: 443–47.

2. The report was correct, although it was another day before Washington received convincing reports of the sighting.

General Greene's Orders

[Coryells Ferry, N.J., 30 July 1777. Commanding officers of Muhlenberg's[1] and Weedon's brigades are to check the state of men's arms and ammunition. Detachments forming Col. Morgan's rifle corps, now at Trenton, to be paid through May.[2] Stewart Orderly Book (Typescript: NjP) 1 p.]

1. John Peter Gabriel Muhlenberg (1746–1807), a tall handsome man of thirty, had been, like his German-born father, a Lutheran minister. As a member of the Virginia House of Burgesses, he had early espoused the patriot cause. In January 1776 he was appointed colonel, and after preaching a legendary sermon ("there's a time to pray and a time to fight"), he recruited his famed German regiment in Virginia. After one year in the South, he was made brigadier and joined Washington's army at Morristown. Put in command of a brigade in NG's division in May 1777, he distinguished himself as a courageous, stubborn, and dependable leader at the battles of Brandywine, Germantown, and Monmouth. After serving with Lafayette at Yorktown in October 1781, he stayed on in Virginia to recruit units for NG in Carolina. See Paul A. W. Wallace, *The Muhlenbergs of Pennsylvania* (Freeport, N.Y.: Books for Libraries Press, 1950).

2. Daniel Morgan (1735–1802), one of the most colorful officers in the war, was greatly beloved by his men. A tall, muscular frontiersman from western Virginia and veteran of Indian wars, he first met NG when he led his company of riflemen to Boston

in August 1775 after a march of six hundred miles in twenty-one days. In a career that involved him in numerous engagements from Canada to Carolina, he became a master of light infantry tactics while advancing from captain to brigadier general. He is especially remembered for his role in Burgoyne's defeat at Saratoga and for his slashing victory at Cowpens in January 1781, which marked the beginning of NG's successful southern campaign. Illness forced him to retire shortly thereafter. His biographer, Don Higginbotham, calls him "the outstanding combat officer" in the war, with the "possible exception of Benedict Arnold." (Higginbotham, *War*, p. 102; see also his *Daniel Morgan: Revolutionary Rifleman* [Chapel Hill: University of North Carolina Press, 1961].)

General Greene's Orders

Warwick [Pa.][1] July 31st 1777

The Assembly to beat at half past 5 in the Morning, to march exactly at 6; before the march begins the Baggage guard to be reduced as small as possible, and those that are appointed to that duty, must be of such Soldiers as are unfit for Service, such as are unable of marching in the Line are to be left under the care of a Subaltern Officer to be appointed from each Brigade to take charge of the whole. All the Invalids are to march in the rear of the Baggage of the whole of the division. Colo Abeel is desired to furnish Waggons to take up such as fall sick on the Road. The Troops in the Line are to march by Plattoons and none of the men suffered to straggle. The Invalids are to keep together and march by files, the order of march as heretofore. We take the route to German Town.

"Muhlenberg Orderly Book," reprinted from *PMHB*, 34 (1910): 188.
    1. Warwick was halfway between the camp at Coryells Ferry and Philadelphia. NG and his division had arrived at the campsite near Little Neshaminy Creek after an exhausting day that had started at 9:30 A.M. with the arrival of an express rider from Congress, bearing news that Howe's fleet had been sighted the day before (30 July) off the Delaware Capes. Even before the express arrived, the British fleet had left their brief anchorage off the Capes and had set sail for Chesapeake Bay, but Washington, having no way of knowing this, had immediately set the army in motion toward Philadelphia.
    Half of NG's division had crossed the river into Pennsylvania two days earlier (see note, NG to Cooke, 29 July, above). Washington now ordered the rest to cross, as well as Stephen's and Lincoln's divisions (both under Stephen's command) four miles upstream at Howell's Ferry. Unaware that Sullivan's division marched without its ill commander, Washington ordered it to proceed at once to Coryells. He also directed Putnam at Peekskill to send two brigades from the west shore of the Hudson, keeping 2,000 continental troops in case there was still a British move up the Hudson. When most of the army had crossed the Delaware, Washington left NG in charge and hurried off to Philadelphia. (Fitzpatrick, *GW*, 8: 501–7, 9: 1–4; Freeman, *GW*, 4: 447–48)

From George Washington

1st Augst 1777
Dear sir
City Tavern Philadelphia
We have not recieved any certain Intelligence that the Fleet have got within the Capes. By the last accounts they were beating in, the wind unfavorable. It was supposed they would get in about three oClock yesterday Evening.[1]

I would wish you to collect and bring up your rear, as soon as may be, to German Town or to proper Grounds contiguous to it where the Troops are to remain untill further orders. If they can be got on this side the better.

You will reduce the division to a proper arrangement in all its parts, and as the Brigades arrive, you will order them immediately to set about cleaning their arms and putting them in the best possible fix.

Neither officers or Soldiers are to be permitted to leave their corps and come to this place.[2] The Soldiers (not a man) is to be allowed to load. To prevent these things you'll issue the most peremptory orders. I am Dr Sr Your most hum Servt

GO: WASHINGTON

p s You'll place Guards on the ways leading to this [place] to prevent the Soldiers from passing.

LS (John F. Reed, Valley Forge, Pa., 1972). The draft in the Washington Papers, DLC, does not have the postscript.
1. Washington had arrived from Coryells Ferry about ten o'clock the evening before, having left NG in charge of the army. (See note, NG's Orders, 31 July, above.) News of Howe's having left the Delaware Capes did not reach Philadelphia until the next day.
2. He feared if troops entered the city "it would only serve to debauch them." (Washington to Gates, 28 July 1777, Fitzpatrick, GW, 8: 490)

General Greene's Orders

Head Quarters [German Town, Pa.][1] August 1st 1777
By express from his Excellency Genl. Washington received a few Hours past, the Genl. is directed to acquaint both Officers and Soldiers that they are not to go into the City of Philadelphia without a permit from a Genl. Officer, any Officer that disobeys will be arrested, and any Soldier that goes without leave will be severely punished. All the Genl. Officers are requested not to grant permission to any person unless it be to execute business of real necessity. The Commanding Officers of Regiments are directed to have a return made out immediately of the Arms out of repair in their Regiments and the

number wanting to furnish every Man fit for duty. The Arms in the Regiments that want no repair to be cleaned and put in the best order for Action, none of the Guards to be loaded 'till further orders all the Arms that are loaded of each Regiment to be drawn up at some proper place under the direction of the Commanding Officer of the Regiment, or one of the Field Officers and discharge all at once, and the General desires the officers of each Company to see that the Men dont load for the sake of firing, such a wanting waste of Ammunition cannot be Justifiable. The Quarter Masters of each Regiment are directed to see the Men are provided with wood for Cooking, the Quarter Master Genl. of each division will direct the Regimental Quarter Masters where to cut wood. No fence to be burnt on any account. All the officers of every rank are requested to protect the Inhabitants from personal Insults, and their property from being plundered.

Field officer for to morrow for the Brigade Major Nicholas, Adjutant for the day, to morrow Fowke.

Stewart Orderly Book (Typescript: NjP).
1. NG had set up camp for the army near Germantown—on a plateau a mile from the falls of the Schuylkill River in Roxborough Township, where the army remained during the first week of August and to which it returned for two days in September, after the battle of Brandywine. (Baker, "Camp," pp. 28–41)

From George Washington

Dr Sir   Chester [Pa.] August 1st 1777[1]

I have just received information by express that the enemys fleet have disappeared from the Capes yesterday morning about eight oClock.[2] This unexpected event makes it necessary to reverse our disposition and I have accordingly sent orders to Sullivan's division and the two other brigades on the other [east] side the Delaware to return and recross the North River. You are immediately to complete your men with two days provisions and hold them in readiness to march at further orders, and you are to give similar directions to the other divisions and corps. You will also be pleased to give the necessary orders to the Qr Mr General and Commissary General respecting their departments, desiring them to make proper arrangements for provisions and forage on the rout. I am Dr Sir Your most Obdt serv

                                                                G W

Df (Washington Papers: DLC). Alexander Hamilton, who drafted the letter, first signed the draft, then crossed out his signature.
1. Washington had spent a good part of the day inspecting fortifications on both sides of the Delaware as far south as Chester—fifteen miles below Philadelphia—where he spent the night. (Reed, Campaign, p. 46)
2. Washington was never more mystified by the enemy's action than at the disappearance of the British fleet from Delaware Bay. (On Howe's decision to go by

sea, see note, Council of War, 12 June, above.) The sighting two days earlier had ended weeks of speculation as to Howe's destination; there had seemed no doubt that it was Philadelphia. To learn that the fleet was now withdrawing was not only mystifying but a shock that seemed temporarily to leave Washington in a near panic for fear that Howe had merely feinted toward Philadelphia and was headed back northward to the Hudson. To Putnam in Peekskill, he dispatched an express to say that he was ordering Sullivan to recross the Hudson at once and that he would "forward on the rest of the Army with all the expedition in my power." (Fitzpatrick, *GW*, 9: 1). By the time he wrote NG later in the day, however, he had apparently recovered somewhat from his initial shock and suggested only that NG hold his men "in readiness to march." Perhaps, on reflection, Washington reasoned that even the unpredictable Howe would not expose his men and horses to two gruelling weeks at sea in July heat in a roundabout feint to screen an attack up the Hudson. In any case, without any further sightings or apparent suspicions that Howe might be heading for the Chesapeake, Washington two days later stopped the rush for the Hudson that he had initiated. He ordered Sullivan's division to stop where it was, unless Gen. Preudhomme de Borre (the ill Sullivan's temporary replacement) had "certain information, that the Enemy's Fleet were arrived at the Hook [Sandy Hook, N.J.]" (Fitzpatrick, *GW*, 9: 7) The army would freeze in its various locations until time brought further sightings.

General Greene's Orders

[Germantown, Pa., 2 August 1777. Troops to be in readiness to move "in a Moments warning"; no officer or soldier to absent himself from camp. Stewart Orderly Book (Typescript: NjP) 1 p.]

General Greene's Orders

[Germantown, Pa., 6 August 1777. Wants fatigue parties and camp coulour men to cleanse camp; unsanitary conditions and "stench" threaten camp health. Gens. Muhlenberg and Weedon to appoint an officer from each brigade to examine provisions that "Officers refuse to take." Troops to be exercised twice a day. "Muhlenberg Orderly Book," reprinted from *PMHB*, 34 (1910): 337.]

Memorial of Board of General Officers[1]

[Camp at Germantown, Pa., 7 August 1777. Asks Washington to recommend repeal of congressional resolve that obliges officers to draw provisions with the men, which deprives officers of a convenience. At the same time (perhaps to make it sound less selfish), they added that the practice "oppresses the men, the officers picking out all the best bits for their own consumption." Recommends that regiments form themselves into messes of no more than twelve to each regiment with liberty to draw from "Commissaries Store."[2] Failure to settle the back rations causes complaints. DS (Washington Papers: DLC) 1 p.]

1. NG signed for all the officers.
2. After Congress reorganized the Commissary Department in June, it became

customary for commissaries to interpret article twenty-four (*JCC*, 8: 443) as obliging them as Congress later said to "issue provisions indiscriminately to the officers and privates." (*JCC*, 8: 732) Washington forwarded the request to Congress on 9 August, pointing out that it could cause no injury "to the Public, and is what, I believe, is allowed, in most Armies." (Fitzpatrick, *GW*, 9: 38) On 4 September, Congress empowered Washington, if he thought proper, "to order the Officers of the several Regiments to receive their Rations in Messes, notwithstanding any Resolutions of Congress to the Contrary." (*JCC*, 8: 711) A resolution was introduced a week later to formalize officers messes, but it was referred to a committee, which, in view of the imminent take-over of Philadelphia by the British, apparently never reported back. (*JCC*, 8: 732–33; Fitzpatrick, *GW*, 9: 38n, mistakenly says "the matter was settled by the resolves of September 11.")

To George Washington

[Camp at Germantown, Pa., 7 August 1777. A meeting of general officers, called by Washington to consider four matters, was attended by Maj. Gens. Greene and Stephen; Brig. Gens. Maxwell, Knox, Muhlenberg, Weedon, Scott, and Woodford. The following recommendations were made:[1]

Wagon master general (Joseph Thornburgh) and those under him are to govern "themselves agreeable to the Rules and Regulations of the Army." If any misbehave, the field officer of the day or brigadier or major general may order them confined.

Five ounces of soap per week to each man are "absolutely necessary to keep the soldiers decent and Clean"; those selling their soap to be severely punished.

No officer has appeared to "shew cause" why abstracts cannot be made out agreeable to general orders.

Congress had allowed each soldier one suit of clothing (on enlistment) or $20.00 if he furnished his own. With inflation the board recommends an annual issue of clothing from regimental allotments with no charges, as long as regimental allowance is not overdrawn.[2] DS (Washington Papers: DLC) 4 pp.]

1. NG signed each recommendation as "President of the Board."
2. In a somewhat confused resolution about clothing on 28 August, Congress did not accept the officers' recommendations. (*JCC*, 8: 690–92)

From Colonel Joseph Ward[1]

[Camp at Germantown, Pa., 7 August 1777. He lists "The causes of Delay in mustering the Army" as the lack of, or the sickness of, deputies; "frequent motions" of the army; want of vouchers; lack of knowledge or attention on part of many officers; the need for certification by a general officer, as well as "Many other Causes."[2] DS (Washington Papers: DLC) 1 p.]

1. Joseph Ward of Massachusetts, formerly an aide to Gen. Artemas Ward, had been named muster master general of the army with the rank of colonel in April 1777. (JCC, 7: 252) In April 1780 he became commissary general of prisoners—a post he held until the end of the war. (Heitman, *Register*)

2. In his orders of 6 August, Washington had requested Ward to appear before the Board of Officers with an explanation. (Fitzpatrick, *GW*, 9: 28) Ward addressed the document to NG as president of the Board of Officers.

From Colonel Richard Humpton[1]

[Germantown, Pa., 7 August 1777. After some delays, payrolls and muster rolls of Eleventh Pa. Regiment have been settled. Officers of Second Brigade of Lincoln's division are of opinion "that 20 lb of good Soap would not be more than sufficient to Wash 100 Soldiers Linnen &c pr week." ALS (Washington Papers: DLC) 1 p.]

1. Humpton, commander of the Eleventh Pa. Regiment, addressed the letter to NG as President of the Board of General Officers.

From Colonel Francis Johnston[1]

[Germantown, Pa., 7 August 1777. Settlement of regimental pay records delayed because paymaster only appointed in March and many accounts are "long standing" and attended by "intricate Circumstances." Bills for arms and equipment not the regiment's responsibility. ALS (Washington Papers: DLC) 2 pp.]

1. Johnston, commander of the Fifth Pa. Regiment, addressed his letter to the Board of General Officers, not to NG.

To George Washington[1]

[Germantown, Pa., 7 [?][2] August 1777. It is necessary to guard Philadelphia against attack by land and water because of "the prejudices of the people in the surrounding States so strong in its favour." Also its manufactures and supplies for the army are numerous enough that "the loss of it would so effect the Country (and) the Army that very great injury would arise (to) the common cause of America." The only security by land is a superior force to stop the enemy's army.

He then discusses at great length his ideas for protecting the city from ships coming up the Delaware. The Delaware is so long and its channel so narrow and crooked (accommodating no more than two ships abreast) that the following defenses would prevent a British fleet from reaching Philadelphia: the three existing rows of "Cheveau de Frize" across the river at Mud Island (discounting the one at Billingsport); Ft. Mifflin on Mud Island, especially when strength-

ened by some 8 or 10 additional cannon and manned by 180 can-
noniers and 300 to 500 men (the fort being protected by the possibility
of flooding the approaches on the Pennsylvania side and by its distance from the New Jersey shore); the use of xebeques, floating
batteries, and frigates posted "behind the upper Cheveau de Frize"
and armed row galleys ready to move up and down the river; and
finally the additional defense of fire rafts and fire ships, which, if
favored with "a good gale and quick tide," could set fire to a fleet
sailing upstream. He would not deplete the army to man the fortifications at Billingsport, Red Bank, or Derby Creek, but in lieu of strong
fortifications at those points, he would place a "number of half moon
Batteries" to annoy the shipping and a "few Eighteen pounders on
travelling carriages to move from place to place." He would, in fact,
recommend demolishing the fort at Billingsport were it "not for the
prejudices of the people, and the reproach it would bring."[3] As for
fortifications "in general" he wrote:

> All fortifications in America except for the security of
> particular objects, considering the nature of the country are
> rather prejudicial than useful: the country is taught to expect
> security and always loose their confidence upon any unfortunate
> event. The Enemy getting possession of our works they serve
> them for strongholds to keep in awe all the circumjacent country.
> By the assistance of our Garrisons the Enemy is enabled to keep a
> much greater extent of country in subjection. If they had no
> Garrisons to protect their troops they would be oblig'd to keep
> their forces more together. If they were to attempt to erect those
> works themselves it must necessarily fatigue their troops and
> Delay their operations. The country cannot be conquerd and
> held in subjection but by Garrisons. It should be our policy
> therefore to have as few as may be. The Enemy gains little or no
> advantage by marching through the country. The inhabitants
> from their cruelties and abuses generally grow more obstinate
> and Confirm'd in opposition.
> If we build strong fortifications the continent must be subject
> to great expence to support the Garrisons besides that of erecting
> and furnishing the fortress with cannon, Military Stores &c.
> These Garrisons only serve to secure a small part of the Country
> which security is purchased by a prodigious drain of men and
> materials from the Army. I could wish that only a few principal
> passes and Capital Citys should have any fortifications about
> them. The security of the country must depend upon our su-
> periority in the field; if our force is divided and appointed to the
> defence of particular places, the Enemy will be masters of the

field and the country loose their confidence in the Army; and notwithstanding the Garrisons at particular places may delay the Enemys operations a little, these advantages are far overballanc'd by the pannick their loss generally strikes upon the Country; and the advantage they give to the enemy to hold the circumjacent country in subjection.[4]

He adds a final strong reason for not multiplying fortifications on the Delaware: cannons cannot be spared from other places. His report has "swell'd much beyond the size I intended," so he has been forced to omit some explanations. ALS (Washington Papers: DLC) 10 pp.]

1. Washington also had opinions from Gens. du Coudray, Wayne, and Knox and from his aide, Joseph Reed. (Their letters are also in the Washington Papers, DLC). In his recommendations to Congress, Washington agreed essentially with Greene and Reed in emphasizing the importance of Ft. Mifflin, the cheveaux de frise, and the use of frigates, row galleys, and fire ships; but he also favored erecting a small "work" at Red Bank to protect American galleys. It should be stressed, however, that all of the recommendations were predicated on Philadelphia's being in American hands when attacked by water, which was entirely different from the situation that faced the courageous defenders of Ft. Mifflin and Red Bank in October and November of 1777, when the British had occupied Philadelphia. (See below, Council of War, 28 September; Washington's letter to Congress of 10 August is in Fitzpatrick, GW, 9: 45–53.) On 11 August, Congress ordered the Board of War to carry out Washington's "plan of defence" (JCC, 8: 630), but there it lay until Howe was upon Philadelphia by land. Since the attack on Philadelphia by water never came to pass, NG's extensive recommendations have been abstracted. His comments on the value of American fortifications, however, have been printed in full at the end of the abstract.
2. The date is conjectured from the opinions of the other men.
3. Washington had recently spent a day examining the river defenses, but NG had to rely on the memory of his visit to Philadelphia the previous March and on what information he had gleaned from conversations with those familiar with the river, such as Commodore John Hazelwood of the Pennsylvania Navy and NG's friend Joseph Reed.
4. The lesson of Ft. Washington's fall was never far below the surface of NG's mind. (See above, vol. 1: 352n) Nowhere has he summarized so convincingly his opinions on the essential uselessness of fortifications and on the dependency of the country's security upon "our superiority in the field."

To Jacob Greene

Camp Cross Roads [Pa.][1] 11th August 1777.
Your favours of the 12th and 19th of July I have received.[2] I am exceedingly alarmed at the ill state of health you appear to be in.

The calamities of the war, the late misfortunes and the common depression of spirits that accompanies every species of indisposition, generally prey upon the imagination, and perhaps may have taken an ungenerous advantage of you in the present case. However, I would recommend great attention to your diet and exercise. Nothing contributes more to health than seasonable and light diet, accompanied with moderate exercise. You must learn to be the philosopher—to behold misfortunes without repining, limit the passions, the appetites and desires to the state of the body, and the necessity of the times. However unfortunate things may appear, let us console ourselves with reflecting that the greatest good often springs out of what we consider as the worst of evils.

General Burgoyne's triumphs and little advantages may serve to bait his vanity and lead him on to his total ruin.[3] This is not improbable when we consult the temper of the human heart, the history of mankind, and the dispensations of divine providence upon the rise and fall of men and kingdoms. The campaign opened with a very fortunate train of circumstances. General Howe was foiled in all his manoeuvres, and disgraced in every movement. Our success was equal to our utmost wishes. The northern department has brought disgrace upon the American arms, and a cloud over New England. But even all *these misfortunes may be a necessary prelude to General Burgoyne's final overthrow.* I agree with you that there is something very mysterious in conducting the military operations to the northward. There must have been a want of judgment in the choice of the posts and extent of the works, or some great negligence in fairly representing the true state of things. We were all led to believe the situation of the place so strong by nature and so improved by art, that the garrison was sufficient to defend itself against any number that might be brought against it. Whatever may be the source of the misfortune, it is not owing to cowardice. I have been with General St. Clair in two actions, and know him to be a man of bravery; and it is agreed on all hands, that the garrison was in high health and full of spirits, and left the place with great reluctance. Charity obliges me to suspend my opinion until there is a fair and candid inquiry made into the cause of the evacuation of Ticonderoga, and if it was necessary to evacuate it, why it had not been done earlier. If the stores and garrison had been saved, the loss of the place would have been inconsiderable.[4]

We have been in and about the city of Philadelphia for near a fortnight past, ignorant of General Howe's destination. I hope it will not be against New England, but I have my fears. We were marching towards Coryel's Ferry from the city, expecting the fleet was gone eastwardly, when, by an express from the president of congress last night we learned that the fleet are bound westwardly.[5] I wish it may be true. It was said that two hundred sail were seen off the coast, between Delaware and Chesapeake Bays, but I doubt the intelligence; for I cannot persuade myself *that General Burgoyne would dare to push with such rapidity towards Albany, if he did not expect support from General Howe.*

You lament the ruin of trade, the depreciation of money, and the discontent of the people as so many sure marks of the downfall of our cause. It is true, our trade is greatly injured, but remember whilst it rains upon us, the sun does not shine upon them. Our trade is perhaps not more injured than theirs; we must balance accounts in national suffering. If the diminution of their force and resources equal our misfortunes and losses, then we are not sufferers on the great scale of national gain. The depreciation of money is rather a temporary, and in some respects, a local evil. The increase of trade and a proper attention to taxation will soon correct the evil. The army are the greatest sufferers. All the other parts of the community regulate their conduct and prices by one another. But the wages of the army are fixed and unchangeable. There is a fund of hard money now establishing in Europe, sufficient to pay the interest of all our loans.[6] This cannot fail of establishing the credit of the money abroad and at home. This is a good piece of policy. The discontent of the people is not greater than is to be expected in every revolution, when robbed of the blessings of peace and plenty, and forced into a long and distressing war to obtain some future advantage that they have but an indistinct conception of. *I have no doubt of a happy issue, although we may experience many calamities in the course of the dispute.*

You distress me exceedingly in committing to my charge the care of your family. God grant you may long live to discharge the duty yourself. I feel the force of brotherly affection equally strong with yourself. I have been equally happy in our mutual good understanding. The sweet pleasures of social fellowship have ever been one of the greatest sources of my happiness. Few misfortunes in life, however tender my other connexions may be, could equal the loss. Although I should esteem this charge one of my greatest misfortunes, yet I trust I should discharge my duty to the survivors of the family with such a brotherly affection as to leave no cause of a blush when we meet in another world. But heaven avert so great an evil to them and to me, and grant you long life and better health shall be my constant prayer. . . . Mrs. Greene tells me she is marked with port wine.[7] Be pleased to send some to the nurse, and direct her to wash the part and give the child a little. This, however simple it may appear, has been often known to remove the marks.

Excerpt reprinted from Johnson, *Greene*, 1: 98–100. The italicized sentences are Johnson's.

1. On the move to Cross Roads, see note 5, below.

2. Letters not found.

3. NG could not suspect how prophetic his words were. Ironically, at the very time he was writing to Jacob, Gen. Burgoyne had just given new orders to Col. Friedrich Baum of the Brunswick dragoons: instead of marching to Manchester, the Germans were to go directly to Bennington—where five days later they (and indirectly Burgoyne) were to meet with a stunning defeat at the Battle of Bennington. See Nickerson, *Turning Point*, pp. 240–63.

4. NG had learned more about the fall of Ft. Ticonderoga since he had written to Jacob on 13 July, but as noted there it was some time before all the facts were in.

5. He means toward the south. For a week after the British fleet left the Delaware Capes on 31 July, the Americans had no inkling that it was headed south. (See note, Washington to NG, 1 August, above.) Washington could "only conclude" that Howe was headed back north to cooperate somehow with Burgoyne. (Fitzpatrick, *GW*, 9: 34) On this premise he ordered the army to start marching back northward to Coryells Ferry on the Delaware at 2:00 PM on Friday, 8 August. They had reached Upper Dublin Township on Sunday evening after two days of intense heat when an express arrived from Congress to report that a fleet—presumed to be Gen. Howe's—had been sighted on 7 August off Sinapuxent, Md., "about 16 leagues to the Southward of the Delaware Capes." (Fitzpatrick, *GW*, 9: 55) Still not suspecting Howe's Chesapeake objective, Washington decided, until he got further word, to camp at Cross Roads, Pa. (also called Bucks County or Camp Neshaminy after the adjoining creek), twelve miles short of Coryells Ferry and some twenty miles north of Philadelphia. There the army stayed until 22 August, when word reached the camp that Howe's fleet had entered Chesapeake Bay. (Fitzpatrick, *GW*, 9: 54–124)

6. NG was being far too optimistic here.

7. Referring to a birthmark of the infant Martha, born the previous March. A good example of his penchant for recommending remedies.

General Greene's Orders

[Camp Cross Roads, Pa.,[1] 13 August 1777. Gen. Muhlenberg to "order a Guard over Mr Millers Oats." Returns of all armorers in the regiments to be made as soon as possible. From "Muhlenberg Orderly Book," *PMHB*, 34 (1910): 351]

1. The camp on Neshaminy Creek was also called by the name of the creek as well as Bucks County Camp.

To General James M. Varnum

Camp at the Cross Roads [Pa.]
Sir   Aug. 14th 1777

Yours of the 8th of this instant I have recd.[1] You are much mistaken respecting the destination of Sir William being known before yours reach'd me. I am totally ignorant yet. This manoeuvre of General Howe is so strange and unaccountable that it exceeds all conjecture. General Bourgoyne's rapid marches into the country is a strong proof to me that he expects to be supported from some other quarter. This leads me to conclude that General Howe's designs are ultimately against New England, notwithstanding his excentric movements. I am glad to hear you are so well prepared to defend the Highlands.[2] I fear the obstructions in the River will scarcely prove sufficient to check the enemy's progress with their ships. Your observations are very just respecting Gen. Schuyler. If he has lost the confidence of the people his talents will be useless. The Congress were made sensible of that and have appointed Gen. Gates to the command.[3] I hope he will succeed better. I think it an object of the first importance to give a check to Bourgoyne, and the very plan you mention has often been proposed both with respect to Bourgoyne and New York. Philadelphia is the American Diana; she must be preserved at all events. There is great affection paid to this city.[4] It is true it is one of the finest upon the continent, but in my opinion is an object of far less importance than the North River. Our position in the Jerseys was calculated to cover the North River and Philadelphia and afford protection to the State of New Jersey, but the cry was so great for the salvation of Philadelphia that the General was prevailed to leave Coryell's Ferry contrary to his judgment, and march down to the city, and I expect to have our labour for our pains.[5] We are now within about 20 miles of the city, waiting to get better information. There have been several expresses from Sinepuxent, an inlet about half way between the Cape of Delaware and Chesapeak Bay, who confidently assert the fleet has been seen off there for several days; but I cannot credit it. I shall mention to the General the Rhode Island troops are without commissions and also the detachment that is detained at Rhode Island contrary to your orders. I am sir your most obdt and humble servant

N. G.

Tr (GWG Transcript: CSmH).
 1. Letter not found.
 2. Varnum was at Peekskill, N.Y., with his brigade.
 3. A command for which Washington had apparently considered NG. See letter and note, NG to Catharine, 17 July, above.
 4. See his comment on Philadelphia in his letter to Washington, 7 [?] August, above.
 5. See note, NG's Orders, 31 July, above.

General Greene's Orders

[Camp at Cross Roads, Pa., 17 August 1777. Gens. Weedon and Muhlenberg and their regimental officers to meet at NG's quarters tomorrow to pick armory site for the division and to report the number of armorers in each regiment.[1] The two brigades to alternate in supplying guards for commissary stores. From "Muhlenberg Orderly Book," *PMHB*, 34 (1910): 357]

 1. In Washington's general orders of 12 August, he requested the major generals to consult their brigadiers, to "fit up as many Armorours as are sufficient to keep the Arms of their divisions in repair," and to provide one or two traveling forges for the purpose. The order is not in Fitzpatrick but is printed in *PMHB*, 34 (1910): 348–49.

To General James M. Varnum

Camp at the Cross Roads [Pa.]

Sir   Aug 17th 1777

Your favor of the 15th is before me.[1] I readily acknowledge the propriety of your observation that delays are dangerous and that the prime of the season is wasteing while we are basking in the Sunshine of Pensylvania; but repentance often comes too late. Could we have divind how General Howe would have directed his future operations some part of your plan might have been carried into execution. The destruction of General Burgoynes army is one of the first objects upon the continent; but how to effect it is the question. You see he moves with caution notwithstanding our army flies before him. It is near a month since he landed at Skenesborough, his advance parties have advanced only about twenty or thirty miles and nothing or next to nothing to oppose him.[2] Sure I am he never would have dard to penetrate an inch if he had met with a serious opposition. It is said our troops are pannick struck: this is strange; they have met with no misfortune. I am confident if there is a formidable force collects under the command of General Gates, that Burgoyne never leaves sight of his shipping. His retreat is secure while he has the command of South Bay;[3] in that situation he will rest unless he can bring over a great part of the country to join him. How that might encourage him I cannot pretend to say. Could I perswade myself that Burgoyne would not retreat upon the Northern army's being reinforced, I would run all hazzard to attempt his destruction. But I am well perswaded he would retreat immediately to Ticonderoga, where it would be out of our power to do him any great injury.[4] I wish the party that is coming by the German Flatts would be defeated; I am much afraid of the consequences of their successes: the disaffected people joind by the Indians will render that a troublesome neighborhood.[5] There is a corps of Rifflemen detacht to combat these Indians, under the command of Col Morgan.

I am under no apprehension about the troops at Rhode Island unless they are joind by General Howes forces; they are as innocent and harmless as can be expected. The greatest injury they do us is the distressing trade and alarming the fears of the people on the surrounding shores.

Our situation is not a little awkward, buryed in the country out of hearing of the Enimy. His Excellency is exceeding impatient; but it is said, if Philadelphia is lost all all is ruined. It is a great object to be sure but not of that great magnitude that it claims in the measure of the American police. Rest assured we shall not remain idle long. This is a curious campaign: in the Spring we had the Enimy about our ears every hour. The Northern Army could neither see or hear of an Enemy. Now they have got the enimy about their heads and we have lost ours, compeld to wander about the country like the Arabs in search of em.

I think there is force enough gone and going to the Northerd if they are well directed and led on with Spirit, but without that they will be idle and useless.

I am glad to hear your forces are healthy. Ours are growing more so than they were. I can assure you I was no advocate for coming so hastily here, for I ever thought Gen Howes motions very equivocal, but the loss of Philadelphia would injure us more than our takeing New York would them, and it is not certain our rapid march did not hinder the Enemy from coming up the Bay to the City. They were hovering about the coast for several days is very certain.[6]

My compliments to all friends. I am with regard your most obedient Servt

NATH GREENE

ALS (NNC).

1. Letter not found.

2. NG, of course, had not yet heard of the defeat of Burgoyne's German units at Bennington two days earlier.

3. The southern neck of Lake Champlain.

4. If Burgoyne had possessed the military astuteness with which NG credited him, he would have retreated when the American forces ahead of him began to outnumber his troops, instead of stubbornly advancing into crushing defeat at Saratoga.

5. German Flats was an area along the Mohawk Valley in New York. The "party" was Col. Barry St. Leger's force of two thousand men (half of them Indians), which had left Oswego on Lake Ontario in late July with the objective of joining Burgoyne at Albany. A week after NG wrote, St. Leger was forced to retreat from Ft. Stanwix by the approach of Benedict Arnold's relief unit. (Nickerson, *Turning Point*, pp. 193–223, 264–76)

6. Washington's rapid march, in fact, did contribute to Howe's decision to withdraw from the Delaware for Chesapeake Bay. See note, Council of War, 12 June, above.

To General Anthony Wayne

[Camp Cross Roads, Pa. (18 August 1777),[1] Monday morning 11:00 A.M. Wishes Wayne to attend meeting of general officers on settlement of rank of Pennsylvania officers, if not to vote, then for consultation. ALS (PHi) 1 p.]

1. Letter undated, but the Board of General Officers met Tuesday, 19 August. Wayne was among those present. (See General Officers to Washington, below.)

Board of General Officers to George Washington[1]

[Camp Bucks County (Cross Roads), Pa., 19 August 1777. Recommends that the "German Battalion" and Col. Hazen's regiment rise "Regimentally," while the "Sixteen additional Battalions" should rise in the line.[2] On subject of back pay, would have officers draw pay from the time of their "right of promotion." DS (Washington Papers: DLC) 1 p.]

1. NG signed as president of the board.
2. The so-called German Battalion was raised in Maryland and Pennsylvania by congressional resolution, 25 May 1776. In 1777 it became one of the sixteen "Additional Continental Regiments" authorized on 27 December 1776 and commanded after March 1777 by Baron de Arendt. Hazen's "own" regiment, composed of Canadians, was recruited from Albany.

Board of General Officers to George Washington

[Camp Bucks County (Cross Roads), Pa., 19 August 1777. Present: Gens. Greene,[1] Stirling, Stephen, Maxwell, Knox, Muhlenberg, Weedon, Wayne, and Woodford. Meeting to discuss the rank of Pennsylvania officers, the board declares there is no principle so generally acceptable as "giving Rank according to their former standing." Since many officers feel "injur'd by Colo (Joseph) Wood's *extraordinary* promotion,"[2] board recommends this principle be applied, unless Congress feels "under some obligations to Colonel Wood for special services." Recommends that Congress grant new commissions to all field officers "agreeable to their Claim from their former Rank and right of promotion," which will do justice to Pennsylvania officers and to the army in general. There follows a recommended new arrangement.[3] ALS (Washington Papers: DLC) 4 pp.]

1. NG as president of the board signed the document.
2. Congress had made Joseph Wood colonel of the Second Pa. Regiment in September 1776, apparently passing over several field officers of higher rank. (*JCC*, 5: 746) He became colonel of the Third Pa. Regiment in January 1777. According to Heitman, *Register*, he resigned a few weeks before this council met.
3. Docketing on the back of the document noted that Congress agreed to the principle adopted by the board on 13 November and that the president had written the same day to say that new commissions were being granted to Pennsylvania officers. The letter is in the Washington Papers, DLC.

Council of General Officers

[Neshaminy Camp (Cross Roads), Pa., 21 August 1777. Having heard nothing of the British fleet since it was sighted off the Maryland coast two weeks before, Washington put three questions to the council, which they answered unanimously as follows: (1) Charleston, S.C., was the most probable destination of Howe's fleet; (2) it was inadvisable for the army to march southward, as it could not possibly arrive in Charleston in time to defend the city; and (3) the army should march immediately towards the North River.[1] The document was signed by Gens. Washington, Greene, Stirling, Stephen, "The Mqui de Lafayette,"[2] Maxwell, Knox, Wayne, Muhlenberg, Weedon, Woodford, Scott, and Conway. DS (Washington Papers: DLC) 2 pp.]

1. Aware that moving the army to the north would leave Philadelphia unprotected, Washington wished Congress's approval. He sent Hamilton to Philadelphia at once to present the decisions of the council, and at 5:00 P.M. the same day, Congress approved the plan and authorized Washington to act as circumstances required. (JCC, 8: 663) President Hancock notified Washington accordingly in a short letter written at 7:00 A.M. on 22 August. In the meantime Washington prepared to break camp. See NG's order below.

2. The nineteen-year-old marquis, who had been commissioned a major general on 31 July, stood out from most of the foreign officers who had presented themselves to Congress. Though young and inexperienced, he was there, he said, to learn and not to teach. He was ambitious and hungry for glory, and even at times something of a schemer in advancing his career, but American officers found him modest and generous. Since he was also wealthy, his generosity was especially appealing to those in Congress and the army. Freeman has written that he had "the rare quality of a personality that first disarmed and then captivated." Washington soon regarded him with almost as much affection as he "could have shown a son of his own." (Freeman, GW, 4: note opposite portrait, between pages 461 and 462) NG had met him for the first time when Lafayette was with the army from the eighth until the seventeenth of August. They soon became friends and remained such until NG's death, at which time Lafayette took NG's ten-year old son, George Washington Greene, into his home in France to educate him. There the boy remained for four years, until the French Revolution forced his return to America. Fifty years after NG's and Lafayette's friendship began, NG's grandson, George Washington Greene, spent a summer with Lafayette at La Grange.

An outstanding study of Lafayette's role in the American Revolution is Louis Gottschalk's three volumes published by the University of Chicago Press, *Lafayette Comes to America* (1935), *Lafayette Joins the American Army* (1937), and *Lafayette and the Close of the American Revolution* (1942). See also Idzerda, *Lafayette Papers*.

General Greene's Orders

Neshaminy Crossing [Pa.] 21 August 1777

Every thing to be in readiness to march early to morrow morning agreeable to the orders of the Day—[1] The Commanding Offrs of Regts are to see that their Regts are properly furnish'd with baggage Waggons and that those Waggons are Well provided with Horses, The Commanding Offrs of the Artillery of each Brigade will take care that their Pieces & Ammunition Waggons are well found, Those Regts that have Sick, Incapable of marching must apply to Col Abeell and QM Gl. for Waggons to transport them in, Such as ought to be sent to the Hospital to be by the Surgeons of the Regts immediately reported to the Director of the flying Hospital—

It is expected after this notice every thing will be in readiness for the march without Confusion or Delay–[2] The Genl observes with concern, many Centries sitting on their Posts, a Practice no less dangerous than disgraceful & considering the severity of the Punishment Inflicted on those found sleeping on their Posts it cannot be too carefully guarded against and more especially as it is consider'd an Evident mark of want of Discipline.

N GREENE

Reprinted from *Weedon Orderly Book*, p. 11.
    1. On breaking camp, see note, Council of General Officers, above.
    2. NG's division never began their northward march on 22 August. At 7 o'clock that morning, President Hancock in Philadelphia had sent off the approval of Congress for the army to move "towards Hudson's River," but until that approval arrived in camp, no tents were struck or wagons loaded. Not long after Washington received the approval, an express pulled in from Congress with news that the British fleet had "advanced high up the bay of Chesapeake, and, therefore, that it is probable the enemy have the city of Philadelphia in contemplation." (*JCC*, 8: 666) Washington immediately notified Congress he would "halt upon my present ground, till I hear something further." (Fitzpatrick, *GW*, 9: 111; Washington misdated the letter as August 21, and it is not corrected by Fitzpatrick.) A few hours later, Hancock followed this first letter with another, enclosing additional details of the sighting. He also said that Congress was ordering the immediate removal of stores and prisoners from Lancaster and York—a fortuitous move, for the supplies at York and Carlisle had been Howe's first objectives when the fleet dropped anchor in Elk River. (Gruber, *Howe Brothers*, p. 238)

To General Anthony Wayne

Dear Sir   Camp [Cross Roads, Pa.] August 22d 1777
    General Knox and myself are going a small Jorney of about thirty Miles and wish as the weather is exceeding hot to go in a carriage. If there is a Phaeton belonging to the family where you Quarter I beg youl use your friendly offices to obtain the loan of it for twenty or thirty hours. The family may depend upon its being well used.[1] I am dear Sir with sentiments of regard your obedient Servt

N GREENE

ALS (PHi).
    1. In a letter to his wife on 25 August, Knox tells of an overnight trip to Bethlehem, Pa., that he and NG made on 22 August to "purchase some things for my dear, dear Lucy." What NG's errand might have been he does not say.
    It is almost inconceivable that either man could have left camp on 22 August for such a whimsical objective with the army waiting only for the arrival of congressional approval (as noted above) before setting off for the Hudson. Obviously the men left before the second message arrived from Congress with the news of Howe's fleet having ascended the Chesapeake.
    Upon their arrival in Bethlehem, they were met not only with that news from Washington but also with word that the army was on its way south to put itself between the British army and Philadelphia. Instead of returning to camp at once, as might have been expected, Knox and Greene "first visited all parts of this singularly

happy place." On their arrival in Philadelphia next day (24 August), they must have been chagrined to find that just an hour earlier the troops had completed an impressive parade through the streets of that city en route to Wilmington, and that they—two of Washington's eminent generals—were not with them. Washington must also have been chagrined. Concerning the Bethlehem trip, see Francis S. Drake, *Life and Correspondence of Henry Knox* (Boston, 1873), pp. 46–47. The army's march through Philadelphia is covered in Fitzpatrick, *GW*, 9: 124–27 and 128n, and Freeman, *GW*, 4: 462–64.

General Greene's Orders[1]

[Darby, Pa.] August 24, 1777

The Division to be in readiness to move precisely at 4 o'clock tomorrow Morning. The Genl expects the D.Q.M.G. will see the Waggons provided with Horses and that every Thing in the Department be in Readiness.

Reprinted from "Muhlenberg Orderly Book," *PMHB*, 34 (1910): 446.
    1. After their jaunt to Bethlehem, Pa., as noted at NG to Wayne, 22 August, above, Greene and Knox rejoined the army, which was encamped a few miles south of Philadelphia en route to Delaware.

General Greene's Orders

Camp at White Clay Creek [Md.][1] Augt 28, 1777

Genl Muhlenburgs and Genl Weedens Brigades each to furnish 100 men that are good marksmen to form a Light corps for the Division as this is meant only for a temporary establishment & as the utility will depend upon the goodness of the men and Officers for such a Service, the Genl desires the Commanding Officers of Regts to send none but such as may be depended on.[2] Lt Col. Parker is to take the Command, Genl Muhlenburg will furnish a Major, two field Officers being necessary.

Reprinted from "Muhlenberg Orderly Book," *PMHB*, 34 (1910): 450.
    1. Earlier that day NG had marched his division from Wilmington southward into White Clay Creek Hundred, Md., camping some ten miles north of the British camp, well in advance of the main American army. (Fitzpatrick, *GW*, 9: 140) His division, in fact, had been in advance of the rest of the army since he rejoined it on the twenty-fourth at Darby. On 25 August, NG's and Stephen's divisions had marched from Darby to within a few miles of Wilmington, while the rest of the army reached Darby. Washington was not certain what he would do, but he needed to learn more about the enemy, and it would appear that he hoped to block Howe from advancing to Philadelphia—even if it meant a general engagement that he had avoided for so long. Riding a few miles ahead of NG's division, he received word at Wilmington on the evening of 25 August that Howe had been disembarking troops all day on the west shore of Elk River, a few miles south of the settlement called Head of Elk. Early on the twenty-sixth, NG's division set out for Wilmington, while he and Lafayette accompanied Washington and a "strong party of Horse" to reconnoiter the British operations. (Fitzpatrick, *GW*, 9: 452) They reached Grey's Hill, Md., within a few miles of Howe,

but they learned little from what they saw, except that Howe was still disembarking troops. They did learn that the local militia had fled at the sight of the longboats filled with the scarlet-clad British. A rainstorm that night forced Washington's party to take shelter in a farm house, one which Washington later admitted was owned by a "disaffected" person. Although Greene and Lafayette were worried that an informer might lead a British party to surround the house as they had done in capturing Gen. Charles Lee in December 1776, they arrived safely back in Wilmington on the morning of 27 August. (See Lafayette's *Memoirs* in Idzerda, *Lafayette*, 1: 92) The following day Washington ordered NG's division forward to the White Clay Creek Camp, where they could not only keep an eye on developments in Howe's camp but could aid in removing stores in the path of the British. The local militia, unfortunately, had failed in this elementary precaution. On arriving, NG sent 150 men from Weedon's brigade to observe the enemy. (McMichael, "Diary," p. 148)

2. Although nearby militia units were joining Washington's army, they were a poor substitute for Daniel Morgan's riflemen who had been sent to the Northern Army. Thus Washington drafted one hundred such men as NG described from each brigade to be placed under the command of Gen. William Maxwell. While not the equal of Morgan's corps, the unit of more than seven hundred men proved their usefulness in the coming weeks. (Fitzpatrick, *GW*, 9: 145–49; Reed, *Campaign*, pp. 88–89; the period from 24 to 28 August is covered in Fitzpatrick, *GW*, 9: 129–42; Freeman, *GW*, 4: 467; and Reed, *Campaign*, pp. 80–88.)

General Greene's Orders

Camp at White Clay Creek [Md.] Augt 29th 1777
A Gill of Spirits to be drawn for the men, this to be continued every morning while the men lay out of their Tents.

Reprinted from "Muhlenberg Orderly Book," *PMHB*, 34 (1910): 450.

General Greene's Orders

[Camp at Red Clay Creek, Dela.,[1] 30 August 1777. Party of twenty men to receive orders from General Weedon. From "Muhlenberg Orderly Book," *PMHB*, 34 (1910): 451.]

.   1. According to Gordon, *History* (an account which he had gotten in part from NG in 1784), NG preferred to remain where he was at White Clay Creek Camp in Maryland, but a council of war back at Wilmington had decided he should be pulled back to near Newport, Dela., east of Red Clay Creek, where the rest of the army would join him later. NG's objections presumably were that they would have their backs to the Delaware at the Red Clay Creek site. Some thought Howe would by-pass them en route to Philadelphia, but NG was convinced Howe's first objective was the defeat of Washington's army. (Gordon, *History*, 2: 494–95) For whatever reasons, NG's division broke camp at 3:00 A.M. and marched from the Maryland camp northeastward to Lancaster Road, thence to the "heights of Newport," where they took post. The division was still south of the rest of the army. The night march is described in McMichael, "Diary," p. 148.

To Jacob Greene?[1]

Wilmington in the Delaware State[2]
August 31, 1777

Dear Sir

I embrace this opportunity by a Providence gentleman to write you. General How after manouevreing about for upwards of Six Weeks has at last landed at the head of Elk in Chesepeake Bay. They have marched a few miles into the country. We have light parties hovering round them. They have been out but three days and there has been upwards of an hundred deserters and Prisoners from them. One single Troop of light Horse commanded by Capt Lee took forty three prisoners in two days.[3] Our Army are drawing together at Wilmington. I am about four miles advanced and about ten miles distant from the Enemy, three hours march brings us to blows which is dayly expected. However I am in hopes Mr How will give us a little time to collect and then we dont care how soon he begins the frolick. There is no place upon the Continent where a greater force can be drawn together than at this place and the country in general appears spirited and active. The face of the country is favorable to the Enemy, being very flat and leavel. However I have the greatest hopes if Providence dont think proper to punnish us further with the calamities of war to give General How a deadly wound. The Army is in good health and high Spirits but is not numerous as you very justly observe in your letter, yet I believe not inferior to Mr Howes. The Troops we have aided by the Militia will form a formidable force.[4]

I am now in hopes your apprehensions are a little quieted respected [respecting?] Burgoynes opperations. Despair not. Under misfortunes we are short sighted beings. We consider every evil as an evil, not as a previous preparation to some great good. The Physician to restore his Patient increases his sickness; so Providence to give a radical cure to Moral and Political evils often increases the calameties of the People but I doubt not he will save them at last.

I wish you may have recoverd your health. I am anxious to hear. You will favor me with a line by the Post. How is your family and all friends? How is my children?[5] I am desirious to know. Mrs Green is at Mr Lotts and enjoys a much better State of health than she did when she came there. The little opportunity we have had to see each other is but a poor compensation for the fatigues of the Jorney. However she dont repent coming.

The Troops at Rhode Island I am told hangs over you as a threatning rod.[6] I am much afraid they will until Winter, if no longer, but I cannot think their numbers as great as represented.

Remember me kindly to all freinds and beleive me to be Affectionately Yours

N GREEN

ALS (MWA).
   1. The addressee is not given, but the contents point to his brother Jacob.
   2. On the campsite, see note, NG's Orders above.
   3. Washington reported to Congress the same day that Lee had brought in twenty-four prisoners. (Fitzpatrick, *GW*, 9: 148) Henry Lee (1756–1818) was henceforth better known as "Light-Horse Harry." Though less celebrated than his son Robert E. Lee, he was a crack cavalryman who, as commander of "Lee's Legion" (a mixed battalion of light infantry and cavalry), won fame at Paulus Hook, N.J., in July 1780 and during the last years of the war as one of the mainstays of NG's Southern Army. The voluminous correspondence between him and NG testifies to their close relationship. From 1792 to 1795 Lee was governor of Virginia but fell soon thereafter upon hard times. It was while he was in debtor's prison in 1809 that he wrote his *Memoirs*, much of it in praise of NG. He went to the West Indies in an attempt to regain his health, and on his way back in 1818 asked to be put off at Cumberland Island, where he died at the home of NG's daughter. He was buried near Catharine Greene, although his remains were removed to Washington and Lee University in 1913.
   4. It is impossible to determine with any accuracy the total number of continental and militia troops. Although Washington ordered a muster "with the utmost expedition" the same day NG wrote, Lesser (*Sinews*) has found no returns for Washington's army between 21 May and 3 November 1777. See estimated numbers of both sides, note on battle of Brandywine, NG's Orders, 13 September, below.
   5. Martha ("Paty"), now five months old, and George, going on two years, lived with Jacob and Christopher during Catharine's year-long visit in New Jersey.
   6. The British in Newport.

General Greene's Orders

[Camp Red Clay Creek, Del., 1 September 1777.[1] Gens. Muhlenberg and Weedon to distribute 278 tin cartridge boxes among their regiments. Boxes divided among "the Messes" are to be examined daily. From "Muhlenberg Orderly Book," *PMHB*, 34 (1910): 452.]

   1. This same day Washington happily announced to the troops the lifting of the siege of Ft. Stanwix, 22 and 23 August, by Gen. Arnold. See above, note, NG to Varnum, 17 August.

General Greene's Orders

[Red Clay Creek, Del., 2 September 1777. Those officers and soldiers of Fifth Va. Regiment now in Virginia are to join their regiment "without loss of time" or they can "expect to be apprehended as deserters." From *Virginia Gazette*,[1] 19 September 1777.]

   1. Most of NG's division were Virginians. It was unusual to publish such an order in a newspaper.

General Greene's Orders

[Camp Red Clay Creek, Del., 2 September 1777. Division to furnish three hundred men ready to march and receive orders from Gen.

Muhlenberg at 3:00 A.M. tomorrow.¹ From "Muhlenberg Orderly Book," *PMHB*, 34 (1910): 452.]

1. See below, NG to Washington, 2 September.

From Levi Hollingsworth¹

Dear Genl
Newmunster 6 Miles above Elk [Md.]
2d Sept 1777

I arrived here last night and find this side of the Country open to the Enemy, and that they are daily driving off stock and removing publick stores from Elk Forge,² 4 miles above the landing and as this side of the Country is by nature strong and well supply'd with stock and forage, besides its being the deposit for all the Corn and salt provisions of our army provided at the head of Elk, I cannot omit mentioning it to your Honour, that unless a detachment of 1500 or 2000 men be speedely sent to Support the removing the Stores with Waggons they will fall into the hands of the Enemy.³

The Iron Hill may be a good advanced post to Wilmington, as it lais in a Line of direction between that post and the Head of Elk, but as the Body of our Magazines are in the several mills of Elk and Nottingham distant from 4 to 10 Miles North and West of the Head of Elk, it would be of great service to have Troops posted in this Quarter. My Brother Zebulon Hollingsworth hath now several Teams Collected at Capt Amos Alexander, ready to remove what Stores may remain at the Forge but as the Enemy have been there in small parties he cannot proceed without troops to Cover his Wagons. Mr Jno Rudulph⁴ was there yesterday and says he Could have Loaded any number of Waggons with Corn, Salt &c and believes it may be done yet. Your Honour will make what Use of this Letter you may think proper should it appear an object worthy your notice. I would recomend the Troops being posted at or near Major Strawbridge, on the road from Newark to Notingham and at Nottingham⁵ I have the Honour to subscribe myself Your Obliged Friend and Humble Sert

LEVI HOLLINGSWORTH

NB Elk Forge Lais 4 miles North of the Head of Elk on that Streem, where are Corn Wheat and Salt of the public with some Salt provisions of privet property. Robert Evans Mill 2 Miles higher up said streem, where are salt provisions and Corn belonging to the Public and some Wheat and Flour privet. Alexander Mills 2 Miles higher, Corn salt provisions public, and wheat and Flour privet. Kirks and other mills in Nottingham with Corn distant from 9 to 12 miles from the Enemy. Zebulon Hollingsworth hath a few Collected Teams and is well acquainted with the General state of Stores but says he must be supported with Troops &c &c

L H

David Wallace 7 Miles up Little Elk a Magazine of corn. Mr Jno Rudulph who was reconoitering with Capt [Henry] Lee yesterday near the Head of Elk says they saw signs of a Detachment of Troops from the Enemy haveing gon towards Nottingham. Capt Lee supposed them by their tracks to be about 500, horse and foot

L H

ALS (Washington Papers: DLC). This was enclosed with NG to Washington the same day.

1. On Levi Hollingsworth, see above, 4 March 1777. He had apparently come from Philadelphia to help his brothers Henry (quartermaster for Maryland) and Zebulon in removing stores. It was an area with which the Hollingsworths were long familiar. A map of "The Province of New Jersey," published by William Faden in London in December 1777 from a survey made in 1769, gives "Hollingsworth" as the alternate name of "Elktown."

2. On the success of the enemy's foraging, see Ward, *War*, 1: 338.

3. As noted in NG to Washington below, NG's and Stephen's divisions could furnish only six hundred men to Maxwell. Unfortunately, horses and wagons were in even shorter supply. Washington estimated several thousand bushels of corn and oats could have been saved from the enemy "had not most of the Teams in the Country been employed by private persons in bringing off very valuable goods." (Fitzpatrick, *GW*, 9: 146) When the British moved on past the captured magazines, they destroyed what they could not use. (Ibid., 9: 196)

4. John Rudulph (also spelled Rudolph) was a member of Lee's light horse. See postscript of Hollingsworth's letter.

5. Newark was in Delaware, Nottingham in Maryland.

To George Washington

[Camp Red Clay Creek, Del., 2 September 1777. Encloses Hollingsworth letter (above). Gen. Muhlenberg "has marched with his detachment to cover the removeal of the Stores."[1] If Washington thinks "additional force" is needed it will be sent at once. ALS (Washington Papers: DLC) 1 p.]

1. The day before, Washington had promised Gen. Maxwell, commander of the new light infantry unit camped near the British, that he had ordered six hundred men from NG's and Stephen's divisions to assist in removing stores, rounding up cattle etc. (See his two letters to Maxwell of 1 September, Fitzpatrick, *GW*, 9: 153–56.)

From Colonel Robert H. Harrison

Wilmington [Del.]

Dr Sir   2 Septr 1777 9 oClock P. M

I am directed by his Excellency to inform you that Genl Maxwell by a Letter from him dated at 6 oClock this Evening, is more and more of opinion from the intelligence he received this afternoon, that the Enemy will be in motion in the morning.[1] His Excellency leaves it to your discretion to send down or not the Two Hundred men mentioned this afternoon, and to give Genl Muhlenburg such orders as you may think necessary. I am Dr Sir Yr Most Obed Servt

ROB. H. HARRISON

ALS (Washington Papers: DLC).

1. The enemy's move was not as significant as Washington implied. Gen. Howe, having sent his supply ships back around to meet him along the Delaware River, was in no hurry to arrive in advance of them. On the morning of the third, however, his two columns under Cornwallis and Knyphausen did set out for Aiken's Tavern—four miles east of Elk River inside Delaware. There was a skirmish at Cooch's Bridge on Christiana Creek between Gen. Maxwell's light infantry and Cornwallis's German vanguard, in which each side inflicted some casualties before Maxwell's troops fled back toward Greene's encampment. Knyphausen joined Cornwallis at Aiken's, but they advanced no further, for Howe was content to idle away a few more days. (Gruber, *Howe Brothers*, p. 240; Reed, *Campaign*, pp. 98–103; Montresor, *Journals*, 445–46)

General Greene's Orders

[Camp Red Clay Creek, Del., 4 September 1777. The division is to furnish 250 men for "Fatigue Party." From "Muhlenberg Orderly Book," *PMHB*, 34 (1910): 455.]

General Greene's Orders

[Camp Red Clay Creek, Del., 5 September 1777. Twenty-four men under a subaltern to march to Newport. From "Muhlenberg Orderly Book," *PMHB*, 34 (1910): 455.]

To Catharine Greene

My dear   Camp near Wilmington [Del.] Sept 7, 1777

I hope you are well. Pray how did you endure the fatigues of the Jorney? Give me a long History.

Nothing new in camp since I wrote you last, only that the army are advanced in line with me .[1] It is said this morning the Enemy are coming out. A note this moment receivd from Capt [Henry] Lee of the light Horse favors the opinion. I am just going out upon a reconnoitering party.[2] You must excuse a short letter.

I have inclosd you two letters, one from Capt Gooch,[3] the other from Sister Nancy [Littlefield]. These will serve to supply the shortness of my letter. My compliments to all the family. Believe me to be affectionately yours

N. GREENE

ALS (NjP).
    1. NG, despite the dateline, was still at Red Clay Creek near Newport. In Washington's "After Orders" of 4 September, he ordered the rest of the army at Wilmington to be ready to march to Newport at 5:00 A.M. the next morning "if the weather permit," NG's division remaining "where it is." (Fitzpatrick, *GW*, 9: 179) The weather apparently did not permit until 6 September. Howe's intentions were still unclear, but Washington was obviously preparing to challenge his advance.
    2. With Washington. (Fitzpatrick, *GW*, 9: 195)
    3. John Gooch, an old Rhode Island friend, was assistant deputy quartermaster at Boston. His letter from there of 20 August tactfully asked Mrs. Greene to intercede for him with NG on a matter of back pay. The letter is at NjP.

General Greene's Orders

[Camp Red Clay Creek, Del., 8 September 1777.[1] One hundred men to report to "the Generals Quarters" with a days provision. Fatigue party of one hundred to report to the engineers. Remainder to pitch their tents "at 10 o'clock if the Enemy are not advancing at that Time." From "Muhlenberg Orderly Book," *PMHB*, 34 (1910): 461–62.]

    1. The entire British army on the morning of 8 September, wrote Capt. John Montresor, "moved 2 hours before daylight—a remarkable borealis" (*Journal*, p. 448). By afternoon they had marched twelve miles—to within two miles of Washington's main army. Anticipating a British attack, Washington had roused the men from bed at 3:00 A.M. The army was drawn up on the east side of Red Clay Creek "with Gen Greene's division to the right." (McMichael, "Diary," p. 149) Howe's purpose, as Washington gradually perceived, was "only meant to amuse us in front, while their real intent was to march by our Right and by suddenly passing the Brandywine . . . get between us and Philadelphia." (Fitzpatrick, *GW*, 9: 197) During the early morning hours of 9 August, therefore, the Americans started for the Brandywine, arriving at Chads Ford that evening after a strenuous march. (See below, NG to Catharine, 10 September.)

To Catharine Greene

Chadsford on the Brandywine [Pa.]
My dear   Sept 10th 1777
    The Enemy marcht out day before yesterday. They took post in a position to turn our right flank, the Cristian [Christiana] being on our left. The General thought our situation too dangerous to risque a battle as the Enemy refusd to fight us in front. The General orderd the army to file off to the right and take post at this place.[1] A general action must take place in a few days. The army are in high spirits and wish for action.[2]
    I have had no letters from home since I wrote before. If you receive any accounts please to transmit me the particulars. I wish to hear your Bethlehem account and know how you are since your return.[3]
    Here are some of the most distressing scenes immaginable. The

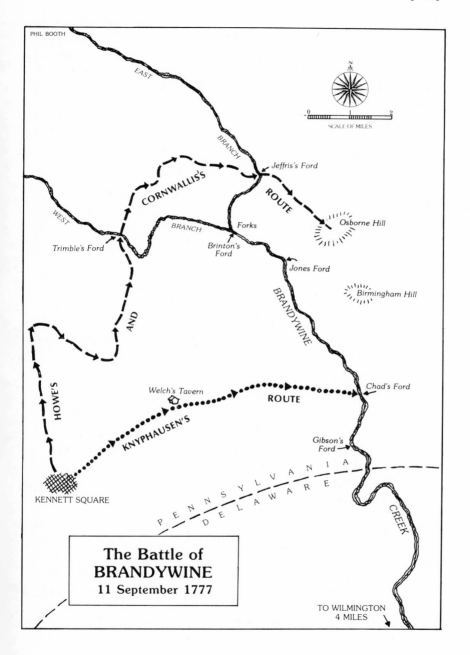

PHIL BOOTH

EAST

BRANCH

Jeffris's Ford

CORNWALLIS'S ROUTE

Osborne Hill

WEST

BRANCH

Forks

Trimble's Ford

Brinton's Ford

Jones Ford

Birmingham Hill

AND

BRANDYWINE

HOWE'S

Welch's Tavern

ROUTE

Chad's Ford

KNYPHAUSEN'S

Gibson's Ford

KENNETT SQUARE

PENNSYLVANIA

DELAWARE

CREEK

The Battle of
BRANDYWINE
11 September 1777

TO WILMINGTON
4 MILES

SCALE OF MILES
0   1   2

Inhabitants generally desert their houses, furniture moveing, Cattle driving and women and children traveling off on foot. The country all resounds with the cries of the people. The Enemy plunder most amazeingly.[4] The militia of this country are not like the Jersey militia; fighting is a new thing with these, and many seems to have but a poor stomach for the business.

I am exceedingly fatigued. I was on Horse back for upwards of thirty hours and never closd my Eyes for near forty. Last night I was in hopes of a good nights rest, but a dusty bed gave me Astma and I had very little sleep the whole night, but little as it was I feel finely refreshd this morning.

Tell Mr Lott I would write him but I have but little leisure, and I direct Major Blodget to transmit him everything material in the army. Make my Compliments to all the family and believe me to be your affectionate

N GREENE

ALS (NjP).
    1. See note, NG's orders, 8 September, above.
    2. On the battle of Brandywine, see note, NG's orders, 13 September, below.
    3. Catharine had gone to Bethlehem, Pa., where NG and Knox had gone on 22 August. See above, note, his letter to Wayne that day.
    4. Plundering went on from both sides. See, for example, Washington's admonitions to his own troops in his orders of 5 September. (Fitzpatrick, *GW*, 9: 178) Citing such orders, Reed (*Campaign*, p. 105) comments: "Whig and Tory civilians alike dreaded the appearance of either army."

General Greene's Orders

Camp at German Town [Pa.][1] 13th Septr 1777
The Genl. takes the earliest opportunity to return his warmest thanks to the Officers & Soldiers of Genl. Weedons Brigade engag'd in the late Action for their Spirited & Soldierly behaviour, A Conduct so worthy under so many disadvantages cannot fail of establishing to themselves the highest Military reputation, The Genl. also thinks himself under an obligation to return his thanks to all the other Officers & Soldiers of his Division for the firmness & alacrity which they have discover'd upon every Occasion in the Course of the Day to Engage the Enemy, The Genl. has the pleasure to Inform the troops, that notwithstanding we gave the Enemy the ground, the purchase has been at much blood, this being by far the greatest loss they ever met with since the commencement of the War. The Genl. recommends an immediate Attention to be paid to the state of the Arms & Ammunition, that the Arms be put in the best order & that each man be furnish'd with a full supply of Ammunition, not less than 40 rounds–[2]

Reprinted from *Weedon Orderly Book*, pp. 45–46.

1. The camp where they had stayed the first week in August. On Friday 12 August, the troops had marched back through Darby and crossed the Schuylkill on the floating bridge at Middle Ferry. (Baker, "Camp," p. 39)

2. As noted above, NG's orders of 8 September, when Gen. Howe bypassed the Americans at Red Clay Creek, Washington immediately ordered the army northward some twelve miles, where it encamped the evening of the 9 August on the east side of Brandywine Creek near Chads Ford. Brandywine Creek, which in many regions would have qualified as a river, flowed in a southeasterly direction into the Delaware just below Wilmington. It was formed by two smaller streams, called East and West Branches, that joined at the "forks of the Brandywine" (the plural was always used) about five miles above Chads Ford. Chads was one of the shallower fords along the lower reaches of the stream. When the water was high, travelers relied on a nearby ferry. Now in September the water was no more than knee-deep, although it was up to a man's waist at other times. Between the shallows the stream was too deep for an army to cross without boats or temporary bridges. On either side of the Brandywine, the land was hilly, with the higher hills standing two to three hundred feet above the small streams that drained them. The area was generally wooded, with enclosed fields and farmsteads here and there.

The Brandywine was the last natural barrier before the Schuylkill River, which, in turn, was the last obstacle before Philadelphia. If Howe chose to cross the Brandywine, Washington had only to concentrate his forces at the fords in order to make the British pay dearly for their advance. As the American army made camp, they learned that the British had reached Kennett Square, just six miles west of Chads Ford. It was apparent that Howe did not plan to bypass Washington's army again.

In the same spirit, it was Washington's firm intention to meet the British head-on; and in this determination he had the wholehearted support of virtually the entire army, bored and restive with months of marching and countermarching. At an earlier time, Philadelphia might have been sacrificed without a fight—indeed, few knowledgeable Americans had even considered that its capture would determine the outcome of the war—but the army and civil population shared a widespread conviction that the time had finally come for an all-out defense of the nation's capital. Washington's army was not without confidence that they could defeat the British; Howe, no less confident of his superb army, readily accepted Washington's challenge.

The battle of Brandywine, in which NG played a brief but significant role at the end, was one of the largest engagements of the war, with some twenty-five thousand men involved. Not since the battle of Long Island in August 1776 had two principal armies met. For two hours or more it was a fiercely fought, bloody battle—more properly, two battles—with severe casualties on both sides. In the end, the British gained the field and suffered fewer losses, but it was far from the overwhelming defeat that Howe had hoped to inflict.

Actually, the British victory owed less to the superiority of its fighting units and to the brilliant strategy of Gen. Howe (as some have called it) than to good fortune. Luck is a frequent companion of victorious commanders, and Howe and his subordinates made the most of the breaks that came their way.

It was their good fortune to camp in a region whose predominantly Quaker inhabitants were either neutral or pro-British, the few ardent patriots having fled. It was Howe's further good fortune to be joined by the Philadelphia loyalist, Joseph Galloway, who brought in local Tories that were intimately acquainted with the terrain. Some of these men not only helped Howe's engineers to lay out accurate maps of the Brandywine Valley but also offered to serve as guides. One such informant was reported to be "a veritable geographical Chart" by the Hessian commander of Howe's vanguard, Capt. Johann Ewald. (Smith, *Brandywine*, p. 13) The British had arrived at Kennett Square early on 10 September knowing little of the country. By evening Howe and his staff were thoroughly familiar with it.

Howe's strategy called for a flanking movement around the American right, a maneuver he had used so successfully (at Gen. Clinton's suggestion) around the American left on Long Island in 1776. Knyphausen was to march with over six thousand British and Hessian troops early next morning along the road to Chads Ford to distract American attention from other fords, while Cornwallis and Howe would proceed northward with the principal army of some eight thousand men along the Great Valley Road to a point above the forks of the Brandywine, where they would cross the West Branch at Trimbles Ford, then turn eastward and cross the East Branch at Jeffris Ford in order to turn the American right. When the time was right, Knyphausen would cross the Brandywine at Chads and join in a pincer's movement against the Americans. It was a bold, adventurous plan, even a dangerous one, for it involved a march of over fifteen miles on a September day that promised to be very warm; and it left Knyphausen's army increasingly out of range of any help from Howe. Thus at the midpoint of Howe's march Knyphausen was vulnerable to an attack by Washington's main army, assuming that Washington's intelligence would keep him abreast of Howe's progress. With the advantage of shorter inside lines, it would be possible for Washington to cripple Knyphausen and still meet Howe with equal or superior numbers at Howe's crossing. Such was the risk that Howe took. As he gave his final approval to the plans for the following day, he could scarcely imagine the extent to which fortune would continue to favor him.

The obverse of Howe's good luck in being among sympathetic inhabitants was, of course, Washington's bad luck. Being unfamiliar with the area he appeared to do little on the tenth to offset Howe's advantages. Not only was he unfortunate in the few informants with whom he did confer, but he was remiss in not querying them more closely. Nor did he learn much from his mounted dragoons. Thus, as he deployed his troops, he was uncertain of the names or precise locations of several fords and did not even know of the existence of others. In assigning Sullivan the American right wing, for example, Washington assured him he need not be concerned with threats from above the forks of the Brandywine (Buffentons Ford) because the next ford upstream (to Sullivan's right) was twelve miles away, with virtually impassable roads leading to it from the British camp. This was disastrous misinformation. Jeffris Ford, which Howe planned to cross, was less than two miles above Sullivan's right.

By sundown of the tenth, Washington had completed the deployment of his troops. Sullivan, in addition to guarding Buffentons Ford on the far right, was also assigned Jones and Brintons Fords, which were down stream from Buffentons a few miles toward Chads. Lord Stirling's division was placed in reserve behind Sullivan. The American center near Chads Ford was assigned to two divisions: Greene's, consisting of Weedon's and Muhlenberg's brigades, and Lincoln's under Anthony Wayne (Lincoln being at Saratoga). They were backed up by Gen. Adam Stephen's division. Col. Thomas Proctor's artillery was emplaced on high ground near NG's division to cover Chads Ford. Downstream at Gibsons Ford, Washington placed Gen. John Armstrong's two brigades of Pennsylvania militia. Gen. William Maxwell's light corps was sent across to the west side of the Brandywine in order to delay any offensive directed at Chads. Washington commanded approximately fourteen thousand troops, including militia, many of them untrained; Howe had perhaps fifteen thousand well-trained troops. (Troop figures are taken from Smith, *Brandywine*, pp. 29–32.)

The first glimmer of daylight found a heavy fog settled over most of the area. Howe's good fortune was holding. In the first gray light, Knyphausen set off with his units along the road to Chads Ford. Shortly thereafter, Howe and Cornwallis followed with their larger army. In two miles they turned north and soon hit the Great Valley Road, carrying them away from Knyphausen. The fog shrouded them and muffled the sounds of marching in case there was a patriot informant in the area.

Accounts of what transpired in the next eight hours are generally sketchy, confused, and conflicting, sometimes based on supposition. But there is no disagreement on the essentials. Knyphausen performed his role perfectly. Although Maxwell's men managed to slow Knyphausen's advance somewhat by firing from behind rocks and trees, in little more than an hour the German general and his army were just where they had planned to be—on high, wooded ground, a few hundred yards west of Chads Ford. Soon their artillery was answering the American barrage from across the creek. Washington's divisions, meanwhile, were immobile until Howe's intentions became known. Incredibly, during the next six or seven hours, Howe's main army marched fifteen miles as planned, crossing to the east side of the Brandywine and nearing Sullivan's position from behind before the Americans became aware that the British had in fact stolen a march on them.

American ignorance of the terrain, of course, was basic to the success of Howe's strategy. But ignorance was compounded by the incompetency of Washington's reconnaissance commander, Col. Theodorick Bland, and by the failure of Washington and his immediate staff to analyze seemingly contradictory reports that came in during Howe's march. Shortly after Knyphausen's appearance near Chads Ford, Washington received a vague report of a British flanking march, but one of Col. Bland's dragoons assured Washington through Sullivan that none of the enemy was to be found near the American right. At 10:00 A.M. Col. Moses Hazen, Sullivan's reliable commander stationed at Jones Ford, sent word of an English flanking movement. Washington waited impatiently for confirmation of the report from Colonel Bland but to no avail. From early morning until after 1:00 P.M., in fact, Col. Bland and his mounted scouts on the west side of the Brandywine failed to spot a single British soldier!

At noon Washington received a message via Sullivan from a Pennsylvania Militia Colonel, James Ross, written at 11:00 A.M. from Great Valley Road, reporting that his unit had been close to the rear of an army of at least five thousand men under Gen. Howe, with sixteen to eighteen artillery pieces. For the first time, Washington was convinced that Howe had indeed divided his army. Washington acted at once. He gave orders to his commanding generals for an attack on Knyphausen, but they had little more than received the orders when fresh intelligence seemed to contradict Hazen's and Ross's reports. Under the circumstances he dared not launch the attack. There is some confusion as to how far advance units had gone in carrying out Washington's order when he countermanded it, but Knyphausen must have had some uneasy moments with Howe, by this time, a ten-mile march from him.

The fresh intelligence that caused Washington to countermand his order came from Maj. Joseph Spear of the militia. Washington's interpretation of Spear's report was critical to the outcome of the battle. Sullivan sent Washington a written account as told him by Spear, then sent Spear to elaborate upon his letter. Since Spear's intelligence appeared to contradict Hazen's (as well as Ross's, which Sullivan had not seen), Sullivan sent a scout to "know whether there is any foundation for the Report." (Hammond, *Sullivan*, 1:451. Freeman, *GW*, 4: 476n, who had overlooked Hammond's careful transcription as well as the original in the Washington papers, takes Jared Sparks to task at some length for taking liberties with Sullivan's letters. Freeman would have been embarrassed to learn that Sparks's rendition was more accurate than the version he printed.)

Spear, who had ridden down from near the forks earlier in the morning, reported he had see nothing of the enemy. Washington always blamed the militia major for misleading him. Some writers have assumed Spear was a Tory who deliberately tricked Washington, but two modern authorities, Reed (*Campaign*, p. 125) and Smith (*Brandywine*, p. 13) have shown that at a certain time Spear could have traveled the route he described without seeing a British soldier. We can only surmise that, since Washington and his staff were ignorant of the roads and other landmarks (including fords), they could not intelligently interrogate the major. It was a crucial failing. It not only aborted an attack on Knyphausen that could have been successful, but it threw the Americans off guard against Howe's imminent crossing above the forks.

The same charge could be made against Washington's immediate aides, who should have questioned Spear. By this time, it appears, all of those at headquarters were convinced that any appearance of Howe along Great Valley Road was a ruse to trick the Americans; that he had since marched back to join Knyphausen and was waiting quietly nearby for Washington to take the bait and attack. So firmly were they convinced of this that when John Eustace carried Sullivan's report that it was "the enemy's intention to turn our Right flank," Washington and Knox, according to Eustace's sworn testimony, laughed and sent him back with no comment. (Smith, *Brandywine*, p. 13.) NG, with his own division, knew nothing of Spear's report.

By this time Cornwallis and Howe had crossed the West Branch at Trimbles Ford and were nearing the East Branch at Jeffris's. Capt. James McPherson, of Howe's vanguard, sent Capt. Johann Ewald and his mounted jaegers to reconnoiter with Ewald's aforementioned "veritable geographical Chart." Ewald reported a twisting defile leading southeasterly from Jeffris's of over a thousand paces in length. They worked their way slowly up the defile lest Americans be lying in wait. Ewald was amazed that "the pass had been left wide open for us, where a hundred men could have held up either army a whole day." (Smith, *Brandywine*, p. 15). Soon the rest of the British army was streaming through the defile with no opposition.

Not long after, Col. Bland, who had crossed over to the east side of the creek, spotted the British vanguard for the first time. He dispatched a rider with a hurried note to Washington at "1/4 past one o'clock." (Washington Papers, DLC) Despite Washington's recent rejection of Eustace's report and his disenchantment with Bland's earlier performance, he did not dispute the information. Perhaps the pieces had at last fallen into place in his mind.

He immediately ordered Stirling's and Stephen's divisions, which were closer than Sullivan's, to march toward Birmingham Meeting House. Bland, in a subsequent note to Sullivan (who forwarded it to Washington at 2:00 P.M.), reckoned there were two British brigades—an estimate far too low, of course, but sufficient for Washington to order Sullivan to join Stirling and Stephen. It was 2:30 when Sullivan received his orders. Howe and Cornwallis in the meantime had assembled their troops on Osbornes Hill, a mile north of Birmingham Meeting House and to Sullivan's rear, to refresh themselves. They had walked fourteen miles. By the time Sullivan got orders to his brigades, Cornwallis's advance units were already approaching Birmingham Meeting House along Forks Road. The battle of Brandywine was about to begin.

The battle that swirled for almost two hours in and around Birmingham Hill involved only the divisions of Sullivan, Stirling, and Stephen. Despite the impatience of Greene and Wayne to join the fight, they had orders to remain at Chads Ford to watch Knyphausen. Washington remained impatiently with them. The action around Birmingham Hill was extremely confused.

Before Sullivan joined Stirling and Stephen, they had miraculously gotten small cannon and ammunition to the top of the hill and had begun an artillery barrage that struck the British advance troops with great effect. On the American right, Woodford's Virginia brigade of Stephen's division had settled themselves behind stone walls and trees near the Meeting House and were laying down a murderous small arms fire against the British left, with little loss to themselves, at least initially.

It was at the west end of Birmingham Hill that confusion soon reigned. As Sullivan's division moved back from the Brandywine to close the gap with Stirling's division, British advance units were approaching. In taking overall command, Sullivan left his division with a sixty-year old French brigadier, Preudhomme de Borre. The advance unit, the First Maryland, was caught in a narrow lane by Hessian grenadiers with bayonets. The regiment's commander, Col. John Stone, was thrown from his horse and injured; soon twenty or more of his men lay dead. The rest of the regiment took to their heels. Soon the panic spread to other Maryland regiments and eventually to all of Sullivan's division except for Hazen's, Ogden's, and Dayton's regiments. Officers were helpless to rally them as a thousand men streamed down the back of the hill. Among them was Gen. Preudhomme de Borre, who resigned three days later rather than face charges of cowardice.

Despite later criticism of Sullivan, he remained cool as commander of the remaining troops on Birmingham Hill. The fierce fighting see-sawed back and forth, sometimes hand to hand, the Americans retreating and then coming back, until for the last time they had to fall back half a mile to a hill behind Birmingham, later called Battle Hill. Gen. Conway, the French veteran of many battles, was reported as saying he "never Saw So Close & Severe a fire." (Ward, *War*, 1: 352.) If any regiment deserved highest honors in this part of the battle, it was Col. Thomas Marshall's Virginia regiment around Birmingham Meeting House. Marshall had his horse shot from under him but withdrew the rest of his regiment to Birmingham Hill. The Virginians had paid heavily for their defense: 5 officers killed, 13 noncommissioned officers and 60 privates wounded or dead out of 150 men. Their brigade commander, Gen. Woodford, was wounded. After the British took Birmingham Hill, they began an assault on the American second position at Battle Hill. There they also met stiff resistance, but the Americans' ammunition was running low. This time, Scott's brigade of Stephen's division was thrown into confusion when struck on the flank by crack British light infantry and Hessian jaegers.

Before this happened, the incessant firing had drawn Washington toward the fighting. He left Wayne in command at Chads Ford (with Maxwell and Proctor's artillery) and ordered NG's division to follow him. Washington arrived to see Stephen's division begin to scatter; then the British concentrated their attack on Conway's brigade. At this point Lafayette, in his baptism of fire, joined Conway in an effort to get the men to stand up to the British bayonets, but he took a musket ball in the leg and had to be removed.

Soon NG arrived with Weedon's brigade. A brief account he wrote ten months later in a letter to Henry Marchant (see below, 25 July 1778) is the only description of his part in the battle: "I marched one brigade of my division, being upon the left wing, between three and four miles in forty-five minutes. When I came upon the ground I found the whole of the troops routed and retreating precipitately, and in the most broken and confused manner. I was ordered to cover the retreat, which I effected in such a manner as to save hundreds of our people from falling into the enemy's hands. Almost all of the park of artillery had an opportunity to get off, which must have fallen into their hands; and the left wing posted at Chadsford got off by the seasonable check I gave the enemy. We were engaged an hour and a quarter, and lost upwards of an hundred men killed and wounded. I maintained the ground until dark, and then drew off the troops in good order. We had the whole British force to contend with, that had just before routed our whole right wing. This brigade was commanded by General Weedon." Many writers have put NG's other division—Muhlenberg's—in the thick of the battle, but there is no evidence that the brigade participated. No participants mention Muhlenberg. Sullivan specifically wrote that "Weedens Brigade was the only part of Greens Division which was Ingaged." (Hammond, *Sullivan*, 1: 473). Muhlenberg's most recent biographer makes no mention of his participation or of the apocryphal story that the Anspacher jaegers shouted: "Hier kommt Teufel Piet!" (See Paul A. W. Wallace, *The Muhlenbergs of Pennsylvania* [Freeport, N.Y.: Books for Libraries Press, 1950]). Muhlenberg would have his day at Germantown. (See below, note, NG's orders, 7 October.)

From all the evidence, NG's account is accurate. Unfortunately, Weedon's is both overly modest and overly brief. In a letter written several days later, he has only this to say: "About 6, General Green's Division arrived to cover the Retreat. One of his Brigades (Weedon's) gave the Enemy such a check as produced the desired Effect." (Weedon added his name in parentheses. The account, erroneously dated "Sep'r the 11th," along with a map that bears little relation to the topography, are in ICHi.) NG explains in his letter to Marchant of 25 July 1778 why Washington could not single out Greene or Weedon and his fellow Virginians for commendation.

While Weedon's brigade was holding back Cornwallis, Wayne had been confronted by Knyphausen, who crossed just below Chads Ford under sharp American fire. Col. Proctor lost all of his artillery and a number of his men. Wayne's troops, who fought furiously against great odds, managed to slow Knyphausen's advance but not to stop it. After a disorganized retreat, they were able to escape in the growing darkness and make their way to Chester, towards which the rest of Washington's army were straggling. Howe showed no inclination to have Cornwallis or Knyphausen follow the weary Americans. His men, too, were weary after a long day's march and battle, and he had his own wounded to care for as well as those the Americans had had to abandon. Howe's superiors, perhaps unfairly, criticized him for not exploiting his victory. Lord North declared himself "very melancholy notwithstanding our victory." (Gruber, *Howe Brothers*, p. 272.)

There was no doubt of Howe's victory. His army had gained the field and had suffered fewer losses. Peckham, *Toll*, p. 40, estimates American casualties at 200 dead, 500 wounded, and 400 captured, compared with 90 British killed and 448 wounded. Yet Howe had not defeated Washington's army. He had, in fact, gained a new respect for the fighting qualities of the American soldier, if not, in this case, for its commander in chief. Despite their weariness and disappointment, the Americans had gained a new respect for themselves. Howe had not seen the last of them.

Secondary accounts of the battle of Brandywine are generally as confusing as the battle itself. In part this is because there are few primary accounts on either side by men in a position to observe more than their immediate surroundings. Gens. Howe, Cornwallis, and Knyphausen, for example, gave only the most cursory descriptions of the battle. Washington wrote nothing at the time; the brief and uninformative account he sent Congress at midnight after the battle was written by Timothy Pickering, Washington being too tired (Fitzpatrick, *GW*, 9: 207–8). Sullivan treated the day's events at greater length, but he waited two and three weeks to do it and his accounts were essentially defensive in response to congressional criticisms of him—unjustified, it should be added.

Reed, *Campaign*, pp. 117–40, is a generally reliable account and well told. Smith, *Brandywine*, has covered the ground thoroughly and has made especially good use of Capt. Ewald's manuscript journal. (This excellent account, translated and edited by Jospeh P. Tustin, was published as *Diary of the American War* by Yale University Press in 1979 as this volume goes to press.) Freeman's chapter, "The Intelligence Service Goes Astray" (*GW*, 4: 471–89), covers aspects not treated by others. Ward, *War* (pp. 341–54) distills the essence of the battle but has gaps and inaccuracies.

General Greene's Orders

[Camp at Germantown, Pa.]

[13th September 1777]

A return to be made out immediately of Shoes and Stockings wanting for the Troops and such other Articles as are necessary and Comfortable for the Soldiers, necessary steps are taken to have them supplied.

Stewart Orderly Book (Typescript: NjP).

To Catharine Greene

Camp at German Town [Pa.]

My dear   Sept 14th 1777

I had just time to write you yesterday to acquaint you I was well. I have been exceeding busy ever since and am preparing now to march. Therefore you must content yourself with a short letter again.

General How sent in a flagg yesterday acquainting General Washington that it would be out of his power to do Justice to such of our wounded as fell into his hands.[1] I suppose he has full employ in taking care of his own. He sent out and got all the Country Doctors for Ten miles round to assist his surgeons. From those circumstances and from several accounts of people that has seen the field of action, there must have been a terrible carnage among his troops. I expect the next action to ruin Mr How totally. We should have done it now if the Troops could have got up seasonably. You may expect to hear of another Action in a few days. Our troops are in good health and high Spirits and wish for action again. I have full confidence the Lord of

Hosts will give us Victory. The villinous Quakers are employd upon every quarter to serve the enemy. Some of them are confind and more deserve it.[2]

Pray how does all my good friends do at Mr Lotts. I suppose you have all Long faces and fearful apprehensions. Tell them to chear up and fear not, all things will go well. These are only so many preparatory steps to Mr Hows ruin. We are gathering about him like a mighty cloud chargd with destruction and by the blessing of God I hope its execution will be dreadful.

Many reinforcements are coming in. Mr How will find that another Victory purchased at the price of so much blood must inevitably ruin him.

O My sweet Angel how I wish, how I long to return to your soft embrace. The endearing prospect is my greatest comfort amidst all the fatigues of the campaign. I am sensible your situation in doubtful suspense must be exceeding distressing. How happy should I be could I administer consolation to you in a distressing hour. Rest assured my dear, nothing but the great duties of my station, the loud calls of my Country, the peace, liberty and happiness of Milions, should keep from those social and endearing pleasures ever to be found in your society. Comfort yourself, a few Weeks will terminate the Campaign (If kind fortune continues propitious and carries me through showers of leaden deaths unhurt, as hither too she has done, we will be happy again). Until which God bless with every comfort. My kind love to Mr and Mrs Lott and all the family. Your affe[ctionate]

[signature missing]

I receivd your letter wrote by Mr Buncombe how could you think it would be disagreeable to me? The sentiments were beautiful.

AL[S] (NjP).
    1. On the battle at Brandywine, see note, NG's orders of 13 September, above.
    2. This was not the first time he was critical of his erstwhile fellow Quakers; see above, NG to Jacob, 4 June 1777.

Proceedings of a Council of General Officers

At a Council of War held at
the Camp near Potts Grove
the 23d day of Septem 1777.[1]

Present His Excellency the Commander.

Major Generals	Sullivan	Brigadiers General	Knox
	Green		Weedon
	Lord Stirling		Nash
	Stephen		Scott
	Armstrong		Conway
			Potter

Besides the above Major Genl St. Clair and John Cadwalader Esquire were also present.

His Excellency informed the General Officers that the Reason of his calling them together was to acquaint them that the Enemy had, the preceding night, crossed the Schuylkill by several Fords about twelve miles below and by the best accounts were proceeding towards Philadelphia. He also informed them that the Troops under Generals Smallwood and Wayne had not yet rejoined the Army and that a Brigade of Continental Troops under the command of General McDougal might be expected in a few days from Peekskill and about one thousand Militia from Jersey under Genl Dickinson in the same time. He therefore desired the opinion of the Council whether it would be most advisable to advance upon the Enemy with our present Force or wait till the Reinforcements and detachments above mentioned should come in.

Previous to taking the Voices upon the foregoing Question His Excellency begged leave to inform the Council of the present state of the Army and the Reasons which had induced him to make the late Movements which (tho' well known to most of them) were not so fully to Major Genl Armstrong and Brigr. Genl Potter who had been detached from the main Body of the Army. This being agreed to, His Excellency proceeded to inform the Council that when the Army left Germantown upon the 15th instant it was with a determination to meet the Enemy and give them Battle whenever a convenient opportunity should be found; that they advanced the same day to the Sign of the Buck and the day following to the Warren Tavern upon the Lancaster Road.[2] On the 17th in the morning intelligence was brought that the Enemy were advancing upon which the Army were paraded and a disposition made to receive them, the pickets had exchanged a few shot when a violent Storm of Rain which continued all the day and the following night prevented all further operations. Upon examination of the Arms and Ammunition on the 18th it was found that the former were much impaired and all the latter that was in Cartouch Boxes, was intirely ruined, wherefore it was judged expedient to withdraw the Army to some place of security untill the Arms could be repaired and the Ammunition recruited.[3] Before this could be fully effected advice was received that the Enemy had quitted their former position near the White Horse Tavern and were marching down the Road leading to the Swedes Ford but the Army not being in a condition to attack them owing to the want of Ammunition, it was judged most prudent to cross the River at Parkers Ford and take post in the Rear of the Fat Land Ford opposite to the Enemy. In this Position the Armies continued for two days when on the 20th instant that of the Enemy appeared to be in motion, and from our own observation and the accounts of our reconnoitering parties, were marching rapidly up the Reading Road; this induced us to move up likewise, to hinder them from crossing above us and by getting between us and Reading, take an opportunity of destroying a large collection of military Stores deposited there. On the Night of the 20th the Army decamped and marched up to the Trap and on the 21st to within four Miles of Potts Grove, the Enemy's Van then being at French Creek upon the West side of Schuylkill. In the night of the 22d advice was received that the Enemy had crossed Schuylkill at Gordons Ford below us, but the account was again contradicted, but in the morning of the 23d, certain accounts came to hand that they really had crossed in large Numbers and were moving towards Philada.[4] His Excellency further informed the Council that the Troops were in no condition to make a forced March as many of them were barefooted and all excessively harrassed with their great Fatigue. The Question being then put, The Council were unanimously of opinion.

That, from the present State of the Army it would not be advise-able to advance upon the Enemy, but remain upon this Ground or in the Neighbourhood till the detachments and expected Reinforcements come up.[5]

FC (Washington Papers: DLC).

1. Potts Grove (also Pottstown) was on the Schuylkill, some fifteen miles above Valley Forge and forty miles above Philadelphia. On Howe's immediate strategy, see note 5 below.

2. In a somewhat different summary of the meeting, the last two pages of which are in NG's hand, Washington was reported as saying at this point that on the sixteenth "he intended to go on towards the Enemy; But found Considerable part of the Army was still unprovided with provisions thru' the neglect of some of the Commissaries and the Confusion in that department. To remedy this, Greatest part of that day was lost, by which means the Enemy had time to gain Intelligence of our motions, and were preparing to Attack us the next day, which rendered it necessary to Alter the position of our Army, during which came on a Voilent Storm of Rain.'" (Cy, Record RG 93, WRMS, Ms 29573; DNA; the document is endorsed in Washington's hand as "Sentiments of Board of Genl Officers taken near Potts Grove.")

3. The other summary reads here: "The Arms put in very bad order, and the men much fatigued and distressed to remedy which it became necessary to retire over French Creek and towards Reading Furnace."

4. At this point the other summary reads: "That this morning [23 September] he has received intelligence that a part of the Enemy's Army has Crossed the Schuylkill at or near the Fat Land Ford, and by other Intelligence appeard that a Considerable part of the Army was still on the other side of Schuylkill near French Creek Bridge but that numbers on other side was not yet ascertained, that he had dispatched several parties in order to gain further Intelligence, and had wrote repeated letters to hasten the March of General MackDougal with the Troops from Peeks Kill, to Genl Dickenson with the Jersey Militia and had ordered Genl Wayne and Genl Smallwood to Join this Army with the Troops under their Command." (Montresor recorded that just past midnight on the twenty-third, the whole British army crossed to the north side of the Schuylkill at Fatlands Ford, *Journals,* p. 457.)

5. Howe's recent biographer has written that, after the battle of Brandywine, Howe "astonished the rebels and angered his subordinates by failing to press his

advantage. He had lost the best chance he would have in 1777 of destroying the Continental army." (Gruber, *Howe Brothers*, p. 241) Washington's army was in no condition, as he said at the meeting, to give battle, but he had been convinced that for the moment (because of the Schuylkill) Howe would not make an attempt on Philadelphia from the south. When Howe did start upstream along the southern bank toward one of the fords above Philadelphia, Washington could well fear, as he told the council, that Howe had in mind cutting off his supplies at Reading, for when the British landed at Elk River, it had been Howe's plan to first cut off American supplies at Carlisle and York. (Gruber, *Howe Brothers*, p. 238) On 21 September the British started building a bridge across the river near Valley Forge as a feint before crossing at Fatlands Ford, in foot-deep water. There was little that Washington could now do to stop their march downriver along the north side to Philadelphia. See note at Council of War, 28 September, below. The complicated maneuvering is well covered in Reed, *Campaign*, pp. 141–67.

From Colonel John Duyckinck[1]

Sir   Easton [Pa.] Septemb 26, 1777

Having yesterday received orders to make my self ready to march for Dumfries in Virginia, I have Determined previous thereto to solicit your good office, that the order may be staid, and that I may be permitted to remain at my own home.

I beg leave with as much truth and candour as I am master of to lay before you my situation from the moment I was taken, and the Course which induced me to decline the proposal made me at that period.

I was a Militia officer in your service for a considerable time during which peri[o]d I Challenge mankind to Charge me with any breach of duty, and I flattered my Selfe my Conduct was Such as procured me the approbation of the leading people in the State in which I resided. When the British Army came into Jersy and in actual possession of the most Considerable part of my property, I went within their lines and got a Protection and took the oath of allegiance to the British Gov't. While there I remained peaceable, with this fixed and unalterable determination not to bear arms against my Countrymen, with whom I had been so long in the field, and many of whom were my friends and raylations. My reasons for coming out of the British lines were purely in expectation, that being in, Consequence of the oath I had taken, rendered incapable of assisting my Countrymen, any farther in the field, they would have permitted me in Consideration of my former Service, and of my then peaceable and friendly disposition towards them, to have remained quietly and peaceable with my family. It was thought proper to take me in Custody after I came out, and I was soon after caried to Philidelphia Prison, where I remained upwards of four months; by the friendly interposition of Major General Miflin I obtained a Parole to Reading, and from thence was removed to this place. The thoughts of being

Conveyed to Dumfries in Virginia a Country so far distant from this; and thereby excluded from any intercourse with my family and tenderest connections has filled me with much uneasiness. I am however in hopes that you will be kind enough to assist me in this unhappy Situation, by which you will lay me under an eternal obligation. My request is therefore that I may be permitted to go to my farm at Lam[b]erton on my Parole, within as limited a Circle as you and His Excellency General Washington may think proper, and I am parifectly disposed to swear that I will there remain without giving any kind of connivance whatever to the British Cause, and lay my Selfe by oath under any other reasonable obbligation, and if it would be any Sadisfaction to my Countrymen I will likewise make oath, that I Came out of the British lines with no intention of injuring them and that I Had no view or desire whatever for taking such a Step than the hopes and Expectations of living inoffensively among them. Col'l Hooper has been kind enough to Stay [with] me here till your Answer arrives. This letter comes to you by Express, and I must trust in your goodness in giving me an answer, and indeed in Every other respect, for I have no other dependance. With due respect Your huml Srt

JOHN DUYCKINCK

ALS (Elias Boudinot Papers: DLC). Boudinot was sent the letter as commissary of prisoners.

1. In February 1777 Gen. Philemon Dickinson of the N.J. Militia had reported Duyckinck as a British sympathizer. When NG examined him, at Washington's request, he asked the colonel why he had not taken the oath under Washington's proclamation but received "such evasive answers" that NG and Washington were convinced "he only came out to get intelligence." Washington thereupon ordered him confined in Philadelphia and told Gov. Livingston in April he was too "dangerous" a man to set at liberty. (Fitzpatrick, GW, 7: 415; Fitzpatrick mistakenly identifies him as Christopher Duyckinck.) Gen. Dickinson reported that Washington's answer gave "great Pleasure to the Militia who are best acquainted with him." (Letter of 16 February 1777, Washington Papers, DLC)

NG's answer to Duyckinck's moving letter has not been found, but NG must have responded favorably to it, for the prisoner was paroled on 19 November at Easton. On 16 January 1779 Washington restored his liberty "to return to the former place of your abode." (Washington Papers, DLC)

Proceedings of a Council of General Officers

At a Council of War held at
Head Qs at Pennibeckers Mills[1]
the 28th day of Septr 1777.[2]

Present: His Excellency, the Commander in Chief
Majors Genl Sullivan
Greene
Ld Stirling

Wayne
Muhlenberg
Nash

	Stephens	Weedon
	Armstrong	Scott
Brigadr Genls	McDougal	Conway
	Maxwell	Potter
	Smalwood	Irvine
	Knox	

Besides these, John Cadwalader and Joseph Read [Reed] Esquires were present.

His Excellency informed the Board, that the main body of the Enemy, by the last Accounts he had obtained, lay near German Town, and that part had marched into the City of Philadelphia.[3] Whether to remain there or not he could not learn. That their whole force from the best accounts he could get and from a comparative view and estimate, amounts to about 8,000 men.[4]

That a Detachment of Continental Troops from Peekskill, under the command of Brigadr Genl McDougal consisting of about 900 men had joined the Army; That Genl Smallwood, with the Militia of Maryland, amounting to about 1100, had also arrived, and that Brigadr Foreman with about 600 Jersey Militia, would be near the Army to day on the Skippack Road. That of Continental Troops, at this time in Camp, exclusive of the Detachment under Genl McDougal and that under Genl Wayne at the Trap,[5] there were returned present fit for duty 5,472, to which is to be added the light Corps lately under Gen Maxwell, supposed to amount to 450 Men, and the militia of the state of Pensylvania under the command of Major Gen Armstrong. That upon the whole, the Army would consist of about 8000 Continental Troops Rank and file, and 3000 Militia.

His Excellency further informed the Board, that a Body of Militia was coming from Virginia and that part had arrived at Lancaster. That he understood from Report, that the number of 'em amounted to near 2000 men, but that from good authority he was advised they were badly armed and many of them without any at all.

His Excellency also informed the Board that on the 24th Inst he dispatched an Express to Genl Putnam with a Letter dated the day before ordering a Detachment to be sent immediately from Peekskill to reinforce the Army under his Command, which detachment, in addition to the Corps then on the march under Gen McDougal, should make the Whole Force directed from that post amount to 2500 Effective Rank and file.

Under these circumstances he had called a Council of War to consult and resolve on the most advisable measures to be pursued; but more especially to learn from them, whether with this Force it was prudent to make a general and vigorous attack upon the Enemy, or to wait further Reinforcements, upon which he prayed their opinions.

The Board having taken into consideration the whole circumstances and the Question propounded, are of opinion, that an immediate attack should not be made; but they advise that the Army should move to some Grounds proper for an Encampment within about 12 Miles of the Enemy, and there wait for a further Reinforcement, or be in readiness to take advantage of any favourable opportunity that may offer for making an Attack.

ALEXR MC DOUGALL

H KNOX

F. NASH

P. MUHLENBERG

T. CONWAY

JNO SULLIVAN

NATHL GREENE

STIRLING

ADAM STEPHEN

JNO ARMSTRONG

The subscribers being of opinion our Force was sufficient to attack with but being overuled concur with the above.

W. SMALLWOOD

ANTHY WAYNE[6]

JAS POTTER

JAMES IRVINE

CHS SCOTT

DS (Washington Papers: DLC).

1. To be closer to Philadelphia, Washington had ordered a campsite laid out at Pennypackers Mills on Perkiomen Creek, some twelve miles east of the Potts Grove camp. The army marched there on 26 September.

2. The men were cheered by the arrival that day of a somewhat exaggerated account of Gates's strategic victory over Burgoyne at the battle of Freeman's Farm (or the first battle of Saratoga), 19 September. There was no exaggeration, however, in the casualty figures: almost six hundred British compared with three hundred American. Washington ordered a "gill of rum a man, and . . . a discharge of *Thirteen* pieces of artillery at the park." (Fitzpatrick, *GW*, 9: 276–77; the battle is covered in Nickerson, *Turning Point*, pp. 304–18.)

3. The same day that Washington's army reached Pennypackers Mills, Cornwallis marched into Philadelphia "amidst the acclamation of some thousands of inhabitants mostly women and children." (Montresor, *Journals*, p. 458) Philadelphia and immediate surroundings were now under British control, but Howe could scarcely crow over the achievement. For one thing, the loyalists that he had expected to flock to his banner on the way from Head of Elk had proved disappointingly few; then, too, American defenses along the Delaware still prevented much-needed supplies from reaching Philadelphia by water; and finally, Washington's army, though in need of supplies, was still nearby—undefeated.

4. If Washington was speaking literally of Howe's "whole force," his estimate was far too low. Reed (*Campaign*, p. 239) estimates that British and German forces amounted to fifteen thousand. Even if Washington meant the number available that day, the figure was still too low, for of the fifteen thousand men Howe had available, all could oppose Washington but three thousand men who were transporting supplies by land to Philadelphia and four battalions Howe had sent across the Schuylkill to help subdue the American defenses on the Delaware.

5. He was speaking of Trappe, Pa., six or seven miles south of Pennypackers.

6. Anthony Wayne was always a daring, impulsive man ready to take the offensive, but he may have been especially anxious to wipe out the memory of his humiliating defeat at Paoli on 21 September when Gen. Charles Grey made a surprise night attack on his sleeping troops. To prevent the roused Americans from spotting the British by their musket fire in the dark, Grey had ordered an attack with bayonets and insured their use by having the men remove the flints from their guns. The carnage was terrible. American losses in dead have been estimated at 200, with another 100

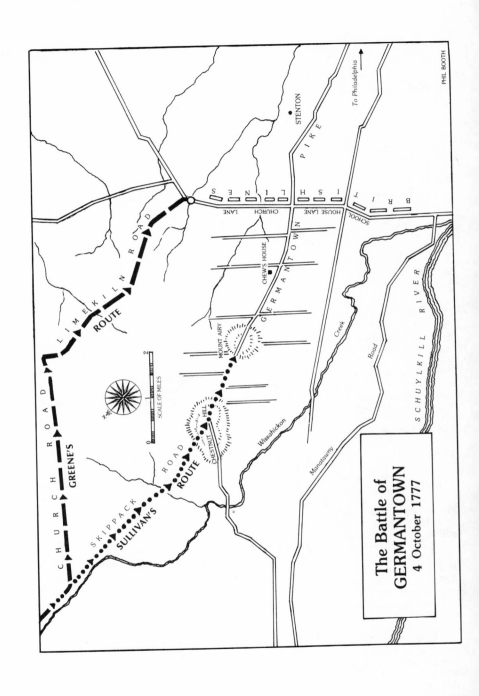

The Battle of
GERMANTOWN
4 October 1777

PHIL BOOTH

wounded and 71 captured. The British lost only 6 killed and 21 injured (Peckham, *Toll,* p. 41). American propagandists dubbed the British general "No-flint Grey" and misnamed the one-sided British victory the "Paoli Massacre." Stories that the British gave no quarter were refuted by the prisoners they took. Wayne was later acquitted by a courtmartial. (Reed, *Campaign,* pp. 168–79)

Advertisement

Hd. Qrs. Skippack [N.J.] 30th Sepr. 1777[1]
General Greene lost at new Hanover Camp, a brass pistol, both Stock & barrel mark'd H. . K . . . Any Person who has found it, & will return it to the General shall receive twenty Dollars.[2]

Reprinted from *Weedon Orderly Book,* pp. 63–64.

1. On 29 September the army had marched the five miles eastward from Pennypackers Mills to Skippack, where they encamped near the Mennonite Church until 2 October.

2. New Hanover, just north of Potts Grove, was apparently Weedon's name for Potts Grove Camp. The initials "H.K." suggest that Henry Knox might have given the pistol to NG.

General Greene's Orders[1]

Camp at Perkioming [Pa.] Octr. 7th 1777
The Genl returns his sincere thanks to the Officers and Soldiers in general of his Division for their behaviour on the Action at German Town. Nevertheless he has the Mortification to hear some few behav'd ill who are arrested and reported to his Excellency. The Genl has the highest Confidence in the Troops of his Division and in the Spirit and good Conduct of the Officers. He from the best information has the mortification to assure the Troops they fled from Victory, and he wishes most ardently, that the Troops may be convinced of the necessity of retreating and rallying briskly, and that a Partial Retreat to change a position is often necessary, and therefore a particular Retreat is not to be Considered general without the order is such. Notwithstanding the Fog depriv'd us of the Opportunity of seeing how to Conduct our near approaches at the Enemy's confusion and giving them a Compleat route which beyond a Doubt we should have done if the Weather had been Clear, nevertheless he has the satisfaction to assure the Troops, the Enemy suffer'd very severely.

The Arms and Ammunition are to be put in good order as soon as possible and everything got in readiness for Attack and defence.

Manuscript Orderly Book, Muhlenberg Papers (PHi)

1. Although five of Washington's generals, as we have seen, voted at the Council of War on 26 September to attack the British immediately, the other ten, including NG, favored moving within some twelve miles of Howe's army at Germantown to await

promised reinforcements. By the thirtieth the army was at Skippack; on 2 October it moved five miles east and encamped on Methacton Hill in Worcester Township. They were now a little less than twenty miles northwest of Philadelphia and, hence, about fifteen miles from the British at Germantown. Washington established his headquarters at the Peter Wentz house. There the battle of Germantown was planned.

With the additional troops in camp, Washington did not hide his eagerness to avenge the defeats at Brandywine and Paoli and the humiliating occupation of Philadelphia. The news of Gates's victory at Saratoga, by contrast, had given an even unhappier complexion to the affairs in Pennsylvania.

Since 28 September Washington had received additional intelligence of the enemy. Cornwallis had several brigades in Philadelphia, and because the American forts on the Delaware still blocked water transport, some three thousand British troops were involved in bringing supplies overland into the city. On 2 October Washington received two intercepted letters indicating that the British had sent a detachment across the lower Delaware into New Jersey to subdue the fort at Billingsport. This left approximately nine thousand men in the main army under Howe at Germantown. Washington's intelligence must also have informed him that Howe had not bothered to fortify his position, apparently unconcerned about the possibility of an attack by an army that he had defeated three weeks earlier and that he knew to be low on supplies of all kinds. Howe did not know that recent reinforcements had offset Washington's losses at Brandywine and Paoli. As one student of the war has written: "The crucial point about the depletions on both sides was almost always this: though his losses were greater than Howe's, Washington could scrape up reinforcements, the Briton could not." (Higginbotham, *War*, p. 186).

To Washington the time seemed propitious for an attack. On 3 October he communicated the latest intelligence to his general officers, who, as he later told Congress, "were unanimously of Opinion, that a favourable opportunity offered to make an Attack." (Fitzpatrick, *GW*, 9: 308–9). Minutes of a council have not been found, but Gen. Smallwood, who was present, commented a few days later on the unanimous decision of "his Excellency in Council with the other General Officers on the 3d Inst." (*PMHB*, 1 [1877]: 401).

Germantown, as the generals knew (most having been in the vicinity twice in a month) was five miles northwest of Philadelphia on the road to Reading. It consisted of a string of widely separated houses, mostly stone, that lined both sides of the road for two miles. The road here ran roughly parallel to the Schuylkill River (a mile to the west) and was known locally as the Germantown Pike. All the houses fronted on the road in fenced enclosures that ran back some distance. Here and there the enclosures were separated by lanes that extended back at right angles on either side of the road. About midpoint in the village stood the market house.

At the south end of the town, Howe had camped his army along a line that crossed Germantown Pike at right angles and extended on either side for more than a mile. The British left wing, under Gen. Knyphausen, was situated along the south side of School House Lane; his far left, comprised of Hessian jaegers, reached to the Schuylkill. The right wing, under Gen. Grant, was camped along the south side of Church (or Limekiln) Lane. The far right was held by the Queens Rangers. Although Howe had spurned any fortifications, the rough topography and the many fences in the village were effective defense barriers against an attack from the north.

On 3 October, Washington perfected his plan of attack. Although it was reminiscent of the nighttime march and dawn attack on Trenton in December 1776, it was far bolder, because the target now was not fourteen hundred Hessians but the main British army of nine thousand men. Timing and coordination, moreover, were more critical than at Trenton.

The plan called for dividing the army of some eight thousand continentals and three thousand militia into four attacking prongs (Washington called them wings or columns), which would approach the British camp from four directions, reaching their staging areas at precisely the same predetermined time and making a coordinated surprise attack at dawn. The long marches were to be made entirely in the dark. For such an intricate maneuver to succeed, the army would need all the luck that accompanied it at Trenton. There is no evidence, however, that even the most conservative generals showed any hesitancy in approving the proposal. NG, who had helped plan and execute the Trenton attack, may very well have helped devise the strike against Germantown.

One wing under Sullivan was to advance down the Skippack Road to the Bethlehem Road, thence south to Chestnut Hill and the Germantown Pike, a march of some fourteen miles. In addition to Sullivan's own division, the column would include Lincoln's division, still under Wayne, with Conway's brigade in the vanguard and Stirling's division as a reserve. NG was to command his own and Stephen's divisions, the lead to be taken by McDougall's brigade, which had recently arrived from New York. Washington had assigned over half of the continental forces to NG's wing because the British right wing was reportedly the strongest. (Figures are not available for 3 October, but a month later NG's and Stephen's combined divisions reported about four thousand troops fit for duty. McDougall's nine hundred thus would have given NG almost five thousand men on the left compared with Sullivan's three thousand on the right. Sullivan later said: "Two Thirds of the Army at Least were Detached to oppose the Enemys Right." Hammond, *Sullivan*, 1: 543. The 3 November reports are in Lesser, *Sinews*, pp. 50–51).

The route NG was to take branched off to the left (and east) of Sullivan's onto Church Road, thence south on Limekiln Road, from which he would strike the British right wing from the north. It was a more difficult route than Sullivan's and longer by several miles. The other two prongs were to be formed by militiamen. Smallwood's Marylanders and Forman's New Jersey Militia were to swing in a wide arc off NG's left in order to flank the British far right, even coming in upon their rear. Not only did these militiamen have the longest march, but Washington's orders to Smallwood and Forman, both of them strangers to the area, were enough to confuse a native. His orders read in part, "Smallwood and Forman to pass down the road by a mill formerly Danl. Morris and Jacob Edges mill into the White marsh road at the Sandy run: thence to white marsh Church, where take the left hand road, which leads to Jenkin's tavern, on the old york road, below Armitages, beyond the seven mile stone half a mile from which turns off short to the right hand, fenced on both sides, which leads through The enemys incampment to German town market house." (Fitzpatrick, *GW*, 9: 307). The fourth prong, consisting of Gen. John Armstrong's Pennsylvania Militia, was to strike off to Sullivan's right and, staying close to the Schuylkill, attack the Hessian jaegers on the British far left "in flank and rear." They, at least, could not stray further west than the banks of the Schuylkill.

The four columns were to "endeavour to get within two miles of the enemys pickets on their respective routs by two oClock and there halt 'till four and make the disposition for attacking the pickets." This was to be done "precisely at five oClock with charged bayonets without firing." Final instructions called upon every officer and soldier to have "a piece of White paper in their Hatt" to identify them and for the columns to "communicate with each other from time to time by light horse." (Fitzpatrick, *GW*, 9: 308). Since none of the columns would be closer than a mile from the next and the outside ones would be five miles or more apart, the mounted messengers riding in the dark across rough countryside would have their work cut out for them.

In a moving and lengthy general order on 3 October, Washington did his best to rouse his troops to fighting pitch. In recounting Gates's victory at Saratoga he said, among other things, "The main American Army, will certainly not suffer itself to be out done by their northern Brethren . . . Covet! my Countrymen, and fellow soldiers! Covet! a share of the glory due to heroic deeds!" They should never let it be said in a day of action, he continued, "that you turned your backs on the foe." He ended with a peroration: "Our dearest rights, our dearest friends, and our own lives, honor, glory and even shame, urge us to the fight. And My fellow Soldiers! when an opportunity presents, be firm, be brave; shew yourselves men, and victory is yours." (Fitzpatrick, *GW*, 9: 305–6.)

The British still did not suspect the impending attack. Thomas Paine, a former aide to NG who had spent the night in NG's quarters, observed the troops the morning before the battle fortifying "the camp as a deception." It was 7:00 P.M. and well after dark when NG's division, with the furthest to go, set off down Skippack Road. Paine wanted to accompany the column, but "Gen. Green," Paine later wrote, "desired me to remain there till morning." (Paine to Benjamin Franklin, 16 May 1778, *PMHB*, 2 [1878]: 287–88) Sullivan's column, accompanied by Washington, followed later. (Sullivan said they left at 9:00 P.M., Hammond, *Sullivan*, 1: 544) Although Sullivan's column had a direct road, Washington had not allowed sufficient time for poorly shod men who had marched incessantly for weeks. It was daybreak before they reached Chestnut Hill, still a mile from the British outposts at Mt. Airy and almost four miles from the main British line. (Ibid.) Thus it was past sunrise by the time a regiment from Conway's brigade and one from the Second Maryland brigade attacked the British outposts. (Fitzpatrick, *GW*, 9: 309)

Meanwhile, other hitches developed in Washington's plans. In the darkness a local guide had inadvertently led NG's column off on the wrong road, a loss of precious time for a column that had the longest route. Furthermore, the light horsemen that were to keep the columns in touch with each other found their task impossible. Washington, who was with Sullivan, thus knew nothing of NG's difficulties. He had also, of course, lost contact with Smallwood's and Forman's militiamen on the far left, as had NG, who was closer to them. The battle of Germantown would be fought, in fact, without the aid of the two outside militia wings. Smallwood and Forman did not reach the area until the battle was over, while Armstrong's Pennsylvania militia on the right never crossed an intervening creek to make contact with Knyphausen's left. This loss was not as severe as it might have appeared on a diagram of Washington's plan, for he had not envisioned a genuine pincers movement by these two weakest prongs.

Until NG's column finally reached the village, which was at least an hour after sunrise, the fighting fell entirely upon Sullivan's wing along the Germantown Pike. Despite delays and the breakdown in communications, Sullivan's vanguard managed to surprise both the outposts at Mt. Airy and the several hundred light infantry that Howe had stationed more than a mile north of the British lines. Howe himself had been awakened at 4:00 A.M. with a report that a captured American flanker had told of an approaching detachment, but Howe was half a mile behind the main British line and three miles from Mt. Airy. He mounted his horse at once, and although he alerted his main army as he passed through, he was too late to warn the light infantry.

Sullivan's attack upon the light infantry was not only a surprise, but it turned out to be extremely effective. He moved Conway's brigade and Moylan's light horse to his right and formed his own division along the right side of the road, with Wayne's division on the left side of the road. The British light infantry made a stand at every ditch and every fence. Despite the Americans' weariness, they fought fiercely. Wayne's troops were energized by the prospect of avenging their bloody defeat at Paoli. (See note, Council of War, 28 September, above). The British light infantry continued to give ground slowly, until suddenly they turned on their heels in a complete rout as the Americans overran their encampment. It was the first time since the battle of Harlem Heights that Washington's army had seen the backs of the enemy. By this time the fighting had gone on for more than an hour, during which time a fog had begun to drift in, slowing the American advance.

Howe arrived in time to witness what he considered a shameful retreat from a mere American patrol, but he soon discovered that it was more than a patrol from which his troops were fleeing. Narrowly escaping a charge of grapeshot from American artillery, he wheeled his horse and hastened back to the British lines to prepare them for what they were up against. Col. Thomas Musgrave's Fortieth British Regiment, which had come to the aid of the light infantry, found themselves surrounded during the American advance. Musgrave took refuge with 120 of his men in a large stone house on the east side of the road, half way between the British outposts at Mt. Airy and their main camp—a house abandoned earlier by its owner, Judge Benjamin Chew. They barricaded the heavy front door, reinforced the first floor shutters, and from the upstairs windows their best marksmen began to pick off some of Stirling's men, who were bringing up Sullivan's rear. In thus taking refuge in the Chew House (also known as Cliveden), Musgrave could scarcely have imagined the damage he would be able to inflict on the American offensive.

As Wayne and Sullivan advanced beyond the Chew House, the fog thickened, cutting visibility in spots to as little as thirty yards. The closer they got to the British lines, the rougher the ground became; by this time, moreover, Grant's brigades were moving up to meet them, firing blindly at times into the fog. By firing wildly both sides were wasting ammunition but also suffering heavy casualties. Meanwhile, to Wayne's rear, there was disagreement among the American officers as how best to cope with Musgrave's force in the Chew House. Some of those present (with whom later military writers have sided) favored bypassing the house, posting a guard at a distance in case Musgrave attempted to leave. But Henry Knox, the chief of artillery who was well versed in classical military theory, insisted that an army should never leave an armed "castle" to its rear. He persuaded Washington that they should bring artillery to bear on the house. For an hour or more, cannon balls from three- and six-pounders bounced off the thick stone walls; the house proved to be, in the words of Knox's biographer, "the most immovable object in the military career of Henry Knox." (Callahan, *Knox*, p. 119) It also proved impregnable to individual sorties. Efforts to storm the door or to set fire to the house were costly in American lives: Maxwell's and Nash's brigade from Stirling's division took the brunt of the sharpshooting from the upper windows. In all, more than a hundred Americans lay dead or wounded before the foolish attempt to take it was abandoned.

More was involved, unfortunately, than the lives of the besiegers. The sound of the firing in Wayne's rear led him to believe that Sullivan was in trouble. Not knowing, because of the fog, that Sullivan's division was actually abreast of him on the west side of the road, Wayne turned his division back in order to help. In so doing he unknowingly exposed Sullivan's left to British fire. The retrograde move did more than that; by now NG's column was approaching on the left down Limekiln Road. When Gen. Stephen heard the intense firing around the Chew House to his right, he moved his division in that direction without consulting NG. The usual explanation for Stephen's action is that he was drunk, but whatever caused him to leave his appointed route, the effect was all but disastrous. In the fog his men mistook Wayne's backtracking troops for the enemy and began firing at them. Wayne's men, thinking it was the British right wing, reciprocated. No one knows how many casualties resulted, but suddenly Grant's British brigades were advancing against a disorganized sector. Soon there was utter confusion among troops in both Stephen's and Wayne's divisions, followed by panic. Ignoring their officers' attempts to rally them, the men ran northward along the Germantown Pike.

Then Sullivan's troops began independently to retreat. A regiment of North Carolinians and one from Conway's brigade, which had been in the forefront of the fighting, ran low on ammunition. In the fog the British were close enough to hear the men discussing the shortage and immediately British units took advantage of the American plight. Sullivan thought the "Cry of a Light Horse man on the Right that the Enemy had got round us," plus the sight of "Some Troops flying on our Right," caused his division to retire with "as much precipitation as they had before advanced." (Hammond, *Sullivan*, 1: 546)

At one point Washington rode up dangerously near the front to discover what was wrong, withdrawing only upon Sullivan's insistence. He was completely in the dark as to what had caused the sudden reversal, although he had earlier warned Sullivan's men to be careful of their forty rounds of ammunition. Only gradually did he become aware of Stephen's and Wayne's divisions running in panic. With victory seemingly in his grasp, Washington could scarcely believe, much less account for, the turn in his fortune. From the left the sounds of NG's guns continued to reach him as they had for an hour, although only later would he learn what had been happening in that sector.

The wrong turn that NG's column took during the night had cost him almost an hour, but he had made up perhaps half of it. Lambdin (cited below) on good authority says NG's advance units made contact with Sir George Osborn's light infantry near Bettons Woods only half an hour after Sullivan's attack on Mt. Airy. NG had not expected to meet the enemy until he reached Lukens Mill, a mile to the east, but later testimony of Osborn reveals that his battalion had advanced the night before in front of the British right wing and that "there can be no doubt" he was stationed north of a line that ran east of the Chew House. (Alfred C. Lambdin, "Battle of Germantown," *PMHB*, 1 [1877]: 383n) NG halted his column after reaching Limekiln Road to make a disposition of his troops. Stephen's division was ordered to the right of the road, NG's to the left, with McDougall's assigned the far left. Leaving the road meant that all the units were marching through fence lines, woods, and marshes. When Stephen's division pulled off to the right toward the Chew House, NG's division proceeded to the left of Limekiln Road, meeting heavier and heavier fire from Gen. Mathew's brigade. The fog was hampering NG as it was Sullivan and Wayne to the west. McDougall's brigade had gotten separated because of the rough ground, leaving NG's division exposed on the left to the Queens Rangers. McDougall, like Smallwood and Forman, never got into the action.

Muhlenberg's brigade, which had not participated in the fighting at Brandywine, found themselves in the thick of the fight as they forged ahead, Weedon's brigade following. The entire division advanced for some two miles past their first contact with Osborn's light infantry. One of Muhlenberg's lead regiments, Col. George Mathews's Ninth Virginia, acquired such momentum that they actually reached the area just abandoned by Wayne near Market Square behind the British lines, capturing a hundred prisoners in the drive. Unfortunately, the regiment had isolated itself and was soon surrounded by the enemy. Mathews not only lost his hundred prisoners but surrendered with four hundred of his men.

The rest of NG's division found rough going off to the left of the Limekiln Road. What happened to the division after Mathews's capture is extremely confused. Col. Walter Stewart took three cannon from the enemy and had reached almost as far as Mathews before he had to beat a hasty retreat (Lambdin, p. 386). With Wayne's and Sullivan's divisions on the run, Gen. Grant could concentrate against NG's scattered and weary division. NG ordered a retreat just in time. He was able to save several cannon, but he also lost a good many men before he could withdraw his two brigades in the fog with some semblance of order. In the meantime, Cornwallis had appeared with his Philadelphia brigades, and Washington reluctantly approved what had already become a general retreat. Panic, however, had given way to a more orderly falling back as the men streamed north. All around them lay the dead and wounded, but they had to leave their own wounded and dead for the British to care for or bury. The British followed the retreat in an almost leisurely fashion, slowed in part by an occasional burst of American artillery that had been hastily set up for a few shots; but perhaps also, in part, because their hearts were not in any more killing. Thus they kept a safe distance behind. Washington did not stop the army at Methacton Hill but kept the weary men marching another five miles to their old camp at Pennypackers. When the men finally set foot in camp they had marched over thirty-five miles since the previous evening and had fought for more than two and a half hours. Muhlenberg, reportedly, fell asleep in his saddle. His men needed only a horse and saddle to follow suit.

The battle of Germantown in the end was a British victory. Although Howe's light infantry had given way and his lines were penetrated, his troops had repulsed the American offensive and with fewer losses. Peckham (*Toll*, p. 42) estimates 152 Americans killed, 500 wounded, and 438 captured (most accounted for by Mathews's Ninth Virginia Regiment). He lists British casualties at about 550. Reed (*Campaign*, pp. 238–39) makes similar estimates. He points out that casualties were especially heavy among American officers, listing some 117 wounded and 30 killed. Both sides lost a general: Francis Nash, a North Carolinian just NG's age, was mortally wounded and died three days later; British Gen. James Agnew was also mortally wounded but more fortunate than Nash, for he lived only fifteen minutes.

The American forces, surprisingly, were not as disspirited by the loss as might be supposed. They had, after all, attacked the finest British army head-on, had fought them to a standstill for almost three hours, had seen the British light infantry turn tail and run, had penetrated their lines, and finally, from the commander in chief downward, they believed they had come within an inch of driving Howe back across the Schuylkill and completely defeating his army. Most historians, however, are inclined to believe Howe when he later testified he had no intention of fleeing. Granted that Howe had not considered a retreat and that the Americans had essentially failed in their attack, as Boatner has pointed out, "There can be no disputing the paradoxical fact that this failure boosted their morale and self confidence. *They* thought they had almost won." (*Encyc.*, p. 430) Weedon said that "though the enterprise miscarried, it was worth the undertaking." (Cited by Freeman, *GW*, 4: 517) Many Americans applauded Washington and his army for their audacity in attacking the cream of the British army. Congress resolved unanimously on 8 October that "the thanks of Congress be given to General Washington, for his wise and well concerted attack upon the enemy's army near Germantown . . . and to the officers and soldiers of the army, for their brave exertions." Congress was satisfied that "the best designs and boldest efforts may sometimes fail by unforeseen incidents." A medal was then ordered to be struck and presented to Washington. (*JCC*, 9: 785) Washington's audacity was likewise praised on the European continent.

Unfortunately in the eyes of a growing group of domestic critics, such as Benjamin Rush and John Adams, Washington's audacity and execution were greatly overshadowed in the blaze of Gates's victories at Saratoga. (See "Conway Cabal" in note, NG to Jacob Greene, 7 February 1778, below.)

Soon these critics were also at NG for unduly influencing Washington and for his delayed arrival at Germantown. The fact that the criticism was based on ignorance and was completely unfair made it no less difficult for NG to endure. He was still smarting from the critics' barbs months later as can be seen in his correspondence with McDougall of 25 January and 14 and 28 February 1778 and in his letter to Marchant of 25 July 1778 below. Even as late as 18 February 1782, in a letter in which he was offering solace to Lighthorse Harry Lee for lack of public recognition, the criticisms still burned in NG's memory. "At Germantown," he wrote, "I was evidently degraced [disgraced], altho I think if ever I merited anything it was for my exertions on that day. . . . But I never murmured or complained, notwithstanding I was held in indignation for faults and misfortunes I had no direction of." (ALS, CSmH)

Both primary and secondary accounts of the battle are numerous. Many, however, reflect the confusion that existed on the foggy battlefield, and none is complete. They also are contradictory. In all of the secondary accounts, there is considerable guesswork as to just which units were where and at what time. A carefully documented older work that is still useful is Alfred C. Lambdin, "Battle of Germantown," *PMHB*, 1 (1877): 368–403. Three good modern accounts, each using essentially the same sources, but with some differences in both sources and interpretation, are: Ward, *War*, 1: 362–71; Freeman, *GW*, 4: 490–519, and Reed, *Campaign*, pp. 214–39. Boatner (*Encyc.*, pp. 426–30) is a succinct and thoughtful account, based on secondary accounts, to which he applies sound judgment and keen insight.

From Colonel Walter Stewart, Colonel Lewis Farmer and Major John Murray[1]

Sir   Camp [Towamencin, Pa.][2] Octo 11th 1777

I think it my Duty to Inform you of the Conduct of two of my Officers for some time past, in walking both from the dangers and duty their Brother Officers are expos'd to.

Captain Patrick Anderson when we left Morris Town July 6th, pretended sickness and stay'd behind the Regiment; he being determin'd never to encounter a Northern Campaigne. Finding his disposition, I order'd him on the recruiting service, but Instead of doing his duty in this way he has never got one man or Indeed left his house to Attempt it.[3]

I have twice Order'd him to Join the Regiment but can have no Answer from him, except what he has told some of the Officers, that he was determin'd not to serve untill made a Major; this Post must say I think him by no means qualified for, and could wish his Excellency would appoint a Worthy Young Gentleman Lieutenant Joseph Finley[4] (the 1st L't in my Regiment) in his place; as he seems determin'd not to attend for a regular Tryal.

Jacob Metz Lieutenant to Captain Anderson left us at Germantown Sep'r 19th, went Home and is now Working at his trade of a Black Smith; Make no doubt both these Gentlemen would willingly Join the Regiment, should we get into Winter Quarters; as I find they both play'd the same Game last year: but immediately Join'd the Regiment when they got to Philadelphia. We are Sir your Most Obt Servants

WALTER STEWART

LEWIS FARMER

JOHN MURRAY

ALS (Washington Papers: DLC).

1. The three officers signed the letter, but Col. Stewart wrote it. Stewart (1756–96), born in North Ireland, was said to be "the handsomest man in the American Army." He was an aide to Gen. Gates until June 1777, at which time, at age twenty-one, he was appointed colonel of a Pennsylvania militia regiment and as such, fought at Brandywine and Germantown. On 13 November his regiment was annexed to the continental line as the Thirteenth Pa. Regiment. While NG was in the South, Stewart corresponded with him, and in January 1782 Catharine Greene stayed with the Stewarts in Philadelphia on her way south. He was a merchant after the war and, at the time of his death, major general of the First Pa. Militia. (*PMHB*, 47 [1923]: 275) Farmer and Murray remained with the regiment when it became the Thirteenth Pa. Continental.

2. After retreating from Germantown, Washington camped the army on the west bank of Perkiomen Creek (opposite Pennypackers) at Pawlings Mills in order to "rest and refresh the men." (Fitzpatrick, *GW*, 9: 320) By the eighth they had sufficiently recovered to move a few miles eastward to Towamencin Township. (Reed, *Campaign*, p. 249.)

3. Both Anderson and Metz were suspended in Washington's orders of 15 October "for their non-attendance." (Fitzpatrick, *GW*, 9: 378–79)

4. Joseph Lewis Finley had been a second lieutenant in the First Pa. Rifle Regiment. He was made a captain in Stewart's regiment the day after Anderson's suspension. (Heitman, *Register*).

To George Washington

[Towamencin, Pa., 15 October 1777.[1] Recommends acceptance of Capt. Hugh's resignation due to sickness. Will also permit Col. Stewart to reduce his companies to ten. ALS (RG 93, WRMS, Vol. 169: DNA) 1 p.]

1. It was the fifteenth when word reached Washington of the Northern Army's signal victory over Burgoyne in the second battle of Saratoga on 7 October, although it was later before Burgoyne's surrender was confirmed. (See Nickerson, *Turning Point*, chapters 11 and 12.) Washington swallowed the envy he must have felt, and in a general order warmly congratulated the army for again triumphing over "veteran troops." It was his hope, he added, that "it will prove a powerful stimulus to the army under his immediate command; at least to equal their northern brethren in brave and

intrepid exertions where called thereto." (Fitzpatrick, *GW,* 9: 377–78) Gates's dereliction in pointedly not informing Washington of the victory was the beginning of what came to be called the "Conway Cabal." See below, note, NG to Jacob, 7 February 1778.

General Greene's Orders

[Methacton Hill,[1] Worcester Township, Pa., 16 October 1777, 9:00 P.M. The Second and Fifth Virginia Regiments and Pennsylvania State Regiment to be ready with one day's provisions to march tomorrow with Gen. Weedon. From *Weedon Orderly Book,* p. 94.]

1. The army had just moved that day from Towamencin to Methacton Hill in Worcester Township, where it had camped just before the battle of Germantown. Washington again had his headquarters at the Peter Wentz house. (Reed, *Campaign,* p. 262)

General Greene's Orders

[Methacton Hill, Worcester Township, Pa., 17 October 1777, 11:00 P.M. A regiment each from Muhlenberg's and Weedon's brigades to be ready to march at sunrise with "Colonel Greene."[1] From *Weedon Orderly Book,* p. 95.]

1. Col. John Green of the First Va. Regiment. See NG to Col. Christopher Greene, 18 October, below.

To Colonel Christopher Greene[1]

Camp at Metuchin [Methacton Hill, Pa.]
Dear Sir   Octo 18, 1777
This will be handed you by Lt Col Greene[2] who commands a detachment from my division sent down as a reinforcement for the forts on the Delaware—they are exceeding good troops and are to be depended on as much as any troops in the Army—I am in hopes with this additional strength you will be able to baffle all the attempts of the enemy to dislodge you—the Barron Arandt[3] Col. of the German Battallion an Officer of experience and ability is coming down to take the command at Fort Mifflin agreeable to the determination of the council in the first instance—he is thought to be an officer of great spirit—Remember me to all friends. Your affectionate

N GREENE

Tr (Typescript: RPJCB). A transcription is also in the GWG transcripts at CSmH, but the typescript appears to have been more carefully copied from the original and left unedited.
1. Col. Christopher Greene, NG's third cousin, commanded a regiment in Varnum's R.I. brigade. On Washington's orders the brigade had come down from Peekskill

just after the battle of Germantown, but before it reached camp, Washington ordered Varnum on 7 October to detach Col. Greene's and Col. Israel Angell's regiments "with orders to throw themselves into the Fort at Red Bank upon the Jersey Shore." He added that "Genl. Greene has wrote a particular letter to Colo. Greene, in which he will find instructions," but the letter has not been found. (Fitzpatrick, *GW*, 9: 326–27)

With the battle of Germantown behind him and the British thoroughly entrenched in Philadelphia, Washington realized the critical necessity for the British to clear the Delaware of American defenses so that their supply ships could come up stream. He was determined to do everything possible to prevent this.

Howe, of course, was no less aware of the need to clear the river, although he left it up to subordinates to expedite it. Soon after occupying Philadelphia, the British captured the lower fort at Billingsport, but the principal barriers were the three rows of chevaux-de-frise stretched across the river at the mouth of the Schuylkill (five miles below Philadelphia) and the two forts that defended the barriers—Ft. Mifflin on Mud Island and Ft. Mercer at Red Bank, N.J. Upriver from the chevaux-de-frise, was a motley American flotilla composed of a brig, a schooner, and a number of galleys, half galleys, sloops, xebeques, rafts, and miscellaneous craft. The entire fleet, a few of them continental vessels, was under Commodore John Hazelwood of the Pennsylvania navy.

The principal British objective in early October was the reduction of Ft. Mifflin on Mud Island. Capt. John Montresor, the British engineer who had built the fort some years earlier, began preparations for a siege that started on 15 October and was not to end for a month. It was 20 October before Howe showed sufficient interest to inspect Montresor's bridge across the Schuylkill and the batteries on Province Island. It was Montresor's activities that had led Washington to detach Greene's and Angell's regiments to Red Bank. When the siege of Ft. Mifflin began on 15 October, Washington asked Col. Greene to send over as many men from Ft. Mercer as he could spare to Col. Samuel Smith in command at Ft. Mifflin. On 19 October, Col. Greene sent a 150-man detachment under Maj. Simeon Thayer—a former subordinate and friend of NG's, a veteran of the French and Indian War, and a leading participant in Arnold's march to Quebec in 1775. Col. Angell's regiment and the rest of Col. Greene's remained at Red Bank, along with some 8 artillerists and a Virginia regiment of only 150 men. The scene at both forts was laid for heroic action that was to bring legendary fame to the defenders—especially NG's one-time R.I. regiments. The siege of Red Bank did not begin for three days. (See below, NG to Col. Greene, 26 October.)

The first phase of the Delaware campaign is thoroughly covered in Reed, *Campaign*, 269–86. More detailed is Smith, *The Delaware*, pp. 5–18, which has excellent maps—old and new.

2. John Green of the First Va. Regiment.

3. Col. Henry Leonard Philip, Baron d'Arendt, was a French engineer who proved less able than Washington or Greene expected and whose withdrawal because of illness led to Col. Samuel Smith's reinstatement as commander of Ft. Mifflin on 28 October. (Fitzpatrick, *GW*, 9: 458).

General Greene's Orders

[Methacton Hill, Worcester Township, Pa., 22 October 1777. Several regiments in the two brigades to be ready to march at 6:00 P.M. "without Blankets, or any kind of Encumbrance" and with forty rounds of ammunition.

After Orders

The whole division to be ready to move at 6:00 P.M.;[1] each man to have "forty rounds of Ammunition, a Gill of rum, & a Blanket." From Weedon Orderly Book, p. 100.]

1. The army moved somewhat closer to the Delaware, to Whitpain.

To Colonel Christopher Greene

Dr Sir

Camp [   ] 26 Octo 1777

With the greatest pleasure I congratulate you on your late brave and successful defence, the attempt was bold and the defence noble. Honnor and laurels will be the reward of the garrison.[1]

Cousin Griffin[2] informs me you are in great fear of a siege and that it will be impossible to defend the place any length of time should the enemy lay siege to it. I am sorry to learn that the garrison are growing sickly, their labor and fatigue must be intollerable.

A strong reinforcement will be sent you immediately; I believe three hundred have marched today, and more will march tomorrow. You may depend upon my influence, so far as it extends, shall be exerted to relieve the anxiety of the Garrison. My compliments to all the officers of the garrison. Affectionately yours

N. GREENE

ALS (Varnum House, East Greenwich, R.I.). Right-hand portion of original has been torn off; the missing words have been supplied from GWG transcript, CSmH.

1. For background, see above, NG to Christopher, 18 October. The troops under Christopher had won a brilliant victory in their defense of Red Bank. Count Donop, in order to wipe out the shame of the Hessian defeat at Trenton, had asked Howe for the honor of capturing Ft. Mercer. He crossed from Philadelphia above Red Bank with some two thousand Hessians, and on 22 October attacked the fort. He was unaware that the Chevalier du Plessis, a French engineer and aide to Gen. Knox, had been reducing its size, so that Col. Greene's four hundred men could defend it, and had been strengthening it in other ways. The Americans held their fire until the Hessians were at the walls; then with muskets and artillery, cut them down with devastating fire. Against 14 Americans killed and 23 wounded, the Hessians suffered 153 killed, 200 wounded (many of whom later died), and another 50 lost or captured. The rest retreated, abandoning the wounded Donop, who died three days later in Col. Greene's headquarters.

To frustrate British plans even further, the Americans set fire to the 64-gun *Augusta*, which had been grounded while aiding Donop. The explosion of her magazine could be heard for thirty miles. On top of this, the crew of the grounded *Merlin* set her afire. Washington, who had been overshadowed by Gates's victory at Saratoga, took some comfort in the spectacular achievements of the few men at Fts. Mercer and Mifflin and even in Hazelwood's navy. (See Reed, *Campaign*, pp. 287–304; Smith, *The Delaware*, 18–25.)

The men at both forts were secure for the moment, but brave as they were, they could not forever stop the full British force that was soon to be leveled against them.

(See note, NG to Washington, 14 November, and NG to Washington, 21 November, below.)

2. Cousin Griffin Greene, who was at Red Bank, was married to Col. Christopher's sister, Sarah. He was a business associate and close friend of NG.

George Washington to the General Officers

[Whitpain, Pa., 26 October 1777. "You will, very shortly, be called to a Council of War, when your Sentiments on the following questions will be asked." He then posed the questions that are repeated, in the Council held 29 October, below. AdfS (Washington Papers: DLC) 2 pp.]

To Jacob Greene

Upper Dublin[1] 15 miles from Philadelphia

Dear Sir   Oct 27, 1777

I had the pleasure to receive a line from you some few days since by the hand of Major Ward.[2] I am sorry to hear you are still in a weakly way. I hope with you the cold weather will restore your nerves to a firmer tone. What is the matter with brothers Bill and Kitt? I find that sickness and death are in other places besides the army. I can hear of many friends in private life that have taken a leap in the dark since I left home. I hope neither Bill or Kitt are dangerous. I wish them and all the families better health.

I beg leave to congratulate you upon the good news to the Northerd.[3] You may remember that [I] wrote you sometime since that what we at times conceivd to be the greatest misfortunes often terminateed in peculiar blessings; had not the fort at Ticonderoga been given up, this glorious event in all probabillity had never happend. I wish we had been as fortunate here as the Army to the Northerd. Altho we have not been as successful we have not been less industrious. We have fought two general actions, both of which I have wrote you an account off.[4] We march'd down to this place a few days since with a design to make another attack on General How at Germantown. He immediately retird from that place into Philadelphia under cover of redoubts he has been forming for some time. I think he will decline another general action until he makes further attempts to open passage for his shiping. On the 22d Count Donop with 1500 Hessian Grenadiers made an attack upon Red Bank fort upon the banks of the Delaware in the Jerseys about nine miles below the city of Philadelphia. The attack was very severe and lasted forty minutes. The fort is [a] garrison with Rhode Island troops. Both regiments are there and commanded by Col Greene. They made a gallant defence and beat off the Hessians with considerable loss; near one hundred was left dead upon the field and about as many wounded that could not get off. [It is] said from very good authority that besides these, between two and three hundred were carried over the river into the city; the whole loss of the enemy is thought to be between four and five hundred. Count Donop was wounded in the hip and made a prisoner. Next morning the enemy brought up their fleet to attack Fort Mifflin that covers the Cheveau de frieze that formd the obstruction in the river, which fort is built on a little Island called Mud Island. Red Bank and this fort communicates with each other.[5] The attack began about break of day. There was a most furious cannonade for several hours; at last the Ships were obligd to give way. In their retreat one sixty four and one thirty two gun frigate run aground and were both burnt. Several others narrowly escaped.[6]

I lay close upon the Enemies lines that morning. A large party of the enemy had encampt a day or two before over the Schuylkill, and McDougall had a detachment from the army to attack them, but the enemy retird the evening before and when our troops came upon the ground they found the enemy gone. General Sullivan and myself were detacht to make an attack upon the enemy near Philadelphia, to favor Gen McDougalls attack and prevent any reinforcements being sent but were obligd to retire without fireing, the signal to begin the attack never being given on account of the enemies being gone from the other side of the Schuylkill.[7] I am not able to form any Judgment how the Campaign will terminate here, but I am apt to think General How will leave the City of Philadelphia if Lord How is not able to get up his Shiping, which at present remains very doubtful. I wish our force was able to pen him up in the city of Philadelphia but am sorry to say it is not. We should be glad to fight them, but dare not divide our force for fear of some cappital misfortune. It is an unhappiness to be obligd to magnify your own strength and cry down that of your enemies to keep up the spirits of the people: more is expected than can possibly be executed. Everything has been and will be done to give a happy issue to this campaign, but we have a formidable force to contend with. We want the aid of the N E [New England] militia to compleat the destruction of General Howes army.

The Enemy have burnt Esopus and are commiting most horrid ravages up the North River.[8] I am in hopes General Gates force will soon put a stop to their career. Cousin Griffin was here yesterday and was in the action. He sais the Rhode Island troops behavd with great bravery and all the officers distinguished themselves.

The enemy are greatly Distrest in the city; beef is 2/ Sterling per lb and flour [illegible] and very little of either to be had. The Inhabitants are almost starveing. They leave the city day[ly]. The Quakers voluntarily lent General How 5,000 [£] sterling at his arrival in the city a few days since. It is said he laid them under the necessity of lending him 20,000 more. I wish he may increase in his demand. A gentleman of undoubted truth sais he has heard several of the Friends say they wish G Washingtons army was cut [in] pieces that there might be peace. These are lamb like wishes, and breathe that universal benevolence they profess for all mankind. I am sure the Friends with us are a better order of people than they are here; if they are not, the lord have mercy upon em. Remember me to all the brothers and their families and all enquiring friends. Mrs Green is well at Morristown.[9] Your affect

N GREEN

N B I beg youl pay particular attention to the wants of my children during Mrs Greenes and my absence. I trust [them] wholely to your care and beg you will not let them want.

ALS (NjMoW).
    1. This was probably another name for adjoining Whitpain, where the army was then camping.
    2. Letter not found.
    3. Saratoga.
    4. Brandywine and Germantown.
    5. Mud Island was near the Pennsylvania shore, Red Bank in New Jersey. He must have meant that they communicated by water or, possibly, he spoke of the chevaux-de-frise across the river between them.
    6. Donop's attack and the burning of the ships is discussed in note, NG to Col. Christopher Greene, 26 October, above.
    7. Despite the enterprise proving "fruitless," Washington lauded McDougall, Sullivan, Greene, and their men "for the fortitude and chearfulness with which they went thro' the night marches and fatigues." (Fitzpatrick, GW, 9: 422)
    8. Gen. John Vaughan was headed up the Hudson in mid-October in a vain attempt to relieve Burgoyne. He burned the village of Esopus, but the next day his heavy transports were stopped when his pilots refused to proceed in shallow water. (Willcox, Clinton, p. 188.)
    9. She was still with the Abraham Lotts.

Council of General Officers

At a Council of War held at Head Quarters at Whitpain [Pa.] 29th October 1777.

Present His Excellency The Commander in Chief

Major Generals	Brigadier Generals
Sullivan	Varnam
Greene	Wayne
Stephen	Mughlenberg
Marquis Fayette	Weedon
McDougall	Huntington
Brigadier Generals	Conway

Maxwell   Pulaski
Smallwood
Knox

His Excellency informed the Board That the ⟨Enemy's⟩ whole force, according to best estimate he could form, founded on general returns of their army, which had accidently fallen into his hands, bearing every mark of authenticity, and from probable calculations of such changes as may have happened since the date of them, amounted to about 10,000 rank and file, present fit for duty. That their main body by the last accounts were in and near Philadelphia. That they had established several batteries on Province Island, opposite to Fort Mifflin, from which, they continually annoyed the garrison there; but hitherto without any material effect. That they had on the 22d instant attempted to carry Red Bank by storm, but were repulsed with considerable loss.[1] That the day following several of their ships of war drew up against Fort Mifflin, which in conjunction with their batteries beforementioned began a severe attack upon the fort; but were compelled to quit the entreprise and retire with loss. That, however, notwithstanding the obstacles they encounter in the River obstructions, they have found means to open a communication with their ships by way of Tinicum Island.

He further informed them, That our whole force at this time amounted by the last returns to 8313 Continental Troops and 2717 Militia, rank and file, present fit for duty. That besides these, were the garrisons at Fort Island and Red Bank; the former consisting of about 300 Continental Troops, the latter 350: in addition to which a detachment of three hundred militia marchd the 26th to reinforce the two posts, also the troops on the other side the Schulkill in number about 500 Militia, under Brigadier General Potter.[2]

That this force was likely soon to suffer a diminution of 1986 Militia, by the expiration of the term of service for which those from Virginia and Maryland engaged.

That on the other hand, He had called upon the State of Pensylvania in the strongest terms, to afford all the assistance and reinforcement in its power to this army; and that he had also written to Generals Dickinson, Foreman and Newcomb, pressing them in the most earnest manner, to endeavour to collect all the militia of the State of New Jersey, that can possibly be spared from other objects in the neighbourhood of Red Bank, as an additional aid and security to that post; but was uncertain what degree of success these different applications might have.

He finally informed them that by advices from the Northward, it appeared that General Burgoygne and his whole army had capitulated to General Gates, on condition of being permitted to return to

Great Britain, and not bearing arms again in North America during the present contest. That by a letter of the 25th instant from General Dickinson, there was reason to beleive Sir Harry Clinton and the forces with him had returned down the North River; and that the Troops heretofore stationed at Rhode Island were arrived at New York.[3] That he was not able to afford any precise information of the dispositions made by Generals Gates and Putnam, in consequence of the forementioned events; but had heard that General Gates had detached two brigades to join Governor Clinton at Esopus.

Observing that under these circumstances, he had called a council to consult and resolve upon the measures best to be persued; He accordingly requested the sentiments of the Gentlemen present on the following subjects—

Question   Whether it will be prudent in our present circumstances and with our present strength to attempt by a general attack to dislodge the enemy from Philadelphia?

Answer   It will not.

Question   If prudent, and in case we are unsuccessful, where shall we retreat to?

Answer   Precluded by the above answer.

Question   If not thought eligible, what general disposition of the army had best take place, till the season forces us from the field?

Answer   The army should take post on the ground a little to our left, which has been reconnoitred and reported by the Engineers: and sufficient reinforcements should be sent to the garrisons of Red-bank and Fort Mifflin to complete the number of men requisite for their defence.

Question   Supposing the enemy to keep possession of the City, where, and in what manner, shall the Continental troops be canntoned, when they can no longer keep the field?

Answer   Deferred.

Question   What measures can be adopted to cover the country near the enemy and prevent their drawing supplies from it during the Winter?

Answer   Deferred

Question   Can any, and what succours may with propriety be drawn from the Northern armies at this time?

Answer   Succours should be drawn from the ⟨Northern⟩ armies to consist of twenty Regiments: fifteen of Massachusettes, three of New Hampshire and Lee's and Jackson's regiments.

The deliberations on the foregoing subjects finished, The Commander in Chief proceeded to the following questions.

Question   As the whole time of the Adjutant General seems to be engrossed with other duties, Will the office of Inspector General to our army for the purpose, principally, of establishing and seeing practiced one uniform system of manual and manoeuvres, be adviseable?

Answer   Such an officer is adviseable. The manual, manoeuvres, or any regulations to be established; previously to be settled or agreed to by the Commander in chief, or a board of officers, appointed by him for that purpose.

Question   Should Regimental promotions extend only to the rank of a captaincy or to that of a Majority?

Answer   Promotions should be regimental as high as captains inclusively. All from that rank in the line of the state.

Question   Will it be consistent with propriety or policy to allow soldiers the reward offered to others for apprehending deserters?

Answer   The reward should be allowed to soldiers.

Question   The commissaries complain of the number and disproportion of the rations issued to the troops and at the same time of the exorbitant price of all kinds of spirits, owing to the impositions of the suttlers on the soldiery. What regulations or remedies can be applied to rectify these abuses?

Answer   Deferred[4]

Question   Col Frazer, in a letter of the 9th instant ⟨having⟩ represented that he had "liberty to ⟨mention⟩ it as General Howes earnest ⟨desire,⟩ that a general exchange of prisoners should take place on equitable terms, or that the officers, prisoners of war on both sides should be released and have liberty to go to any place ⟨in⟩ possession of their friends on their paroles." What measures might be ⟨proper⟩ for us to take in consequence of ⟨that⟩ information?

Answer   Deferred[5]
  Jno Sullivan   J. M Varnum
  Nath Greene   Ant'y Wayne

Adam Stephen   P. Muhlenberg
Le Ma'quis de Lafayette   G. Weedon
Alexr McDougall   Jed Huntington
W. Smallwood   T. Conway
H Knox

DS (Washington Papers: DLC). Portions in angle brackets taken from Varick
Tr., Washington Papers, DLC.
    1. See note, NG to Christopher Greene, 26 October above.
    2. Washington's totals are considerably smaller than he reported in his official
returns on 3 November. (Lesser, *Sinews*, pp. 50–51)
    3. This was false.
    4. This question was answered later to the effect that sutlers should not continue
in the army after 5 November, and in the meantime the commissaries should take all
liquor from sutlers "at a reasonable price," or if sutlers do not agree on price, liquors
should be removed. (Washington Papers, DLC)
    5. This question, too, was answered later: if Gen. Howe is not willing to go into a
general exchange, an exchange of officers should follow; if this cannot be agreed on,
they should be released on parole. (On the problem of prisoner exchange, see above,
Washington to NG, 18 and 22 March 1777.)

Report of a Court of Enquiry

Camp [Whitpain, Pa.] Nov 1st 1777

The Court of enquiry having fully examined into the Charges exhibited against Major Genl Stephens,[1] for Unofficer like behavour on the march from the Clove; In the actions at Brandywine and Germantown; Also for drunkeness. Beg leave to report the substance of the Evidences, as follows:

To the first charge there are several unquestionable Evidences of their being great confusion upon the march from the Clove to the Delaware, that General Stephens frequently contradicted by verbal orders his own written ones. He issued in orders that the first Brigade which got ready to march in the morning should march in front; this produced some altercation and great confusion. On this March the Genl was often seen intoxicated, which was generally supposed the cause of the confusion and disorder which pr[e]vailed. At Howels Ferry the General was seen in open view of all the soldiers very drunk taking snuff out of the Boxes of strumpets.

To these positive Evidences the General produced many positive ones of good repute, who say they were with the Troops on that march and neither saw the confusion afforementioned or the General in the least intoxicated with Liquor, altho they saw him at the very places where he was said to be drunk. Most of his Family and several others who frequented his Table declare they have not seen the General intoxicated this Campaign.

The Evidences produced in support of the second Charge against the General in the Action of Brandywine and those he brought in justification of himself, all serve to prove the General did not pay that general attention to his Division which might be expected from an officer of his Command.

The Evidences produced in support of the third Charge respecting the Generals conduct in the Action of Germantown and those which the General brought in justifycation, all serve to prove that the General was not with his Division during the Action. The Evidences also prove their stand might have been made on the retreat at White Marsh Church, and that it was necessary to cover straglers which were coming in. General Stephens was the oldest Officer on the Ground to whom application was made by General Scott and others to have the Troops formed and to post some Artillery to check the Advances of the Enemy; But the General went off under pretence to reconoitre ordering off the Artillery at the same Time and left his Division behind; for want of this necessary Disposition tis supposed many Stragglers fell into the Enemys Hands.

The General produced many Evidences to prove he did not shrink from danger in the actions at Brandywine and Germantown, and that he always appeared cool and delivered his orders with deliberation and firmness becoming the dignity of an Officer and shew no uncommon fear of personal Danger.

NATHANIEL GREENE PRESIDT   WM RICHARDSON

WM SMALLWOOD   WM RUSSELL

HENRY KNOX

Cy (NcD).

1. Gen. Adam Stephen (often miscalled Stephens by his contemporaries) had been in trouble with Washington before these charges. (See note, Council of War, 2 May 1777, above; his role at Germantown is discussed in note, NG's Orders, 7 October 1777, above.) Stephen was tried by a courtmartial, Gen. Sullivan president. After several sessions the court found him guilty "of unofficerlike behaviour, in the retreat from Germantown, owing to inattention, or want of judgement; and that he has been frequently intoxicated since in the service, to the prejudice of good order and military discipline." (Fitzpatrick, *GW*, 10: 89) On 4 December, Washington put Lafayette in command of his division. The dismissal of Virginia's highest ranking officer led to months of jockeying for rank among the Virginia brigadiers. See note, NG to Weedon, 27 April 1778, below.

To Catharine Greene

Camp at Sandy Run [Pa.][1] 12 miles from Phi[ladelphia]

My dear   No 2d 1777

Col Cary by whom I write tells me [he] had the pleasure of spending several days very agreeably at Mr Lotts[2] at whist that you was his partner and that you was in a good state of health. I am very happy to hear you are so agreeably employd. I wish the campaign was over that I might come and partake of your diversions but we must first give Mr How a twiging and then for a joyous winter of pleasant Folly.

There is a report that General Spencer has made a dissent upon Rhode Island and taken 800 prisoners, near thirty pices of Artillery, a large quantity of stores, provisions, salt &c &c. I wish it may be true.[3] I think its probable, yet I fear the Authenticity of the report. We have been advanceing towards the enimy today and I feel exceedingly fatigued in rideing about to reconnoiter the new camp. It is said the enemy were in motion today. Perhaps we may get to fisty cuffing of it in the morning. They have made no further attempts upon our forts as yet altho they threaten em dayly. Count Donop the Hessian General is dead of his wounds, he lamented before his death, his folly in being concernd in the American war.

Our Head Quarters are at one Mr Emlens close in the Neighbourhood of my quarters, there are several sweet pretty quaker girls. If the spirit should move and love invite who can be answerable for the consequences. I know this wont alarm you because you have such an high opinion of my virtue. It is very well you have. You remember the prayer of the Saints, tempt me not above what I am able to bare. But I promise you to be as honest as ever I can.

I have enclosd you Sixty Dollars please to pay Mr Darby the Doctor for the Spurrs Mr Lotts sent me and tell him I am greatly oblige to him as I was in a Hudibrastick state before with one spur for ⟨two⟩ heels. General Weaden was in the ⟨same situation⟩. We are now both made whole, and I can assure you repairs in the camp are very difficult. Remember me kindly to Mr and Mrs Lott to Mrs [Living]ston[4] and all the young ladies.

[*Not signed*]

AL (NjP). Portions in angle brackets from Nightingale transcripts.
1. The army had just moved from Whitpain to Sandy Run (or Whitemarsh) that day, a strong defensive position on three hills, along which the troops began to dig trenches and build huts. The army remained there until 11 December. (Reed, *Campaign*, 363–80)
2. She had been a guest at the Abraham Lotts since July.
3. Gen. Joseph Spencer had been poised to attack when a storm intervened. See note, NG to his brother Christopher, 5 January 1778, below.
4. The Lotts's daughter, wife of NG's former aide, William Smith Livingston.

To Major John Clark, Jr.[1]

Dr Sir   Camp at Sandy Run [Pa.] Nov 4th 1777

This moment accidentally I fell in with Martin your boy, by whom I learn you are at Col Thomases. By Martin I have the pleasure to hear also your wound is got well and your state of ill health recoverd, of which I am heartily glad. I wrote you sometime since in answer to yours covering the Samples of cloth of Col. Donaldsons. I directed the letter to the care of the Col. agreeable to your direction and doubt not it has come safe to hand before this. I wrote for a coat of the blue and a pattern for a Jacket and breeches of the buff, and a pattern for a pair of breeches and waiscoat of the buff for General Varnum. Please to get the whole and trimings for mine. I have got my saddle repaird at Bethlehem and will give you no further trouble about it; and am much oblige to you for the attention you paid already to the affair. If you are not necessarily detaind where you are, and your health permits I could wish you to join the family as its very probable there will be some very serious operations before the close of the campaign. I dont wish you to run any risque to the injury of your health, of which you can best judge whether you are in a condition to under go the fatiguing duty of an active campaign. I am Sir with sinsere regards your most obedient and humble Servt

N GREENE

ALS (RG 46, Records of the U.S. Senate, 15A-G1: DNA).
    1. Clark, NG's aide, had been gathering intelligence for Washington, as is seen in NG's letter to him below on 5 November.

To Major John Clark, Jr.

Dr Sir

Camp at Sandy Run [Pa.] Nov 5th 2 O Clock
PM [17]77

    Yours of last evening was this moment handed,[1] I have receivd but one letter from you since you left me, neither have I wrote you more than once, not knowing where to direct to you. I saw your letter to His Excellency yesterday and am glad you are so usefully employed, intelligence is the life of every thing in war, your letter containd the most accurate state of the enemies situation and intentions that I have seen or heard off. I dont wish you by any means to quit your station as long as you remain infirm, or you can procure necessary information for the General.[2]

    There has been a long and severe cannonade in the river. It has ceast about half an hour since, the result we shall not learn perhaps until tomorrow. I hope the garrison will remain firm. The happy change in the Northern affairs promises us an agreeable issue to the campaign in this quarter.[3] Strong reinforcements will speedily be drawn to the aid of this Army, which I hope will enable His Excellency to give the enemy a decisive blow.

    I wrote you respecting the cloth for a coat and Jacket and breeches for myself and a pattern for a Jacket and breeches for General Varnum, if you can procure the whole and send me, you will oblige me. Make my compliments agreeable to Mrs Clarke and believe me to be with sincere regard your most Obedient and very humble Servant

N GREENE

ALS (Rosenbach Museum, Philadelphia).
1. Letter not found.
2. Washington was especially grateful to Clark for seeing that Gen. Howe received a letter giving false figures on American troop strength. (Washington to Clark, 4 November, Fitzpatrick, *GW*, 10: 8–9.)
3. Burgoyne's surrender.

To [　　　　　]

Camp [Whitemarsh, Pa.] near Philadelphia Nov 7 1777
These may certify that the report circulated about camp that Lieutenant Colonel Guerney carried on a correspondence with the enimy is entirely without foundation.[1] I being directed by His Excellency General Washington to examin into the circumstances of the report was astonished to find it so wholely groundless so as not to leave the least trace for suspicion, and this I declare upon my honor, given under my Hand the day aforesaid[2]

NATH GREENE

ADS (PCarlD).
1. Francis Gurney, a prominent Pennsylvanian of the Eleventh Pa. Regiment, had resigned 22 October. After the war he held important civil and military posts, including that of brigadier general of the militia. (*PMHB*, 47 (1923): 175–76)
2. Col. Richard Humpton, Gurney's superior, was present at the examination and noted at the bottom of the document that "nothing appear'd that could give the least ground to suspect that Col. Gurney had ever given any intelligence or assistance to the Enemy." The rumor arose, he said, from some British soldiers telling a woman in Germantown that their army received intelligence from a general officer, a lieutenant colonel and a captain. The woman mentioned that a Lt. Col. Gurney had recently resigned; someone in her presence confused him with the supposed traitor.

Council of War

[Whitemarsh, Pa., 8 November 1777. Present in addition to Washington: Maj. Gens. Sullivan, Greene, Lafayette, and McDougall; Brig. Gens. Maxwell, Knox, Wayne, Weedon, Woodford, Scott, Conway, Huntington, and Irvine. Washington reported that among reinforcements coming from Peekskill were 1,600 Massachusetts Militia under Gen. Jonathan Warner. If the enemy should make an attack on the Delaware forts, he asked if it "would be proper with our present Force to fall down [i.e., go down the river] and attack the Enemy in their Lines near Philadl?" The answer was "In the Negative unanimously." FC (Washington Papers: DLC) 1 p.]

General Officers to George Washington

[Whitemarsh, Pa., 10 November, 1777[1]]
The Board of General Officers assembled at General Greenes quarters by order of the Commander in chief beg leave to represent to His Excellency that the Rations allowd to the Army in future ought to be as follows. Vizt.

2/.	One Pound and one quarter of a Pound of Beef, or One Pound Pork or 1¼ lb Salt Fish
/5d	1¼ lb Flour or soft bread, or 1 lb hard bread
/7d	Half a Gill Rum or Whiskey pr day in lieu of Beer
/4d	Half a Pint Rice, or a Pint Indian Meal pr week
3/ 4	Three Pounds Candles to 100 Men pr week. Soap agreeable to the late Regulation of Congress.

They also beg leave to represent that upon Inquiry from the Commissary, they find that a Ration according to the above establishment will amount at the lowest Rate to three Shillings and four pence, exclusive of the Soap and Candles, which ought to be paid by the Commissaries for each Ration retain'd since the 1st of May last. The exhorbitant price at which the necessaries of life are purchased by the Army, will render the above Establishment absolutely necessary, otherwise the Officers whom Congress designed should draw four Rations, will not with the Ration-money heretofore allowed them, be able to purchase one, and the Soldiers will suffer in proportion. This has already had a pernicious effect, and caused a number of valuable Officers who have found themselves unable longer to subsist in the Army to resign their Commissions. Many others are complaining of the hardship occasioned by the former Regulations and unless a Remedy is applied, will follow the example of others by quitting the service. The Price of the Rations was formerly fix'd by calculating what the several Articles which Compose a Ration could be purchased for. This inequity should ever be the standard for fixing the Price of Rations, and the Commissary should be directed to pay every Officer and Soldier who have Rations due to them, so much money as those Rations would have cost the Continent if they had been purchased and deliver'd out. They also beg leave to recommend that the Commissaries be order'd to keep their accounts ready posted up, that the Officers who are order'd upon Detachment, or to a separate

Department, may not be delayed in drawing the money due for their Rations.

The purchasing Commissary should once every three months deliver in a Return at Head Quarters of the medium Price at which he has purchased Provisions for the three months preceding—such Return with an Estimate of the Price of Rations should be published in the Army that no Dispute may arise respecting the Price of Rations. That in all settlements with the Commissaries for back Rations, the Article drawn in part by the Officer or Soldier shall be reduced to Rations and deducted out of the whole he was intitled to receive and the Remainder paid for at the price established at the time they became due, except those which have become due since the 1st May last.

It is recommended that the Provision Returns particularize the number of Officers, as well as Soldiers for whom provisions are to be drawn, and what number of Rations to each Officer, that these Returns may be compared with the weekly Returns.

Sign'd

JNO SULLIVAN	A'Y WAYNE
NATH GREENE	P MUHLENBERG
STIRLING	G WEEDON
AR ST CLAIR	WM WOODFORD
W MAXWELL	JED HUNTINGTON
W SMALLWOOD	TH CONWAY
H KNOX	

DS (Washington Papers: DLC).

1. The report is undated, but in his general orders of 9 November, Washington directed the Council to meet at 10:00 A.M. the next day "at General Greene's quarters, to settle the rations. The General Officers will attend this, in preference to any other duty, and make report as soon as they have finished it." (Fitzpatrick, *GW*, 10: 32) He enclosed their report in a letter to Congress on 11 November with the notation that the regulations they proposed "appear to me to be just and necessary." He added that for want of changing the old valuation he believed several officers had left the service. (Ibid., 10: 38)

To Miss Susanna Livingston [?][1]

Dear Miss   Camp near Philadelphia Novem 11, 1777

I was much pleas'd with the receipt of your letter of the 27th of October.[2] I kindly thank you for your charitable allowance for my not writing, and at the same time can with great truth assure you that you have not been more liberal in your opinion than I deserve.

This has been an active and a severe campaign, few officers that have discharg'd their duty have had many leisure hours to indulge the pleasures of private friendships. I have wrote to but four persons since the enemy landed at the Head of *Elk*.[3] Before that period I had a numerous correspondence. I have not even wrote a letter to a member of Congress since, so busily have I been employ'd. I found myself under the necessity to quit the pen or neglect my duty and of two evils I chose the least.

I hope you dont think I have a british Soul, that feels no more of friendship than profession, tun'd[?] to time and place. I have not arrivd to that degree of politeness, neither do I wish I ever may. Altho I have not wrote you I have thought on you thousands and thousands of times. I trust I have too grateful a heart to be forgetful of the civilities received from your family.

I perfectly agree with you in Sentiment that the glorious events to the Northerd leaves us but little room to repine at the loss of Ty-conderoga. General Gates has immortalliz'd himself. General Schuy-ler has been peculiarly unfortunate; the foundation of all General Gates successes were pland under G Schuylers direction, and some important events had absolutely taken place. General Gates came in just timely to reap the laurels and rewards.[4] Great credit is due to all the Northern Army, but that army has been much stronger than ours and a far less force to contend with. The New England and York Militia deserve the thanks of the whole continent for their spirited and gallant behavior. If the Southern Militia had lent the same aid to his Excellency that the Northern Militia did to General Gates Mr How never could have got possession of the Rome of America. We have had two severe and general actions besides many warm skirmishes in the course of the Campaign. Our force has been too small to cover the country and secure the city. The Inhabitants so very unfriendly, has render'd the task still more difficult. The inhabitants from the Head of Elk to Philadelphia in general are as much the friends of G How as one britain can be to another.[5]

The enemy are greatly distresst in Philadelphia and the Inhabit-ants still more so. Our forts and fortifications in the river proves greater obstacles to their plan than they ever dreamt off. God only knows how the campaign will terminate, but I expect some very serious events will take place notwithstanding it is late in the season.

The Enemies scandulous expedition up the North River justly characterises the people; their foot steps are mark't with desolation; like the true instruments of vice they spread misery where ever they go.[6] America, like virtues fair form, is chequerd with their polluted hands. God grant they may soon meet (if possible) with a punishment propotionable to their crimes.

I am very sorry for the sufferings of your friends, but nothing has given me such a contemptable opinion of the enemy as their malice towards the lady of the great Montgomery;[7] their ruining her fair dwellings and adding new distress to the poor widow, betrays the bitterness of their souls and its malice in its true colours. I wish as many curses may attend em, as was marshall'd out by old Emulphies mentiond in Tristram Shandy by Doc Slop.

By some very late accounts from Europe there is the greatest reason to think there is a french war.[8] Capt Weeks commanding one of the continental Vessels with a number of french Ships with American commisions took fifty Sail in the Channel of England of [off] the Jamaca fleet and carried them into France. Lord Hornsby made a peremtory demand of the Ships and thier Captors and was as peremtorily refusd, upon which he was recald. This intelligence comes by the way of the West Indies.

I just escaped an inglorious exit yesterday by a very vitious Horse with tory principles. He first started and then set to kick up as if the devil was in him. This he repeated and kept gaining ground towards a large stone mill; when he got within about ten or twelve feet of the building, he kickt up behind and fell upon his fore knees and threw me over his Head with my head within eight inches of the wall. One foot farther would have given me a passport. Dont you think this betrays a tory principle? This accident has given me an oportunity to write you as I am renderd incapable of doing field duty.

I long to Visit Morristown and relax a few weeks from the horrors of war. Make my complements agreeable to all the family. I have a volunteer aid with me from Maryland, one Mr Loyd, a young Gentleman of family and fortune.[9] He is a fine young Gentleman. Tell all the young ladies of the neighbourhood that stand candidates for matrimony to hold themselves in readiness. Major Blodget is well and hearty. He is as brave as Hector. Major Blodget unfortunately got wounded about the time the enemy landed. Major Burnet got part of his Hair shot away in the action at Germantown. Yours affectionately

N GREENE

If your brother[10] wishes to continue in the army and there is a vacancy that I can serve him in obtaining I shall readily aid his application with my small influence.

ALS (MHi).
1. The contents of the letter indicate the probable recipient to be the daughter of Gov. William Livingston of New Jersey and the sister of William Smith Livingston, a former aide to NG. (For NG's influence on his army career, see Livingston to NG, 23 October 1778, below.) NG and Catharine had met Susanna at the home of Lord Stirling, her uncle, and had visited her at the Abraham Lotts, whose daughter married her brother. Susanna later married John Cleves Symmes. (DAB)
2. Letter not found.
3. On 25 August.
4. NG shared Washington's pique that Gates had by-passed the commander in chief in reporting the victory at Saratoga. See note, NG to Washington, 15 October, above.

5. Howe had not found them so. Neutral would have been a more fitting word; many of them were pacifist Quakers.

6. He apparently refers to the destruction of Esopus; see note 7 below.

7. Mrs. Janet Montgomery was the widow of Gen. Richard Montgomery, who had been killed at Quebec in 1775. The daughter of Robert R. Livingston, and a relative of Susanna's, she had continued to live on her estate of "Grassmere" near Esopus, which the British had burned in mid-October. (*DAB*; see note, NG to Jacob, 27 October, above.)

8. The reports were premature; the French did not enter the war until the summer of 1778.

9. In his orders of 22 September 1777, Washington had confirmed James Lloyd's appointment as a voluntary aide. (*PMHB*, 34 (1910): 473.)

10. William Smith Livingston; see note 1 above.

To George Washington

Dr Sir

At Mr Morris [Pa.][1]

Nov 14th 8 oClock PM 1777

We have just returned from reconnoitering the grounds about Darby, the Islands below and up to the middle ferry. We purpose to go out again in the morning. From the present view Darby appears the only eligible position for the army for the purpose of their crossing the river. It is the opinion of several of the gentlemen that the enemy may be best dislodged from the Islands by [a] detachment, others are of opinion that it would be dangerous unless the party was coverd by the army, but all are of opinion it is practicable either the one way or the other and considering the good consequences that will result from it, it ought to be attempted. Darby is not the most eligible post I ever saw, but it is not so dangerous as to discourage the attempt to relieve Fort Mifflin.[2]

The flag was flying at Fort Mifflin at sunset this evening. There has been a very severe cannonade today. Inclosd is a letter from Col Greene respecting the condition of the fort.[3] The enimy have got up two or three vessels into the Schuylkill. They were attempting to get up a two and thirty gun frigate between Hog Island and Province Island. By the best observation we could make her guns were taken out and follow'd her in a sloop. She did not get up, but what was the reason I know not. The Comodore[4] should be directed to sink a vessel or two in the new channel as soon as possible and the fort encouraged to hold out to the last. There is but one bridge over the Schuylkill and that is at the middle ferry. I examined the river myself from the falls to the mouth.

The enimy have got a chain of redoubts with abatis between them from one river to the other, part of this is from information and part from my own observation. The Schuylkill is very deep and [ra]p-aid, too deep for foot to ford it. The bridge at Mattisons [Matsons] Ford is not in so great forwardness as I could wish, the commanding

officer sais it will be done in three days, but a bridge of waggons can
be thrown over for the foot to pass if that should not be done.

The enimy are greatly discouraged by the forts holding out so
long and it is the general opinion of the best of the citizens that the
enimy will evacuate the city if the fort holds out until the middle of
next week.

There is plenty of forage in this country especially about Darby.
We purpose to examin the ground a little more about Darby tomorrow
and if possible return tomorrow evening. From the best accounts we
can get there is but five Ships with troops on board in the river. I am
[with] great respect your Excellencies most Obedient Servt

NATH GREENE

ALS (Washington Papers: DLC).
    1. Morris has not been identified, but his house was probably near Darby (south of
Philadelphia), since NG planned to return to the Darby area the following morning.
    2. Washington had sent NG to observe the siege of Ft. Mifflin on Mud Island from
as close a vantage point as he dared go. Although only a week before, the Council of
War had voted against the army's going to the aid of the fort, Washington wanted NG's
opinion on whether something still might be done from the Pennsylvania shore. NG
ran considerable risk from British patrols in carrying out the mission.
    Ft. Mifflin, unbeknown to NG, was nearing the end of one of the most gallant
defenses of the entire war. His mission was too late. The crude fort, considered by
many as a "burlesque upon the art of fortification," had been under increasingly heavy
bombardment for the past three weeks. (Reed, *Campaign*, pp. 342) Except for a brief
interlude under Baron d'Arendt, the fort and its four hundred weary, rain-soaked men
had been under the command of Lieut. Col. Samuel Smith, with the aid of a resourceful
and tireless French engineer— François Louis de Fleury. By seniority Smith was under
Col. Greene at Ft. Mercer, but he was essentially independent. To Washington the forts
had become objects to be held with fierce determination. If they could hold out, the
British would be unable to maintain their army in Philadelphia. Washington took over
the general direction of the river defense from his headquarters at Whitpain, but on 28
October he sent Gen. Varnum across to New Jersey to take charge of the entire shore
defenses. Varnum's orders, however, were cautiously written so as not to interfere too
closely with Christopher Greene's and Samuel Smith's on-the-spot judgment. (Fitzpatrick, *GW*, 9: 455–57) Commodore Hazelwood's relation to Varnum was not clear.
The Pennsylvania navy, in fact, seemed at times to be operating independently of
Washington.
    On 7 November the British began to step up their bombardment. It was the
following day that the Council of War at Washington's headquarters voted against
sending the main army to Ft. Mifflin's defense. (See Council of War, 8 November,
above.) On 10 November the assault began in earnest. From floating batteries, from
artillery on Province Island, and from ships of the line down-stream from the chevaux-
de-frise, there was incessant cannonading night and day. One shallow-draft ship, the
Vigilant, came up and fired point blank from twenty yards. Varnum complained that
Hazelwood's navy was of little help, but, in truth, there was little that Hazelwood's
heterogeneous collection of small vessels could do to help at this point. When NG
went to observe on 14 November, he was too far away to see that little was left of the
fort but piles of mud and heaps of splintered debris, behind which the cold, hungry
men huddled, still firing an occasional cannon with their dwindling ammunition. That
night the ill Smith and his weary men were removed to Red Bank and replaced by fresh
troops from Connecticut. Thayer and Fleury stayed on the island.
    Varnum still believed the men could hold out longer, but on 15 November what
was left of Mud Island was turned into a virtual hell. The indomitable Simeon Thayer,

NG's friend and subordinate from the early days of the war, agreed with his council that they must abandon Mud Island, and Varnum had to go along with the decision. That night (the fifteenth) boats took them across to Red Bank. Thayer was the last one to leave. The heroic defense had, at least, kept Howe from taking any other action. It also restored some pride to Washington's army, which was badly in need of such a lift in the face of their defeats and Gates's spectacular victories in the North. (The defense of Ft. Mifflin is covered thoroughly in Reed, *Campaign*, 320–50; see also Smith, *The Delaware*, 28–36.)

3. Letter not found.
4. John Hazelwood.

To Henry Marchant[1]

Dr Sir   Camp [Whitemarsh] near Philadelphia Nov 17, 1777

Since you left Philadelphia I have neither seen or heard from you—a line from you when at leisure will be very acceptable. I am glad to hear you have almost got through the difficult business of confederation.[2] I wish it may serve as a lasting cement to the union of the states.

The operations of this campaign have been various—the successes to the northerd glorious—the struggles of the army great, and altho' we have not been as fortunate as that to the northerd, when the comparative force to each is known and considered, the difference of the country and the people where the operations have been carried on, the merit of the one will not be found inferior to the other. I am very sorry to find the public so illy informed with regard to the operations here, both with respect to men and events. We fight by main strength. It would give me pleasure if some of your body were always with the army. It would enable them to judge of men and measures, to reward merit, and remedy evils. Private friendship often sounds the trumpet of praise and imposes upon the credulity and good nature of your board.[3]

The successes to the northerd have given great relief to the northern states; but the American affairs are in a most critical situation, owing to the universal dislike to service. I think I never saw the army so near dissolving since I have belonged to it. The officers cannot maintain themselves, and from the present temper prevailing in general determine to leave the service at the close of the campaign.

Military rank being conferred upon people of all orders so lavishly has rendered its value of much less importance than formerly. It was once considered a jewel of great value, but it now begins to be held in light esteem.[4] I shall write you fully upon several matters in a few days, and shall only add for the present that I am with sincere regard, Your most obedient, humble servt,

N. GREENE

From an unidentified newspaper clipping among GWG transcripts, CSmH.

1. Marchant had asked for a leave of absence from Congress the day NG wrote him; he did not return until June 1778. (*JCC*, 9: 932; 11: 575)

2. After a year of haggling, Congress on 15 November finally approved the Articles of Confederation and submitted them to the states for ratification. (*JCC*, 9: 932–35) It was 1781, however, before the last state—Maryland—approved them.

3. The Board of War.

4. A reference no doubt to the promotion of James Wilkinson; see NG to Laurens, 12 January 1778, below.

To Catharine Greene

My dear   Fort Lanes End near Bristol [Pa.] No 21 [20], 1777[1]

I am now on my march for Red Bank fort. Lord Cornwallis crost over into the Jerseys day before yesterday to invest that place with a large body of troops. I am in hopes to have the pleasure to meet his Lordship.[2] This excentrick movement will lengthen out the campaign for some weeks at least and it is possible may transfer the seat of war for the winter. The enemy are now geting up their Stores and fortifying the city of Philadelphia as strong as possible. The weather begins to get severe and campaigning of it disagreeable, but necessity obliges us to keep the field for some time.

I wrote you in my last that Major Abales [Abeel's] boy would get you a pattern for a cloak. If he does not you must try to get one for yourself.

I had a bad fall from my horse some time since, but have got entirely over it, all except a sprain in my wrist.

How does Mrs Livingston bare the absence of her husband? Is she as much of a philosophess as yourself?

I lodge in a fine country House tonight. I could wish for your company if you could return in the morning. The Marquis of Fyette [Lafayette] is in company with me. He has left a young wife and a fine fortune of 14,000 pounds Sterling per annum to come and engage in the cause of liberty. This is a noble enthusia[s]m. He is a most sweet temperd young gentleman. He purposes to visit Boston this Winter. If so youl have an opportunity to see him.

How is Mr and Mrs Lott? I wish to spend an evening by their social fireside and dance with the young ladies. Your brother I am told behavd the hero the other day in the attack on Red Bank. Present my complements to all the family and believe me to be with affect your

N GREENE

ALS (NjP).

1. The date should be 20 November; by 21 November NG was in New Jersey. Bristol was on the west bank of the Delaware, some thirty miles due east of the camp at Whitemarsh.

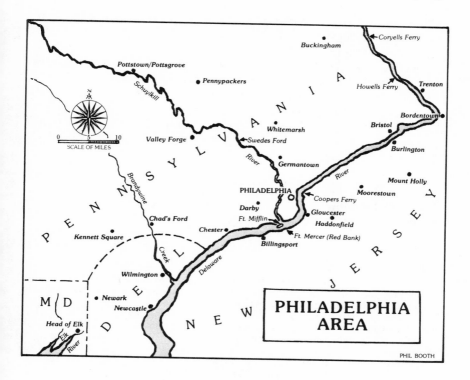

PHIL. BOOTH

2. After the capture of Ft. Mifflin, Gen. Howe sent Cornwallis across the river at Chester (twenty miles below Philadelphia) in order to assault Ft. Mercer at Red Bank from the south. At Billingsport, N.J., he was joined by four thousand troops that had come from New York in transports. (Gruber, *Howe Brothers*, p. 260) The same day that Cornwallis left, Washington put NG in command of all the forces on the Jersey side of the river, which included the brigade of NG's old friend and companion-in-arms, Gen. James M. Varnum. NG took Weedon's and Muhlenberg's brigades with him. By the time they had crossed the river, however, Cornwallis was already within a few miles of Red Bank. Unbeknown to NG, Col. Greene and Gen. Varnum had decided to save what stores they could and to blow up the fort. The same night, Commodore Hazelwood, to the chagrin of the army, burned seventeen of his vessels. It had taken the British two precious months to clear the river of American defenses. Howe took consolation that Philadelphia at last could be supplied by water; Washington and his army could only swallow their bitter disappointment. (See Reed, *Campaign*, pp. 351–58; Smith, *The Delaware*, pp. 38–40.)

To General James M. Varnum

Sir   Burlington [N.J.] 12 oClock Nov 21, 1777
    I make no doubt you are acquainted with the marching of the troops of my division to join you. I am at a loss respecting your

situation, the condition of Fort Mercer, or the operations of the Enemy in the Jerseys. A report prevails here this morning that Fort Mercer is evacuated and the fleet below burnt.[1] Youl please to inform me as to the truth of the reports, where you are, where the enemy is,[2] and where you think a junction of our forces can be easiest form'd, and also if you think an attack can be made upon the enemy with a prospect of success. General Glovers Brigade are on their march to join us and Morgans Corps of rangers. General Huntingtons Brigade I immagin will be with you today.[3] I am Sr with respect Your most Obedient Humble Servt

N GREENE

N B I am a stranger to all the lower part of the Jerseys [which] makes me be so particular.

ALS (NNC).
    1. See note, NG to Catharine, above.
    2. After the evacuation of Red Bank, Varnum had marched to Mt. Holly, some ten miles southeast of NG's quarters at Burlington. Cornwallis's troops were at Red Bank, where they were in the process of destroying the fortifications; the rest of the British troops were between Red Bank and Billingsport to the south.
    3. Washington had earlier recalled Gen. John Glover's brigade and Daniel Morgan's riflemen from Saratoga; Glover himself had remained to help with the British prisoners. Gen. Jedediah Huntington was coming from Washington's main army at Whitemarsh. Lafayette, whose leg wound from Brandywine was not entirely healed, left headquarters on 20 November with a "detachement under Mjor. Gral. Greene." (Lafayette to Henry Laurens, 20 November, Idzerda, *Lafayette Papers*, 1: 155)

To George Washington

Dr Sir   Burlington [N.J.] 5 oClock PM Nov 21 1777
    General Varnum this moment acquaints me that Fort Mercer was evacuated last evening. Comodore Hasselwood [Hazelwood] informs me also that the greater part if not all the fleet except the thirteen Gallies were burnt this morning; one or two of the smallest vessels attempted to pass the city and could not effect it, one was set on fire and one other fell into the enemies hands owing to the matches going out. The People made their escape. My division arrivd on the other side of the river about ten this morning but the want of scows to get over the Waggons will prevent our marching until the morning. The greater part of the Night if not the whole will be employd in geting over the baggage and artillery.
    General Varnum has retreated to Mount Holly. I purpose to see him and General Huntington early in the morning. If it is practicable to make an attack upon the enemy it shall be done; but I am afraid the enemy will put it out of my power as they can so easily make us take such a circuitous march by takeing up the bridge over Timber Creek. I

cannot promise any thing until I learn more of the designs of the enemy their strength and the position they are in. If it is possible to make an attack upon em with a prospect of success it shall be done. Col Shrieve[1] was with me this afternoon about turning out the Militia. I wish he may succeed, but from the temper of the People there appears no great prospect. I have heard nothing from General Glovers brigade. I hope Col Morgans Corps of light troops will be on in the morning and Capt Lees troop of light Horse.[2]

The fleet are greatly disgusted at the reflections thrown out against the officers; the Comodore[3] thinks the officers are greatly injurd, he asserts they did their duty faithfully. I am with great respect your Excellencys most obedient Servt

N GREENE

N B the Comodore this momt [moment] informs me there is three sloops and a Brigg past safe by the city.

ALS (Washington Papers: DLC).
1. Possibly Col. William Shreve of the New Jersey Militia.
2. On Col. Daniel Morgan's and Gen. John Glover's progress, see below, NG to Washington, and Washington to NG, 22 November.
3. John Hazelwood.

To Colonel Joseph Haight[1]

Sir   Head Quarters Mt Holley [N.J.] 22d Novr 1777
You will remove from hence to Morestown[2] with the Troops under your Command. There you will take Post till further Orders. Keep your Out Guards and Videts advanced so as to annoy, and gain the best Intelligence of the Enemy, Information of which you will from Time to Time give me. Do all in your Power towards removing the Stores from Morestown towards this Place. Keep always two Days Provisions ready cooked beforehand. Make Return of your Troops as soon as possible, and of their Guns, Ammunition, Flints and Accouterments. Relying upon your Activity and Vigilance, I am Sir your most obdt Servant

NATH GREENE

N B You are fully empowered to raise and appoint as many Horse Men from the Militia and others in your Neighborhood as you can to act as Videts. Send them as soon as possible.

ALS (RPB).
1. Haight was a colonel in the N.J. Militia.
2. Moorestown was roughly half way between Mt. Holly and Philadelphia.

To George Washington

Sir   Mount Holly [N.J.] Novr 22d 1777

I came to this Place yesterday morning. The Difficulty of crossing the Baggage over the River prevented its coming up last night. The Boats and Scows at Burlington are under very bad Regulations. Gen. Varnum had retreated as I wrote your Excellency before to this place. He left a party of militia at Haddonfield. I am afraid there was a very considerable Quantity of Stores fallen into the Enemies Hands, but principally belonging to the Fleet. The Enemy and the militia had a small Skirmish at Little Timber Creek Bridge. The Enemy crossed there in the afternoon and encamped. They say they are going to take Post at Haddonfield to cover the lower Counties and open a market from thence. Those Counties are some of the most fertile in the State, from whence great Quantities of Provisions can be drawn. A large number of Boats went [up] to Philadelphia from the Shiping yesterday morning. There were some Soldiers on board of them.

Colo Morgans Corps of Light Infantry advanced this morning for Haddonfield. If the Troops can be got in Readiness I intend to put the whole in motion this afternoon. We are greatly distrest for want of a Party of Light Horse.[1] I must beg your Excellency to forward some as soon as possible.

I have heard nothing from Glover's Brigade.[2] I sent an Express to the commanding officer yesterday, but from the present Situation of things I believe it will be best not to wait their coming up.

Every Piece of Intelligence necessary for my Information with Regard to the movement of the Enemy in the city I must intreat your Excellency to forward to me by Express.

Colo Shreeve will attempt to turn out the militia, but the Commissary's Department is in such a bad Situation and the People so unwilling to furnish Supplies that it will be difficult to subsist a large Body.

A considerable Body of light Horse would be very useful here.

Your Excellency's Letter of the 22d is just come to Hand. You have in this all the Intelligence which I have received. I am with the greatest Respect your Excellency's obdt Servant

NATH GREENE

LS (Washington Papers: DLC).
 1. Washington had ordered Capt. Henry Lee's dragoons to join NG in New Jersey. See Washington's letter to NG the same day, below.
 2. See Washington's second letter, below.

From George Washington

Dear Sir   Head Qurs Whitemarsh [Pa.] 22d Novemr 1777

I am favoured with yours of Yesterday afternoon from Burlington. As you have crossed the River, an attack upon the Enemy's Detachment if it can be made with success, would be a most desirable object. But I must leave the propriety of it entirely to your own judgment. I have heard nothing more of Glover's Brigade than that they were advancing down the Road from Morris Town, I sent an Express to meet them, and to turn them down towards you, but I think you had better dispatch one of your family or an Officer to guide them to you. There are not more than one hundred and seventy of Morgan's Corps fit to march, as they in general want shoes, they went yesterday and will join you I suppose this day. Captn Lee's Troop are not yet come from the other Side of Schuylkill, but they are expected every instant, and will be sent immediately over to you.[1] If you can procure any account that you think may be depended upon of the number that the Enemy detached from Philadelphia, I beg you will send it to me. Or if they send any part of their force back, let me know it instantly. I shall be anxious to hear of every movement of you or the Enemy and I therefore wish to have the most constant advices. I am Dear Sir yours &c

G WASHINGTON

⟨PS I shall order an Express to be stationed at Bristol to bring on your dispatches.⟩

Df (Washington Papers: DLC). Portion in angle brackets taken from Fitzpatrick, GW, 10: 96.

1. Capt. Lee wrote Washington from near Chester, Pa. (south of Philadelphia), the following day. He believed that Cornwallis had recrossed the river to Philadelphia, but he was mistaken. (Lee to Washington, 23 November, Washington Papers; DLC).

From George Washington

Dear Sir   Head Quarters [Whitemarsh, Pa.] 22d November 1777

I have received your Letter of this days date. It does not appear from any account worthy of credit that any part of the Detachment which cross'd the Delaware under Lord Cornwallis has return'd to Philadelphia. I am inclined therefore to wish that you would advance to meet it as much in force as possible and that for this purpose you would use every means to hasten the junction of Glovers Brigade. I am at a loss to account by what mistake Capt Lees Troop is not with you, that was originally intended for the service you mention as it was esteemed the best calculated for it.[1] As a party of horse appears so essential, that or some other will be order'd to join you immediately. I am Sir your Obedt Servt

By an Officer from Glovers Brigade I was informed that it reached Morris Town the evening of the 20th. I sent a message to him to urge them forward and have reason to think they are by this time in your Neighborhood.

DF (Washington Papers: DLC).
1. On Lee, see Washington's first letter of 22 November.

General Greene's Orders

[Mt. Holly, N.J., 23 November 1777. Arms to be put in order, number of tents to be reported. Approves one hundred lashes to each of three men who deserted. *Weedon Orderly Book*, p. 139.]

General Greene's Orders

Head Quarters [Mt. Holly, N. J.]
Nov. 24th 1777.

Majr Boman is to take the Command of the Artillery & all Returns from the different Companies & from the conductors of military Stores to be made to him a Reserve to the Guards consisting of 100 men properly officer'd under the Command of the Majr of the Pickets are to be Posted at the Qr Meeting House who are to Reinforce & support any of Guards that should at any time be attacted. The returns Ordred the Day before Yesterday to be made immediately. All Officers who have any Continental or Impress'd Horses are to make returns to the Qr Mr Genl. The Detachment of Colonel Foremans Regiment to be added to Genl Varnums Brigade. Mr. Chs Lyne is appointed to act Principal Commissary for this Department untill one shall be appointed by Colo Stewart, & the Difft Commissarys are to take Notice accordingly. A serjeant from the Genl Staff Department is Daily to call at Orderly time at the Deputy A. Genls Office that all delays may be avoided as much as Possible & every Order Immediately Executed.

After Orders.

All the Troops to hold themselves in Readiness to march by 7 o'clock Tomorrow morning.[1]

Reprinted from "Muhlenberg Orderly Book," *PMHB*, 35 (1911): 185–86.
1. The after orders were countermanded in his orders of the following day, below.

Colonel William Davies[1] to Colonel Joseph Haight[2]

[Mt. Holly, N.J., 24 November 1777. Has sent "8300 musket cartridges" to be forwarded to Col. (Joseph) Ellis at Haddonfield. Gen. Greene wishes Davies to appoint new guard to conduct them. In a postscript the general (NG) desires officers of First and Sixth Va. Regiments at Moorestown to be ready to march at shortest notice. ALS (RG 93, WRMS, Ms 31887: DNA) 1 p.]

1. Davies was lieutenant colonel of the Fifth Va. Regiment.
2. The address sheet reads "To Colonel Hoit at Moor'stown," but apparently it should have been Haight. See NG to Haight, 22 November, above.

From Colonel Joseph Ellis[1]

Dear Sir   Haddonfield [N.J.] Novr 24th 1777

In complyance with your Letter of yesterday, I send you a state of the Militia under my command, which is about 400 Effective at this place, and about 100 in the neighbourhood before Mantu[a] Creek; the time of Service for which they came out will for the greater part expire in a few days; orders are out for assembling the other Classes so that I hope to keep up the number. As to the Enemy, from the best discoveries we have been able to make, their main strength is at Woodbury, and their lines extend from Manto Creek to Little Timber Creek, an extent of six or Seven miles: their whole force about 5000 Consisting of Brittish, Hessians, and Marines. The Marines are employ'd in distroying the Works at Red Bank; when that is effected they give out they intend moveing their Army upwards to Burlington and Mount Holly. Their Post at Woodbury is advantageous and difficult to attack. Thus you have an account of matters in this quarter. If anything interesting comes to my knowledge I shall transmitt it with all possible speed. I am Sir yr Hb Servt

JOS. ELLIS

N. B. The Enemy have 8 or 9 Field pieces on the different Roads near Woodbury.

Just now receiv'd Intelligence by a person who came thro' part of the Enemy's lines on the upper side of Great Timber Creek who says there is about 300 at and between the two Timber Creeks. Yrs &c

JOS. ELLIS

Cy (Washington Papers: DLC). The letter was enclosed in the first of two that NG wrote to Washington on 24 November, below.
1. Ellis was a colonel in the N.J. Militia.

To George Washington

Dr Sir   Mount Holly [N.J.] Novr 24, 1777

I have nothing new to communicate to your Excellency with Respect to the Motions of the Enemy. They remain or did last night at Woodbury, with a Guard at Timber Creek, consisting of about six hundred men.[1] The Boats that went up, mentioned in my former Letter, I conjecture had on Board the Baggage of the Army; the Soldiers seen on board were the regimental Guards to the Baggage.

The Militia of this State is dwindling to nothing. Gen. Varnum says there was upward of 1400 a few days since; they are reduced now to between seven and eight. Colo Shreeve is gone out to see what Impression he can make upon the People, and to endeavour to draw together as large a Number as possible;[2] but I cannot flatter myself with any considerable reinforcement. I will endeavour to inclose your Excellency a Return of our Strength in Continental and Militia, this afternoon if possible.

We are all ready to advance; but the General Officers think it adviseable, to wait the Return of the first Express sent to Glover's Brigade; to learn the strength and time the Junction may be formed with that Brigade. I have heard nothing where it is, notwithstanding I have sent three Expresses. Capt Lee[3] is not arrived, neither have I heard any thing of him. I could wish if possible, some Horse might be sent, as every Army is an unweildy Body without them; and in this Country, they are more immediately necessary to prevent the Enemy from sending out theirs to collect Stock.

Colo: Cox[4] who is with me at this Place, says, if the Enemy can open a Communication with the three lower Counties, they will be able, independant of all the surrounding Country, to draw Supplies of every kind necessary for the Subsistance of the Army, and Inhabitants of the City of Philadelphia.

Your Excellency observes in your last, you must leave the Propriety of attacking the Enemy to me. Would you advise me to fight them with very unequal Numbers? Most people, indeed all, agree they are near or quite 5000 strong.[5] Our Force is upwards of three, exclusive of the Militia, which may be from seven to eight hundred at most. The situation the Enemy are in, the Ease with which they can receive Reinforcements, and the Difficulty of our knowing it, will render it absolutely necessary, whenever we advance from this Place, to make the Attack as soon as possible. I had much rather engage with three thousand against five, than attack the Enemy's Lines, and there is a much greater prospect of succeeding, but still I cannot promise myself Victory, nor even a Prospect of it, with Inferior Numbers. I have seen of late the difficulty your Excellency seemed to labour under, to satisfy the Expectations of an ignorant Populace, with great Concern.

It is our misfortune to have an Extent of Country to cover, that demands four times our Numbers. The Enemy so situated as to be very difficult to approach, and from pretty good Authority, superior to us in Numbers. Under these Disadvantages, your Excellency has the choice of but two things, to fight the Enemy without the least Prospect of success, upon the common Principles of War, or remain inactive, and be subject to the Censure of an ignorant and impatient populace. In doing one you may make a bad matter worse and take a Measure that, if it proves unfortunate, you may stand condemned for, by all military Gentlemen of Experience; in pursuing the other you have the Approbation of your own mind, you give your Country an opportunity to exert itself to supply the present Deficiency, and also act upon such military Principles as will justify you to the best Judges in the present day, and to all future Generations. For my own Part, I feel Censure with as great a Degree of sensibility as is possible and I feel ambitious of doing every thing that common Sense can justify; but I am fully persuaded, in attempting more you may make a temporary, a lasting Evil. The Cause is too important to be trifled with to shew our Courage, and your Character too deeply interested to sport away upon unmilitary Principles.

For your Sake for my own Sake and for my Country's Sake I wish to attempt every thing which will meet with your Excellency's Approbation. I will run any Risque or engage under any Disadvantages if I can only have your Countenance if unfortunate. With the Publick I know Success sanctifies every thing and that only. I cannot help thinking from the most dispassionate Survey of the Operations of the Campaign that you stand approved by Reason and justified by every military Principle. With Respect to my own Conduct, I have ever given my Opinion with Candour and to my utmost executed with Fidelity whatever was committed to my Charge.

In some Instances we have been unfortunate. In one I thought I felt the Lowr of your Excellency's Countenance when I am sure I had no Reason to expect it.[6] It is out of my Power to command success but I trust I have ever endeavoured to deserve it. It is mortifying enough to be a common sharer in misfortunes but to be punished as the author without deserving it, is truly afflicting.

Your Excellency's Letter of the 22d but I suppose it was of yesterday, this moment came to hand. As I have wrote so fully upon the Subject I have nothing to add only, that to advance from this place before Glovers Brigade joins us unless we attack the Enemy without them will rather injure than facilitate our Designs. But if your Excellency wishes the attack to be made immediately, give me only your

Countenance and notwithstanding it is contrary to the opinion of the General officers here I will take the Consequences upon myself.

Inclosed is a Copy of a Letter from Colo Ellis at Haddonfield.

The Hospitals in the Jerseys are greatly complained of. They prove a grave for many of the poor Soldiery, principally owing to the Negligence of the Surgeons who have the Care of the Hospitals. How far these Complaints are well grounded I can not pretend to say, but I would beg leave to recommend the sending of a good trusty officer to inspect the management of the Hospitals and to remain there untill regularly released.[7] I am with great Respect your Excellencys most Obdt Servt

NATH GREENE

Major Burnet has just returned from Glover's Brigade. They will be at the Black Horse to Night, Eight miles from this place. Half past three oClock.

LS (Washington Papers: DLC).
    1. Woodbury, N.J., was below Red Bank and back from the river a few miles.
    2. Getting the N.J. militia to cooperate, especially in the lower counties, was a constant problem. Washington attributed the trouble partly to "the pernicious practice of hiring substitutes for the Militia." (Fitzpatrick, GW, 9: 486) Lundin believes the large farm population shared the blame by preferring to pay fines to "entering into the military service" and that many who did turn out were more interested in "looting their neighbors." (Cockpit, p. 239)
    3. NG reported to Washington on 25 November, below, that Lee was in the area.
    4. The next year John Cox became NG's assistant quartermaster general.
    5. British Capt. Montresor recorded that Cornwallis had six thousand men on 20 November (Journals, p. 478)
    6. He refers to what he considered unfair criticism of him at the battle of Germantown. See note, NG's orders, 7 October above.
    7. On NG's concern over hospitals, see below, Rush to NG, 2 December.

From George Washington

Dr Sir   Head Qrs [Whitemarsh, Pa.] Novr 24th 1777
    If you have not moved from Mount Holley when this comes to hand, I wish you to wait there till you see Colo Meade[1] who will set off immediately, charged with some important matters which I thought it improper to commit to paper.[2] This However you are to understand under this restriction that I do not mean to prevent you a moment from prosecuting any Object you have immediately in view that promises success. I am Dr Sr Yr most obed Sert

GO: WASHINGTON

LS (Washington Papers: DLC).
    1. Col. Richard Kidder Meade of Virginia had become an aide of Washington in March 1777.

2. The matter is discussed in NG's letter to Washington at 9 o'clock that night, below.

To George Washington

Dr Sir

Mount Holly [N.J.] 9 oClock Nov 24, 1777

I receivd your favor by Col Mead who has communicated to me the design of an attack upon Philadelphia.[1] The consequences if successful are so desirable that I wish it appeard to me more practicable. In war there must be always something left to chance and I would always recommend to trust some consequences to the Spirit and bravery of the Troops. An excess of caution which councils of war are generally productive of often deprives a country of the advantages of a due exertion of the spirit and bravery of the troops, but I have viewed this subject in and out of council. I have weighed the good and the bad consequences. I have surveyd it in a Historical point of light. I have examind it from my own observation in the course of the war and I cannot thing [think] there is that degree of probabillity of the attempt succeeding that will warrant the undertaking. I have not time without detaining Col. Mead too long to give my reasons against the attack in full detail, but I think it a hassardous attempt and will terminate to the injury of the Continent and disgrace of the army. I am sensible that many things pronouncd impracticable before they were attempted have been crownd with success in the undertaking. But prudence forbids that being made a principle which necessity alone can justify. I wish that it was in our power to give that Army some capital wound. The reputation of the Army and the happiness of the country loudly call for it, but in consulting our wishes rather than our reason we may be hurried by an impatience to attempt something splendid into inextricable difficulties.

The depreciation of money, the corruption of the people, and the dislike to service that prevails throughout the Army, will justify measures at this day that might wear the complexion of rashness under different circumstances. How far these considerations may authorise the attempt I cannot pretend to say. One thing I would beg leave to recommend; that is, if your Excellency thinks of attacking the city this winter, improve the present moment; for sure I am whatever reinforcements of Militia may be drawn in to aid the army, they cannot render it so formidable and equal to the attempt as it is at this hour. I am very willing to lay aside my own private Judgment and second the attempt. You may depend upon it, Sir, that I will as freely embark in the attempt, if your Excellency thinks it warrantable, as if I was of the same sentiment, and whatever may be the event my opinion never shall be known.

The troops here are under marching orders. Glovers Brigade will join us in the morning. I intended to advance in the morning at nine, but Col Meads coming and recommending the postponing the march until I hear further from your Excellency, and as the troops coming in will want one days rest, I thought it best to countermand the orders for marching until I hear from your Excellency. And I am farther inducd to the measure because I dont apprehend the difficulties of attacking Lord Cornwallis will be increasd from one or two days delay. The Enemy give out they are 10,000 Strong and that they intend to march to Burlington.[2]

I wish your Excellency to weigh the subject coolly and take your measures accordingly. I shall be perfectly satisfied be the result what it may. I am with the sincerest regard [your mo]st obedient [Servt]

N GREENE

ALS (Washington Papers: DLC).
    1. Meade must have ridden hard from Whitemarsh with the report on a council of war held there earlier in the evening. (The minutes for the meeting have not been found, but several of the generals' opinions written on the twenty-fifth speak of the meeting held "last night.") NG actually wrote his opinion and sent it back by Meade before those who attended the meeting had written theirs. The majority who attended were in agreement with NG not to attack Philadelphia. Gen. Maxwell pointed out, for example, that even before NG and Huntington left the main army with their troops for New Jersey, the officers had thought it unwise to attack. With all of those troops still in New Jersey it seemed to Maxwell even less wise. But five of those attending—De Kalb, Scott, Stirling, Wayne, and Woodford—argued that with Cornwallis in New Jersey the loss would be offset, and there would not be a better time. (Their letters are in the Washington Papers, DLC.) Washington, as he makes clear in the next few days, feared Cornwallis's imminent return from New Jersey.
    2. NG to Washington, 24 November, above, thought the number near five thousand.

General Greene's Orders

Head Quarters [Mt. Holly, N.J.]
November 25th 1777.

The order of Yesterday for marching at 7 o'clock is countermanded, three Days Provisions is immediately to be Drawn & Cooked & the Troops to hold themselves in Readiness to March on the shortest Notice.[1]

After Orders.

All the spare stores belonging to the Qr Mr Genls departmt are to be delivered up to the Deputy Qr Mr Genl. The Deputy Commy Genl of issues is as soon as possible to Inquire into the state of the stores of his Department & take care that a sufft Quantity of Provn is always in Hand. The Conductor is to make his Returns of the Military Stores in his Possessien to Majr Boman of the Artillery. Doctor Tenny of Colo Angels Battalion in Genl Varnums Brigade is appointed to act as surgeon Genl to this Army untill one shall be properly authorized by Dr Cockran. Returns of the sick are to be made to him & fit Places to be Provided for their Reception. The surgeons are to apply to Dr. Tenny for sulphur for their Regiments. A return of the Bakers in the Army to be made as soon as possible.

The Following is the order of Battle.

General Varnums and General Huntingtons Brigades form the Right wing, General Varnums Brigade on the right of the wing, Huntingtons on the left. The right wing to be commanded by General Varnum. General Muhlenburgs and General Weedons Brigades form the left wing, General Muhlenburgs the left of the left wing and General Weedons the right of the left wing. General Muhlenburg commands the left wing.

General Glovers Brigade forms the second line. Colo Haits and Colo Hathaway's militia form upon the right flank. Colo Ellis Militia and Morgans light Corps cover the left flank. In posting the officers in the Regiment the Officers are to be posted with their men without regard to rank, there being great Inconveniency resulting in action by the officers being remov'd from their own men.

In marching to action the Brigades are to march in Regimental columns. The officers leading the Regimental columns are to take special care in advancing that they preserve their proper distances from each other so as to be able to form the line if necessary. A Company to be ⟨Detached as an advanced Guard to the Heads of the Columns.⟩ The Reserves to the wings to march in Columns in the rear of the center of each Brigade and to be in readiness to Join for the Support of either Brigades or to act seperately for the Support of the Brigades from which they were detach'd.

The Second line to march in Regimental columns in the rear of the center of the first line, about four hundred yards, ready to support any part that should be hard prest.

The Artillery to be immediately under the direction of the Commanding officers of the Brigades to march and take post where they direct. The Militia and light troops are to endeavour to gain the flanks of the Enemy, but more especially to prevent them from gaining ours.

The orders and the first paragraph and sentence in angle brackets of the "After Orders" are reprinted from "Muhlenberg Orderly Book," *PMHB*, 35 (1911): 186–87. A slightly different version of the order of battle (last five paragraphs) is also in "Muhlenberg," but the version printed above was drawn up by NG's aide and enclosed in his letter of 26 November to Washington, along with his drawing of the arrangement. Both documents are in the Washington Papers, DLC. Washington docketed the order of battle as "intended Battle agst Lord Cornwallis Novr 1777."

1. NG's battle plan was never put into operation, as he relates to Washington in his letter written at 4:00 P.M. on 26 November, below.

From General George Weedon

Hatonfield [Haddonfield, N.J.]

Dr Genl　　　　　　　　　Novr 24 [25] [1777] 7 oClock[1]

We only arrived here a few minutes ago. Some of our parties have taken Nine prisoners, which will get to you Early tomorrow. From them we have had I believe pretty Exact Accounts of their Numbers which the marquis will inclose you a particular Acct of. They Amount to 4250, Sixteen pieces of Artillery and one hundred Light Horse. The Infantry and Artillery may be Nearly right, but Doubt the information respecting their Horse. They have this Day Advanced on this side Great Timber Creek with their main Body, and have [pitcht] on this side of Little Timber Creek also. Some of the prisoners were taken within two miles of This Town. They have no Troops at Red Bank and but few at Billingsport. The prisoners say they intend Crossing the Delaware at Coopers Ferry.[2] We shall look about us in the morning and shall Communicate anything of Importance. I am yrs Very Sincerely

G WEEDON

I have this moment recd your Orders to return. Myself and Horse is so much fatigued that cant get further than Moors Town tonight. Shall join you Early in the morning.

G W

ADfS (PHi). Postscript in Weedon's hand was found on the address sheet in the Washington Papers, DLC, attached to a later copy of the letter.
1. The date should be 25 November as corroborated by Blodget to Weedon, 25 November, transmitting NG's order for Weedon and Lafayette to join him that same night and by Weedon's postscript here, acknowledging the order.
2. Weedon's intelligence was not as accurate as that given to Col. Comstock by the "smart young woman." See his letter, below.

From Colonel Adam Comstock[1]

Sir　　　　　　　Haddenfield [N.J.] 25 Nov 1/2 past 12, 1777

This moment I arrived from a reconnoitering tour near Little Timber Creek Bridge, sent a smart young woman who had a sister in Gloster [Gloucester] as a spy to Gloster: She has returned and I believe has rec'd no other damage than receiving a Kiss from the Hessian General (this is as she says). She reports that a very large number of British and Hessian troops are in Gloster, that they are embarking in boats and going to Philada, and that her sister there informed her they had been embarking ever since early in the morning.[2] That Lord Cornwallis quartered at Col Ellis' house and the Hessian General in a house opposite, who asked the young woman where the Rebels were. She answered she could not tell, she had seen none of them. She said she passed many Sentrys before she came to Little Timber Creek Bridge where she passed the last.

I doubt not this information. I fear they will be too quick for us. Col Harts Regt is here. With great esteem, yr humble servt.

ADAM COMSTOCK

ALS (Washington Papers: DLC). Enclosed in NG's second letter to Washington, 25 November.

1. Comstock had been one of the founders, with NG, of the Kentish Guards in Rhode Island in 1774. Since the first of January, he had been lieutenant colonel of the First R.I. Regiment, serving under Gen. Varnum.

2. Cornwallis had decided against crossing at Cooper's Ferry, opposite Philadelphia, because he was more vulnerable to an attack by NG's army. (Reed, *Campaign*, p. 359) At Gloucester, five miles downstream, Cornwallis was well protected by natural barriers, as NG describes in his letter to Washington written at 4:00 P.M., 26 November below.

From Colonel Adam Comstock

Hadenfield [N.J.] 25th Novemr 1777

Sir

3oClock PM

Seven prisoners just arived here from the Enemy taken by the Militia about 3 Mile from this place on the Road to Gloster. The prisoners I have examined. Two of them are Guners and 2 Matross belonging to the first Regt of Artilary. The other 3 belong to the 33d Regt. They were about 1/2 a mile from their Picket plundering. Those belonging to the Artilary had 3 of the Artilary Horses with them Mark'd G R which are also taken. This Express rides one of em. The Prisoners on Examination say the Main Body Lyes about 4 Mile from this on the Gloster Road encamp'd; that their Line form a Tryangle; that they are to wait there till they have imbark'd all the Stock for Philadelphia, which will take em all Day and that the Army expects to imbark tomorrow and go into winter Quarters; that they have 2 6 pounders in front, 2 Ditto in the Rear and Some smaller in the Center; that they were not in the least apprehensive of any of the American Army being within 10 Miles of them, otherwise they should not have been taken in the Manner they were. This Moment 7 Hessian Prisoners Arived here taken in the same Manner. I have not examind them. I could wish your Army was here now for I think they may be supprisd very easy. They give various Accts of their Numbers from 5 to 8 Thousand. They mostly agree that Billings Fort and Fort Mercer are Leveled. O how I want to give em a Floging before they Leave the Gerseys. With every sentiment of Esteem and Respect I am your Honour humble Servt

ADAM COMSTOCK

ALS (Washington Papers: DLC). Enclosed in NG's second letter to Washington, 25 November.

To George Washington

Mount Holly [N.J.]
Dear Sir   Nov 25th [1777] 4 oClock
This moment receiv'd intelligence the enemy are embarking from Glouster and crossing over to Philadelphia. Col Comstock sends the intelligence and since it may be depended upon I have orderd General Varnum and General Huntingtons brigades to advance immediately to fall upon the enemies rear and prevent their geting off their stock.[1] I wait your Excellencies orders to march where you may think advisable. Colo Sheppard got into camp about noon. The whole body of the troops will be ready to move at a moments warning. The Riffle[2] Corps and about 600 militia are upon the enemies flanks.

A detachment from Capt. Lees Horse[3] took nine prisoners yesterday, the first account I ever had of their being in this quarter. I am with great esteem your Excell[encies] obed Servt

N GREENE

ALS (Washington Papers: DLC).
1. Order not found.
2. Daniel Morgan's Corps.
3. NG had been waiting for several days for Henry Lee to come to his assistance.

To George Washington

Mount Holly [N.J.] Nov 25th [1777]
Dear Sir   12 oClock [midnight]
I wrote your Excellency this afternoon that the enemy were crossing from the Jerseys to Philadelphia and that the intelligences came from Col Comstock. He is stationd at Haddenfield to collect intelligence. I have receivd two letters from the Col today: the first dated at 12 o Clock, the last at three, both of which I have inclosd. It appears to me the enemy are crossing their Cattle but I much doubt whether any part of the troops have crost the river perhaps they may begin in the morning. I am divided in my mind how to act. If your Excellency intends an attack on Philadelphia our moveing down to Haddenfield will prevent our coopperateing with you but if the enemy are crossing, the attack upon the city would not be warrantable now, if before, without our whole collective force at least and as part is below and part here I wish to move forward for the support of the troops below and attack the enemy if [practicable?].

I expected before this to have receivd your Excellencys further

Orders but as I have not, and from the intelligence there appears a prospect of attempting something here, I have ventureed to put the troops in motion.[1] If I should receive orders to the contrary I can speedily return.

If the enemy cross to the city they may be attackt at any time hereafter as well as now. If they have not crost and are in a situation to be attackt we shall have an opportunity to attempt something. I am anxious to do every thing in my power and more especially as the people seems to be dissatisfied at the evacuation of Red Bank fort. I am with sentiments of regard your Excellencys most Obedient Servt

N GREENE

ALS (Washington Papers: DLC).
    1. See his orders above for 25 November.

William Blodget to General George Weedon

[Mt. Holly, N.J., 25 November 1777. NG directs him to tell Weedon that Glover's brigade will be within a few miles of Mt. Holly tonight. As he has ordered troops out at eight tomorrow morning, wishes Weedon to be here with Lafayette tonight if not too fatigued. Should the "Marquis be fatigued," he had "better join us in the morning."[1] From Balch, *Maryland Line*, p. 95.]

    1. According to the printed document, Blodget sent this by express to Weedon "at or near Morristown." It should have been Moorestown.

From George Washington

Dr Sir   Head Qrs [Whitemarsh, Pa.] 25 Nov 1777 8 OClock PM
    Colo Mead delivered me Yours this Morning[1] as I was upon my way to reconnoitre the Enemys Lines from the West side of the Schuylkill. I had a full view of their left and found their works much stronger than I had reason to expect from the Accounts I had received.[2] The Enemy have evacuated Carpenters Island and seem to be about doing the same by Province Island. Accounts from the City say Lord Cornwallis was expected back to day or tomorrow which corresponds with the information sent you by Gen Weedon. All these movements make me suspicious that they mean to collect their whole force while ours [is] divided and make an Attack on the Army on this side. I therefore desire (except you have a plan or prospect of doing something to advantage) that you will rejoin me with your whole force as quick as possible.[3] I have ordered all the Boats down to Burlington to give you dispatch and when you have crossed, All

those not necessary for the common use at the Ferries should be immediately sent up to Coriels [Coryells] again.

Your's of yesterday that appears to have been written before that sent by Col Meade, has reached me since I got Home. The Hospital at Burlington deserves your consideration; If you leave it uncovered and Lord Cornwallis should detach a party, the patients will certainly be made prisoners. I therefore beg you would endeavour to have them removed or think of some way of giving them protection by posting some Militia or leaving some Other Troops while the Enemy remain in that Quarter. The Hospital at Princetown also will be left naked if the Enemy should move farther up, you will therefore leave them some cover, if you think there will be occasion. I am Dr Sir Yrs

P.S As leaving a Guard at Princetown will still divide our force if the patients could be removed further from thence, I think it would be for the better. I told Dr. Shippen when he fixed it there it would be dangerous.[4]

Df (Washington Papers: DLC).
    1. The letter NG had written at 9 o'clock the previous night, with his opinions on attacking Philadelphia.
    2. Washington summarizes his estimate of Howe's defenses around Philadelphia in a letter to Gen. Gates, 2 December. (Fitzpatrick, GW, 10: 130–33)
    3. It was 28 November before NG's army moved back. See his orders below for that date.
    4. On removing patients, see NG to Washington, 27 November, below. Dr. William Shippen was director general of hospitals; see below, Rush to NG, 2 December 1777, and Rush to NG, 1 February 1778.

To George Washington

Haddonfield [N.J.]
Dr Sir   Novr 26th 4 o'Clock P. M. 1777
    Your Excellency's letter of the 25th reached me at this place. I halted the troops on the reciept of it, those that had not got into the town.[1] Genl Varnums and Huntington's Brigades got to this place before the letter came to hand. I am sorry our march will prove a fruitless one. The enemy have drawn themselves down upon the Peninsula of Gloucester: the ships are drawn up to cover the troops. There is but one road that leads down to the point, on each side the ground is swampy and full of thick underbrush that it makes the approaches impracticable almost. These difficulties might have been surmounted but we could reap no advantage from it, the Shipping being so posted as to cover the troops, and this country is so inter-sected with creeks that approaches are rendered extremely difficult and retreats very dangerous. I should not have halted the troops, but

all the Genl officers were against making an attack, the enemy being so securely situated and so effectually covered by their Shipping.

We have a fine body of troops and in fine spirits, and every one appears to wish to come to action. I proposed to the Gentlemen drawing up in front of the enemy and to attack their Picquet and endeavour to draw them out but they were all against it, from the improbability of the enemies coming out. The Marquis with about 400 militia and the rifle Corps attacked the enemies Picquet last evening, kill'd about 20 and wounded many more and took about 20 prisoners. The Marquis is charmed with the spirited behaviour of the militia and Rifle Corps. They drove the enemy above half a mile and kept this ground untill dark. The enemy's picquet consisted of about 300 and were reinforced during the skirmish. The Marquis is determined to be in the way of danger.[2]

From the best observations I am able to make and from the best intelligence I can obtain it is uncertain whether any of the enemy have crossed the river. The boats are constantly going but I believe they are transporting stock. There is as many men in the returning boats as there goes over. By tomorrow it will be reducd to a certainty. I believe the enemy have removed the great Chiveaux de frize.[3] There went up 60 Sail of Vessels this morning. If the obstructions are removed in the river it accounts for the enemies evacuating Carpenters and Province Islands as they are no longer necessary. The prisoners say the enemy are going into Winter quarters as soon as they get up the river.

Inclosed was our order for battle, with a plate agreeing to the order.[4]

I purpose to leave General Varnums brigade and the rifle corps at this place for a few days, especially the rifle men who cover the country very much. Genl Varnum's brigade will return to Mount Holly tomorrow or next day. I will make further inquiry respecting the hospitals and give such directions as appear necessary.

My division, Huntington's and Glover's Brigades, will proceed with all dispatch to join your Excellency. I could wish the enemy might leave the Jersies before us.[5] I am your Excellency's most Obedient Servant

NATH GREENE

LS (Washington Papers: DLC).

1. They had marched the fifteen miles southward from Mt. Holly that day. Haddonfield was a few miles east of Cornwallis's embarkation point at Gloucester.

2. In a letter to Washington the same day, Lafayette gave a joyful and detailed account of what he called "a little event." (Idzerda, *Lafayette Papers*, 1: 156–58) The rifle corps of which NG speaks consisted of some 150 of Daniel Morgan's men under Col. Richard Butler. (Ibid.) The British admitted "31 Jagers killed, wounded, and missing" (Montresor, *Journals*, p. 479).

In a letter to Congress the same night, Washington quoted the portion of NG's letter on Lafayette in support of his recommendation that Congress assign a division to Lafayette, who had been "pressing in his applications for a Command," and who, he feared, might otherwise "return [to France] in disgust." (Fitzpatrick, *GW*, 10: 109–10)

3. NG was correct. Lord Howe, in the *Eagle*, accompanied by sixty-two other ships, reached Philadelphia.

4. See the last part of his after orders of 25 November, above.

5. By 27 November all of Cornwallis's troops had crossed back to Philadelphia. (Montresor, *Journals*, p. 479)

From George Washington

Dear Sir   White Marsh [Pa.] Nov 26th 1777

My letter of yester night (wrote after I returnd from a view of the Enemy's Lines from the other side Schuylkill) I must refer to. Our Situation as you justly observe, is distressing, from a variety of irremediable causes; but more especially from the impracticabillity of answering the expectations of the world without running hazards which no military principles can justify; and which, in case of failure, might prove the ruin of our cause; patience and a steady perseverance in such measures as appear warranted by sound reason and policy must support us under the censure of the one, and dictate a proper line of conduct for the attainment of the other, that is the great object in view. This, as it ever has, will I think, ever remain the first wish of my heart, however I may mistake the means of accomplishment. That your views are the same, and that your endeavors have pointed to the same end, I am perfectly satisfied of, altho' you seem to have imbibd a suspicion which I never entertaind.

I can forsee Inconveniences, I can forsee losses and I daresay I may add that I can forsee much dissatisfaction that will arise from the withdrawing the Continental Troops from the Jerseys. But how is it to be avoided? We cannot be divided when the Enemy are collected. The evils which I apprehended from throwing Troops into the Jersey's now stare me more forcibly in the face and a day or two, if you cannot join us in that time, may realize them. For my mind scarce entertains a doubt but that Genl Howe is collecting his whole force with a view of pushing at this army.[1] This, especially under the information you have received of Lord Cornwallis's recrossing the Delaware, induces me to press dispatch upon you, that our junction may be formed as speedily as possible and the consequences of a division avoided.

The Current sentiment as far as I can collect it, without making it a matter of question, is in favour of our taking Post on the other side Schuylkill.[2] In this case the Jersey's will be left totally uncovered, consequently all the craft in the River with their Rigging, Guns &c, the Hospitals on that side of the River, the Magazines of Provisions which the Commisaries are ab't establishing in the upper part of

Jersey &c. Think therefore I beseech you of all these things and prepare yourself by reflection, and observation (being on the spot) to give me your advice on these sevl matters. The Boats (those belonging to the Public, and built for the purpose of transporting Troops &c across the River) ought in my judgment to be removd, so soon as they have served your pres[en]t calls, up to Coryales Ferry at least if not higher. I am almost Incline[d] to think (if we should cross the Schuyl-kill) that they ought to be carted over also.

I shall only add that your Letters of 12 o'clock and 4 yesterday have both come to hand and since I began this, and that I am with sincere regard and affectl Dr Sir Yr most Obed

G. WASHINGTON

It has been proposed that some of the Galleys should fall down to, or near the mouth of Frankfort Creek, in order to prevent Troops coming up by Water and falling in the Rear of our Pickets near the Enemy's Lines.[3] Will you discuss with the Commodore on this subject? Will you also ask what is become of the hands that were on board the Vessels wch were burnt?[4]

Tr (GWG transcript: CSmH). The original, in Washington's hand, is in the Greene Papers, DLC, but is badly damaged. It was transcribed by G. W. Greene while it was still in good condition.
1. Washington's apprehensions, rather than any intelligence, were the basis for his expecting such an attack. John Clark, NG's aide whom Washington praised for his intelligence work, reported nothing about an impending attack in his letter to Washington on 26 November. Three days later he reported to Washington that his informant (a "very Communicative" friend on whom he could rely) said that British officers "give out that they intend making an attack on your Army but have made no preparations." (Clark to Washington, 26 and 29 November 1777, Washington Papers, DLC)
2. That is, the south side. The "Current sentiment" was that among the general officers.
3. Frankford Creek emptied into the Delaware about five miles above Philadelphia.
4. NG did not apparently learn from Commodore John Hazelwood what had become of the men who had set fire to their galleys the previous week.

To Colonel [Joseph Haight][1]

Haddonfield [N.J.] 27th Novr 1777
General Greene Orders that the Militia take Post at and about Moors-town and Haddonfield. That they do all in their Power to annoy the Enemy and prevent them from making Incurtions into the Country. That they cause all the live Stock to be drivin back from the Creeks, and that the Bridges be taken up so as to prevent crossing from Creek to Creek near the Deleware and prevent any communication with the enemy as much as possible. The Militia of the eastern part of the State of New Jersey to be aiding and assisting to the Western Militia.

NATH GREENE[2]

LS (RPB).
1. NG's aide addressed the letter to "Colo. Hoits." NG spelled it correctly in his letter of 22 November, above.
2. Because Haight was in the N.J. militia, NG signed his letter as major general "in the Continental Army." It is questionable whether a colonel of the N.J. militia was obligated to carry out such peremptory orders of a continental officer. Whether Haight did carry out the orders is not known.

To George Washington

Dr Sir   Mount Holly [N.J.] Nov 27 1777

Your favor of yesterday I receivd last night about 12 oClock. The greater part of the troops returnd to this place last night and marched early this morning to cross the Delaware.[1] I staid at Haddenfield myself with General McDougals division to give the necessary Orders to the Militia. I have left the rifle Corps at Haddenfield and Capt Lees troops of light Horse to encourage the Militia and awe the enemy, to prevent their coming out in small parties. Col Olney had orders to make an attack upon their Piquet this morning but they drew them in so close to their main body and there being but one road he could not effect it. Their Picquet consisted of about 300 men. I am much afraid the withdrawing the troops will greatly alarm the Country. Any position below this with any considerable force would be very dangerous the country is exceedingly intersected with creeks and lies so contiguous to Philadelphia. I think any body of troops may be surprisd from the city at Haddenfield in five hours and at almost any place in its neighbourhood.

The Hospitals will be in some danger at Burlington, Burdenton [Bordentown] and Princetown if all the troops are withdrawn from this state, but if the sick were orderd to be immediately removd it would still increase the alarm in the country, for which reason I would risque what are there at present and order the Director General not to send any more there.

I shall set out immediately for Burlington. I have given Lt Col Abale[2] orders to procure Waggons and send off all the spare ammunition to Huntington, the heavy cannon to Bordenton. At my arrival at Burlington I will enquire of the Comodore respecting the matters by you directed.

General McDougals division will quarter here tonight and march at five in the morning for Burlington. I think there are as many troops gone forward as will be able to get over today.

I shall push on the troops as fast as possible without injuring their healths.[3] I sent forward one of my Aids to Burlington early this morning to supertend the embarkation of the troops and baggage.

I am with sinsere regard and due respect your Excellencies most Obedient Sevt

N GREENE

ALS (Washington Papers: DLC).
1. They would cross the river at Burlington, seven miles from Mt. Holly and some twenty miles above Philadelphia.
2. James Abeel.
3. Their destination was Whitemarsh, Pa., where Washington's army had been camped since 2 November and from which NG had left for New Jersey on 19 November.

General Greene's Orders

Head Quarters Mt. Holly, N.J.
November 28th 1777.

Such of the Troops as are not already Provided with cooked Provisions for Tomorrow are to Draw & Cook it this Night. At Day break a Cannon will be fired as a signal for the whole Army to Parade ready to March when the whole are Completely Formed. They are to Ground their Arms but be ready to take them up again at a Minutes Warning. If it should Rain or Snow the Men are not to Parade.

Reprinted from "Muhlenberg Orderly Book," *PMHB*, 35 (1911): 290.

To George Washington

Burlington [N.J.] Nov 28th
9 o Clock 1777

Dr Sir

These Brigades are now on their march for Head Quarters, my division and Glovers brigade. General MDougalls division is not yet come to town. They had orders to march at four this morning and I was in hopes they would have been in town by the time Glovers brigade got over the River. I am afraid the want of provision has detaind them this morning. It is with the utmost difficulty we can get bread to eat. The Commisary of purchases of flour is very ill managed. There is no magazines of consequence, and the Army servd from hand to mouth. The Baggage cannot be got over by tomorrow night. Mr Tench Francis an uncle of Col Tilghman was brought to me a prisoner this morning.[1] He was taken at Glouster. He sais Lord Cornwallis detachment consisted of about 6000 that none embarked until yesterday. He also adds that the reinforcement consisted of about 2500 from New York. General How designs to make an immediate attack upon the Army unless the weather is bad. This is the general conversation of the Officers of all ranks. Mr Francis says he thinks the enemy design to burn and destroy where ever they go.

Germantown is devoted [i.e., doomed] to destruction. The enemy plundered every body within their reach and almost of every thing they had. It is the common conversation among the officers of all ranks that they design to divide our lands as soon as the Country is conquerd. The obstinate resistance they say made at Mud Island[2] has broke the campaign. I am with great respect your Excelly most Obdt Sevt

N GREENE

ALS (Washington Papers: DLC).
    1. NG's statement implies that Tench Francis (Jr.) had been captured by an American while he was fighting with the British. He must have been a British prisoner, however, whom the Americans liberated. Uncle of Washington's aide, Tench Tilghman, Francis had been a prominent merchant in Philadelphia, an early patriot, and a colonel of a Pennsylvania militia unit. (*PMHB*, 49 (1925): 82–83)
    2. On the defense of Ft. Mifflin on Mud Island, see above, note, NG to Washington, 14 November.

George Washington to Major General Nathanael Greene or Brigadier General James Mitchell Varnum or Jedediah Huntington

Head Quarters
Dear Sir   28th Novemr 1777 7 oClock P. M.
    Capt Duplessis has just delivered me yours of this morning from Burlington. Every account from Philada confirms the Report that the Enemy mean to make a speedy move. I shall not be disappointed if they come out this Night or very early in the morning. You will therefore push forward the Rear Brigades with all possible expedition and the moment that the Troops and Baggage have all passed, let the Boats be instantly sent up the River to Coryells Ferry, for one part of my information is that the Enemy are preparing to send Boats up the Delaware and it cannot be for any other purpose than to destroy the remainder of our Water Craft. I shall be glad that you would come on immediately upon the Receipt of this and send word back to the Brigadiers to hasten their march. I am &c

If Genl Green should not be found Genl Varnum or Huntington will be pleased to do what is directed above[1] And send word to the Captains of the Gallies to fall lower down the River to meet any Boats that may be coming up to annoy the passage of the Troops or Baggage.

Df (Washington Papers: DLC).
    1. Whether NG received this before he crossed the river to Pennsylvania on 29 November is not recorded. He had posted Varnum at Haddonfield, N.J.

To George Washington

[1 Dec. 1777]

Agreeable to your Excellency's command I shall in a few words give my Sentiments with respect to the necessity of puting the troops into winter quarters and the properest place to canton them in. Everyone that views the Condition of the army and is acquainted with the severe duty they have gone through will readily agree that good, warm, comfortable quarters are necessary to supply the defect of cloathing and that some relaxation is essential to give a proper tone to both men and officers to prepare them for the ensuing campaign. In doing this we must have regard not only to the army but [to] the country. An army without a country is like an Infant incapable of feeding or cloathing itself. Every part of the country, whether Whig or Tory, that we suffer to be ravaged is a diminution of our strength and an increase of theirs. Men are essential in war but provisions, cloathing and accoutrements are equally so. The first and great object in cantoning the troops is to take a position secure from surprise. The next is covering; the third is a situation convenient for drawing forage and provisions for the subsistence of the army and the cattle belonging to it. These are the great principles to be attended to in quartering the troops and cannot be dispensed with without certain and inevitable ruin to the whole military machine. There are other secondary considerations such as covering the country and distressing the enemy in drawing their supplies. Where a position can be found to answer all those valuable purposes is the subject of inquiry.

It is said by many that a total relaxation is necessary [for] the good of the army, to enable the officers to recruit their Regt and to give the men time to recover their spirits. I must confess if I was to speak from my feelings and declare my wishes instead of my sentiments I should be of that opinion. Pleasure is ever agreeable to human nature but never more so than after long and severe duty. An opportunity to unbend the mind must be the wish of every one and it is not very difficult to accommodate our reasong [reasoning] to our wishes, but whether a total or a partial relaxation will be for the general interest of the army is worth inquiring into.

If we retire so far back as to be totally out of danger, pleasure and dissipation will be the consequence. Officers of all ranks will be desirous of visiting their friends. The men will be left without orders, without government—and ten to one but the men will be more unhealthy in the spring than they now are and much worse disciplined.

The health and discipline of troops can only be preserved by constant attention and exercise. We must not flatter ourselves that going into quarters will recover the health and discipline of the troops without regard is paid to one and attention to the other.

It is said we must carry on war upon the great Scale and that particular interest must not be brought in competition with the general interest and that by attending to the minutiae we will sacrifice the principle object. I readily agree that it is perfectly consistent with the maxims of sound policy for the lesser to give place to the greater, but is it necessary for us to throw open a great extent of country to give a necessary relaxation to the army? It is the country that feeds, cloaths and furnishes us with troops. If the substance of the Inhabitants is destroyed they will be incapable of giving us the necessary aid. If the army in the winter season leaves the country unprotected, will it not be a discouraging circumstance to sending recruits to join us which will be a diminution of their local security if they can expect no protection from the collective force? I am no advocate for taking measures from popular opinions, but it is necessary to preserve the confidence of the country; for by the union and spirit of the people alone can the opposition be continued.

The Legislator is in some measure under the necessity of accommodating his measures to the prejudices of the people. Mankind will only be subservient to your purposes in proportion as they conceive their interest and happiness connected with your measures. I have heard it remarked that the sufferings of the army, spread in all directions throughout the continent, alarms the people and prevents them from entering into the service. The same may be said with regard to the poor plundered inhabitants. It is true the eyes of all the continent are upon us for protection, but it is natural for men to reason: what is my neighbours condition may bye and bye be mine.

If the army seems disposed [to] exert its force to shelter the country from ravage, it is natural to expect the people will be anxious to strengthen its hands, but if the enemy are left at liberty to ravage at large, as the inhabitants of one State make the condition of another their own, it will be an alarming consideration. Therefore I think some regard should be had in taking our measures to afford as much cover to the country as possible without militating with the principal design, not for the sake of the particular spot that is covered, but to prevent the disagreeable influence it will have upon the surrounding Inhabitants.

I cannot conceive a total relaxation to be necessary to recruit the army or recover its spirits. I am fully persuaded that recruiting by voluntary inlistments is in a great measure at an end. The enormous bounties that are given so far exceed the american funds, and the continental bounty now allowed falls so far short of private bounties that few if any recruits are to be expected through that channel. If this be granted then the recruiting Service will wholly depend upon the exertion of the civil authority of the respective States, and this exertion doubtless will be in proportion to the reputation and confidence the legislative bodies place in the army. For it cannot be expected from the local prejudices of mankind that the several legislative bodies will be willing to strip themselves of their inhabitants and lessen their own internal safety unless they are well persuaded the measure is essential to their own happiness and security.

It is absolutely necessary the army should have an opportunity to relax and recover its spirits. But there is a great difference between constant duty and total relaxation; a proper medium between these two extremes will be found better adapted to restore the spirits of the army and preserve its discipline. We must be in a situation to take off that constant watching and yet not so remote from danger but that some attention to duty is necessary.

Men are naturally apt to sink into negligence without there is something constantly to rouse their attention. The objects of pleasure are so much more inviting than those of Duty that without a restraint is laid on one and a necessity imprest to attend to the other it is ten to one that the objects of Pleasure steal the mind wholly from the discharge of its duty. I do not mean to urge these reasons for taking a position near the enemy to oblige us to be constantly on the watch but to shew that a total relaxation may be dangerous. Remember Hannibal's army in Capua.

The general discontent among the officers of almost all ranks renders winter quarters essential to redress the prevailing grievances and new[ly] organize the army for the spring, but the fatigues and hardships of the campaign and the want of rest and relaxation are not the great sources of the discontent that prevails. It springs from a different fountain. It is the pay and subsistence which are found to be incompetent to the necessary demands of the officers to preserve their dignity and support their families. This is the great evil and this must be remedied or else this army must and will dissolve. There are some other things complained of, Such as Rank, that military Jewel being confered on almost all orders of men to the disgrace of rank, and great mortification of officers who find themselves often reduced to a level with persons they despise from the prostitution of military dignity.

The manner of cloathing the troops is a subject of complaint. There is no provision made proportionable to the demand of the army; and the difficulty of obtaining that which is provided has given great disgust to some and discontent to others.

These are some of the principal subjects of complaint; and a partial relaxation from military duty is necessary to put every thing in a proper train for opening the next campaign.

It is necessary that an appearance should be kept up as much as possible of besieging the enemy, not only to cover the country but to preserve the credit of our currency which will always rise and fall as our army appears superiour or inferior to the enemy. The enemy will also draw out of the country many recruits without they are kept within bounds. All these are objects worthy our attention.

There have been two places proposed for cantoning the troops. One from Bethlehem to Lancaster, the other at Wilmington and its environs. There can be great objections raised to both. It is said (with how much truth I know not) that all the back towns are crowded with inhabitants, refugees from Philadelphia. If that be true, to turn them out to make room for the Soldiery will bring great distress upon the inhabitants and be productive of no small discontent. I have no doubt in my own mind but that there can be quarters procured in the proposed Line of cantonment from Bethlehem to Lancaster but there appears to me to be many evils attending it. It is a great distance back in the country and leaves the Enemy a great range in front and upon each flank. It must distress the back inhabitants. We shall be consuming the substance in the bowels of the country which should be always held as a reserve against a misfortune. In withdrawing ourselves to so great a distance it will be improved abroad into a kind of dispersion into the mountains and among ourselves it will wear the complexion of a retreat, and many will be suing for Protection.

I must confess however that if safety and relaxation are the only objects under consideration the geography of the country from Bethlehem to Lancaster is more favorable for a Cantonment than Wilmington, but I cannot help thinking that quarters can be got at Wilmington with much less distress to the Inhabitants of the State, that the position will be secure enough with the force cantoned in and about it, that provision and forage can be got easier and cheaper in that position than in the other, that from this Position we can draw it from the enemy while the other will leave it for them; that this gives us a better opportunity to protect the lower Jersey, and not less the upper; that this will distress the enemy in drawing supplies, and upon the whole cover a greater extent of country than any other. For these reasons I am for the Position of Wilmington, and if any part of our Stores are insecure I would immediately have them removed. I would have about a brigade of continental Troops in the Jerseys and about one thousand militia between the Delaware and Schuylkill, and about a thousand more at or near the Gulph, and an advance post at Chester of continental troops.[1]

NATH GREENE

ALS (Washington Papers: DLC).

1. A Council of General Officers was held on 30 November, but no minutes of the meeting have been found. Fitzpatrick notes from Harrison's summary of the letters (which are in the Washington Papers, DLC): "Greene, Lafayette, Armstrong, Small-wood, Wayne, and Scott—in favor of Wilmington; nine—Sullivan, De Kalb, Maxwell, Knox, Poor, Muhlenberg, Varnum, Weedon, and Woodford—for the Lancaster-Reading line; Lord Stirling for the Great Valley; Du Portail and Irvine for hutting in a strong position; and Pulaski for a winter campaign." (Fitzpatrick, *GW*, 10: 133n)

General Greene's Order

[Whitemarsh, Pa., 2 December 1777. "Most unfit" man to go with each wagon. Each regiment to be "told off into Grand and Sub Divisions"; each man to have forty rounds of ammunition. *Weedon Orderly Book*, p. 147.]

From Doctor Benjamin Rush[1]

Dear Sir   Princetown [N.J.] Decemr 2, 1777

We have in the hospital of this place, near 500 sick and wounded soldiers many of whom have complaints so trifling that they do not prevent their committing daily a hundred irregularities of all kinds. The physicians and surgeons of the hospital possess no power to prevent or punish them. The design of this letter is to beg that you would send immediately two or three officers, or even one, if more cannot be spared to take the command in this place.[2] The sick cannot be governed without military authority. But if the sick as patients derived no advantages from being subject to military rules, I am persuaded your army will benefit by it hereafter. A Soldier should never be suffered to exist a single hour without a sense of his having a master being imposed upon his mind, nor the fear of military punishments. It is no purpose to train your men to subordination in the field or camp. In one month they will loose in our hospitals the discipline of a whole year without officers to command and govern them. In the British army the hospitals constantly feel the influence of military Authority.[3] An Officer of note is always stationed near a hospital who is called a *Military Inspector*. His business is to appoint guards, have a roll called, visit the wards, and finally to report all deficiencies to the commander in chief. It is in consequence of this, and some other useful regulations made use off in the British army that Mr Howe has at this time only 1000 sick and wounded in his hospitals at Philada: while we in the *same* time, and with no *more* battles and hardships have filled our hospitals with near 4000. Let me conjure you my dear Sir by your love of human nature to direct the attention of the army more towards the health of the soldiery. The character of our officers, nay even our cause suffers by the many monuments of sickness and distress which are left by our army in every village in New Jersey and Pensylvania. I am Sir yours sincerely.

B RUSH

Cy (PPL).
1. From this letter it is hard to believe that a few weeks earlier Rush had noted in his journal that NG was "a sycophant to the general, timid, speculative, without enterprise." (Cited in Hawke, *Rush*, p. 206). The shock of attending the wounded from Brandywine and Germantown in the overcrowded, makeshift hospitals and the disappointment over Washington's failures in the face of Gates's successes had been too much for the emotional, hypercritical Rush. No one escaped his lashings—not his superior, Dr. William Shippen, Jr., or Washington, or any of those close to him. Now, on sober second thought he must have considered his earlier judgment of NG unfair. Perhaps he had been softened by his knowledge of NG's humane concern for the sick and wounded (see above, NG to Rush, 3 May 1777). Hawke sees this letter as an indication that Rush now considered NG "an understanding friend." (Ibid., p. 211) Rush, however, did not soften his criticism of Shippen or Washington. (See below, Rush to NG, 1 February 1778, and "Conway Cabal," NG to Jacob, 7 February 1778.)
2. He made the same request to Shippen that day (Butterfield, *Rush*, 1: 169–70). On 12 December, Shippen asked Washington for an invalid regiment to guard the hospitals, which Washington granted two days later. (Washington Papers, DLC; Fitzpatrick, *GW*, 10: 152)
3. Since the battle of Princeton, Rush had favored the British hospital system. He examined British medical practices at first hand two days after Brandywine when Washington arranged for Rush and other physicians to go behind the British lines to treat wounded Americans. In a letter to John Adams of 1 October, he praised the British for their concern for the diet and general health of their soldiers as well as for British hospital practices. (Butterfield, *Rush*, 1: 154–57)

George Washington to the General Officers

Sir   [Whitemarsh, Pa.] Decr 3d 1777

I wish to recall your attention to the important matter recommended to your consideration sometime ago, namely, the advisability of a Winters Campaign, and practicability of an attack upon Philadelphia with the aid of a considerable body of Militia to be assembled at an appointed time and place.[1] Particular Reasons urge me to request your Sentiments on this matter by morning, and I shall expect to receive them in writing accordingly by that time.[2] I am Sir Yr Most Obed Sr
Circular   G W

ACyS (Washington Papers: DLC).
1. At a meeting of general officers at Whitemarsh on 24 November, a majority of those present voted against an attack on Philadelphia at that time. In a letter from New Jersey, dated 9 o'clock, 24 November (above), NG voted with the majority.
2. The "Particular Reasons" for which he needed their latest opinions by the next morning was because of the special committee appointed by Congress on 28 November. The three members—Robert Morris, Elbridge Gerry, and Joseph Jones—had arrived at Whitemarsh that day with instructions to hold "private confidential consul-

tation with General Washington, to consider of the best and most practical means for carrying on a winters campaign with vigour and success, an object which Congress have much at heart, and on such consultation, with the concurrence of General Washington, to direct every measure which circumstances may require for promoting the public service." (*JCC*, 9: 972) NG's opinion follows.

To George Washington

Camp [Whitemarsh, Pa.] December 3d 1777[1]
The Subject under Consideration before the board is whether a plan to draw together a large Body of militia in aid of the continental Troops in the dead of winter to attack General Howe in his winter quarters is eligible or not. However desirable the destruction of General Howe's army may be and however impatient the public may be for this desirable event, I cannot recommend the measure. I have taken the most serious View of the subject in every point in which I am able to examine it and cannot help thinking the probability of a disappointment is infinitely greater than of Success. We must not be governed in our measures by our Wishes. The love of glory natural to men often prompts them to exceed the bounds of human nature in their enterprizes. I am sensible in many instances that things pronounced impracticable have been crowned with success in the attempt. I know it is justifiable in war to leave something to chance, yet prudence forbids that being made a principle which necessity alone can justify; I am by no means inclined from an excess of caution in a council of war to rob my Country of the happy consequences that may result from a due exertion of the spirit and bravery of the Soldiery, but at the same time let us not flatter ourselves from the heat of our zeal that men can do more than they can. To judge properly upon the subject we must first consider what human nature is capable of when aided by all the powers of art, and what is to be expected when unsupported by those necessary assistants. In the second place we have to consider how reluctantly people will leave the pleasures of domestic life and engage in a hard and dangerous enterprize at such a rugged season of the year, especially after being out [a] great part of the summer.

In the third and last place, let us consider what a combination of circumstances are necessary to give success to the enterprize; weigh this in the Scales of probability and see how far we can promise ourselves a happy issue to the design.

In the first place, supposing our soldiery the best of veterans, capable of the boldest attacks, are they cloathed, are they appointed with every thing necessary for such a severe and difficult attempt? Let any body examine the Condition of the troops, one half without breeches, Shoes or stockings, and some thousands without Blankets, and judge how far men in this situation are capable of enduring the severity of a winter's Campaign. The continental troops must be out in the field during all the time the militia are drawing together, and in the natural order of things there must be a great diminution of their Force. The troops must be subject to this evil or else go into winter quarters untill the militia are collected, in which case the officers will be dispersed, which will render it very difficult if not impracticable to draw the troops out of quarters in a condition to undertake the attack. I would not wish to spare either blood or treasure necessary to work the destruction of General Howe's army. The object is so important that it demands every sacrifice that human nature or national policy can justify, but to make a great sacrifice of men and money without accomplishing the design will be disgraceful to the Army and discouraging to the Country.

The militia perhaps may come together something better cloathed than the continental troops but the different manner of their living in camp to what they have been accustomed to, together with the extraordinary hardships they must be necessarily subject to in the undertaking, cannot fail of producing a great mortality, or at least some thousands may be expected to frll sick and be rendered incapable of duty. This will not only produce a great diminution of Strength but a numerous Sick must be very distressing to those that are well.

In Europe where they are much older in war than we can pretend to be and where there are as hardy a race of men as are on the Globe; where the severity of the season little exceeds that of ours and where necessity, and ambition and military Glory all conspire to produce winter campaigns, yet they are never undertaken without the soldiers being well cloathed and each furnished with a good watch coat and Blanket. Experience is the best of schools and the safest guide in human affairs, yet I am no advocate for blindly following all the maxims of European policy; but where reason corresponds with what custom has long sanctified, we may safely copy their Example. It must be confessed and the fatal effects of last winter's campaign will confirm it, that unless men are well cloathed they must fall a sacrifice to the severity of the weather when exposed to the hardships of a winter's campaign. The successes of last winter were brilliant and attended with the most happy consequences in changing the complexion of the times, but if the bills of mortality were to be consulted, I fancy it would be found we were no great gainers by those operations.

There is not only the difficulty of cloathing, but that of covering also. Tents cannot be procured, houses in the country are too scattering to quarter the troops in, either for attack or defence. If the troops lye out in the weather they must soon, very soon, be rendered unfit for duty. Such a numerous body of men, hastily drawn together, all unconnected, cannot be speedily so arranged as to cooperate in one great and general design. To these difficulties may be added that of subsisting such a numerous body of troops without having large magazines previously established for that purpose when such a cold and rigid season and the variableness of the weather will render transportation by land and water very difficult and uncertain.

Hospitals proper to receive such a number of sick as we may reasonably expect there will be, will increase the distresses of the army and add to the complaints of the country, especially if the event should be unfortunate.

The second objection I have to the measure is the difficulty of drawing out such a body of militia from the different States as will be necessary to ensure Success to the enterprize. Those States which are remote from dangers, whose militia have been harassed in the Course of the Campaign will be unwilling to call them out without the most pressing necessity, and supposing the Legislators to feel all the military enthusiasm we could wish, we cannot flatter ourselves that that Spirit will pervade all orders of men, which will be necessary to draw out such bodies as will be requisite for the Design.

Every one that has attended to the difficulties of calling out large bodies of militia, the uncertain success of the most spirited exertions, the impatience they discover to be gone, and the trouble of manageing them when here, may form a good judgement what success we can promise ourselves when we have all those difficulties to encounter in the different stages.

It is highly probable that a requisition from the Congress to the neighbouring states may produce a resolution in each to furnish their quota, but out of the number demanded perhaps not two thirds would actually march and out of the number that did march, ten to one whether more than three fifths ever arrive at camp.

The time of the troops being drawn together and forwarded on to camp depends on the coercive power of Government, some being stronger and some weaker, those that arrive first will get out of patience before the arrival of the others. Desertion and disgust will be the consequences, and if either the one or the other should prevail to any considerable degree, the whole plan would be defeated. I would ask any one if these observations are not founded in truth and human nature, and whether it is not the true history of the militia? If it is, what can we promise ourselves from the attempt, when if the whole force was to arrive safe at camp, still there is a great combination of circumstances necessary to compleat the work? The failure of either may render abortive the whole scheme.

The best way of judgeing of men and measures at a future period is to recur to their past conduct under similar circumstances. How difficult have we found it to draw the militia of one State to the aid of that of another, even where it was necessary to give a check to the enemy from entering the State to which they belong?

This measure must go recommended to Congress. From the Congress after a week or ten days' consultation a resolve will take place, recommending it to the different States. The assemblies of each are to be called together, their Deliberations and judgement to be had upon the propriety of the measure and then an order after ten or twelve Days issues to assemble the militia. If the officers are slow and tardy as usual, to collect and march them to camp will be the business of a month. The continental troops must be out in the field near two months on the most moderate calculation before the Scheme will be ripe for execution. We shall all this time be wasting the very vitals of the army, and risquing a certain evil for an uncertain good, dependent upon too many contingencies for us to be very sanguine of success.

The different States will be put to no small difficulty to provide arms for a numerous militia which must protract the time for collecting it. Consider likewise what delays great and heavy Storms will produce. How distressing they must prove to those that are coming to camp as well as those waiting their arrival there.

The third and last objection I have to the measure is the great combination of circumstances necessary to crown it with success, and the improbability of such a multitude of circumstances ever harmonizing together that are independant of each other and originate from such different springs.

There is in the first place a sufficient [insufficient?] force so appointed as to be able to execute the plan of attack. It is highly improbable that such force can be put in motion, and still more improbable that they will be properly equipt. Supposeing the necessary force to meet properly appointed, they will be a very unwieldy machine, and it must take up a very considerable time to organize the whole in such a manner as to move in concert. Such a numerous militia cannot be drawn together very near the Enemy where their force is collected and always ready to take advantage of circumstances without being very liable to Surprize and defeat. Therefore if they must be drawn together at a considerable distance from the enemy's Lines, and first organized, and then move to the attack, the variableness of the weather may interfere. Heavy storms of either rain or Snow will put a total Bar to the operations for a time, and more especially the former. But suppose neither of these difficulties interferes, still the operations will be dependant upon the temper of the weather which must be neither too severe or too moderate to enable us to prepare and execute the manoeuvre. If the weather is very severe the men cannot live out in the Field long enough to prepare and execute the attack. If the weather is not so severe as to freeze the rivers hard enough for men and artillery to pass over, there can no attack be made, only in front of the Enemy's lines—and how far such an attack can be expected to succeed I leave every one to judge. I am told the weather is very variable here and that Storms are frequent, both of which must ruin the platform of our operations; our whole success depending upon the Rivers being sufficiently frozen to enable us to pass over on the ice.

But suppose all these circumstances should happen to combine to give success to the design—which by the bye is scarcely within the limits of possibility and far out of the bounds of probability—can we promise ourselves a victory? Does history afford us an instance as a foundation for such a hope? It is agreed on all hands that there is a very formidable force in Philadelphia and every house is a fortification. Can it be expected that young troops unaccustomed to such enterprizes will have steadiness enough to push the Enemy from place to place untill they are totally routed from the City? To make the attack and not totally defeat them will fall far short of the importance of the design or the expectations of the public.

What aid can be expected from the militia? Will they come up to storm the houses? Let us recur to past experience of the militia, and such a militia too as we cannot expect for the present attack, and see how far we can hope for success with such troops opposed by such as we have to attack. I must confess I think it right to trust every thing to the spirit and bravery of troops that is warranted by human nature, History or our own observation. Has the present Scheme these Sanctions? Are we not rather drawn into the attempt by the brilliancy of the object than by the probability of its Success, founded in either nature or Reason?

The King of Prussia, the greatest General of the age, strongly protests against attacking troops by storm in villages, much more in large regular brick cities. He observes, it often piques the ruin of the best part of an army; this was verified in several attacks he made upon towns and villages last war. Philadelphia is a great object, but I wish our reason may not be seduced from its importance to take measures to repossess it that are not warranted by history or our own observation. An attack of this nature will not depend upon the multitude that attacks, but upon their bravery, for the greater the multitude, the worse the confusion when once they are thrown into disorder; and we have no reason to expect any thing else from our own or others experience. Men who are brought from home with all their family feelings about them, commanded by officers who in general have little or no ambition for military glory, are not fortified for such scenes of carnage as are generally exhibited in attacks made upon towns defended by a large body of veteran troops.

I am not against a winters campaign if the temper of the officers and the conditions of the troops would admit of it, neither have I the least objection to making an attack upon Philadelphia if there was a probability of succeeding founded in human nature or the experience of mankind.

Let us consider the consequences that will result from a disappointment in a measure of this nature. In the first place, it will be attended with a vast expence and the loss of many lives to no valuable purpose. It will prove a great obstruction to the recruiting service, and a defeat will give a general alarm and spread universal discontent throughout the continent. It will expose the weakness of our militia to the enemy, and not only to them but to all Europe who now consider them much more formidable than they really are.

A winters campaign in the present discontented state of the officers, and an attack upon the city of Philadelphia appear to me like forming a crisis for American liberty which if unsuccessful I fear will prove her grave. If the army goes through a winters Campaign and the recruiting service is as much injured as I expect from calling out the militia, it will be in a miserable plight to open the campaign within the spring; and we may reasonably expect that Great Britain will rake all the kennels of Europe for troops to repair their affairs in America.

I have wrote my mind so fully upon the subject of winter quarters and with respect to a winter campaign that it is unnecessary [to] add any thing further here. I would beg leave to recommend the measure suggested in that paper for recruiting the army, and filling up the continental Battalions. If the measure is adopted the army can be recruited nearly or quite as soon as the militia can be got together. The attack can be made with much more hopes of success and if we are defeated we shall still have a force to carry on a regular Seige as soon as the military apparatus can be prepared and the season will permit us to open batteries against the enemy's lines.

These are my sentiments Sir upon the subject which with all due deference are submitted to your Excellency's consideration, but if your Excellency thinks a winters campaign a necessary measure or an attack upon Philadelphia an eligible plan I will lend every possible aid in my power to carry it into execution; notwithstanding that this is the third year since I have paid the least attention to my own private affairs.[2]

NATH GREENE

ALS (Washington Papers: DLC) 32 pp.

1. The midnight oil must have burned in all the officers' quarters the night of 3 December as they wrote in response to Washington's peremptory circular of that day (above). NG's lengthy answer is dated 3 December, but it is likely he did not finish it until the early hours of 4 December. If he suffered from the cold and fatigue, his writing does not reveal it.

2. Washington received twenty other opinions, including those from two militia generals and from his sometime aide and adjutant, Joseph Reed, who was familiar with the area. All agreed with NG on the impracticability of attacking Howe's strongly entrenched position—including the five who had favored such an attack in November. (See note, NG to Washington, 24 November, 9 o'clock above; their opinions are in the Washington Papers, DLC, but have been printed in Worthington C. Ford, "Philadelphia Defences," PMHB, 20 [1896]: 521–51; 21 [1897]: 51–70. Rhode Islanders Varnum and Greene wrote half as much as the other nineteen combined.)

Armed with these unanimous opinions, Washington sat down with the committee to discuss the hopes that Congress held for an attack on Philadelphia. (Congress was then at York, where it remained until the evacuation of Philadelphia in June 1778.) The committee was fully persuaded by the arguments, which they summarized for Congress at a meeting on 16 December. They came to the following resolutions (which they also sent in a letter to Washington): "That an attempt on Philadelphia with the present Force under Genl Washington, either by storming the Lines and Redoubts, crossing the Schuylkill, or by regular approaches to the City, is an enterprise under the circumstances of the Army attended with such a variety of difficulties, as to render it ineligible." They went on to elaborate upon the impossibility of gathering a militia force from distant states, upon the need for Congress to determine "on the properest mode of reinforcing the Army," and, until reinforcements could be obtained, declared that the army should take a post the "most likely to overawe the Enemy, afford supplies of provision, wood, Water, and Forage, be secure from surprise, and best calculated for covering the Country from the ravages of the Enemy, as well as provide comfortable Quarters for the Officers and Soldiers." (JCC, 9: 1029–31) Looking back from Valley Forge, the final admonition seems especially ironic.

By the time Congress had heard the report and laid it on the table, the army had been searching for that ideal "post" for a week (see below, Order of March, 10 December), but in the meantime Gen. Howe had decided to leave his cozy quarters in Philadelphia in order to challenge the American army at Whitemarsh. If, on his arrival, an attack appeared inadvisable, he hoped at least to lure Washington from his lair as he had tried to do in June when Washington was ensconced in the Watchung Mountains of New Jersey. (See note, Council of War, 12 June 1777, above.) On the night of 4 December, Howe set out with columns under Gens. Cornwallis and Knyphausen.

Washington, who had feared an attack by Howe while NG's army was in New Jersey, now welcomed it—confident that the army, in its strong position along the hills above Sandy Run Creek at Whitemarsh, could defeat Howe if he dared attack. When word came of Howe's departure, Washington put NG in charge of the left wing of the army, Sullivan the right wing. On NG's left, and somewhat forward, were Daniel Morgan's rifle corps and Col. Mordecai Gist's Maryland militia; on Sullivan's right was Gen. James Irvine's Pennsylvania militia corps.

Several hours before daylight on 5 December, the British were sighted at Chestnut Hill, three miles in front of the American right. The Americans had lit many fires so that to the Hessian Major Baurmeister "it looked as if fifty thousand men were encamped there." (Baurmeister, Revolution, pp. 135–36) Just before noon, British advance units met with Irvine's militia. It was a minor skirmish, but Irvine was wounded and captured. No further action ensued that day. After facing the American left for a day, Howe began to shift his army during the night of 6 December by way of Germantown toward NG's sector on the left. At mid-day on the seventh, Gen. Charles Grey advanced but met up with Morgan's rifle corps and Gist's Maryland militia. A hot exchange followed along a wooded area, with the Americans falling back. Morgan had a horse shot from under him, but he and Gist got their men to the rear in good order. Morgan's losses were probably heavier than he had suffered in the entire Saratoga campaign, but Grey's losses were sufficient to cause him to retire. (Higginbotham,

Morgan, pp. 80–81; Peckham, *Toll,* lists thirty Americans killed, forty wounded, and enemy casualties "as heavy"; p. 45.)

As Howe surveyed the entrenched American lines stretching along the tops of the hills—the slopes of which bristled with abatis and scattered artillery emplacements—he was dissuaded from attempting a frontal attack. He had hoped that Grey's advance would draw Washington down to fight, but as Washington later told Congress, disappointed as he was that Howe would not attack, "I must add that reason, prudence, and every principle of policy, forbad us quitting our post to attack them." (Fitzpatrick, *GW,* 10: 144) Some of Howe's officers favored a wide flanking movement, but he vetoed the suggestion and "returned dejectedly to Philadelphia." (Gruber, *Howe Brothers,* p. 266) Thus ended Howe's campaign of 1777. It was, as Gruber has written, "disastrous for the British—primarily because Sir William Howe had been obsessed with recovering Pennsylvania and incapable of taking prompt or consistent action." (Ibid.) His failure was a victory of sorts for Washington, but one that was completely overshadowed by the spectacular victory of the Northern Army over Burgoyne.

Assured that the British had returned to Philadelphia, Washington turned to the problem of finding winter quarters. (See below, Order of March, 10 December.) The action at Whitemarsh is covered in Reed, *Campaign,* pp. 370–80. Robertson, *Diaries,* pp. 158–61, clears up questions of chronology.

To Robert Morris

Dr Sir   Camp [Whitemarsh, Pa.] Decem 4th 1777

This will be handed you by Col Barton[1] from Rhode Island the Gentleman that took Major General Prescot prisoner. He waits upon you Sir by my advice in a delicate affair. The Congress were pleasd to honor him with a Sword. His fortune is not so liberal but that he would wish to feel their bounty in some thing more substantial. Providing you thought there was not an indelicacy in the application or that it would be fruitless, if made. I shall esteem it a favor Sir if youl give him your opinion upon the subject. He was going on to Congress. I thought it most advisable to consult you on the business. The enterprise was bold and hazzardous. The Congress are the best Judge how far Wisdom and prudence dictates a liberal reward to be necessary for encouraging such bold and hardy attempts. I am Sir with great respect Your Most Obedt Servt

N GREENE

ALS (PCC, Item 155: DNA).

1. On Col. Barton's exploit, see above, NG to Catharine, 17 July 1777.

Order of March from Whitemarsh, Pa.

[10 December 1777]

To his Excellency Gen. Washington Commander in Chief of the American Army.

Pursuant to your Excellency's orders We have considered upon a proper order of March for the Army in crossing the Schulkill and recommend that the Troops march first in the following order Viz. Part of Pennsylvania Militia under Potter.

1st Maryland Brigade	Huntingdon
2d do do	Varnum
1st Pennsylvania	North Carolina
2d do	Glover
Poor	Learned
Maxwell	Patterson
Conway	Weedon
Woodford	Muhlenberg
Scott	Maryland Militia, Rifle Corps

The Baggage, Stores and Park of Artillery to cross at Sweeds Ford setting off at least two hours before the Army marches. The Baggage to march in the following order Viz. 1st   Quartermasters Stores. 2dly   Commissary's Stores. 3dly   The baggage of the respective Brigades in the same order as the Troops march. The whole to be preceded by the Artillery Park and attended by the Artificers of the Army. One Brigade to cross before the Army and pass down some Miles towards the Enemy on the other Side Schulkil and take post on the Road leading from the middle Ferry between the Enemy and the main Army. Two covering Parties of five hundred Men each to pass down the Ridge Road and German Town Road to watch the Motions of the Enemy. One Regiment to go with each of those parties. The other two Regiments to march in front of the main Army.

JNO SULLIVAN
in behalf of the whole[1]

A party of one hundred men under the command of a major to precede the Army after the rout is fixt; and repair the little foot bridges, and cover the wet places, the party to be furnished with axes for that purpose.

The brigade that is to be sent into the Jerseys to serve as a covering party on this [east] side the Schuylkill and if there is no intelligence that renders it necessary for them to cross the River to remain on this side until orderd into the Jerseys.

The first days march the head of the Column to reach the Lancaster road, the Engineers and Major General of the Day to examin the ground to encamp upon, to set off tomorrow morning if the army marches tomorrow. G—Potters militia to cross with the Army over the Schuylkill, but to recross it again when the Brigade of Continental troops leaves the ground to go into the Jerseys, the whole of the Pensylvania militia to act collectively between the Delaware and the Schuylkill. Head Quarters to be near or at the Cross Roads. Guards to be established to cut of [off] Provision going into the City.

The boats fited for carriages to be brought to Wilmington on Carriages, the others to be carried to Easton.

The troops sent into the Jerseys to take post at Mount Holly.

The baggage to cross the River under the direction of the quarter master at the most convenient fords to keep the back roads in the rear of the army.

Ferries to be established with slideing roaps upon the Bethlehem plan, across the Schuylkill about twenty or thirty miles above the City.[2]

The following disposition to be made of the Horse: one Troop in the Jerseys, the remainder of a Regiment to act with the Pensylvania Militia, the rest of the light Troops to be with the main army on the other side of the Schuylkill.

The Army to march at four in the morning.[3]

DS (Washington Papers: DLC).
    1. Sullivan signed as senior officer; the remainder of the document is in NG's hand.
    2. NG had apparently observed the ferry when he and Knox were in Bethlehem. (See note, NG to Wayne, 22 August, above.) Twenty years earlier the resourceful Moravians had equipped the ferry that ran across the West Branch of the Delaware with what NG calls "slideing roaps." Where it had previously taken four men half an hour to pole a boat across at high water, a chronicler wrote, it "now crosses the river by rope usually in *ninety seconds*." (John W. Jordan, "The Bethlehem Ferry," *PMHB*, 21 [1897]: 109)
    3. When the officers worked out the order of march across the Schuylkill, they had not reached agreement as to where the army should camp for the winter—except that a majority had voted against the location at Wilmington, Del. (the choice of NG and others), in favor of some place on the Lancaster-Reading line. (See above, NG to Washington, 1 December and note.) Washington was no nearer a decision, when on the morning of 11 December he put the army in motion. Some eleven thousand cold, weary, half-shod men left the cold comfort of their tents or shacks at Whitemarsh and set off—precise destination undetermined. Sullivan, in the vanguard, had gotten part of his division across a bridge of wagons at Matsons Ford when they ran into a foraging party, the advance troops of some two thousand men under Cornwallis. Sullivan immediately got his men back across the river with the help of a Pennsylvania militia unit that skirmished with Cornwallis's vanguard.
    Washington then ordered the army upstream four miles to Swede's Ford, where they camped in the open on the east side of the river the night of 11 December. The next day (the twelfth) was spent bridging the river at Swede's Ford, and during that night most of the army crossed to the west bank. Cornwallis, meanwhile, had headed back to Philadelphia with the spoils of his foraging expedition. Washington now decided to go back downstream to the Gulph, which Cornwallis had evacuated and where Sullivan first started his division across. There the army camped without tents (which were still on the east bank of the river) for several days. A slushy snow covered the ground and the men.
    Washington had still not decided on a location. He favored moving further back from Philadelphia where provisions were more plentiful, but when the Pennsylvania Assembly and Executive Council received word at Lancaster that the army had crossed to the west bank of the Schuylkill, they suddenly became gravely concerned that Washington was abandoning the area east of the river to British depredations. They were especially fearful the army might consider moving to Wilmington as NG had recommended. In a formal remonstrance to Congress, they declared that with the "removal

of our Army" it would "be impossible to recruit the Regiments of this State" or to raise taxes to support the "War for the Ensuing Year." It would also, they threatened, "give a fatal Stab to the Credit of the Continental Currency throughout this State." (*Pa. Archives*, 6: 104–105)

Congress, which had permitted Washington to choose his winter camp, received the remonstrance on 17 December while Washington was still at the Gulph; they sent it to him by express, requesting that he inform Congress whether he had "come to a fixed resolution to canton the army," and if so, how he planned to protect the area east of the Schuylkill or the State of New Jersey. (*JCC*, 9: 1036) Washington had already gotten wind of the not-so-subtle message from the Pennsylvania legislature. He realized that he dared not camp any further west than the neighborhood of the Gulph. In finally choosing the west side of the Schuylkill at Valley Forge, twenty-five miles north and west of Philadelphia, he had the advice of two Pennsylvanians who were familiar with the area—Gens. Wayne and Muhlenberg. Considering Washington's own requirements that he be able to keep an eye on the British in Philadelphia (while at the same time being in a good defensible position) and considering the Pennsylvania legislature's threats against removal any further from Philadelphia, Valley Forge was probably as good a choice as could have been made.

On 18 December as the army prepared to move, it rained. On the morning of the nineteenth, the army broke camp for the last time—until June 1778. The interminable marching from June to December was over at last; the hardships at Valley Forge would now begin. (See note, NG to Jacob, 3 January 1778, below. The period from 10 December until the arrival at Valley Forge is discussed in Reed, *Campaign*, pp. 381–96. The location of the brigades at Valley Forge is in Reed, *Valley Forge*, pp. 5–6; Du Portail's map of Valley Forge, as well as modern location symbols, are on pp. 20 and 21.)

To George Washington

[Valley Forge, 29 December 1777. Col. Gibson of Virginia Staff Regiment asks that three of his officers be sent to "collect the straglers deserters and recruits," thinks it "necessary for the publick good." ALS (Washington Papers: DLC) 1 p.]

To George Washington

Dear Sir   Camp Valey Forge January the 1st 1777 [1778]

It gives me the greatest pain to hear the murmurs and complaints among the officers for the want of spirits. They say they are exposd to the severity of the weather, subject to hard duty and nothing but bread and beef to eat morning, noon, and night, without vegetables or anything to drink but cold water.[1] This is hard fare for people that have been accustomd to live tolerable. The officers observe however disagreeable their situation they would patiently submit to their hard fortune if the evil in its own nature was incureable. But they think by a proper exertion spirits may be procurd to alleviate their distress until they have an opportunity to provide for themselves.

Lord Sterling was mentioning yesterday that he had made a discovery of a considerable quantity *of spirits* sufficient to supply all the officers. Supposing His Lordships information to be true, will it not be consistent with good policy to sieze it and distribute it among the Regiments for the use of the Officers about thirty or forty Gallons for each Regiment. This would give a temporary relief and the present dissatisfaction seems to be so great it is absolutely necessary to take some measures if possible to silence as many of the complaints as may be. Col Abeel has just returnd from Bethlehem and sais there is 16 hogsheads of spirits at that place belonging to the old Commisary department. It is in the hands of Mr Oakley and was sent there by Mr Ervin. Col Abeel thinks it will be disposd on [of?] for private property if not sent for immediately. Col Abeel also observes there is great quantities of Whiskey sent into the Jerseys at Easton and that a full supply might be had for the use of the Army if some person was sent there to sieze it.[2]

I have got a very disagreeable pain in one of my Eyes or else I should have waited upon your Excellency.[3] I am with great respect your Excellences Obedient Sevt

N GREENE

ALS (Washington Papers: DLC).
    1. Washington had started the new year by issuing a gill of spirits to the soldiers at Valley Forge. Meanwhile the commissioned officers, who had to fend for themselves, had been unsuccessful in buying spirits. A few days later, spirits that Washington had ordered to be seized—probably from loyalists—were distributed to them. (Fitzpatrick, GW, 10: 225, 242–43, and 272)
    2. Liquor was reported as plentiful around York, Pa., where Congress was meeting. See below, John Clark, Jr., to NG, 10 January.
    3. His eye bothered him off and on for the rest of his life.

To Samuel Chase[1]

[Valley Forge, 2 January 1778. Asks Chase's help if John "Clarke," NG's former aide, should wish an appointment—one that was "consistant with the true interest of the Continent" since he, NG, was "an enimy to court party and favoritism."[2] ALS (PCC, Item 41: DNA) 1 p.]

    1. NG probably addressed his letter to Chase because at this time he was an extremely active and influential member of Congress who had a warm admiration for Washington, some of which undoubtedly spilled over to NG. A signer of the Declaration of Independence for Maryland, Chase had been a radical leader of the Sons of Liberty. He served in Congress until 1785—except from 1778 to 1780, when he had not been reappointed because of questionable business dealings. He later sat on the U.S. Supreme Court.
    2. See Clark to NG, 10 January, below.

To Jacob Greene

Camp Valley Forge 3d January 1778
Our army are tenting themselves at this place;[1] they are almost worn out with fatigue and greatly distressed for want of clothing,

particularly the articles of shoes and stockings. The present mode of clothing the army will always leave us without a sufficient supply. The change in the commissary department has been a very distressing circumstance; the army has been fed from hand to mouth ever since Mr. Trumbull left it. Our operations have been greatly retarded from the situation of the commissary department. The quarter-master-general's department also has been in a most wretched condition.[2] General Mifflin, who ought to have been at the head of the business, has never been with the army since it came into the state. He was unwell the early part of the season, but it is said he is disgusted with the general for not paying such mighty deference to him as his vanity leads him to think himself entitled to. I am credibly informed, he has been endeavouring to wound the general's reputation, in order to bring in General Gates at the head of the army; and for fear I should be an obstacle to his measures, he has thrown out some insinuations to my prejudice. I am but little afraid of his insinuations. He may possibly poison the public mind for a time, but he cannot injure me in the army, where my conduct is best known.

The congress have lately appointed Colonel Wilkinson to the rank of a brigadier and Brigadier General Conway to the rank of major general. Both these appointments are exceedingly disgusting to the army; the first to the colonels, the last to the brigadiers. The army is exceedingly convulsed by these appointments, and God knows what will be the issue.[3] Almost all the colonels in the army will resign in consequence of Wilkinson's appointment. General Gates is exceedingly blamed for recommending the measure.

General Conway is a man of much intrigue and little judgment. He is a great incendiary, of a restless spirit, and always contriving to puff himself off to the public as an officer of great consequence. He left the army under pretence of going to France, alleging for reason that there was the greatest probability of a French war, and that he should injure his interests by staying here. Every body in the army thought he was gone. But he stole away to congress, announced his intention of going to France, got in with some of the court faction to trumpet his consequence to the congress, and they hastily appointed him a major general, to the prejudice of the brigadiers, who to a man will resign their commissions if he holds his rank and remains in the army. This appointment appears to have been obtained by such low artifices that every body in the army despises him for it. The Marquis La Fayette, and all the other French gentlemen, will scarcely speak to him. He is the greatest novice in war, in every thing but disciplining a regiment, that ever I saw. He is by no means of an enterprizing military turn of mind, and of very little activity. This is the true character of the man, and yet he is palmed off upon the public by little arts, as the first military man upon the continent.

Our cause is sure, if we do not get divided among ourselves. But there is great danger that we shall. Men of great ambition, and without principle or virtue, will sacrifice every thing to their private views. The army in general has been very well united; but I am afraid the injudicious appointments made in congress will ruin it.

You mention my letter to Governor Cook, in which I pronounce the division of the British force as a fortunate circumstance for America. The events of the campaign have verified it. And had our force been equal to General Howe's, or at least as much superior as the northern army was to Burgoyne's, he must have shared the same fate. But alas! we have fought with [i.e., against] vastly superior numbers, and although twice defeated,[4] have kept the field. History affords but few examples of the kind. The people may think there has not been enough done, but our utmost endeavours have not been wanting. Our army with inferior numbers, badly found, badly clothed, worse fed, and newly levied, must have required good generalship to triumph over superior numbers well found, well clothed, well fed and veteran soldiers. We cannot conquer the British force at once, but they cannot conquer us at all. The limits of the British government in America are their out-sentinels.

Reports prevail very strongly again of a French war. I honestly confess to you I do not believe it; for France can have no pretext for declaring war, and certainly it is not the interest of Great Britain to do it. But nevertheless it may happen.[5] I wish congress may not be lulled into security from their late successes to the north, and their hopes of a French explosion. It is our business to levy a new army as soon as possible; each state to furnish its proportion by a draft. There is no such thing as filling the army by voluntary enlistments as speedily as will be necessary to open the campaign to advantage. Each state will be compelled hereafter to furnish clothing for their own troops. The present mode of clothing the army is ruinous. We have had 3,000 soldiers unfit for duty for want of clothing, this fall and winter. The Rhode Island troops have done themselves great honour this campaign. Col. [Christopher] Greene's character is in high estimation. Major Thayer distinguished himself at Fort Mifflin, and has acquired universal applause. Your troops are generally exceedingly well officered from the northward this year. General Gates is a child of fortune, the successes to the northward are all-glorious. General Arnold and General Lincoln are in high esteem; and it is said General Burgoyne gives Arnold the credit for the successes obtained over him.

I am happy that the work is but done; I do not care who does it. But I should like to have [had] a hand in the mischief.

I have no hope of coming home this winter; the general will not grant me permission. Mrs. Greene is coming to camp. We are all going into log huts—a sweet life after a most fatiguing campaign.

Johnson, *Greene*, 1: 160–62.

1. It would be another twelve days before the last of the army were in huts. Logs had to be cut and hauled to the site, and most of the soldiers to erect them were without skill or adequate tools. The windowless structures were planned to be fourteen by sixteen feet, with bunks for twelve men around the sides and a chimney and fireplace at one end that smoked incessantly. As they took shape, the huts varied in size and arrangement. (Trussell, *Valley Forge*, pp. 19–21, 94, 96) The green-log walls were chinked with mud or clay, the floors were earthen, the steep roofs covered with whatever the men could contrive. Damp and uncomfortable as they were, they were an improvement on the tents the troops had lived in for several weeks. Washington made a point of quartering himself and his officers in similar log huts—at least for a while.

2. NG's comments in these few sentences are a restrained indictment of the clothier, commissary, and quartermaster departments; their virtual collapse was soon to make Valley Forge a lasting symbol of suffering and hardship. It is difficult to exaggerate the misery endured by the incredibly patient men who stayed on during January and February. The winter itself, it is true, has been exaggerated in the popular mind; fortunately it was less severe than most winters during the war. If, indeed, it had been as cold as the severe winter at Morristown two years later, few men would have survived Valley Forge. (See Ludlum, *Winters*, pp. 100–107, 111–17, 123–33.) As it was, the toll was measured not so much by deaths from starvation and freezing as by the tortures of hunger and malnutrition, of bone-chilling cold and of lingering illness—too often ending in death. Several thousand men deserted, which probably spared from starvation some who stayed on. The horses were not so fortunate; hundreds died from lack of forage.

The hardships at Valley Forge were extensively recorded by both officers and enlisted men. The letters below are a small part of that documentation: NG to Christopher, 5 January; to McDougall, 25 January; to Knox, 26 February; to William Greene and to George Weedon, 7 March; and from Varnum, 12 February. See also the exchange of letters between NG and Washington from 12 to 20 February on foraging. Washington's letters and orders are among the best sources. His daily concern for the army and his unflagging efforts to alleviate the suffering are evident in his writings from December to March (Fitzpatrick, *GW*, 10: 192–531). Many other primary accounts have been printed. A collection of excerpts from such accounts is found in John Joseph Stoudt, *Ordeal at Valley Forge* (Philadelphia: University of Pennsylvania Press, 1963). Two good secondary accounts, with comprehensive bibliographies, are Reed, *Valley Forge* and Trussell, *Valley Forge*. A good popular account is Noel F. Busch, *Winter Quarters: George Washington and the Continental Army at Valley Forge* (New York: W. W. Norton & Co., 1974). It should be noted that these works record a happier Valley Forge between March and June, as do the letters below for that period.

The basic cause of most of the misery at Valley Forge—the collapse of the supply system—has not been thoroughly documented. The incompetency of the heads of the supply departments—Clothier General James Mease, Commissary of Purchases William Buchanan, and Quartermaster Thomas Mifflin—was a prime factor, but incompetency alone did not account for the breakdown.

Part of the blame lay with Congress, which was responsible for the organization of the supply systems. It is noteworthy that although NG, like most people, was critical of Mease, his criticism in this letter is directed at the "mode" of clothing the army that Congress had established. Although Congress had appointed a committee on the clothing department on 25 November 1777, the committee never made a report (*JCC*, 10: 12n). Washington, who was equally critical of Mease, had refused to accept his resignation in December—probably because he could find no more suitable person to administer the chaotic department. Mease's letter of resignation of 16 December 1777 is in the Washington Papers, DLC; when he finally did resign in August 1778, Washington agreed he had been "by no means fit for the business" (Fitzpatrick, *GW*, 12: 278).

Commissary William Buchanan was similarly denounced for the food shortage, but Congress had contributed to his failures by splitting the department into Commissary of Purchases and Commissary of Issues the previous summer. Joseph Trumbull, the capable commissary, had resigned at that time because he considered the reorganization unworkable—a judgment amply borne out at Valley Forge, although he would undoubtedly have done better than the incapable Buchanan. (Buchanan as commissary of purchases was replaced in April by Jeremiah Wadsworth, but Charles Stewart, the commissary of issues, stayed on until 1781.)

There were, however, additional causes for the shortages of food and clothing that were quite independent of the organization of the two departments or the men who administered them. One was a lack of horses and wagons to haul supplies from distant points where supplies were available—a responsibility of the quartermaster general. There were fifty wagonloads of clothes, for example, at Lancaster, Pa., that never reached Valley Forge. (Reed, *Valley Forge*, p. 14) Another cause, given the lack of transportation, was the locating of the camp where the British were competing for food and forage. The British had a great advantage: silver specie. A nominal patriot, having seen nothing but depreciating currency, could not always resist specie, while British raiding parties were more than willing to use force on those patriots who refused enemy money.

The depreciation of the currency, which by January had fallen to a third its face value, was a factor even where British sterling was not in circulation; suppliers everywhere were increasingly reluctant to exchange their goods for dubious paper. And, finally, after almost three years of war there was less and less willingness among the civilian population to make sacrifices for the army and more and more concern for private interests. In many citizens, at all social and economic levels, this private concern took the form of profiteering, cheating, or even stealing. To the hungry soldier at Valley Forge, of course, it made no difference whether food was denied him by merchants who refused to sell to the army or by the wagoner who drained the brine off the salt pork in order to get more barrels on his wagon—barrels of spoiled meat by the time he reached camp.

Fortunately for the American cause, the army was never again so desperate for basic articles of survival—due in large part to the appointments of NG as quartermaster general and Jeremiah Wadsworth as commissary general. (See NG to Reed, 9 March, below.) As is evident in the correspondence, NG's success reflected personal qualifications rather than any improvement in the conditions. Conditions, in fact, worsened throughout his tenure. Depreciation continued until the dollar was worth one and a half cents. During the same period, there was a growing shortage of everything—men, horses, supplies. War weariness, indifference, profiteering, and cheating, moreover, went on apace.

3. Wilkinson's and Conway's promotions are the subject of NG's letter to Henry Laurens, 12 January, below. Their role in the "Conway Cabal" is related in note, NG to Jacob, 7 February, below.

4. At Brandywine and Germantown.

5. NG could not know that France had already recognized the independence of the United States and was prepared to form an alliance; treaties of commerce and alliance were signed in Paris on 6 February.

To Christopher Greene[1]

Camp at the Valley Forge
Januy 5th 1778

Dr Sir

Your favor of the 27th of November from Westerly came safe to hand.[2] I am much obligd to you for the information you give me respecting domestick matters, the state of your business and the Policy of Administration. It seems that fortune is no freind of ours in the Privateering business.[3] Pray what affront have you given her ladyship? Have you been wanting in a blind confidence in her bounty and generosity or have you insulted her by indeavoring to take your measures from the Laws of reason or the rules of prudence? It is almost immaterial from what quarter her displeasure originates she is determind to be cruel. Let her go on and do her worst, we can surmount all her embarassments by honest industry and free use of common sense.

Col Sherburne gives a drole description of your Legislator [i.e., legislature]. Ignorance, confidence and obstinacy are the true characteristicks of the spirit and genius of Administration. God preserve you from the mischiefs attending such councels and measures. It is an antient proverb that when the political Pot boils the scum rises, and I am told there are many that have jumpt into surpriseing fortunes of late who are creeping into Government, determind not to crawl out of life with the same degree [of] obscurity they entered it.

General Spencer I find is universally censurd for the late unfortunate expedition against Newport.[4] I was always an enemy to that scheme. I always thought it a dangerous attempt; but the force was none [not] large enough to have gone on upon the most certain footing. I never had an Idea of raising a force of such consequence for the expedition. I always thought the object upon the Island too small to draw together a sufficient force to ensure success and if there went on a small force, the risque was greater than the object. I immagin the plan for attacking Newport is a Providence hobby Horse.

I observe you think the suffering of those troops were very great while it lasted. Gracious God if you had been with this Army and been a witness to its suffering and distress, you would not think the suffering of them troops deservd to be mentiond in the same year, much more in the same day. If you could see a defeat, follow a long and tedious nights march, hear the screams of the wounded that are going of [off] the field, see the labour and difficulty of geting them off, have to march forty miles without victuals or sleep, you would hardly think your sufferings worthy nameing. This has been one of the severeest Campaigns America ever felt, and I wish it may be the severeest she may ever feel.

The campaign is now closd, and the Army gone into Huts upon the banks of the River Schuylkill about twenty miles from Philadelphia. The troops are worn out with fatigue, badly fed and almost naked. There are and have been some thousands of the Army without shoes for months past. It is difficult to get sufficient supplies to cloath the Army at large. The demand is multipled by the negligence of the under officers but too little attention is paid by the Clotheir General to the business of his department.[5] I am sorry to say but it always appeard to me to be fact that the Congress had an eye more to the gratification of individuals than to the common interest of the Continent. Experience will teach them better in time. There are many deserving charactors in the House, but they are often led astray by the artful and designing.

There has been two most extraordinary promotions lately: Wilkinson and Conway; the first a Brigadier from a Col, the other a major General from a Brigadier. They were both the youngest officers in the line. In consequence of these appointments almost all the Col[s] and all the Brigadiers will resign. The Army is exceedingly convulsed. I dread the consequences. I have been employd all day in drawing up a representation to the Congress.[6]

The Rhode Island troops have done themselves great honor. The reputation of the Officers is in high estimation. The Soldiers of the two Regiments are put into one and Col Greene and all his officers are coming home to recruit a negro Regiment. Will they succeed or not?[7] Sammy is anxious to get to his Phebe.[8] He is a mighty honest lad. It is a pity so good a lad should get into the road of corruption.

I am exceedingly obligd to you for your Polite offers to wait on Mrs Greene home. She is coming to camp to spend the Winter. I expect her in today. Your observations are very just respecting the disagreeable situation of the officers and soldiers from the depreciation of money and the enormous prices things go at. We must get along as well as we can but God knows how, for I dont. My love to your beloved wife and to all friends in the neighbourhood. Your affect

N GREENE

I write to you with freedom about men and things and therefore must beg you not to expose my letter.

ALS (MWA).
    1. NG's brother.
    2. Letter not found.
    3. On the brothers' privateering business, see below, Griffin Greene to NG, 28 November 1779.
    4. Since December 1776 several thousand British troops had occupied Newport and Aquidneck Island. Although Congress and the R.I. Assembly had urged Gen. Joseph Spencer to attack in the spring of 1777, it was October before he had mustered a

motley army of some nine thousand men—mostly militia—at Tiverton, R.I., for an assault across Mt. Hope Bay. After ten days of stormy weather, during which time half the militia drifted home, Spencer called off the expedition. The sixty-three-year-old Spencer, though not noted for bold leadership, was exonerated by the R.I. Assembly and later by Congress. He tendered his resignation in December; Congress accepted it 13 January 1778. On Spencer's part in the planned attack, see Arnold, *R.I.*, 2: 400–408; Bartlett, *Records*, 8: 154–55, 214–15, 313–14; *JCC*, 10: 47, 322n. The abortive assault has been thoroughly covered in Nathaniel N. Shipton, "General Joseph Palmer: Scapegoat for the Rhode Island Fiasco of October, 1777," *New England Quarterly*, 39 (1966): 498–512. It was August 1778 before the Americans mounted another attack on Newport.

5. On Clothier General James Mease, see note on Valley Forge, NG to Jacob, 3 January above. Even had he been competent, his task would have been overwhelming. In the summer of 1778, the Board of War virtually took over the clothier general's functions.

6. See below, NG to Laurens, 12 January, on Wilkinson's and Conway's promotions.

7. Col. Christopher Greene, NG's third cousin, was the prime mover in organizing the first Black regiment in the Continental army. With the blessing of Gen. Varnum and the tacit approval of Washington, Col. Greene, Lt. Col. Jeremiah Olney, and Maj. Samuel Ward, Jr., NG's long-time friend, were en route to Rhode Island for this purpose. In February, Gov. Cooke and the Rhode Island legislature, faced with a shortage of white recruits, overrode the opposition of the South County slave-holders and pushed through a law that offered freedom to all slaves who were found acceptable to the recruiters, with promises of reimbursement to their owners. The regiment of some 130 men, officered by whites, served with distinction until the end of the war. Upon Christopher Greene's death in May 1781, Col. Olney took command. On the regiment's participation in the battle of Rhode Island, see below, NG to Washington, 28/31 August 1778. (Varnum's and Washington's roles in forming the regiment are seen in letters from Varnum to Washington and Washington to Cooke on 2 January 1778, and Cooke to Washington, 23 February 1778, Washington Papers, DLC; see also Lorenzo J. Greene, "Some Observations on the Black Regiment of Rhode Island in the American Revolution," *Journal of Negro History*, 37 [1952]: 142–72), and Gary A. Puckrein, *The Black Regiment in the American Revolution* (Providence: R.I. Black Heritage Society, 1978).

8. Maj. Samuel Ward, Jr. (see note 7 above) was married on 8 March to Phebe, the daughter of William and Catharine Ray Greene. (See below, NG to William Greene, 7 March.) William Greene became governor of Rhode Island two months later.

From Major John Clark, Jr.

My dear General   Col: Donaldsons York [Pa.]
                                                 Jany. 10th 1777[8]

I arrived here two Days ago. You shou'd have heard from me e'er this, but bad Roads and want of sufficient matter to fill my letter prevented. This Day I delivered His Excellency's Letter to the President. I was politely received, yours to Mr Gerry also, am to have an interview with him at noon. Mr Chase is not here but soon expected.[1]

I am informed Congress have rescinded their late resolve in the appointment of the late Brigadier, and have offered him an appointment as Secretary to the Board of War.[2] There are great debates in and out of doors with respect to Conways late promotion, great indeed. I'm told the remonstrance of the officers is look'd on as too peremptory and wish that some other mode of application to have those kind of grievances which do and are likely to exist, cou'd be fallen upon. Mr Laurens thinks the last above named Gent. has used His Ex—cy Gr W—n very ill, and appears much incensed at his conduct.[3] I've often, since my arrival, been asked my opinion with respect to the propriety of his promotion, and the sentiments of the Army. I have I hope candidly given them in the following words: "Gent. you may as well attempt to change the System of the Universe, as the disposition and services of the Army where Officers in the same line behave equally well, the promoting one of them over the next, is lessening them in the esteem of the public and checking that Spirit which fires the breast of a Military character, which is the grand source of an innumerable train of Evils ever attendant on these occasions. The Officers wish a regular line of promotion and when any *distinguish* themselves that are in the *line of Fire*, those to be mark'd by His Excellency and recommended to Congress accordingly, promotion thus will create a Spirit of emulation, and not disgust, and Officers will endeavor to out vie *each other* in their Profession. At present the Army is convulsed to a great degree, and in this Situation the most disagreeable consequences are to be apprehended, the Officers acknowledge the *Authority* of Congress and argue they, when agrieved, have a right to retire if not redressed and the same Spirit will animate those who succeed them, and so you may go on to infinitum." Warm words have passed from my lips. I've hinted that designing Persons are at the bottom of the whole—indeed 'tis publickly talked of. Various reports have been circulated thro' this Country to prejudice the People against His Excellency and you. You are said to lead him into every measure and that he had wrote if he fell, to have you appointed to the command of the Army.[4] But all these among the sensible and Virtuous have no weight. Many other disagreeable things have been told which I cannot at present relate: they in turn, will also vanish into nothing and brand the propagators with *eternal infamy* and shame. Pursue the same line of conduct and you will thro *divine* favor live to see your Enemies your Friends. I think a duel or two will soon put a period to those injurious reports; indeed, I have cautioned some against them [reports], assuring 'em the Gent. of the Army (*friends to the Gen'l*) wou'd not hear them abused without calling the persons to account in a public manner. Therefore I believe they will sing small; indeed I believe a few Oz's [ounces] of Gunpowder diffused thro [*illegible*] channels will answer a good purpose.

Take the Sentiments of the President before mentioned, and you may guess those of Congress with respect to the promoting.

Liquor is very plenty in this country at 15/ per Gall. Captn Bittinger assures me he can furnish (if sufficiently empowered and suitable Commissions) the Army in a short time with 10000 Gals. We want only proper Persons to make purchases and have those Articles delivered to proper persons and the Army will be well supplied.[5] If a proper encouragement was given to the Farmers in this and Neighbouring Counties they wou'd raise vast quantities of Cabbage and supply the Army with Sour Crout, an excellent thing for Troops, as also Potatoes. Dr Rush is here. I mention'd it [to] him and he assures me 'tis much wanting and wou'd have the happiest effects.[6]

If a prudent Active Officer was dispatched among the Quakers near the Enemy with Orders to engage a few Farmers as Spies on this Condition, that they shou'd be excused from all Military Service and fines for non attendance or not providing Substitutes, it wou'd enable His Excellency to get every information of the Enemy's designs etc. and there is not one in ten of those Farmers but wou'd be happy to serve America in that station, permit 'em to carry marketing and give them a *few Dollars* on *extraordinary* occasions and I'll pawn my life, you succeed. Pray communicate this to His Excellency and write me (by the first Express directed to the care of Col. Donaldson at York) on that head, to whom be pleased to give my love. Compt to Mrs Greene and all Friends and think me yours

JNO CLARK JUN

Gen'l Knox equally shares the censures of individuals for having the ear of His Ex—y.

P. S A Brigade of Waggons from Williamsburg with Blanketts Cloathing etc this moment has just arrived.

I beg you so soon as you read this to destroy it.

ALS (MiU-C).
1. Clark, who had done double duty as aide to NG and spy for Washington, was in ill health and had carried letters of introduction in search of an easier assignment. (See above, NG to Chase, 2 January, and Fitzpatrick, *GW*, 10: 250.) A few weeks later, he was appointed as auditor to the army. For a biographical note, see above, vol. 1: 342n.
2. He speaks of the scheming James Wilkinson, whose promotion, along with Conway's, is discussed below, NG to Laurens, 12 January.
3. For Conway's relations with Washington see "Conway Cabal," NG to Jacob, 7 February, below. Henry Laurens (1724–92), the president of Congress, was a strong supporter of Washington. Laurens was a successful South Carolina merchant and planter, who, on returning from a three-year stay in England in 1774, became active in the patriot cause. He was elected to Congress in January 1777 and was unanimously elected by that body to the presidency on 1 November 1777, resigning a year later in a conflict over the Silas Deane—Arthur Lee quarrel. (*DAB*; Philip M. Hamer, "Henry Laurens of South Carolina," Mass. Hist. Soc., *Proc.*, 77 [1965]: 3–14.) The first volume of the *Papers of Henry Laurens*, edited by Philip M. Hamer and George Rogers, Jr., appeared in 1968. The series has reached Volume Six thus far, which takes Laurens's career to August 1769. The last three volumes were edited by Rogers and David R. Chesnutt.
4. This was not the first or last time that Washington was rumored to have said that should something befall him, he wished NG to succeed him. Two years later Gen. Schuyler reported a delegate as having told Congress that NG "was the first of all the

Subordinate Generals In point of Military knowlege and ability, that in case of an accident happening to Gen: Washington he would be the properest person to Command the Army, *And that General Washington thought so too.*" (Schuyler to Washington, 5 April 1780, Fitzpatrick, *GW*, 18: 185n) James Flexner, Washington's recent biographer, has written: "Washington may well have believed that Greene would make his most promising successor, but, all legend to the contrary, no unimpeachable document indicates that Washington ever said so. He would undoubtedly have regarded any such statement as an encroachment upon the prerogatives of Congress." (Flexner, *GW*, p. 368n)

5. See above, NG to Washington, 1 January.

6. Clark knew of NG's long-standing concern that the troops eat vegetables. Sauerkraut, as Dr. Benjamin Rush knew, was a staple winter food among Pennsylvania Germans. He may also have been acquainted with its earlier use by Capt. James Cook, the English explorer, to prevent scurvy among his crews.

To Henry Laurens, President of the Continental Congress

Sir   Camp at Valley Forge January 12th 1778

I would take the liberty of addressing Congress through you, upon a subject which appears to me of great importance, and which in my opinion deserves their most serious attention; It is the present prevailing discontent among the Officers in two capital lines of the Army; to wit, the Colonels and Brigadiers. I am sorry to say this discontent has arisen to such a height and is so general as to forebode the most alarming consequences.

This dissatisfaction proceeds principally from some promotions which have taken place lately, by which the Officers in those lines respectively concieve themselves most materially and esentially injured in their rank: the first more particularly in the promotion of Col. Wilkinson, the last in that of Brigadier General Conway to the rank of Major General. They feel the force of the injury doubly in these instances, from being superceeded by those who had served in subordinate stations. I cannot pretend to say upon what principle those Gentlemen were promoted, but I doubt whether the advantages resulting from their rise will answer the flattering expectations of Congress in their appointments. I do not wish to lessen their merit, but I believe it is generally thought their promotions have been to the prejudice of others at least as deserving as themselves and who had superior claims in every other point of view.[1]

The Officers of this army say they engaged in the service of their Country, not only from a sense of duty as Citizens, but with the fullest confidence that the justice of Congress would secure to them their rank and the rights of promotion according to the rules which prevail in all well regulated Armies. If they concieve these principles to be violated, if they loose their confidence in the justice of Congress it is easy to foresee the fatal effects that will result. Military ardor will languish, a spirit to enterprize cease, Men of honor will decline the service, art and cabal will succeed, and low intrigue will be the characteristick and genius of the Army.

I am persuaded Sir, the Army is not blind to merit, neither are they averse to measures calculated to promote their true political interest, the interest and happiness of their Country; the former they wish to be rewarded, and the latter ever attended to: But with difficulty they will be brought to confess merit in Officers from their appointments, which never has been discovered in the field.

That the Congress should have the power to reward is acknowledged by all, and that great political reasons will justify the introducing Officers in some instances and promoting them in others out of the common line, none can deny. However, Merit and the reasons of State in such cases should be obvious; If they are not, the promotions will be viewed with disgust. Under the above distinction, I am happy to mention the Marquis de la Fayette. This Nobleman's generous, disinterested conduct, his sacrafices to our cause and his great merit, gave him a just claim to an honorable Notice.

I have delivered my sentiments with great candour on this important occasion. The subject demanded it, duty required it. I am not personally affected by the injuries complained off nor am I immediately interested in any manner but as a man, whose only wish is to promote the happiness of his Country.[2] I am with great respect Your Excellencies most Obedt and very humble Serv

NATHANAEL GREENE

LS (PCC, Item 155: DNA).

1. Congress had resolved on 6 November 1777 that Col. James Wilkinson, Gen. Gates's twenty-year-old adjutant general at Saratoga, having been strongly recommended by Gates as a "gallant officer, and a promising military genius," be brevetted a brigadier general (*JCC* 9: 870). Congress soon regretted its hasty action in promoting the troublesome Wilkinson over many senior and more deserving colonels, and after Gates learned early in January of Wilkinson's part in the Conway affair (see below, NG to Jacob, 7 February), he also lost his admiration for the young man. When the new brigadier, reacting to the "dissatisfaction in the army," resigned his commission, Congress wasted no time in accepting it. (*JCC*, 10: 226; for Wilkinson's controversy with Gates, see Nelson, *Gates*, 181–84, 195–96.) For the denouement of Conway's equally unpopular promotion, see below, NG to Jacob, 7 February.

2. This letter touched off no such furor in Congress as had NG's letter to President Hancock the previous summer over du Coudray's promotion (see above, 1 July 1777). As noted there, Congress considered at that time that Sullivan, Greene, and Knox were trying to influence Congress's vote on a future action; here NG was reporting the effects of past action. Judging from Clark's letter above, moreover, NG could count on Laurens's sympathy over Conway's ill-considered promotion.

To Governor Nicholas Cooke of Rhode Island

Valley Forge

Sir   [Before 13 Jan.] 1778

I had the pleasure of your favour of the 4th of Novr[1] by Col. Barton, and take the oppertunity by his return to acknowledge it. That brave officer has lately waited upon Congress, and I have the pleasure of informing you that They have shown a proper sense of his merit by appointing him a Colonel in the Continental service.[2]

I am very sorry for the late unsuccessful expedition against Rhode Island. The best concerted enterprises often fail through some unforeseen accidents; but from whatever principles that attempt miscarried, I hope the blame may not justly be charged either to the Civil or military departments in the state.[3]

I am sensable that many and the greatest blessings will flow from the successes at the Northward [i.e., Saratoga], and heartily congratulate you and all my Friends upon the occasion. A superior force if well directed will always ensure success. Though we have been sometimes unfortunate the Efforts of this army have been almost unparralled. They have attempted everything that their strength would permit. Good Policy makes it necessary to conceal the misfortunes we have met with.

As the success of the ensuing Campaign must depend upon the preparations made this winter, the greatest exertions are necessary to raise the Levies and to compleatly equip the Troops, that we may take the field early and in the most advantageous manner. It is not improbable from appearances that a French war may soon take place. Such an event would be attended with agreeable consequences. However it would be highly impolitick and imprudent to relax our preparations upon so uncertain a principle. We ought to make use of the resources within our own power to call forth our own strength, and then we may expect success, whether France declares war against Great Britain or not.[4] The last Campaign open'd with unpleasing prospects, but our vigorous measures have closed it with advantage. Similar Efforts for the ensuing Campaign may close the war.

The badness of the present establishment gives the greatest uneasiness to the officers of the army, and ought to be remedied. The depretiation of money has reduced their Pay to almost a Cipher so that far from being able to lend their Families any assistance, They can scarcely subsist themselves. Justice demands that their situation be made more agreeable. There are but few men who can serve with alacrity and chearfulness, when Their Families are in want of the common necessaries of Life.

We shall find if we take a review of past times, that those who have been intrusted with the supreme power [i.e., Congress] have been too often actuated by motives of private Interest, or an Illiberal attachment to favourites and flatterers. Innumerable are the disadvantages that have resulted from this conduct—not to mention the squandering of the Public moneys, their jealousy of great and good characters, the Cabals and intrigues to ruin them often deprives a Country of the services of the best of men, and greatly endangers the common safty. 'Tis necessary to guard against those evils in these states, for I am fully convinced that we have nothing to fear while we have honest Councellors and preserve Unanimity amongst ourselves.

The army is now posted for the winter near the Valley Forge on the Banks of Schuylkill. They have been busy for some time past in building their Hutts, which are now nearly compleat, and will be very comfortable. In the course of the Campaign the army has sufferd the greatest hardships with patience and have encounterd the greatest Dangers with alacrity and chearfulness. They have twice fought with [i.e., against] superior numbers, and tho' defeated have always kept the Field.

It is very necessary that large supplies of Cloathing be procured and sent forward for the use of the officers as well as the Soldiers. They suffer very much for the want of Cloaths. 'Tis peculiarly hard that added to all the necessary hardships of a soldiers life we should suffer so much in this respect. But exclusive of the sufferings of the soldiers 'tis of great public disservice for 'tis impossable to make any movement with Troops that are barefoot at this season of the year, the operations are greatly facilitated by having the soldiers well cloathed, and the health preserved. If cloathing cannot be procured thro' the common Channels, let each Town be rated for its proportion; there can be no difficulty in manufacturing a sufficient Quantity and supplying the Troops without distressing the country. I am Sir with great respect Your most obedient and very humble Servt

N GREENE

LS (Valley Forge Historical Society).
1. Letter not found.
2. On Col. William Barton's exploit, see above, NG to Catharine, 17 July 1777. NG's letter to Robert Morris of 4 December 1777, above, undoubtedly aided in his promotion.
3. See note, NG to Christopher, 5 January, above.
4. On the French alliance, see above, NG to Jacob, 3 January.

General Greene's Orders

[Valley Forge, 13 January 1778. On fortifying left wing. Febiger Orderly Book (Vi) 1 p.]

From Governor Nicholas Cooke of Rhode Island

Dear Sir   Providence [R.I.] January the 13 1778
    Yours by Cornl Barton I Received this Evening. Am glad to hear you are well. I hope God will bless you with health and Enable you to go through all those firey Tryals with a truly heroick Spirit and in the End Crown you with Lorels that shall last in the annels of America till time shall be no more. As for the Rhodisland Expedition it was not planed in this State but when it was concluded upon in the other States, we did Everything in our Power to carry it into Execution Efectualy although I must confess at the same time my own private opinnion was that if we proved sucksesfull and drove them from the Island on Bord their Ships we could not Keep it long without a very great Expence as the Ennemy were masters at Sea and could Saile all Round the Island with their Ships. I hear the Congress have orderd another inquirey to be made into the Reasons of the failer of the Expedition. I hope it will be done Efectually and the Real cause may be Serched out. I dare Say it will be agreeable to the inhabitants in this State in generall both of the Civil and milletary Departments.[1]
    I am Sorey to hear that our Brave troops have Sufferd So much in the field for want of Comfortable Cloathing. We have done Every thing in our Power to Cloath them Comfortabley, we have Now obtained a considerable Quantety. I hope they will soon be made comfortable on that account. We have two waggons going of[f] Tomorrow with 1000 pair Stockings, 600 Pair Shews, 300 Shirts, 120 pair Briches, 50 coats, 100 hats &c. I hope they will come Safe to hand. His Excelency General Washington is very Pressing in his letter for our Compleating our two contenential Battalions which will be Exceeding difficult under our present situation.[2] There is now in the harber of Newport Lord How with nine Ships of the line and fourteen or fifteen friggets with as many more Smaller vessels, tenders to the men of war, and one hundred and Eighty Saile of transports which must at the lowest computation have of mercenaries and Sailers a body of near 8,000[3] men besides the land forces that have been there all Summer which by all accounts are between three and four thousand men. They are now meditating some decent on the maine [land] Supposed to [be?] this town. They have collected a larg Number of Boats at Coasters Harber and have made a larg Draught of their troops to hold them Selves in Readiness to imbark at the Shortest Notice.
    We have not now in the State 500 troops besides those that belong to the State. We have had none from Conecticut Since last Spring Except what came for 30 days on the late Expedition. Consider our cituation: 100 miles Sea cost, a larg Bodey of the Ennemy in allmost the middle of the State, more in Number than Every man in

Letter from Nicholas Cooke, 13 January 1778
(Courtesy of the Rhode Island Historical Society)

the State able to bear armes, with arms and Every Nesesary, fit for war in the best manner, and we but a handfull Scattered all Round the Borders of the Shore for 100 miles togather. When Boston was in the Possession of the Ennemy and their Numbers did not Exceed the Number now in this State they had 20000 men lay Round them to keep the Ennemy from Breaking into the Contry. This little State at that time sent them more than three times the Number that we have now from them, although there is none of the Ennemy now in New England but in this State. But I must leave the matter; the Subject is two Panfull To dwell upon.[4] I must conclude dear Sir with my best Respects to my Worthy friend General Washington yr Selfe and the officers in the Rhodisland Regments

NICHS COOKE

ALS (RHi).
    1. On the Rhode Island expedition, see note, NG to Christopher, 5 January, above.
    2. On raising Black troops to help fill the state's quota, see note, NG to Christopher, 5 January, above.
    3. Cooke probably exaggerated the numbers. Of the eighty-five ships under Lord Howe's command in American waters, at least thirty, according to Gruber (*Howe Bros.*, pp. 292–93), were unfit for service. The rest were scattered at three bases besides Newport or were engaged in the blockade along the Atlantic coast. Many of the crews and soldiers aboard the vessels at Newport, moreover, were sick. There is no evidence of "one hundred and Eighty Saile of transports" in the harbor.
    4. Although Gov. Cooke's fears are understandable, it was the considered opinion of Washington and Greene, substantiated in retrospect, that the enemy had no serious intentions of attacking the "mainland." Their continued occupation of Newport, moreover, effectively removed the garrison's three or four thousand men from Howe's New York or Philadelphia armies. (See quote from Trevelyan, above, vol. 1: 366n.)

General Greene's Orders

[Valley Forge, 18 January 1778. Party to make fascines. Febiger Orderly Book (Vi) 1 p.]

General Greene's Orders

[Valley Forge, 20 January 1778. Commander in chief asks camp be put in "defenceable condition as soon as may be." Febiger Orderly Book (Vi) 1 p.]

To Henry Bromfield[1]

[Valley Forge, 24 January 1778. Introducing Abraham Lott. From Colonial Society of Massachusetts, *Transactions*, 10: 73]

    1. Henry Bromfield (1727–1820) was an influential Boston merchant who had served on the Massachusetts Board of War in 1776, at which time NG probably met him

for the first time. (Mass. Hist. Soc., *Proc.*, 3 ser., 50: [1917] 437n; 63: [1930] 328n; 69: [1947–50] 180)

To Governor Nicholas Cooke of Rhode Island

[Valley Forge, 24 January 1778. Introducing Abraham Lott, whose "politeness and hospitality has endeared him to all the Officers of the Army." Tr (GWG transcript: CSmH) 1 p.]

To General William Heath

[Valley Forge, 24 January 1778. Introducing Abraham Lott. ALS (MHi) 1 p.]

To General Alexander McDougall

Camp near Valley Forge
January 25th 1778

I am happy to hear you are recovering your health very fast. I exceedingly regret your being absent from the Army at this time, there are many new regulations requisite to put the Army upon a proper establishment. I wish for your aid and assistance.[1]

The severity of the last campaign, the amazing expence which Officers are subject to, to subsist in the Army, and the disagreeable prospect that lies open to their view at the close of the war, has produced a general discontent; and among many of the Officers a resolution to leave the service. Great numbers are gone and others going daily.[2]

There is but one radical cure for this evil; that is to put the Army upon the British establishment, or at least to grant the Officers half pay for life. We have always flattered ourselves that a love of liberty and a thirst for military glory was such predominant principles that there never would be want of Officers; but we find the spirit of Patriotism and the splendor of military glory vanish into nothing when a person is obliged to sacrafice all the solid comforts of life, for empty sounds only, which are the creatures of a day and then sink into contempt the remainder of life. This will be the case of all those who have not an interest independant of the Army sufficient to support their military character after the war is over. There are few instances of public gratitude where the present moment is not improved, while the heart is warm with a sence of your services. The Officers say they cannot see why they should be made a certain sacrafice of, for the common good; they are willing to support the burden in common with others, but the load is too heavy for the few that bear it. I have been silent upon the occasion, but there is great justice in the Officers demands; and I very much doubt whether there can be any measures adopted that will give the Officers a fondness for service and engage them to execute the duties of their profession with chearfulness unless there is some ample provision made them for life.[3]

I suppose you have heard of the appointments of Colonel Wilkinson to a Brigadier and General Conway to a Major General. Is it possible to conceive the policy or justice of these appointments? The Army has been greatly convulsed—the Colonels and Brigadiers have sent in a memorial to Congress representing their greviances. If these appointments are not recinded, there will be a general resignation of two capital lines of the Army; but it is said Wilkinson is appointed Secretary to the board of war; what will be done with Conway I don't know.[4] I think him a very dangerous man in this Army; he has but small talents, great ambition, and without any uncommon spirit of enterprize, naturally of a factious make and of an intrigueing temper. It is said (and I don't doubt the truth of it) that he wrote to Genl Gates that he believed God almighty favoured the American Army or else they must have been destroyed, for there never was an instance of such a weak General at the head of an Army, aided by such an ignorant council, that did not fall a sacrafice. Can you believe it? This Gentleman is puffd off to the public as one of the *greatest* Generals of the Age; and that the Army is indebted to him for every judicious movement they have made; but by the bye this is done by a certain faction that is said to be forming under the auspices of General Gates and General Mifflin, to supplant his Excellency from the command of the Army and get Genl Gates at the head of it.[5] How success swells the vanity of the human heart? This Gentleman [Gates] is a mere child of fortune; the foundation of all the Nothern successes was laid long before his arrival there; and Arnold and Lincoln were the principal instruments in compleating the work. I do not wish to detract from his glory, but could wish for his own sake as well as that of the continent that he had known himself better. Several pieces have been thrown out in the papers to sound the wishes of the public upon such a measure but I am happy to find them universally condemned as far as their intentions are known. I think the faction will make no great head. General Mifflin and his creatures have been endeavouring too wound my reputation. It is said I govern the Genl and do every thing to damp the spirit of enterprize. Pray Sir, did you ever discover the least inclination in me to check that spirit, or did you ever know me to impress my sentiments upon the General in Council? I always gave my opinion with candour and left the General to take his measures as he thought proper. I have been also told there has been some insinuation to my prejudice respecting the Germantown battle. You had the best opportunity to see the greatest part of my conduct that day, and to know my reasons more fully than any one. You will oblige me very much to favour me with your opinion (with the candour of a friend) respecting my conduct that day. I wish to know whither I shewed a want of activity in carrying the troops on to action, a want of judgment in the disposition, or a want of spirit in the action or retreat. If you think me blameable in any instances, be so good as to point them out.[6]

The winter is wasting away and little or nothing done to recruit the Army; there seems to be a strange lethargy taken hold of Administration. I am afraid the Spring will approach before any thing is done to put the Army upon a proper footing. A Committee is coming from Congress to regulate all matters in the Army in conjunction with the Board of war whereof General Gates is president and General Mifflin vice president, but I fear in passing through the forms there will be no time left for Execution.[7]

The Quarter Master General, Commissary General and Clothier Generals departments are in such a wretched condition that unless there are some very great alterations in those departments, it will be impossible to prosecute another Campaign. Our Troops are naked, we have been upon the eve of starving and the Army of mutinying. Our horses are dying by dozens every day for the want of Forage, and the men getting sickly in their Hutts for the want of acids and Soap to clean themselves. I am Dr Sir your most obedt humble Servant.

NATH GREENE

N B   I write with freedom and in confidence.

LS (NHi).
1. On 8 February, Washington spoke of McDougall's "late severe illness and present feeble state" (Fitzpatrick, GW, 10: 428). Ill health seemed to plague the Scottish-born general. Douglas S. Freeman thought that with better health "his place among American commanders might have been near the top." (Freeman, GW, 4: note opposite portrait, preceding p. 618) Although ten years older than NG, McDougall was a close friend.
2. Washington had warned Congress on 23 December of the need for "binding the officers by the tye of Interest to the Service (as No day, nor scarce an hour passes without the offer of a resignd Commission) otherwise I much doubt the practicability of holding the Army together much longer." (Fitzpatrick, GW, 10: 197)
3. The officers were as tireless in pressing for half pay for life as Congress was in resisting their importunities. To most members a system that created a group of "pensioners" smacked of a professional, standing army—an idea equally abhorrent to the average civilian. (For NG's defense of a standing army, see his letter to William Greene, 7 March, below.)
4. On these promotions, see above, NG to Laurens, 12 January.
5. See the "Conway Cabal," NG to Jacob, 7 February, below.

6. On NG's part in the battle, see above, note at his orders of 7 October 1777.

7. The desperate supply problems had prompted Washington to write Congress 23 December, underscoring a proposal made by one of their committees that two or three members of the Board of War or another committee come to camp to work out with him "the most perfect plan that can be devised for correcting all abuses." (Fitzpatrick, *GW*, 10: 197) Congress, always receptive to appointing another committee, on 10 January delegated Francis Dana, Joseph Reed, and Nathaniel Folsom (later adding John Harvie) to visit Valley Forge with a broad agenda for improving the army. (*JCC*, 10: 39–41) The committee had its work cut out for it. When they took up quarters at Moore Hall near Valley Forge in late January (without the Board of War), little did they suspect they would still be there in April; even less did NG suspect that within a month they would have persuaded him to become quartermaster general. See below, NG to Reed, 9 March.

To the Reverend John Murray

[Valley Forge? January, 1778?][1]

Once more, on the close of the campaign, I am to announce to my very dear friend, that I am still an inhabitant of this globe. We have had a hard and bloody campaign, yet we ought rather to dwell upon the mercies we have received, than to repine because they are not greater. But man is a thankless creature: yet you, dear Murray, know, that the mercies of God are happily proportioned to our weakness. Retired to winter quarters, the social passions once more kindled into life. Love and friendship triumph over the heart, and the sweet pleasure of domestic happiness, call to remembrance my once happy circle of friends, in which you, my dear Sir, appear in the first rank. My Friendship for you is indeed of the warmest description. My attachment was not hastily formed, and it will not easily be relinquished. I early admired your talents; your morals have earned my esteem; and neither distance nor circumstances will diminish my affection.

Excerpt reprinted from Murray, *Life*, 255–56.

1. The date is conjectured from Mrs. Greene's visit ("sweet pleasure of domestic happiness") to winter quarters after a "hard and bloody campaign." The description fits no other winter during the war.

To George Washington

[Valley Forge, January 1778.[1] To George Washington. Abstract of a 42-page discourse by NG, portions of which are quoted verbatim as indicated by quote marks or by indentation.

The commencement of the American war was so singular, its duration so uncertain, the hopes of reconciliation so strong, that our defence began and has been continued rather by temporary expedients, than from any proper and fixed establishment.

In the early stages of the dispute the novelty of war was so great, the spirit of patriotism so high and the abhorrence of slavery such that the people flew to arms regardless of their families, fortunes and pleasures which they were about to give up, to engage in the service of their Country. Every body expected a short and speedy issue to the unhappy dispute, and every one felt a perfect freedom to make the necessary sacrifices to bring about a proper reconciliation: that the basis of our future freedom might be so grounded as to admit of no more political shocks. With these flattering hopes the Army struggled through the first campaign and necessity obliged them to persevere in the second.

The third has been prosecuted upon an establishment laid in the second and altho it made more ample provision for the Officers than had been before, yet it is found to be very unsatisfactory.[2] The duty as Citizens, the glow of patriotism and the honors of the field are found insufficient to bind people [i.e., officers] to a service that subjects them to a loss of fortune, to give up all the pleasures of domestick life and engage them in a hazardous and fatigueing line of duty, with but very few of the common comforts of life. However melancholy the consideration, it is a serious truth, that there is a greater disinclination to the service at the close of this Campaign than has ever been discovered before. It is true the campaign has been severe but not more so than may be expected while the war continues. People begin to think coolly, they compare their condition in the field with that at home, the situation of their families and their future prospects grow into objects of importance. To return into private life with a ruined fortune, with a broken constitution after years of hard servitude, there to sink into neglect and almost contempt are comfortless considerations to every mind that looks forward to the natural consequences that will result at the termination of this war. I believe Sir, the Officers of this army begin to view their situation in this light; they cannot concieve themselves bound by any ties either private or publick that oblige them to continue in a service that makes a certain sacrafice of a few, for the common benefit of the rest of the Society. They cannot concieve either the justice or policy of this measure; every Officer sais he is willing to bear a part of the common burden, but a very few have resolution enough to engage under such a hopeless prospect as the present institution exhibits to the view of every one in the service.

NG argues that, faced with a lack of spirit and resolution and a love of pleasure and wealth among Americans, it is necessary to fix upon a plan satisfactory to the officers and least expensive to the public. Men are often influenced more by security than by a liberal provision of a short duration. To silence complaints of officers, to reward their services, to make commissions more valuable and their owners more attentive to duty, to promote stricter discipline, and to render the army more respectable, the following is recommended: put officers on a regular establishment for life similar to that of the British;[3] allow a commission from a captaincy downward to be sold (after first offering it to officers in the regiment)—provided the commanding officer approves and the purchaser is from the state where the regiment was raised.

Congress or Board of War should decide, with advice of generals they choose to consult, whether the establishment of the army is to be based on principle of "force or oeconomy." It is almost a maxim in Europe that the longest purse will remain master of the field. If Great Britain cannot triumph by superior force, she will leave no stone unturned to subjugate America with her wealth. The hopes for a "speedy issue" from the discontent of the British people has not been realized.

> Pride and Ambition are so deeply rooted in British politicks, and the Court are so united in their measures, and the Ministers so much masters of the national wealth, that one may with great reason expect the whole national strength to operate against us untill their finances fail, or some European power interposes.

The present militia—because of short terms, desertion, the numerous sick, wastage of ammunition—is far too costly compared with an established army. Men unacquainted with camp life are doubly exposed, and mortality is higher than in regular army.

> Every thing is due[4] to the spirited exertions of the Militia since the commencement of the war, but it is much against our national interest to prosecute it upon a plan, that multiplies our expences, stagnates all kinds of business and deprives society of many of its most usefull members.

There is more reason to fear a shortage of funds and military stores than a lack of men.

Recommends regiments of 504 rank and file, 29 commissioned and 48 noncommissioned officers, in 9 companies, a lieutenant colonel to command. One of nine companies should be light infantry since experience has shown such troops "give a favourable turn to an action" that would be impossible if they were scattered through a regiment.[5] Only a small portion of an army engages in battle; rest stand by to help. "The fate of the day commonly declares in favour of those who push their advantages in the first of the action."

Clothing, arms, and accouterments are as necessary as men. If the states completed the full complements of men now requested, it would be all that could be equipped. Present battalions have far too many supernumerary officers.

> Military rank is of such a nature and of such consequence in the army that to preserve order and promote good government, to silence faction and discourage intrigue, to restrain vain glory and stimulate to an honest ambition, it is of the highest importance that its true principles be ascertained and known. Altho rank may be said to have no substantial good in it separate from command, yet as it is considered a badge of military distinction no Officer can give it up without incurring such a degree of military contempt, as must render him truly unhappy. Rank under this consideration is an object of such attention, that it becomes one of the strongest motives to great and dignified actions the human breast is capable of feeling. The hopes of obtaining and the fear of loosing it, is a continual spur to ambition and military enterprize.

NG favors progressive rank (i.e., advancement by seniority) although admittedly it may promote men without special merit; an officer totally without merit should not be promoted. Promotion by merit only, may open up advancement to men through artifice. Unless an officer has very conspicuous merit, his promotion out of line causes envy and often renders him "contemptible" among officers. "To confine the line of promotion to the respective States independent of one another, destroys a necessary cement among the whole. . . . Our true policy would be to consider the army but as one body." If a general officer can rise only in the line of his own state, he has only to "make his court" to them, without regard to the common interest. In summary NG would recommend progressive rank in the continental line, Congress reserving the right to reward particular merit.

Recommends two principles in promoting colonels to brigadiers: (1) oldest to be promoted to vacancies, although in some cases the right of the state may overbalance this; (2) the states to have officers in the same proportion as they furnish regiments.

Rank is a badge of distinction that is cheapened if granted lavishly to staff officers. The staff officer, unlike the line officer, has not paid the proper price of "being subject to the dangers of the field."[6] The line officers despise titles that can be had so easily. Rank must not be degraded. Men are often "fonder of honors than pecuniary rewards." Sees no justification for rank in staff department functions except possibly for aides-de-camp already serving. Most of the staff serving with the army (as opposed to those behind the lines) may be taken from among line officers, keeping their same rank. For a brigade he would have only one commissary, one quarter master, and one forage master with rank. The quartermaster general should be with the army and employ contractors to procure all kinds of materials for its use. Many men in these departments are "without principle, without honor or honesty." The clothier general's department is one continual disappointment. Every state must clothe its own troops.

As to recruiting, if the states can "bring the Militia to a draft," there will never be a lack of men. Drafting is "perfectly consistant with the strictest principles of liberty, where all are put upon the same footing, and every body must allow that Society has a claim to the personal services of every individual, and when the security of the State requires it, the legislatures must have a right to tax accordingly." Some states will probably be able to fill quotas by voluntary enlistments, but NG would like to see drafting established, if only as a precedent. D (Washington Papers: DLC) 42 pp.]

1. The document is unsigned, unaddressed, and undated. Washington docketed it as "Maj. Genl. Greene's Opinion on a proposed new Establishment." It is in the hand of NG's aide, Ichabod Burnet. The document is dated in the Washington Papers (DLC) as [Jan. 1778], which is a reasonable conjecture that cannot be narrowed further. NG was at Valley Forge throughout the month.
2. The three campaigns refer to the years 1775, 1776, and 1777.
3. On half pay for life, see note, NG to McDougall, 25 January, above.
4. The phrase appears to be the equivalent of "all praise is due."
5. The new establishment approved by Congress on 27 May 1778 was similar. A regiment was to consist of 9 companies, one of them of light infantry, numbering 477 privates, 54 noncommissioned officers, and 27 commissioned officers. (*JCC*, 11: 538–42)
6. The staff officers to whom NG refers were mostly serving "behind the lines" in such departments as those of the commissary, quartermaster, or clothier general. NG believed they should be civilians. When he became quartermaster, however, he was not averse to having one of his deputies, Udny Hay, have a military rank. (See below, NG to Laurens, 1 May 1778.)

From Doctor Benjamin Rush

Lancaster [Pa.]
Dear Sir   Feby 1st 1778
I set down in the name of our unfortunate countrymen to acknowledge the obligations of the hospitals to his Excellency Genl Washington and to the General Officers of the army for sending military Inspectors to see that the sick are properly attended, and provided with every thing necessary for them. The advantages resulting from having gentlemen *independent* of the officers of the hospitals

constantly in their neighbourhood, are so obvious that I wonder it has been so long neglected especially as the Director General informed a Committee of Congress that he had *repeatedly* applied for them together with a small body of guards to the principal Officers of the Army but to no purpose. I was happy in being able to inform the same committee that I had been much more successful in my Applications to the General Officers of the Army, for that my first letters to the commander in chief, and to yourself had immediately procured a field officer to visit all the hospitals, and a determination to keep up guards and the discipline of the army among them.[1]

I find from examining Dr Shippen's return of the numbers who die in the hospitals that I was mistaken in the accounts I gave of that matter in my letters to you. From his return of December last I find very few have died in proportion to the number I have mentioned. All I can say in apollogy for this mistake is that I was deceived by counting the number of coffins that were daily put under ground. From their weight and smell I am persuaded they contained hospital patients in them, and if they were not dead I hope some steps will be taken for the future to prevent and punish the crime of burying the continental Soldiers alive. It is a new evil under the Sun, and I hope a new punishment will be discovered for it.[2]

As most, if not all the Abuses which have prevailed in the hospitals during the last campaign have been ascribed to a want of harmony between the Director General and myself I have (to prevent the future operation of that Apollogy for murder) resigned my commission. Nothing can be more unjust than the insinuation. I Sacrificed my feelings and judgement to harmony till my conscience grew uneasy with my Silence. I complained with delicacy. I laid nothing to the direct charge of Dr Shippen in my letter to Genl Washington. I have always blamed his officers and the System for the principal Abuses which prevailed in the department, and if I was forced into any personal charges of ignorance and negligence in Dr Shippen they were extorted in defending myself from his charges against me. I am so much Absorbed in the great Object of the war, and in the means of carrying it on, that I have not a moment's leisure to be angry, or dispute with any thing but putrid fever, or with any body but General Howe.[3]

Apropos—I have made a discovery—a sure and certain method of destroying Howe's whole army without powder or ball, or without any of the common implements of death. Lead them thro' any of the Villages in Lancaster County where we have a hospital, and I will ensure you that in 6 weeks there shall not be a man of them alive, or fit for duty.

The board of war have ordered 4000 copies of an address published last spring in a newspaper containing directions to officers for preserving the health of the Soldiers. I know from your humanity and attention to the poor fellows you will not be wanting in your endeavours to circulate and enforce it. I bequeath it as my last legacy to my dear countrymen in the line of my profession.

I am not disgusted, or distressed with the opinion of our superiors concerning the cause of my complaints, or of my resignation. My dear country—freedom and independence, are words as big with charms to me as ever. I shall therefore join the army in the Spring as a Volunteer, and while there are 500 men in arms in America I shall never keep back the mite of my labours and life from the service of my country and posterity. With great esteem I have the honor to be Dr Sir yr sincere frd and Hble Sert

[signature cut off]

AL[S] (PPL).

1. This was a slap at Dr. William Shippen, the "Director General" whom Rush had by-passed in writing directly to NG on 2 December, above, and to Washington on 26 December. (Butterfield, Rush, 1: 180–82)

2. Shippen had opened himself to this slashing sarcasm by understating the number who had died in hospitals. Rush took his count from an affidavit signed by the carpenter who delivered the coffins. (Hawke, Rush, p. 221)

3. Rush was scarcely truthful in saying he blamed the system, not Shippen. Since early December, in fact, his attacks on his superior to friends in Congress had been unrestrained. At Rush's request Congress called a session the last week in January to hear Rush's charges, but he went too far at the hearing in making his testimony a personal attack against Shippen. Even Rush's friend, John Witherspoon, told him that Congress would be satisfied only with his resignation from the medical department. Rush resigned the day before he wrote to NG.

For two years he joined Dr. John Morgan intermittently in an attempt to get Shippen dismissed. After Shippen was acquitted in a lengthy courtmartial in the summer of 1780, Congress held its own hearings, also exonerating him; and in October 1780 the legislature slapped both Morgan and Rush by reappointing Shippen. In January 1781 Shippen finally resigned, but not without a commendation from Washington. Rush's role in the Shippen affair is carefully considered in Hawke, Rush, chapters 11 and 12; Morgan's role is discussed in Bell, Morgan, chapters 12 and 13. See also NG to Morgan, 10 January 1779, below.

From General James M. Varnum

Sir   Camp Valley Forge Febry 1st 1778

The Time of Service of the State Troops in Rhode Island will expire soon. If I remember right, about the first of March next. The State are about raising them again for the Term of one Year. This Measure will tend to impede filling the continental Battalions. The Practice of forming intermediate Corps, partaking in some Degree of the nature of regular Troops, and in some sort of Militia, is very prejudicial to the Interest of America.[1] For, wanting a Stability and Duration adequate to every purpose of War, we find ourselves weakest when Circumstances demand our greatest Exertions. Militia are sufficient to repel a sudden Decent, or check the Progress of an Enemy 'till an Army can be marched to their Relief. They never can be prevailed upon to keep the Field for any length of time; And, being called out for a few Weeks, they return home the moment their term expires whither relieved or not. Consequently the Stores and everything else must be exposed unless there are some Troops formed upon a different Principle.[2]

It is upon this Account that the State of Rhode Island are obliged to raise Battalions; And, at a most enormous Expence. They have no other Alternative but certain Ruin. They find themselves neglected by the Continent, altho' called upon to furnish their full Quota of men for the common defence. They have been censured for attempting their own salvation when it was totally neglected by others. Had they not exerted themselves in raising the three Battalions last winter, in all probability the five Villages upon the River and Bays would long before this have been in Ashes. They were censured because it obstructed filling the continental Battalions; Yet had the Continent at large kept as many men in the Field according to their Proportions, the last Campaign would have closed the War. They were censured for not filling their continental Battalions when it is evident they were to receive no immediate Benefit from them. When they solicited that these Battalions might remain in the State they were told that all Considerations must give Way to the general Interest, And that if the main Body of the Enemy could receive an important Wound, its Detachments would fall of Course. With this Reasoning have they been quieted for upward of a Year.

Their Distress has been great beyond Example. They feel it increase daily without the least Prospect of mitigation. They feel like men who think themselves injured. Their Reasoning must correspond to their Feelings. They are not insensible to the Rights of mankind, nor ignorant of the mutual obligations existing in political Society. They expect some degree of Protection in Return for their obedience to the public Laws. They consider the united Strength of America as collected for the Defence of all its parts. Why should they contribute to this without sharing in the common Benefits? In Proportion to what they surrender into the public Stock they are weakened as an individual State: Of Course, the less able to defend themselves.

They well know that War is ever attended with Calamities. They are willing to receive a full Share of them; but cannot be reasoned into the Propriety of such an unequal Distribution, which tends to their total Destruction. There has not been an Instance similar to theirs. Whenever any other State hath been seriously invaded, Troops have been sent to their Relief. Why should Rhode Island be thus discriminated [against]? Is it because they are small in the general Scale or because they have less Virtue than others? If the former, they stand in greater need of Assistance. If the [latter] let those which are faultless bring the Accusation. However small their Territory, however few their Numbers, they are a part of the whole, and united, by every Tie that is sacred, in one great and glorious Cause.

It is said the Troops cannot be spared; Our Army is small, and the State of Pennsylvania would be ravaged were Detachments to be made. If the Continent at large is deficient in furnishing Troops, why should our State in particular be pointed out and made to suffer? Why were our Calculations so formed as to be able to fight a part of the British Army only? If our united Force is a match for theirs, as it ought to be, how are we weakened in opposing their Detachments? But why shou'd this particular Sacrifice be made when seven Battalions are quartered at and about Albany, without the possibility of opposing an Enemy? Surely two Battalions could be better detached to give some kind of Security to a State which has struggled with Difficulties beyond rational Expectation.[3]

Was Rhode Island at [a] State in Alliance only, the continent would attempt supporting them from Principles of Policy, As well to increase their own Power as to prevent the Enemy from making a valuable Acquisition. But certainly what is just and honorable is of far more Estimation than what is merely convenient. Feeble indeed is that Policy which prefers not Justice for its own sake. And ill framed or badly administered that Government which provides not equally for all its parts.

An essential part of the Controversy between Great Britain and America was concerning Property. How far this might be called our own was the material Question. Rather than hold it upon the precarious footing of being at the discretionary Disposal of a Foreign Legislature we embarked even Life itself in the Contest. How painful then must it be to those who are exposing themselves for the general Safety to reflect in a moment whatever they possess may be destroyed, while others reap all the Benefits of their Toils! We cannot wholly deprive ourselves of an Attachment to private Interest. We enter into Society for its Preservation. We give no more into the public Stock than is absolutely necessary for that Purpose. No Individual has an Interest in Society unconnected with his own Safety. Disinterested Patriotism is but a name, and public Virtue is the genuine Offspring of self Love, founded in the unalterable Feelings of the human Heart. Tell us that the Love of our Country should controul every other Attachment, and that we are bound to manifest the same by a Course of Actions that tend immediately to the Destruction of our Wives, our Children, our tenderest Concerns; And that we may expect in the End to reap the blessed fruit of all our Labors, Want, Misery and Wretchedness; Who would not be fired with Indignation and invoke the Justice of heaven to witness the Absurdity of such unnatural Doctrine?

Rome never wanted Soldiers while they were convinced that they fought for their Wives, their Children and their Household Gods. But whenever they found that others were to receive all the Spoils, while they partook only in the Burthens of War, they became turbulent, mutinous, and finally disbanded themselves. But to have no prospect of personal Advantage, and be under the Necessity of seeing the little we now possess exposed to almost inevitable Loss, fills us with Inquietude, and strongly insinuates our fate is cruel.

The State of Rhode Island must sink under the present mode of defence. One Third of their Militia are continually in the Field, besides their State Battalions. The necessaries of Life have risen so high that they are obliged to pay the Troops in the Produce of the Country at former Prices. Taxes must therefore equal, in a short time, the total amount of Property. When their Credit fails they must either become a Prey to their own Soldiers or the British Army, or both. Let therefore the Remains of their two Battalions be detached to them. Let the State know that these Troops shall remain with them while the Enemy remain in Possession there. From this Assurance they will immediately fill the Battalions to their full Establishments and be freed from the necessity of raising State Troops. The Continent will be doubly served. In the first Place they will defend a part of their Empire; And in the second, will have two compleat Battalions ready to march to any part of the Continent whenever Circumstances may require it.

Upon the present System it cannot be rationally expected that they can be compleated. The proportion was too great before the Enemy took Possession of any part of their Territory. They hold one Quarter, and that the most valuable part. They have deprived the Inhabitants of the Benefit of their Harbours, formed by Nature for Commerce and on which they principally depended for Support. Their distress must now be the greater and therefore cannot, being left to defend themselves, give Troops to the continental Army unless in the Ways posed.

Every Principle of good Policy would justify this measure. Militia are not calculated effectually to oppose a formidable Body. A few regular Troops are sufficient for them to collect to: And, in Case of a Decent upon the main, the two Battalions would be of infinite Service.

I have been explicit upon this Subject. I could enter largely into the Consequences. But your Feelings, if not your Opinion, must be similar to mine. Should these Observations appear rational, I must beg you to urge the Proposal to his Excellency. I have wrote and spoke my Mind freely to him heretofore, tho' my standing in the Army forbids my making Use of that degree of Freedom, which with you I do not esteem a Crime. Your Rank, your steady Attachments [to] the Cause of America, and your known Regard for his Excellency may add Weight to your Application.[4]

I know the great General in [this] as in all his other Measures, acts from a Goodness of Soul and ar[rives at?] a View only to the public Weal. But the best may err, and it is a dishonor to retract where convinced of the Impropriety of an Opinion.

You have often heard me say, and I assure you I feel happy in the Truth of it, that next to God Almighty and my Country, I revere General Washington. And nothing fills me with so much Indignation as the Vilainy of some who dare speak disrespectfully of him! I fear, I greatly fear his Character will suffer in that State which you and I hold most dear! The People may begin to think his Ear is deaf to the Cries of the distressed; That he feels no Sympathy in the Misfortunes of others, and that his Attachments are too confined. Forbid it gracious Heaven, And suffer not private Motives to influence us to condemn what we do not fully comprehend! I am Sir with great Respect, your very obedient humble Servant,

J M VARNUM

ALS (R-Ar).

1. On 19 December the R.I. Assembly had voted to raise three battalions of 1,500 men "for the defence of the United States in general, and of this state in particular." (Bartlett, *Records*, 8: 345–46) Whether, in the event of British abandonment of Newport, they could be sent outside the state for the defense of the rest of the United States the Assembly did not say.

2. He spoke from experience; a year earlier he had headed the R.I. Militia for two months.

3. Varnum was much closer to the plight of his home state than NG. Not only had he spent some months there since the war began (compared with NG's two days), but during most of that time he had also commanded Rhode Island's two continental regiments, whose families kept them informed of being constantly beset by British coastal depredations and by fears of a full-scale invasion of the "mainland" by British troops from Newport.

4. Although NG spoke to Washington, the commander in chief seemed unmoved by Rhode Island's predicament. He kept Col. Israel Angell's regiment at Valley Forge, and he maintained that the state was one of several that were fully competent to raise their quota for the army at Valley Forge. When asked by Congress on 21 February to name a successor to Gen. Joseph Spencer as commander in Rhode Island, he tried to palm off either Gen. Heath or Gen. Putnam—neither of whom he greatly respected. Only when the Committee of Congress objected, did he name John Sullivan. (Fitzpatrick, *GW*, 11: 31, 57–58) NG would have liked the assignment himself, but by this time (10 March) he had agreed to accept the quartermaster post.

Letter from James M. Varnum, 1 February 1778
(Courtesy of Rhode Island State Archives, Providence, R.I.)

To Governor Nicholas Cooke of Rhode Island

Dr Sir   Camp Valley Forge Feb. 5th 1778

I wrote you a short letter a few days since by one Mr Windsor that Mr Ellery had wrote to me[1] that Genl Spencer had resigned and that he wanted to know whether it would be agreeable for me to take the command at Rhode Island.

I have consulted the Genl [Washington] upon the subject but find him very averse to such a measure. I have acquainted Mr Ellery accordingly, therefore expect some other person will be appointed to the command. It would have been perfectly agreeable to me had it been consistent with the views of the Genl and the interest of the Continent; but as the proposition was founded upon his approbation I could only write agreeable to his answers to me. I shall use my influence with the Genl to obtain leave for the Rhode Island Troops to return home and to remain there as long as the enemy continue in the State.[2] Upon these conditions I imagine the Regts will be soon fill'd up to thier full compliments. I think it a very great cruelty upon our State that the troops have been idle so long at Albany when the State was in such a jeopardy; while the operations of the campain were going on necessity obliged the Genl to leave Rhode Island naked, but he always expected the forces at Newport would have been with drawn to reinforce Genl Howe. But why you have not been reinforced since the Convention at the Northward I cannot imagine.

There is an expedition now on foot to be commanded by the Marquis de la Fayette against St John's and Montreal; I must confess I do not see the policy or utility of the measure.[3] It cannot change the seat of war, neither can we hope to obtain many stores. To leave our own property exposed for novel and excentrick movements does not seem to be warranted by sound policy. An attempt to destroy the enemies Shipping on the lakes might be an eligible plan, any thing further is pursuing a measure without an object; or at least there is no object to ballance the probable injury that may arise by depriving the Country of the necessary force to protect it, but more of this hereafter.

There is a Committee of Congress now at camp to put the Army upon a new establishment. I wish they may do the business effectually. I am with great esteem Your most Obedient and very humble Servant

NATH GREENE

LS (R-Ar).
    1. Neither letter has been found.
    2. See above, note, Varnum to NG, 1 February.
    3. On the still-born Canadian expedition, see note at NG to McDougall, 5 February, below.

To General Alexander McDougall

Dr Sir

Camp Valley Forge Feb 5th 1778

The Marquis de la Fyette is appointed to command an expedition against St Johns and Montreall, the force order'd upon this duty is the Continental troops at Albany and the Militia of the [New Hampshire] grants under the command of General Starks.[1] *Major* General Conway was appointed the second in command, but the Marquis at his special request has obtain'd leave for you to accompany him provided your health permits. If not the Baron de Calb[2] is to go. I wish the plan appear'd to me ellegible and you in a condition to undertake the execution with the Marquis; he is a very cleaver honest fellow; he wishs you to go exceedingly for many reasons, but I am confident your health is not sufficiently restor'd to undertake such an arduous piece of business. The force that is to go upon the expedition is to consist of about 3000 men, much too large for the importance of the object. A *coup de main* upon the shiping might be attempted with some propriety, but what can be the object at Montreall I can't conceive. I have great reason to think this plan is a creature of faction, calculated to serve Gen Conway who the faction intended should have had the command of it, but the Marquis was proposd; and as the reasons that had been urg'd for giveing the command to Conway was his being a french Officer which might give him great influence over the Canadians, those reasons operated doubly in favor of the Marquis from his superior importance; therefore the faction was oblig'd to consent altho reluctantly to the Marquises appointment. If you are not able to undertake the expedition, the Marquis desires you to give him such advice and information as you may think necessary to direct his conduct. If you have any acquaintances that may be useful to him he begs you'l favor him with some Letters.[3]

The designs of a certain faction which I mention'd to you some days since in a Letter unfold themselves more and more every day. The Principals begin to be most horridly frighted. The poor and shallow politicians unmask'd their batteries, before they were ready to attempt any execution, but more of this hereafter. Great pains has been taken to give the Publick an Idea the General was about to resign, and that I governd him in all cases. Could you have conceiv'd that Ambition was so predominant among people struggling for life and everything that is dear and valuable? We seem to have imbib'd the conception of European Politicks, without the least pretention to their policy. God grant us more wisdom and virtue or else I shall begin to despair of our cause. I wish you would publish the Battle of Germantown, I think it would answer some valuable purposes, but if you are free I must beg a compliance with the request in my last Letter.[4]

The Committee of Congress are here and upon the business of new arrangeing the Army. They came to Camp with Parliamentary prejudices, but stubborn facts and the condition of the Army has wrought a wonderfull reformation; they seem now to be in ernest to put every thing upon a proper establishment but I am afraid whether the Congress can be brought to confirm their proceedings.[5]

The Army is growing more healthy. The Virginians are exerting themselves to fill up their Regiments early in the Spring. Mrs Washington arrivd in Camp this evening, and brings the agreeable intelligence that 5000 Volunteers engag'd for six or twelve months from April next are to join us from Virgina under the command of Col Spotswood now made a Brigadier General. These are to be over and above their propotion of Continental troops. I am with great respect your Obed Srt

N GREENE

ALS (NHi).

1. Gen. John Stark of the New Hampshire militia, the hero of the battle of Bennington, had been appointed brigadier general in the Continental army in October.

2. Johann Kalb (1721–80), of German peasant background, assumed the title of "Baron de Kalb" while in the French army. In a career of thirty some years, he fought in two wars, retired twice, and visited America on a secret mission. In 1777, as a newly named brigadier general, he accompanied Lafayette to America. After some delay Congress made him a major general in September 1777. Although an able soldier, he served most of the war without distinction. He was mortally wounded while leading a hopeless attack under General Gates in the battle of Camden, S.C., in 1780. (*DAB*; for previously unpublished letters, see A. E. Zucker, *General De Kalb: Lafayette's Mentor* (Chapel Hill: The University of North Carolina Press, 1966.)

3. The Canadian expedition, although urged on Congress by Gen. Gates, was scarcely a "creature of faction." On 22 January the majority of Congress, mistakenly convinced that the French Canadians were ripe for revolt, ordered an "irruption" into Canada and named Lafayette to head it, with Conway as his second in command. The twenty-year old marquis, viewing Conway as Washington's enemy, insisted that either McDougall or DeKalb be placed over Conway. McDougall's poor health led Congress to name De Kalb. (*JCC*, 10: 84, 87, 107; on Lafayette and the "Conway Cabal," see below, NG to Jacob, 7 February.)

Most military men agreed with NG that the "irruption" was a dubious operation at best. Washington called it a "child of folly," and those generals most familiar with the invasion route—Schuyler, Lincoln, and Arnold—considered it too late for an invasion that was planned over the ice of Lake Champlain. It was also McDougall's opinion as seen in his letter of 28 February, below. When Lafayette arrived in Albany in mid-February, it was not only too late, but he also found the militia had not been called, the army was unpaid and almost naked, and supplies were nonexistent. Disappointed as he was that his road to glory was temporarily blocked, Lafayette informed Congress of the impossibility of carrying out the mission. On 2 March they suspended the invasion "for the present." (*JCC*, 10: 217) The "present" was to stretch into the following autumn, when once again the Canada bug bit Congress and certain of the military. (See below, NG to Washington, 28 October 1778.)

The best secondary account of the expedition is Gottschalk, *Lafayette*, chapters 7 and 8. A full account is found in the annotated documents in part IV of Idzerda, *Lafayette*, 1: 243–385.

4. On the battle of Germantown, see above, NG to McDougall, 25 January.

5. The committee is discussed in a note at NG to McDougall, 25 January, above.

To Jacob Greene

Valley Forge February 7th 1778

Governor Cook wrote me a few days since a most alarming letter respecting the situation of Rhode Island. Mr. Ellery proposed to me to take the command there, provided it was agreeable to his excellency; but he is totally averse to the measure. General Spencer has resigned; who will take command I know not; I wish General Sullivan may, as I can think of no person who will do it more justice. I am in hopes to prevail on the general to let the Rhode Island troops return home, and there continue until the enemy leaves the state. I flatter myself they will fill up their ranks very soon if they go home with that understanding.[1]

A horrid faction has been forming to ruin his excellency and others. Ambition, how boundless! Ingratitude, how prevalent! But the faction are universally condemned.[2] General Mifflin is said to be at the head of it. And it is strongly suspected that General Gates favours it. Mifflin has quarrelled with the general, because he would not draw the force off to the southward last summer and leave the New England states to themselves, before the enemy's object was ascertained. It was uncertain whether he intended to go up the North River, to Newport, or to the southward. The general thought it his duty to take a position to give the earliest support to either. Mifflin thought Philadelphia was exposed by it, and went there and raised a prodigious clamour against the measure, and against me for advising it. But the general, like the common father of all, steadily pursued the great continental interest, without regard to partial objects, and the discontents of individuals. This faction has been the offspring of that measure. See upon what a monstrous principle the general is persecuted. To injure his reputation, and prejudice the country and army against me, General Mifflin has been endeavouring to persuade them that I governed the general in all things. . . . I hope my little children are well. Money becomes more and more the Americans' object. You must get rich, or you will be of no consequence.

Excerpt reprinted from Johnson, *Greene*, 1: 162–63.

1. See note, Varnum to NG, 1 February, above.

2. The "faction" of which he speaks was also called a "party" or the "Junto," but it was best known at the time as the "Conway Cabal," a term that historians have generally also used. Not until Bernhard Knollenberg published his *Washington and the Revolution, a Reappraisal: Gates, Conway, and the Continental Congress* in 1940 did most historians begin to qualify the Conway Cabal as the "so-called" Conway Cabal or the "Conway Cabal." Before this study appeared, many reputable historians accepted George Bancroft's interpretation of the "cabal" as a well-planned conspiracy to replace Washington with Gen. Horatio Gates, whom Bancroft called a "petty intriguer." The chief plotters, according to such accounts, were Gens. Gates, Conway, and Mifflin, working hand in glove with such members of Congress as James Lovell, John and Samuel Adams, Richard Henry Lee, and certain other shadowy members.

Certainly Bancroft and his successors were not without documentary evidence in the papers of Washington's loyal subordinates that something underhanded was thought to be going on—the purpose of which was to unseat their chief, or, at the very least, to remove Greene and Knox, who were thought to influence Washington unduly. Mifflin especially believed that NG had dissuaded Washington from making a proper defense of Philadelphia. If Bancroft had consulted nothing more than the dozen letters to and from NG during this period (cited below), he would have had sufficient basis for constructing a tentative premise of such a plot. But, of course, historians were by no means limited to NG's letters; equally revealing was the correspondence of other loyal associates of Washington: Lafayette, Lord Stirling, Henry Knox, James M. Varnum, Anthony Wayne, John Cadwalader, Daniel Morgan, and aides John Laurens and Alexander Hamilton. And this does not exhaust the list.

Few historians are entirely immune to the ancient truism that where there is so much smoke there must be some fire. But Bernhard Knollenberg was convinced after studying the matter thoroughly that there was little or no fire. A brilliant lawyer as well as a learned historian, Knollenberg wrote what amounted to a lawyer's brief, in which he succeeded in convincing most readers that the conspiracy was largely in the eyes of the beholders—chiefly those loyal subordinates of Washington—and that they either persuaded Washington of a plot against him or greatly strengthened his own suspicions. Before the bar of history, lawyer Knollenberg found Gates and Conway innocent of the charges against them, although not necessarily innocent of certain vanities and weaknesses.

A better balanced and less argumentative account, based on recent scholarship, is Don Higginbotham's chapter entitled "Civil-Military Tensions, 1777–1778" in his *War of American Independence*, pp. 204–25. The reader who would fully understand the "cabal" in its historical context should read the chapter. The summary that follows (taken largely from Higginbotham) does not do justice to the subtleties and complexities of the affair.

Against the backdrop of growing civil-military tensions, Higginbotham describes the widespread criticism of Washington and his generals in the "grand army" that arose after the discouraging setbacks at Brandywine, Germantown, and the Delaware forts—especially when contrasted with the triumph of Gates's army over Burgoyne at Saratoga. Such criticism was not unnatural, particularly in a country struggling toward democracy and in its third winter of war. While Congress shared full responsibility for the shortage of men and supplies, it was within its rights—and even its obligation—as the legislative and executive branch of government to criticize the army and the officers it had appointed. To Washington and his men, however, who had given everything they had in defending Philadelphia against a much stronger army than Gates had faced, who had sent Daniel Morgan's riflemen to aid in Gates's victory (though their army could ill spare them), who were weary from marching and were poorly fed and clothed—to those men, such criticism seemed unfair. It also, however, struck sensitive nerves, for their sense of failure was much with them.

But criticism by members of Congress was a far cry from conspiracy. The harshest criticism, as Higginbotham has pointed out, came from outside Congress. There was probably only one member (James Lovell of Massachusetts) who actually favored replacing Washington. Benjamin Rush, for example, who was Washington's particular nemesis, was no longer a member of Congress. Delegate Eliphalet Dyer of Connecticut declared there was never "the most distant threat of removing Genl. Washington"; Henry Laurens, the president of Congress, though disturbed by the criticisms of Washington, agreed with Dyer.

Where, then, did Conway and Gates fit into the affair? (On Conway's career, see note, Adams to NG, 2 June 1777, above.) Shortly after Saratoga, Conway had written a personal letter to Gates congratulating him and criticizing Washington's army. Several weeks later, Washington received a letter from Lord Stirling (who had been the victim of Conway's sharp and ready tongue) containing what Conway had purportedly written, a letter that James Wilkinson (Gates's aide) had seen while nosing about in Gates's files and had "quoted" to Stirling's aide. Without checking into the reliability of this dubious source, Washington wrote a curt letter to Conway, quoting Conway's purported words as Stirling had written them to Washington: "Heaven has been determind to save your Country; or a weak General and bad Councellors would have ruind it." (9 November 1777, Fitzpatrick, *GW*, 10: 29)

What Conway had written was "What pity there is but one Gates! But the more I see of this army, the less I think it fit for general action under its actual chiefs and actual discipline. I speak to you sincerely and freely, and wish I could serve under you." (Knollenberg, *GW*, p. 51) Conway protested to Washington that he had not used the words that Washington had ascribed to him, though he granted that he had found fault with several army measures as European officers did with their armies, and he offered to show Washington the original letter.

The matter might have ended there but for several developments in the following two months—developments that seemed to confirm Washington and his circle in their suspicions of an intrigue between Conway, Gates, and Mifflin with some influential members of Congress. On 7 November, the day Washington received Stirling's letter, Congress appointed Mifflin to the War Board. On 24 November, Mifflin proposed Gates as president of the board, in which Congress confirmed him a few days later. (*JCC*, 9: 874, 959, 971) The board was expected to pay particular attention to Washington's army. In November, Conway had offered to resign, but instead of accepting his resignation, on 13 December, Congress made him inspector general of the army and advanced him to major general. This not only convinced Washington and his circle that Conway would be scrutinizing them but also annoyed all of the brigadiers that had been passed over, creating new enemies for Conway. (On Conway's promotion, see above, NG to Laurens, 12 January 1778.) It now appeared to the officers at Valley Forge that Washington's critics were being deliberately put in a position to oversee him and his staff; and when Conway appeared at Valley Forge in his new capacity, he met a cool reception from Washington.

Gates in the meantime, though involved in no intrigue to replace Washington, responded to Washington's accusatory letter about the Wilkinson report in such a flustered manner that he seemed to implicate himself. "Washington and Gates," writes Higginbotham, "exchanged a series of letters . . . that would have been better left unwritten." And of Washington's strained relations with Conway, Higginbotham writes: "Rarely was Washington ever so ill-tempered, disposing of Conway as 'one capable of all the malignity of detraction and all the meanesses of intrigue, to gratify the absurd resentment of disappointed vanity, or to answer the purpose of personal aggrandizement, and promote the interests of faction.' It was anything but Washington's finest hour." (Higginbotham, *War*, p. 219)

But time and suffering at Valley Forge gradually pushed the affair into the background. Congress replaced Conway as inspector general with Baron Steuben and sent Conway under Lafayette on the abortive Canadian expedition. (See note, NG to McDougall, 5 February 1778, above.) In late March it confirmed Gates as subordinate to Washington; and in April the unpopular Conway resigned. (After suffering a painful facial wound in a duel with John Cadwalader in July, he returned to France.) As Washington told his friend Landon Carter in May, he was not inclined to say whether any members of Congress were privy to the scheme of removing him, but he was "well informed, that no whisper of the kind was ever heard in Congress." (Fitzpatrick, *GW*, 11: 494) He even treated Gates with civility when Gates was sent north to the Highlands.

For references in NG's correspondence to the "Conway Cabal," see above, John Clark to NG, 10 January; NG to McDougall, 25 January and 5 February; and below, NG to Knox, 26 February; McDougall to NG, 28 February; NG to Smallwood, 16 March, and William Greene to NG, 6 March; NG to William Greene, 7 March; NG to Jacob Greene, 17 March; NG to McDougall, 28 March; and George Lux to NG, 28 April and 26 May.

From General Alexander McDougall

[Morristown, N.J., 7 February 1778. Will answer NG's letter of 5 February more fully later. His "backward" strength did not permit him to accompany Lafayette to Canada.[1] ADf (NHi) 1 p.]

1. See above, NG to McDougall, 5 February, on the proposed expedition.

From General James M. Varnum

Sir   Camp Valley Forge Feb 12th 1778

Inclosd you'll receive the Report of yesterday.[1] I must add to that the situation of the Camp is such that in all human probability the Army must soon dissolve. Many of the Troops are destitute of Meat and are several Days in Arrear. The Horses are dying for want of Forage. The Country in the Vicinity of the Camp is exhausted. There can not be a moral Certainty of bettering our Circumstances while we continue here. What Consequences have we rationally to expect? Our Desertions are astonishing great. The Love of Freedom which once animated the Breasts of those born in the Country is controuling by Hunger, the keenest of Necessities. If we consider the Relation in which we stand to the Troops we cannot reconcile their sufferings to the sentiments of honest men. No political consideration can justify the Measure. There is no local Object of so much moment as to conceal the obligations which bind us to them. Should a blind Attachment to a preconcerted plan fatally disaffect and in the End force the Army to Mutiny, then will the same Country, which now applaudes our Herritage, curse our Insensibility. I have from the Beginning viewd this situation with Horror. It is unparalelled in the History of Mankind to establish Winter Quarters in a Country wasted and without a single Magazine. We now only feel some of the Effects, which Reason from the beginning, taught us to expect as inevitable.[2] My Freedom upon this Occasion may be offensive; I should be unhappy but Duty obliges me to speak without Reserve. My own Conscience will approve the Deed, when some may perhaps look back with Regret, to the Time when the Evil in Extreme might have been prevented. There is no Alternative, but immediately to remove the Army to places where they can be supplied, unless effectual Remedies can be applied upon the spot which I believe every Gentleman of the Army thinks impracticable.[3] I am Sir with great Respect your very Obedient Servant

J M VARNUM

ALS (Washington Papers: DLC).

1. The report (on guards at Valley Forge) is in the Washington Papers, DLC.

2. On locating the camp at Valley Forge, see above, note, Order of March, 10 December 1777. Varnum was not alone in criticizing the location, but other factors were chiefly responsible for the suffering he described. (See NG to Jacob, 3 January, above.) "From the strategic and tactical point of view," Mark M. Boatner has written, it was "a good place for winter quarters." (*Encyc.*, p. 1136)

3. Varnum's letter, which NG gave to Washington the same day, undoubtedly spurred the commander in chief to issue the order immediately following.

From George Washington

Sir   Head Quarters [Valley Forge] Feb. 12, 1778

The good People of the State of Pennsylvania living in the vicinity of Philadelphia and near the Delaware River having sufferd much by the Enemy carrying off their property without allowing them any Compensation, thereby distressing the Inhabitants, supplying their own Army and enabling them to protract the cruel and unjust war that they are now waging against these States. And whereas by recent intelligence I have reason to expect that they intend making another grand Forage into this Country, it is of the utmost Consequence that the Horses Cattle Sheep and Provender within Fifteen or Twenty miles west of the River Delaware between the Schuylkil and the Brandywine be immediately removed, to prevent the Enemy from receiving any benefit therefrom, as well as to supply the present Emergencies of the American Army.

I do therefore authorise, impower and Command you forthwith to take, carry off and secure all such Horses as are suitable for Cavalry or for Draft and all Cattle and Sheep fit for Slaughter together with every kind of Forage that may be found in possession of any of the Inhabitants within the Aforesaid Limits Causing Certificates to be given to each person for the number Value and quantity of the horses Cattle Sheep and Provender so taken, Informing them that notice will be given to the holders of such Certificates by the Commissaries and Quarter Master General when and where they may Apply for Payment that they may not be disappointed in calling for their money.

All Officers *civil* and *military*, Commissaries, Quarter masters &ct, are hereby Orderd to obey and assist you in this necessary business.

All the Provinder on the Islands between Philadelphia and Chester which may be difficult of access or too hazardous to attemp carrying off, you will immediately Cause to be destroyed, giving Directions to the Officer or Officers to whom this Duty is assign'd to take an account of the Quantity together with the Owners Names, as far as the nature of the Service will admit.[1]

Given under my hand at head Quarters this 12th day of Feby 1778.

GO: WASHINGTON

DS (PHi).

1. The conditions described above in NG to McDougall on 25 January had, as described by Varnum, greatly worsened—especially in the matter of forage for horses and food for the men. A heavy snow storm on 8 and 9 February virtually stopped all food from entering camp for several days. There was no meat, and for some troops not even flour. It was as close to starvation as the Continental army would ever come. (Trussell, *Valley Forge*, pp. 21–26; Freeman, *GW*, 4: 574–77)

A slightly different version of this letter by Gen. Anthony Wayne, dated 9 February, is found in the Washington Papers, DLC. It is docketed in Washington's hand as "Instructions for a Forage Party" and is noted as being intended for Wayne. One can only surmise that it was Wayne's idea to scour the country between the Schuylkill and the Brandywine, an area with which he had been familiar all his life and where he had just spent a month at home on sick leave. Washington must have asked him to draw up the order, then decided to direct the order to NG as the magnitude of the operation appeared too great for a brigade. Wayne was ordered to help, as noted by NG's letter to him below.

As is apparent from NG's letters to Washington, he spared nothing during the next eleven days to carry out the order in an area that had already been thoroughly gleaned. His operations in Pennsylvania and Wayne's and Henry Lee's in New Jersey and Delaware nevertheless helped many men and horses to survive the bleakest period at Valley Forge. NG assessed the effectiveness of his operation in his letter to Knox below, 26 February. (Wayne's foraging is covered in Wildes, *Wayne*, 150–57.)

To Colonel Clement Biddle

Moorhall [Pa.][1] 12 Feb 1778

Colonel Biddle Commissary General of Forage is hereby directed to issue the necessary warrants and Instructions for the execution of this Service and to superintend the Commissaries and Quarter Masters

NATH GREENE

DS (PHi). This order was appended to Washington's order above.

1. Moore Hall, three miles west of Valley Forge, was the home of William Moore, a seventy-eight-year-old farmer who had rented his house to the Committee of Congress at Camp, which had invited NG to discuss the quartermaster general's post. (See below, NG to Reed, 9 March) The committee stayed in the house from January to April. (On Moore's difficulties in getting paid for their use of his house, see below, Moore to NG, 10 November 1778, and William Smith to NG, 28 January 1779.) NG and Catharine moved to Moore Hall shortly after 30 March because he found his hut at Valley Forge "very inconvenient for the Q M Generals department." (NG to Biddle, 30 March, below; see also his letter below to Catharine, 23 June.)

To General Anthony Wayne

More Hall [Pa.] Thursday morning

Dr Sir   [12 February 1778][1]

Inclosd is a line from Capt Lee; youl observe what he says. His Excellency thinks we had better make the experiment nevertheless. Col Biddle waits upon you this morning to consult and fix upon the plan for execution. I will call upon you by and bye, as soon as the Committee dismisses me.[2] Yours

N GREENE

ALS (PHi).

1. The date is determined by NG's 12 February conference as seen above at his order to Biddle. The conference is noted in the committee minutes, Burnett, *Letters*, 3: 83.

2. The precise subject of this letter is unclear, but it is concerned with the foraging expedition outlined above in note at Washington to NG, the same day. Henry ("Light-horse Harry") Lee was to lead his dragoons on a foraging expedition to Delaware (Lee to Washington, 19 February, Washington Papers, DLC, and Washington to Lee, 25 February, Fitzpatrick, *GW*, 10: 513–14)

To Colonel Clement Biddle

Head Quarters Springfield [Pa.] Meeting House
Feb 14, 1778

Sir

We are posted at this place and purpose to collect all the cattle carriages &c &c in and about the neighbourhood today. Tomorrow we purpose to take post at one Edwards about six miles in our rear. We have orderd all the collections made today to Edwards tavern tonight. I must beg you to exert yourself in collecting forage otherwise the business will go on slow. Tell all the Waggoners and the Officers that have the superintendande [superintendence] of the Waggons that I will punnish the least neglect with the greatest severity. You must forage the Country naked, and to prevent their complaints of the want of Forage we must take all their Cattle, Sheep and Horses fit for the use of the Army. Let us hear from you and know how you go on. I am your most obed Servt

N GREENE

Tr (GWG transcript: CSmH).

From General Alexander McDougall

Sir

Morris Town [N.J.] 14th Feby 1778

I have endeavored to recolect your conduct in Councils of war, but do not remember your dictating to the General or to useing any other means to impress your sentiments on his mind, than are common on such occasions, and which were used by every member who spoke his sentiments.[1] Nor do I remember your checking the spirit of enterprise, by any part of your conduct which has fallen under my knowledge. And I have reason to believe that the contrary insinuations are vile groundless Calumnies. Equally so are any charges to your disadvantage, respecting your conduct in the German Town Battle.[2]

I did not see the least indication of your want of activity or spirit in carrying on the Troops that day but the contrary. Those of your and Genl Stephens Divisions marched so brisk or ran to the charge that they were some minutes out of sight of my Brigade, altho we formed and marched immediatly behind your division, when its rear passed the corner of the Fence where the new disposion was made. And as to the retreat your endeavors were not wanting to bring off the Troops in order; but could not effect it, as the panic had seized them, and your conduct was far from showing any signs of fear. I am Sir, your Hble Servant

ADf (NHi).
1. On these charges, see above, note, NG to Jacob, 7 February.
2. NG had asked him in his letter of 25 January, above, about Germantown. On NG's part in the battle, see above, note, NG's orders, 7 October 1777.

From Colonel Robert Ballard[1]

Sir   [Valley Forge] Sunday Morning [15? Feb 1778][2]

I am sorry to inform [you] that my Scheme has prov'd ineffectual, the enemy had by some means got knowledge of our march, indeed we saw a Light horseman ride on to give the news when we had approach'd within about 500 yds. We then push'd on as hard as possible but found them secur'd in the Stone house. They began a very heavy fire before we got within 100 yds, which was very warmly returnd on our part till we got within 50 yds, but conceiving it impracticable to force them out of the house, I ordered my Men to retreat. They behav'd exceeding brave and would, I believe, have attempted Staving the Doors. Major Cable's [Samuel Cabell] party who went on the lower side next the Schuylkill fell in with a small party. He thinks he killd Several of them.

The poor fellows are exceeding fatigued and woud be glad of Some Whiskey. I directed the Officers of each respective corps to make out a return for Whiskey. Many of them say they haven't had a mouthfull of meat this 4 days. I am so worsted I cannot wait on you at your quarters.

My party met with but little loss, 4 or 5 Slightly wounded and I believe 1 or 2 killed.[3] I am with respect your obedt Servt

ROBERT BALLARD

ALS (Washington Papers: DLC). Enclosed in NG to Washington #1, below.
1. Ballard was lieutenant colonel of the First Virginia Regiment, later transferred to the Fourth Virginia (Heitman, *Register*).

2. The date is established by NG's reference to the raid as "yesterday" in his letter below to Washington. Ballard dated it only "Sunday Morning," which was the fifteenth.

3. The unsuccessful foray was typical of hundreds of such incidents, accounting for thousands of deaths on both sides by war's end.

To George Washington

Head Quarters Springfield [Pa.] Meeting House
Sir   Feb 15 1778

We are in want of some of the Deputy Q M Generals to conduct the business of that department. Please to send us one. I receivd two Letters from Col Biddle. He has got but few Waggons. The Inhabitants conceal them. The Col complains bitterly of the disaffection of the people. I sent out a great number of small parties to collect the Cattle, Horses &c &c yesterday but the collection was inconsiderable, the Country is very much draind. The Inhabitants cry out and beset me from all quarters, but like Pharoh I harden my heart. Two men were taken up carrying provisions into the Enemy yesterday morning. I gave them an hundred [lashes?] each by way of Example. I have sent of [off] all the Cattle Sheep and Horses. I will send on the forage and all further collections that may be made as fast as possible. I determine to forage the Country very bare. Nothing shall be left unattempted.

As Provision will be scarce especially of the meat kind, if the Commisaries could purchase a quantity of sugar, the troops with Wheat might make a fermity, a diet that would contribute to their health, be palatable and nourishing to the troops. I think it would be a very good substitute for meat, and not much more expensive if any.

Lt Col [Robert] Ballard was out on the foraging business yesterday down about Darby and got intelligence of the Enemies Bridge being removd and that it was with difficulty they relevd their Guards being some hours about it. He selected a party to attempt the Guard, upon his earnest entreaty I granted his request. Inclosed is his report by which you will see the attempt was unsucessful.[1]

I hope the Committee of Congress wont loos sight of Col Cox. There is no man will serve their purpose better. Your Excellency may remember I mentiond Mr Lott for that department; please to name him to the Committee.[2] I am with great respect your Excellencies most Obedient Servant

NATH GREENE

ALS (Washington Papers: DLC).
1. See above.
2. It is likely he is recommending possible assistants should he accept the quarter-

master general post. John Cox and his friend Abraham Lott were both merchants. See below, NG to Joseph Reed, 9 March.

To George Washington

Sir   Providence Meeting House [Pa.] Feb 15 8 o Clock [PM[1] 1778]

Col Biddle is here and informs me there is but a poor prospect of geting Waggons. I wish all those at Camp that can be spard from the ordinary duties of the Camp may be forwarded to us as fast as possible. We have a great number of small parties out collecting to day of Cattle, Horses and carriages. Their success has not been reported this evening, but I am afraid there will be nothing considerable as the Country appears much draind. Hay is the plentifulest article that there is in the Country, sixty or seventy tons may be had in this neighbourhood.

If your Excellency thinks proper as soon as the Bridge is passable I would recommend a forage in Bucks County and in the mean time have forageing parties up about Reding [Reading]. General Wayne thinks it advisable to destroy all the forage upon the Jersey shore. Col [Richard] Butler will undertake it and cross the River from Chester. I shall wait your Excellencies instructions respecting the matter. To morrow we shall mount a press party on Horses to press Waggons the back of Brandywine. The Inhabitants hereabouts if they have any Waggons or Harness they conceal them. I am with great respect Your Excellencies most Obedient Servant

NATH GREENE

ALS (Washington Papers: DLC).

1. The evening hour is determined by NG to Washington, 16 February, below, where he speaks of writing "last evening" and burning the hay.

To George Washington

Sir   Providence Meeting House [Pa.] Feb 16 1778

I receivd your Excellencies answer by Col Hambleton to mine of yesterday morning.[1] I wrote you again last Evening proposing the burning the Hay on the Jersey shore, also another forage in Buck County. Upon revolving the matter over in my mind, I think the following would be the best plan to execute it upon. Waggons cannot be got in this Country [county] and to attempt to collect them in Bucks County will explain our intentions too early for the safety of the party. I would therefore propose a press Warrant to be sent to Col Smith now at Lancaster and for him to apply to the Executive Council for an hundred Waggons to be got ready in three Days, and in case they dont furnish them by that time, that Col Smith collect the

Waggons with his press Warrant; but if your Excellency thinks our situation will justify dispensing with an application to the executive Council, the press Warrant will be the most speedy and certain method of geting the complement of Waggons seasonably. These Waggons when collected to be loaded with forage in some of the best Hay Towns between Camp and Lancaster and at their arrival in Camp to be immediately taken upon a forage into Bucks County.[2] The business in this way can be conducted with so much secrecy and dispatch, that it will be difficult for the Enemy to defeat it. I will do everything in my power here but the face of the Country is strongly markt with poverty and distress. All the Cattle and most of the best Horses have been carried into the City. The few Whigs that are here say there has been great numbers drove along for Philadelphia [British] market. We take all the Horses and Cattle, Hogs and Sheep fit for use but the Country has been so gleand that there is but little left in it.

Your Excellencies Letter of this day this moment came to hand. I have given Orders to all the press parties to bring the Inhabitants prisoners that conceal their Cattle or Carriages, and examples shall not be wanting to facilitate the business I [am] out upon.

Capt Lee this moment writes of the increasing distress of the Army for want of provisions. God grant we may never be brought into such a wretched condition again. General Wayne will cross over into the Jerseys from Willmington to execute the design of destroying the Hay and driving in all the stock from the shores, which he proposes to forward on to Camp by the shortest and safest rout. But this will not afford an immediate relief. I shall send into Camp this Night everything I can collect. By this detachment my party will be much diminished. Great numbers have already been sent home that have fallen sick and got foot sore amarching. I think it will be best therefore to send two of my field pieces to Camp, they being altogether useless to me. I am with great respect your Excellencies most obedient Servt

NATH GREENE

ALS (Washington Papers: DLC).
1. Washington's letter via Alexander Hamilton not found.
2. Washington did not go through the Pennsylvania Executive Council as noted in his answer to NG, below.

From George Washington

Sir   Head Quarters [Valley Forge] 16 Feby 1778
I have received your Letter of yesterday and have given instructions to the Quarter master to supply your demand of Waggons by sending forward as many as can be spared from the Camp and

pressed in the neighborhood. However, I would not have your exertions abated by a Reliance on Success in this quarter.

As it is impossible to secure the Hay on the Jersey Shore for our own use it is certainly advisable to destroy it that the Enemy may derive no benefit from it; and the sooner Colonel Butler affects this business the better. An Express has been sent to Colonel Cox on the subject you mention. I am with great regard Sir yr most obed Serv

G W

P S If there is any good reason to believe that the Inhabitants have carriages and withhold them make severe examples of a few to deter others. Our present wants will justifie any measures you can take.[1]

FCS (Washington Papers: DLC). The draft is in John Laurens's hand; the postscript is in Washington's hand.
    1. In his desperation Washington had left nothing to chance. The day before, he had ordered Col. Clement Biddle (through an aide) to "impress every Carriage that can be found" and load them with forage, or "we shall not have a Horse left alive to eat it." The deputy quartermasters and commissaries of purchases, he demanded, were to round up forage and find meat supplies for the men as "fast as you can get them," for the troops "must have instant relief." He cautioned them on the need for secrecy lest the enemy learn of the army's plight. (Fitzpatrick, GW, 10: 463–64) He also, as NG suggested, issued warrants to Gen. Smallwood and Capt. Henry Lee, authorizing them to impress wagons. (Ibid., 10: 467–68)

To George Washington

Providence Meeting House [Pa.]
Sir   Feb. 17, 1778
    I sent on to Camp yesterday near fifty Head of Cattle. I wish it had been in my power to have sent more, but the Inhabitants have taken the alarm and conceal their stock in such a manner that it is very difficult finding any. They have done the same with their Waggons and Harness. Our poor fellows are obligd to search all the woods and swamps after them and often without success. I have given orders to give no receipts for everything they find conceald and to notify the people accordingly.

    Col Harmer is gone with a party on the back of the forks of the Brandywine a little above the rout [route] of the enemy.[1] General Wayne is gone to Willmington in order to cross over into the Jerseys, but if the ice wont permit him to pass he is to make a large circuit and come in by the way of Goshen.[2] Col Spencer is gone to the Township of Goshen to rendevous at the meeting House to collect Cattle &so.[3] I shall continue here until the impressed Waggons and all those from Camp are loaded, but I am afraid there will be but few to what our wants demands, and what might be Loaded here with Hay. Grain there is but little to be got.

The business I am upon is very disagreeable, but I should be happy in executeing of it if our success was equal to our wants. The teams that come into Camp that are not for the ordinary duties of it should never be sufferd to continue there all night if it can possibly be avoided. If they can only get a few miles into the Country they can get forage for their Cattle. The transportation has become one of the most difficult parts of the business of forageing, for forage is really plentier than teams.

We have collected a considerable number of Horses, but the Officers in spight of everything I can say to them, will bring in many that are unfit for our purpose. All such we shall notify the Inhabitants to come and take again. The Whigs here are afraid to give any information respecting the Tories for fear when we are gone they will be carried prisoners into Philadelphia.

I am afraid we have lost one of our small parties that was sent out to collect Cattle from Springfield Meeting House. The party was sent from Col Sheppards division, commanded by one Ramsdel, an exceeding good officer, Col Sheppard sais, and consisted of twenty odd men. They went out day before yesterday morning and have never returnd. How they could have fallen into the Enemies hands I cant immagin, for I have never heard of their being out. I think the Officer must have got lost and fallen in with the Enemies Piquet at the ferry before he knew where he was, or else his men must have made him a prisoner and carried him into the enemy, which I dont think improbable, for most of his party were Virginia Convicts. If the Enemy had been out and attacked him its ten to one but some of the party might have got off. Its possible the Soldiers might kill the officer and go in themselves, but by what means he or his party has fallen into the Enemies hands I am not able to conjecture. But I am well convinceed they have, by their not returning and by an account I have from the City of such a party being marched through it the evening of the day they went out. The Intelligence sais there was no officer with the men which makes me apprehend foul play, but its all conjecture.[4]

Col Ballards report did not prove true; there was not a man of his men kild, five were slightly wounded. He kild one Hessian and mortally wounded another; two of his men on their march deserted.[5]

The Enemy are geting ready for a grand forage some where. The Inhabitants thinks from many circumstances they intended it on this side, but I immagin they will alter their plan now if they designd it before. I have no doubt of Bucks County being their object.

We have burnt all the Hay upon Tinecum Island and the other

little Islands about it; the quantity was very considerable. We got a number of very good Horses from off the Islands. I am with great regard your Excellencies most Obedient and very Humble Servt

N GREENE

ALS (Washington Papers: DLC).
1. Josiah Harmar (1753–1813) was lieutenant colonel of the Sixth Pennsylvania Regiment. In 1781 he served under NG in Lee's Legion during the Southern Campaign. (See his correspondence with NG below, 1782 and 1783.) He was engaged for five years after the war in subduing the Indians north of the Ohio river, for which he was brevetted a brigadier general, and from 1789 to 1791 he was commander of the U.S. army. (*DAB*)
2. Since the Delaware River was ice-free, as it had been most of the winter, Capt. John Barry transported Wayne's regiment in row galleys. (Reed, *Valley Forge*, p. 35)
3. Oliver Spencer was colonel of a New Jersey regiment.
4. Ramsdel, in Col. William Shepard's Fourth Massachusetts Regiment, has not been identified. As can be seen in NG's follow-up to Washington, his fears were unjustified.
5. See Ballard's letter of 15 February, above.

To George Washington

Providence Meeting House [Pa.]
Sir   Feb. 18, 1778
I wrote your Excellency yesterday I was afraid we had lost one of our small parties, but they came in a few minutes after I sent the Letter off. Has there been any great desertions from Camp, or any report of prisoners made on the other side of the Schuylkill? I am persuaded there was some of our prisoners paraded for some purpose. If there has been no report of any being lately taken, they have paraded some of our prisoners from the Goals [jails] to make the Inhabitants believe they had taken a considerable part of the party that attackt their Piquet.

The time for which I came out expires tonight, but as the forageing business has been greatly obstructed for want of Waggons it will be necessary for me to continue a few days longer. I wish to know your Excellencies pleasure respecting the matter, that I may govern myself accordingly.[1]

I am told by the Inhabitants that one Mr James that lives a few miles from this place has enlisted near an hundred men from this County.[2] There has gone fifteen from the town of Goshen. This Corps is for Cavalry, most of them have found means to get Horses. These are the reports of the Whigs here.

I am persuaded there has been too little attention paid to the branding the Continental Horses; brands would prevent their being Stole or exchanged, but the Waggon Masters and Waggoners must be stricktly forbid exchangeing the branded Horses for others only for a temporary releif; both parties often suffers by the exchange. The Country man often has his branded Horse taken from him, and the Waggoner sells the other or sends it away by some of his comrades after a few days service. Indeed I think if every Horse that belongs to the Continental teams that fails upon the road and others pressed to supply their place were immediately branded and paid for, the Continent would be subject to less expence than they now are, and the Inhabitants receive less injury. One of the Waggon Masters told me there was forty or fifty teams expected into this neighbourhood from Camp last night. I am very glad of it, as few are to be got about here. I am your Excellencies most obedient Servant

NATH GREENE

ALS (Washington Papers: DLC).
1. The questions NG raises in this letter are answered by Washington this day (below).
2. Jacob James tried to raise a troop of Tory dragoons for the enemy in Chester County, Pa. (Fitzpatrick, GW, 10: 476n)

From George Washington

Sir   Head Quarters [Valley Forge] 18th February 1778
I have received your two favors of yesterday and today. There has been no considerable desertion from this camp to my knowledge within a few days past, nor have the Enemy made any number of Prisoners on the other side of Schuylkil. The persons said to have been paraded in the city were perhaps defenceless Inhabitants that have been seized upon by the traiterous parties who style themselves Royal Refugees.

If you have any prospect of making it worth the while I would by all means have you continue foraging a few days longer. If the matters alleged against Mr James are founded in truth, and he is within reach, he ought immediately to be secured.

Your observations with respect to the branding Continental Horses are exceedingly just but the proper arrangements and regulations in that department can only take place when there shall be an active and intelligent head to it. I am Sir Your most obedt Servt

FC (Washington Papers: DLC).

To George Washington

Providence Meeting House [Pa.]
Sir   Feb. 20, 1778
General Wayne wrote me last Evening that all his troops had crost over the River Delaware into the Jerseys. He intends to collect all the Stock and burn all the Hay along the River that will be within the reach of the Enemy. If he executes the business effectually the only chance the Enemy will have of forageing will be between Schuylkill and the Delaware. I am told there is considerable Hay upon the Delaware at a place cal'd Point-no-point which may be burnt.[1] The Enemy have got a great part of it away, but there is still remaining a large quantity. It would be well worthwhile to attempt to destroy, for everybody that comes from the City agrees they are short of forage.

Col Biddle wrote me last Evening he had Loaded forty Waggons yesterday. We want nothing but Waggons to make a grand forage. There is great plenty of Hay a little below Marcus Hook. Capt [Henry] Lee was at Willmington yesterday. He said he was out after Cattle. Col [Oliver] Spencer wrote me from Goshen last night there was but few Cattle to be got there. I have not heard from Col Harmer since he set off for the Forks of the Brandywine but I have heard of Cattle going to camp from that quarter and therefore suppose they were sent by him. Many people in this Country refuse certificates for their Horses and Cattle. The next move I make from here I shall order home all the troops except one division; they will be so remote from the Enemy that there will be little or no danger from them, and the Country will be pretty well gleaned. One division will be a sufficient cover against any attempts of their light Horse, and they will be too remote for the foot to attempt any thing by surprise.

I have quartered the troops constantly in Houses that they have sufferd very little, only from the heavy marches they have gone through in collecting Cattle &so. I am with great respect your Most Obedient very Humble Servant

NATH GREENE

ALS (Washington Papers: DLC).
1. Gen. Wayne did burn some of the hay in New Jersey. Although nearly cut off by a strong British contingent, he managed to drive some cattle north to Coryells Ferry, where they were ferried across the Delaware to provide beef for Valley Forge for several days. (Wildes, *Wayne*, pp. 152–57)

Petition of Nathan Sellers

[(   ) 23 February 1778. Begs return of his mare (with foal) as she "is all the Horse Kind" he has; promises to keep her from enemy. ADS (PPAmP) 2 pp.][1]

1. Robert Forsyth, NG's aide, noted on the petition that it was "General Greenes wish" the mare be returned. Alexander Hamilton, Washington's aide, located the horse and so ordered it.

To General Henry Knox

Dear Sir   Camp Valley Forge Feb 26, 1778

I receivd your favors from Mr Lotts and from Boston the 5th of this instant.[1] I have just returnd from forageing in Chester and its environs. My orders were to collect all the Horses fit for Cavalry or draft, the Cattle, Sheep and Hogs fit for killing, together with the Carriages and Harness fit for the Continental use. I executed my orders with great fidelity. I was out ten or Eleven days which prevented my writing you by the last Post. I must beg your pardon for not writing you before; but I have put it off from time to time to learn the determination of the Committee of Congress respecting the establishment of the Army. The matter is now gone to Congress, and I beleive strongly recommended by the Committee, but I am well perswaded from many circumstances that it will be rejected. A mystical darkness has spread over the Councils of America and prevents her councillors from seeing her true interest. The Army has been in great distress since you left it. The troops are geting naked, and they were seven days without meat and several days without bread. Such patience and moderation as they manifested under their sufferings does the highest honor to the Magnanimity of the American Soldiers. The seventh day they came before their superior officers and told their sufferings in as respectful terms as if they had been humble petitioners for special favors; they added that it would be impossible to continue in Camp any longer without support. Happily releif arrivd from the little collections I had made and some others, and prevented the Army from disbanding. We are still in danger of starveing; the Commisary department is in a most wretched condition; the Quarter Masters, in a worse. Hundreds and Hundreds of our Horses have actually starvd to death. The Committee of Congress have seen all these things with their own eyes. The faction is in great discredit and prodigiously frighted. Several very humiliateing Letters have been wrote to the General [Washington]. Conway has wrote to the General disavowing the contents of a Letter wrote to General Gates and another actually appears in a different stile. But the artifice is too barefac'd to deceive anybody, General Gates has censurd General Wilkinson for betraying family secrets, and has refusd to admit him as Secretary to the board of War where the Congress wanted to place him to get him out of the way of the Colonels, but more of this hereafter.[2]

General Gates and some others who wanted to serve Conway

and to sanctify his appointment proposd an expedition against St Johns and Montreal.[3] The reasons urged for appointing Conway to this command was his being a Frenchman which must necessarily give him great influence over the Canadians. The Marquis [de Lafayette] was namd as being a fiter person upon that principle than the other. He accordingly was appointed to the great mortification of some others who had party purposes to answer. I look upon the whole plan to be a creation of faction [leekt?] into a publick form, to increase the difficulties of the General. An attempt upon the enemies shiping was worthy the publick attention in a partizan way, but the bare parade of this enterprise was sufficient to defeat it. However the Lakes have not been froose, and consequently nothing could be attempted.

I have been urged to take the command of the troops at Rhode Island, but the General objects to it so strongly, that I am obligd to refuse the appointment. The Committee of Congress have been urging me for several days to accept of the Q M Generals appointment; His Excellency also presses it upon me exceedingly. I hate the place, but hardly know what to do. The General is afraid that the department will be so ill managed unless some of his friends undertakes it that the operations of the next campaign will in a great measure be frustrated. The Committee urge the same reasons and add that ruin awaits us unless the Q Masters and Commisary Generals departments are more oeconomically managed for the future than they have been for some time past. I wish for your advice in the affair, but am obligd to determin immediately.[4] The Congress orderd G Mifflin to account and he was greatly netled at it.

My best respects to Mrs Knox, in behalf of myself and Mrs Greene who is very unwell and unable to sit up. The bridge is finished all but planking, and G. Sullivan is coming to the Northerd.[5] I shall write you in a few days again. In the interim believe me to be your affectionate friend

N GREENE

ALS (NHi).
1. Knox had left camp in mid-January for Boston. Neither of his letters has been found.
2. On "Conway Cabal," see note, NG to Jacob, 7 February, above.
3. See above, note, NG to McDougall, 5 February.
4. On his accepting the post, see below, NG to Reed, 9 March.
5. Sullivan had volunteered to oversee the building of the bridge across the Schuylkill on 21 December, optimistically expecting to finish it within a week. (Fitzpatrick, *GW*, 10: 190, and Hammond, *Sullivan*, 1: 604–5.) Sullivan's "coming to the Northerd" may have referred to Washington's plan to send him to Rhode Island, although it was 10 March before he so ordered him.

From General Alexander McDougall

Sir

Morris Town [N.J.] 28th Feby 1778

I acknowledged the receipt of your favor of the 5th instant in my last. As I have not the particular Detail of the opperations of the right wing of our Army at the Battle of German Town, I am not therefore possesed of sufficient materials to publish it.[1] I have heard much of the machinations of a certain Juncto to intrigue our Chief out of the Command but I want such proof of it as will bear the Public Eye.[2] If this could be obtained, we might soon take such measures as would not only put a period to their wicked and ambitious hopes, but render them odious to the Continent, which their conduct justly merits. I am not surprised that European wickedness in politicks appear among us nor am I discouraged at it, for in a Contest so important requireing so many instruments to support it, we could not expect (considering the great depravity of Human Nature) but that some would engage in it under the mask of Patriotism to serve their private Ends. While I am on this subject permit me to ask you to answer these Questions if you can. Was there not a considerable Quantity of Arms, stores plunder &c taken at Trent Town? Was there not General orders that those articles taken from the Enemy should be sold for the Benefit of the Captors? If so have the soldiers been paid their shares? If not, who has the possesion of what of right belongs to those Hardy Gallant Fellows? Should not the Possesor of the Proceeds be exposed for His fraud or delinquency?

I am of opinion with you, that the Force going into Canada is much too great for a Coup de main on the shipping and I cannot conceive on what principles or information the Congress or Board of War have carried their views any farther, while we are unable by our Supineness to expel the Enemy out of our states. This I confess appears to me a new Maxim of carrying on a war. I think our penetrating as far as Montreal with 3000 is subject to two Capital objections, the danger of wanting subsistance and a certain retreat; for there are large sums due to the Canadians, contracted by our last opperations in that Country and there is a season of the year in which Lake Champlain is not navigable with boats nor passable on the Ice; occasioned by the latters being too strong for the one, too weak for the other. If the Juncto expect by this expedition to raise a Pillar for their ambitious fabric, I fear they will be dis-appointed. I wish therefore, for the sake of the Marquis and the other Honest fellows who are to accompany him that the object of the expedition had not been so extensive.[3] I am glad the Army is growing more healthy, and of your information of 1500 volunteers under General Spotswood being to join the army. I wish the latter may be confirmed. I have still to

Lament that I cannot learn any decisive measures are taken to the Eastward of Virginia to fill up the Army; the season of action is approaching fast.

This affords but an unpleasing Prospect, while the House of Commons on the 5th December last in a Committee of Supply have voted an addition of 20,000 men to their Army. And altho I do not think it probable they will be able to raise or hire that number, Yet I think (we have reason to fear) they will a considerable reinforcement. It is confidently asserted in the Papers that 11,500 men are already negotiated for with five petty German Princes. Their names and Quotas are enumerated. That vote was occationed by their receiving private intelligence via of Quebec of General Borgonyne's Fate which was then not anounced to the Public. His misfortune was greatly Lamented by the House, and chiefly ascribed to the Minister who planned the expedition, for which he was much censured and inveighed against. I have perused the Debates of the House of that date, and General Howe's official Letters relative to the Battles of Brandwine and German Town.[4] In the latter He informs the Ministry, that his Patroles discoved our army advancing at 3 A M on the 4th october, that the Granadiers did not come up in time. But Lord Cornwallis came early to German Town. From the stream of his Letter it appears that a considerable part of their Army was not Engaged. We have various accounts here of the release of General Lee.[5] Some say that he is to be exchanged for General Prescot, while others affirm that he is to be out only on Parole for a month. I cannot see on what principles we can agree to a general exchange, if he is excluded when we have an officer of theirs of equal Rank why should we agree to a Proposition which will give them a large reinforcement and allow them from mere caprice to hold a General officer of ours in Captivity? This would be a Conduct too Humiliating to America, and an act of injustice to the General, which I hope will never be agreed to. I shall be obliged to you for what information you have on this matter. The advertisements in the late Boston Papers contain a great variety of Goods Suitable for the Army. Fine and Coarse Cloths Blankets, shoes &c. It is inhumane and unpardonable in the Country to let their Army suffer so much as they have for want of these necessaries. His Excellency has pressed me to hold an Enquiry into the loss of the Posts in the High Lands. I have determind to essay it; altho those Courts are contrary to my Judgment, because they seldom answer any valuable purpose, and often produce mischief. I wait for the Commission which I expect every moment. If the chief Commissary of purchase or issues is at or near Head Quarters, I shall be much obliged to you if you can get direction or information from either of them, How I shall come at a supply of some of the considerable Quantity of Spirits and

wine purchased by the late Commissary Trumbul; and which I imagine are not brought forward to the Army. I have by this time tres-
pass'd on your patience, and shall only add that I am Dear [Sir] with
much Esteem your friend and very Hble Servant

Df (NHi).
1. This is in answer to NG's question of 25 January, above.
2. See "Conway Cabal," NG to Jacob, 7 February, above.
3. On the Canadian expedition, see NG's letter of 5 February, above.
4. On Brandywine and Germantown, see notes at NG's orders, 13 September and
7 October 1777, above.
5. On Gen. Charles Lee's exchange, see below, Meade to NG, 4 April.

The General Officers to George Washington

Lord Stirlings Quarters [Valley Forge]
March 4th 1778
The Board having Taken into Consideration the Relative Rank of
Generals Woodford, Mulenburgh, Scott and Weeden and after Ex-
amining the Papers Reffereed to Them, are unanimously of opinion
That in the original promotions of Those Gentlemen to the office of
Brigadiers They ought to have been arranged in The following Man-
ner viz Woodford, Mulenburgh, Scott, Weeden: This Arrangement
ought to have Taken place agreable to the Rank Those Gentlemen had
held in the Army previous to their promotions To the Rank of Brigadier Generals but as their appointments by Congress were Different
The Board Cannot give any further opinion upon the matter.[1]

JNO SULLIVAN	WM MAXWELL
NATH GREENE	J M VARNUM
STIRLING	J HUNTINGTON
LACHN MC INTOSH	

DS (Washington Papers: DLC).
1. For the background of this meeting and a discussion of the various points of
view, see below, NG's letters to Weedon, 7 March and 27 April.

From General Benjamin Lincoln

[Boston, 5 March 1778. Returns linen he had borrowed. His leg
almost healed. ACyS (MiDbF) 1 p.]

From William Greene

Dr Sr   Warwick [R.I.] 6th March 1778
I receivd Your Kind favor and am much Oblig'd to you for
forwarding to me so large a Share of the Scituation of Affairs in your

Quarter. Although many of them Appear Very Disagreable.[1] I am Desierous of Knowing the foundation we have to build upon and I flatter myself if the Other parts of the Contenant have Done their propotion as to Cloathing the same that we have, the Army are Now much more Comfortable in that respect then when you wrote me, and I have heard lately by persons from the Army that they are Now well fed which has Afforded me much Satisfaction as I am Convinc'd and that long Since that under God our all Depends by making them Comfortable so as to Create in them Chearful Inclination to Carry on our Reasonable and Very Necessary Defence.[2]

It gave me much pain to hear that there was an unreasonable party Forming Against General Washington.[3] I say unreasonable as I amagine it was Carried on without the least foundation, and for any man or Set of men to undertake a matter of so Dangerous a Consequence must have lost Sight of our Grand Cause, but I was much pleas'd to hear by your letter to your Brother Jacob that the Affair had Vanish'd for I Sincearly believe there is Know [no] greater Earthly

Letter from William Greene, 6 March 1778
(Courtesy of American Antiquarian Society, Worcester, Mass.)

Instrument that promises Greater probibelity of Success at the head of our Grand Cause then General Washington. May the Almighty prosper him and all under his Command with that Degree of Success which so Just an undertaking Merits.

As to our Scituation it is reather Disagreable as we are Dependent upon our Sister States for Troops to Guard the Sea Coast. It has often Happen'd and Indeed Now is the Case that we have not One of the Other States Troops to Assist us and we have been Oblig'd at this busy Season to Call out the Militia, there being Only about four or five Hundred of what we Call Year men in the Service and many of them out upon parole as they are Now recruiting; but notwithstanding our Dangerous Scituation I am Sencible the Grand Army is of much Greater Consequence to the whole Then any thing I can Say of this State, but I heartily wish to hear the States in General may send forward a much larger reinforcement the Insuing Campaign then what were in the field the last, as I think there was a Very Great Neglect somewhere when I consider the Number we had in the Grand Army Exclusive of our fifteen Months men and Often Times a large propotion of our Militia in the Field, but I hope for better Times.[4] As to the State Bill I dare say you have as Great a liking for it as many have this Way but as it was Earnestly recommended by Congress to make a Trial the Convention thought proper to adopt the measure as the Former regulating bill was but a partial One and the State of Conecticut has thought proper to Carry it Into Execution; but what the Other States will Due I at present am at a loss but hope they will due for the [illegible] as that is much Easier then to point out a Method although I heartily Join with you in Sentement in regard to Taxation.[5] As to the Connection you mention'd it has taken place in my Family and I pray God to bless their undertaking. It affords me much pleasure to hear so respectful a Carector of him from One who is so good a Judge and discover'd from Sentiment of Sincerity.[6] Your Son is Charmingly but your Daughter, my Wife was a Telling me the Other day when she came from there, was Very backward of baring her weight upon her feet.[7] My Wife is now gone into Potowomut or perhaps She wou'd have had something to say as well as I and perhaps she may yet at her return. I Wrote this now as I am a Going from home. Sammy Sets out tomorrow. I hope if it will not be two much Trouble you will be good Enoughf to let me Know the Scituation of Affairs by the next conveyance but I fear as you are so much Ingag'd in the Wrighting way to a large Number of Others it will be reather an unreasonable request and therefore am willing to give way untill it will Sute Your conveniency. Please to remember me Very Kindly to General Vernum [Varnum] and believe me to be your Sincear Friend.

WM GREENE

Mr Green left his letter for me to add a line and I find it Nessasary as he had Neglected mentioning Caty in it. Must Be throw [*illegible*] He was Just going to Little Rest [Kingston] and was interrupted while writeing you. Will then Both [of you] axcept his and my love and believe me with every Wish for your health and happiness your friend and aunt

C GREENE[8]

ALS (MWA).
1. Letter not found.
2. Such optimistic reports on Valley Forge were unjustified at this time.
3. See "Conway Cabal," note, NG to Jacob, 7 February, above.
4. On Rhode Island defenses, see above, Cooke to NG, 13 January, and Varnum to NG, 1 February.
5. What William Greene calls the "State Bill" was but the latest of several attempts to stem the rising tide of inflation. (See above, vol. 1: 121n, and NG to Unknown Person, 20 May 1777.) On 22 November 1777 Congress had proposed that delegates from the various states meet in regional conventions to recommend corrective steps to their respective states. (*JCC,* 9: 956–57) Delegates from New England, New York, New Jersey, and Pennsylvania met in late January 1778 at New Haven, Conn. It required no greater perspicacity by the gentlemen in New Haven than by those sitting in Congress to assess the major cause of rising prices: namely, the flood of paper money and bills of credit that poured off the presses. The solution was equally self-evident: retire most of the paper in circulation and severely limit its future emission by taxation and loans. After days of deliberation, the delegates so recommended, but, knowing there was little likelihood of the states, either individually or collectively, hearkening to such harsh advice, they recommended as an interim measure a schedule of maximum prices allowable for most goods, wages, and services in daily trade, to take effect after 20 March. Prices were generally pegged at not exceeding 1774 prices by more than 75 percent (textiles by 100 percent). Only certain vital imports were exempted. (Ms minutes of the convention are in R-Ar and are printed in Hoadley, *State Records,* 1: 607–20.)
Connecticut passed a regulating bill on 12 February 1778—the only New England state to do so. Gov. Trumbull fruitlessly put pressure on Rhode Island and Massachusetts to follow suit. According to Gen. John Sullivan as late as June 1778, Connecticut was withholding militia from Sullivan's army at Providence in hopes of forcing Rhode Island to comply. (Hammond, *Sullivan,* 2: 70) Pennsylvania, New York, and New Jersey passed similar acts, although Pennsylvania soon rescinded theirs. On 4 June 1778 Congress reversed its position, resolving that limitation of prices had proved to be "not only ineffectual" but "productive of every evil Consequence." It recommended that the states repeal or suspend such laws. (*JCC,* 11: 569).
6. Two days later Samuel Ward, Jr., married Phebe, Gov. Greene's daughter.
7. On the health of NG's one-year-old Martha, see below, Jacob to NG, 12 April.
8. Catharine Ray Greene, the aunt of NG's wife, Catharine.

To William Greene

Dr Sir   Camp Valley Forge March 7, 1778
     Your favor of the 2d of February came safe to hand.[1] I thank you kindly for the family information. The distance is so great and the opportunities so seldom, that family occurrences are extreem welcome. It gives me a peculiar pleasure to hear my children are well, not only for my own satisfaction but it relieves Mrs Greens anxiety for

their welfare. Necessity obliges me to do great violence to my own feelings. I have spent but a short hour at home since the commencement of the War. I never saw but one of my children and that but once. I was absent eighteen months from Mrs Greene, six days excepted.[2] I have totally neglected my interest, and every measure to cultivate or increase its consequence. I have in a great degree deprivd myself of all the pleasures of domestick life. I am wearing out my constitution and the prime of life. It is true I shall have the consolation of exerting my small abillities in support of the Liberties of my Country, but that is but poor food to subsist a family upon in old Age. And publick gratitude you know would be a novelty in modern politicks. However I am determind to persevere in the same Line of conduct that I have been pursueing and trust my fortune with my *friends* and *Country*.

I am glad to find there are some few who sympathise with the Army in their distress. We are almost ready to think sometimes that our services are despisd and that our Country are determind we shall struggle with cold and hunger without their aid. I am perswaded the sufferings of this Army is but little known, or else every sentiment of humanity, private virtue and publick spirit have left the States. We have been upon the eve of starving and disbanding. Thousands of our poor fellows are without cloathing, especially shoes and stockings. Hundreds of our Horses have starved to death in Camp for want of forage. The Q M General, Commisary General and Clothier Generals departments have been so incompetent to the demands of the Army that we have been in the most wretched condition immaginable. But I am in hopes nevertheless to conquer and surmount all our difficulties.

There is a Committee of Congress here at Camp to establish the Army anew. They were astonished at our situation and declare they had no conception of our condition altho they were within sixty miles of us.[3] They seem to be very sensible of the great inattention *paid to the Army* and of the mismanagement of the three great departments. They are strieving to correct and amend them as fast as possible, but it will be a work of time to bring about a general reformation. They have recommended to Congress the puting the officers of the Army upon half pay for life, but I am perswaded the measure will be rejected as being incompatible with *Civil Liberty*: but however disagreeable the system, necessity will oblige them to adopt it, for the Officers will not continue to serve under such a hopeless prospect. All the Citizens of America like those of Rome must agree to serve in turn or else satisfaction must be given to those that are now engagd.[4] There has near a thousand officers resignd since the close of the campaign, and the much greater part of the rest are only waiting to know the result of the report of the Committee.[5] Nothing but such an establishment can give force and energy to our Army. To expect decipline from discontented Officers is a folly. To commit Soldiers to their care is devoting them to certain destruction, and what success can we hope from a disjointed Army, organnizd with murmuring members.

Four things are necessary for the establishment of American Liberty. The confederation of the States. The establishment of the Officers upon half pay. Taxation to keep pace with our emissions and expenditures, and drafts from the Militia to fill up the Continental battallions as shall become necessary from time to time. If these measures were all to take place they would be a sure foundation for our independance, and no system short of this can warrant it with certainty.

This war I am perswaded will terminate in a War of funds, the longest purse will be triumphant. I am perswaded there are resources of every kind in America if prudently and oeconimocally manageed to answer all the great demands of the States for men and provisions of every kind. But the Militia are such a constant drain upon our Provisions and military Stores of all kinds that our Magizines and Arsenals are all together inadequate to our consumption. We are paying and subsisting thousands and thousands of men that scarsely render the least shadow of advantage to the cause; these men are consuming our provisions, wasting our Arms and Ammunition, incrasing our expenditures of every kind, draining our funds, and depreciating our currency. I am confident from my own calculations that the present mode of procecuting the War will ruin our cause if the Enemy does nothing at all, which in fact they cannot do if we are wise and United. We must have a cleaver little snug Army, well cloathed, well fed, and well deciplind; such an Army will be able to do infinitely more than a great unwieldy mass of people without order or connection. Troops can do nothing unless they are well cloathed and well fed. We have had some thousands in our Army for months past that have been rather a burden than an advantage, for want of cloathing, and their sufferings have been intollerable.

The groundless jealosies of the great National council [i.e., Congress] respecting the dangers of establishing a regular Army hath been productive of an endless expence and other innumerable evils. If this disposition continues I will undertake to prophecy that sooner or later it will bring on the ruin of our cause. A standing Army is undoubtedly an enemy to Civil Liberty, but when the Liberties of a people are invaded from abroad there is no other alternative but to submit to one or establish the other, where the force of the invader is so equal to the strength of a country as Great Britains is to ours. Could the opposition be supported upon a safer system for our

Liberties, sound policy would dictate it, but we had much better trust the Liberties of the People in the hands of our own Army than in that of the Enimies.

There is another great evil which I very much dread, that is factions and parties among our selves. Ambition, that seven headed monster, begins to mingle its poison in our politicks to spread detraction through the Country, to lessen the confidence of the people in the commander in chief and hurt the reputation of his subordinate Officers.[6] General Mifflin is said to be concernd in such a plan, but with what Justice I cannot pretend to say. Should such a disposition prevail we have everything to fear, for the publick good is always sacrificed to gratify private resentment, but I am happy to find at this time little to fear from this evil. All those dissatisfied spirits are sinking in their consequence and the Congress begins to find their credulity and confidence have been greatly abused. General Conway has been a great incendiary in our Army. He is a man of great ambition and little tallents. He is a man of intrigue and without principle. He wishes to be thought a hero but wants the enterprise. He had the most consumate impudence to publish General Washington deficient in every point of Generalship. He was lately made a Major General which he obtaind by the most dirty artifice. The Brigadiers of the whole Line are all disgusted at it. He was lately sent upon a Donquixote expedition to the northerd which I am perswaded was pland to serve some party purposes.

Mr Ellery lately wrote me that General Spencer had resignd and that they wanted me to take the command at Rhode Island. General Washington would not consent to my leaveing this Army. The command would have been very agreeable to me; to give protection to my own Native place must have been a grateful employment. I am astonished that Rhode Island hath been left so naked this Winter. In the active part of the Campaign there seemed to be a necessity to strip them of the necessary security, because more important objects were in view, but since the convention to the Northerd they ought to have had a better guard. Several regiments have been left at Albany [illegible] all Winter, while you lay exposd to every danger. It is strange to me General Gates never once thought of you. Mr Ellery is very anxious for your safety and is by no means satisfied with General Washingtons refusal.[7] The Committee of Congress here, and the General too, have been urging me for some time past to accept the Q M Generals place. It is a very disagreeable department, render'd still more so by mismanagement, by depreciation of our currency and the resources of the Country being inadequate to our immediate wants. I wish to decline the business but they will compell me to accept the appointment whether I am willing or not. Rhode Island will be called upon for only one Regiment while the Enemy continues in the State. General Varnum and myself have been endeavoring to get liberty for this Regmt that is here to return home, but cannot prevail as yet, but I make no doubt if the enemy remains with you Liberty will be obtaind as soon as the recruits join the Army.

I observe you flatter yourself great benefit will result from your regulating bill; I wish there may, but I must confess I have but little hopes from such a measure.[8] The only radical cure lies in taxation, lessen the quantity of money, and that will soon reduce every thing to the proper standing. Correct monopolies and carry on taxation and all further regulations will be unnecessary and without them they will be ineffectual.

Major Ward by this [time] I suppose has become a branch of your family. I beg leave to congratulate you upon the ocasion. He is in high estimation in the Army as well as at home. You will be blest with a good son in Law and Cousin Phebe with a good husband. I most heartily wish you all every possible happiness.[9] Mrs. Greene has been with me for several weeks past. She has been very ill for about a fortnight with a fever, but is geting better. My complements to all freinds. Mrs Greene desires her Love. I am your most Obedient Servt

N GREENE

ALS (RHi).
    1. Letter not found.
    2. He had been home briefly in early April 1776 en route from Boston to New York. The eighteen months separation was from early 1776 in Boston to July 1777 when Catharine joined him in New Jersey. The "six days" would have been scattered throughout June and July 1776, the period she was in New York City and he was deeply involved in the fortification of Long Island.
    3. Congress was at York, Pa., during the British occupation of Philadelphia.
    4. On the half-pay issue, see note, NG to McDougall, 25 January, above.
    5. The number was not reported, but his figure was exaggerated, as was his prediction that the rest would quit if half-pay were not voted.
    6. On the "Conway Cabal," see above, NG to Jacob, 7 February.
    7. On Washington's refusal, see note, Varnum to NG, 1 February, above.
    8. On the regulating bill, see note, William Greene to NG, 6 March, above.
    9. See also William Greene's letter above on the marriage.

To General George Weedon

Dr Sir   Camp Valley Forge March 7, 1778

The Army hath been more wretched since you left[1] it than it ever was before; the Troops were near starving, nothing savd the Army from disbanding, but the collections that I made upon a foraging party: On this ocasion the Soldiery discoverd more patience and fortitude than was ever manefested by common soldiers under such distressing circumstances.

The Committee and the General impress'd me so strong to accept of the Quarter Master Generals department, that I have consented upon certain conditions, providing they can engage certain persons to act under me, but I am heartily sorry that I ever gave the least encouragement for I am perswaded my greatest efforts and utmost industry will not give satisfaction, every thing in the department is in such a bad train, and the resources of the Country so inadequate to the demand of the Army.[2]

There are Commissioners appointed to settle a Cartel between America and Great Britain for the exchange of Prisoners &c &c Cols Harrison, Grayson and Hambleton are the men.[3]

General How has wrote to the General the most impudent and abusive Letter you ever saw—he calls us rebels and what not, and taxes us with the most studied barbarity to his Prisoners, and exclaims against our civil authority, as void of virtue, honor or honesty.[4]

The settlement of the rank of the Virginia General Officers was submited by the Committee of Congress to a board of General Officers, who sat upon the business at Lord Sterlings day before yesterday.[5] Most of the board were for establishing the rank according to your former claims, and some urged the justice and equity of the measure with great warmth, but it was my Opinion that no power short of that power which created could derange the establishment. They could if they were so dispos'd. A report was made how you ought to have rankd if justice had been done in the first appointments—Woodford, Muhlenburg, Scott and yourself. The reason why Woodford is placed first, it evidently appears he had injustice done him in the appointment of General Stevens [Adam Stephen], and as that may happen to any one by the undue influence of some intrigueing spirit, his resignation did not cancel his claim. I attended carefully to the Sentiments of the Officers and find they are all of oppinion, that it will not be inconsistent with the man of honor, for you to serve under General Woodford and Scott. I advise you to one of two things, to oppose the alteration in Congress with all your influence and quit the Service upon it being carried, or else to make a virtue of necessity and generously subscribe to Woodfords and Scotts ranking before you. I am pretty certain the matter will be carried in Congress and therefore wish you to adopt the latter measure as I should be very sorry to have you leave the Army at all, and much more against the General voice of the Officers of the Army. General Muhlenburg is here and does not seem disposd to oppose the matter with any spirit. I have advisd him to the same Line of conduct that I do you. I will advertize you as soon as I can get his determination. You will both appear to a great disadvantage to give a slight opposition, just sufficint to discover your disapprobation and then, serve afterwards. It will betray a little selfish spirit and want of resolution and true dignity.

The Committee have recommended to Congress the establishment of the Army, but I am well perswaded their report will be
rejected. The plan is infinitely more oeconemical than the former, but
the Idea of sallaries in a free state are alarming.

I have not time to add more, Major Forsyth is just going, and I
have been obligd to write upon the gallop.

My compliments to Mrs Weedon and all Virgina friends. I am
your most Obedient Servt

N GREENE

Mrs Greene has just opend her Eyes. It is early in the morning and
desires her compliments to you and your Lady.

ALS (PHC).
  1. Weedon had gone home to Fredericksburg, Va., on leave.
  2. His acceptance of the quartermaster post is discussed at NG to Reed, 9 March,
below.
  3. Robert H. Harrison and Alexander Hamilton were Washington's aides, Col.
William Grayson of Virginia was a former aide. A fourth member was Elias Boudinot,
commissary of prisoners. The commissioners met with Howe's deputies on 31 March
and again on 11 April, but the negotiations for a general agreement on the exchange of
prisoners collapsed principally because the Americans would not accept Howe's authority as sufficient guarantee. Succeeding negotiations were almost as fruitless, and it
was not until near the end of the war that the two sides could agree on anything more
than partial exchanges. (Bowman, *Captive Americans*, pp. 107–15)
  4. In a long letter to Washington on 21 February, Gen. Howe was especially
concerned over mistreatment of prisoners by Gen. Smallwood's troops, who had
captured the British ship *Symetry*. (See below, NG to Smallwood, 16 March.) In a letter
to Washington on 9 March, Smallwood denied the accusations, saying, among other
things, that because the weather was very cold several prisoners were accidentally
frostbitten. Howe's letter is in PCC, Item 152; see also Washington to Smallwood,
6 March, Fitzpatrick, *GW*, 11: 32–33; and Smallwood to Washington, 9 March 1778,
Washington Papers, DLC.
  5. The bickering among the Virginia brigadiers had gone on since 21 February
1777, the day on which they were all advanced to the rank of brigadier (*JCC*, 7: 141).
Normally, in simultaneous commissioning of equals, Congress decided on relative rank
by seniority among them. This time, however, Congress voted to settle the rank the
next day. When they could not agree the following day, they left the matter up in the
air; and there it stayed for a year. In the meantime, Weedon had enjoyed a kind of *de
facto* rank above the others because he was arbitrarily named first in the resolution, with
Muhlenberg and Woodford listed after him. (Charles Scott was not made brigadier
until 1 April.) The matter was brought to a head by the dismissal in November 1777 of
Gen. Adam Stephen, who had been the senior Virginia general. Since Woodford had
been the first Virginia colonel commissioned and Weedon the last, Woodford threatened to resign unless Weedon would relinquish his claim. At this point, in late
February 1778, Congress asked the generals at Valley Forge for advice. (See their
opinions, 4 March, above.) NG gave a resume of this meeting and his part in it in a
long letter to Weedon on 27 April, below.

To Joseph Reed[1]

At my own Quarters [Valley Forge]

Dr Sir   One oClock March 9, 1778

I found your favor of this morning at my Quarters on my return from Head Quarters where I went with an expectation of meeting the Committee.[2] You are very right, it is absolutely necessary to have a right understanding respecting the profits of the Q M Generals department. While I was at Head Quarters I wrote you a line upon the subject. I am perfectly willing to share the profits equally with Col Cox and Mr Pettit, or in other words I am willing to leave two thirds to be divided as they can agree: but I could wish for the satisfaction of the whole that all were equally interested, then there could be no complaints. Col Cox and Mr Petit cannot wish or expect any thing more generous and equal than this. I am appointed principal in the department, made responsible for all the branches. I am taken out of the Line of splendor. I shall be subject to as much fatigue as any one, and more expence. I only agreed to accept the department upon Col Coxes being joind. I would gladly relinquish it to him if practicable, but if not, I am ready to act providing the Col engages, but I cannot engage upon the conditions of the present appointment upon any other terms than the foregoing. I wish Mr Petit to engage because I have a great opinion of his integrity. I am perswaded Col Cox will agree for Mr Petit to be joint sharers.

Mrs Greene is very unwell or else I would have waited upon you. I shall see you at Head Quarters in the morning. In the meantime let the express go off for Col Cox that the matter may be brought to some issue. My compliments to the Gentlemen of the Committee. I am with truth and sinserity your most Obedient Servt

NATH GREENE

ALS (NHi).

1. Joseph Reed (1741–1785) and NG had been friends since July 1775 when Reed came to Cambridge as Washington's secretary. They were to remain good friends throughout Reed's life, although after the fall of Ft. Washington, he was briefly one of NG's severest critics.

Reed had difficulty in choosing between a military and civilian career during the Revolution. Son of a New Jersey merchant, educated at the College of New Jersey (Princeton), and in the law at the Middle Temple in London, he had established himself as a leading young lawyer in Philadelphia before the war. After serving as Washington's secretary, he was elected in the fall of 1775 to the Pennsylvania Provincial Assembly. In June 1776, at Washington's urging, he returned to the army as adjutant general with the rank of colonel but resigned after taking part in the battle of Princeton. Washington wanted him as head of the cavalry, but when Congress belatedly offered him a general's commission, he refused it. While with Washington in the Philadelphia campaign, he was elected to Congress, and in January 1778 he was made chairman of the committee at camp. As noted below, he was largely responsible for NG's appointment to and acceptance of the quartermaster general post.

In December 1778 he became president of the Pennsylvania Executive Council—the equivalent of Pennsylvania's governor. By aligning himself with his erstwhile political adversaries—the radicals—he remained president for three terms. Because of his English relatives and his early efforts to reconcile England and America, his political enemies accused him of disloyalty, charges totally without foundation. His contentious and sometimes suspicious nature tended to feed such malicious charges. He was again elected to Congress in 1784, but ill health prevented him from serving. It was his intention, had he lived longer, to write a history of the war in the North, collaborating with NG on the southern campaign. He also contemplated writing a biography of NG.

The collections of his papers in the New-York Historical Society contain a wealth of material on the era. The two-volume biography by his grandson (Reed, *Reed*) is still useful; a readable, short, scholarly biography is Roche, *Reed*.

2. As noted at NG to McDougall, 25 January, above, the committee from Congress had settled in at Moore Hall at the end of January to study the problems of Washington's army, especially those concerned with supply. Heading their list of areas to be examined was the quartermaster department. In their first recommendation to Congress on 28 January, the committee declared, after consulting with Washington, that "the Appointment of a Qr Master Genl is a Matter of great Importance and immediate Necessity." (PCC, Item 33. The final committee, minus the War Board members that Congress first proposed adding, consisted of Chairman Francis M. Dana of Massachusetts, Joseph Reed of Pennsylvania, Nathaniel Folsom of New Hampshire, John Harvie of Virginia, and Gouverneur Morris of New York. Charles Carroll of Maryland, the final appointee, never served. No formal secretary was named, but Joseph Reed wrote most of the letters to Congress.)

During the next four weeks, the committee worked long hours studying the quartermaster department. By its own testimony, it examined the "widest Circle of Acquaintances" for possible quartermasters, and it assured Congress (without apparent exaggeration) that "not a Moment hath been spent unnecessarily." (Letter of 25 February, PCC, Item 33)

In the committee's first letter to Congress of 28 January was a half-hearted recommendation of Gen. Philip Schuyler for the post, a recommendation saddled with qualifications that virtually eliminated him from consideration. Not only did they question whether he would accept it (although they had not asked him), but they pointed out he was still under "an Accusation" (for the loss of Ticonderoga) and that a strong objection was his rank next to Washington, whereby "Fortune may throw in his Hands the supreme Command." What weight Congress might give these considerations the committee could not say; as for the committee, however, they assigned them great weight. If Congress thought Schuyler's appointment "inexpedient," it should notify the committee at once, since it had "other Persons under consideration." (PCC, Item 33)

Congress apparently gave equal weight to Schuyler's disadvantages. Although it received the committee's letter on 31 January (*JCC*, 10:103), it chose not to answer it, concentrating, instead, on a new arrangement suggested by the former quartermaster, Thomas Mifflin, now of the War Board. In its second letter, of 12 February, the committee, fearing its letter had "miscarried," again stressed the appointment of a quartermaster "as an Object of the last Importance," referring to him as the "great Wheel in the Machine." The committee emphasized at great length the waste that had gone on—tents, tools, supplies of all kinds going to ruin around the countryside or fallen into greedy hands. Col. Henry E. Lutterloh, Mifflin's deputy at camp, had been recommended, but the committee objected to him on two counts: first, they pointed out the possible "Danger of intrusting so confidential an Office to a Stranger whose Attachment to this Country must be light and transient" (he had come from Brunswick, Germany a few years earlier, *PMHB*, 23 [1899]: 483); but, more importantly, they judged his "Talents or Activity" not equal to the job. (To Congress, 12 February, PCC, Item 33)

On the morning of the twelfth, before Reed started this long letter, the committee had spent some time at Moore Hall, according to their minutes, conferring "with Genl.

Green abt the Qr. Mastr. Gen. Departmt." (Burnett, *Letters*, 3: 83) They had first conferred with Washington, but they did not name NG, saying only that a "Character has presented itself, which in a great Degree meets our Judgment and Wishes; we have opened the Subject to him, and it is now under his Consideration, when we are at Liberty we shall introduce him to your Notice, but Delicacy forbids our doing it, untill he has made up his Mind on the Subject, and given his Consent to the Nomination." Another gentleman of "comprehensive Genius" was also under consideration but he was in civil life and at some distance.

A few hours after the committee conferred with NG, Washington sent him on the foraging expedition, but in the rare minutes he had to spare during the next week, he thought of little else. He was never more torn over a decision in his life. Reasons for rejecting the appointment were almost overwhelming. The committee listed some general reasons for anyone's hesitancy: "the advanced Season, the Confusion of the Department, the depreciation of our Money, and exhausted State of our Resources." (Letter of 25 February 1778, PCC, Item 33) This was in addition to the dire report they had just given Congress on the immoral men in the department—the "little, piddling, pilfering Plunderers in the character of Deputies, and Deputies Assistants"—numerous enough "almost to form an Army." (Ibid.) In the same letter, the committee relayed two special reasons for NG's reluctance: the first was that he "was very unwilling to enter into this large Field of Business." Although he had headed the family anchor business, the brothers calling themselves "merchants in company," in truth he had been a small businessman even by eighteenth-century standards. In the end, however, his reluctance on this score was overcome by the willingness of the committee to appoint John Cox and Charles Pettit as his two assistants. Cox, a Philadelphia merchant who had carried on an extensive iron and salt business, was qualified to make purchases, said the committee, because of his "Knowledge of the Country, and of Business," while Charles Pettit, the New Jersey secretary of state, would "attend to the keeping of Accounts, and of Cash," which, the committee added, "is not as heretofore to be intrusted to any Deputy."

NG's principal reluctance however, was a second one listed by the committee: that he would be prevented from "doing the active Duty of a General Officer." He would, as the committee promised, continue to hold his rank of major general (as Mifflin had done), but he would be a staff officer, not a line officer. NG put it somewhat differently in his letter above to Reed. "I am," he said sadly, "taken out of the line of splendor." The yearning for battlefield glory was no romantic affectation on the part of NG or most of his colleagues in the War for Independence. Twentieth-century historians who minimize such sentiments fail to understand the men who led the fight for independence. In a letter to his friend McDougall (28 March below), NG poured out his heart: "All of you will be immortallising your selves in the golden pages of History, while I am confind to a series of druggery to pave the way for it." A year later he bemoaned to Washington that "No body ever heard of a quarter Master in History as such or in relateing any brilliant Action." (24 April 1779, below)

What, then, led him to accept a post that he had declared in all honesty to Henry Knox only a week before that he hated? Despite accusations by George Bancroft and others, it was not money. Although, under the arrangement discussed below, Greene and his two assistants had prospects of drawing handsome commissions, the well-established commission system was suggested by the committee—not by Greene. When, in fact, with the greatest reluctance, he finally accepted the appointment, he offered to take the post for a year at his current salary. (When he was later criticized for profiteering, he told James Duane in a letter of 16 April 1779, below, that Washington and the committee would remember "that I offer'd to serve a year . . . without any additional pay to that which I had as a Major General." Washington later corroborated the offer, saying he remembered that in one of their conversations on the subject NG had "offered to discharge the military duties of it, without compensation for the space of a year." (Letter of 3 September 1779, below)

During the latter part of February, the pressure on him to accept the post increased. The energy and effectiveness that he had displayed on the foraging expedition served only to strengthen the committee in its choice. To Knox, NG wrote on 26 February (above) that the committee "have been urging me for several days to accept" and that "His Excellency also presses it upon me exceedingly." To McDougall he later confided that the committee and Washington had been at him "Night and Day." (28 March, below)

In the end it was his fear for the very survival of the patriot cause that was one of the two compelling reasons for his acceptance. The same inducement, said the committee, motivated Pettit and Cox. "Nothing but a thorough Conviction of the absolute Necessity of straining every Nerve in the Service, could have brought these Gentlemen into Office upon any Terms." (Letter of 25 February) For NG there was another equally compelling inducement: his extraordinary regard and affection for Washington. A year later he reminded Washington: "I engag'd in this business as well out of compasion to your Excellency as from a regard to the public. I thought your task too great to be commander in chief and quarter master at the same time." NG recalled that Washington had been so desperate he told the committee he "could stand quarter master no longer." (24 April 1779, below)

It was not without some misgivings that Washington pressed the post upon the man that many people thought closest to him. NG, unlike Mifflin, would remain near headquarters where Washington could still seek his advice, but the responsibilities of the new post would prevent him from performing the special tasks that Washington had previously assigned him. Yet who else could do the job? On 1 January, Washington had endorsed Col. Udny Hay for the post, on the strong recommendations of Gens. Sullivan and Wayne (Fitzpatrick, *GW*, 10: 244); but Congress had failed to act, and conditions in the meantime had worsened so much that Washington would not recommend anyone with whom he was unacquainted.

With NG's acquiescence the committee set about to work out a financial arrangement agreeable to Pettit and Cox, which it reported in its long letter to Congress on 25 February. (PCC, Item 33) Though NG was willing to work for his old salary, Pettit and Cox required greater remuneration. Cox, the committee wrote, would be giving up a "very lucrative" private business, while Pettit would lose "a genteel as well as permanent Provision for his Family" from the state of New Jersey. To pay NG a salary commensurate with that demanded by Pettit and Cox would cause every other officer in the army to "expect a similar Increase," which would end in "publick Banktruptcy."

The committee thus proposed that the quartermaster and his two assistants receive 1 percent commission on all purchases, to be divided among themselves as they saw fit. Admittedly such a commission (though time-honored among the British and more recently paid NG's predecessor) was "a Temptation to enhance the Price of Articles purchased; and it is possible enough that this Temptation will have its Effect." Suppose, however, the committee argued, that a quartermaster was "inclined to defraud the Publick of 1000 Dollars." Would he do it by giving $200,000 for goods worth only $100,000, "thereby giving an alarm?" Or would he do it by reporting the ostensible loss of articles in his department in that amount "for which a thousand opportunities would daily present themselves, without the Possibility of Detection?" "The Fact is," the committee continued, "if those at the Head of it are not vigilant and honest, the publick may, nay, must be defrauded of immense Sums by an Infinity of Ways in Spite of every Check which the Ingenuity of Man can devise. . . . There is therefore no Possibility of obviating Peculation, but by drawing forth Men of Property, Morals, and Character—these are the only solid Basis of Security."

If even those safeguards did not entirely satisfy Congress, however, the committee pointed out that the three men, after all, would be watching each other. With this final bit of insurance, they believed they had taken "all the Precautions which the Nature of the Case will admit."

It was more than enough, for in the end, as the committee had first stressed, honesty and character were the most certain guarantees that the public good would come first. NG was fortunate, as was the army, in the selection of his two civilian assistants. The fact that John Cox was Joseph Reed's uncle and Charles Pettit was Reed's brother-in-law undoubtedly brought them to NG's attention, but they were able men of integrity who contributed substantially to NG's success during the following two years. Favoritism in appointments, common to all ages and places, rarely was so fortunate.

If honest men at the top level insured against "Peculation," the insurance unfortunately did not extend downward to the lower levels. Within months the same charges the committee had levelled at the "piddling, pilfering, Plunderers" were being aimed at underlings in NG's department. And although there was not the slightest evidence that NG or his assistants ever tried to increase their commissions by overpayment on purchases, the sheer amount of commissions the next year—especially as measured in devalued dollars—aroused envy and brought down criticism on NG's head. However much the barbs might hurt, however, they were no reflection on his successful handling of a virtually impossible job.

Congress, having ditched Mifflin's proposed rearrangement of the quartermaster department, had authorized the committee to make the new appointments, but committee members favored final congressional ratification of their arrangements and confirmation of the nominees.

On 2 March 1778 Congress put the committee's recommendations into a resolution, although Pettit and Cox had not actually given their final acceptance. NG was to be quartermaster general, Cox and Pettit "assistant quarter masters general." The three were to be "allowed, for their trouble and expence, one per cent. upon the monies issued in the department, to be divided as they shall agree." As a condition of NG's acceptance, Congress resolved that "forage masters, waggon masters, and other officers in the department, be in the appointment of the quarter master general," who, Congress added, "is to be responsible for their conduct." It proved to be a troublesome phrase. Finally, Congress spelled out that "Major General Greene retain his rank of major general in the army." (*JCC*, 10: 210)

There was still the matter of how NG and his assistants would split their commission. In a letter of 5 March, Pettit told Reed that he and Cox were each to receive three-eights of the 1 percent. This would leave NG two eights of the 1 percent plus his pay as a major general. (Pettit to Reed, 5 March 1778, NHi). By the time NG wrote the above letter to Reed on the ninth, however, they had agreed that each would take one-third of the 1 percent commission. Pettit's letter of the fifth to Reed detailed other important arrangements that the committee and Congress had left up to the three to work out. The 1 percent commission, for example, was "to extend to the whole Department throughout America including Forage, and all necessary Officers to be paid by the Publick so that the Commissions come neat and free from Deductions." Pettit was to keep track of "Cash and Accounts, to be stationed at Head Quarters or where the Com'r in Chief shall direct." This left Cox with the "Circuitous Business of purchasing, transporting and collecting &c." It was an arrangement that was to hold until NG resigned in the summer of 1780. Although not spelled out, it was agreed that Pettit should be in charge of the department when NG was detached, as he was while serving in Rhode Island from July to October 1778 (see below).

What was the nature of the department that NG had inherited? Congress had created the office of quartermaster general on 16 June 1775, two weeks before Washington took command of the grand Continental Army in Cambridge. (*JCC*, 2: 94). In mid-August, Washington named one of his aides, thirty-one-year-old Thomas Mifflin, to the post. Although in the late summer of 1777, as we have seen, the department began to suffer seriously under Mifflin's leadership, in 1775 he was a fitting choice. Scion of a well-to-do Philadelphia Quaker family, Mifflin was a graduate of the College of Philadelphia who had apprenticed himself for four years to one of Philadelphia's leading merchants. Thereafter he and his brother managed a much smaller mercantile house in Philadelphia. His abilities and interest, however, lay primarily in politics. He had risen rapidly in the Pennsylvania Assembly and served in the first and second Continental Congresses before joining Washington's army. His appointment as quartermaster was roundly applauded by Congress, an approval that was undoubtedly anticipated by Washington. (Rossman, *Mifflin*, pp. 5–46)

Congress, lacking previous experience in such matters, had established the office with the British model in mind. The post of quartermaster general had first appeared in the British Army in 1689, when the two earlier offices of scoutmaster general and provost marshal general were combined. (R. W. Scouller, *The Armies of Queen Anne* [Oxford: Clarendon Press, 1966], p. 62) Americans became familiar with the office during the French and Indian War, and veterans of that war helped the young Mifflin and Congress to shape the department that NG eventually took over.

From the beginning, one major difference with the British model was in the powers and position of the quartermaster general himself. The British counterpart was virtually a chief of staff, serving as the right-hand man of the commander in chief. Mifflin occupied no such position, partly because of his youth and inexperience and partly because the latter two-thirds of his tenure were spent in Philadelphia, away from Washington's headquarters. Otherwise the department developed along lines similar to the British model. (The British quartermaster's functions during the war are dealt with in R. Arthur Bowler, *Logistics and the Failure of the British Army in America, 1775–1783* [Princeton: Princeton University Press, 1975].)

The American quartermaster department was only one of several army supply services. It was responsible for acquiring and distributing those supplies that did not fall within the categories of food, clothing, arms and ammunition, or medical supplies. The partial list in Appendix II suggests the extent and variety of the quartermaster's responsibility in this area.

The quartermaster was also responsible for two vital services, without which the army was helpless. One was the transportation of all supplies. Not only was it the most vital function of his office, but it was also the most costly and troublesome. (Transportation problems are discussed in a note at NG to Biddle, 23 March, below.) The other service he provided was to move and encamp the army. Moving an army involved transportation, of course, but it also required extensive knowledge of the country, intelligence of the enemy, and foresight in the location of supply magazines en route. Encamping an army even temporarily required a familiarity with the topography and a knowledge of water supply, drainage, and sanitation. Laying out a permanent encampment for the winter was comparable to planning and building a city of fifteen thousand people—and doing it within weeks.

Although the camps around Boston had been laid out before Mifflin took office, he was responsible for getting the men into barracks for the winter of 1775–76 and for moving the army to New York in April 1776. In May, when Mifflin was named brigadier general, he resigned his post in order to take an active command. Stephen Moylan, Washington's muster-master general, was appointed in Mifflin's place. In September a committee from Congress, critical of Moylan's handling of the department, persuaded Mifflin to accept the post again. (The most thorough study of the quartermaster department during the War for Independence is a manuscript by Dr. Erna Risch, to be published by the Center of Military History, Department of the Army. The following summary is taken by permission largely from Dr. Risch's manuscript, designated as Risch MS.)

Although Mifflin and Moylan held the title of quartermaster general, it should be noted that Congress had also helped to shape the department. It had, for example, appointed a deputy quartermaster for the Northern Department a month before Washington named Mifflin to the post of quartermaster general in Cambridge. When Sullivan went north to Canada in May 1776, he was authorized to name Udny Hay as deputy quartermaster. In September 1776 Congress confirmed Gates's appointment of Morgan Lewis as deputy quartermaster for the Northern Department. (Risch MS, p. 40) In the South, Congress named William Finnie as quartermaster for Virginia and Nicholas Long for North Carolina. Although Finnie requested instructions from Mifflin, he never received any; thenceforth he and Long were virtually independent of the quartermaster general.

Despite Mifflin's lack of enthusiasm for the job and despite the time he spent raising volunteers in Philadelphia in December 1776, he did apply considerable energy to the post for six months. Soon after his reappointment, he and the committee presented Congress with a long list of needs, toward which Congress appropriated $300,000 on 2 October. (*JCC*, 5: 839–40) Mifflin managed during the winter to have a number of wagons constructed, although Washington kept a close watch over their progress. With the help of Washington and several deputies, Mifflin also equipped the army for the rigorous campaign of 1777. (Risch MS, pp. 96–97)

After December 1776 Mifflin was rarely with the army. He persuaded himself,

Washington, and Congress that he was more useful in Philadelphia; and although Washington needed him at headquarters, at one point he even suggested that Mifflin stay in Philadelphia to help protect military stores. In February 1777 Congress rewarded him for his success in raising militia by making him a major general. He preferred to return to the military line, but neither Congress nor Washington responded to his hints.

Perhaps Mifflin's greatest contribution was a revised plan for his department, which, with Washington's approval, Congress passed on 14 May. The plan, as Risch has written, "essentially incorporated the Quartermaster experience gained in the campaigns of 1775 and 1776." (Risch MS, p. 47) Separate forage and wagon departments were established under the quartermaster. In consultation with the commander in chief, Mifflin was to appoint all deputies and assistants and to make whatever arrangements deemed necessary. Most of the deputies who continued under NG were Mifflin appointees. The new plans also called for an elaborate system of monthly returns. Deputies were to report to Mifflin, who, in turn, was to combine their monthly figures in one general return to the Board of War and Washington. Unfortunately, few deputies complied, and Mifflin himself became so bogged down in his accounts that he failed to enforce the system. Detailed rules were also laid down to prevent "the loss and embezzlement of intrenching tools, and other military stores." (JCC, 7: 356. The entire resolutions are printed on pp. 355–60.)

Once Mifflin's recommendations were adopted, he did little to implement them. During the summer of 1777, much of it was left up to Washington. He appointed Col. Henry E. Lutterloh deputy quartermaster with the main army, and on 1 July he named Col. Clement Biddle to be commissary general of forage. Biddle was an able man who did much to bring order to the new department. Washington was less fortunate in his appointment of Joseph Thornburgh as wagon master general. Thornburgh did little, and the responsibilities continued to fall on Washington. Not until December was the capable James Thompson made acting wagon master general, a post he took over fully under NG. (Risch MS, pp. 104–6)

There are no figures on the number of people in the department when NG took over, but with deputies, assistant deputies, agents, clerks, wagoners, conductors, artificers, etc., the number ran into the hundreds. The financial arrangement for deputies and agents is equally unclear. In 1775 Congress had voted to give Mifflin a 5 percent commission on purchases "for his trouble." (JCC, 3: 473) This compared with 1 percent that Greene, Pettit, and Cox were to receive, but Mifflin obviously shared his commission with others. Some agents reputedly received 5 percent, but at least one—Hugh Hughes—worked for a salary. (See his correspondence with NG in March and April 1778, below.) Whatever Mifflin's commissions, they were not enough to prevent him from resigning on 8 October 1777. Although he was accused of profiteering, as NG was later, there is no evidence that Mifflin was ever dishonest in his job. It was unfortunate that he did not insist on resigning in May of 1777 when he wished to do so, for it was the succeeding months of chaos that marked him as an inept man.

To Colonel James Abeel[1]

Sir   Camp Valley Forge March 11, 1778
    I receivd yours of the 3d and 9th of this instant.[2] I am sorry to find Mr Lotts sugars in such a bad condition, and still more so that they are not likely to sell to advantage. I am confident if they are put in good order and proper pains taken they may still be sold at a good advance. Sugars cannot fall in and about Camp. Capt Gibs denies that he wrote to have the sugars sent forward. He only mentioned the offer he had for them and that they were to be taken at Morris Town. I wrote to Mrs Lott respecting the sugars also and advised her to send

them on, to the best of my remembrance, but I founded my advice
and opinion upon your information, for I desird you to enquire par
ticularly and told you I wanted to write Mr Lott respecting the matter
You gave the highest encouragement at your return from Bethlehem
and Potts Grove. If there is any loss or fault you are to blame for no
representing things in their true state. But I would not have you be
too hasty in the sale of the Sugars. If they cannot be sold any other
way they can be brought to Camp and retaild out by being put in the
hands of some good trusty person. I must beg you to exert yourself to
the utmost, both you and myself are under obligations to serve M
Lott at all times. You will oblige me by endeavoring to make the best
of the sugars.[3]

I wish you to minute down at every place where you find publicl
Stores, what they are and in whose hands. There has been great
losses sustained for want of attention, but more of this hereafter.

I observe what you say respecting the contractorship of N Jersey
I can give no answer to the matter as its altogether new to me. If you
appointment to any post depended upon my recommendation to M
Morris, you will have the benefit of it, but dont be in haste, hav
patience, and see how the tide of affairs goes on.[4]

Let me hear from you every opportunity. I think the several
brigades will take great part of the Sugars. Major Burnet is endeavor
ing to find A market. Your most Obedt

N GREEN

ALS (RHi).
1. Though he became one of NG's most diligent deputies, little is known of James
Abeel (probably pronounced Abale, the phonetic spelling that NG and others gave it in
early letters). He was born in Albany in 1733, the grandson of an early mayor, Johannes
Abeel, and died in 1825 at the age of ninety-two. (Furman, *Letters*, p. 126n) As a major
in a New York militia unit, he fought in the battle of Long Island in August 1776; by
1777 he was a lieutenant colonel in the quartermaster corps. (See above, NG to
Washington, 27 November 1777 and *JCC*, 9: 1040.)

It is apparent from reading his extensive correspondence with NG that he had had
a mercantile background, associated in some way with NG's friend, Abraham Lott, the
former New York merchant with whom Catharine Greene had recently been staying.
When NG finally accepted the quartermaster post, Abeel was probably the first hold
over to be reappointed. As deputy quartermaster in charge of purchasing all camp
equipage for the army, he would occupy a special position in relation to the staff
deputy quartermasters under NG. Abeel seemed at times, in fact, to serve virtually as
an adjutant. His surviving letter books in several repositories constitute in themselves
a comprehensive record of supply problems during the war.
2. Letters not found.
3. Abraham Lott had not returned from Boston. (See NG's letters of introduction
24 January, above.) The sugar business, as NG makes plain, was not concerned with
the quartermaster department.
4. Although NG relates in his letter below of 16 March that he still had not
accepted the post of quartermaster, he sounds in this paragraph as if he were already
directing the department.

To Colonel James Abeel[1]

Sir   Camp Valley Forge March 16, 1778
    Your favor of yesterday morning has just come to hand. In
answer to that part of your Letter which respects the QM Generals
department, I have no objection to Mr Butler or any other Gentlemen
belonging to the department reaping any advantage from their honest
industry. The Congress have thought proper to appoint me at the
Head of the business, and the Committee and the commander in
cheif urges my acceptance, but I am by no means determin'd yet.
However I am much obliged to you in behalf of the publick for searching out their stores where they lye conceal'd or neglected. You will
oblige *Me* also by sending a copy of all the QM throughout the
Continent. Please to send this by express.
    I am sorry you meet with such poor encouragement respecting
the Sugars. I wish Doctor Potts would take the Sugars for the Continent providing he will give a price that will answer Mr Lotts wishes
and the Continent be no sufferer. Tell Doctor Potts he will oblige me
by takeing the Sugars if he can do it consistent with his duty.
    Mr Lott has returnd home. I receivd a Letter from him last Night.
I beg youl exert yourself to the utmost to make the best of the Sugars.
    Mrs Greene is much obliged to you for the Coffee Mill; and I am
also for the Stand and Wax. I wish you would send me some good
paper.
    I am not solicitous about the profits of the Office of QMG. If the
publick business is but well executed, that will be all that I shall be
solicitous about if I accept. I wish Officers of every denomination and
in every department was more attentive to the publick good and less
so to their private gain. Your further enquiries and information respecting the department will be very acceptable. I am your most
Obedient Servt

                                                    NATH GREENE

ALS (N).
    1. The letter is unaddressed, but the content leaves no doubt about the addressee.
(See NG to Abeel, 11 March, above.)

To General William Smallwood[1]

Dear Sir   Camp Valley Forge March 16, 1778
    I receivd your favor of the 15th of [Feb.?], and am greatly obligd
to you for the Hyson [torn] and Sugar.[2] I will transmit you the amount
when ever the prices are fixt, or at the prices you mention in your
Letter. Mr[s] Greene is much oblige to you for the Hyson as it is
difficult to get that, that is good and as you was so Polite as to spare it
out of your own stock.

There was sundry things taken on board of the prise Ship that would have been agreeable to me [torn] purchase runs so high, that I am glad you did not bye any thing.[3]

General Sullivan is appointed to the command of the troops at Rhode Island, he is now a happy man. [torn] subordinate command is not agreeable to his taste. The Committee of Congress are still siting here, the establishment of the Officers upon half pay remains a doubt. The Congress have appointed me QMG, the Committee and the Commander in chief urges my acceptance. I am at a stand to know what to do. If I dont accept I am afraid all our operations the next Campaign will be retarded by the mismanagement of the department, but if I do accept I am sensible of the druggery and difficulty of the business. I should be glad of your Opinion.

The States in general appear very dilatory in filling their Battallions. The Campaign will open soon, and we shall have nothing but the shatterd remains of the Army of the last Campaign to begin it with. The people of America are too sanguine in their expectations of the good effects of the Northern Convention.[4] British pride will prompt them to attempt our subjugation as long [torn] and money can be procurd. It appears more than probable to me this dispute will terminate in a War of funds. Four things are necessary to secure our Independance; Consideration and agreement among ourselves, the establishment of the Officers upon half pay, Taxation in each State to form funds to defray the Annual expence which will preserve the [illegible] money and drafts from the Militia to fill the Continental Battallions. Upon this plan with proper oeconemy ile engage America can prosecute the War an hundred Years if necessary. Nothing would induce our Enemies to quit their mad policy like such a system. But upon our former plan we should defeat ourselves. The Militia are so expensive, their waste of Arms and Ammunition so great that neither the funds or resources of the States can support the drafts.

The late faction that has been the subject of speculation for sometime past vanishes like a mist before the warming beams of the Sun in a summers morning. It begins to be a doubt whether there ever was any such thing if the party chargd were to be credited.[5] I am with sinsere regard Your most [torn] very Humble Servt

N GREENE

ALS (NHi).

1. William Smallwood (1732–92) had fought in the French and Indian War and had served in the Maryland Assembly. In early 1776 he was a colonel in the Maryland line; by October that year, a brigadier. When this letter was written, his brigade was at Wilmington, Del., charged with keeping open the supply lines from Head of Elk.

When he was assigned to NG's southern command in 1780, NG employed him in raising men and supplies in Maryland, a task for which he was better suited than a field command. The Maryland line was held in high esteem for their fighting qualities, but Smallwood was given little of the credit. His men, in fact, criticized him as a drillmaster and for his willingness to sacrifice them. After the war he served for three years as governor of Maryland. (*DAB*)

2. The letter accompanying the sugar and hyson (a Chinese green tea) has not been found.

3. A unit in Smallwood's brigade had captured the armed British brig, *Symetry*, in the Delaware. The men claimed the prize, with its rich cargo, on the basis of a resolution passed by Congress in October 1777 (*JCC*, 9: 802). Washington thought the prize should be shared by the men at Valley Forge, but Congress upheld the rights of the captors. (*JCC*, 10: 88; Smallwood's letter of 30 December 1777 describing the cargo is in the Washington Papers, DLC; Washington's opinion can be found in Fitzpatrick, *GW*, 10: 302.) Those men at Valley Forge who finally shared in the cargo did so only by paying for the coveted objects. In the Washington Papers, DLC, there is considerable correspondence between Smallwood and Washington on selling the cargo.

4. Probably New Haven Convention. See above, note, Wm. Greene to NG, 6 March.

5. See the "Conway Cabal," note, NG to Jacob, 7 February, above.

To Jacob Greene[1]

My dear Sir   Camp Valley Forge March 17, 1778
Your agreeable Letter of the 26 of Feb came to hand last night.[2] Thank you kindly for your care of my little shavers. I am greatly obliged to Sister Peggy for her goodness. I am sure by the manner of your writing they are not well situated at Coventry. I have wrote Cousin Griffin respecting the matter. I wish you and Sister Greene to pay some attention to them until Mrs Greene returns home which will be in May.[3]

I have the pleasure to inform you that the faction raisd against General Washington has sunk into contempt. The party charged denies they had any intentions of the kind, but the symtoms have been too visible to doubt the truth. Ambition is a dangerous evil in a free State when it happens to rage in an unprincipled boosom, but we must expect such little ebullition of discontent and partial views to mingle in our National Politicks.[4]

It is very true what Cousin Griffin told you that I wanted to retire to private Life again, providing it was consistent with the publick good, but I never will forsake the cause of my Country to indulge in domestick pleasures.[5] Nevertheless it would be agreeable to retire if no injury was to follow to the public, for the Splendor of the Camp is but a poor compensation for the sacrafices made to enjoy it.

I observe you think the spirit of patriotism is ready to expire in the Army among the Officers from their demand to be put upon half pay. Can you think the obligation rests upon those that first engaged to go through the dispute without any further provision than a bare subsistence for the time being? If the dispute was just and necessary than [then] the obligation rests upon all equally, but if not, then there is no obligation to support it. These being the simple and natural principles upon which the question stands, take into consideration the situation of the officers and se[e?] how far their demand is founded in justice. The Officers of the Army at the begining of the dispute flew to Arms regardless of their families or fortunes, expect ing at the same time that peace and reconciliation would soon take place. Few expected the dispute would be carried to such extremity but the contest has been growing warmer and warmer from first to last, that there never has been the most distant opportunity to bring about a reconciliation.

If it is necessary to maintain our cause, if our present safety and future happiness depend upon its support, it is the duty and interes of every individual to lend his aid. Then it becomes a common obli- gation upon all. Why therefore should a few zealous officers be made a certain sacrafice for the common good? Those that are in the Army are wasting their fortunes, impairing their constitutions, depriveing themselves of every domestic pleasure and if they continue a few years longer in their present situation what is to become of them after the War? Out of business, out of credit, without connexion in the way of trade, Military distinctions or charactors to maintain, numerous acquaintances contracted without the means to be civil to them, hereafter must render the condition of the officers infinitely more wretched than other parts of Society. Is it reasonable that men should be exposd to all the hardships of war, be constantly exposed to sudden death and broken bones without any compensation? Is this makeing the business of Society equal? There never was a Nation under the Sun where a set of officers were left without support after a long and cruel war unless it was where all the Inhabitants did equal duty in the civil and military departments. But waveing the Justice of their claim, good policy demands the measure for the Continent can- not support the War upon the present system. Niether our funds or magazines are equal to our present demands. We must have a good regular Army subject to good dicipline, well fed and well cloathed, with a small force; upon such a basis more can be done than twice their numbers, where they are badly fed badly cloathed and without order or dicipline. Our Taxes are five times as great as are necessary to carry on the War. A numerous Militia always coming and going from the Camp, swells our expenditures to an enormous size. The draft upon the funds, the consumption of Provisions, and the waste of ammunition [*remainder of letter missing*]

ALS (MWA); letter incomplete.
    1. Addressee determined by contents of the letter.
    2. Letter not found.
    3. In June 1777, when Catharine left Rhode Island to be near NG in New Jersey, she had left her two children with Jacob and his wife, Peggy. The oldest, George Washington, was then sixteen months old; the youngest, Martha Washington, three

months old and unwell. In the intervening nine months, most of which she had spent as a guest of the Abraham Lotts, she enjoyed an exciting social life. To all who knew Catharine it was apparent her concerns were rarely centered on her children. In a letter to Christopher of 22 April, below, NG refers to his "almost fatherless and motherless" children.

4. See note, his letter to Jacob of 7 February on the "Conway Cabal."

5. The letter to Griffin has not been found, but judging from other letters he wrote at this period, such sentiments were in the nature of complaints, not to be taken literally.

To Colonel Clement Biddle[1]

Dear Sir   Camp Valley Forge March 23, 1778
We have been looking over your plan for the forage Master Generals department. We wish to have a plan of the relative State the Forage Masters department stood in to the Q M Generals heretofore. You will give us an account of your former conditions of serving who were paid by the month, who receivd a Commission, what it was, and on what it arose. Give us as full a history of the matter as may be necessary for our full information to compare the two plans.[2] I am my dear Sir with great respect Your most Obedient Sert

N GREENE

ALS (PPIn).

1. NG was fortunate that Clement Biddle, a friend since 1776, agreed to stay on as forage master general. He had been appointed in the summer of 1777 but had had little direction or support from Gen. Mifflin.

No problem that faced the new quartermaster general demanded more urgent attention than transportation, on which all supply services depended. By stopping most coastal shipping, the British blockade had forced the American army into dependence on land transport. Not only were roads inadequate—often mere trails or even nonexistent—but there was a never-ending shortage of all the components of land transport: carts, wagons, sleighs, sledges, oxen, horses, harness, packsaddles, wagoners, carters, and forage. Forage was scarcest of all, and without the hay (or pasturage) and grain that provided a draft animal's motive power, nothing moved. Forage was to the revolutionary army what oil is to the twentieth-century army. Forage, moreover, had to be hauled, and the beasts that hauled it had to eat, sometimes consuming much of what they hauled. (See NG's estimate of the number of horses needed just to haul forage, NG to Washington, 18 October 1778, below.) In the more than 2,500 letters that have survived from NG's two and a half years as quartermaster, no refrain is sounded oftener than the want of forage—with the possible exception of the want of money. NG expended great effort, not only in helping Biddle search for new supplies of forage and ways to conserve supplies on hand, but also in seeking alternate means of moving goods.

The most obvious alternative was water transport, the mainstay of colonial trade. NG, who had spent most of his life within sight of Narragansett Bay, never lost sight of the advantages of water transport. As disastrous to American coastal trade as the British navy had proved to be, he demonstrated that, should only one transport out of four get through the blockade, it was still cheaper than land transport. (NG to Washington, 27 October 1778, below.) In the summer of 1779, it was largely at his insistence that several vessels slipped through the British blockade to bring rice from Charleston, S.C., to Boston—an unthinkable undertaking by land transport. Often, of course, a destination was not reachable by salt water.

He also made use of river transport wherever feasible. In the spring of 1778, for example, he ordered a warehouse built at Reading, Pa., on the Schuylkill, whence supplies could be boated down to Valley Forge. (See Abeel to NG, 10 May, below.) As water levels dropped in the river, he ordered a survey of the shallows and a plan for the state to use in improving them. (See Pettit to Wharton, 16 May 1778, *Pa. Archives,* 6: 513–14.)

Too often the rivers were more of a hindrance than a boon to transporting supplies. Running as they did to the ocean, they lay athwart many of the principal land routes that paralleled the coast. Although a few smaller streams were bridged, most had to be forded, or if too deep, they had to be crossed by ferry boats, as did all the larger streams. If roads, bridges, or ferries did not exist where the army needed them, it was the quartermaster's responsibility to see that they were constructed and kept in repair. (On the repair of roads near Valley Forge, see below, NG to Pettit, 11 April.)

In coping with the problems of transportation during his tenure as quartermaster general, NG laid the foundation for his successful southern campaign, one that depended above everything else on mobility.

2. Neither plan has been found.

To Colonel John Davis[1]

Camp at the Valley Forge
March 23, 1778

You are hereby appointed and authorized to act as Deputy Quarter Master General of the American Army, on the western Side of the Susquehannah in the State of Pennsylvania, with the Privilege of making Purchases on the Borders of Maryland and Virginia.[2] You are to purchase as many Waggons and Horses suitable for the Use of the Army as you can meet with, preferring Teams completely equipped for the Service where they are to be had, and such other Articles as you shall from Time to Time be instructed to purchase by the Quarter Master General, and the Assistant Quarter Masters General, or either of them. You are allowed to employ such Clerks and Assistants as shall be found necessary for making the Purchases and collecting the Horses and Teams for the ensuing Campaign, taking Care to keep no such Clerk or Assistant on Pay longer than shall be necessary and making constant Returns to the Office of Quarter Master General, of the Appointment and Dismission of such Clerks and Assistants. And for your Trouble and Expences you are to be allowed a Salary of Fifty Dollars per Month, and a Commission of one and a Half per Cent on the Purchases you shall make and on all other necessary Disbursements.[3]

Given under my Hand at Camp at the Valley Forge the twenty third Day of March in the Year of our Lord One thousand seven hundred and seventy eight

NATH GREENE

LS (John Davis Papers: DLC).
1. In 1774 Capt. John Davis joined a militia unit near his home in the frontier

county of Cumberland, Pa. In 1776 he served as commissary of the Sixth Pennsylvania Battalion, and by 1777 he was in the quartermaster department at Carlisle, Cumberland County, with the rank of major and the title of barrack master and deputy quartermaster. In June that year he was promoted to colonel in charge of acquiring supplies in western Pennsylvania and in the border areas of western Virginia and Maryland, a post he held throughout the war. His papers at the Library of Congress, from which this biographical information was taken, constitute a detailed record of supply problems in what was then a remote section of Pennsylvania.

2. Davis's area was later reduced somewhat, as seen in NG's letter to him of 9 May, below.

3. With some exceptions, such as amount of reimbursement, similar wording was used in the appointments of all deputy quartermasters.

To Henry Laurens, President of the Continental Congress

Sir   Camp Valley Forge 26th March 1778

I received my Appointment as Quarter-Master-General through the Hands of the Committee of Congress here at Camp, by whose special Solicitation I engaged in the Business of the Department.[1] I am very sensible of the importance of the Trust, and the Difficulty of putting the Business upon a Tolerable Footing at this advanced Season. My utmost Exertions, however, shall not be wanting to answer the Expectations of the Congress and to accomodate the Army; and I am sensible the Gentlemen who are appointed my Assistants will give me all the Aid in their Power. The Demands are so extensive, and the Resources so few that the Shortness of the Time in which we must provide the necessaries for the ensuing Campaign will not leave us at Liberty to make the most advantageous Contracts. This is an Inconvenience to which the Publick must be subject in Consequence of the Business of the Department being taken up at so late a Period, and will necessarily call for a large and immediate Supply of Cash. Col. Cox will wait upon Congress in a few Days and give them further Information upon this Head. I hope by this Time they are impressed with proper Ideas respecting the Situation of the Department; and they well know how essential it is to the Operations of the ensuing Campaign that the most speedy Preparations should be made. If I am not properly supported; if I am not aided with all the Influence of the Congress in the several States, I am fully persuaded our utmost Endeavours will fall vastly short of the desired Effect; the Army will be distressed; the Public disappointed, and our Reputations ruined. I hope therefore as I engaged in the Business of the Department from Necessity and not of Choice, and the Gentlemen also that are with me, that every possible Encouragement will be given to enable us to answer the Demands of the Army.

I have not received any Returns from General Mifflin, and therefore can only conjecture as to the full Extent of our Wants. I have seen some Returns from Col. Butler, Agent for Camp Equipage, by which I find a great Deficiency in the Article of Tents.[2] The like Deficiencies also appear as to Horses, Carriages and other Capital Articles. We are taking every Method in our Power to draw in Supplies as fast as possible, and shall be obliged to extend our Views to the Neighbouring States, which renders our immediate Demand for Cash very great.

I find there are very large Demands against the Quarter-Master-Generals Department now outstanding. It will be necessary to appoint Commissioners for the Settlement of these Accounts, or to authorise us as a Board for that Purpose. But unless we are to be furnished with Money fully equal to the former Claims and the present Demands, I could wish to be unconnected with the Business, as it will be attended with the most destructive Consequences to cramp the present Preparations.

You cannot be insensible that the present depreciated State of our Currency and the extravagant Prices Things are sold at, must greatly increase our Demand for Money. The Publick Expenditure will always be proportionate to the Depreciation of Money; for the Prices of Commodities are regulated entirely by that. And as our Contracts must be paid in Cash, the Publick will suffer the whole Loss. Those who have one Thing to barter for another suffer no Injury from the advanced Prices. Nothing can correct this Evil but a heavy Tax.

I find Waggoners are not to be got under Ten Pounds per Month. This is a most extravagant Demand, but Necessity will oblige us to comply with it; for that appears to be the current Price given for private Business. Good Waggoners will be a valuable Acquisition. Horses are scarce and difficult to be got, and Hundreds are lost for Want of good Conduct in the Drivers. The Loss of one Horse amounts to almost a Drivers Wages for a whole year. Those that have been drawn out of the Line have been very ignorant of their Duty; and besides, it gives great Discontent to the Officers and keeps up a kind of perpetual Warfare between the Staff and the Line.

It may be not improper for me to assign to Congress the Reason why I did not somewhat sooner take upon me the Exercise of the Office. It was a preliminary Condition of my Acceptance that the Gentlemen appointed as Assistants should accept also; they were at a great Distance from hence when the Appointment arrived, and it necessarily took up a considerable Time for them to receive the Notification and make the necessary Preparation for coming to Camp so that they did not arrive till Saturday last, and we entered on Business immediatly afterwards. I have the Honour to be with great Respect, Sir your most Obedient humble Servant

NATHANAEL GREENE

LS (PCC, Item 155: DNA).
1. See above, NG to Reed, 9 March.
2. Anthony Butler had also served as Mifflin's chief deputy from the time of Mifflin's illness in September 1777 (*JCC*, 12: 971). A week after NG wrote this letter, Butler requested in Mifflin's name that all deputies send returns with the "utmost dispatch." He prefaced one such request with the declaration that "various malicious Reports . . . [have] been circulated by a Sett of Men enimical to the late Quarter Master General to the prejudice of the Deputies, Assistants and the general conduct of the late Department." (Butler to John Davis, 1 April 1778, Davis Papers, DLC). Before Butler left the department, he gave NG and his deputies additional trouble. (See below, Abeel to NG, 12 May.) Mifflin never turned over an adequate accounting to NG; it was two years, in fact, before his accounts were straightened out to the satisfaction of Congress. (Rossman, *Mifflin*, p. 160)

To Thomas Rutherford[1]

[Valley Forge, 26 March 1778. Asks his help in procuring horses and wagons in Berkeley, Dunmore, and Frederick Counties, Virginia. LS (Vi) 1 p.]

1. Rutherford was in the quartermaster's department in Virginia. (See his letter of 18 June 1778 in the Washington Papers, DLC) An answer to NG's letter has not been found.

To George Washington

[Valley Forge, 26 March 1778. Acknowledges Washington's letter[1] on suggestions for obtaining wagons in Virginia and asks for introductory letters for his agent. Needs them soon, since "time is so short" for putting his department in readiness. LS (Washington Papers: DLC) 2 pp.]

1. Letter not found.

To General James M. Varnum

[Valley Forge, 27 March 1778. Asks permission to send "Mr Littlefield" with urgent letter to Rhode Island.[1] ALS (NNC) 1 p.]

1. William Littlefield, NG's brother-in-law, was a lieutenant in Varnum's brigade. The urgent business has not come to light.

To General Anthony Wayne

[Valley Forge, 27 March 1778. Horses that Wayne wanted are not available. ALS (PHi) 1 p.]

To the Inhabitants of the United States

Camp, Valley-Forge, March 28, 1778.
From the great number of Deputies and Agents necessarily employed in the Quarter-Master-General's department; and from the unavoidable hurry in which much of the business has been transacted,—which has greatly increased the number of those Deputies and Agents, and, in some instances, has occasioned the employment of improper persons, many irregularities have taken place in the department. That order and regularity which is necessary to the well-conducting a business so important and extensive, has been much broken in upon; and many of the good people of the country have complained of disappointments and ill treatment. In order to remedy the manifold inconveniences arising from these causes, and, as much as possible, to guard against abuses in future, great care will be taken to engage such persons in the department who are the best adapted to the business of their several employments, and the most likely to preserve a proper deportment and to give satisfaction to the well disposed part of the community, in the respective districts assigned them. To this end punctuality in payment for such articles as shall be purchased, will be highly necessary; and we mean to preserve it as far as possible: But as it will be impracticable to make such a distribution of cash as will enable every person employed in purchasing to pay as he goes, regular printed certificates will be put into the hands of the Deputy-Quarter-Masters to be filled up and delivered out to the people from whom purchases shall be made.[1] In every State where these certificates are distributed, persons will be appointed to attend and pay them off at certain short periods, and at such places as will best accommodate the inhabitants; of which public notice will be given. This mode, it is imagined, will relieve the sellers of produce from the difficulties and disappointments so much complained of. The certificates, having a settled form, and being put into the hands of none but those who will have authority to sign and pass them, will at once save the receiver from the delay and difficulty frequently happening from the want of form, and from the doubt and uncertainty of the authority of the signers of them; and, as they will be paid to any person who may possess them, having the first proprietor's name thereon endorsed by himself, they may be negociated as cash in the intervals of payment, or at least be presented at the pay-office with the less trouble to the proprietor.

As it is our earnest desire, and will be our constant endeavour to accommodate the whole business of our department to the ease and convenience of the inhabitants of the country, as far as shall be consistent with the good of the service, we hope to receive their

cheerful aid and assistance on all occasions in promoting the common cause of American Freedom, and the rights of mankind.
Camp, Valley-Forge, March 28, 1778.

NATHANIEL GREEN,

JOHN COX,

CHA. PETIT

Reprinted from the *Pennsylvania Packet*, 15 April 1778.

1. The certificates described in this proclamation were drafts against future funds of the quartermaster department, issued in exchange for goods or services. They were also used by the other supply departments. The journals of Congress do not record when they were first authorized, but they had been in use at least since 17 June 1776, at which time Congress instructed Washington "that no certificates be given in future by any but brigadiers, quartermasters and their deputies, or a field officer on a march, or officer commanding at a detached post." (*JCC*, 5: 451) The first ones were crude hand-written promissory notes, often hastily and haphazardly drawn up and difficult for an honest holder to redeem in cash, yet easily forged by the dishonest citizen. The printed forms specified in this proclamation were an improvement, but they were often signed by unauthorized persons and they too were subject to being forged. To correct such problems, the following year NG recommended a set of stringent rules that required full names and identifications of the officers issuing them, a list of commodities or services provided, their supposed value, and the time and place of the transaction. (NG to Washington, 15 February 1779, below)

Throughout the war, but especially before August 1780, holders of certificates found that redeeming them was far more difficult than indicated by the facile promises made in this proclamation. Pay offices of necessity often operated in a hit or miss fashion, and when they *were* set up, they soon ran out of currency. Holders were sometimes shunted from office to office. As a consequence, the original holders would often take less than face value for a certificate by endorsing it over to someone else for cash.

Even when there were no obstacles to redeeming them, it was imperative during this inflationary period that the holder get to a pay office as soon as possible since they were redeemable only in rapidly depreciating continental currency. (After August 1780, when NG was no longer quartermaster, Congress made them payable in new emission money at specie value while old ones were redeemable according to a sliding scale. Henceforth they also bore interest.)

Although the above proclamation implied that the quartermaster department expected sellers to accept certificates willingly, the truth was that they were only a substitute for currency, and they were so considered by the public. Less than six weeks after the issuance of this proclamation, for example, Pres. Thomas Wharton of the Pennsylvania Executive Council reported to NG on 7 May (see below) that the use of certificates had had "a very mischievous effect, by rendering the Service disagreeable to the people, in consequence of which force becomes necessary to compel them into it." From that time onward, certificates found their normal use in paying for supplies that were being impressed. To the unwilling seller, the choice was a certificate or nothing. British sympathizers whose goods were impressed would have been happy to receive even such reimbursement.

If certificates had disadvantages for the holders, so had they for the army. Aside from the extra work involved in redeeming them, as compared with paying out currency, they often raised the price of impressed goods, as Robert Morris later pointed out. Officers, he wrote, "who are compelled to the melancholy duty of plundering their fellow-citizens" try to make up by overpricing the goods. Not only did deputies or agents salve their own consciences in this fashion, they also increased their own commissions. (The Morris quote is from William Graham Sumner, *The Financier and the Finances of the American Revolution*, 2 vols. (New York, 1892), 1: 287. Ferguson, *Power of Purse*, pp. 57–68, treats certificates as one of the means employed to finance the war.)

To General Alexander McDougall

Dear Sir   Camp Valley Forge March 28, 1778

I am favord with yours of the 14th, 17th and 27 of February and 22d of March.[1] I beg leave to congratulate you upon your appointment to the command at the North River. I cannot agree with you that you enter upon the command under disadvantages. The late misfortunes will pave the way for the public to be satisfied with any thing short of a series of similar blunders.[2]

I am appointed Q M General, and am vexed with myself for complying with the pressing importunity of the Committee and the General. They were at me Night and Day. However now I have accepted I will do the best I can. In answer to your request respecting Mr Bostwick, I can only say I shall always esteem myself happy to oblige you, and shall take care to recommend him to the principal of the forage department who will have the appointment of all those that acts under him, and made accountable for their conduct.[3]

I wish you would recommend all Persons fit to fill the Q M General department at Peeks Kill that I may compare them with others that are given in.

I have not time to enlarge upon Politicks but I think the regulating bill[4] will be attended with the most destructive consequences. The regulation of the Army has been in the hands of the Committee for some Weeks and I believe is now gone to Congress, but little is to be expected from a body who are determined not to profit by experience. Jealousy is the worst of curses; it seals up every generous purpose of the Soul either in private adventures or public administrations. All of you will be immortallising your selves in the golden pages of History, while I am confind to a series of druggery to pave the way for it.

The faction has expird for a time, but I expect they are lying conceald until a more favorable opportunity—but more of this hereafter.[5] I am with the Sincerest wishes for your health and prosperity. Your most Obedient Servt

                                                            NATH GREENE

ALS (NHi).
1. Only the letter of 14 February has been found.
2. Two weeks earlier, Washington had ordered McDougall to assume "chief command" in the Hudson Highlands (Fitzpatrick, GW, 11: 91). On 15 April, however, only two weeks after McDougall had arrived at Fishkill, Congress placed Gates in command of the troops in the "whole northern department." (JCC, 10: 354) Although Pres. Laurens saw this as a "pretty little attempt" to make Gates independent of Washington, three days later Congress made it clear that Gates would be subordinate to Washington. (Nelson, Gates, pp. 186–87) After first ordering McDougall to return to New Jersey as soon as Gates arrived, Washington decided in mid-May to leave him there. He was to remain in the Highlands during most of the war.

3. Andrew Bostick became deputy quartermaster of forage at Fishkill, N.Y.
4. The regulating bill, which is discussed above at William Greene to NG, 6 March, is not to be confused with the regulation of the army referred to in the next sentence.
5. On the "Conway Cabal," see above, note, NG to Jacob, 7 February.

To Colonel Clement Biddle

Sir

Camp Valley Forge March 30th 1778

I agree with you there is not a moments time to be lost in fixing upon proper places for magazines. I have been thinking upon the subject and am of opinion that the following must be the great outlines of the chain of magazines; the quantity to be laid in of particular Stores upon the River and at intermediate posts to form a proper communication must be regulated by circumstances.

200,000 bushels of Grain upon the Delaware and as much Hay as can be got.

200,000 bushels of Grain upon the Schuylkill and as much Hay as can be bought.

200,000 bushels of Grain at the head of Elk and the intermediate posts to camp and as much Hay as can be bought within forty miles to Camp upon that route.

100,000 bushels of grain upon the line of communication from the Susquehannah to the Schuylkill from Reading through Lancaster to Wrights ferry and as much Hay as can be got

100,000 bushels of grain from the Delaware to the North River to be proportioned to the consequence of the several posts forming the communication and a necessary quantity of Hay.

40,000 bushels of grain round about Trenttown within a circle of Eight or ten miles and as much Hay as can be got. As there had been a post kept at Trenton it is more than probable the forage must be principally drawn from Burlington or Monmouth. The forage at the North River must be proportioned to the number of troops to be kept there. I am ignorant of that at present, but believe it will amount to five thousand and as it is on the direct rout of communication from the Eastern States the quantity must be considerable—the River will enable you to form that Magazine very easy.

In forming your magazines give all sorts of grain the preference to wheat.[1] Oats first, Corn next, Rye next and so on. You must get a number of Screws made to Screw all the Hay and employ Hands to do it either at the farmers barns or at the Magazines. You cannot get about this too soon. There must be a number of forage carts provided to be employed in no other business. I shall call upon you this afternoon if possible. I find my present Situation to be very inconvenient for the Q M Generals department and purpose to remove to More Hall as soon as possible.[2]

I Intend to construct some boats as soon as may be to transport forage and Stores upon and down the Delaware and Schuylkill. I am Sir your most Obedient Servt

N GREENE

Tr (GWG transcript: CSmH).
    1. Wheat was to be reserved, if possible, for making flour.
    2. On Moore Hall, see NG's letter to Biddle of 12 February, above.

To Colonel Clement Biddle

[Valley Forge, 31 March 1778. He is to carry out the plan as approved by Washington's letter of 31 March, below. Tr (GWG transcripts: CSmH)1 p.]

To Colonel Hugh Hughes[1]

Sir   Camp Valley Forge March 31st 1778
    You will probably have heard before this reaches you, of my Appointment to the office of Quarter Master General and as I would wish to Continue in their respective Stations, all such Officers as I find in the Department, whose conduct has manifested their fitness for the employment, I should be glad to know how you are disposed on that subject, as speedily as may be; and if you are inclined to continue, you will be pleased to inform me of the Terms and Conditions of your former Appointment, and what are your Expectations under a new one. In the meantime I doubt not you will be careful that the Bussiness of the Department does not suffer. Considerable supplies are Expected from the Eastern States which will be directed to your Care, particularly from Colonel Chase and Mr Benjamin Andrews of Boston, and from Jacob Greene Esqr of Warwick, Rhode Island, which I beg you will forward on to Camp with all possible Care and despatch, as fast as they arrive.[2] I am Sir, Your most Obt Humble Servt

NATHL GREENE

PS If Mr Wadsworth should be appointed to the Office of Commissary General there will be a deputy Quarter Master wanted to Supply his place. In such case I should be glad you would mention to me a Suitable person.

Cy (NHi).

1. Hugh Hughes (1727–1802) was the only deputy to refuse reappointment by NG. (See letters of 8, 16, 23 April and 3 May, below.) Before the war Hughes operated his father's business in New York City and taught school. Although his brother John was appointed Stamp Collector in Pennsylvania in 1765, Hugh was an outspoken opponent of the Stamp Act and became an articulate leader of the New York Sons of Liberty. In 1776 Mifflin appointed him deputy quartermaster for New York with the rank of colonel. During the New York campaign of 1776, Hughes served Washington as virtual quartermaster general, although the title was held by the inefficient Stephen Moylan, Mifflin's temporary successor. It was then that NG met Hughes and came to appreciate his ability and integrity. Washington credited Hughes with rounding up the boats with which Gen. Glover evacuated the army after the battle of Long Island. With Mifflin again quartermaster general, Hughes proved to be one of his ablest deputies and acted in the capacity of an assistant. After refusing NG's appointment, he became deputy quartermaster for New York state. In 1780 Pickering appointed him to the post he had held under Mifflin, which he kept until near the end of the war. A biographical sketch is found in Anna M. Holstein, *Swedish Holsteins in America* (Norristown, Pa., 1892), pp. 70–75, 84–85.

2. See Hughes's reply, 8 April, below.

From George Washington

[Valley Forge, 31 March 1778. Essentially approves NG's 30 March proposal on magazines. Advises no more than six months supply be stored, since the "theatre of War may change and taxation must reduce the price of every commodity."[1] FC (Washington Papers: DLC) 2 pp.]

1. Despite his prediction, the states showed no inclination to fund the war with taxation, and prices continued their upward spiral.

To General William Heath

Sir   Camp Valley Forge in Pennsylvania [March 1778][1]

Having been lately appointed to the Office of Quarter-Mr General, I have sent a considerable Order for Goods and Stores in that Way to be purchased by Mr Benjamin Andrews, Merchant in Boston; since which I have heard his Character has been called in Question respecting some dealings with General Burgoine's Officers.[2] I had conceived so good an Opinion of him as to think him a suitable Person to be employed; but at the same Time I would not choose to continue him in the Employ if his Character is so far injured as to hurt his Usefulness, or is even become doubtful. I shall therefore be much obliged to you to furnish me with the History of this Charge against him, together with your Sentiments concerning his Fitness to be employed as Deputy Quarter-Master-General at Boston. I am told Col. Chase has been employed in that Department.[3] I am not certain that I even know his Person as there are several of the Name with whom I am perfectly unacquainted; you will farther oblige me by Giving me his Character and your Opinion of his Fitness for the Employment.

You will perceive from the Nature of this Letter that it is confidential, and you may rely on my Care that no ill Use shall be made of the Information you may give me. My Aim is to have the Business of the Department well executed, and having been so long absent from Boston it will be impossible for me to form a right Judgment of Characters at so great a Distance without the Aid of this Kind of Intelligence, which no Person is better qualified to give than you. Any farther Aid which it may be in your Power to give me in the Department of Quarter Master General will be a Favour done to the Publick, and will be thankfully received by, Sir, your most obedient humble Servant.

NATH GREENE

LS (MHi).

1. Approximate date is established by NG's recent appointment.

2. Benjamin Andrews was a partner in the Boston firm of Otis and Andrews, which had done business with the quartermaster department. Heath's answer has not been found, but his opinion of Andrews must have been favorable since NG continued to deal with the firm. Andrews was accidentally killed by a friend the following winter (described in Samuel A. Otis to NG, 10 January 1779, below). From the tone of Otis's letter, it is apparent that NG had gotten to know Andrews during his stay in Boston in September 1778. On Otis, see below, note, NG to Board of War, 27 May.

3. Thomas Chase, a Boston merchant, had been a member of the Sons of Liberty in 1769 and a major in Thomas's brigade during the siege of Boston. (Mass. Hist. Soc., *Proc.*, 1 Ser., 11 [1869]: 140; 15 [1876]: 144) He had served in Boston as deputy quartermaster for the Eastern Department under Mifflin, a post he continued to hold during NG's tenure despite some criticism from NG's family and his friend John Gooch. (See below, for example, letter from cousin Griffin, 24 May and from Gooch, 24 October 1778.)

To Henry Laurens, President of the Continental Congress

Sir   Camp Valley Forge 3d April 1778

You will have been informed by my Letter of the 26th of March, that a large Sum of Money is absolutely necessary for the Quarter-Master's Department, to enable us to make due Preparation for the ensuing Campaign, and I expect before this reaches you, Col. Cox will have stated that Necessity to you in a still more pointed light.[1] Hitherto, however, we have not received a single Shilling, tho' we have daily Demands for large Sums, not only for Expenditures here, but to be distributed into different Parts of the Country from whence we expect to draw Supplies; and until these Distributions are made, our utmost Efforts will not have the desired Effect. I have therefore drawn on the Treasury Board for Fifty Thousand Pounds in Favour of Robert Lettis Hooper junr Esquire, an active and useful Deputy Quarter Master for the District in the Neighbourhood of

Easton, who I expect will lay it out to good Advantage; I therefore hope the Draught will be duly honoured.[2] I have directed it to "the honourable the Board of Treasury of the United States." I do not know whether the Address is right, and should be glad to have Directions in that respect; but however that may be, I hope Mr Hooper will not be disappointed in his Expectations of receiving the Cash, as such a Disappointment would be greatly injurious to the Service. I have the honour to be with great Respect, Sir, Your most obedient humble Servant

NATHANAEL GREENE

LS (PCC, Item 155: DNA).
1. NG had asked Cox to go to York to discuss matters with Congress.
2. Robert Lettis Hooper (1731–97), the grandson of a chief justice of New Jersey of the same name, had speculated in frontier lands in Pennsylvania and had turned his hand to surveying and map making. As a deputy quartermaster in 1777, he made numerous political enemies. (See below, Thomas McKean to NG, 9 June.) Against the advice of these enemies, NG refused to discharge him. (Joseph Reed's criticism of Hooper is in a letter of 5 November 1778, below.) NG later assured his deputy that Sullivan's 1779 Indian expedition "must have faild without your particular aid and assistance." (Letter of 21 September 1780) After the war Hooper married the widow of Surveyor-General Robert Erskine. He was judge of a New Jersey common pleas court for some years and served as vice-president of the Council of New Jersey from 1785 to 1788. See Charles Henry Hart, "Colonel Robert Lettis Hooper," PMHB, 36 (1912): 60–91; see also Heusser, Erskine, pp. 233–44, and Furman, Letters, pp. 9–10.

Colonel James Abeel to William Lowry[1]

[Raritan, N.J., 3 April 1778. Is directed by Gen. Greene to ask for an account of all stores. ALS (Nj) 1 p.]

1. Lowry, Mifflin's deputy quartermaster for New Jersey, was replaced by Moore Furman on 25 April. (See below, NG to Furman, 20 May.)

To General Anthony Wayne

[Valley Forge, 3 April 1778. Asks him to suggest a man of correct "political principles" as captain of guides. ALS (PHi) 1 p.]

From Colonel Alexander Hamilton

[Valley Forge, 3 April 1778. As an aide to Washington, he asks for two teams to pick up Gen. Charles Lee's baggage.[1] ALS (NNS) 1 p.]

1. On Lee's parole, see below, Meade to NG, 4 April.

From Colonel Richard K. Meade

[Valley Forge, 4 April 1778. One of wagons ordered by Hamilton on 3 April to report to Meade for directions.[1] ALS (PHi) 1 p.]

1. Washington had arranged with Gen. Howe for the parole of Gen. Charles Lee in exchange for the parole of Gen. Richard Prescott, an American prisoner since July 1777. Washington sent Col. Meade with a small group of horses to escort Lee from the British lines outside Philadelphia to Valley Forge. A few days later, Lee and his baggage were moved to York. (See below, Meade to NG, 6 April.) Lee's exchange for Gen. Prescott, which permitted both men to rejoin their armies, was arranged 21 April. (Alden, Lee, pp. 180–93)

To Colonel Clement Biddle

[Valley Forge, Sunday evening, 5 April 1778. Requests copy of Pennsylvania law "respecting the Waggon department." ALS (PPIn) 1 p.]

From Colonel Richard K. Meade

[Valley Forge, 6 April 1778. Washington requests Gen. Lee's baggage be taken "up the country" and Lee provided with "two of the best Horses you have."[1] ALS (PHi) 1 p.]

1. See above, Meade to NG, 4 April.

From Colonel Tench Tilghman[1]

[Valley Forge, 6 April 1778. Washington requests a horse from Col. Carlton. ALS (PHi) 1 p.]

1. Tench Tilghman (1744–86) was born into an influential family in Talbot County, Md. He attended schools in Philadelphia and on graduation became a successful young merchant in that city. After serving one month as a captain in the Flying Camp, he joined Washington's family as a volunteer aide in August 1776, a position he kept through the war, serving a great part of the time without pay. As Washington's hardworking military secretary, he was given a special commission of lieutenant colonel by Congress in April 1777. Washington honored Tilghman by delegating him to carry the news of Cornwallis's defeat in October 1781 to Congress. After the war he was for a short time a business associate of Robert Morris, until ill health forced him to withdraw. (DAB)

Power of Attorney

I do hereby constitute and appoint Griffin Greene Esqr my attorney with full powers to act transact, negotiate and settle the division of my Interests and Stocks now in company with my five brothers Messrs Jacob Greene, William Greene, Elihue Greene, Christopher Greene and Perry Greene, and that I shall hold myself bound in manner and form to all agreements made in consequence of these powers.[1]

Given under my hand at Camp Valley Forge April 7, 1778.
Chester County Pennsylvania
NATHANAEL GREENE

ADS (MWA).
1. In signing this, NG was anticipating the division of his father's estate, which is discussed below in a letter from Elihue, 12 April, but which was not actually carried out until the summer of 1779. In the meantime, cousin Griffin or one of the brothers must have misplaced the document, for on 30 April 1779 NG signed another power of attorney. (See his letter to Griffin on that date, below.)

To Colonel Henry Hollingsworth[1]

[Valley Forge, 7 April 1778. Recommends John Hall, the bearer, as an assistant; requests horses for hauling stores from Head of Elk. ACyS (NHi) 2 pp.]

1. Henry Hollingsworth (1737–1803) had served as a colonel in the Maryland militia in 1776. He was a brother of the successful Philadelphia merchant, Levi Hollingsworth, who had purchased anchors from Nathanael Greene and Company before the war. In early 1777 Gen. Mifflin appointed Henry deputy quartermaster for Maryland, with an office at Head of Elk, a trading center strategically located at the headwaters of Chesapeake Bay. He continued in the post as long as NG was quartermaster. (See William B. Hollingsworth, *Hollingsworth Genealogical Memoranda* [Baltimore, 1884]; *JCC*, 7: 29, 95; 8: 670.) Hall had been recommended to NG by Gen. Smallwood, as seen in NG to Smallwood, 9 April, below.

From Captain John Gooch[1]

Dear Genl   Boston April 7th 1778
I shall often trouble you with Letters tho' I have nothing to write of any Consequence. Soon I'm determined to quit the Department as I find my present pay will no way support me. I have the miss-for[tu]ne to be placed on the extreem posts of the Departm where my expe[nce]s have always exceeded my pay. My situation in these Posts being so uncertain that I could [not?] carry my family with me, I have apply'd to Genl Heath either to be at Liberty intirely to quit the service or eles [else] be enabled by increase of pay to maintain myself. My pay at present being only 12 £ per month and my board cost me 5 Dollrs per week I must think I'm hardly treated, and if I know myself I'm not unreasonable or apt to Complain. Genl Heath refuse[s] absolutely to let me resigne, and it is not in his power to Augment my pay, that I have but one way left; that is by refuseing to act, render myself a subject to be cashired. The first Law in Nature, self preservation, will oblige me to it.

I'm as ready and willing as any man to sacrifise to my Country, but there can be no Virtue in starving, which must certainly be my

Case if I continue longer in the service. There is no piece of service to be transacted in this Department but I'm the Poor Culprit that must go. If I remonstrate the Genl tells me he has nobody eles [else] he can send. That my Wages is bearly sufficient to make good the Ware and Tare of my Clothing, occationd by my frequent Journies, these are my Griefencies (Grievances) and I think not small ones, and I know no way to rid myself from them but by Quiting the service wholy.

My most Respectfull Compliments to Mrs Greene and belive me with the Greatest Esteem Your most Obedt and most Hble Servant

JOHN GOOCH

ALS (MiU-C).
1. Gooch, an old Rhode Island friend, had been assistant deputy quartermaster in Boston since the previous summer. NG retained him in the post as long as he was quartermaster.

From Colonel Hugh Hughes

[Fishkill, N.Y., 8 April 1778. Acknowledges NG's letter of 31 March and the "Politeness shewn to me upon this and every other Occasion"; congratulates him on his appointment as quartermaster but begs "leave to acquaint you that I cannot continue any longer in the Department than till relieved."[1] Difficult to forward stores, especially when a "late Act of State, restrains the Impressing [of] Teams," as in New Jersey. As for suggesting a deputy for Connecticut, not so "competent to that Business as Colonel Wadsworth." Cy (NHi) 2 pp.]

1. Hughes was the only deputy quartermaster who refused NG's reappointment, a rebuff that led NG to write what he hoped was a persuasive letter, 16 April, below.

To General William Smallwood

Dear Sir   Camp Valley Forge 9th April 1778
Your Favour of the 5th Instant[1] was delivered to me by Mr Hall to whome I gave a Letter of Recommendation to Mr Hollingsworth at the Head of Elk, who had been appointed to act in the Quarter Masters Department in that District before I heard of Mr Hall, and as there is much to be done in that Quarter I doubt not he may be usefully employed as well to the Publick as to himself.

As to the Appraisement of the Prize Goods at Foggs Manor, the sooner it is done the better, and I have no objection to the Officers or their Agent's joining in their appointment of the Appraisers.[2] The present Stock of Tents and Marquees, and the prospect of speedy Supplies do not admit of allowing more than one Marquee for the Field Officers of a Regiment at present; I therefore hope the Gentlemen will rest satisfied with that Allotment. Respecting the Exchange of the old Tents for new ones on the terms you mention, I must claim some further Time to ascertain the state of our Stock and Resourses before I can with Propriety give an answer; and for the same reason I cannot now determine what Part of the New Tents at Foggs-Manor may be assigned to the Division under your Command. I suppose Foggs-Manor to be a suitable place for the New Tents to remain in Store till they are wanted for use, they may therefore remain there for the present. All the old Tents I would wish to have sent to Colo Jacob Morgan, D.Q.M. at Reading to be repaired,[3] as a Company of Sail Makers are employed there in Business of that kind. As to the Arms you mention, I shall give notice of them to the Commissary General of Military Stores, who will take the proper steps concerning them.

You may be assured that neither His Excelly nor myself had the least Suspicion injurious to you. What I said to you respecting the Appropriation of the Tents and Marquees was intended merely to give an early Restraint to the Expectations of the Gentlemen under your Command which, however natural, and perhaps just in them, could not with propriety be gratified. I am Sir with great respect your Most Obedient Humble Servt

NATH GREENE

LS (Mr. John F. Reed, Valley Forge, Pa., 1972).
1. Letter of 5 April not found; on Hall, see NG to Hollingsworth, 7 April, above.
2. The capture of the *Symetry* is discussed at NG to Smallwood, 16 March, above.
3. Jacob Morgan, Jr. (1741–1802), is often confused with his father, a prominent man who was a colonel in the Pennsylvania militia in Berks County. Young Morgan had fought in the French and Indian War and was an early patriot. (*PMHB*, 4 [1880]: 98) In 1777 he served on the Pennsylvania Executive Council but resigned on 4 April 1778 to accept NG's appointment as deputy quartermaster of Berks County, stationed in Reading (*Pa. Archives*, 6: 399). NG considered him an able deputy. After leaving the department, he was appointed superintendent of the Pennsylvania Commissioners of Purchases (*Pa. Archives*, 2 ser., 3: 431).

To Colonel Clement Biddle

[Valley Forge, 10 April 1778. Asks Biddle to accompany him to Lancaster, Pa., as "I am almost a stranger to all the Assembly." ALS (NjMoW) 1 p.]

To Colonel Charles Pettit

Dear Sir   At the Red Lion [Lionville, Pa.] April 11, 1778
The road from Camp to this place is exceeding bad and as it is the great communication between Camp and Lancaster and between Camp and the Yellow Springs where our principal Hospitals are, It is our interest to set about mending it as soon as possible. Apply to His Excellency for fifty men to work upon this road and fifty upon the

Reading road. I met and overtook several Waggons that were stall'd yesterday—the sick that were removing in distress and the Cattle almost ruined by repeated strains in attempting to get through the most difficult part of the Roads. More attention must be paid to the Roads than has been heretofore to favor our Cattle and save Waggon hire. We must get some good man to survey the roads and to direct the operations of the fatigue parties.

We have the misfortune to have a rainny morning which I am afraid will detain me here today as it is now past twelve oClock. I am Sir your most obedient very humble Servt

NATH GREENE

ALS (NHi).

From Colonel John Davis

[York Town, Pa., 11 April 1778. Has purchased horses, linen, writing paper; says he "Shall allways Make it my Study" to keep NG informed. ACyS (Davis Papers: DLC) 1 p.]

From Elihue Greene

Dear Sir　　　　　　　　　　　　　Coventry [R.I.] April the 12th 1778

Your long Silence when I know you have Received my letters is One of the Reasons that induced me to write in this way to Inquire the Reasons of A neglect that I Am not Consious of Deserving any more now than formerly when you Said it was A pleasure to you to answer mine.[1] Now dear Sir I am not Desirous of Draging alonge a Correspondence that you have an avertion too. I must bege of you that you will be Candid with me in this matter. In your letter to Brother Jacob you Requst a Division.[2] You offer for one Reason that [it] is not Agreable to Some of [the] Company fore you to be in it. This Charge we all Deny and I Should be glad to know for what Reasons you Think so; for my part I [ever?] wisht to make your Situation in the Arme [Army] as Agreable as I Could. In Regard to Your family, how Ever Short my Indevours may have Prooved, I Still wish to doe the Same as far as it is in my Power, but I find from the Difficulty of the Times and the Situation I now Stand [in?] to make Every thing as Agreable as I could wish, a matter that I have not fully Accomplish or at least that the Company has not done it. This apears in your Letter to Brother Jacob. I Trust that opinion Arises from a wrong Information but dont think it is any one of the Company that has given it. Your Cander [candid?] Generossity I Trust will bring to light from what Principals that opinion was formd.

The Situation of our affairs in Company Brother Tells me he has wrote you fully. From that Information you will let us know your Inclination in Respect to Company Matters.

I Congratulate you on your late Appointment. May you and the Publick obtain Every blessing that Could be wished and Expected from it.

Your little Washington is well. He Apears to have a good Temper and very active for Child so fat as he is. He is Continual in motion. Your little Patty has not been blest with the Same healthyness as Washington. She is little Rictte [rickety] the Docter says.[3] He Proposes dipping hur. Docter Senter has prescribed 2 months. Mrs. Mecam [Mecom] and Jenny desires ther Respects to be Presented you and Sister Catey.[4] I also Joine with them with my love to you boath. I am with regard Your Friend

ELIHUE GREENE

P s   I hear that Si[s]ter Caty is Comeing home. Tell hur that we Shall be v[er]y glad to See hur and will make hur as happy as we can while she is from you. Molley desires me to write to youer Wife if she Could get Somthing that was Good and hamsome [handsome?] for the Children for Couple of frocks, she shoul be glad. She has Sent in pay a Couple of locks of the Chldren[s'] hare.

ALS (NjP).
    1. This is the only letter from brother Elihue to NG that has been found. Since his letters undoubtedly contained "family secrets," NG probably burned them. (See NG to Christopher, 22 April, below.) Many of Jacob's letters were kept because they often discussed business.
    2. The letter to Jacob has not been found, but a year earlier he had told NG it was the brothers who wanted their father's estate divided. (Jacob to NG, 7 May 1777; the family business is discussed at note 3.)
    3. If Patty (Martha) did have rickets, she was apparently not affected in later life.
    4. Mrs. Jane Mecom, the sister of Benjamin Franklin, was grandmother of Elihue's wife, Jenny Flagg Greene.

From Griffin Greene

Dear Sir   Coventry [R.I.] April 12, 1778
    Your Letter by Cousin Bill came safe to hand.[1] The inclination that He has to serve the Publick drove him on so heard [hard?] that He is allmost down Sick. I find the Baking business is put upon a plan that you think will not answer the purpose intended, and that the General wants to put it upon the footing you proposed, but their is a doubt whether it will be altered from it[s] present mode.[2] I am of your sentiments in the matter. The interest that the Managers will have in this affair will be the same whether they due much or little and their will be nothing to stimelate.
    I wrote you by Majr [Samuel] Ward what I had undertaken and

desired your sentiments which I beg you to give and I will pursue to a little [to the letter?].[3] My offer I still wish to fulfill when it may be in my powar. As you observe the regulating bill has put a stop to all kinds of business at present without its for the Army. You have givven Brother Jacob an appointment somthing simerlar to what I proposed in my last.[4] I think this will add much to that plan and that will furnish us with Waggons to forward the goods to camp, and if you was to Authorise to purchase Horses it would serve still to expedite business. I will help to assist Him in the purchasing way untill I hear further from you. I think their appears a probabillity in the plan of driving cattle from North Carolina of its being good business if you are determined upon that plan. I will go upon it as you may direct.

Cousin Bill sayes Cousin Caty is a comming home. If she comes I am at her commands if she will please to call on me. Little Patty [Martha] is much as she was when I wrote last. Dr Senter is giving Her medicine for the Ricketts and thinks She shall soone be able to have the better of the disorder. His little Excellency is well and hearty and grows finely. Please to make Sally's and my Complyments agreable to Mrs Greene. We hope She has had an agreable Jorney to Maryland and expet to have the plasure of having a discrption of that Country and the Manners and Castumes [customs?] &c. Sally is much obliged to you for your kind remembrance of her and desires her respects to you. With wishing you Health and Happiness and all the other Blessings of Heaven to attend you I conclude your Affectionate Friend

GRIFFIN GREENE

P. S. Please to let me know how to subscribe so as not have my Letters opened for publick letters.

ALS (MiU-C).
1. NG's letter not found. On William Littlefield, see above, NG to Varnum, 27 March.
2. Griffin had been baker to Rhode Island troops in 1776. (See vol. 1: 213 and n)
3. Letter not found.
4. See letter from Jacob, below, on his appointment.

From Jacob Greene

Dear Sir   Warwick [R.I.] April the 12h 1778
I Received your Letter of the First of this Instant And the Inclosed Invoice With An Appointment To Be A Contractor For your Department In the Army.[1] I am Much obliged To you For the Apointment But My Being Limmited To Sertain Places To the Westward of Bedford Will Make it Imposible For Me To Procure the Articals Contained In

the Invoice as the Several Places Where I am To Purchase Are Draned of Such Articals As their is No Arrivals Here Nor Very Few To the Westward, only the Ship you Mention Whos Goods Are All Ingaged By the Continental Agent. It is utterly out of My Power To Be of Any Great Servise To you Except My Apointment To Joine With Mr Andrews, As the Greatest Part of the Knifes Are Carryed Into the Eastward [i.e. to Boston].[2]

Griffin Sets out Tomorrow Morning To Consult Him upon the ocation As their May Be A Sufficient Quantity of Goods Within His Limits To Compleat Both Invoices. But If He Refuses To Be Concerned With Me And I Cannot Be Authorised To Purchase Within His Limits My Invoice Must Fail. If you Can Consistantly Let My Appointment Be At Large I Am Sure It Will Be To Better Effect as We Shall then Indeavor to out Vie Each other In Purchaseing, Haveing Perticular Regard At the Same Time Not To Give the owner Any Advantage By Biding one upon the other. You Must Be Perticular In Giveing Instructions. You Have ordered Fifteen Thousand Canteens. I am At A Loos [Loss] To Know Where [whether] They Are To Be Wood or Tin. Should Be Glad you Would Inform Me per First oppertunity. In Mean Time I Will Inquire Where Tin is to Be Had And Shall order A Quantity of Woden ones Made. The Great Distance I am From Camp Seems to Determin Me that you Mean Tin As Those Made of Wood Might Be Had Much Nigher Camp.

The Artical of Duck [canvas] is Very Scarse. I Much Question Whether It is to Be Had as Private Property. I am Informed that their is Large Quantitys of that Artical In the Sevoral Continental Agents Hands. As We Have No Authority To Draw it out of Their Hands And they None To Send it Forward And We Cannot Purchase it, the Army May Be Greatly Distrest For Want of it. I Mention this as you May Hit upon Sum Effectual Means To Git it out of their Hands.

As I am Sure If We Cannot Purchase it their Will Be Great Difficulty In Any Way Near Compleating your Invoice As Tradesmen And Artificers, As Well as the Raw Material, Are Very Scarse. I Shall Do My Best For it Being Compleated as Quick as Posible. As I only Received your Appointment Last Night am Not Able To Really Inform you What Can Be Done only From Here Say [hearsay].

This Will Be Handed you By Capt Dexter Who Sets out this Day For Camp. I Thought it My Duty To Give you the Earliest Inteligence that I should Accept of the Appointment though I Hardly think Myself In a State [of] Health Sufficient For Such An undertakeing. But Griffin And the Brothers Are Very Antious [anxious] I Should Accept And Promise Me All the Assistance In their Power Which Will Enable Me, I Hope, To Answer your Expectations. I Must Be Furnished With Money Pun[c]tualy as the Publick Credit Runs Low At this Time. They Cannot Be Credited upon So Good Conditions As

Present. This is owing To the Great Fa[i]llure In Almost All Publick Payments For Some Time. The [Napsacs?] you Mention, I Cannot Find Any Person that understands What they Are or Can Inform Me How they Are Made. I Shall Procure the Duck And Endeavour To Find Sum Person that Can Direct How they Must Be Made. For Fear I Should Not Be Able Please to Give Directions In Your Next How they Are Made.

You Mention you Will Inable Me To Make Good All My Contracts By Either Giveing Me orders on the Loan offices[3] or Transmiting the Money From the Treasury Board, Which Will Be the Most Sertain as the Constant Demands upon the Loan offices Keep them Short of Cash. They have Not Money for Recruiting and I fear your orders Will Fail If Given.

The Great Difficulty in Procureing of Teams At this Season Will Be Almost Insurmountable For Such Long Journeys, As Teams Are Worn out With the Springs Servise. Your Appointment Is three Months To Late To Open the Campaign With Necessary Articals Forthcomeing To Advantage. Great Industry and Activity Must make up For the Lost Time, But it Has Been Known All Winter That the Articals Must Be Had and Now are Wanted on the Spot. They Are To Be Picked up And Transported Four Hundred Miles Which Will Make them Two [too] Late To Answer the Purpose Intended.

I Fear We Shall Be obliged To Make A Number of Second Hand Purchases As Goods By Whole Sale Are Very Scarce [and] Are Catched Up As Soon As they Arrive By People Who Intend to Make A Profit of them, But I Shall Do Everything in My Power For the Advantage of the States. I Fear Billy How [General Howe] is A preparing To Give you A Fatal Blow in the opening of the Campaign As he is A Calling Part of His Troops From Newport And New York. Two Reigments Are Gone From Newport.[4]

Your Brother [in-law] Simon Littlefield Was Hear When Billy [Littlefield] Arrived. They and Nancy Set out Tomorrow'ng For Block Island. Simon Told Me He Saw J[oseph] Wanton [Jr.] in Newport About A [Fortnight?] Since And He Told Him that Twenty thousand Troops Was to Sail the First of March. He says the Cornell [Colonel] Has But Little Notice Taken of Him. He Seemed to Appear Like A Person in a Dijected State as If Much Disappointed. I hope He is And May Return [?] Every Such Sco[u]ndrell Who Joines the Enemy Against their Country.[5] The Enemy Have Fortifyed Newport from Carrington Cove to Easons Pond And It is Not At All Probable that they Will Leave the Island. The arrival of G[en] Sullivan will Have No Effect upon them As they Are Secure on An Island And their Ships to Guard them. Since My Last We have Recevd Sertain Accounts of the Sloop Florida and the Sloop General Greene Being Taken. It is Mad-

Letter from Jacob Greene, 12 April 1778
(Courtesy of William L. Clements Library at the University of Michigan)

ness to Venture to Sea Now as Nine Vessels out of Ten Gets Taken.[6] I
Will Not Ing[age?] Again. I Expect to Hear Every Day that this will Be
the Fate of the Privateers.

Your Children are In the Same Way as When I Wrote Last. Patty
Seems to Be Inclined To the Ricts [rickets]. Senter Think it Will Be
Necessary to Dip Her. I Intend to Carry Her to Potowomut And Have
Her Diped In Salt Warter. I Am Very Sorry For this Misfortune. I fear
Molly Has Kept Her two Still. My Wife is A Prepareing A Sirrup For
Her Simalar To one She Thought Cured Varnum. I Hope you Make
yourself Easy as Everything Shall Be Done For Her Recovery. She is
Not Bad Nor, I hope, in No Danger of its Affecting Her Shapes. It
Seem to Lye Principaly In Her Stomach. Give My Best Respects To
Mrs Greene And Believe Me To Be your Most Affectionate Brother

JACOB GREENE

P S The State Bill is on in Coneticut And In the Masecuset [Massa-
chusetts].[7] This Will Retard our Purchaseing Very Much As We Shall
Not Dare To Give Any More than the Stated Prise And their Will Be
Nothing To Be Had At that. I Expect this Will Be Ruinous To us As the
Authority [i.e. Congress] Will Not Countnence our Giveing Any
More Notwithstanding the Case is So urgent. Govener Trumbull is so
opposed Becaus He is Against A State Bill. This Mat[t]er is urged
[Principally?] By the Priest. It Effects His Salery. The[y] Preach the
Necessity of it Taking Plase In their [?] Pulpit. I See We Shall Be In
[confusion?].

J G

ALS (MiU-C).
1. Letter not found. His appointment of Jacob as contractor in the quartermaster
department was later to bring down a great deal of criticism on his head.
2. Benjamin Andrews was a partner in Otis & Andrews of Boston. (See above, NG
to Heath, end of March.)
3. He refers to the certificates described above, NG et al to Inhabitants, 28 March.
4. On receiving news of the French alliance, the British cabinet in March had
authorized the evacuation of Rhode Island if necessary, but there is no evidence that
they withdrew a substantial number of troops at this time.
5. Col. Joseph Wanton, Jr., was the son of the last colonial governor of Rhode
Island, who had remained loyal to the crown.
6. The Greenes' vessels had run into bad luck as well as into the increasingly
effective British blockade. See Gov. Cooke to NG, 19 April, below, and letter from the
mate of the *Florida*, Holderby Langford, 28 May, below.
7. On the "State Bill" see William Greene to NG, 6 March, above.

To Colonel Hugh Hughes

Sir   Head Quarters Valley Forge Apl 16th 1778

I am favored with yours of the 8th Instant, wherin you congratu
late me upon my being appointed to the Office of QM General. Wha

can induce you to think my Appointment is agreeable, especially when one of the principal Officers of the Department discovers so strong an Inclination to decline his further Services I know not. My rank in the Army and the Splendor of Command, which I am obliged to discontinue for a time, are no inconsiderable sacrafices. And what have I in return, a troublesome Office to manage, and a new set of Officers in the different districts to seek for.

I had not the least Idea of your resignation, as you would have the same Command as heretofore, and continue to enjoy all the profits and Emoluments of the Office. I cannot think your reasons for resignation are well grounded. You can settle your Accounts without resigning, and the motives that first engaged you to enter the department operate still and claim your continuance.

I would wish you therefore to reconsider the matter. I am induced to request this from your general Character and the Satisfaction you have given in transacting the business of the Department. Your situation is both Honorable and profitable, as least as much so as any one branch of the Department. If you are not wounded on the one Hand, and are not too wealthy to regard profit on the other, I should think you an Enemy to your own Interest to reject so considerable an Appointment. I cannot imagine a place of so much consequence can go beging a very long time. I shall not look out for a person to fill your place, untill I hear further from you.[1] I am with sincere regard, Your Most Obt Servant

NATHL GREENE

Cy (NHi).

1. See Hughes's answer below, 23 April.

To General Alexander McDougall

[Valley Forge, 16 April 1778. Predicts "establishing the army" will be referred to states and killed;[1] although "Cabal" has broken up, a New York member is "extreme inamical to the Commander in chief";[2] cartel on exchange of prisoners not settled. ALS (NHi) 2 pp.]

1. "Establishing the Army" was primarily the proposal, backed by the Committee at Camp, to put officers on half pay for life. It continued to be the contention of general officers, including Washington, that without such an establishment, officers would continue to resign. On 21 April, Washington noted the "violent shock" to the Virginia line from the ninety officers who had resigned already. (Fitzpatrick, GW, 11: 285) On the outcome of the half-pay issue, see note, NG to McDougall, 25 January, above. Congress did on 27 May pass a resolution entitled "Establishment of the American Army." It specified 9 regiments of 477 men for each brigade, but it was largely taken up by a higher pay scale. (JCC, 11: 538–43)

2. As Freeman points out, James Duane is the only member this fits. (GW, 4: 610n)

To Doctor Jonathan Potts[1]

[Valley Forge, 16 April 1778. Requests list of wagons and other articles needed and an account of any items ordered through other channels. LS (Valley Forge Historical Society) 1 p.]

1. Dr. Jonathan Potts (1745–81), a relative of Dr. Benjamin Rush, was among the first group of doctors to be graduated from the College of Philadelphia (later the University of Pennsylvania). He joined the Northern Army as surgeon in June 1776 and succeeded Dr. Samuel Stringer the following year as deputy director general of hospitals in the Northern Department. In February 1778 Congress transferred him to the same position in the Middle Department. (JCC, 10: 131) A brief sketch is in PMHB, 1 (1877): 175–80.

From Colonel James Abeel

[Beverwyck, N.J.,[1] 16 April 1778. Has sent for tin and copper from Hackensack; when some residents refused to give up army horses, magistrate sent "proper Persons to take them away"; no assistant needed at Pompton; New Jersey man who furnished iron and other articles is still owed $10,000. ALS (PPAmP) 2 pp.]

1. Abeel wrote from the home of Abraham Lott, a friend of his and of NG.

To Colonel James Abeel

Sir   More Hall [Pa.][1] April 17th 1778
     I have seen your Letter with the returns of the QMG Stores in New Jersey; when it came to hand I was from Home at Lancaster. Mr Pettit wrote you a short answer to the several matters. Before you proceed any farther I want to see you at Camp, you will therefore come as soon as you possibly can. In the meantime give orders for collecting and repairing all the broken Waggons, and order on to Camp all the Canteens, knap and Haversacks there are in the Jerseys belonging to the QM Generals department.
     Mr Slotts of Middle Brook has orders to sell all the Horses that are unfit for further service and to account for them accordingly.
     If there are any public stores, Horses or other Articles of any kind dispersd among the Inhabitants, please to give the necessary Orders to have them collected. I am sir your most Obedt Humble Servt
                                                        NATH GREENE

ALS (RHi).
     1. Although NG and Catharine were living at Moore Hall, he usually headed his letters "Camp at Valley Forge."

To General James M. Varnum

[Moore Hall, Pa., 17 April 1778. Varnum's brigade may keep axes NG had called in; Col. Bowen reports people of Rhode Island want R.I. Regiment to return home.[1] ALS (MiU-C) 1 p.]

1. See Varnum to NG, 1 February above.

From Governor Nicholas Cooke of Rhode Island

Sir   Providence [R.I.] Aprill the 19, 1778
    Yours of the 16 March by Major Morris Came to hand last Evening.[1] General Sullivan took the Command hear yesterday.[2] I make no dout he will give good Satisfaction in this department. It was more than we Expected that Either you or he could be Spared from the grand army.
    It gives me pains to hear how slowly the Recrutes come in to you there. General Washington, whom God long preserve, had need like Moses of old to have the assistance of a son and her [heir] to asist him in this trying day, but I trust in God as his day is, so his Strength shall be, for I believe he was Raised up on purpose to stand up for the defence of his bleding Country in this day of tribulation, and I trust God will support him and proteckt him against all his Ennemies.[3]
    None would wish to have so destructive a cruel war come near there own dwelings where there wives and Children and there all that is worth living for is setteled down, but I Serely [Surely] beleive had Generall How piched [pitched] with his army in New England last Summer as he did in Penselvany, General Washington would have found a sufficient force come to his assistance when Caled for to put him in as bad or worse situation than Burgoye [Burgoyne] was put in by General Gates. We are at present Extremely bare hear for troops, have had none from the Neighbouring States Except about 20 from the Masechusits Since the first of this month. General Sullivan informs that the 300 Expected from Nwhampshear will be along soon. Common Report says we are to have none from Conecticut till we comply with the State acht.[4] It would be very agreable to have our own troops sent home if they can be spared from the grand army.
    We are very much at a loss to know what steps to take respecting the State Bill but Expect if Boston comes into it we shall be obliged to comply, they on one side and Conecticut on the other will have no trade with us nor give us no assistance. A large part of the Ennemies forces in our Cappitall [Newport] and a fleet that Blocks up our harber and Cuts of [off] all trade by sea [means] that we have no Choice left but are obliged to do as our Neighbours do. Things had

began to alter much for the better in Nw England till the last star about the State bill began to make a Noyse again. We had taxed largly This little State had taxd itselfe to the amount of 128000 pounds in the Course [?] of one year. As money grew scarce other things grew plenty and began to fall very fast, and Every body that had any thing to sell preferd the money to any other pay, but since the State bill is in agitation again there seems to be a stagnation to all business, and when we shall get matters in their propper channel again I am at a loss to tell. Sure I am taxation if it were followd closely would bring things to Rights again. Whether it would be so spedy a Remdy as is necesary I cannot say, but it would be a certain one in time.

Your observation upon South Kingston in Respect to the Negro Rigment is very Just; they are not pleased with it at all and grumble a goodeal.[5] There is many disafected parsons in that and North Kings town, and the towns Round there. About 30 have gone over to the Ennemy this Spring allready. Our trade in this State is intirely at a Stand, at present we are so blocked up by water [i.e., blockaded] that no vessels can get in or out without so great a Risk that nobody cairs to venture their intrest and indeed I think it would be best to stop all trade at present. The Ennemy have so lind the coast with their Shipping from Carolina to Nova Scotia that there is hardly any such thing as to Escape them. We by sending out not only loose our intrest but our men, and supply the Ennemy with many things that it would be very difficult for them to get if they were not supplyed this way If we were to imply [employ] our men in the army instead of send ing them to sea[6] I think by Gods blesing we might prevent their penetrating the Country if we did not drive them Quite out of it.

They bost much in the papers of the larg armyes and fleets that are a coming over. Man may appoint but it is Easey with God to disapoint all their Scheams. I am not free from fears that we shall want amunition and arms both this campain for I doant hear of any importations of Either and I am Sure very great Quantetyes must have been Expended and lost the last Campain. And it appears to me that people in general are got very cairless about it; I could wish those at the head of afaires would make Some inquirey into [it so that it?] might be known before it is two late to Remedy an Evil of that kind.

Since I rote you last there has Raised a considerable party in the State and put out an oposet prox to Mr Greenes with Governer Bradford at the head of the prox and Mr Greene for second.[7] By what I can hear it will be a very Cloast Vote between them but as yet have no certain account from all the towns, am not able to say which has got most proxes but I believe Mr Greene has from what I hear. Many towns had but few proxes in; the inhabitants in generall did not vote

I am Sir with great Respect and Esteem your most obedient Humble Servant

NICHS COOKE

ALS (RHi).

1. Letter not found.
2. See note, at Varnum to NG, 1 February, above.
3. See "Conway Cabal," note, NG to Jacob, 7 February, above.
4. The State Act or State Bill, as the governor calls it in the next paragraph, is discussed above, William Greene to NG, 6 March.
5. Most slave owners were in that area. The Black Regiment is discussed in note, NG to Christopher, 5 January, above.
6. Even with the tightened blockade, privateering still lured low-paid army privates with hopes for a rich prize.
7. The R.I. prox as used here was the ticket or list of candidates. As used in the next sentence it was a ballot. William Greene defeated William Bradford in the upcoming election.

To Henry Laurens, President of the Continental Congress

Sir
Camp Valley Forge 20th April 1778
Having received Information from Joseph Borden Esqr, the Loan Officer for the State of New-Jersey, that he has on Hand a considerable Sum of Money which he wishes to be called out of his Hands as he thinks his Situation at Bordentown not safe;[1] and as Col. Cox did not obtain a sufficient Quantity of Cash from your Treasury to distribute through all the Channels which immediately call for it, and a large Sum is wanted in New Jersey to give Vigour to the Purchasing of Horses and other necessary Supplies; I shall hope to receive by the Return of this Express an Order on the Loan Officer of New-Jersey for One hundred and fifty thousand Dollars. Near one half of that Sum he has on Hand; the rest we will draw from him as it comes in, or take in Certificates which we can negotiate in the Country.

I hope this Business will meet with no Delay as the Agent for purchasing in New-Jersey will wait the Return of this Express.[2] I have the Honour to be, with great Respect, Sir, your most obedient humble Servant

NATH GREENE

LS (PCC, Item 155: DNA).

1. The threat to the money was a possible British raid from nearby Philadelphia.
2. For the response of Congress, see below, Laurens to NG, 24 April.

George Washington to the General Officers

Head Quarters [Valley Forge]
April 20h 1778

Questions for the consideration of the General Officers[1]

There seem to be but three general plans of operation, which may be premeditated for the next campaign: one the attempting to recover Philadelphia and destroy the enemy's army there; another the endeavouring to transfer the war to the Northward, by an entre-prise against New York; and a third the remaining quiet, in a secure fortified camp, disciplining and arranging the army, 'till the enemy begin their operations and then to govern ourselves accordingly. Which of these three plans shall we adopt?

If the first, what mode of execution shall we persue, and what force will be requisite, estimating the present numbers of the enemy in Philadelphia at 10,000 men, exclusive of marines and seamen whose aid may be called in? Shall we endeavour to effect the purpose by storm, by regular approaches, or by blockade, and in what particu-lar manner?

If the second, shall we attempt to take New York by a *coup de main*, with a small force, or shall we collect a large force and make an attack in form? In either case, what force will be necessary, estimating the number of the enemy in and about New York at 4000 men, and what disposition shall we make so as to effect the enterprise, and, at the same time, to protect the country here and secure our stores?

If the last, what post shall we take, so as to keep the army, in a state of security, to afford cover to the country and to our magazines, and to be in a situation to counteract the future motions, of the enemy?

The Commander in chief thinks it unnecessary to make any comments on these questions, as the General officers, will, no doubt, weigh every circumstance proper to be considered, and sensible of the importance of the objects, to which their attention is called, will make their opinions the result of mature deliberation.

Df (Washington Papers: DLC). The original, in Hamilton's hand, is damaged Some words have been filled in from Fitzpatrick, *GW*, 11: 282–83.

1. Congress had resolved on 18 April that Washington be "authorized and di rected" to convene a council of major generals to help in forming a plan for the "general operations of the campaign as he shall deem consistent with the general welfare of these states." (*JCC*, 10: 364)

It was on his own initiative, however, that Washington called this conference of all the generals at Valley Forge three days before receiving the gratuitous advice of Con gress. NG answered 25 April, below.

Delegate Gouverneur Morris warned Washington from Congress that if anything were decided at the council to "let Congress know nothing about it. A secret should never be trusted to many bosoms. I will forfeit anything, except reputation, that it will not be well kept, even by those necessarily confided in." (Sparks, *Morris*, 1: 165)

To General John Lacey[1]

Sir   Camp Valley Forge April 21st 1778
    The wife of Mr Jacob Brick complains that some of your people have taken from her husband one of their horses, which they are in want of to enable them to move up to Reading. I wish you to enquire into the matter, and if there is no capital objection, to order the beast to be delivered to the owner again. The war is a sufficient calamity, under every possible restraint; but where people are influenced by avarice and private prejudice, they increase the distresses of the inhabitants beyond conception. These evils can only be restrained by the Generals whose duty it is to protect the distressed inhabitants, as well as govern and regulate the affairs of the army. I hope you will pay particular attention to this affair; as the age and distress of the complainants appear to claim it. I have the honor to be your most obedient humble servt

NATH GREENE

Tr (GWG transcript: CSmH).
    1. John Lacey (1755–1814) was a twenty-three-year-old brigadier general of a Pennsylvania militia unit. When he received this letter he was at Crooked Billet, Pa., near Philadelphia, where a few days later he and his men were surrounded by a surprise British attack, from which they extricated themselves only after heavy losses. After helping to harass Clinton's march across New Jersey in June, he turned over his command to Gen. James Potter and returned home. In 1781 he was again in command of a militia unit. (DAB)

To Christopher Greene

Dr Sir   Camp Valley Forge April 22d 1778
    I am favord with yours of the 8th of this instant.[1] I observe the anxeity you feel and the suspicions you have that there is some mischievious correspondent employed to creat jealosy and mistrust among the brothers. I can assure you to the contrary, there is no person with whom I correspond but brother Jacob and Cousin Griffin, neither of whom ever wrote anything to the prejudice of the family.
    I would gladly gratify you respecting Jacobs Letter by its return; but I make it a constant rule to burn all that contain family secrets, as soon as I have read them. There was two paragraphs in Jacobs Letter that led me to make some of the observations in mine; one appeard to be the Sentiment of distress, flowing from a heart full of trouble, the other of kind benevolence extended from the father to the Children.
    As far as I can recollect the following were the purport of the two Sentences: "I have been exceeding unwell. My constitution is sinking fast, but I chuse to do everything in my power, sick or well, for fear the Brothers should think hard of me."[2] The other sentence was "Your children are at the great house in Coventry, but if you had

rather have them at Potowomut they shall live with me."[3] Alth
these were innocent and unmeaning expressions in him, and appea
to be the genuine offspring of an honest pride and brotherly affection
in the one case striving to do all in his power to live independant, an
in the other offering his friendly attention towards my poor almos
fatherless and motherless children. I say altho these were the produc
of a full heart in him, they excited a train of very different Ideas in me
People in public life learn from necessity to interpret peoples design
and intentions, more from little incidents than open declarations; an
it is natural for one to transfer the same modes of reasoning upon
subjects in one state to that of the other; from hence I was led t
conclude if it was necessary for brother Jacob to exert himself whil
he was afflicted with a bodily infirmity to give satisfaction to th
company, Their indulgence would not be greater to me than to him
and it was natural to suppose they were not better pleased with m
situation than with his, reaping the benefit of their Labours withou
contributeing anything to the common stock. I have understoo
frequently from you and you have mentioned it in several of you
Letters that there was a discontent among the brothers respecting th
company concerns. Cousin Griffin has hinted the same to me. A
these circumstances put together inducd me to conclude that a dis
solution of partnership was the secret wish of all, but no one wa
willing to demand it as a matter of right, for fear of being reproache
with a want of generosity and brotherly affection.

With regard to the children I could not see why he should offer t
take them to Potowomut if they were well accomadated at Coventry
whether they were or were not I cannot pretend to say; but I canno
help thinking there was some circumstances of discontent.

Now Sir I appeal to your candor in the first place to knov
whether there was not a dissatisfaction in the company respecting m
and mine.[4] I am well persuaded there has been. If I have sufferd m
suspicions to run too far or made any conclusions injurious to trut
and the family feelings I am sorry for it; but my pride however poor i
above being dependant. I was anxious to know the true history o
things, and as I considered brother Jacob nearly in the same predica
ment with myself I concluded he would give me the most satisfactor
accounts of anyone. All men have a view to their own interests and i
was natural to suppose if you wished a seperation of the Stocks yo
would wish an advantagious one for the same cause that led you t
desire the one would induce you to pursue measures necessary t
obtain the other.

It is very possible I may have been too free in my observations.
wrote in haste, surrounded with cares and applications of every kind
I have no copy of my letter and therefore cannot tell what it contains.

Before I enterd the Army there was no one of the brothers that had made so great sacrafices to serve the family as I had. Who undertook the disagreeable task at Coventry? Who was always obligd to settle all litigateed matters? It is true I have been out of the company for sometime but I trust not altogether useless to its interest.

Necessity almost compeld me to engage in the Army; the same necessity constrains me to continue, but I did not dream that the additional weight of manageing the companies concerns would be productive of a single wish for its dissolution. Many in the Army have their domestick affairs manageed by their friends and relatives at home, which made me the less apprehensive that the burden would be that greivious to the family.

With respect to procecuteing business in company again, it is a matter perfectly indifferent to me. I leave you all at full liberty to consult your own inclinations. If it is more agreeable to include my interest in the Stocks and procecute business jointly together I am satisfied; but if on the contrary a seperation is more your wish, I am easy and contented. I wish you to act with freedom and candor.

You mention in some of your Letters Brother Bill and Elihue were uneasy because I dont write them. All the Letters that I have every wrote to you or Jacob I considerd as wrote to the whole family except the one you mention. I have the same Love and affection for all the brother[s] that I ever had, and am sorry that brother Perry continues to persecute his own reputation. My Love to Sister Greene and all friends.[5] In haste yours Affectionately

N GREENE

ALS (MWA).
1. Letter not found.
2. Jacob worried a great deal about his health, but he lived for another thirty one years—to the age of sixty-nine.
3. The children had been living recently with Elihue in the house where NG and Catharine lived when they were first married.
4. For background on the division of the "company," see above, Elihue to NG, 12 April.
5. On Perry, see above, vol. 1: 38. Sister Greene was Christopher's wife, Catharine.

From General Edward Hand

Ft. Pitt, Pa., 22 April 1778. Introduces Col. Archibald Steel,[1] deputy quartermaster for the Ft. Pitt garrison; Steel needs money for old debts and new contracts. Cy (RG 93, WRMS: DNA) 1 p.]

1. Steel, a veteran of the Pennsylvania Rifle Corps and of Arnold's expedition to Quebec (where he was prisoner for a year), was reappointed by NG to his remote post t Ft. Pitt on 22 May (see below). Although Hand considered him an "active indus-rious good Officer," he turned out to be less than an efficient deputy. When after a

year he had sent no monthly returns, NG wrote, "This is pure negligence which cannot excuse." (See below, 6 July 1779.) Three months later NG was still waiting. (See below, 29 September, 1779.) Steel continued to be better at producing excuses than monthly returns, but NG kept him on, partly because Steel had the support of NG's old friend, Gen. Hand, but also undoubtedly because he found it difficult to discharge anyone. It is quite possible, of course, that no one at that remote outpost on the Ohio River would have done any better. (See also Heitman, *Register* and *PMHB*, 45 [1921] 391; 53 [1929]: 381.)

To Christopher Greene

[Valley Forge, 23–30 April 1778.[1] Cannot accept his offer to escort Mrs. Greene home because she plans to be home before he can get to Valley Forge. Gen. Howe is returning to England; Gen. Lee is exchanged. ALS (MWA) 1 p.]

1. Date is determined by recent news on Howe and Lee.

From Colonel Hugh Hughes

Sir   Fishkill [N.Y.] 23d April 1778
Your Favor of the 16th Instant came safe to hand the day that Colonel Hay set off for Head Quarters. I would then have written, but observing your request to reconsider the affair, deferr'd it to this time when, I assure you, there· is not the least Alteration, as to my Continuing in the Department.

You Ask, what can induce me to think your Appointment agreeable? I answer, the very Sacrifice you mention. "The splendor or Command" not "Sacrifices" for your Rank is retained. And was not this as natural a supposition, as that I would continue when superseded, deprived of Rank, and left at the will and pleasure of those put over me?[1]

You speak of Profits and Emoluments. That I am an entire stranger to, I assure you Sir. I never derived any benefit from the Office but my Wages and Rations.[2] I have heard that the Gentlemen of the new Arrangement are so happy as to have it in their power to enjoy very great Profits and Emoluments, which if so, may perhaps have given Rise to the Idea of others having had the same or similar advantages, and as to the Honorary Part, whatever was, is now done away, as far as concerned me.

I perfectly agree with you that the Department will not go a beging very long, and am happy to find those are your Sentiments, as it affords me the pleasing Prospect of a speedy relief, which the service really requires, it being impossible to acquit myself in the Mannor I could wish, in my present situation.

Please to accept my Thanks for your politeness in giving me

further Time to reconsider the Matter, and believe me to be, Sir Your very Humble Servt

HUGH HUGHES

Cy (NHi).

1. Congress had just decided to allow staff officers to retain their rank only if they had been commissioned previously as line officers. (See note, NG to Laurens, 1 May, below.) Hughes, therefore, would have lost his rank as colonel. As for his being "left at the will and pleasure" of those over him, he was undoubtedly referring to NG's assistants, Charles Pettit and John Cox, who had the same titles, if not the same responsibilities, as Hughes had had.

2. Some deputies, at least in Pennsylvania, had received commissions under Mifflin. (See above.) If Hughes had been aware of this, one would have expected him to have insisted on the same arrangement.

From Colonel John Davis

Dr Genl

Conidoguinet [Pa.][1]
April 24th 1778

I have Sent by James Rowney Wagon Master ten teams fully Equipt with 100 bags 240 Bushels of Chopt Grain for Forage to be Delivered to Col Biddle. I have Sent 60 Single Horses by Robert Riddle for the Artillery. In two Days I shall Send ten Wagons and teames more. The greatest part of what horses I have Sent in teames will answer the Artillery. When the[y] arive at Camp you may Cull them as you think proper. Wagoners are verry hard to be got. As fast as I can Equipt teames and Engage Wagoners I shall Send them forward. I Have yet on hand 180 horses 60 of which are pack horses, about 30 of them will Require 4 weaks keeping before the[y] go to Camp. Let me know by Bearer if I Shall Send the pack horses to Camp or Detain them here till the[y] are Equipt with Sadles. I have Sadlers at work for that purpose.

Horses and Linnen Cloth are Much Higher than I Expected. Good young Wagon horses are from 100 to £150 and Linnen Cloth from 10 to 12/ per yd. I have Contracted for a Large Quantity of tarr. As fast as it is Ready I Shall Send it to Camp. I was under the Necessity of sending the Horses Or I Should have Lost the half of them. I gave Col Cox the Names of all my Assistants and the Names of the Different Posts where Magazines of Forrage will be Wanted for the Use of the pack horses Employed in Carrying Stores and Provision to Genl Hand. I have been informed by Sundry Respectable Men that there is Great Complaints for Want of a proper person to Superintend the pack Horses to the Westward.

I should be glad to know if it come within the Line of my Duty to appoint men to Lay in the Magazines of forrage at the Different posts and appoint a man to Superintend the pack Horses. If it Come under my Direction I am sure I can appoint a man that have a general knowledge of the Business and will have Justice Done. I am told the Horse Masters lies to [too] [much?] in one place Consuming forrage and Rendering No Service to their Contry. They ware formerly under the Direction of Col Steel, But Now are Entirely Within the Limits of my District.[2] Col Steel are Confined at Fort Pitt with Genl Hand and Cannot See or know the Neglects of the Horse Masters; therefore it is absolutely necessary to have some p[r]oper person to Look after them. He will Save the Publick five times his Sallery and prevent many Reflections [i.e., criticisms].

Please to Send me Your instructions fully Respecting Every Matter and the[y] Shall be Executed as far as lyes in my power. I am Dr Genl your Obed Humble Servant

JOHN DAVIS

NB I have sent allong with the Artillery horses one wagon and team fully Equipt with 14 Bags to Hawl forrage for the horses on their way to Camp. My asistant in York Town wrote me he had some horses fit for the artillery which I have Desired him to send on Emediately.

J D

ACyS (Davis Papers: DLC).
1. Conoduguinet was in Cumberland County, near Davis's post of Carlisle, where a large depository of military stores was built up. (See Council of War, 17 June, below.)
2. His district included that part of Pennsylvania west of the Susquehannah River and the border areas of Maryland and Virginia. Two weeks later the western part of the region was put under Archibald Steel (NG to Davis, 9 May, below).

From Henry Laurens, President of the Continental Congress

[York, Pa., 24 April 1778. In response to NG's request of 20 April above, Congress approved a warrant for only $50,000 on Bordentown office because other drafts have been made on that office. LB (PCC, Item 13: DNA) 1 p.]

To Moore Furman[1]

[Valley Forge, 25 April 1778. Appointment as deputy quartermaster general for New Jersey, except for Sussex County.[2] Document is worded essentially like appointment of Col. John Davis, printed above, 23 March, except Furman's commission was 2 percent, out of which he was to pay an assistant. DS (Nj) 1 p.]

1. See biographical note, NG to Furman, 20 May, below.

2. Sussex County, in the western part of the state, was within the jurisdiction of Col. Robert L. Hooper at Easton, Pa. Furman's headquarters were variously at Trenton, Pitts Town, and Lamberton.

To George Washington

Sir

[Valley Forge 25 Apr. 1778][1]

The only hope that the Enemy can ever have of subjugating this Country is by possessing themselves of our *Capital Cities*, distressing our trade, destroying our Stores, and debauching one part of the Comunity to lend their Aid to subjugate the other.

These appear to be the great out lines of their plan, upon which they have hitherto regulated all their Operations; and they have never varied from this system but when their force was unequal to the business. The enemy began with possessing themselves of New York, Rhode Island and now Philadelphia. New Jersey was only evacuated because their force was found to be incompetent to their Operations in Pensylvania and the security of their Troops there.

The loss of our Sea-ports is a distressing circumstance notwithstanding we affect to dispise it. Many thousands of comfortable Citizens are drove into the country without the means of support, or places to shelter themselves from the weather. If the Citizens evacuate the Cities this is their fate; if they stay, they are made subservient to the Enemies designs: that in either case Their situation is distressing; besides these injuries the Army is deprived of a great variety of articles necessary to it's operations and convenience.

The Romans did not always make rapid conquests, but they always took care to secure their advantages: and partly by force and partly by distress compelled the people to submit to their yoke. This I apprehend will be the British system if we may form any judgment from the instances of their ravages committed in the latter part of last Campaign. The greater distress the Enemy bring upon the Country the more difficult it becomes for us to support an Opposition; neither the Virtue of Citizens or Soldiery are equal to constant sufferings. The distresses of the Army has induced many to abandon it. The distresses of the Country will engage many in the Enemies service. The great difficulty the Enemy labour under is to continue and secure their conquests at the same time: could they debauch such a part of the Inhabitants as to secure their Posts, their conquests would be almost certain.

One of the kings of France finding it difficult to raise Soldiers found means to possess himself of all the magazines of bread in the kingdom. This put the people so much in his power that they were compelled to engage in his service. If our enemy pursue a similar policy, they will by ravaging the Country constrain many to engage in their service.

They are now in possession of New York, Long Island, Rhode Island and Philadelphia. This enables them to hold in subjection a considerable part of the circumjacent country and three of the places are Capital objects and command great part of the Navigation in the Middle States. To compleat their plan I apprehend they will push their conquests to the Southward, unless we can fall upon some measures to make them act defensively. It is probable Maryland and South Carolina will be their objects. New England will remain untill the last. If these States continue firm after feeling the loss of their Capitals and ravages of their Country where there is not that degree of union which prevails in New England, they [i.e., the British] can have nothing to hope for from that quarter. But if they can bring some of the Middle States to abandon their union and disavow the present Government, then with their own force and such aid as they may be able to draw from the Middle States, New England may be attacked to advantage. From hence I conclude they will exert themselves to compleat the subj[ug]ation of the Middle States first.

Hitherto the enemy have gone on possessing our Cities one after another, and altho' their progress has been slow, their Operations have been sure. This has made a deep impression upon the minds of many well affected Inhabitants who reason from the past to the future and conclude that we must be finally conquered notwithstanding it may take time to affect it. Both civil and military government depend in a great measure upon opinion; therefore it is of the highest importance to give a proper bias to the public sentiment and a favourable opinion to the Army. Prejudices early imbibed and in some instances confirmed by experience and observation gain such an ascendancy over the mind as to influence from opinion to action.

The Enemy have been endeavouring to impress upon the minds of the Inhabitants their certainty of conquest, and urge as a proff that in every place where they get possession they hold their ground. It will be of importance to convince the public that this opinion is not well founded; to do this we must dispossess them of some of the places they now hold. An event of this sort will remove the impression of certain conquest, revive the hopes of general expulsion, confirm the weak and wavering among ourselves, stagger the confidance of the Inhabitants now in the power of the Enemy and incline them to favour our designs.

It will also have a great affect upon the people of Great Britain and upon all the courts of Europe. The task will be endless to conquer and be reconquered; the business of one campaign lost in the next must damp the hopes of [British] Administration and breed discontent among the people for pursueing such a fruitless and expensive war.

Our Governments are gaining a firmer tone, our currency increasing it's value,[2] there is nothing wanting to establish both but to convince the public that their prejudices and prepossessions are groundless, and that the enemy cannot go on to conquer and hold their conquests.

It is not the real value of Cities as places that gives the public a good or bad impression but the imaginary estimation given them. The real injury by the loss of Philadelphia bears but a small proportion to the effect it had from the imaginary estimation given it by the public. That was the case with New York and Rhode Island. To repossess any of those places will have just an oposite effect to that which was felt at their loss, and nearly in the same proportion.

I have said thus much not directly connected with the subject before me, but to explain my Ideas of the Enemies plan and the principles upon which they regulate their operations and the effect it has upon the country, as well as to shew the necessity there is of counteracting them either by beseiging some of the places they have in possession, or, if our force is not equal to that, by taking a position to prevent their further conquest.

Your Excellency demands my opinion upon the following questions:

There seem to be but three plans of operation which may be premeditated for the next campaign. One, the attempting to recover Philadelphia and destroy the Enemy's Army there. Another, the endeavouring to transfer the war to the Northward, by an enterprize against New York. And a third, the remaining quiet in a secure, fortified camp, disciplining and aranging the Army, 'till the Enemy begin their operations and then to govern ourselves accordingly; which of these plans shall we adopt;

If the first, what mode of execution shall we pursue, and what force will be requisite, estimating the present numbers of the enemy in Philadelphia at 10,000 men, exclusive of marines and seamen, whose aid may be called in? Shall we endeavour to affect the purpose by storm, by regular approaches or by blockade, and in what particular manner?

If the second, shall we attempt to take New York by a coup de main, with a small force, or shall we collect a large force and make an attack in form? In either case, what force will be necessary, estimating the number of the enemy in and about New York at 4,000 men, and what disposition shall we make so as to affect the enterprise, and the same time to protect the country here and secure our Stores?

If the last, what post shall we take so as to keep the army in a state of security, to afford cover to the country and to our magazines, and to be in a situation to counteract the future operations of the enemy?

Philadelphia is undoubtedly the most flattering object. The City is great, the army in it an important one, besides which the Stores are numerous. But to invest this city properly, to secure the passages of the river, and at the same time keep the enemy within their lines will require a great force, especially if the enemies strength is estimated at 10,000 men; which may be occasionally aided by all the marines and Sailors belonging to the fleet. To obstruct the passage of the river both Billingsport and Darby must be taken possession of. The force at Billingsport should be near 5,000 men, and they securely fortified, the post at Darby about 4,000 securely fortified; the main Army should consist of at least 15,000 who should take post between Delaware and Schuylkill [rivers], all to take post nearly at once. There should be a number of flatbottomed boats at Billingsport to draw reinforcements from Darby in case the enemy should attempt to invest that place. A bridge of communication will be necessary on [the] Schuylkill near Germantown. A few gallies will also be wanting to keep the enemy from ravageing the country upon the banks of the river. All the bridges of communication from Cooper's Ferry to Billingsport should be cut down that there may be no approaches made but by the heads of the Creeks. There will be wanted a number of flat boats above the City to cross our Army into New Jersey in case the enemy should attempt to retreat through that State by the way of Amboy. Without such a force and such a dispostion little more will be obtained by the investiture of Philadelphia than the repossession of the City.

Magazines and military stores should be prepared to aid the operations. And if we do not trust in the blockade to starve the enemy out, twenty or thirty pieces of heavy cannon will be wanted and eight or ten mortars. However, I am very doubtfull whether we shall be able to make regular approaches to the City as the enemy have superior mettle [metal?] and will be able to command our approaches by counter batteries, besides which it will require such a great consumption of powder as may ruin the State of our magazines. Should we attempt the city by regular approaches and meet with a defeat by counter batteries, we must raise the seige or it must terminate in a blockade.

The Continental troops will not be equal to a blockade, neither can the Militia be brought to their aid in such numbers and for such a time as will be necessary to starve the enemy into a surrender, and the impatience of the Militia is too great for the slow operations of a blockade. It will be a folly to attempt to beseige the City unless you can count upon a certain force and for a certain time. To attempt to

Storm the City will be madness. The Enemy have a body of men sufficient to man their works, with proper reserves to bid defiance to a force much superior to yours. Tens of thousands of Militia will avail nothing. The success of a Storm will depend upon the steadiness and bravery more than the number of the troops. I think therefore as our number of regular troops is not likely to be equal to a blockade, and as we may be foild in attempting to approach the city by counter batteries, and as a storm is impracticable by a numerous host of Militia the best plan will be, for this Army to remain in its present position and pursue the system of diciplining the troops; our position is well situated to cover the country and to draw supplies for our own support. While this army remains here growing stronger by recruits and perfecting its dicipline from day to day, the enemy will not dare to make any considerable detachments. If they continue where they are they will waste the campaign to no purpose. The Militia of the country will not be harrassed; our troops will become formidable for any enterprize. And if the enemy think proper to come out to meet us in the field we shall be ready to meet them upon any terms. These are my thoughts upon the first and third questions.

The second question which is an attack upon New York is the most promising plan. The Militia of New England are numerous, compact, well arrmed and equiped and can be easily called out for a sudden enterprise. There should be for this expedition about 4000 men of the regular troops and about 8,000 or 10,000 Militia. The Rhode Island troops may be detached from this Army under pretence of returning home for the security of that State. The New York troops may also be detached for the security of the North River. These with what troops are now at the North River and at Albany will compose a body sufficient for the purpose. Greater detachments cannot be made from this army without explaining our intentions and if it was possible to do without these I should prefer it, as I could wish to have this country in perfect security and because any detachments may serve as a clue to explain our intentions. I am sensible much greater numbers of Militia may be had from New England should they be thought necessary. The glow of patriotism and the spirit of enterprise runs so high since the capture of Burgoyne and his Army that almost any numbers may be brought out.

My plan for this enterprise should be to avoid the enemies works; my disposition, as follows: Four thousand men to assemble at Norwalk in Connecticut and cross over to Long-Island, these to be principally Militia, to advance first and move rapidly over the Island in order to take as many prisoners as possible and draw the enemies attention that way. Six thousand to move down by the way of the White Plains with light boats to throw a bridge over Harlam creek, plank and boards to be prepared also. This division should march next and move down a little wide of Kings-bridge.

The third and last division should consist principally of the regular troops and embark at Peekskill in boats to be provided for that purpose, and run down the North River and land a little above the city of New York. On this Corps I would principally depend for the reduction of the City. The troops on Long Island should have boats ready to cross over to N. York Island upon a signal to be given them upon the landing of the troops upon York Island from Peekskill at the same time the troops upon Hearlam [Harlem] River should cross and push down to the City. Fort Washington and the works at Kingsbridge will fall of themselves if we get possession of the City, but if they should still attempt to hold their ground they can be reduced at leasure. I foresee as much difficulty in putting the Militia in motion without explaining the design, as in any part of the execution for want of some ostensible reason. The most speady and secret mode would be for the Congress to give you (if you are not now intrusted with such powers) authority to call out as many Militia and at such places as you shall think proper. Your influence in New England is such that it will enable you to call forth as many Militia as you please. I would demand 2,000 from New York to be under the command of Governor Clinton, 5,000 from Connecticut, 4,000 to asssemble at Norwalk, and 3000 from that part of Massachusetts Bay that lies the most continguous to Fish-Kill; Then the New York troops and the remaining 1,000 of the Connecticut forces to assemble at Fish Kills.

The forces should be engaged for one month after they arrive upon the ground:

A descent upon Rhode Island may be talked of, and not so publicly as to betray our real intention; the troops raised in New York, it may be given out, are to secure the passes while a detachment is made from the regular forces to attack the troops at Newport.

I should recommend that your Excellency command this expedition as much will depend on personal influence.

General Lee may be left with the command here.[3] A body of New Jersey Militia may be put in motion to cooperate with the New England forces and make a descent upon Staten Island; doubtless there will be some stores and some prisoners to be taken there. It will all tend to increase the enemys confusion, and if they answer no other purpose, they will serve as a check to prevent the Enemy from attempting to throw reinforcments from Philadelphia into New York by the way of New-Jersey.

The Quarter Master General should go into New England to prepare for the enterprise some time before it is ripe for execution, but your Excellency should not make your appearance untill the troops are assembling; you may leave this army under a pretence of a conferrince with the commanding Officer at Fish Kill, and a few days before you set out let it be reported about the Country that the whole body of the Militia are to be collected together to make an attack upon Philadelphia.

I should recommend that there be some good Continental Officers picked out to command bodies of Volunteers to be drawn from the Militia: these Corps will be little inferior to regular troops.[4]

If this plan is adopted and does not succeed it will not materially injure the grand Army; and if it does succeed agreeable to our wishes, many advantages will result from it, but whether it succeeds or not, I am persuaded it will confine the operations of the next Campaign to the limits of the Enemy's present possessions.

If the enemy should have a number of Ships so stationed that [the?] party proposed to come down the North River could not get by them, they might join the party that marches by Hearlam.

The reasons I would wish to avoid the Enemies works are, it will give an air of confidance to the expedition, spirit up our own party and damp the hopes of the Enemy. The slow operations of regular approaches do not agree with the impatience of the Militia, and to approach regularly will give the enemy time to remove the Stores and prepare themselves for a regular evacuation of the place.

The time that I would fix for this expedition should be about the middle of June.

Almost all the troops may be drawn off from Fish Kill as it will be impossible for the enemy to attempt any thing while the operations are going on against New York.

I have not time to go more minutely into the subject.[5] The business of my department claims too much of my attention to be more particular upon the questions. I have said sufficient to comply with your Excellency's commands, tho' I have not been so explicit as I could wish.[6] I am with great respect Your Excellencys most Obedt humble Servant

NATHANAEL GREENE

LS (Washington Papers: DLC).
    1. The date is docketed in Washington's hand.
    2. The continental dollar, which had depreciated steadily from October to March, had actually increased in value during April, possibly from confidence inspired by the very survival of Washington's army and the improvements made by Steuben. If so, such confidence soon withered; in May the dollar started on its long downward slide that was not to stop until it was worth less than two cents. See Appendix I.
    3. Gen. Charles Lee's exchange had been arranged only four days earlier, permitting him, as his parole had not, to rejoin the army. (See above, Meade to NG, 4 April.)
    4. Although NG thought the militia normally too costly, often ill-disciplined, and seldom to be depended upon over long periods of time, he was always ready to affirm

their fighting qualities when they were employed in a limited engagement close t their homes and under good officers. During the southern campaign, he went so far a to call the militia the "great palladium of American liberty." (NG to Joseph Reed 6 August 1781)

5. NG's response concentrated so on the hazards of attacking Philadelphia or Nev York that he scarcely did justice to his preference for Washington's third option– "remaining quiet in a secure, fortified camp." Although he spoke of the army's remair ing in its "present position" while strengthening itself, he did not preclude moving th camp for a mile for sanitary reasons. (See below, Washington to NG, 8 June.)

6. As usual, Washington received a variety of conflicting opinions—seventy page of them, in fact. According to Fitzpatrick, Wayne, Paterson, and Maxwell approved a attack on Philadelphia. Knox, Poor, Varnum, and Muhlenberg favored an attack o New York. Stirling favored both New York and Philadelphia. Lafayette, Steuben, an Duportail deemed any operation against the British inadvisable, but that the arm should be "strengthened and better trained." (Fitzpatrick, GW, 11: 283n) At some poin in the spring of 1778, Washington wrote ten pages of "Thoughts upon a Plan o Operation for Campaign 1778," listing the advantages and disadvantages of each of th three options outlined in his 20 April circular. Fitzpatrick dated the document som time in March 1778 (Fitzpatrick, GW, 11: 185–94); Freeman (GW, 4: 630 n) placed i before the 20 April circular, although he granted there was a slim chance it could hav been an expansion of that circular. On close examination, however, the "Thoughts" seem less like an expansion of the circular than a blending of Washington's ideas an assessments with certain of those submitted by the generals after 23 April. Som proposals and even some of the wording, for example, are remarkably similar to part of NG's letter above. Whatever the source of Washington's thoughts, they wer apparently intended for his eyes alone, and he seemed resigned to doing nothing mor than waiting for the enemy's first move.

To Thomas Wharton, President of the Pennsylvania Council

[Valley Forge, 26 April 1778. Asks delivery of horses for Col. (George, Baylor's "light Dragoons." From Pa. Archives, 6: 444]

To General George Weedon

My dear General   Camp Valley Forge April 27th 1778

I have received three Letters from you since I wrote;[1] I am sc exceedingly hurried with Publick Business, that I have scarse a mo ment that I can call my own time, otherwise I should not have beer silent so long.

The Congress agreeable to my former apprehensions (communi cated to you in my last,) have deranged the Officers of the Virginia Line.[2] You mistook the Report of the General Officers, respecting your Relative Rank, they carefully avoided saying any thing about the Rank, after the Congress had appointed and Ranked you: but re ported how you ought to have been Ranked in the first Instances. This Report was founded upon the following Principle; and upon the following facts being granted. "That General Woodford was the old est Officer in the Virginia Line, and was superceeded, and compel'd to go out of the Service. That Regular promotion shou'd always take place when the Persons are fit for it. That a sense of honor will constrain a person to leave the Army, where he is superceeded by a younger Officer of the same State. That every Officer that has been Promoted to the Prejudice of another, should be willing to do justice to the Injured party." But this in my opinion can only be a voluntary concession, for I have no Idea that the Congress have any more right to De-range Officers of the same Rank, than I have; They may give superior Rank to an inferior Officer because they claim and exercise the right of Promotion upon different Principles.

I wrote you in my former some of the General Officers were for giving General Woodford his Rank, and for recommending it to Congress for confirmation, but others of us were against it; We fore-saw the danger of the Precedent, if it could be exercised in one instance, it might in more, and then no Officer would have any security for even his own standing in the line of the Army, much less for his claim of regular Promotion. I look upon the exercise of such a power dangerous, arbitary, and unjust; The Congress have a right to create in the first instance as they please, they have a right to promote as they shall think proper: but to alter the standing of Officers of the same Rank, is a doctrine that I never can subscribe to.

The General Officers in giving in their Report, only meant to shift the Business off their hands, and leave the Congress to correct their own errors. It was the opinion of some of the General Officers, that the Congress could not make an alteration without the consent of the Officers who were to be effected by it. It was my opinion. I told the Committee of Congress (then sitting at Camp) the reasons for our Report and that we could not undertake to recommend an alteration, where a Plan had been fixed and sanctified by Congress.

All the General Officers agreed that if General Woodford was injured, and compel'd to leave the Service, that, those who had been promoted to his prejudice ought to do him Justice: but it must be done by their own voluntary consent. Every body agrees that General Woodford was injured, and all the General Officers seem to wish from a fellow feeling with a Brother injured Officer, that Justice might be done him: but there was a difference in opinion respecting the mode; some were of opinion that the Congress could do it, others, that nobody but the Party themselves voluntarily agreeing to the alteration, and confirmed by Congress could warrent an alteration; This was my opinion, which made me write in the stile and manner I did in my former Letter: but I was apprehensive of the alteration by Congress, and therefore was anxious that you should pave the way by your own voluntary Consent, this wou'd have given an air of Justice to your proceedings, removed the embarassments of Congress and laid General Woodford under an obligation for such a condesention.

The Congress have taken the matter up in such a Humiliating manner to the Officers affected, giving no reasons for the change and new arrangement, but only declaritive of their good will and pleasure, and in the Language of the Creator. Let there be light and there was Light. Let the Officers Rank as follows, and they shall Rank so. I say the alteration has been made in such a Humiliating way to the Officers affected, and in so alarming a manner to others subjected to the same decisions, that I can give you no further advice upon the Question. I know your value and usefulness in the Army. I feel for you the warm attachment of a faithfull Friend, and am sorry the Publick should be depriv'd of your Services, and your Friends of your Society: but I cannot advise how to act; If you feel yourself degraded! I wish you to come to Camp nevertheless, be your determination what it may.

I shall curse the Quarter Masters Department before [*torn*] the years about.

[*Torn*] All [?] things remain much in the same [situation?] as when you left us; The Army recruits slow, Lord North and the Ministry are endeavoring to sound the Americans once more upon the subject of reconciliation; Genral Howe is going home,[3] and Genl Lee is exchanged. My and Mrs Greene's Compliments to Mrs Weedon, and Mrs Greene desires to be remembred to the Danceing General. I am with great Regard your most Obedient Servt

NATH GREENE

LS (NjMoW).

1. None of the letters Weedon wrote while home on leave in Fredericksburg has been found.

2. For background, see above, NG et al. to Washington, 4 March and NG to Weedon, 7 March. On 19 March, Congress had granted new commissions to the four Virginia brigadiers, with Woodford in first rank, followed by Muhlenberg, Scott, and Weedon. (*JCC*, 10: 269). For months thereafter both Weedon and Muhlenberg fumed. (See Fitzpatrick, *GW*, 11: 173, 239.) Despite NG's stand on Weedon's rank, they were to remain good friends. After refusing to accept Weedon's resignation in April, Congress permitted him in August to retire with his rank as brigadier, to be called back into service "whenever, from a change of circumstances, the inconveniences he now labours under can be removed." He was not to be paid in the meantime, nor to receive half pay after the war unless he had been called back. (*JCC*, 11: 807) In June of 1780 (possibly related to Woodford's capture at Charleston on 12 May), Washington arranged for his old Fredericksburg friend to come back into the service. (See Weedon to Washington, 30 June 1780, Washington Papers, DLC and Burnett, *Letters*, 5: 163–64 and n.)

Meanwhile, in December 1779 Muhlenberg requested that his case also be reconsidered, but Congress stuck with its resolution of 19 March 1778. (*JCC*, 15: 1418–19) Muhlenberg remained in the service until the end of the war.

3. Within a few days after 9 April, the day Howe received word in Philadelphia that he was to be replaced by Gen. Henry Clinton, the rumor reached Valley Forge;

within two weeks the intelligence was confirmed. (Fitzpatrick, *GW*, 11: 302). Howe's recall and departure, including the extravagant festivities in honor of his leaving (called a *mischianza*), are covered in Gruber, *Howe Brothers*, pp. 274–300.

From General John Lacey

[Crooked Billet, Pa., 27 April 1778. Answering NG's 21 April letter, the person who took a citizen's horse is to appear before him. Has ordered his "parties not to distress the inhabitants unless they be found favoring the enemy." Various people this winter have committed the "most villainous robberies imaginable under the character of Militia." Tr (GWG Transcript: CSmH) 1 p.]

To Colonel Henry Hollingsworth

[Valley Forge, 28 April 1778. Approves his taking (by force) the wheat that is "in the Enemies power"; he should send all horses and wagons he can buy;[1] hopes he has not forgot need for portmanteaus. Excerpt in *Charles Hamilton Catalog* of 25 January 1968.]

1. On the same day, Congress authorized Maj. Henry Lee to take by force as many horses in Hollingsworth's area north of Chesapeake Bay as needed for his dragoons. (*JCC*, 10: 401–2)

From Henry Laurens, President of the Continental Congress

[York, Pa., 28 April 1778. Encloses extract (now missing) of letter from McDougall to Congress. LB (PCC, Item 13: DNA) 1 p.]

From George Lux[1]

Dear Genl   Baltimore [Md.] 28 April 1778
I did myself the pleasure of writing you a long Letter by Lieut. Moore of Moylans Regt, which you must long e'er now have received.[2] Although I have not received any answer to it, yet as I know your time is engrossed by Public Business I cannot with propriety stand upon Ceremony, but chearfully emb[race] the opportunity of paying my Comp'ts to you by Col'l Ballard of the 1st Virginia Regt, who I know will deliver this in prop[ria] person[a], and [thus?] I will write you fully.
Col'l [Robert] Ballard tells me that you are [appointed?] Q M G and have accepted the Post. I really pity you, as it is so important a Post, and must have been much neglected by the late Q M G,[3] [who?] scandalously permitted private Pique to have more Influence

on him than the Public Good. Genl M. has said (as is *reported* for I never have heard it *directly* asserted) that this was a Proof of your having *engrossed* His Exc'y's Confidence, as you wished to keep out of the way of Bullets. I learn, that Genl M. has publickly declared, that he looked upon His Exc'y as the best Friend he ever had in his Life, so that it is a plain Sign, that the Junto has given up all Ideas of supplanting our [*indecipherable*] General from a Confidence of the Impracticability of such an Attempt.[4] It was currently reported here and firmly believed that an Attempt was made in Congress for removing the Genl and that the 4 Eastern States and Virg'a voted for it, i.e., Messrs F. [Francis Lightfoot] Lee and Jo. [Joseph] Jones for it and Mr Harvey [Harvie] against it. I then wrote to a Gentn there of my Acquaintance, telling him of the Report, and that I thought the Gentlemen ought to be informed of it in order to vindicate themselves if unjustly accused, but if justly, that they ought to be excluded from our Public Counsels as men unworthy of Confidence, since which I have been favoured with a Letter from Mr Jones wherein he denies the Charge, and upon Enquiry I since find, that no such motion was ever made in Congress, and that Messrs Jones and F. Lee were warm advocates for the Genl. I wish I could say as much for his Brother R H [Richard Henry] Lee, who, if he is not much altered, since Congress sat here, would be much averse to him—dark, subtle and designing, he never will openly appear in any point which he wishes to carry, it is impossible to detect him in the prosecution of his Schemes.

However, if I am not misinformed, his Existence in Congress is very short, for a Letter is at last detected from him to his Steward, in which he orders him to decline taking Continental money on the Terms prescribed by Law, a behaviour not to be forgiven in any man, who pretends to call himself a Friend to American Liberty. No man could be more uneasy than myself at the Prospect of Gen W's Station being rendered uneasy to him, and I am confident such a Scheme would have been prosecuted, were it not for the high Confidence the Continent reposes in him. R.H.Lee was always for placing [Charles] Lee in his Room. I almost fear therefore that he will be rendered factious. God grant my Apprehensions may be groundless.

We hear here that Genls Arnold and Lincoln are to serve this Campaign under Genl W. They certainly will be useful Coadjutors to him. Arnold, it is said, is to command a chosen Cour [Corps] of Light Infantry with Genls Wayne and Scott under him as Brigadiers. Much therefore may be expected from such Excellent Officers and picked Troops. Our Division of Marylanders at Wilmington, from what I can learn, are declining fast, for their numbers are much reduced, and several of our best Officers were wounded at Germantown, and what is worse than all, Genl Smallwood is very unpopular among them, owing to his Stateliness and excessive Slowness of Motion. I am credibly informed, that he lately issued out in orders, that no Officer shall presume to intrude upon him on any pretence whatever, but between the Hours of 3 and 6 in the Afternoon—a pretty Condition he would be in, were the Enemy to attack him in the morning. I am pretty confident, that he is not liked by a single Officer in the Division, and when that is the case a General Officer ought to resign; I really like him much, as he has been very friendly to me and cannot concieve, what could have caused this Alteration in him. However, I have several times known him to keep his Soldiers 6 and 8 Hours together under Arms, before he would determine what he would do—this alone will render a Genl unpopular, let his Accomplishments be ever so exalted. The Division now regrets the Loss of Genl Sullivan, who has been amazingly popular with them since the Battle of Germantown.

I imagine Genl Sullivan will render the Enemy's Situation uneasy to them in Rhode Island, as Alertness and Activity are his Characteristicks. His Predecessor in that Command was certainly a mere Cypher. It is said Genl Putnam has resigned.[5] I wish he and Genl Heath would and then our Cour of M Genls would be excellent. Genl Gates, I am informed is to command at Peekskill with Genls McDougal and Conway under him. I should be glad, they could make a Descent upon N York and try to release our Officers, who are Prisoners in the Enemy's hands. McDougal will be useful in tempering the factious and turbulent Spirits of Conway and I hope Genl Schuyler will preside in the Board of War, in order to curb Genl M. a little. We have had it reported here, that Col Pickering was one of Conways Party and that all the Board of War in short were. Can it be believed?

Please to forward the Inclosed to Bob Gates (the Genls Son) at Peekskill; or if you cant, Col'l Wat [Walter] Stewart will, as he corresponds with Genl Gates's Family. Genl Gates's Family and ours have long been intimate, and as the Genl has assured *he never even wished* to displace His Exc'y, I still keep it up. I have however, wrote freely to Bob telling him that his Fathers weak side is too strong Attachments to those he thinks his Friends and [too?] violent Resentments against the Persons he deemed his Enemies; that he has suffered by it in the case of Wilkinson and may hereafter [*rest of sentence illegible*]

Our Assembly have determined to try if they cant make up our Quota of Troops by Substitutes before they proceed to a Draught, and they come in so fast, that I expect they will be able to do it.

Col'l Ballard tells me, that Mrs Green is now at Camp. Although I am not acquainted with her, please to present my best Comp'ts to her, as I expect to be so, if she stays this Summer near the Camp.

Our Governor [Thomas Johnson] was well 2 days ago and as busy as usual. I shall always be glad to hear from you, when convenient, and am Dr Sir Yr oblig'd huml Servt

GEO LUX

ALS (NNC).
1. George Lux is something of a shadowy figure. His public career was limited to serving briefly as secretary to a congressional committee. At this time he was living with his parents on the family estate of Chatsworth, near Baltimore, which he shortly inherited. (His father died before he wrote NG on 26 May, below.) Thenceforth, he seems to have concerned himself chiefly with its management and with entertaining the important people of his time. The next year he married Catharine Biddle, daughter of Edward Biddle of Reading, Pa., former speaker of the Pennsylvania Assembly.

Lux had first met NG in 1777. It is clear from the ten surviving letters to NG over a five-year period that he was an indefatigable gossip. Unfortunately for the historian, he did not discriminate among fact, rumor, and opinion. During the spring of 1778, Lux undoubtedly added fuel to NG's suspicions of Mifflin and the "Cabal," but time seems to have taught NG to take Lux's letters with a pinch of salt. (None of NG's letters to him has been found.)

Lux's interest in people was not limited to America. Alexander Graydon said that Lux was acquainted with the "ramifications and affinities" of the great families of Europe. Graydon considered him "shamefully negligent of his person," with only a "very moderate share of judgment or discernment." (Graydon, Memoirs, pp. 345–47)
2. Letter not found.
3. The reference here and in following sentences is to Gen. Mifflin.
4. See "Conway Cabal," note, NG to Jacob, 7 February, above.
5. Sullivan's predecessor in Rhode Island was Gen. Joseph Spencer. In 1779 Gen. Israel Putnam suffered a paralytic stroke that ended his military career.

To Colonel John Davis

Sir   Camp Valley Forge April 29th 1778

I am favour'd with yours of the 12th and 24th of this Instant, with three or four others that its unnecessary to be particular in mentioning; I should have answer'd them before, but my time is so taken up in answering other Letters more pressing than your, that I have been under the necessity of neglecting you. I wish you to continue writeing from time to time, whether I answer you or not.[1]

I am happy to find your conduct answers to the character given of you; your industry and attention to business full equals my expectations, and is perfectly satisfactory.

I am sorry to find Waggoners so difficult to be got. I was in hopes I should meet with no difficulty in procureing a sufficient number, after offering such liberal pay and promising those engaged to be excused from Militia Duty and Fines. You cannot engage too many.

As fast as you can get your Teams compleated forward them on to Camp; You may detain the Pack-Horses untill the Saddles are ready: but forward all the Artillery Horses. Forward the Tarr as fast as it comes to hand; we are in great want of some to compleat a number of Waggons, and for repairing Boats.

You did perfectly right in branding the Horses; make it a constant rule for the future to brand all you purchase upon the four [fore] Quarters. I make no doubt the States have lost some hundreds of Horses, for want of proper attention being paid to the branding the Cattle [i.e., livestock] that have been purchased from time to time.

You will take the direction of the whole Business belonging to the Quarter Master Generals department, upon the communication from York to Fort Pitt. Form the necessary magazines, and account to Colonel Biddle for the Forage Department, and appoint such persons to conduct the Pack-Horses as shall be necessary to correct the abuses complain'd off: and to manage the public Business to the best advantage.

I shall do everything in my power to supply you with Cash; but I am afraid from what you write to Colonel Cox, there will be no small difficulty in procureing the necessary supplies.

Get all the Linnen you purchase made up into Baggs, Knapsacks, and Haversacks.

Before this will reach you, I hope the money directed by Colonel Cox to be forwarded to Mr Smith will be on its way. If it should not, I must beg you to stay by Mr Hilligas,[2] untill he furnishes you with the necessary Sums.

I received a Letter yesterday from Mr Smith, who says he is, and will be unable to do anything considerable, untill the money comes to hand, and if he fails us, we shall fall short of our demand for Teams. I am Sir Your Hble Servt

NATH GREENE

NB Make the Pack-Saddles upon the old Indian Traders plan, without covers.

LS (Davis Papers: DLC).
1. Davis's letters of 11 and 24 April are the only ones that have been found.
2. Michael Hillegas was treasurer of the United States; his son Samuel was an assistant.

From Henry Laurens, President
of the Continental Congress

[York, Pa., 30 April 1778. NG's messenger is dangerously ill with smallpox. Asks by "what means the growing expense is to be reimbursed." LB (ScHi) 1 p.]

From the Pennsylvania Executive Council

[Lancaster, Pa., 30 April 1778. Encloses circular to commissioners in counties appointed to buy horses for army. They will follow NG's directions. Twenty-one horses to be delivered to Maj. (Henry) Lee. Df (PHarH) 1 p.]

From Charles Tillinghast[1]

[Fishkill, N.Y., 30 April 1778. Col. Hughes, who has a "violent cold," asks him to enclose copy of his letter to Samuel Ogden. ACyS (NHi) 1 p.]

1. The letter from Col. Hughes to Ogden, agent at Boonton, N.J., declared that the department would need at least four thousand camp kettles, that if the enemy should move up the Hudson it would be very difficult to get them later. He could expect to receive orders from "General Greene." Tillinghast was Hughes's aide.

To Henry Laurens, President of the Continental Congress

Sir   Camp Valley Forge 1st of May 1778
    This will be handed to you by Lt Colonel Hay who acted as Deputy Quarter Master General to the northern Army the last Year by an Appointment from Congress. Upon my offering him a new Deputation, he informed me that, as Congress had been pleased to give him the Rank of Lieutenant Colonel in the Army with his former Appointment, and he could not, without acknowledging that to be cancelled, accept of a new one, he could not with Propriety accept it at present; that he was ready, nevertheless, to act either under his old Appointment or a new one, provided his military Rank were preserved; but wanted to know the Mind of Congress on these Points previously to his entering on Business, and therefore would wait upon you for an Explanation.[1]
    The Business of a Deputy Quarter Master General is so distinct from any Idea of military Rank, that I apprehend they have no necessary Connection nor Relation. I believe Colo Hay to be a very good and active Officer, and I doubt not he will bring strong Testimonials of his merit from former Services. It may therefore be very proper that his military Rank should be continued to him; but this is a matter that, as Quarter Master General, I pretend not to interfere in. So far, however, as relates to the Quarter Master's Department, I conceive the Appointment of all Subordinate Officers to be clearly within my Province, as well from the Nature of the Business, which requires an Orderly and regular Subordination throughout the Department, as from the Resolution of Congress on my Appointment in

which it is expressly mentioned and which makes me responsible for the Conduct of my Deputies to a Degree that would be incompatible with any other Mode of Appointment.[2] I have therefore concluded that it was undoubtedly the Intention of Congress in that Resolution that all former Appointments were wholly superseded on the Appointment of myself and my Assistants, and I rest assured that Congress will give it no other Interpretation to Col Hay. Were it necessary I could mention many Inconveniences that would arise from different Modes of Appointment: it would give Birth to Disputes very injurious to the Service, were Precedence to be claimed by Appointments coming through different Channels, and the Respect arising from some Degree of Dependence, and which is necessary to the Preservation of due Subordination and Discipline, would be totally lost. A Person lately applied to me with an old Appointment from Congress as Deputy Quarter Master General at Baltimore, which I was obliged to disregard, not only because I conceived it to be extinct, but because I had, before I had any Knowledge of it, appointed another Person whom I esteem more fit for the Office, in the same Place.[3]

As other Instances of the like Kind may arise, I have thought it proper thus to explain my Ideas of the Powers Congress have been pleased to invest me with, and of the Propriety of my appointing all subordinate Officers in the Quarter Master's Department. At the same Time I shall always be ready to gratify their Wishes in favour of any particular Person, or on any Occasion, when it may be in my Power consistent with that Order which must necessarily be preserved in a Business of so much Importance, and for the well conducting of which I am in so great a Degree responsible. I have the Honour to be, with the highest Respect Sir, Your most obedient humble Servant

NATH GREENE

LS (PCC, Item 155: DNA).

1. In 1775 Udny Hay (d. 1806) was a lumberman and timber merchant in Quebec, hiring, he said "a great number of the lower class of *Canadians* at and about Quebeck" to cut and load timber. When war broke out, he lost most of his lumber, horses, and rafts to the British. After Ticonderoga fell in May 1775, he made his way south to join Benedict Arnold. The following year he was made assistant deputy quartermaster in New York. On the recommendation of Gen. Gates, Congress named him assistant deputy quartermaster at Ticonderoga and appointed him a lieutenant colonel "by brevet" in January 1777. (*JCC*, 7: 23; for his career as a timber merchant, including the quotation, see his letter to Gates in Force, *Archives*, [5] 3: 744–45; see also *PMHB*, 8 [1884]: 375.) On the advice of Gens. Wayne and Sullivan, who were acquainted with his work, Washington had recommended him as quartermaster general at the beginning of the year, but Congress had already decided the committee to camp should choose Mifflin's successor. (See Washington to Congress, 1 January 1778, Fitzpatrick, *GW*, 10: 244.)

NG reappointed him as a deputy but could not guarantee that Congress would permit him to keep the lieutenant colonelcy. NG, in fact, had gone on record in January as disapproving the granting of commissions to staff people (such as Hay) who had not paid the price of "being subject to the dangers of the field" as had the line officers. (NG to Washington, end of January, above.) He was willing to make an exception because of Hay's abilities; it was Congress that denied Hay's request, using the occasion to proclaim that "no persons, hereafter appointed upon the civil staff of the army, shall hold or be entitled to any rank in the army by virtue of such staff appointment." (*JCC*, 11: 555, and NG to Hay, 17 June, below) Hay did not carry out his threat of resigning, and he remained throughout NG's tenure, serving the department faithfully, as almost two hundred surviving letters between him and NG testify. Hay kept his title, moreover, though denied the rank by Congress.

2. Congress had declared in the resolution appointing NG on 2 March that the "forage masters, waggon masters, and other officers in the department, be in the appointment of the quarter master general, who is to be responsible for their conduct." (*JCC*, 10: 210) They reaffirmed this in the preamble to the resolution about Hay on 29 May, but did not respond directly to NG's elaboration on the point. (*JCC*, 11: 554)

3. The reference is to John Hall; see above, NG to Hollingsworth, 7 April and to Smallwood, 9 April.

From Nehemiah Hubbard

[Hartford, Conn., 1 May 1778. Can hire teams more cheaply than buying. Asks NG's judgment. LB Excerpt (RG 93, WRMS: DNA) 1 p.]

From Colonel John Davis

[Carlisle, Pa., 2 May 1778. Has sent wagon teams and pack horses; will send more; has harness leather; Col. Cox has agreed on $80.00 monthly for wagon masters. ACy (Davis Papers: DLC) 1 p.]

To George Washington

Sir   Camp Valley Forge 3d May 1778
    From the Situation in which I found the Quarter Master General's Department on my entering upon the Office, which is not unknown to your Excellency, It appeared to be absolutely necessary to make very extensive and speedy Preparations for the ensuing Campaign, especially in Horses, Teams, Tents, and other Articles of high Price. In Consequence of this apparent Necessity, I have given extensive Orders, almost without Limitation, for the Purchase of these Articles; apprehending, from the Prospects at that Time, the utmost Exertions we could make would not procure more than a Sufficiency for the necessary Accomodation of the Army.[1]
    From the Intelligence lately received, the Aspect of our Affairs is essentially changed;[2] and it may be that in Consequence of this Change the Plan of military Operations may undergo such material Alterations as may, in a considerable Degree, abate the Demand for

those expensive Preparations which some Weeks ago were thought indispensibly necessary. And as I would not willingly enhance the Expences of the Quarter Master's Department farther than Prudence and good Oeconnomy absolutely require, I take the Liberty of addressing Your Excellency on the Occasion, to request the Favour of your Advice and Direction whether the Plan above mentioned for obtaining Supplies ought to be retrenched, and in what Degree; or, in other Words, in what Degree the Plan of Preparations ought to be continued: And, particularly, as the Prospect of the local Situation of the Army may be greatly altered by these Changes, what Alterations should be made in the Plan lately approved by Your Excellency for establishing Magazines of Forage in the Different Parts of the Country.[3] I have the Honour to be, with the Greatest Respect, Your Excellency's most obedient and most humble Servant

NATH GREENE

LS (Washington Papers: DLC).

1. For background on the transportation problem, see note, NG to Biddle, 23 March, above. It is evident from NG's correspondence after he took over in late March that he had attacked the transportation problem with vigor. The correspondence tells only part of the story, however. Many letters between him and his deputies have been lost, while those written to others by Col. Cox or Col. Biddle that reflect NG's policies have not been sought out for inclusion in these volumes.

2. He is probably referring to the two hundred British transports that Washington reported to have sailed down the Delaware during the past week. (Fitzpatrick, GW, 11: 351–52) The officers at Valley Forge could not know their significance for several weeks. See below.

3. For Washington's answer, see below, 5 May.

From Colonel Hugh Hughes

Sir

Fishkill [N.Y.] May 3d 1778

Being greatly indisposed some Days past, I order'd my Clerk to inclose You a Copy of a Letter, sent to Col Ogden, at Boonetown, in answer to one he favored me with some time before that, by which you will see that the Department is in want of a further supply of the Article therein mentioned, or, at least that is my Opinion. When I dictated that Letter, I had scarce the powers of Recollection, which will account for my Silence concerning Nail rods being wanted in Store as well as Camp Kettles. There ought at all times to be 10 or 15 Tons of them kept as a Deposit on this side, If I may be allowed to offer my Sentiments. But they could not be procured from that Gentleman, any otherwise than as mentioned in my Letter to him, or I should have laid them in.

However, the Wants of the Department are not confind to those two Articles. Sir, they are many and pressing, occasion'd more by the loss, daily use, and Consumption of them, than an omission in

Providing. I will mention the most Capital: such as Horses, Oxen, Waggons, Forage, Tents, Cordage, Duck, Canteens, Timber, Boards, Tar, Bricks, with many others of less Importance, but yet necessary, and which I really cannot enumerate just now, being far from a State of Health.

But, to crown all, Cash is wanted, and your Deputy to deal it out, as I have none but what is procured by negotiating Loan Office Certificates, where a Friend can be found that has a little to Spare, and that is call'd for much faster than collected, by public Creditors of long standing.

Besides, several Persons offer to Contract for different Articles, whom I refer to you, Sir, but they will not bear the Expense of going so much farther on uncertainty, which, in my situation, I am unable to remedy. Nay, if I had power to contract, unless I could pledge myself for the pay being made according to agreement, it would not avail. Such is the wretched situation the Department is bro't to, by not having had a suitable and timely supply of Cash, and this has been the case ever since the Main Army cross'd Hudson's River, and has rendered it, at this time, almost impossible, without a very ample Supply to answer the demands of the service.

The Duty I owe my Country induces me to apprize you of those Circumstances, which, at the same Time, will convince you that I am not insensible to its Claims, which you mentioned in a former Letter, and that, tho' I quit the Department, it does not follow, I shall the Country, or cause. It is well known in this State, and Several others, that I was among the first who espoused the American Cause. It is equally true, that my Efforts were Feeble, but they were unremitting and Consistent, to the time of my entering the Service, since when, I have been lucky enough to procure a General Approbation of my public Conduct, which I have ample Testimony of, and, indeed, which you yourself have been so generous as to acknowlege, Sir.

I accepted when the Prospect was gloomy and almost every thing to look for. I resign when there is little to fear, but from the intrigues of an insidious Enemy, whom Congress seem to have anticipated. And if it be remembered, that we have made, at least, five precipitate Retreats, and twice burnt out, besides the loss of three Forts in this Department, it will be found, I expect, by the Return made General Mifflin, that we have as many stores as any of our Brethren, who have as often been put to the route, and suffered by fire. I acknowlege my Tediousness, but as I have mentioned chiefly Facts, it is imagin'd my Vanity will be the more pardonable, especially when it is done to show, that whatever Opinion I entertain of my present Situation, I am by no means going to desert the Cause of my distress'd and bleeding Country, tho' at the same time, I will not serve under Men who were never of the line nor Staff before me, let their Merit be what it may.[1]

Colonel Biddle has amus'd himself with my Continuation, and written a long Letter, with Instructions for the Forage Department &c., in consequence of it, which I have not been able to answer. It is a pity that any Time should be lost just now, and, as somebody else will take the Department, that Person ought to be possess'd of them, not I.

As I have been ingeneous with you from the first, Sir, I must now intreat your Candour in relieving me very shortly, as the situation of my Family, not having had a Furlough since I entered the service. My Concerns with General Mifflin, and my Health require it. And I beg Leave to remind you, that I cannot after this reaches you be answerable[2] [one or more pages missing]

Cy (NHi).
1. See note at Hughes to NG, 23 April, above.
2. Hughes returned to the quartermaster department under Pickering in 1780. Despite his unwillingness to serve as a deputy under NG, there is no evidence that Hughes bore him any ill-will. On the contrary, in an exchange of correspondence in October 1780 (when NG temporarily commanded at West Point), Hughes's letters are most amicable.

NG reluctantly accepted this letter as Hughes's final answer, and he assigned the post to Udny Hay. (See below, NG to Gates, 15 May 1778.)

From Colonel John Laurens[1]

[Valley Forge, 5 May 1778. Washington wishes "proper quarters" for Gens. Gates and Mifflin.[2] ALS (PHC) 1 p.]

1. John Laurens (1754–82) had been an aide to Washington since September 1777. The son of South Carolina's Henry Laurens, president of the Continental Congress, young Laurens had returned to America in 1777 after five years of schooling in England and Switzerland. Fluent in French he served also as an interpreter for Washington. He was one of the officers that saw themselves as Washington's defenders against the "Conway Cabal." (See note, NG to Jacob, 7 February, above.) In December 1780, at the age of twenty-six, he was sent to France as a special envoy, but returned in time to fight at Yorktown.

He then joined NG's army in South Carolina, where he played an important part in driving the British from the backcountry. Some sixty of his letters to NG from that period have survived and reveal a warm bond of affection and mutual respect between the two men. In August 1782 Laurens was killed in what NG called a "paltry little skirmish," a fate that he was led to by "love of military glory." (NG to Otho Williams, 17 September 1782, below) For a sketch of his brief life, see DAB and Sara B. Townsend, An American Soldier: The Life of John Laurens (Raleigh: Edwards & Broughton Co., 1958).
2. Gates and Mifflin came as members of the Board of War, although Gates was soon on his way to the Hudson and Mifflin henceforth was absorbed in his own affairs.

From George Washington

Sir   Head Quarters [Valley Forge] May 5th 1778
In answer to your favour of the 3d. I give it clearly as my opinion that no change has happened in our affairs, which will justify the least relaxation in our military preparations and consequently that the provisions you have been and are making in your department ought to be continued in their fullest vigor and extent.

Whether any or what change may happen in the local situation of the army for the ensuing campaign, or what dispositions in your department may be necessary in consequence, are matters which, for particular reasons, I cannot yet determine. A council will soon be held in which will be decided a general plan of operations for the army.[1] When this is done you shall receive your instructions accordingly. In the mean time you will proceed in the plan already on foot. With great Esteem I am Sir Yr huml Ser

FC (Washington Papers: DLC).
1. See below, 8 May.

From Colonel Alexander Hamilton

[Valley Forge, 7 May 1778. Asks NG to order saddle, bridle, holsters —better than the first set which "was of a coarser kind that would only do for my servant." ALS (MiU-C) 1 p.]

From the Pennsylvania Executive Council

In Council, Lancaster [Pa.]
Sir   May 7, 1778.
The great and repeated complaints which are made by the people whose Waggons have been in the publick service compels us to mention this subject to you. It is said, that when the accounts of these people are settled, they receive only certificates expressing the Sums Due to them instead of their money; this has had a very mischievous effect by rendering this service disagreeable to the people, in consequence of which force becomes necessary to compel them into it, which not only encreases the dislike and sours the minds of the people, but is also attended with a very considerable expence which is a dead loss to the publick.

The earnest desire we have to do every thing which may tend to bring forth the whole strength of this State, in aid of the common cause, induces us to solicit your attention [to] these complaints, from a firm persuasion that you have undertaken the Quarter Master Department with a resolution of removing every just ground of com-

Letter from Alexander Hamilton, 7 May 1778
(Courtesy of William L. Clements Library at the University of Michigan)

plaint, as well as every false pretence which may have been used to countenance the disaffected in their unwillingness to serve the United States.[1]

[THOMAS WHARTON]

Df (PHarH).

1. By the time Wharton's letter arrived at Valley Forge, NG had left on a trip to Fishkill. In his absence, Charles Pettit answered Wharton, readily admitting the justice of the complaints. "We have therefore, with unabated Attention, endeavored to remedy this Mischief, as well for the sake of the People, who are the immediate sufferers, as with a view to facilitate the Publick Service." He went on to say that their endeavours had been successful and that he believed such complaints would not rise again. "It was some time after we came into the Department," he said, "that we obtained our first supply of Cash; we were therefore obliged, for a time, to encounter the Difficulties that Opposed us with the Shattered Remains of Credit." The department now has more ample funds, which, he hopes, will "pay all our Current Contracts and . . . clear off the incumberances which have arisen since our Commencement . . . the 2d of March last." (For background on the use of certificates, see NG et al. to Inhabitants, 28 March, above.)

In the same letter, Pettit requested with NG's blessing that the Pennsylvania Council help to improve the shallow fords in the Schuylkill, so that boats might use the river. (Pettit to Wharton, 16 May 1778, Pa. Archives, 6: 513–14; printed with the letter is a list of the shallows, their distances, and the depth of water at each. As for providing funds, the council sent a discouraging reply on 19 May, ibid., p. 525.

Council of War

In a Council of War held at Head Quarters at Valley Forge the 8th day of May 1778, agreeable to two Resolutions of Congress dated the 18th and 27th of April[1]

Present

His Excellency The Commander in Chief

Major Generals	Gates	Brig: Generals	Knox
	Greene		Du Portail
	Stirling		
	Mifflin		
	De la Fayette		
	De Kalb		
	Armstrong		
	Steuben		

The Commander in Chief informs the Council—

That the enemy's whole force within these States is distributed into three divisions, one at Philadelphia, one at New York and its dependencies, and one at Rhode Island amounting, according to the best estimate he can form, to between sixteen and seventeen thousand rank and file fit for the field, exclusive of horse and Artillery.

Their whole force in Philadelphia, consisting of the flower of their army is about 10,000 rank and file, exclusive of Marines and new levies, fortified by a strong chain of redoubts from Schuylkil to Delaware, with a small detached work at Bilingsport.

At New York, Long Island and Staten Island they have about 4000 rank and file, composed of a few British regiments, some German corps and new levies. The city is secured by shipping in front and on both flanks, and in the rear by Harlem River, by the forts Independence and Washington, and by a country difficult of access.

At Rhode Island they have about 2000, mostly Germans. What fortifications they may have raised for their defence is not particularly known, but they derive their principal security from the insular situation of the post and the protection of their Shipping.

He is not sufficiently acquainted with the general complexion of European intelligence, to be able to form any precise judgment of the reinforcements which the enemy may expect this Campaign, or at what time they will arrive. But from such appearances as have fallen within his view, and supposing that England will be in some measure governed by the rules of prudence, and by a regard to her own honor, interest and safety and to the safety of her possessions abroad, He is led to conjecture they will probably not be very large, nor very early.

The Commander in Chief further informs them—

That the whole of our Continental force hitherto assembled lies in the States of Pensylvania and Delaware and on the North River and amounts to about Fifteen thousand rank and file, fit for the field, besides horse and Artillery.

The main body lies at this post, Valley Forge and in its vicinity, amounting to about 11,800, rank and file, capable of service, comprehending such of the sick present and on command, as might be called into action on any emergency, as per general return herewith submitted dated the 2d instant.

The detachment at Wilmington in Delaware state is about 1400, comprehending a like proportion of sick present and on command as above.

From the best judgment he can form not having had any late returns from that quarter, he imagines the force on the North River at Fish Kill and its dependencies, may be about 1800, rank and file, fit for duty.

With respect to the reinforcements of Continental troops to be hereafter expected, he is destitute of any information, from the different states, on which dependence may be placed; but judging of the future from the past, there will not be more in the field from every quarter, than ab't 20,000 rank and file, fit for duty; unless the favourable events, which have lately taken place, in our political system, should stimulate the states to greater and more successful exertions, than have been heretofore made.[2]

The succours of Militia, which may be occasionally drawn to the aid of the army, will not admit of an exact calculation. Notwithstanding the most pressing applications, a greater number could not be collected at any time in the course of the last campaign to reinforce the Southern army, than between three and four thousand men; and generally there was far short of three thousand. With the Northern army there was about [*left blank*]

What quantity of ordnance, small arms and military stores our magazines will afford for the use of the ensuing campaign, He is unable to decide; but imagines there will not be a sufficiency for any regular siege, if there is for the contingencies of the field.

In regard to supplies of provisions, The Commissary's department has been for some time past in such a defective and disordered state, that no accurate estimate can be formed. The Gentleman lately appointed to the head of it, reports that his prospects are tolerably good, though he cannot with any precision ascertain their extent.[3]

Having stated these particulars for the consideration of the Council, The Commander in Chief requests, that after a full and candid discussion of the matter in council, each member would furnish him with his sentiments in writing on some general plan, which, considering all circumstances ought to be adopted for the operations of the next campaign.[4]

D (Washington Papers: DLC).
1. The 18 April resolution is discussed in a note, Washington to General Officers, 20 April, above. On 27 April, Congress authorized Washington "if he thinks proper" to call in the commander of artillery (Gen. Knox) to the council that it had suggested on the eighteenth. (*JCC*, 10: 397)
2. The camp at Valley Forge had celebrated the alliance with France only two days before.
3. Jeremiah Wadsworth.
4. For the response of the general officers, see document below, 9 May.

From General Peter Muhlenberg

[Valley Forge, 8 May 1778. Needs wagons for his division and huts for new recruits. LS (PHi) 1 p.]

To Jacob Greene

[Valley Forge After 8 May 1778][1]
. . . and the brothers. Have you made a final seperation of the Interests; or have you come to some agreement again?[2] If you seperate business and you, Cousin Griffin and my self carry on trade together I think it will be a folly for you both to live at Coventry as one is full equal to the business by the assistance of a good Clerk.

I shall be for Griffins going abroad [i.e., leaving Coventry] and wish him to prepare himself for it. The interest at Coventry under the best improvement will not produce more than a decent support for two families and it will be a folly to spend the prime of life in such triffleing employments.[3]

I wish to know the State of our Stocks, the number of Vessels we are concern'd in, the amount of our debts due and from us. I think we have been peculiarly unfortunate in Navigation; but I am not for quiting yet. It is a long Lane that has no turn. However this is almost like the Gamesters Hope: Many of the great speculators will be confoundedly taken in in this part of the World. Goods are falling here very fast; but they will rise again by and bye.

I am told there is forty Sail of French Merchantmen Arrivd in Boston. If so Goods will fall with you. A few Weeks hence will be a good time to speculate there but you must wait a little and not too long neither.

Pray how goes on Sullivan among you?[4] Does he give good satisfaction? Does he call himself the second Alexander? He is fond of flattery and if you wish to please him that is the key that will unlock his heart. Praise him highly; and he will do you every favor in his power. I wish you to Court him and Governor [William] Greene also for he will give you a Charactor[5] as you pay your court. Who would not spend a little flattery in Merchants shop where it has such a current coin? My love to all your family and friends. I am dear Sir yours

N GREENE

AL[S] (MWA); one or more pages are missing at beginning; signature is partially destroyed.
1. The earliest date is established by his reference to Gov. William Greene, who took office on 8 May. The letter was probably written not long thereafter, for there is no indication in it of the impending evacuation of Philadelphia or the army's subsequent march across New Jersey.
2. On the division of the brother's interests, see above, Elihue to NG, 12 April.
3. At this time the business at Coventry consisted essentially of the iron works. Their anchor business had been curtailed because of British control of Newport and Narragansett Bay.
4. Sullivan had been commanding the troops in Rhode Island since 17 April.
5. One of Samuel Johnson's definitions of "character" was "a representation of any man as to his personal qualities."

Nathanael Greene et al. to George Washington

Valley Forge May 9th 1778

Having maturely considered the state of facts and representations submitted to us in Council, by His Excellency the Commander in Chief, with a request that "each member, after a full and candid discussion of the matter in council would furnish him with his sentiments on some general plan, which considering all circumstances, ought to be adopted for the operations of the ensuing campaign."[1]

We beg leave to offer it as our opinion, after a free and un- reserved discussion of the subject, that the line of conduct most consistent with sound policy, and best calculated to promote the interest and safety of the United States, is to remain on the defensive and wait events; without attempting any offensive operation of con- sequence, unless the future circumstances of the enemy should afford a fairer opportunity than at present exists, for striking some success- ful blow; in the mean time employing our utmost exertions, to put the army in the most respectable state possible, both with respect to numbers, appointments and discipline, and to establish and fill our magazines with arms, military stores, provisions and necessaries of every kind; so as to be upon a proper footing more effectually to counteract any measures of offence, which may be hereafter adopted by the enemy or to undertake, at a more convenient season, any offensive entreprise, that may be found necessary against them.

This opinion is founded upon the following considerations:

1st   That the only attempt of importance which can be made, in the present situation of the country, the army, and the enemy must be directed against Philadelphia or New York, either of which would be attended with many certain inconveniences, much difficulty and hazard, and if it should fail in the execution, with the most unhappy consequences.

2dly   With respect to Philadelphia, nothing could be attempted against it, with its present force but in the way of blockade, with an army of not less than thirty thousand men. To carry it by storm, would, in all probability be impracticable. Secured in the rear and on both flanks by rivers and by shipping, and its entrance guarded by a strong chain of redoubts and lines of communication, the force it con- tains, would be fully sufficient to repel any number of men we could bring against it, especially as the principal part must, of necessity, consist of Militia. To reduce it by regular approaches would require a number of heavy cannon and a quantity of stores, to the furnishing which we are utterly unequal. It would be a work of infinite labor and expence, which would be rendered abortive by the enemy's vast superiority in Artillery, and every apparatus of war, which would give them a facility, in counterworking all our measures. The plan of reducing it by blockade is, by far, the most eligible; but there is very little prospect of success even in this way. In addition to our Conti- nental force, we should require fifteen or sixteen thousand militia, and those to be engaged for several months. Past experience will not authorise an expectation of obtaining such a body of militia for the time requisite. The letters received by His Excellency from the Governors of Pensylvania and Jersey give no great encouragements from those states; and the other neighbouring states will probably not do more in proportion. There is still less hope of bringing any considerable body of Eastern Militia to act at such a distance from home, and to continue in service the necessary length of time. Neither is the temper of Militia at all suited to the slow progress of a blockade. We could not reasonably expect from them a degree of patience and perseverance equal to the task; and should be in danger of their abandoning us in the most critical moments, and obliging us to relinquish the project with confusion and disgrace. An essential point also in the plan of a Blockade is the possessing ourselves of Bilingsport, in order to interrupt the communication of the River. The works there are now in the hands of the enemy, and if they should reinforce them with a considerable garrison, as they would in all likelihood do, on discovering our preparations for a blockade, which could not be concealed, it would become a very arduous business to dispossess them.

3d   With respect to New York, it must either be taken by storm, or by regular approaches. The former is practicable with a sufficiency of men, though perilous and difficult. The latter is liable to objections similar to those assigned in the case of Philadelphia. For a storm, it will require more men than the States can, at this time, furnish and equip; at least, to give that chance of success which would justify the attempt. The principal part of the troops for this service should be Continental and must be sent from the army here, and their place supplied by militia, to secure the country and our magazines from the entreprises of the enemy in Philadelphia; for it could not be reconciled to any rules of military prudence to diminish the force in this quarter so as to disqualify it for a vigorous and effectual opposition. It will therefore be necessary in aid of the continental forces, here and against New York, to call out a very numerous body of militia, which will be a measure attended with many obvious disadvantages. The insular situation of New York gives it a vast advantage for the purposes of defence. The enemy there may be so protected by their shipping as to be almost unapproachable except by the entrance from the country. By collecting their chief force to that point, assisted by Harlam River, by strong ground and fortifications, they might be able to withstand numbers much superior to their own. To distract their attention by attacking at different places, and endeavouring to throw a body of troops by the help of boats into the city would require a coincidence of circumstances, which could hardly be relied on. If our design should be suspected beforehand, which notwithstanding any stratagems that could be contrived to prevent it, would be very likely to happen, a considerable reinforcement might be sent from Philadelphia with safety; and with the addition of three thousand men, to their present force, and the signal advantages of situation they possess, We could have but little hope of carrying the city.

4thly   The uncertainty of getting so large a body of Militia together, as would be requisite in either case. The difficulty, if not impracticability of assembling them all at one certain period, which, by the way, would be a clear manifestation of our intentions, and engaging them, for a sufficient term of service. The certain expence that would attend calling them out—The inconvenience of drawing such a number of men from the culture of their farms and other occupations of public utility, at so interesting a season[2]—The immense additional consumption and waste of arms, military stores and provisions to which our Arsenals and magazines are very little competent. The impropriety of bestowing that time and attention and exhausting those provisions in the different departments of the army, which ought to be devoted to preparations for a general system of defence on objects of immediate offence the success of which is not a little precarious, appear to us to forbid any attempt, either against Philadelphia or New York, under our present circumstances and with our present prospects.

5th   If the attempt should be made, and it should succeed, the advantages would undoubtedly be great, in one case, decisive. But if it should fail, as is most probable, and in one case almost certain, the consequences would be deplorable. Besides the disgrace and disappointment, it would serve to deject and dishearten the country, give spirit to the enemy, and would have a very ill influence upon our negotiations in Europe. If we hold our own and keep the enemy on the defensive, without effecting any thing more, it will have rather a good than a bad appearance in Europe, and if we do not gain, we shall not at least lose any of our present consequences—But if we make an attempt and fail in it, it will have a tendency to throw us considerably back. A defeat of such magnitude would turn the scale of the whole campaign against us. Probably, at the moment when we shall have tired out the Militia, in a fruitless and unavailing business, the enemy will be reinforced and ready to take the field with collected strength, which we shall have to oppose wholly with our continental troops, unaided by the Militia and dispirited by recent ill-fortune, our magazines unprovided, and our provision exhausted.

6th   By remaining on the defensive we put nothing to the hazard. Our army will increase in number and improve in discipline. Our Arsenals and magazines will be more respectable and more adequate to the exigencies of the service. A large emission of public money will be saved, which will have a negative efficacy in raising its value. We have the chance of events, resulting from the important treaties lately concluded between France and America, which may oblige the enemy to withdraw their force without any further trouble to us. If this does not happen, and they make a vigorous effort the ensuing campaign, which seems to be a necessary alternative, we shall be in a much better situation to give them opposition. We can then rely on the aid and co-operation of the Militia, who having been left in a state of repose to cultivate their lands, and persue their other private avocations and domestic concerns will more cheerfully come to our assistance. Thus circumstanced, we shall have a much fairer prospect of disappointing the future attempts of the enemy and terminating the campaign, to our own honor and advantage. Unanimously agreed to in Council.

HORATIO GATES	THE BARON DE KALB
NATHANAEL GREENE	JOHN ARMSTRONG
STIRLING	DE STEUBEN
THOMAS MIFFLIN	H KNOX
THE MIS. DE LAFAYETTE	THE CHEVALIER DUPORTAIL

Camp at Valley Forge
May 9th 1778

May the 22d 1778

I being from indisposition absent at the time of the above council of War was held, upon a perusal of the contents do subscribe to the unanimous opinion of the Generals who composed it.

CHARLES LEE

DS (Washington Papers: DLC).
1. The quote is inaccurate. Washington had requested in the document above that "each member would furnish him with his sentiments in writing." (Fitzpatrick, GW, 11: 366) In a rare display of unanimity, they chose instead to sign a joint communication.
2. That is, at a season when their interests were so concerned.

To Colonel John Davis

Sir
                                    Camp Valley Forge 9th May 1778
Having had no Return of the officers appointed in the Different Districts in the Quarter Master General's Department, nor any Information how the Districts had been divided and allotted by my Predecessor in office, I was not aware at the Time of giving you an Appointment nor when I wrote to you on the 29th of last Month, of the Inconveniencies that would arise from making your District so extensive, and I am Willing to believe you was not fully apprized of

the extent of Mr Steels former appointment as I immagine if you had you would have mentioned it to me. I find Mr Steel has been for some time past DQMG for the Garrison of Fort Pitt and the counties o Bedford and Westmoreland in Pennsylvania, Washington in Maryland and Berkely in Virginia; and as I received ample recommendation of his Abilities and good Conduct in office, and have not heard any thing directly nor indirectly against him I feel myself bound, both in Regard to him and to the Publick service, to continue him in the Employ at Least in the same Extent he had it formerly: I have therefore given him an Appointment accordingly.[1] This may perhaps be some Disappointment to your late Expectations, tho I am persuaded your District will remain as large both in Extent of Ground and Quantity of Business as you had in Contemplation in the Beginning. I doubt not you will be so far convinced of the Propriety of this [arrangement?] as to be fully satisfied with it. I may at the same Time mention that as the counties allotted to Mr Steel may furnish many Articles not wanted for the Garrison under his care, and he is to purchase no more than will supply those wants, you are still at Liberty to purchase in those Counties any articles that will not interfere with his necessary demands. On the other Hand if he shou'd want any Article not to be found in his District which yours can furnish, he is to apply to you for it, and you will Comply with his request. The Posts on the Communication within your District you will furnish with every thing necessary, and he will do the like in his These Points being settled I have too good an opinion of you both to suppose any Differences can arise between you, and as I presume you both have the good of the Publick in view I would warmly recommend Harmony and a mutual Intercourse of good offices in the Course of the Business, which will tend much to the Publick Service as well as to your Ease and Convenience.[2] Any Purchase you may have made within Mr Steels District before this reached you will be considered as properly made: and any Assistants you may have appointed there will most probably be confirmed by him, they becoming answerable to him in Future.

Major Blodget whom I dispatched to Congress about ten Days since on purpose to solicit a farther supply of Cash is still waiting upon them on that Business only, and I daily expect to receive Advice of a warrant on the Treasury, out of which you shall receive a due Portion. I am, Sir, you most obed't humble Servant

NATH GREENE

LS (Davis Papers: DLC).
    1. Davis's appointment is printed above, 23 March. For Archibald Steel's appointment, see above, Hand to NG, 22 April, and below, NG to Steel, 22 May. The fou

counties that were removed from Davis's jurisdiction amounted in area to half his district, but they were thinly populated.

2. NG was overly optimistic; Davis found a number of occasions to complain about Steel. In part this was because Steel's appointment did not specify the four counties listed above and in part because of Steel's inefficiency. There may also have been personal reasons for the lack of harmony.

From Colonel James Abeel

Sir

Reading [Pa.][1] 10 May 1778

I have delivered Colo Morgan your Letter and he seems much pleased with my Appointment as it will relieve him of a great deal of Trouble and I can assist and be of service to him in many Respects.[2] You may be fully assured that I will take every Step in my Power that will contribute to the Interest of the Department and pay strict attention to my Duty.

I have also delivered Mr [Anthony] Butler your Letter. He is to deliver me his Stores tomorrow. I shall the moment I have his Return send you a Copy of it, that you may know what Stores are on hand. Colo Morgan has a Number of Lame Horses on hand which will never be fit for Service. If he was ordered to dispose of them it wou'd save the Continent a vast expence as they destroy a great deal of Forrage.

Mr Butler says he has contracted with Mr Sam'l Ogden for 8000 Camp Kettles at four Dollars each, that he has paid Mr Ogden for about 2000. The rest he will relinquish to your Department. Wou'd it not be best the remainder shou'd go thro' my hands as it will save you the Commission? He has also Contracted for a Number of Waggons on which he has advanced a Sum of Money. The remainder he will do with as with the Kettles. A great Number of Stores of every kind are here but scattered about the whole Place and lyable to being Pilfered. Colo Morgan thinks it best to have a proper Store built here and to have all collected. This will enable me to do my Duty with less expence to the Publick. Matterials are Plenty at this Place belonging to the Publick. Cou'd a few of Bruens or the other Artificers be spared they cou'd be of great service here. Many are Idle in Camp or at least do little.

I called upon Mr Mitchell and shewed him my Instructions.[3] I told him it wou'd be necessary, I shou'd have a Return of what stores were on hand and what were purchased that I might know from whence to draw my Supply's and be enabled to Comply with your Instructions. I recieved this Answer that he wou'd recieve nor pay attention to no Orders but what came from Genl Green or his assistants. I shou'd therefore be glad you wou'd write to the Several Deputys to make me monthly Returns that I may be enable to make out a Genl Return as often as required. Mr Mitchell had a Cask of Horse Shoes that he had got made which are by no means fit for the Horses, being Slightly made and too Slender. I told him of the Fault in a genteel Manner at the same time cautioned him to pay the Strictest attention to the manufacturers employed or they wou'd take every advantage in their Power of him. This I thought no crime but he seemed to be offended altho he cou'd easily know it was my Duty to point out any Defect that it might be remedied soon as possible.

Colo Morgan is very attentive to his duty and I am well convinced I shall be happy with him in every Respect.

The Principal Stores at Lebanon are Spades, Shovels and Axes. The Deputy from thence is gone to Camp with his Return, but for fear he shou'd not get there in time I have on the other side made a minute of them. I fear they have blended the two Departments together, Flowers's[4] and the Q M Genl as I am well assured more of our Stores have been sent to that place. However soon as I can get Matters in Order at this Place I shall proceed thither and rectify any mistakes that may have happened.

The Tents Ordered will be sent immediately. I am With Respect Sr Your most Hble Servt

LB (Abeel Papers: DLC).
1. Abeel had just set up headquarters at Reading, Berks County, located on the Schuylkill, where he built up sizable stores in the next month. (See Council of War, 17 June, below.) When the river was high, as it was in late spring, supplies could be boated down to Valley Forge.
2. Jacob Morgan, Jr., was deputy quartermaster in Reading.
3. John Mitchell, a Philadelphia merchant before the war, had been a colonel of militia, commissary of Pennsylvania artillery troops, and mustermaster of the Pennsylvania navy in 1776. (*Pa. Col. Records*, 10: 504, 510, 522) NG appointed him a deputy quartermaster in April 1778. After the British left Philadelphia in June 1778, Mitchell was stationed there, often serving as liaison between Congress and NG or his assistants.

In January 1779 Mitchell became inadvertently embroiled with the Pennsylvania Executive Council over their charges that Benedict Arnold had used army wagons for personal business. (See below, NG to Joseph Reed, 31 January 1779.) Although NG and Pettit were sometimes critical of him (Pettit to NG, 24 September 1779, below), they supported him against strenuous efforts of the Executive Council to remove him, and Mitchell stayed on in the department until 1780. Stationed mostly in Philadelphia, he and his wife entertained many people, including the Greenes and the Washingtons. Over the years, in fact, he did many personal favors for Washington. According to Johnson, *Greene*, 1: 185n, "Poor Mitchell who expended £ 800 in pastry at one entertainment, was actually thought sufficiently dignified by his munificence to be made the subject of a formal impeachment by a great state." Johnson does not give the outcome or his source.
4. Benjamin Flower, commissary general of military stores, was not under NG.

From Colonel James Abeel

Sir

Reading [Pa.] 12th May 1778

I wrote you two days ago since which I have begun to receive the Stores from Mr Butler among which are a large Number of Frows, Wedges, Picks, Shovels, and spades which I shall send on to Lebanon, as they will not be wanted. I am extremely sorry to find Mr Butlers Conduct not so Agreeable as I Expected.[1] He dont seem disposed to Assist me in any respect, and is very dilatary in delivering up the Stores, besides very disobliging Claiming every Desk, Table, Office &ca as his own private property. He ordered a New Horsemans Tent to be reserved for him but as I know it was Continental Property I have taken it away from his Clerk. In short they have so influenced those under them formerly that they will Afford me no Assistance at all. However I will do without him.

It is Scandelous to see the waste that has been made of Public Property. Col Morgan informs me that a large Number of Tents have been suffered to rot for want of proper care. This Day I found laying in a Store which was open between Seventy and Eighty pr [pair] of Duck and four Horsemans Tents which has been exposed a long time. God knows how much has been Pilfer'd. Also in another place between 60 and 70 Shirts fit for the Waggoners. In short no attention seems to have been paid to the Publicks Interest by any Person in this Department. I have employed hands in making and repairing such utensils as may be wanted. The old Tents are repairing and New ones making, Portmantuas, Veleces &ca. No Tent Poles went down with the Tents sent yesterday, but as a Number of Tent Poles are at Potts Grove I have desired Mr Mitchell to send them to Camp. As Nails and Halters were much wanted I have ordered down a Cask of Each to Camp. If paper is wanted I can send you plenty from this place. I have a few Iron Chains for Traces which shall be sent to Camp soon as Waggons can be got.

The Stores are very much scattered about this place in Cellers where they will soon receive damage if suffered to lay, but this I will prevent by removing them. I shou'd be glad to have a few of the Carpenters from Camp at this place as many must have little to do and I have employment Enough for them here. A Number of Carabines, Muskets and Bayonets are at this place which I shall send to Lebanon to be repaired.[2] I shall in a short time point out to you many abuses that will be in your Power to Remedy.

Col [Jacob, Jr.] Morgan affords me all the assistance in his Power and seems disposed to assist me in every respect. He is very Industrious. I herewith send a large Punch Bowl I purchased by desire of Mrs Green for his Excellency which I wish safe to hand. I begin to

want money very much. If any is Arrived please to send me some
soon as possible as without little can be done. You may be assur'd I
will get all the Raw materials manufactured but the Artificers will
want to be punctually paid. Rest assur'd Sir every Step in my Power
shall be taken for the good of the Publick and beleive me to be Sir
your friend and Hble Servt

JA'S ABEEL

LB (Abeel Papers: DLC).
    1. On Anthony Butler, see note, NG to Laurens, 26 March, above.
    2. The quartermaster department was not normally responsible for weapons and
ammunition, but a conscientious deputy, such as Abeel, stepped in if there was no one
else to do it.

Colonel James Abeel to Unnamed Deputy Quartermaster

[Reading, Pa., 14 May 1778. He is directed by NG to ask for monthly
returns. Needs no more iron or entrenching tools, but saddles, harness, etc. are wanted. LB (Abeel Papers: DLC) 1 p.]

To General Horatio Gates

[Fishkill, N.Y., 15 May 1778. Sorry Col. Hughes will not continue
as deputy at Fishkill;[1] has left it in Hay's hands; asks for Gate'
regulations on quartermaster department at Albany. LS (NHi) 1 p.]

    1. NG may have gone to Fishkill as a consequence of Col. Hugh Hughes's resigna-
tion. (See note, Hughes to NG, 3 May, above.)

Colonel Robert L. Hooper, Jr., to Major William Hart

[Easton, Pa., 15 May 1778. Is directed by NG to receive all horses h
has bought for the cavalry by order of Pa. Council. ALS (RG 9
WRMS, Ms 034983: DNA) 1 p.]

To Nehemiah Hubbard

[Fishkill, N.Y., 15 May 1778. Treasury should send him sixty thousand
dollars soon; asks him to expedite purchase of horses for the artillery
at Farmington.[1] (Typescript of original letter furnished by Francis
Brooks, East Weymouth, Mass., 1976) 1 p.]

    1. Hubbard did not respond to this request until 27 June, below.

Colonel James Abeel to Moore Furman

[Reading, Pa., 16 May 1778. Is directed by NG to collect returns; needs saddlery and paper—especially orderly books. Expects to have magazine for storage at Easton. ALS (Nj) 1 p.]

To Elihue Greene

Dear Sir   Fish Kill [N.Y.] May the 16 1778
    I receivd a Letter from you a few days since, desireing to know why I neglected writeing you.[1] Not from any particular disregard, I can assure you. I have generally kept up a correspond[ence] with brother Jacob and sometimes with brother Kitt [Christopher] which I consider'd as family Letters as I supposed they circulated through the whole, and therefore it was unnecessary to write to every individual. I never wrote but one Letter, and that was to brother Jacob, but what I wrote as much for one as another. Several little incidents occurd about that time which led me to conclude the brothers began to think me a burden to the family and I appeal to your candour whether there has not been something of this sort happend among you. I dont wish to be dependant upon anybody, but I could hardly have expected the least discontent among the brothers for my belonging to the Company considering my situation.[2]
    If I have done injustice to the intentions of the brothers or wounded their feelings by ill grounded jealoseis I am sorry for it. I thought from the general complexion of matters it was necessary for me to enquire into the State of matters. I must confess my apprehensions had not the most permanent foundation but a train of incidents awakened a degree of suspicion. How far it was well or ill grounded you can best judge.
    The love and harmony that has always subsisted among us has always been one of the most pleasing circumstances of my life. I hope no little triffleing incident will produce such a convulsion as will estrange us from each other. If a seperation of interest is necessary I am content; when a family gets too extended it cannot preserve its harmony; the members has so many different views, wishes, and designs that it is almost morally impossible to harmonize together. When this gets to be the state of things a seperation becomes necessary. You who are on the ground are the proper judges and I hope you will act accordingly.
    Give my best respects to Mrs Greene[3] and the rest of the family and believe me to be with sincere regard your most obedient Humble Servt

NATH GREENE

ALS (MWA).
1. See above, Elihue to NG, 12 April.
2. See NG to Christopher, 22 April, above.
3. Their stepmother.

From Henry Laurens, President of the Continental Congress

[York, Pa., 16 May 1778. Encloses Act of Congress and extract of letter from Gov. Livingston of New Jersey on reimbursing New Jersey for horses purchased by Committee at Camp.[1] LB (PCC, Item 13: DNA) 1 p.]

1. See JCC, 11: 505.

From George Washington

Dr Sir   Head Quarters [Valley Forge] 16th May 1778
From many concurrent circumstances it appears that the enemy are preparing to evacuate Philadelphia, whether their design is to withdraw altogether from the Continent or to concenter their forces at New York cannot be ascertained, in case the latter should be the case it will be proper to have provision of forage made on the road to the No [Hudson] River for such body of troops as may be ordered to march from hence in consequence.
If you could employ an intelligent confidential person to go into New York and inform you of what passes there, it would be of infinite use in the present conjuncture as any similar preparations on the part of the enemy in that place would evince their intention of generally abandoning the Territories of the United States.[1] I am with great respect

Df (Washington Papers: DLC).
1. It is doubtful that NG received this letter, since he left Fishkill the next day for Morristown, where Washington's letter of 17 May (below) reached him.

From George Washington

Sir   Head Quarters [Valley Forge] 17th May 1778
Every piece of intelligence from Philadelphia makes me think it more and more probable that the Enemy are preparing to evacuate it.[1] Whether they intend to leave the Continent, or only go to some other part of it, must be uncertain. There are some reasons that induce a suspicion they may intend for New York. In any case it is absolutely necessary we should be ready for an instant movement of

the army. I have therefore to request you will strain every nerve to prepare without delay the necessary provisions in your department for that purpose. The most pressing and immediate object of your attention will be the procuring a large number of Waggons for transporting baggage provisions &c, and some good horses for the artillery. You will call upon this State and use every other mean[s] in your power for a supply.

The scarcity of forage will not allow any number of horses being brought into Camp, but it is essential the horses and Waggons should be collected at different places in the vicinity of camp, where they can be furnished with forage and drawn expeditiously to the army. Tents should also be provided and hastened forward with all possible speed; not only with a view to a general movement, but also on account of the advancing hot season, from which we already begin to experience very unhappy effects, and have reason to apprehend worse, if we keep the men much longer in huts. We probably have no time to lose, and I shall rely upon your exertions that every thing will be done on your part to enable us to be prepared for events. Let me know what prospects you have, and when you think you will have it in your power to answer the present exigency. I am &c

GR WN

P s   As we may have to go to the No[rth] River, magazines of forage should immediately be provided on the different routs, particularly those by way of Coryels, Morris Town &c, and Trenton, Boundbrook, Westfield &c; smaller ones should be formed on the road by Howels Ferry, Goshen &c. You will also immediately have the boats on the Delaware inspected and got ready in all respects to transport the army across. Those which want it must be repaired.

Df (Washington Papers: DLC).
    1. NG received this letter at Morristown on his way back from Fishkill, N.Y. (See below, his letter to Gates, 19 May.) On the British evacuation of Philadelphia, see below, Council of War, 17 June.

To General Horatio Gates

[Morristown, N.J., 19 May 1778. Summarizes Washington's letter of 17 May, above. Asks him to advance money to Col. Udny Hay (at Fishkill)[1] since "he is a stranger where he is, and the credit of the department at a low ebb, oweing to bad payment heretofore." ALS (NHi) 1 p.]

    1. Gates had arrived at Fishkill only the week before to take command of the Highland-Hudson area.

Colonel James Abeel to Colonel George Ross[1]

[Reading, Pa., 19 May 1778. Is directed by NG to collect returns. Needs "Iron Traces, Waggon Harness, Knapsacks, Saddles and Bridles, Wooden Pails, Tar Potts, and Forage Bags"; also "500 Blank Orderly Books Bound with Paste Board cont'g a Quire of Paper." LB (Abeel Papers: DLC) 1 p.]

1. Ross was a deputy quartermaster at Lancaster, Pa.

To Colonel Jeremiah Wadsworth[1]

Dear Sir   Morris Town [N.J.] May 19th, 1778

Mr Lott a Gentleman of this place purchased a small quantity of Rum and Salt at Boston, which he cannot get on, owing to the State Laws. I shall be much oblige to you to give him such a pass, that his property may come forward.[2] He wants the Salt for his family's use. Part of the spirits he proposes for Sale.

Mr Lotts character for generosity and hospitallity is too well known to say any thing upon the subject. I am under particular obligations to him; and shall esteem my self so to you, if youl be kind enough to enable him to get forward his property. The propriety and necessary forms you are the best judge off; and therefore submit the matter to your opinion and direction. I am Sir with sincere regard your most Obedient Humble Servt

NATH GREENE

ALS (CtHi).
1. Jeremiah Wadsworth (1743–1804), the new commissary general, was to become one of NG's closest friends and associates. He was born in Hartford, Conn., the son of the Rev. Daniel Wadsworth and was, through his mother, a grandson of Gov. Joseph Talcott. Only four years old when his father died, he was raised under the influence of his mother's brother, Matthew Talcott, a merchant and ship owner. Eschewing an education at Yale, Wadsworth went to sea at eighteen and within ten years was a successful ship captain and merchant in the West Indies trade.
In 1774 he became a commissary in the Connecticut militia through the influence of his uncle Matthew, a legislator and colonel of militia. Joseph Trumbull appointed him as one of his continental commissaries in 1775. Trumbull, discovering the young man was a resourceful finder of scarce supplies and an excellent administrator, advanced him to commissary general of the Eastern Department in 1776. When Trumbull resigned in August 1777 Wadsworth followed him, but he remained a deputy quartermaster, a post he had held also for some time. A month after NG became quartermaster general, the Committee at Camp induced Wadsworth to become commissary general—to be paid one half percent commission.
Washington praised him as "indefatigable in his exertions to provide for the Army." (Fitzpatrick, GW, 12: 277) Under Wadsworth, the army continued to be well fed through 1779, although many people blamed him (as they did Greene) for the exhorbitant prices brought about by inflation. Wadsworth was also criticized for keeping on dishonest agents, although in an unpublished biography, Chester McArthur Destler has shown that much of the criticism was politically motivated, that Wadsworth, in fact, was resolute in dismissing such agents—including one that involved him in a conflict of interest.

NG and Wadsworth were attracted to each other by the criticism directed at them. When Greene sought areas in which to invest the commissions he collected, Wadsworth invited him to become a secret partner (with him) in Barnabas Deane & Co. They remained partners until the war's end.

In January 1780 to Washington's dismay Wadsworth resigned as commissary general. Thenceforth he engaged in a great variety of enterprises, including a partnership with John Carter that supplied the French army. At the end of the war he was a wealthy man. Weathering the depression years, he invested in commerce, shipping, manufacturing, banks and insurance. A strong supporter of the new constitution, he was elected in 1788 to Congress as a Federalist. In his last years he served in the Connecticut Council. He was also a patron of the arts and gentleman farmer with a keen interest in scientific agriculture. As an executor of NG's estate, Wadsworth advanced money to Catharine Greene and her children—a considerable part of which he never recovered. (DAB) Destler's unpublished biography is a detailed, balanced account of Wadsworth's life.

2. The "State Laws" were the laws on embargoes; see above, note, NG to Unknown Person, 20 May 1777. On NG's use of the military waiver on embargoes for friends and relatives, see below, note, Griffin Greene to NG, 24 May 1778.

Colonel James Abeel to Colonel John Davis

[Reading, Pa., 20 May 1778. Letter is similar to one to George Ross, abstracted above, 19 May; he adds "For Gods sake dont let any Axes be made unless it be of good Steel and warranted." LB (Abeel Papers: DLC) 1 p.]

To Moore Furman[1]

Sir [Morristown, N.J.] May the 20th 1778
I came here in hopes to have had the pleasure of seeing you; but unfortunately you was gone. Mr. Pettit write[s] me[2] that he has inform'd you of the Enemies preparation for evacuating Philadelp and of the probability of our armies marching through New Jersey. I have not heard from the General particularly upon the Rout he designs to march; but I expect it will be by Easton, Sherrards and Coryells. The two divisions that march by Sherrards and Coryells ferries will go through your district in New Jersey, and will require forage at 15 miles stages. That division that comes by the way of Sherrads will march by Morris Town; that by Coryells, by way of Boundbrook, Equacananck, Tappan and so to Kings Ferry. But you shall be more particularly instructed upon this head in a few days. In the meantime let there be forage and Waggons engagd upon these Routs without depositing it at any particular place. It will be best to send some good trusty persons to see that your orders are faithfully complyed with—a disappoint[ment] will be attended with the worst of consequences.

You will compleat your purchases as heretofore instructed as fast as possible, for I am really afraid all our exertions will fall far short of supplying the wants of the Army. On your return you will make out a summary account of what we are to expect from you.

I shall write you immediately on my return to Camp if any change or alteration will be necessary. Spare neither pains or expence to put everything in the best situation and forweardness the condition and resources of the Country will admit off.

A free conversation upon the business of your department might have been beneficial to us both; but you must conduct matters as circumstances renders necessary, without waiting for particular instructions. I am Sir with regard your most obedient Humb Sert

NATH GREENE

An appointment will be wanted at Pompton, now in your district, formerly in Hughes, at the North River. For[a]ge will be wanted there too.

ALS (Nj).
1. Moore Furman (1728–1808), deputy quartermaster for New Jersey, had undoubtedly come to NG's attention through his assistant, Charles Pettit, the stepbrother of Furman. (Furman's father, Jonathan, had married the widow of John Pettit.) As a young man, he held several public offices in Trenton and was a partner in a mercantile firm with Andrew Reed, the father of Joseph Reed. In 1772 he moved to Philadelphia, where he joined in forming the importing firm of Coxe, Furman & Coxe with William Coxe, the mayor of the city, and his more famous son, Tench. At the age of forty-seven, Furman was named captain of a battalion in the Philadelphia Associators but left the unit the following year and moved to Pittstown, N.J., where he built a village and established several businesses, including a nail factory and flour mill. His voluminous correspondence with NG in this and the following volume reveals him as a dependable, resourceful deputy. He resigned from the quartermaster department in 1780 when NG left. After the war he was a mayor of Trenton and a successful investor in real estate. (Furman, *Letters*, pp. vii–xi)
2. Pettit's letter to NG not found.

From Colonel James Abeel

Reading [Pa.] 20th May 1778

By the Bearer you will receive 3 hogsheads Containing Twelve Complete Setts of Harness. Those harness are fetched from a Place 7 miles below this so that I cannot inclose you a Receipt for them but will be sent from the manufacturer. I shall send you some more Tent Poles and a Load of Cutting Boxes which please to have Examined as they were contracted for by Mr Butler but he has paid very little attention to see the work well done. I mention this because I think it an impossition on the Public as a Number that Colo Morgan has contracted for came much cheaper and worth double the Sum Butlers are. There is about 60 more here of Butlers all of the same kind. Shall they be ordered on or Shall I receive them and keep them untill wanted? Herewith you will receive four Dozen of Orderly Books, more are making and shall be sent on soon as possible. I am in haste Your most Hbl Servt

JAS ABEEL

I coud send you 9 New Cover'd Waggons but cannot get drivers for them. Cant a few be drawn from the army? The scarecity of Waggons here is a great hinderance to the Service.

LB (Abeel Papers: DLC).

From Timothy Matlack, Secretary of the Pennsylvania Council[1]

[Lancaster, Pa., 20 May 1778. Council wishes him to know that due to lack of forage, horses for light cavalry cannot be cared for properly in Lancaster. ADfS (PHarH) 1 p.]

1. Matlack (1734?–1829) had been secretary of the Executive Council since March 1777 and continued in the office until the end of the war.

Colonel Udny Hay to Assistant Deputy Quartermaster Pynchon at Springfield[1]

[Fishkill, N.Y., 21 May 1778. NG has approved Hay's proposal for building three scows and batteau for transporting horses and he orders it "be put in Execution Immediately." Cy (PPAmP) 1 p.]

1. The state was not identified, but it was Springfield, Mass.

Colonel James Abeel to the Quartermaster General at Yorktown, Pa.[1]

[Reading, Pa., 21 May 1778. Almost identical to Abeel to Ross, 19 May, above. LB (Abeel Papers: DLC). 1 p.]

1. This was probably intended for John Mitchell, who was normally stationed where Congress sat.

To Colonel Archibald Steel

[Valley Forge, 22 May 1778. Appointment as deputy quartermaster general[1] "for the Garrison of Fort Pitt on the Ohio, and the neigh-boring Country west of the Allogana (Allegheny) mountains" and "neighboring Counties in Virginia." Otherwise the wording is es-sentially the same as the appointment of John Davis, 23 March, above. DS (PWcHi) 1 p.]

1. NG wrote John Davis on 9 May, above, that Steel had already been appointed, and he specified four counties in Steel's district. That appointment was never sent. It is not clear why the document above omitted the specific areas enumerated in the letter to Davis. Steel's appointment is discussed in note, Hand to NG, 22 April, above. See also NG to John Davis, 9 May, above.

Oath of Allegiance

23d May 1778

I *Nathanael Greene* do acknowledge the UNITED STATES of AMERICA, to be Free, Independent and Sovereign States, and declare that the people thereof owe no allegiance or obedience to George the Third, King of Great-Britain; and I renounce, refuse and abjure any allegiance or obedience to him; and I do *Swear* that I will to the utmost of my power, support, maintain and defend the said United States, against the said King George the Third, his heirs and successors and his and their abettors, assistants and adherents, and will serve the said United States in the office of *Major General* which I now hold with fidelity, according to the best of my skill and understanding. [1]

NATH GREENE

Sworn before me the 23d May 1778

GO: WASHINGTON

DS (RG 93, WRMS: DNA).
1. On 3 Feb. 1778 Congress had resolved to require oaths of allegiance by army and navy officers and all persons holding civil office in order to "prevent persons disaffected to the interests of the United States from being employed." In addition, those who had the "disposal of public money" or were "entrusted with the charge or distribution of public stores" were to take a performance oath as illustrated in the following document that NG signed as quartermaster. (*JCC*, 10: 114–18) But Washington decided in early February, as he later told Laurens, that there were "strong reasons which made it expedient to defer the matter." (Fitzpatrick, *GW*, 11: 332) A principal reason was the discontent of the officers with Congress's failure to establish the army upon a permanent footing, especially in the matter of half pay for life.
On 27 April, Laurens, goaded by Congress, requested Washington to "immediately require all . . . officers to comply." He softened the harsh request with the news that "Congress had proceeded so far last Night as Resolving that one half the present Pay be continued during Life without exceptions," although Laurens was forced to admit that the matter was "subject to further discussion." (Burnett, *Letters*, 3: 190–91). Indeed it was—for many years, as noted in NG to McDougall, 25 January, above. Washington agreed to comply, not because he believed Congress would take any immediate action, but because he could not stall any longer. He transmitted the request in his general orders of 7 May (Fitzpatrick, *GW*, 11: 360–63) Most officers, though equally cynical about any forthcoming action on half pay, reluctantly signed the oath after some weeks. Perhaps the change in attitudes had taken place simply because spring had come to the Schuylkill.

Oath of Office for Quarter Master General

[Valley Forge] 23d of May 1778

I *Nathanael Greene* do *swear* that I will faithfully, truly and impartially execute the office of *Quarter Master General* to which I am appointed, and render a true account, when thereunto required, of all public monies by me received or expended, and of all stores or other effects to me intrusted, which belong to the UNITED STATES, and will, in all

I *Nathanael Greene* 4
do acknowledge the UNITED STATES of AME-
RICA, to be Free, Independent and Sovereign States, and
declare that the people thereof owe no allegiance or obedience to George the Third, King of Great-Britain; and I renounce, refuse and abjure any allegiance or obedience to him;
and I do *swear*. that I will to the utmoft of
my power, fupport, maintain and defend the faid United
States, againft the faid King George the Third. his heirs and
fucceffors and his and their abettors, affiftants and adherents,
and will ferve the faid United States in the office of *Major
General.* which I now hold with fidelity,
according to the beft of my fkill and underftanding.

Sworn before me *Noth Greene Maj General*
the 23 May 1778.
G. Washington

I *Nathanael Greene* 3
do *swear*. that I will faithfully, truly and impartially execute the office of *Quarter Master
General* to which I am appointed, and render a true
account, when thereunto required, of all public monies by
me received or expended, and of all ftores or other effects to
me intrufted, which belong to the UNITED STATES,
and will, in all refpects, difcharge the truft repofed in me
with juftice and integrity, to the beft of my fkill and underftanding.

Sworn before me *Nathanael Greene QMG*
the 23 of May 1778
G. Washington

Oaths of Allegiance, 23 May 1778
(Courtesy of U.S. National Archives, Washington, D.C.)

respects, discharge the trust reposed in me with justice and integrity, to the best of my skill and understanding.[1]

NATHANAEL GREENE

Sworn before me the 23d of May 1778

GO: WASHINGTON

DS (RG 93, WRMS: DNA).
    1. See note at Oath of Allegiance, above.

From Colonel James Abeel

[Reading, Pa., 23 May 1778. Has sent good axes; horse shoes and "Taylors Tools such as Shears, Geese, Thimbles, 5000 needles and some bodkins." The bearer brings "a pr Shears to Cut money with."[1] LB (Abeel Papers: DLC) 1 p.]

1. Currency was printed in sheets; the individual denominations were then to be signed and cut apart. The treasurer had long since given up signing the endless chits, turning the task over to others designated by the Treasury Board. As the presses speeded up in the following months, the board even authorized low-paid boys to sign them.

From Colonel James Abeel

[Reading, Pa., 23 May 1778. Sending but six dozen orderly books; only "one Book Binder in this Place and he a very old man." LB (Abeel Papers: DLC) 1 p.]

From Colonel James Abeel

Sir   Reading [Pa.] 24th May 1778
    Inclos'd you have Mathew Cochs Rec't for Sundry Horsemens and common Tents which are all that are ready at present. I rec'd a parcell of old Tents from Mr Weise out of which 4/5 will only answer for making paper. The Remainder shall be repaired soon as possible and sent on. Mr Weise mentioned his being in want of Harness. I have likewise sent a parcell down which is all that we have on hand. As so large a Number of horses have gone on within thes few Day's I was afraid you wou'd fall short of Horse Shoes. I have therefore sent you 6 Boxes. A Number more can be sent on if wanted.
    As the Public is at a most heavy expence by employing Artificers in different Parts of this department, it wou'd be a very great saving if Blacksmiths, Wheelrights, or Saddlers cou'd be taken out of the different Reg'ts and sent here to work. Likewise Carpenters. I cou'd

give them Constant employment and save the States a great Expence that they are now at by paying a most Extravagant price f[or] every article they have made.[1] I shou'd be much obliged to Mr Pettit if there are any Letters for me in his office he wou'd deliver them to the Bearer or send them forward to me. I am in hast Sir

LB (Abeel Papers: DLC).
1. If NG responded to this sensible suggestion, it has not been found. The impending British move out of Philadelphia probably sidetracked it.

From Griffin Greene[1]

Dear Sir
                                                    Coventry [R.I.] May 24, 1778
    I have been down at Boston, in order to compleat the Invoice sent to Brother Jacob. I find that Col Chace, D.Q.Master General, of that department has received Orders from the Board of War, to purchase Duck for 4000 Tents, and he is determined to have it at all events if it is to be found, and that he may be sure to have all that is for Market he offers higher than has been given for some time past. He is an illnatured crooked Man. I heard him say that he has authority superior to you, that the Board of War had a right to direct you and he was directed by them. How far this may be true I cannot tel but it is conterary to reason to suppose that a Deputy should have a superior right to him that Deputised him. I find He is disagreeable to many, and Mr Andrews says it will be agreeable to General Heath, to have an other in his place.[2]
    I have reason to think Mr Andrews would be willing to take the place provided he could appoint him an assistant to do part of the business, and to pay him out of what is allowed by the Congress. Mr Andrews dont desire to have any thing to do in that Department if it is in your powar to prevent the business from clashing in the manner it does by his receiving orders from the Board of War. Pray point out how far we have a right to call goods out of the Hands of the Merein [Marine] Board or the Continental Agents for the supplying your Department, And I must also beg you to inform Col. Chase if he is continued what his duty is and let us know his limmits, and ours that the publick may not be injured by our interfearing one with the other.
    We are a going to undertake to make a little Mony by the way of speculation and want you to give us a lift to help us to git our goods through the States of Connecticut, York and Jersey, something to secure us against the Stamp act or State Bills or Imbargoes. Cousen Charles [Ward] is a going to joine in this matter and such assistance as you can give will be greatefully acknoledge by us. General Mifflin has

made a good sum in this way by gitting goods a long at the same time for Private use that publick goods ware brought forward. I don't mean at publick expence but to let all go under one head to avoid impositions.[3] I am a going to Boston to purchase Goods for the above plan and shall forward them to Fairfield whare Charles is to meet them when he returns from you and will then proceed according to your advice. I observe you think Spirits will be a good article. I am of your sentiment and we have concluded to make up our Cargo mostly of that kind of Goods. Spirits may be had for 6 Dollars per Gallon at Boston. If you approve the plan and the price will admit we will have an other fraight at Fairfield by the time Charles can return after his selling the first Cargo.

I must intreat of you to let us know what we shall do respecting purchassing the remaining Duck if Chase should get the 4000 Tents according to the orders to him from the Board of War.

In your Letter by Major [Samuel, Jr.] Ward you said you liked my plan. I suppose it is that plan for establishing a Store hear for Waggons and all kinds of Iron Work. If you have any business in this way or any other let us have the refusal, I mean any you can consistant with your honor.[4] Little George is well, Patty is better and I am in hopes will be well again soon if Molly can be prevailed upon to let her be exercised ennough. Mrs Greene is much obliged to you for your thoughtfullness of her. She desires her compliments to you.

So with beging your patience to find out my meaning I conclude With Sincere regard yr most obedient Humble Ser

GRIFFIN GREENE

P. S. Sir, Pray put it out of the Powar of Col Chace to perplex us in the way he does by raising the price of goods. If he is not stoped and we purchace it will rais the price of goods Cent per Cent [100%]. Sir, their has a Cargo of Heard Ware of all kinds just arived. If you are in want of Tin or any thing Else you can have it.

G.G.

ALS (MiU-C).
1. Cousin Griffin was writing as a member of Jacob Greene & Company, which was serving as an agent for the quartermaster department. (See above, Jacob Greene, to NG, 12 April.)
2. On Andrews and Chase, see above, NG to Heath, end of March. NG passed along Griffin's strictures on Thomas Chase in a letter to the Board of War, 27 May, below.
3. Military goods were allowed to cross state borders without impositions. Whether NG acceded to Griffin's request is not recorded, but he had asked Jeremiah Wadsworth to do the same for his friend Abraham Lott. (See above, 19 May.) Although the practice was common among military officers, it was certainly against the spirit, if not the letter, of various state laws. As for Mifflin's practices, Griffin was repeating rumors, not speaking from first-hand knowledge.

In your Letter by Maj.r Ward you said you
liked my plan and I suppose it is that plan
for establishing a Store hear for Waggons
and all kinds of Iron Work if you have any
business in this way or any other let us have
the refusial, I mean any you can comply with
with your honor — Little George is well, Patty
is better & I am in hopes will be well again
soon if Molly can be prevailed upon to let
her be excused amongst — Mrs Greene is
much obliged to you for your thoughtfullness of
her, she desires her compliments to you.
So with begging your patience to fine out my meaning I conclude

         With Sincear regard so

          most obedient Humble Ser.t

            Griffin Greene

P.S. Sir Pray put it out of the
Powar of Col Chace to perplex us
in the way he does by raising
the price of goods if he is not
Stopd & we purchase it will
raise the price of goods Cent
p.r Cent

Sir their has a Cargo of Heard
Ware of all kends just arived if
you are in want of Tin or any thing
Elce you can have it. G. G.

Letter from Griffin Greene, 24 May 1778
(Courtesy of William L. Clements Library at the University of Michigan)

4. As far as the correspondence reveals, NG's family never asked anything of him that he considered inconsistent with his honor. But how was he to define that standard and how was he to measure himself against it? If the family sold goods to the quartermaster department at no more than the going price, NG could be accused of nepotism (a common enough practice during the war), but not of unethical behavior. There is no evidence that Jacob or Griffin did sell goods at more than the going rate, either for the company's profit or for the benefit of NG and his assistants, whose commissions increased with the price of goods. There is contrary evidence, in fact, that Jacob Greene, at least, was usually a careful purchaser of goods for the department. Granted that such standards of ethics were met, there has still been criticism of NG as quartermaster for purchasing from a family concern in which he had a share, albeit a share that brought him small returns. It is not entirely clear whether he considered this consistent with his honor at all times, although many people at the time would have considered it so. On NG's partnership with Jacob and Griffin, see his letter to Jacob dated "after 8 May 1778."

To Jacob Greene

[Valley Forge, after 24 May 1778][1]

Griffin I find is gone to Boston to make another purchase. I am afraid he was too late. Goods should always be purchaseed when upon the fall. Then is the Time to make great bargains while the partys fears operates in your favor, for as soon as his hopes returns his mind is fortified and reasons upon qute a different scale.

You may be assurd I will give you all the information in my power that I can consistent with my public station. Nothing shall ever induce me to depart from the line of honor and truth in any business commited to my care.[2]

The gloom that has sat so heavy upon the minds of the People of America begins to wear off and its natural for plasures and diversions to succeed. Luxury I am afraid off. Diversions are by no means so dangerous. However I think almost all ranks and orders of men are relaxing too fast from the republican oeconemy; and slideing into Monarchical extravagance. The great Fortunes that some has made and the great plenty of money circulating gives birth to abundance of extravagance. These evils are founded in human Nature and are to be expected in the common order of things as the revolutions of the Times takes place.

The business that Mr Greene [i.e., Gov. William] wrote me upon shall have countenance as far as is in my power [one or more pages missing].

I wish you would write me the public Sentiments respecting the transactions in the quarter masters department, how the public veiws me and my Agents. It is of great importance to know these things seasonably.

You will please to make my kind love to Sister Peggy and the family. I am glad your Sons are studying the Grammar.

You must not let people see my Letters as they contain Sentiments that I would not wish to be made public. I am affect Yours

N GREENE

I am oblige[d] to write upon the full Gallop as people are waiting.

ALS (MWA); incomplete.
1. Date is determined by reference to Griffin Greene's trip to Boston, described in his letter of 24 May above.
2. See note, letter from Griffin, above.

To Griffin Greene

Dear Sir   Camp [Valley Forge] May 25th 1778
    I wrote you from Peeks Kill[1] since which I have not heard from you.
    I find the business of the Q M G department very extensive and very much out of order in almost every part of the Continent. The neglect of some and the designs of others had got things into a most disagreeable train. However I am in hopes to put them upon a better footing by the help of my friends ere long.
    The partiallity that His Excellency General Washington has always shewn to my advice when supported with the strongest reasons, has created me a great many jealous friends and some deadly enemies. Great pains was taken in the course of last Campaign, altho unknown to me then, to ruin my reputation. The most ungenerous insinuations and bare faced falsehoods were th[rown?] out among the People at large. General Mifflin was at the Head of this affair, altho behind the Curtain. [His?] ambition and private views led him to pursue the most wicked line of conduct.[2] There is no doubt there has been many bad impressions made upon the minds of many People, to which I am now a stranger. I find it one of the most difficult things in the World to learn the Publicks sentiments respecting ones self. If they have a bad opinion the information is a disagreeable Office. If a good one, it wears too much the complexion of flattery. However from our long and uninterrupted friendship I am induced to request you to give me the best information upon this head you possibly can, without diminishing the disagreeable or exagerateing the good.
    It has been hinted to me that General Sullivan was among the number of my jealous friends if nothing worse. It is said he has misrepresented the battle of Germantown secretly, but as i have no kind of authority for these suspicions I cannot rely on them. You can give me better information upon this Head, as General Sullivan has been some time at Rhode Island.[3] If the public refuses me that degree

of Reputation due to my services, I have the satisfaction of the approbation of my own Heart; and make no doubt that the impartial Historian will do justice where it is now refus'd.

General Washington has been equally persecuted with myself, and it is confidently asserted [*ms. damaged*] However the opposition has been long since upon the decline, and is now in a manner come to nothing.

General Lee has joined this Army with his usual retinue; and I hope he may be of use. But I apprehend no great good, as the junto will endeavor to debauch and poison his mind with prejudices. He is undoubtedly a good officer and a great scholar. But he is not a little unhappy in his temper.[4]

Mrs. Greene is on her way Home and doubtless will arrive before this reaches you. You will see her situation and condition and I hope accomodate her accordingly. I shall be much oblige to you and brother Jacob to endeavor to render her as happy as circumstances will admit.

William Greene Esqr I am informed is elected Governor. I hope he will give himself an External appearance suitable to the dignity of his station. He must support that or he will lose Reputation from the acceptance of the appointment. He is a man of an upright Heart and supports a fair Character in the circle of his acquaintance; and it will be a pity to neglect the necessary forms and give his Enemies an opportunity to reproach him. From the goodness of his own Heart he may think that he ought not, nor has not, any Enemies; but I hope he wont place too much confidence there in this corrupt age.[5]

The Enemy are upon the very eve of quiting Philadelphia. It is supposed they are going to New York and tha[t] they will go through New Jersey.[6] There has been a hot press in Philadelphia and New York, both, for seamen but they took all kind of characters and conditions of men. The Quakers not excepted. It is confidently asserted there is a French War; if so the Enemy will very probably leave the Continent. I wish they may. But I wish our confederation was compleat to prevent disputes and quarrels among ourselves.

I am anxious to hear how the brethren are settling their affairs. I wish they could have seperated their business without personal disputes. It gives me pain that the long harmony is dissolved. The seperation of Interest I believe will be no disadvantage to any party. The House had got too complex and intricate to go on smoothly long. But the loss of brotherly affection is a disagreeable circumstance.

I wish to know the general plan of your business that you and Jacob have in prospect. The Iron Works is not by any means a sufficient source of profit for two or three extensive families. Trade must be your plan and I would wish to fix it upon an Extensive schale.[7]

Great things may be done yet by speculation, but not equal to what has taken place; but if I was you I would improve every opportunity. Without wealth a man will be of no consequence by and bye. Mark my words for it—Patriotism and every sacrifice will soon [be for]gotten. My love to Sally and all Friends

[*signature damaged*]

AL[S] (OMC).
1. Letter not found.
2. See "Conway Cabal," note, NG to Jacob, 7 February, above.
3. Although William Blodget reported the rumor in his letter of 29 May below, there is no evidence that Sullivan ever made such an accusation.
4. On Lee's rejoining the army, see note, Meade to NG, 4 April, above.
5. NG had advised the governor on this point in his letter below.
6. On British intentions, see below, NG to Washington, 18 June.
7. Griffin was a partner in the iron works in Coventry, R.I.

To Governor William Greene of Rhode Island

Dear Sir   Camp [Valley Forge] May 25th 1778
I am happy to hear you are elected Governor of Rhode Island, and beg leave to congratulate you upon the occasion. I am told Dr. Bradford took some very disingenuous measures to supplant you. The duplicity of his conduct met with a deserved punishment.[1]

I am persuaded you have taken the reigns of government from the best of motives, and that you will discharge your trust with the greatest integrity. Nevertheless don't flatter yourself that the most upright conduct will secure you from reproach. The pride and ambition of some, the spight and envy of others, will allways find occasion through misrepresentation to wound the reputation for a time. But truth and virtue will triumph at last. Therefore don't be surprised at the one nor dispair of the other. You have a very difficult and jealous people to manage. They are feeble in their tempers, variable in their measures. They are warm in their friendships, but subject to sudden and unaccountable changes. But to do them justice I don't think there is a more patriotick or spirited (*people*) upon the continent. They feel for the calamities of their neighbours, and like generous spirits, lend them a helping hand. They have done with more liberallity than they have ever received in return.

Your sallary will go but a little way towards the defraying the additional expenses of your office. Splendor and Dignity are essential among a Mercantile people. Pomp and parade goes a great way towards governing them; for the vulgar are generally apt to admire those things they least understand, and Merchants dispise what don't consist in part of show. You must, in order to support your reputation, make a figure equal to the importance of your station.

There is such a general intercourse throughout the Continent that a person becomes contemptible abroad unless he appears character-istical at home. Having heard many animadversions upon these mat-ters by travellers, I just take the liberty to give you a hint of what you are to expect.[2]

I beg leave to congratulate you upon the Agreeable news from France. Our Political alliance is most excellent. It is strongly reported Spain has acceded to the treaty also.[3] I don't doubt all Europe in a few months, not in alliance with Great Britain, will declare us free and Independent States.

The Enemy are making the greatest preparations immaginable for the evacuation of Philadelphia. Their further intentions and des-tinations is unknown. We have the best intelligence the whole of the British forces are to rendezvous at New York; but whether they are going to leave the Continent or go up the North River, remains yet to be discovered. I must confess many circumstances induce a belief they are going off all together. How happy will America be, like a man just free from a racking pain.[4]

A French war is confidently asserted. There has been the hottest press in New York and Philadelphia ever known. The enemy took everybody they could lay their hands on, *Quakers* and all.

Upon the enemies evacuating Philadelphia we shall move to-wards the North River, where General Gates is now commander.

Pray, how does General Sullivan agree with you? He is a good officer, but loves flattery. That is his weak side, if you only take him by his leading [*indecipherable*], you may govern him as you please.

General Lee has joind this army with his usual train of dogs. I feel a singular happiness at the different Situation of the American affairs between the time he left us and the time he joins us again.[5]

Major [Samuel, Jr.] Ward left this army some time since to join his Regiment in Rhode Island. Mrs Greene is on her way home. Poor girl! she is constantly separated, either from her husband or children, and sometimes from both.

My compliments to Mrs Greene, Mrs Ward, Miss Celia and the rest of your family. I shall be happy to hear from you at all times and wish to know the Political and current conversation of the Eastern States. I am, sir, with sincere regards Your most obedient and humble servant.

NATH GREENE

Tr (G. W. Greene transcripts: CSmH).
    1. NG's distant relative William Greene, who had succeeded the retiring Nicholas Cooke, was to serve eight successive terms. His opponent, William Bradford, had been Cooke's deputy governor.
    2. NG may have been satirizing the times to some extent, but as he makes clear in

is letter above to Griffin, he was also extending some advice to the rough-hewn
William Greene, an intelligent though uneducated farmer, whose simple life style was
not affected by NG's advice or by the high office of governor. Over the years, for
xample, when the Assembly met in Providence, Gov. Greene often walked the ten
miles to and from his home at the edge of East Greenwich.

3. Spain did not ally herself with France until June 1779—and then not with the
United States.

4. See below, Council of War, 17 June.

5. Lee, exchanged in April after being a British prisoner since December 1776, had
ust rejoined the army.

From Colonel Udny Hay

Fishkill, N.Y., 26 May 1778. Asks if barrack master at Fishkill is
independent of quartermaster department.[1] Cy (PPAmP) 1 p.]

1. When Hay wrote on 29 June, below, he had not received an answer. Since the
barrack master was under the quartermaster, Hay presumably got his answer later.

From George Lux

Dear General   Baltimore 26 May 1778
Yours of the 22d Inst was just handed me by Mr Calhoun, and as
now have liesure I sit down to answer it in order to send it by the
first Conveyance.[1] As Mr Calhoun observed, I have really lost a
father in whom the Qualities of Parent, Husband, Son, Brother,
friend and Master shone in the most exalted Degree. No man in this
County was ever so universally beloved, when living, or lamented
when dead, as he was. If you had but known him, you would really
pity me. I have this Consolation, that he died with the Fortitude,
Calmness, and Composure of a Christian, and almost without a
pang. So much do I revere his Memory and so proud am I of being
son to such a Father, that I would not change him, though dead, for
any living Father in America. By his death I am left Master and Head
of a Family, and have much Business to settle which I am unequal to,
having never in my Father's lifetime attended enough to it. I must
now be assiduous and attentive in order to get his affairs properly
arranged, and to evince myself at least a tolerable Son of a very
worthy Father, for accordingly as I conduct myself for the ensuing
twelve months, will my Character for Life be established. I must also
endeavour to console my poor Mother for her irreparable loss, and by
my Dutiful Behaviour try to render the Evening of her days happy.
These Considerations will prevent me from going to Camp this Summer, as I did intend, in order to take an active Part during this
Campaign.
I am glad that the factious and designing Junto, who would
sacrifice everything to their insatiable Ambitions are alarmed at their

Unpopularity on account of their malevolent Machinations, and now deny all their Practices.[2] It shews they will be cautious hereafter. have heard it reported that Genl M[ifflin] has wrote to His Exc declaring he esteemed him above all men both as an Officer [and Gentleman, and his particular Friend, and wondered how so man reports injurious to him could have been propagated. Now I mysel heard him condemn him for his Partiality to You and Genl K[nox]. I is true, he did it in *very oblique Terms*. I never credited his assertion and I believe *very few now do*. I at Cambridge in my own mind se him down as a bad Man, and almost rendered myself hateful to a my acquaintances on my return home by freely saying so, for hi Popularity was then amazingly high.

As for Major Eustis, he is really insignificant. Genl Lee has spoi him by making a man of him too soon; and from an uncommonl smart and sensible Boy, he has become conceited and pragmatical t the last degree.[3] That Genl M[ifflin] said you accepted the Q. M G. Post in order to be out of the way of Bullets I firmly believe and woul readily give you liberty to mention my Name to him, were I the onl Person who should be called upon, as I would very willingly incur hi Contempt and Hatred, for I never wish to be in favor with a Man always disliked and despised. I was told it by a Young Fellow whom love as my own Brother and with whom I have been very intimate fo these 3 Years past, and an Unreserved Correspondence has been eve since carried on between us. Now this Young Fellow is greatly oblige to M. who has conferred *very particular* Favors on him, and I believ the Young Fellow is to mary one of M.'s Relations. However he ha been in the Army and always has been strongly attached to His Exc and totally abhors all the malevolent machinations formed agains him. I'll tell you in confidence his name; it is Major Scull of Patten Regt,[4] but you know it would be the heighth of impious Ingratitud in me to expose him and divulge what he mentioned in confidenc Mifflin has promised to make his Fortune, and will do it. He says h likes M. *as a Friend*, but abhors and detests his Practices and cordiall hates C-on-y and G-s [Conway and Gates]. I only mentioned it t you to *caution* you to be on your guard. Bob Gates *hinted the sam thing to me*.

From the same Quarters I am told that Genl Lee has been tolc but *cannot ascertain by whom*, that you tried to persuade His Excy to le him remain in Captivity, and that your words were "I think your Exc need not be in *an hurry* about Exchanging him." I would have you mention to Genl Lee that such a thing *has been reported*, and exculpa yourself, as I am convinced it is a false and malicious Assertion, bu you must not mention my Name because I should be sory Major S should get Odium from all his Friends, which would undoubtedly b

ιe case, and Major S. would be angry if he knew I mentioned it to
ɔu and anybody else whatever. My only Reason for it is that you
ιay be convinced I have it from good Authority. Another good
Ϲonsequence will arise from your not mentioning this either with
ɾegard to P. S. or Bob G-s,[5] viz: it would be out of my power to trace
ɪny future malevolence, and I can certainly [learn?] any that may
ɦereafter arise, as I keep up a Correspondence with Bob Gs almost
ɪntirely for that purpose. I was very fond of Genl G's till the Pride of
ρrosperity turned his Brain, and it would answer no end for me to
ɋuarrel with him because I have been very intimate with him and
ɾeceived many Civilities from him. I have not the same Obligation
ʋith regard to M. and therefore would not care who told him. I
ɦoroughly disliked him. I wrote to Bob Gates and freely desired him
ɔ tell his Father to beware of C-y and M., else they would lead him
ɪnto a Scrape from which he might with Difficulty extricate himself.

Now I do not think it would be amiss for you (as M. is at Camp)
ɔ take an Opportunity of telling him *in a public Company* that *it has*
ɓen reported (but that you cannot recollect any Author) that he has said so
ɪnd so, and ask him if it is true. If he acknowledges it, you will be
ɑved the Trouble of producing any Author, and if he denies it, it will
ʈamp the Character of a Lyar effectually upon him, as the whole
ɑrmy knows he said so. I wish I could consistently let my Name be
ɹsed on the occasion as I have no reason to care about them, but that
ϗ not the case with regard to Major S., therefore I wish *you may not*
ɾop even a Hint that might lead to the Discovery of your, or my,
ɑuthors.

Our Division[6] still complains bitterly of Genl S—d [Smallwood].
ɪam told he has at last absolutely issued out in orders that no Officer,
ɒn any pretence whatever, shall presume to intrude upon him but
ɓetween the Hours of 2 and 6 in the Afternoon. Were he to be
ʈtacked in the Morning what would be the consequences? He is
ɘrtainly very dilatory in his motions, avaricious, implacable in his
ɾesentments, warm in his Friendships, and haughty and stately in
ɦis Demeanor, and keeps his Field Officers at a more obsequious
Ɗistance than His Excy does even the Ensigns of the Army. I know
ɦim extremely well, having served under him 2 Months as a Soldier
ɪ our Independent Company, in which time he quarrelled with every
Ɱan in it but myself. I was a particular Favourite with him as I made a
ɒint of being strictly obedient to him while under his command.

I imagine Genl Sullivan will render the Enemy [*ms. torn*] Rhode
ϗland, as Activity and Alertness are his Character[istics].

We hear here that Genl P-t-m [Putnam] has resigned. I am glad
ϝ it, as his Ignorance disqualifies him from rendering us any essential
ɘrvice. Genl Sp-e-r [Spencer] has before resigned, and if Genl

H—th [Heath] would also do it, we should have then a C[orps] of N Genls that might be depended upon.

Is not Genl St Clair yet cleared—how hard it is that the Country [etc?] should be deprived of his Services.

[We] hear that Genl Thompson is to be exchanged for Gen Hamilton of Burgoyne's Army, which I am glad of as he will make an excellent *Executive Officer*. He is too violent in his Passions and hi Abilities are not brilliant, but I have the most exalted Opinion of th Goodness of his Heart.[7]

We hear here that Genl Gates is to command at Peekskill witl McDougal under him, and that Lee and Mifflin are to command ir the Jerseys. If so, I almost dread, the latter will render L— rathe factious and turbulent. Has Genl Conway resigned or not? Are Genl Arnold and Lincoln recovering and soon expected at Camp?

I shall write you again next week, and shall be glad at all times t hear from you. I am sincerely Dr Sir Yr Obligd Huml Servt

GEO LU

ALS(MiU-C).
1. Letter not found.
2. On Lux's unreliability as a purveyor of news, see note, his letter to NG 28 April, above.
3. John Eustace had been an aide to Gen. Charles Lee.
4. Peter Scull had resigned from Col. John Patton's Pennsylvania Regiment on January 1778. In November 1778 he was chosen by Congress as secretary to the Boar of War. A year later he was named secretary to the American minister to Versailles bu was lost at sea en route to France. (Heitman, *Register*; *JCC*, 12: 1101, 15: 1115)
5. Robert Gates was the only child of Gen. Horatio Gates. He died in October 178 at age twenty-two, a month before NG replaced his grief-stricken father in the souther command.
6. Maryland's Division.
7. His round-up of reports on various generals was something less than half right Israel Putnam did not resign at this time; Gen. William Thompson, who had been o parole since his capture in Canada in 1776, was not exchanged for the German Ger Riedesel until 1780; Lee and Mifflin were not to command in the Jerseys. Arthu St. Clair, about whom he asked, was cleared by courtmartial in December 1778.

To the President of the Board of War[1]

Sir   Camp Valley Forge May 27, 177

Considering the weighty Affairs which must constantly claim th Attention of the Board of war it gives me no small concern to fin myself in a Situation which Obliges me to ask their Interposition. Bu as it respects a Matter in which the Publick Interest and harmon necessary to the well conducting the Business of our respective De partments are in no small degree concerned, I am persuaded th Application will be accepted.

It has been my constant Aim in the Appointment[s] I have mad

Our Division still complains bitterly of Genl S——d — I am told, he has at last, absolutely issued out in orders, that no Officer, on any pretence whatever, shall presume to intrude upon him, but between the hours of 2 oClock in the Afternoon — Were he to be attacked in the morning, what would be the consequence. he is certainly very dilatory in his Motions, avaricious, implacable in his resentments, warm in his Friendships, and haughty & stately in his Demeanor, & keeps his field Officers at a more obsequious Distance, than his Excly does even the Ensigns of the army. I know him extremely well, having served under him 2 Months as a Soldier in own Independent Company, in which time he quarrelled with every Man in its both ... & I was a particular favourite with him, as I made a point of being strictly obedient to him, while under his com—

I imagine, Genl Sullivan will render the Enemy Rhode Island, as Activity & Alertness are his Character—

We hear here, that Genl P-t-y has resigned — I am glad of it, as his Ignorance disqualifies him from rendering us any essential Service — Genl Sp—n has before resigned, and if Genl H—y would also do it, we should have then a ... of M[ajor] Genls that might be depended upon —

is not Genl St Clair yet cleared — how hard it is, that the C... should be deprived of his Services —

... hear, that Genl Thompson is to be exchanged for Genl Hamilton of Burgoyne's Army, which I am glad of as he will make an excellent Executive Officer — he is too violent in his Passions, & his Abilities are ... but I have the most exalted Opinion of the Goodness of his heart—

We hear here, that Genl Gates is to command at Peekskill with McDougal under him — and that ... & Mifflin are to command in the Jerseys. if so, I almost dread. the latter will ... rather factious & turbulent — Has Genl Conway resigned or not? Are Genls Arnold & Lincoln recovering & soon expected at Camp?

I shall write you again next week, & shall be glad at all times to hear from you & am sincerely

D. Sir Y' Oblg' Ham' Serv't
Geo Lux

Letter from George Lux, 26 May 1778
(Courtesy of William L. Clements Library at the University of Michigan)

to engage such men in the different Branches of my Department as were, in every point of view most Sutable for the Business, giving the preference where I conceived it could be done with Propriety to those I found in office. But having not been Favoured with any Return of those Formerly employed, I may perhaps have made some Changes which might have been Avoided had I obtained better Information. The office of a Deputy Quarter Master General does not, however, necessarily include that of a Purchaser of Stores, nor are the Abilities for the one always attended with a proper Capacity for the other. I have in Some Instances, therefore, thought it expedient to appoint Gentlemen skilled in mercantile Business to make Purchases to whom I have not offered a Deputation in the Quarter Masters Line.

Among these is Mr Benjamin Andrews of Boston to whom in March last I sent a large order for the Purchasing of stores, particularly Duck and other materials for Tents and Knapsacks.[2] I had heard that Col. Chase was Deputy Quarter Master General in Boston and as I knew of no Cause of complaint against him I did not cho[o]se to displace him, but at the Same time, Being wholly unacquainted with his Character and Mercantile abilities, I thought it most prudent to send an order of so much Importance to a Gentleman of whose Character and fitness for the Business I had a more thorough Knowledge. He has Accordingly made considerable purchases and some of the Goods are now on the way from Boston hither. But he and his Partner, Mr. Otis,[3] complain that they have been much obstructed by the Interference of Col. Chase, founded, as is alledged, on A[u]thority derived from the Board of War; that he claims an Authority Superior to mine, and determines to bid as high for purchases as any one; that a Large Quantity of Duck, Tents, Cloths &c lately arived at Boston, which the Navy Board intended to deliver to Messrs Otis and Andrews as Purchasers for the Quarter Masters Department till Col. Chase demanded Sufficient to make 4000 Tents, [for] which he said he had orders from the Board of Warr of a later date than my orders to Mr Andrews, to get made up and forward Immediately, and threatened to purchase at any Rate if this demand were not Satisfied. On the whole they describe Col. Chases Conduct in this Business as favouring more of Resentment and Setting up one Source of A[u]thority in Competision with another than a prudent Regard to the Good of the Services.[4] They have therefore desisted from purchasing Articles of this kind till the matter shall be farther explained, and Consented that Colo. Chase Should receive the Duck from the Navy Board rather than injure the Publick by a Contest.

How far this Line of Conduct may be warrented by Instruction from the Board of war is not for me to determine, but I must, till have more full Information, suppose there is some Mistake in th

1atter. For however necessary it might have been for the Board
ɔ execute the Office of Quarter Master General while the Place
ʌas Vacant I cannot admit the Supposition that so respective [re-
pectable?] a body would continue the exercise of it after they knew it
ʌas filled without at least notifying the Quarter Master General of the
art they had taken, that he might regulate his Conduct accordingly.
ut, from whatever Motive Col. Chase may have been Actuated, this
ind of Competision is certainly injurious to the Publick in a high
egree. The Business is not only retarded by it but must finally
e effected at a Greater expence by Raising the Prices of the Com-
1odities purchased and thwarting the measures taken by either Party.
cannot therefore doubt but the Board will make due Enquiry into the
ʌffair, and give such Directions as will be proper on the Occasion.[5] I
ave the Honour to be with great Respect Sir your most obedient and
1ost humble Servant

NATHANAEL GREENE

yS (NHi).
    1. The Board of War had been without a president since Gen. Horatio Gates left in
ɪrly May to take command at Peekskill. If a congressional resolution of 21 April had
ɛen strictly interpreted, the board would have virtually ceased to exist, since Congress
ɛclared that any member was "authorized, in conjunction with any two or more of
ʌe present commissioners, to manage the business of that department, till an addi-
ɔnal number of commissioners shall be appointed." (JCC, 10: 371). Congress did not
ɔpoint additional members, however, and by mid-May the board was reduced to two
.embers—William Duer, a congressional delegate, and Timothy Pickering. Richard
ɛters was secretary.
    Since Duer was not present from mid-May to mid-August, the meetings were
tended only by Pickering and Peters. The legality of these rump sessions went
nchallenged by Congress until Pickering and Peters criticized Congress in a letter of
August that Pickering signed as "President." Many members, considering this usur-
ation a "high insult" to Congress, reinterpreted their 21 April resolution slightly as
aving required "that not less than three persons be present to constitute a Board of
'ar." (JCC, 10: 761–62; see also Pickering, Pickering, 1: 216–31.) Congress seemed to be
ʌying that the meetings held by Pickering and Peters did not constitute meetings of
ʌe Board of War, but since no one had challenged the legality of the board's decisions,
.ckering and Peters had actually functioned quite effectively all summer.
    2. Andrews was a partner of Samuel A. Otis. (See note 3 below, and NG to Heath
the end of March, above.) NG's complaints, although attributed directly to Otis &
ndrews, were actually by way of his cousin Griffin, whose letter of 24 May is printed
ɔove. NG studiously avoided mentioning that his brother Jacob and cousin Griffin
ɛre also agents, "presumably skilled in mercantile Business."
    3. Samuel Allyne Otis (1740–1814) was a member of the celebrated Otis family of
ʌrnstable, Mass. James Otis, Jr., the fiery patriot of "Writs of Assistance" fame, was
.s eldest brother; Mercy Otis Warren, his sister; and Harrison Gray Otis, the Boston
ɛderalist leader, his son. He was married to a cousin of Abigail Adams. Before the war
tis had proved himself a successful merchant in Boston, willing to take prudent risks.
ɪ 1777 he was deputy clothier general in Boston under James Mease, continuing as an
ɟent for that department in partnership with Benjamin Andrews, and after Andrews's
ɛath in January 1779, with David Henley. Otis and partners were said to have
ɪpplied the army with eighteen thousand uniforms during the war. From 1778 to 1780
ɛ partnership did extensive business with NG as quartermaster general, and at the
me time, Otis and NG had private dealings. They shared, for example, in the

ownership of several privateers. (See the exchange of correspondence on investing in the *Tartar*, 7 and 17 September 1779, below.) In 1782 Otis was elected speaker of the Massachusetts lower house. Although he declared bankruptcy in the postwar recession of 1785, he eventually retrieved much of his fortune. (John J. Waters, Jr., *The Otis Family in Provincial and Revolutionary Massachusetts* [Chapel Hill: The University of North Carolina Press, 1968], passim)

4. As noted above, NG to Heath, end of March, Thomas Chase remained as deputy quartermaster under NG despite these criticisms. There is no record that the Board of War, or Pickering writing for the board, had given any such orders to Chase after NG became quartermaster. Griffin Greene must have exaggerated Chase's short-comings; if not, NG was indeed tolerant of his deputy in Boston.

5. Pickering may well have answered NG's letter, but his answer has not been found. Even though NG's severest critic, Thomas Mifflin, was gone from the board, NG suspected that Pickering was sympathetic to Mifflin and hence critical of him. But NG's aide, William Blodget, reassured him two days later of Pickering's friendship. (See below, 29 May.) Thus, any answer of Pickering's would have been to reassure NG that the board would not interfere. Pickering remained a key member of the Board of War throughout NG's tenure as quartermaster, and although the board virtually ran the clothier general's department at times, it did not unduly interfere with the quarter-master's. Pickering succeeded NG as quartermaster in 1780.

From Colonel John Davis

[Carlisle, Pa., 28 May 1778. Has sent or is sending teams, tents, knapsacks, portmanteaus, pack horses, rye forage to Col. Steel. ACy (John Davis Papers: DLC) 1 p.]

From Holderby Langford

Sir   Phila New Goal May the 28th 1778
By this favourable opportunity Let you know my distrest situation. I was taken in your Vessel, ever since which time have not had any supplies that is hard Cash, which have sufferd much. I am very bare of Cloathing and am Quite distitute of friends or hard money. Should it lay in your Power to supply me with some hard cash, will take it particular favor. If it was in your Power to have me Exchanged, would do any thing that lay in my power to oblidge you as my Situation is very disagreable. Please to Excuse my letter and bad Writing as the flag is a waiting. I am yours Sincerly

HOLDERBY LANGFORD
Mate of the sloop Florida[1]

ALS (MiU-C).
1. Langford was a Rhode Islander. The *Florida*, owned jointly by NG and his brothers, was listed as missing in Jacob's letter of 12 April, above.

From Major William Blodget

[York Town, Pa., 29 May 1778. Congress is surprised at size of NG's demands and at report that NG had determined to hold the department no longer than contracts could be filled with honor;[1] reports Pickering is NG's friend; have "never heard a lisp to your prejudice" on battle of Germantown; believes Sullivan was "original reporter."[2] Abstract and quotations from Stan Henkel's *Catalog* #1005 (1909)]

1. Blodget may have been making the report to goad Congress into action. It would not be the last time NG declared his intention of leaving the department—sometimes seriously, sometimes as leverage.
2. On the Sullivan rumor, see above, note, NG to Griffin Greene, 25 May.

From Henry Laurens, President of the Continental Congress

[York, Pa., 29 May 1778. Encloses Act (of 26 May) requesting that Baron Steuben be provided with "two good horses."[1] LB (PCC, Item 13: DNA) 1 p.]

1. *JCC*, 11: 533.

From Colonel James Abeel

[Reading, Pa., 30 May 1778. John Mitchell sent duck for knapsacks, but women "do not sew with so Stiff a Needle as a man." Must have sailmakers' palm. "Besides it wou'd be a Sin to make use of such Canvas when it is wanted for Tents so much." LB (Abeel Papers: DLC) 1 p.]

To Colonel Henry Hollingsworth

[Valley Forge, 31 May 1778. Requests that teams haul salt provisions from Head of Elk; army is "much more distressed for want of Provisions than forage." Excerpt from Charles Hamilton *Catalog* #24 (25 January 1968).]

Colonel James Abeel to Colonel Henry Hollingsworth

[Reading, Pa., 31 May 1778. Is directed by NG to collect returns of stores. Needs canvas, writing materials, canteens, and knapsacks. LB (Abeel Papers: DLC) 1 p.]

To Colonel Robert L. Hooper, Jr.

Sir   Camp [Valley Forge] May 31st 177!
Your favor of the 29th [is] before me. The Horses you mentio
are arrivd but I am sorry to inform you there are a great many o
them that is barely fit for service and make but a very indifferen
appearance.

I must beg you to be very particular in purchases and order
given to those that purchase for you, That no more bad Horses ma
be brought to Camp.

The public will find themselves saddled with great expence i
the purchase of Horses and if there is but little or nothing to show fo
it, they will thing [think] themselves greatly injurd.

Forward the Valeeses, Portmantaeus, Knapsacks, Canteens an
Axe Slings as fast as possible.

The Enemy still remain in the City of Philadelphia altho there ha
been appearances of their designing to evacuate it from day to day fo
a Week past. I am Sir with regard your most Obedient Servant

N GREEN!

ALS (NHi).

Colonel James Abeel to Colonel Francis Wade[1]

[Reading, Pa., 31 May 1778. Is directed by NG to collect returns. L
(Abeel Papers: DLC). 1 p.]

1. Francis Wade had been victualer to the Pennsylvania navy in 1775. (*Pa. Co*
Records, 10: 423, 485) In 1777 he was a captain in the Continental army, stationed i
Allentown, N.J., where he served in the commissary department and provided intel
ligence for Washington. When complaints of his rough handling of New Jerseyite
reached Washington, the commander in chief granted he might be "a man of warm
temper" but added that he had "a sad disaffected Set to deal with." (Mifflin t
Washington, 9 March 1777, and Washington to Mifflin, 19 March, Washington Papers
DLC) A congressional investigation subsequently exonerated Wade. (Wade to Wash
ington, [?] May 1777, ibid.) NG appointed him deputy quartermaster for Delawar
and, despite difficulties in getting returns from him, kept him on during his tenure. I
1786, when delegated to sign an emission of Pennsylvania currency, Wade kept
considerable sum in an effort to stave off bankruptcy and was prosecuted as a publi
defaulter. (*Pa. Colonial Records*, 14: 631, 633, 640; 15: 374, 482, 524) He died in 1810
(*PMHB*, 38 (1914): 460) See below, NG to Pettit, 16 November 1778, on dispute betwee
Wadsworth and Wade.

From General Horatio Gates

[Robinson's House, West Point, N.Y., 31 May 1778. Col. Morgar
Lewis, deputy quartermaster for Northern Army believes Congres
had not put him under NG. Gates assured him it was so. Advance

him $50,000; with the $50,000 advanced to Col. Hay "your department here is in very bad plight."[1] He adds, "Money! Money! Money!
or all must Stand Still." Cy (PCC, Item 155: DNA) 1 p.]

1. Gates had written Washington on 21 May that the $50,000 advanced to Hay was
"but a trifle" compared to the sum needed, and he asked Washington to "press
General Greene" for a proper supply of cash. (Washington Papers: DLC)

From Henry Laurens, President
of the Continental Congress

[York, Pa., 31 May 1778. Encloses Act on Col. Udny Hay.[1] LB (PCC,
Item 13: DNA) 1 p.]

1. See note, NG to Laurens, 1 May, above.

General Greene's Orders

Camp at the Valley Forge
1 June 1778
I do hereby Authorize and Impower Benjamin Bartholomew,
Lewis Gronow and John Cloyd of the State of Pennsylvania, Gentlemen, or any Two of them, To Hear and Examine into the Damages
which any of the Inhabitants in and about the present Encampment
of the Army may Have sustained By means of said Army, Whether by
Collecting Materials, Destruction of Fences, or Timber or Otherwise:
and to give Certificates Thereof To the People who have sustained
such damages, specifying the Quantity and Quality of the Materials
so taken and by whom, and For what purpose, and the value thereof;
Or the amount of the Damages Sustained by the Destruction of
Fences, Timber or other Property, or by any Depredations Committed
by the Army, Specifying in all Cases where it can be done, by whom
such destruction and Depredation was Committed. You are to keep
an Exact account of your proceedings Herein, and Register the Certificates you shall grant, a Copy of which you are to return To me, and
for your Time and Trouble Herein you shall be paid a Reasonable
Compensation.[1]
Given under my Hand in Camp at the Valley Forge The 1st day of
June Anno Dom: 1778.

NATHANAEL GREENE

Cy (PCC, Item 42: DNA).
1. Although Congress had not specified the reimbursement for damages or ex-
propriation of goods as being the responsibility of the quartermaster, the practice had
grown as a logical extension of his duties in acquiring materials for future use. An
example of Gronow and Cloyd's certificate is abstracted below, 28 December 1778. To

NG, desperate for supplies and short of money, it must have seemed like paying for a dead horse. As time went on, he did not accept the responsibility. (See his letter to John Sullivan, 9 February 1779, below.)

On 17 February 1779 Congress, noting that "allowances have in some instances been made in the Quarter Master General's Department for Damages done by the troops . . . [but] *Resolved,* that such allowances are not warranted by any Resolution of Congress and ought not to be made until some general rule may be established for doing equal justice in all similar cases throughout the United States." (*JCC,* 13: 194)

Colonel James Abeel to Thomas Chase[1]

[Reading, Pa., 1 June 1778. Is directed by NG to collect returns of stores. Also needs stationery and canvas for tents, knapsacks, and haversacks. LB (Abeel Papers: DLC) 1 p.]

1. The letter was headed to the DQMG at Boston.

Colonel James Abeel to Nehemiah Hubbard[1]

[Reading, Pa., 1 June 1778. Is directed by NG to collect returns of stores. Especially needs canvas, linen, stationery, carpenter hammers. Has plenty of other tools. LB (Abeel Papers: DLC) 1 p.]

1. The letter was headed to the DQMG of Connecticut.

To Henry Laurens, President of the Continental Congress

Sir Camp Valley Forge 1st June 1778

In order that the Army might be left in a Condition to move as light as possible, His Excellency the Commander in Chief was pleased, some time ago, to issue General Orders that the Officers of the Army should send out of Camp all the Baggage they could possibly spare reserving only such as could be carried without Chests and Trunks.[1] The effect of this Order will considerably reduce the number of Baggage Waggons. Some Baggage, however must necessarily remain, and as the Chests and Trunks are chiefly sent away Valeeces and Portmanteaus are requisite to supply their Places; and as the officers could not be permitted to leave Camp to provide these Articles for themselves, I thought it expedient, with the Approbation of the Commander in Chief, to procure a number for them. I have given Orders accordingly to draw them from various Parts of the Country. They are in considerable forwardness, and beginning to come in, and as the Army must speedily move it seems necessary they should be delivered out without Delay. On the other Hand, it ought to be previously determined whether they are to remain public lick Property or to be purchased by the Officers, as great Incon venience would arise if the latter should be determined upon after a Distribution under even a faint Expectation of the former. Many of the Officers imagine that, as they submit to much Inconvenience on the Occasion, and thereby save to the Publick abundantly more than the Expence of the Portmanteaus and Valeeces they have some Right to expect these Articles will be delivered to them at the publick Expence. Considering the high Prices of the Necessaries and Conveniences which Officers must purchase for themselves, greatly exceeding a due Proportion to their Pay, this Expectation seems to be founded in Reason. But as it may be doubted whether I am officially authorized to furnish these Articles to the Officers at the publick Expence I should be glad to obtain the Sense and Direction of Congress on this Point as speedily as possible.

Many Officers in and about the Army, as well of [as?] those in the military Line as some in the different civil Departments, are obliged, from the Nature of their Duty, to keep Horses. And though they generally furnish these for themselves, yet from various Accidents, such as their Horses dying, straying, being stolen, falling lame &c, a new Supply becomes necessary; and the like, with some variation in the Circumstances, with respect to Saddles and Bridles. These Officers being not at Liberty to go into the Country in pursuit of Supplies, and the Difficulty of obtaining them when they can go out is so great, they are in a Manner compelled in many Instances, to have Recourse to the Quarter Master General for temporary Supplies. In some of these Cases, under particular Circumstances I have furnished Horses, Saddles and Bridles as Occasion required; in others I have denied them. But as, from the nature of the Business, and the peculiar Circumstances of the Times, these Applications will continue to be made in great numbers, and the Necessity of the Case seems to call for a Compliance in many Instances, I should be glad to have the Sense of Congress on this Subject also, as clearly expressed as the nature of it will admit.

Permit me also to mention to you the great Inconvenience I labour under for want of a Knowledge of the Acts of Congress, many of which probably contain important Directions for the conducting of my Office, and therefore ought to be known and clearly understood by every Person acting in my Department. Some of these Acts I may have seen occasionally as they were published in News Papers or other detached Publications, but not so as to preserve them in Memory; nor can I find that they are anywhere collected in such Manner as that I can obtain a Sight of them. If Congress will afford me the Means of knowing their Laws I will endeavour to have them executed in my Department in the best Manner I can, but if in the mean Time, from unavoidable Ignorance I should happen to do any Act which they forbid, or omit doing what they require should be done, I hope it will not be imputed to me as a Crime.

I am induced to give Congress this Trouble from a sincere Desire to execute the Office to which I am appointed in the Manner most agreeable to the true Intent and Meaning of their Resolutions, and I flatter myself the Questions I have stated will not long remain unanswered, especially when it is considered that unless Congress shall direct the Contrary, I shall be obliged from the Necessity of the Case to distribute many Horses, Saddles and Bridles, and probably all the Valeeces and Portmanteaus, as publick Property.[2]

The Command of Congress to supply Baron Steuben with two Horses, is received, and shall be duly attended to. I have the Honour to be, with great Respect Sir your most obedient and very humble Servant

NATHANAEL GREENE

LS (PCC, Item 192: DNA).
1. Washington's order of 27 March 1778 is in Fitzpatrick, *GW*, 11: 161–62. He had urged the use of portmanteaus and valises made of canvas to save weight.
2. As Laurens noted in his letter of 5 June, below, Congress turned over NG's letter to the Board of War (then consisting of Timothy Pickering and Secretary Richard Peters). The Board ignored NG's letter and Pettit's entreaties. (See NG to Pettit, 18 June, below.) Only when NG appeared before it in February 1779 did it propose and Congress agree to pay for portmanteaus and "valeeces." (*JCC*, 13: 214) NG apparently continued to provide horses without authorization.

To Gouverneur Morris[1]

Valley Forge June 1st 1778

I received your favor of the fifth of May,[2] upon the subject of the Q Ms department, and intend to follow your advice, in order to my own justification, and to silence the faction. I have represented the substance of what I wrote you (only more fully) in a letter to the General, requesting his advice and direction, which he has given much in the same terms as you did. But I am frightened at the expense. I have drawn on the Treasury already for upwards of four millions of dollars, and it seems to be but a breakfast for the department, and hardly that.[3] The land carriage is so extensive and costly, the wants of the army so numerous, and everything selling at such enormous prices that our disbursements will be very great. I dare say they will far exceed your expectation.

I have written to Congress for their sense and direction upon several matters respecting the department. I beg you will endeavor to bring the matter to issue as soon as possible, as I am much at a loss to know how to proceed.[4]

The enemy appear, from every piece of intelligence, to be making all necessary preparation to evacuate Philadelphia. I should be glad of our opinion respecting their future operations. Some of the officers think they are going to the West Indies; others are of opinion that they are going up the North River. There is one objection to this scheme. There is not a sufficient force to cooperate with Sir Henry from Canada. I should think that if Great Britain meant to be serious in her propositions for a reconciliation with America, her forces would be collected together at some secure place, and there wait to see the issue of the commissioners' negotiations.

Sir Henry Clinton sent out a letter to his Excellency a few days ago, respecting certain acts of Parliament lately passed in favor of America, as he terms it. This letter, I suppose, has been before Congress before this time.[5]

General McDougall is not well pleased at the manner of his being superseded in the command on the North River. He thinks the public will form some unfavorable sentiments respecting it. General Gates will not meet with the most cordial reception there. However, he will undoubtedly be treated politely.[6] Governor [George] Clinton showed me several letters respecting the operations of last campaign, which will do him much credit in history.

Pray how came General Mifflin to be ordered to join this army?[7] This is a phenomenon in politics. General Conway is at last caught in his own trap, and I am most heartily glad of it. I wish every such intriguing spirit may meet with the like disappointment in his ambitious designs. He is a most worthless officer as ever served in our army.[8]

I suppose you go on pretty much in the old style, puzzling one another with doubts and difficulties, each striving to display the greatest wisdom and ingenuity. What progress have you made in the establishment of the army? The half-pay you have fixed at seven years. Most of the officers are discontented with it, and I am sorry for it.

r (GWG transcript: CSmH).

1. Gouverneur Morris (1752–1816), scion of a leading New York family, had been elected to Congress at age twenty-five. In January 1778 he was put on the Committee at Headquarters that persuaded NG to accept the quartermaster post. While at Valley Forge, he became, as he told Washington, "an Advocate for the Army." (Mintz, *Morris*, . 101) With a flair for organization, he was especially helpful to NG, serving in November 1778 as chairman of a committee named to aid NG's department. (See his letter of 16 November 1778, below.) His defeat for reelection in 1779 represented the loss of an influential friend in Congress for NG, although they remained personal friends. His nephew, Lewis Morris, was an aide to NG from 1779 to 1782. From 1781 to 1785 Gouverneur was assistant to Robert Morris (no relation). As his correspondence with NG reveals during those years, the men shared a nationalist desire for a strong central government, but NG was not sympathetic with Morris's antidemocratic philosophy. In

the 1790s Morris lived abroad, serving during 1792–94 as envoy to France. Mintz, *Morris*, is a good recent biography.

2. Neither Morris's letter of 5 May nor NG's to which it was an answer has been found. The faction about which Morris wrote was made up of Mifflin's friends.

3. The scrounging for funds and the barbs of Mifflin supporters were offset in part by the commissions that were rolling in. The $4,000,000 represented commissions of over $13,000 each for Greene, Pettit, and Cox. Even with the dollar worth only twenty-five cents, NG earned more in these two months than in any previous two years.

4. As noted at NG to Laurens, 1 June, above, Morris in this case was apparently unable to influence Congress.

5. When Congress received the resolves on 6 June, it haughtily notified Lord Howe and Clinton that it would "attend to such terms of peace, as may consist with the honor of independent nations." (*JCC*, 11: 574–75)

6. See note, NG to McDougall, 28 March, above.

7. To Washington's chagrin, Congress had granted Mifflin leave from the Board of War to rejoin Washington's army (*JCC*, 11: 520). On 11 June, however, Congress ordered Mifflin to Fishkill to Gates's command, the same day it directed Washington to order an inquiry into the conduct of Mifflin as quartermaster. (*JCC*, 11: 590–91)

8. To the surprise of the hapless Conway, Congress lost no time in accepting his resignation on 28 April (*JCC*, 10: 399).

To Thomas McKean[1]

Sir   Camp Valley Forge June 3rd 1778

Colo Robert L Hooper of North Hampton County, one of my Deputies in the QMG's department informs me, he has lately been served with a warrant from under Your hand, charging him with having libeled the Magistrates of this State in a Letter to Gouverneur Morris Esqr. and directing the Sheriff to bring him before you at York Town.[2]

The Colo waited upon me to communicate his situation, and to know if the Circumstances of the Army would admit of his Absence, but as the Army is just upon the Wing, and Part of it in all Probability will march through his district, I could not without great Necessity concent to his being absent, as there is no other Person that can give the Necessary Aid upon this Occasion.

As you wish well to the Army and its Operations, I presume you would not desire to call Colo Hooper from his Post, if it can Possibly be avoided, and the Necessary forms of Law complyd with. He has not the least Objection to entering into a recognizance with ample Sureties to appear at any Court where he is legally Answerable, neither have I the least desire to interrupt the Course of the Law, or to Secure him from its proper operation. Therefore what I would request of you is to direct Some Magistrate in North Hampton County, to take Colo Hoopers Recognizance with Such Sureties as you may think proper and to Transmit the Same to you, which I Presume will answer every Legal Demand and equally Preserve the dignity of

Government.[3] I am Sir with Great Respect Your most Obed Hble
Servt

NATHANAEL GREENE

LS (PHi).

1. Thomas McKean (1734–1817) managed to keep a political foot in both Delaware
and Pennsylvania during most of the revolutionary period. Trained in the law, he was a
member of the Delaware Assembly from 1762 to 1779, part of the time as speaker.
Although he moved to Philadelphia in 1774, he was governor of Delaware for a short
time in 1777. While serving in the Delaware Assembly that same year, he was named
chief justice of the Pennsylvania Supreme Court, an office he was to hold for twenty-
two years. During five of those years (1778–83), he represented Delaware in the
Continental Congress, for five months in 1781 as president. He ended his career by
serving two turbulent terms as governor of Pennsylvania. An able lawyer, he was also
a learned judge. He was honest and unbending and at times harsh and arrogant. (*DAB*;
a recent study that carries his career only to 1780 is John M. Coleman, *Thomas McKean:
Forgotten Leader of the Revolution* [Rockaway, N.J.: American Faculty Press, 1975]

2. For background on Hooper, see note, NG to Laurens, 3 April above, and from
McKean, 9 June, below. As noted there Hooper had attacked the Pennsylvania attorney
general. He described the incident to Gouverneur Morris, saying that he would whip
all the council and would "not stop at the President of the State [Wharton]." Morris,
who thought the letter amusing, showed it to several people at Valley Forge, including
Washington and Greene. When the Pennsylvania council demanded the letter as
evidence aginst Hooper, Morris refused to surrender it on the grounds of its being
private. (Mintz, *Morris*, 95–96)

3. However reasonable NG's request appears in view of the imminent British
evacuation of Philadelphia, McKean did not find it so in his answer of 9 June, below.

To Catharine Greene

Camp Valley Forge June 4th 1778
Capt Bowen is just going and have only time to let you know that
I am here in the usual stile, Writing, Scolding, Eating and Drinking.
But there is no Mrs Greene to retire to spend an agreeable hour with.

Col Hay writes me you past the Fish Kill in great haste. I hope
you got safe home. I receivd a Letter from Billy.[1] He says the Children
are well. I wish it may be so. Pray write me a full History of family
matters; there is nothing will be so agreeable. Kiss the sweet little
children over and over again for their absent Papa. You must make
yourself as happy as possible. Write me if you are in want of any
thing to render you so.

Mr More and the family all enquire after you with great affection
and respect, and I beleive with a degree of sincerity.[2] Col Cox has
wrote a most pompous [i.e., splendid] account of you to Mrs Cox as
appears by her answer. She desires him to prepare you to see an old
fashion plain Woman markt with age and rusticity among the Pines. I
believe there is no necessity for that for every body agrees She is one
of the finest Women of the age. Mrs Washington and the other Ladies

of Camp are dayly asking after you. Col Cox and Mr Pettit desire their most respectful compliments to the *intruding fair*. Mrs Knox is in Camp and lives with the General. She professes great regard for you and often inquires how and where you are. You will judge of the Regard from former circumstances. But she really seems sincere.

I had a Letter from Mr Lott last night. The family are well.

Mr Lebrune [Le Brun] is going to join Count Polaskies [Pulaski][3] Legion, he is gone to Baltimore. He does want to see Mrs Greene very much. He thinks he loves her very well. Blodget is still at Yorktown dun[n]ing the Congress for money. Major Burnet is not yet arrivd. I had a Letter from Major Loyd a few days past.[4] He is still paying his court to Miss Tilghman. Poor fellow he is over Head and Ears in Love.

Betty is gone out of our family and has got married. I wish to know if you mist anything from among your Cloaths. She has deliverd me your Knife.

The Enemy remain much in the same situation in Philadelphia as I wrote you before.

My kind love to all the family, Cousin Griffin and Sally, Mother Greene and all other friends. Yours Affectionately

N GREENE

ALS (NNC).
1. Probably Catharine's brother, William Littlefield.
2. NG and Catharine had stayed at Moore Hall from the end of March. (See note, NG to Biddle, 12 February, above.)
3. Casimir Pulaski (1748–79), a Polish nobleman with cavalry experience, had joined the army in July 1777 as an aide to Washington. In September 1777 he pressured Congress into appointing him as a brigadier general in charge of the dragoons. His career in America was filled with strife and bad luck. His trouble was caused in part by his lack of English and by his insistence that his orders come directly from Congress. In March 1778 he resigned his post as chief of cavalry and formed an independent legion of mounted troops, accepting—against Washington's advice—prisoners and deserters. He was sent south in 1779, where he was defeated in May in a battle near Charleston and killed in October during a brave but foolhardy cavalry charge against Savannah. (*DAB*)
4. William Blodget, Ichabod Burnet, and James Lloyd were aides.

From Henry Laurens, President of the Continental Congress

[York, Pa., 5 June 1778. Has presented NG's letter of 1 June[1] to Congress. Cy (PCC, Item 13: DNA) 1 p.]

1. See NG to Laurens, 1 June, above.

From Colonel James Abeel

[Reading, Pa., 6 June 1778. Has sent iron traces; will send "Blind Bridles." LB (Abeel Papers: DLC) 1 p.]

From George Lux

[Baltimore, Md., 6 June 1778. Salt-water damage of this letter has left only a few complete sentences out of three pages. He has received NG's letter (not since found); he relays gossip about Mifflin; he is off to see his "Dulcinea" in Reading, Pa.[1] ALS (Greene Papers: DLC) 3 pp.]

1. His "Dulcinea" was Catharine Biddle, whom he later married.

From George Washington

[Valley Forge, 6 June 1778. Asks NG to provide sixty-three horses to be ready when men are recruited for newly formed maréchausée[1] and to provide a horse at once for "Capt Van Heer," the commander. Tr (Varick transcript, Washington Papers: DLC) 3 pp.]

1. The maréchausée were mounted provosts, responsible for policing a military camp. Two months later, When Capt. Bartholomew von Heer had been unable to get recruits, Congress authorized him to pay a bounty "for his troops or marechasseurs." (JCC, 11: 729)

From Colonel James Abeel

[Reading, Pa., 7 June 1778. Has sent or is sending bridles, traces, canteens, and chains—mostly by boat.[1] LB (Abeel Papers: DLC) 1 p.]

1. See note, Abeel to NG, 10 May, above.

From Colonel James Abeel

[Reading, Pa., 7 June 1778. Has sent some thirteen tons of iron to various forges. Has "a Number of Artificers of every kind at Work in Town and all about the Country." Can soon "Supply all your wants, as every thing is going on Cleverly here." Will have horseman's tents made when Pettit approves design; is finishing a marquee for Washington; tents reported coming from Boston.

I am Extremely Sorry to tell you that I find a very great abuse in the Waggon Mast'r Gen'ls Department at every place I have been.[1] In the first Place some of the Waggon Masters do not drive there Waggons above Nine and Ten miles a day whereas they can with ease drive 20 miles. Besides if they come in of an Afternoon early instead of Cutting Straw drawing their Fodder and Provisions so as to be ready to set off early Next morning they take the greatest part of that day to load and draw Provisions so that they go only 3 or 4 miles at farthest that day. They make it a Rule to Stop at every Tavern on the Road and Loiter there time away. In short it wou'd take a side of Paper to point out the abuse in that Department. While I was Station'd at Suckasunny Plains I made this Agreement with the Waggon Masters that they shou'd Travel at least 20 miles a Day steadily on and that whatever they went short I deducted from their Wages. This made them do their duty and very few Horses were hurt by being drove too hard, as it [is] often the Case that they Stopt 3 or 4 houses on the Road and then drove as if the Devil was Driving them by which many good Horses are Ruined as they do not give them time to cool before they feed them.

Asks him to examine cutting boxes he sent; he has all the smiths between Lebanon and Lancaster making chains. LB (Abeel Papers: DLC) 2 pp.]

1. The wagon master general, James Thompson, had been kept on by NG and was stationed at Valley Forge. The Pennsylvania wagon master was James Young, who appeared to be answerable to both the executive council of Pennsylvania as well as to NG's department. See, for example, Young to Matlack, 3 March 1778; to Col. Melchior, 4 August 1778; and to Wagon Masters, 27 September 1778, in *Pa. Archives*, 6: 330, 676, and 765.

From George Washington

[Valley Forge, 8 June 1778. Because of "very sickly situation of the camp and the danger of its becoming still more alarming," NG should reconnoiter a new camp nearby with chief engineer at once; should be primarily wholesome situation with wood and water and secondarily in good defensive position.[1] Df (Washington Papers: DLC) 1 p.]

1. Hamilton first wrote, and then scratched, "The expectation of leaving it dayly, has for some time past, prevented a removal, but the arrival of the commissioners at Philadelphia—" As a result of peace feelers by the Carlisle Commission, Washington presumably thought the army might be around for a longer time than he had anticipated. NG and Du Portail located a new camp the same day about a mile from the old camp, to which Washington ordered the army to move on 10 June. The camp was still called Valley Forge. They remained there only ten days before crossing the Delaware in pursuit of the British.

From George Washington

[Valley Forge, 8 June 1778. As stores at Head of Elk will be in danger with removal of Smallwood's troops, he orders NG "without loss of time to have every thing of value in your magasines thereabouts, transported." Df (Washington Papers: DLC) 1 p.]

From Colonel John Davis

Dr Genl   Carlisle [Pa.] 9th June 1778
    I have Sent by Sam'l Purviance Sixty Single Horse with two Wagons and teams fully Equipt and Sundry Other articles, a Rec't of which I have Inclosed you.
    I have a Number of articles in hand which I Shall Send to Reading this week at the Request of Mr Abeel. I have also a number of pack Horse with Sadles and other accoutraments. I Should be glad to know If I Shall Send them to Camp or to the Westard, and What pay I Shall allow Horse Masters and Horse Drivers, and if I am Called on to Hire pack Horses for the Westward What I Shall allow for Each Horse per Day, when found [i.e., fed] by the publick and How Much When the[y] find themself.
    I am geting portmantaues Valices and Havesacks made as fast as possible. I find a great Dificulty in geting Wagoners but I Expect this Week to have as many as will Send of [off] two Brigades.
    As Soon as I have the Wagons I have on hand Compleated with horses and harness I Shall Ceas Purchasing Horses till I Receive your further orders.
    I Can Hire a Number of Wagons Within my District at 30 [dollars?] per Day when found but the Demand for transporting Commissary Stores and the Demands to the Westward Will take all I Can Engage. I am [Sir?] Your Obedient Humble Servant[1]

JOHN DAVIS

ACyS (John Davis Papers: DLC).
    1. NG answers in detail, 14 June, below.

From Thomas McKean

Sir   York-Town [Pa.] June 9th 1778
    I just now received your favour of the 3d instant and am not a little surprized that the Sheriff of Northampton County should have permitted Colo. Robert L. Hooper, after he was arrested by virtue of my Precept, to wait upon you untill he had appeared before me.[1]
    You say, Sir, "Colo. Hooper waited upon me to communicate his situation, and to know if the circumstances of the army would admit

of his absence, but as the army is just upon the wing, and part of it will in all probability march through his district, I could not without great necessity *consent* to his being absent, as there is *no other person* that can give the necessary aid upon this occasion."

I do not think, Sir, that the absence, sickness or even death of Mr Hooper could be attended with such a consequence, that *no other person* could be found who could give the necessary aid upon this occasion; but what attracts my attention most is your observation, that *you* cannot without great necessity *consent to his being absent*. As to that, Sir, I shall not ask *your consent* nor that of any person in or out of the army, whether my Precept shall be obeyed or not in Pennsylvania.

The warrant for the arresting Mr Hooper being special, no other magistrate can take cognizance therefore but myself. The mode you propose of giving bail cannot be adopted for many reasons.

I should be very sorry to find, that the execution of criminal law should impede the operations of the army in any instance, but should be more so to find the latter impede the former. I am Sir with great respect, Your most obedient humble servant.[2]

TMK

ACyS (PHi).
1. For biographical note on Hooper, see NG to Laurens, 3 April 1778. As a deputy quartermaster in 1777, Hooper had refused to take an oath under the radical Pennsylvania constitution and urged others to do the same. When he was falsely accused by two members of the safety council of aiding "Tories," he threatened them with physical violence—they being, as Pres. Thomas Wharton said, "very unequal to H. in power of body." A few weeks before NG took office, Hooper had thrashed one of them, Atty. Gen. John Dickinson Sergeant. (Wharton to McKean, 15 February 1778, *Pa. Archives*, 6: 266–68; Wharton's quotation is on p. 268.) In early March, Hooper had finally taken the oath. (Ibid., p. 344)
2. There can have been few American judicial opinions more magisterial in asserting the supremacy of the civil government over the military than this document from the pen of Pennsylvania's chief justice. McKean's biographer calls it "vintage McKean." (Coleman, *McKean*, p. 225) In his usual court sessions, Coleman tells us, "McKean wore a scarlet gown and an immense cocked hat, which he usually kept on during the entire proceedings of the Court. Occasionally he wore a sword." (Ibid., p. 223) One can imagine him so arrayed and accoutred (with sword) the day he sat down to squelch Nathanael Greene. For a biographical note, see NG's letter of 3 June, above.
Hooper was presumably tried, but the outcome of the trial is not known. He seems to have lost little time from his duties.

To Colonel James Abeel

[Valley Forge, 11 June 1778. Requests he provide tents for Col. Daniel Brodhead's regiment en route to Ft. Pitt.[1] ALS (WHi) 1 p.]

1. See note, Davis to NG, 15 June, below.

To Colonel John Davis

Sir

Camp Valley Forge June 14th 1778.

Your favour of the 9th of this Inst. by Mr Purviance came safe to hand.[1] Inclosed is a copy the reciepts given to Mr Pervyance for the articles delivered, by which you will see the agreement between the reciepts given and recieved.

Send the Pack horses and Pack saddles to the Westward for the use of the Garrison at Fort Pitt.

Horse masters may be allowed the same as Waggon-masters 40 dollars per month, horse drivers L10 per month and for the hire of single horses half a dollar per Day and forage found [furnished] them, and where they find their own forage to be paid the value of it.

Let your Portmanteaus be well lined and the knapsacks painted. You will cease purchasing any more single horses to come to Camp and make up all you have on hand into Teams and let them come properly brigaded with Waggoners compleat.

Engage a sufficient number of hired teams to do all the duty in your district, and let the purchased ones come to Camp.

You will please to make me a return of the number and conditions of the Assistants you have employed under you.

Some of the Teams that come on from Virginia, come empty to Camp. I beg you would give them a load at York Town to bring on. I wish you would give the necessary orders for this purpose. I am Sir Your humble servant

NATH GREENE

LS (Davis Papers: DLC).

1. This is a point-by-point answer to Davis's letter of 9 June, above, a fair example of the administrative burdens shouldered by the quartermaster general. There were similar exchanges with other deputies that have not been found. He complained a week later, for example, when his assistants, Pettit and Cox, were both absent that he was left "with business enough for ten men." (NG to Catharine, 23 June, below)

To Moore Furman

Sir

Moore Hall [Pa.][1] June 15th 1778

Your's of the 9th and 15th are receiv'd.[2] You wrote us some time ago that you could engage any number of teams to do the QMGenls duty in N. Jersey upon hire; in yours of the 9th you mention a condition that the owners of the Teams demand as a matter of right established by common Custom, that each team be allowed five days in a month to recruit.[3] If there ever was such a custom, I do not know it, neither do I approve of it. To pay for five days actual service while a team is laying still, is neither just nor politick. I therefore abolish every such custom; leaving it with you to grant such indulgencies from time to time, as reason and justice may require.

If the Cavalry horses that are broken down are delivered to you for sale, you ought to recieve and dispose of them. But I know of no right we have to demand them, as the Officers are the only proper judges which and when the Cattle [i.e., livestock] are fit for service.

Wherever you hear of Continental property you ought to seize it for the use of the [United] States; but the horse you mention that the British left behind them, I would not meddle with.

If the former QMGenl at Trenton has a continental horse, and you are informed he claims him as his own property, you should speak to him on the subject, inform him it is your duty, as information was given you upon the subject.

Colo Biddle I hope has wrote you fully respecting the manner in which the Light Horse are to forage, as he waited on his Excellency upon the Subject. He will also write you the reason for sending the money to Messrs Lawrence and Ball.

With regard to the prices of things you must settle them upon the best terms you can, every thing is extravagant almost every where; but I hope people are more reasonable with you than here as the demand is not so great.

You must not increase the pay of the Waggon masters; it would fly all the Continent over in a few days. If the boy you mention will answer for a Driver of a continental Team, send him on; I will put him to drive one of the Genl. Officers baggage Waggons.

I have sent you 24,000 Dollars which I hope will quench your thirst, untill we can get a new draught from Congress which Mr Pettit has gone to obtain.

The old accounts you mention we cannot undertake to settle without being duly authorized by Congress; we have fully represented the injustice of keeping the people out of their money so long.

Please to send your large grey horse to Camp.

Colo Cox has made some agreement, or instructed Mr Hagland to engage three or four brigades of Teams[4] to transport public stores for Egg Harbour.[5] You must confirm the contract as far as is possible consistant with the interest of the States. It may be necessary for us under some circumstances to give some special orders with regard to particular posts, within your jurisdiction, in which case you will conform to the agreements made in consequence thereof. In the present case if there are more teams at Bordenton, than is wanted there for the public service, they must be employed elsewhere or dismissed.

Intelligence comes this moment from the Jersey's the Enemy are all over in your State from Philadelphia.[6] I am Sir Your humble servant

NATH GREENE

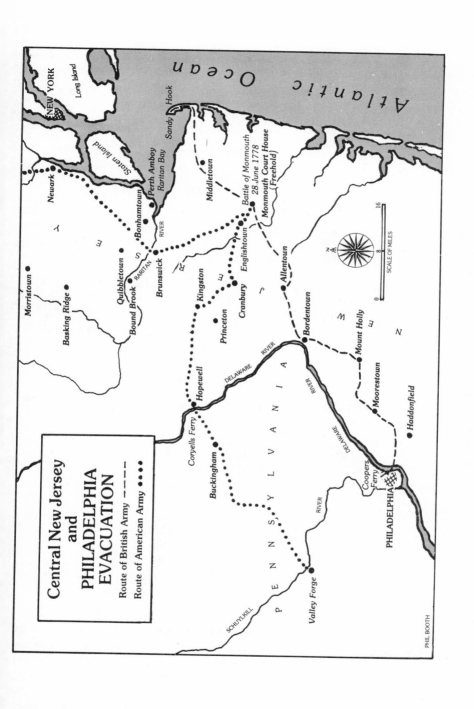

Central New Jersey
and
PHILADELPHIA
EVACUATION

Route of British Army — — —
Route of American Army • • •

NEW YORK
Long Island
Staten Island
Atlantic Ocean
Morristown
Basking Ridge
Newark
Bonhamtown
Perth Amboy
Raritan Bay
Sandy Hook
Middletown
Battle of Monmouth
28 June 1778
Monmouth Court House
(Freehold)
Quibbletown
Bound Brook
Brunswick
RARITAN
RIVER
Kingston
Princeton
Cranbury
Englishtown
Allentown
Bordentown
Mount Holly
Moorestown
Haddonfield
Hopewell
Coryells Ferry
DELAWARE
RIVER
Buckingham
P E N N S Y L V A N I A
DELAWARE
RIVER
Coopers
Ferry
PHILADELPHIA
SCHUYLKILL
RIVER
Valley Forge

SCALE OF MILES
0   8   16

PHIL. BOOTH

LS (Nj).
1. He had continued on at Moore Hall after Catharine Greene left in May. (See his letter to her, 23 June, below.) On Moore Hall, see above, NG to Biddle, 12 February.
2. Letters not found.
3. To be refreshed or restored by rest and feed. NG was not denying the need for "recruiting," only that the owners should not be paid for those days.
4. A brigade of teams consisted of ten teams.
5. Egg Harbor, where ships unloaded, was just above Cape May on the New Jersey coast.
6. On the British in New Jersey, see below, Council of War, 17 June.

From Colonel John Davis

[Carlisle, Pa., 15 June 1778. Has sent pack horses, valises, "Scalping knives, Carpenters tools &c" for McIntosh's Expedition.[1] Has sent NG butter and "four Gammons of Backon and two hams of Vennison." ACyS (Davis Papers: DLC) 1 p.]

1. In early May, Washington had put Gen. Lachlan McIntosh in command, at Fort Pitt and "in the Western Country," to keep the Indians in check. (Fitzpatrick, GW, 11: 379) Many of the supplies assembled by the deputy quartermasters in central Pennsylvania were for that expedition. McIntosh later quarreled with his subordinates, and Washington replaced him with Daniel Brodhead the following March. (Ibid., 14: 193–94)

Council of War

At a Council of War held at Head Quarters Valley Forge the 17th day of June 1778.

Present
His Excellency The Commander in Chief

Major Generals	Brigadier Generals
Lee	Smallwood
Greene	Knox
Arnold	Poor
Sterling	Patterson
Fayette	Wayne
Steuben	Woodford
	Mughlenberg
	Huntington
	Portail

The Commander in Chief informs the council, that from a variety of concurring intelligence, there is the strongest reason to believe the enemy design speedily to evacuate Philadelphia; having actually put all their heavy baggage, cannon and stores on board their transports, which have fallen down the river, and having sent across to the Jersey shore the principal part of their waggons, containing their light baggage and a considerable part of their force, including, according to several recent accounts, almost the whole of their cavalry; their grenadiers and light infantry, a brigade of British and some regiments of New levies being the only troops now remaining in the city.[1] That from every appearance the most natural inference is, they are destined for New York, either by marching through the Jerseys towards Amboy, or down the river to some convenient place of embarkation, and thence round by water, but as it is far from impossible, they may only mean to draw us out of this strong position, throw us off our guard and attack us to advantage or may intend some southern expedition, these objects ought duly to be attended to. That their force amounts to 10,000 rank and file, fit for duty.[2]

He further states to them, that the strength of the army at this post, including those on command, who might be drawn together in time of action, and such of the sick present as might be capable of acting on an emergency is 12500 lang [rank] and file. That of these near 11000 would be able to march off the ground, in a condition for service. That there are now in camp about 2300, who, from sickness and want of necessaries, would be unable to march with the army for the purpose of operating, but would most of them be able to travel moderately to some place of greater security, into the country, in case of a removal of the army. That besides these there are in the rear of this camp within the distance of eight or ten miles twelve hundred who would be incapable of removing themselves in case of necessity; but must be carried away in waggons, if it should become requisite. That there are no very considerable magazines, either in camp, or in its vicinity; but there are some valuable stores, in the Quarter Master General's department at Reading, and two large depositaries of military stores at Lebanon and Carlisle. That there are parcels of flour and other provisions, dispersed in different parts of this state; but no material quantity at any one place.

His Excellency also informed the Council, that there is a brigade of Continental troops in the Jerseys consisting of about 800 fit for duty and that all the Militia of that state have been notified of the probability of the enemy's marching through it, and warned to collect on signals for the purpose, to give them all the annoyance and disturbance in their power, in concert with the Continental troops.[3]

He observes to them also, that on a junction of the enemy's force in and near Philadelphia, and that which they already have at New York and its dependencies, their number will amount to between 14 and 15000. That on our part, when this army shall be united to the one on the North River, we shall have near 14000 Continental troops fit for service.

Having stated these facts, for the information of the Council, The

Commander in Chief requests, after a personal discussion of the subject, that each member will favour him with his opinion in writing,
on the conduct, which it will be adviseable for this army to observe
on the present occasion, and under present appearances, in determining which, though he would not wish to confine the attention of
the Council solely to these objects, He recommends the following
questions to their mature consideration.

Whether any entreprise ought to be undertaken against the
enemy in Philadelphia, in their present circumstances?

Whether this army should remain in the position it now holds,
'till the final evacuation of the city or move immediately towards the
Delaware?

Whether any detachment of it shall be sent to reinforce the Brigade in the Jerseys, or advanced towards the enemy to act as occasion
shall require and endeavour to take advantage of their retreat?

If the army remain on its present ground 'till the enemy quit the
city, and if they march through the Jerseys towards Amboy, will it
be practicable from the obstructions they may probably receive from
the troops already there, in conjunction with the Militia, to arrive in
time with this army, to give them any material interruption? Will it
be prudent to attempt it, or not rather more eligible to proceed to
North River in the most direct and convenient manner, to secure the
important communication between the Eastern and Southern states?

In case such measures should be adopted, as will enable this
army to overtake the enemy in their march, will it be prudent, with
the aid which may reasonably be expected from the Jersey Militia, to
make an attack upon them, and ought it to be a partial or a general
one?

In case of an immediate removal of this army, what precautions
will be proper for the security of the sick belonging to it, and of the
stores in this state?

D (Washington Papers: DLC).
    1. It is a mystery why Washington waited until the last minute to discuss with his
general officers how the army should respond to the British evacuation of Philadelphia.
A month earlier he had told NG that "every piece of intelligence from Philadelphia
makes me think it more and more probable that the Enemy are preparing to evacuate"
(letter of 17 May, above). In the interim scarcely a day passed without fresh intelligence
of further British preparations. Washington's informers, of course, had no way of
knowing what lay behind the external signs of an impending move.
    Shortly after Clinton replaced Howe as commander of British forces he received
word from the British Cabinet that, in order to counter the French alliance, he was to
send five thousand troops to St. Lucia in the West Indies, three thousand to the
Floridas and to move the remainder of his army from Philadelphia to New York.

Clinton's orders did not specify by what means he was to get the troops to New York. He took it upon himself to delay transferring the eight thousand troops to St. Lucia and Florida because of insufficient naval escorts. It was a fortunate decision for the British, since unbeknown to Clinton or Lord Howe, who still commanded the American fleet, Count d'Estaing was nearing American waters with a formidable French fleet. If d'Estaing had intercepted the ill-protected transports, Clinton would have been virtually helpless with his remnant of five thousand troops. Since all available vessels would be engaged in transporting loyalists and invalids from Philadelphia, Clinton boldly planned to march his army across New Jersey to New York, risking an attack by Washington against his train of troops, artillery, and supply wagons that was to stretch out to a length of some twelve miles. (Clinton's instructions and his decision are covered in Willcox, *Clinton*, 222–33, and in Mackesy, *War*, pp. 214–16.)

2. In listing possible alternatives to New York as the destination of Clinton's army, Washington was reflecting opinions that Gen. Charles Lee had expressed two days earlier. Despite the many signs that pointed to New York, Lee was convinced Clinton would choose one of three alternatives, depending on his offensive capacity: strike for Lancaster, Pa., the seat of Pennsylvania government, either directly or by way of New Castle, Del.; shift to the lower part of the Susquehannah River, where they could encourage Indian uprisings on the frontier; or settle in Delaware or the Eastern Shore of Maryland, where they could sustain themselves while still under the protection of the navy. (Lee to Washington, 15 June 1778, *Lee Papers*, 2: 399–402)

A figure on troop numbers, as usual, is elusive. Willcox, *Clinton*, p. 232, puts the number at "some ten thousand"; Mackesy, *War*, p. 214, lists 14,700 in Philadelphia; Smith, *Monmouth*, p. 30, quotes Gen. Howe's figures of 17,600, but he estimates by the time Clinton began his march he had 13,000 men.

3. The continental troops in New Jersey consisted of Gen. William Maxwell's four New Jersey regiments. (Lesser, *Sinews*, p. 68) The New Jersey militia was under Maj. Gen. Philemon Dickinson. Brig. Gen. William Winds, who commanded one unit of the New Jersey militia at Elizabeth Town, had just reported to Gov. Livingston that he had less than six rounds of ammunition per man. (*N.J. Rev. Correspondence*, pp. 117–18)

To Colonel Udny Hay

Camp Valley Forge June 17th 1778

I am very Sorry the Congress have abolished your military rank. I am really of Oppinion that as you left the Line of the Army to engage in the more disagreable business of the Qr Mstrs department and as you have served under an Expectation of preserving your rank without any Extraordinary Emoluments and to the Entire Satisfaction of the Public and the Army, that it would have been but a piece of Justice due to your merit to have Continued you all the Honors and Emoluments due to a Lieutenant Colonel.[1]

There is no Man of whose Activity and Industry I have a better Oppinion, and I persuade myself we Cannot fail to preserve a good Understanding. I am happy to hear your Conduct is Satisfactory to the Army and pleasing to the Country.

NATH GREENE

Cy of extract (PCC, Item 151: DNA).
1. For background, see above, NG to Laurens, 1 May.

To George Washington

Camp Valley Forge June 18th 1778
In order to answer your Excellencys six queries and be clearly understood, I shall first state a query and then give it an answer, and so on
in order untill the whole is answered.[1]

Query the first   Whether any enterprize ought to be undertaken
against Phila.

Answer.   I am clearly of Opinion that there ought not. The
Enemy can recall any part of their force from the other side of Delaware so easily and secretly that it is impossible for us to plan an
attack, and form any tolerable Idea of the force we have to contend
with. It is to be presumed the Enemy have force enough in the City to
defend their Redoubts; and if they have not, they are all prepared for
a retreat, which they can effect with such ease and expedition that it
will be impossible for us to take advantage of it; That in either case we
shall gain nothing by such an enterprize, fatigue the Troops to no purpose and be drawn out of our proper direction, to the prejudice of
operations necessary to be carried on in New Jersey.[2]

Query the 2d.   Whether we should remain in our present position untill the Enemy finally evacuate Phila, or move towards the
Delaware.[3]

Answer.   I concieve it to be both the duty and interest of this
Army to leave it's present position and move towards the Delaware.
It is impossible to reduce the Enemies intentions to a certainty; but I
think the ballance of evidence is greatly in favour of their going
through New Jersy. We must suppose they have some fixed object,
some plan for their future operations; and I cannot believe they
would change their measures, for the little advantages they might
gain, by making an excurtion into this part of the Country with a view
to destroy our Stores or possess themselves of our sick. It is our duty
to cover New Jersey as much as possible, their patriotism merits it. In
this position we cannot do it effectually. I remember it was urged last
night that this was the only secure position the Country affords, that
by moving out of it, we might invite the Enemy to attempt to bring us
to a General action. If they were desirous of that, by moving into the
Country either to our right or left they could oblige us to abandon this
post, or we must give up the Country to be ravaged, which with our
present forces I believe no person would advise to. An Army of
observation in the neighbourhood of the Enemy is always liable to be
brought to a General action; but the General has ever the choice of
two things, either to take a position and defend himself, or retreat out

of their way, and there is no other alternative when the Enemy are determined to bring us to action. If the Enemy wish to bring us to action they can take a position in N. Jersey, and that will compel us to go into their neighbourhood and then the consequences of a general action may follow. For we must not, neither can we, give up the Country to be ravaged. It will be in vain for the Inhabitants to remove their stock, if this Army is not some where in the neighbourhood of the Enemy to protect it.

The State of European politicks and the promising condition of our own affairs forbid our taking any rash measures, or putting anything to the hazard unnecessarily. But moving towards the Delaware is neither rash nor hazardous. It is impossible for us to take any position and not risque something. I know we uncover part of the Country by moving towards the Delaware, but the ballance of evidence is so strong in favour of it as to justify the measure. It is said not to be our interest to be in the neighbourhood of the Enemy in moving thro' the Jerseys. They can oblige us to that by taking a position there. However I am by no means convinced they will wish to fight us in their passage, with their force divided and ours united, their ships at a distance, the Country their enemies and our friends. If they have orders to evacuate the Country, I am persuaded they do not want to risque an action especially upon unequal terms. If the situation of their affairs renders the evacuation of this Country necessary, if they gain a battle of us it would not alter their measures, and if they are going to form a junction of their forces to act in these States we shall never meet them upon better terms.

I would not be understood from what I have said to be an adviser to a general action. I only mean to show that if in affording protection to the Country we are brought to action, it is not upon very unequal terms on our part, and that in making this move we shall do nothing more than the enemy can oblige us to do. The probability of the enemy's possessing themselves of this post is also objected to our moving. I confess the force of that reason does not strike me as I cannot concieve wherein it is elligible for their purposes. But suppose they should if our sick and stores are gone, they will gain no great advantage by the measure. I would move somewhere in the neighbourhood of New Town.[4] I would leave about five hundred men at this place with a Regt of horse to cover the Sick and Stores. But I would order a sufficiency of Waggons to be held in readiness to move off the Sick in case the Enemy should move out. Dr Shippen thinks one hundred will move the whole.

Query the 3d. Whether any detachment shall be made from this army to reinforce the Brigade in New Jersey or the whole Army to advance towards the Enemy to act as occasion may require.

Answer. I would not detach from this Army for in doing that we hazard both parts, and if it's dangerous for the whole army to go into the neighbourhood of the Enemy it must be still more so for a part.

I should be for moveing with our whole force or not at all, and I think even the Brigade and the Militia of New Jersey will fall a sacrafice, if the Enemy have got such a body of horse as we are told, unless they have orders to keep at a respectable distance.

Query 4th. If the Army remain on it's present ground untill the final evacuation of the City; and if the Enemy march through the Jersies, will it be practicable from the obstructions they may probably receive from the Continental troops there in conjunction with the Militia for this army to arrive in time so as to give them any material interruption. Will it be prudent to attempt it or not, or for the Army to march directly to the North River to secure the communication with the Eastern States.

Answer. It is very doubtfull whether this Army if it remains on its present ground could get [i.e., catch] up with the Enemy in passing through the Jersies, and I should not think it worth attempting unless they took post some where and began to ravage the Country. In that case we must of necessity endeavour to protect the Inhabitants. Otherwise I would advise to march immediately for the North River.

Query 5th. In case this Army could get up with the Enemy shall we make a partial, or general attack or none at all.

Answer. I cannot give any possitive answer to this query. The policy of pursuing either the one or the other of the measures depending so much upon circumstances, I would therefore advise if we should get into the neighbourhood of the Enemy to make the attack either partial or general as things may appear at the time. I would not risque a General action if it can well be avoided, unless I had some great advantage from the make of the ground or the manner of attack. Neither would I make any attack at all if it should appear at the time to be against our interest.[5]

Query 6th. How to secure the Sick and Stores in this State if we leave this Post.

Answer. This query has been answered before in the answer to the second query. But it may be said in addition to that: The position at Newtown will not totally uncover this Country, and should it be necessary to regain our present [position] we can easily affect it, or if the Enemy mean to operate against the Lower counties of Delaware and Maryland we shall be only two days longer in getting up with them.

NewTown is a strong situation, abounds with forage, and supplies may be had down the Delaware for the support of the Army. If in taking that position we should oblige the Enemy to change their measures it must ruin their plan of operations and make them waste a great part of the Campaign to no purpose and give the Eastern States an opportunity to fill up their Regiments and effectually secure the North River.

NATH GREENE

LS (Washington Papers: DLC).

1. NG made some changes in paraphrasing Washington's queries as quoted above at Council of War, 17 June. Answers of all those attending the council are in the Washington Papers, DLC. Lafayette's answer is dated 17 June; the rest—including that of Cadwalader, who did not attend the council—are dated 18 June.

2. None of those attending favored attacking Philadelphia.

3. Washington had said move "immediately" toward the Delaware.

4. Before most of the generals had finished writing their opinions, the rest of Clinton's army had crossed the river into New Jersey. Only two of them, however, sided with NG in agreeing the army should move before Clinton's objectives were known. Wayne thought the army should be "put in motion the soonest possible" toward the river to be in a position to cross readily: Cadwalader considered the same move "absolutely necessary."

The others may have been influenced by Charles Lee, who spoke authoritatively and persuasively, although his record for anticipating the future moves of his former English associates was not impressive. As noted at the Council of War, above, Lee was quite certain that New York was not Clinton's destination. Even with the British encamped across the river in New Jersey, he declared in his written opinion to Washington that "on a mere supposition that it is the Enemys intention to march through that State, it would be unjustifyable to leave this Country uncover'd." (Washington Papers, DLC).

5. Wayne and Cadwalader were less cautious in recommending an attack; the others either hedged their answers or favored going directly to the North River.

To Moore Furman

Sir   Head Quarters [Valley Forge] June 18, 1778

The enemy are gone from Philadelphia. Our Army are on the March for Coryells Ferry where the whole are to pass. You will assist us there with a large number of Waggons, straw &c &c.

I have not time to be particular but Waggons and forage, there will be a great cry for. Mr Pettit is at Yorktown and Col Cox is gone to Philadelphia and I am alone without the least aid. I am Sir your humble Sert

NATH GREENE

ALS (Nj).

To Colonel Charles Pettit

Dear Sir   Head Quarters [Valley Forge] June 18, 1778

Intelligence this moment has arrivd from Philadelphia that the enemy have evacuated it. Part of our Army begins their march towards the Delaware this afternoon and the whole will be in motion tomorrow morning. Various are the opinions of the General Officers respecting the enemies further designs; General Lee seems to think they are going to Maryland; but I am fully of opinion they are going to New York. The ballance of evidence at present is much in favor of this conjecture.

I hope you have brought your business to some issue before this, the sooner you can join us the better. Col Cox is going into the City immediately; and I poor soul shall be left all alone to do both the field and family duty.

Stop Col Davis from geting any more Portmantaues made, as the Officers dont like to pay the cost thereof.[1] I hope you will collect the intention of Congress fully upon this point and the Horses and Saddles. I am with sincere regard your most Obedt Hum Sert

NATH GREENE

ALS (NHi).
    1. See above, NG to Laurens, 1 June.

To Moore Furman

Sir   Buckingham [Pa.] June 21, 1778

I want to know what number of Teams and what quantity of forage you can provide us with at Coryells Ferry. We have a great many hir'd and impressd Waggons belonging to this State which I wish to dismiss if possible on this side of the River; and therefore want to know what assistance you can give us that I may regulate my conduct accordingly.

We shall reach the ferry this forenoon and encamp on this side to Night and cross early in the morning. The teams we shall want, will be for the Commisary of provisions and forage. We have nearly baggage Waggons enough.

The ferry at Coryells is attended with a very great expence, if not accompanied with an equal degree of imposition; I wish to know whether it would be agreeable to you to undertake the regulation thereof. I am Sir your humble Servt

NATH GREENE

ALS (Nj).

From Colonel William Smith[1]

[Springfield, Mass., 21 June 1778. Has NG's letter of 12 June; has appointed forage master for Brookfield, Mass. He will soon build scows that NG mentions.[2] Townsmen object to "there being a Continental Ferry here and say a license must first be obtain[ed] from the Court." Town has let ten acres half mile from town, "the place Genl Knox thought conveniant for erecting an Elaboratory &c."[3] Stores less exposed to fire there than in town. ALS (PPAmP) 2 pp.]

1. William Smith (1756–1806) was the youthful deputy quartermaster for western Massachusetts. He remained in the post throughout NG's tenure. He was a merchant for many years after the war in Springfield. (Charles W. Chapin, *Sketches of the Old Inhabitants . . . of Springfield* [Springfield, 1893], pp. 348–49)
2. NG's letter of 12 June not found, but Udny Hay had passed on NG's request for boat building to Smith's assistant, Pynchon, 21 May, above.
3. This was the beginning of the Springfield arsenal. Progress on it was slow, however, for Smith reported in October that it was nothing more than a barn. (Smith to NG, 1 October, below)

To Moore Furman

Dear Sir   Camp Hopewell[1] [N.J.] June 23d 1778
    The Commissary [Jeremiah Wadsworth] comes with a grievious complaint—Not a barrel of flour in Camp and a monstrous family to supply . I must beg you to furnish [him] with all the Waggons you possibly can. The forage department is important but the Army must be fed at all events. You will consult with the Commisary General or the person he shall send and take the necessary steps accordingly. I am Sir your humble Servt.

NATH GREENE

ALS (Nj).
1. Hopewell was ten miles east of the Delaware River, which the army had just crossed. The American army was roughly paralleling the British route.

To Catharine Greene

           Camp Hopewell near Princetown, New Jersey
My dear   June 23, 1778
    I have not receivd a single line from you since you left camp, only that by Mr Lebrune. I am afraid your Letters are stopt and opend by some impudent scoundrel. I have wrote you five or six times.[1] I had the pleasure to hear of you on the Road and that you were well. I hope you got home safe.
    The Enimy have evacuated Philadelphia and are now on their march through the Jerseys. They are at this time about fifteen or

twenty miles distant from us at a place call'd Crossix. We arrivd here last night and shall march for Princetown this afternoon.

Col Cox is at Philadelphia and Mr Pettit at Congress and I am left all alone with business enough for ten men. They both write and desire their compliments to you. They are often paying you the highest complements. This they do by way of pleasing me as well as paying a proper tribute to your merit and worth. They profess great friendship for you.

You cannot conceive how the family at Moore Hall were destrest at my leaving them. They expected every kind of insult and abuse after I was gone. You are their favorite; they pray for you Night and Day.[2]

Mrs Knox has been in Philadelphia and is now gone to Morristown. She is fatter than ever which is a great mortification to her. The General is equally fat and therefore one cannot laugh at the other. They appear to be extravagantly fond of each other and I think are perfectly happy.

Pray write me the first opportunity of everything, particularly about the Children and yourself. My love to all friends. Yours affectionately

NATH GREENE

ALS (NjP).
1. Only one of his letters during this time has been found.
2. On Moore Hall, see above, NG to Biddle, 12 February.

Council of War

At a Council of War held in Hopewell Township, New Jersey, June 24th 1778.[1]

Present
The Commander in Chief

Major Genls	Brigadier Generals
Lee	Knox
Greene	Poor
Stirling	Wayne
Fayette	Woodford
Steuben	Patterson
	Scott
	Portail

His Excellency informs the Council, that by the latest advices he has received, the Enemy are in two columns, one on the Allen Town and the other on the Borden Town road, The front of the latter near the Drawbridge, at which the two roads unite in the main Cranbury road, Their force from the best estimate he can form is between 9 and 10,000 rank and file.[2]

That the strength of the Army on this Ground, by a field return made two days since consisted of 10,684 rank and file; besides which there is an advanced Brigade under General Maxwell, of about 1200. That in addition to this force from the account given by Genl Dickinson there appear to be about 1200 Militia, collected in the neighbourhood of the Enemy, who in conjunction with General Maxwell are hovering on their flanks and rear and obstructing their march.

He further informs the Council, that measures have been taken to procure an aid of Pensylvania militia; which have not as yet produced any material effect. Genl Cadwalader with fifty or Sixty Volunteers and a Detachment of Continental Troops, amounting to about 300 were to cross the Delaware yesterday morning and fall in with the Enemy's rear. General Lacy had crossed with 40 men.[3]

He observes to the Council that it is now the seventh day since the Enemy evacuated Philadelphia during which time they have marched less than 40 miles. That the obstructions thrown in their way, by breaking down Bridges, felling Trees &c was insufficient to produce so great delay, as is the opinion of Genl Dickinson himself, who has principally directed them; and that the opposition they have otherwise received, has not been very considerable.

Under those circumstances, and considering the present situation of our national affairs, and the probable prospect of the Enemy, the General requests the sentiments of the Council on the following questions.

Will it be adviseable for us, of choice, to hazard a general action?

If it is, should we do it by immediately making a general attack upon the Enemy, by attempting a partial one, or by taking such a position, if it can be done, as may oblige them to attack us?

If it is not, what measures can be taken, with safety to this army, to annoy the Enemy on their march, should it be their intent to proceed through the Jerseys?

In fine, what precise line of conduct will it be best for us to pursue?

Answer to the first question. It will not be adviseable. To the second, This is involved and answered in the first. To the third. A detachment of fifteen hundred men to be immediately sent to act as occasion may serve, on the enemy's left flank and rear, in conjunction with the other Continental troops and militia, which are already hanging about them, and the main body to preserve a relative position, so as to be able to act as circumstances may require.

To the fourth. This is partly answered in the foregoing and may be referred to further consideration.[4]

CHARLES LEE	POOR
STIRLING	JNO PATERSON
NATH GREENE	WM WOODFORD
THE MIS. DE LAFAYETTE	CHS SCOTT
STEUBEN	DUPORTAIL
	H KNOX

DS (Washington Papers: DLC).

1. As noted above, NG to Washington, 18 June, most of the general officers were of the opinion that the army should remain at Valley Forge until Clinton's intentions were clearly established. But by 11:30 A.M. on 18 June, while some of them, in fact, were still writing down their opinions, word reached Washington that the last of Clinton's army had crossed into New Jersey. Without waiting for further intelligence, he gave orders at once that put the army in motion. Lee's division was ordered out first, with the remaining divisions under Lafayette, Kalb, and Stirling to follow early on the nineteenth. NG's formal responsibility as Washington's orders put it, lay in "regulating the order of March, encampment and planting of Guards." (Fitzpatrick, GW, 12: 91) The task as described in his letter to Gen. Weedon, 25 July, below, was far from being that simple.

Washington directed Benedict Arnold to take command in Philadelphia and sent units under William Maxwell and Daniel Morgan across the river to harass the enemy and impede their progress. Lee's division completed its crossing of the river at Coryells Ferry in the early morning hours of 21 June. Washington arrived at Coryells at noon, but rain prevented the rest of the army from crossing until 22 June. Although Clinton's forces had advanced less than twenty miles in three days, there was no longer any doubt that New York was their destination. On the afternoon of 23 June, Washington set up headquarters at the Baptist Church in Hopewell, with the army encamped nearby. He called the Council of War for 9:00 A.M. on 24 June. (Freeman, GW, 5: 16; the army's movements from 18 to 24 June are on pp. 11–17. See also Fitzpatrick, GW, 12: 74–117. The progress of Clinton's army is detailed in Robertson, Diary, 173–76; see also Willcox, Clinton, 231–33.)

When NG later took credit with Rhode Island's delegate to Congress for expediting the progress of Washington's army across New Jersey, he was not boasting unduly. (See below, NG to Marchant, 25 July.) It was the magazines he had established that permitted Washington's army to catch up with the heavily ladened wagon trains of the British. With Clinton's change in destination from Amboy to Sandy Hook, N.J., the American army was forced to leave the route where magazines were located, but NG's supply wagons adapted to the change. As Theodore Thayer points out in his Monmouth (p. 27), when the troops arrived at campsites "they found latrines, firewood, and piles of straw for bedding. Springs were walled with stone to keep the water from becoming muddy from constant use. Barrels of vinegar were provided for warding off intestinal disorders."

2. On the various figures given for Clinton's army, see note, Council of War, 17 June, above.

3. Gens. John Cadwalader and John Lacey commanded the Pennsylvania militia.

4. The overly succinct answers to Washington's queries, to which all but Anthony Wayne subscribed, were far from representing the diversity of opinion that prevailed at the meeting, as is clear in NG to Washington, below, and the accompanying note.

To George Washington

Sir   ⟨Hopewell, N.J. June 24, 1778⟩

The delicate situation I am in prevents my speaking in councils of war with that openness I should if I was to take a part in the command.[1] I must confess the opinion I subscribed to, if it is to be considered in confind sense, does not perfectly coincide with my Sentiments. I am not for hazzarding a general action unnecessarily but I am clearly of opinion for makeing a serious impression with the light Troops and for haveing the Army in supporting distance. As I said today in Council, I would have two Brigades to support the light troops and the whole army should be at hand to support them. The attack should be made upon the enemies flank and rear.

If we suffer the enemy to pass through the Jerseys without attempting anything upon them, I think we shall ever regret it. I cannot help thinking we magnify our difficulties beyond reallities. We are now in the most awkward situation in the World. We have come with great rapidity and we got near the Enemy and then our courage faild us and we halted without attempting to do the enemy the least injury. Your Excellency may remember I mentiond this matter at Buckingham. People expects something from us and our strength demands it. I am by no means for rash measures but we must preserve our reputation.

I think we can make a very serious impression without any great risque, and if it should amount to a general action I think the chance is greatly in our favor. However I think we can make a partial attack without suffering them to bring us to a general action.[2] I am your Excellencys obedient Servt

NATH GREENE

ALS (Washington Papers: DLC). Portion in angle brackets from Varick Tr., Washington Papers, DLC.

1. As quartermaster general NG was a staff, not a line, officer. He had no reason to anticipate that he would have a command at the battle of Monmouth four days later. (See NG to Jacob, 2 July, below.)

2. Lafayette, agreeing essentially with NG, also wrote Washington after the council adjourned to say that he had signed the document only "because I have been told I schould sign it and because almost all the others who were of the same opinion as I am also sign'd." He pointed out that six generals—including himself, Steuben, du Portail, Wayne, Paterson, and Greene—were for sending a detachment of 2,500 men to attack the enemy's flank and rear. Steuben and du Portail, neither of whose English was up to Lafayette's, asked him to express to Washington how distressed they were to see that "we were going to loose an occasion which may be reputed as one of the finest ever offered." Lafayette thought he detected that Washington was inclined to go along with this group. (Lafayette's letter, which is in the Washington Papers, DLC, has been printed in Gottschalk, Letters of Lafayette, pp. 46–47.)

Wayne had refused to sign the document and wrote to Washington that day to advocate the same measures that NG and Lafayette proposed (Washington Papers, DLC). Hamilton, who as Washington's aide had summarized the answers at the Council of War, saw Charles Lee as dominating the council with his timid strategy. The results of the council, he confided to Elias Boudinot in a letter of 5 July, "would have done honor to the most honorab[le] society of midwives, and to them only." (Syrett, Hamilton, 1: 510)

To what extent Washington was influenced by the bolder advocates is discussed at the battle of Monmouth, NG to Jacob, 2 July, below.

From Colonel James Abeel

[Reading, Pa., 25 June 1778. Sending "sundry necessary Articles"; off for Philadelphia to see Cox and get money. "God grant you Burgoyne the Enemy." LB (Abeel Papers: DLC) 1 p.]

From Colonel Robert L. Hooper

[Easton, Pa., 26 June 1778. Has sent twelve four-horse teams, spades, pick axes, shovels, bridles, portmanteaus and valises. ALS (PPAmP) 1 p.]

From Nehemiah Hubbard

[Hartford, Conn., 27 June 1778. In answer to NG's of 15 May, will send returns and vouchers; has wagoners and teams for artillery. Since they haul seven barrels to a load they should be paid more than Major Wood's teams, which haul only six. Otherwise it "makes a great deal of uneasiness." Cy of excerpt (RG 93, WRMS: DNA) 1 p.]

From Colonel Udny Hay

[Peekskill, N.Y., 29 June 1778. Asks again if barrack master is independent of quartermaster department.[1] Cy of excerpt (PPAmP) 1 p.]

1. See his letter of 26 May, above.

From Colonel Morgan Lewis[1]

[Albany, N.Y.? June, 1778]

General Gates when President of the Board of War had regularly every month a Return of the Officers of the Quarter Master Branch in the Northern Department. He has had the same since his last accession to the Command. On his arrival I waited on him at West Point. I there informed him there was a superfluous number of Officers in my Department and requested of him to discharge such as I should mention, alledging I never had *myself* appointed an officer and was not invested with a power to discharge any.[2]

At the Same Time I acquainted Genl Gates (as I had done before by Letter when he sat as President of the Board of War) that I was building at Saratoga by orders of the Marquis 100 Batteaux, and gave him the Marquis's Reasons for ordering them to be built there, which Genl Gates upon my Representation highly approved of. At this Time about Sixty of the Batteaux were finished, and I asked the

General if the Carpenters should go on and compleat the hundred. His answer was by all means.

All the officers in the Forage Department, and all in the Barrack Masters Department, one in the latter Dept excepted, were appointed by General Gates after the last Campaign in Novr or Decr without my previous Knowledge.

M LEWIS

Cy (PCC, Item 155: DNA).

1. Morgan Lewis (1754–1844), a graduate of the College of New Jersey (Princeton), was studying law in 1775. A volunteer at the siege of Boston, he was named deputy quartermaster general of the Northern Army at Albany with a colonel's commission in 1776, and during the Saratoga campaign, he was Gates's chief of staff. NG kept him in the Albany post throughout his tenure. After serving as chief justice of the New York Supreme Court, he was elected governor in 1804. During the war of 1812, he was made quartermaster general of the army, retiring as a major general. (*DAB*)

2. For the background of this letter, see below, NG to Laurens, 27 July, with which this was enclosed.

Peter Gordon[1] to Moore Furman

[Camp Spotswood, N.J., 1 July 1778. Entire army stopped here en route to Brunswick. NG asks that he send as many horses as possible, as heat had made it necessary to rest many of those with army. ALS (Nj) 1 p.]

1. Gordon, formerly a major in the N.J. militia, was an assistant quartermaster in Trenton who had accompanied the army to Monmouth and was still with NG. He remained in the quartermaster department until 1780. After the war he was active in public life, serving as New Jersey state treasurer from 1803 to 1821.

From Colonel John Davis

[Carlisle, Pa., 1 July 1778. Concerns wagons, teams, and wagoners for main army and western expedition.[1] Has stopped buying "Horses and Waggons Unless Where I meet With a team fully Equipt and Consider it a bargain." ACyS (Davis Papers: DLC) 2 pp.]

1. See above, Davis to NG 15 June.

To Jacob Greene

Dear Sir   Camp at Brunswick [N.J.] July 2d 1778

It is sometime since I have wrote or rec'd a Line from you. I have been too much engaged to write and I suppose it has been difficult for your Letters if you have wrote to find Me.

The Enemy evacuated Philadelphia on 18th of June and marchd

from the valley on the 20th. The Enemy took their Rout from Coopers
Ferry through Mount Holly, Allentown to Monmouth. We took our
Route to Coryells Ferry, Princetown, Cranberry and to Englishtown
about six Miles from Monmouth where we came up with the Enemy
after a March of near double the[y] Marched. Two Days before the
Action, which was on the 28th, Men was detached from the Line of
the Army near Three Thousand of pickd Troops and officers and Two
other Brigades amounting on the whole to near 5000 Men under the
command of Major General Lee.

Great things was expected from this Detachment. The General
had orders to attack the Enemies Rear wherever he came up with it.
The whole Army followed in supporting Distance. On the 28th in the
morning General Lee came up with the Enemy's rear Guard a Little
out of Monmouth Town. Upon our Troops making their Appearance
the Enemy began to face about and put themselves in a Posture of
Defence. Our whole Army was in full March to support General Lee
in case he began the Attack. However from Want of Confidence in
our Troops either as to their Numbers, Spirit, or Discipline, or from
the Enemes superior Numbers, the General did not think proper to
begin the charge But orderd a Retreat. The Enemy perceiving our
People begin to move off, began to push them in Turn and drove
them back upon the main Army in great confusion. Fortunately the
Main Army had gained a very advantageous Piece of Ground for
covering our Peoples Retreat and checking the Progress of the Enemy.
The Place where the two Armies Met was a little in the Rear of
Monmouth to between that and Englishtown. A Severe Cannonade
began on both sides which continued without intermission for some
Hours. General Lee with the greater Part of the Troops under his
command were orderd in the Rear of the Army, being more spent
with the Heat and Fatigue of the March in the Morning, where they
continud the Remaining part of the Day.

After forming the Line, encouraging the Men and refreshing
them for about Two or three Hours during which time there was a
most furious canonade burst on both Sides, our Infantry began to
advance. There was a few choice Corps selected for the Purpose
under the command of Col. Scilly [Joseph Cilley] of New Hamshire
who did himself imortal Honor. Col. Stewart, General Wayne and
Col. Parker, those were some of the corps that distinguished themselves most. But all our Troops behaved with the greatest Bravery
They began the Charge between 3 and 4 oClock in the afternoon
which lasted about an Hour when the Enemy fled and left us Masters
of the Field. They supported the Attack with the Grenadiers, Kings
Guard and Battalion of Light Infantry and Two Brigades of [*indeci-*

pherable] Men who, to do them Justice, behavd with great Spirit. They had also about 400 Horse in the Field and a large Train of Artillery which kept Shot and Shells flying as thick as Hail. It is supposed the Enemy loss in the course of the day was upward of a 1000 Men killed and wounded. We buried between two and three Hundred of their Men found upon the Field of Action next Day. It is remarkable that the Enemies Loss was more than Two to one of ours notwithstanding our People advancd upon them under many disadvantages.

We encampd upon the Field of Action that night but was prevented from pushing our Advantages from the peculiar Situation of the Enemies Reserves which were posted a little in the Rear of the Field of Battle securd on both Flanks by impassable morasses with only a narrow Defile leading to their Front. The Enemy retreated that night about 12 oClock. As General Lee was detached I had the Honor to command the Right Wing of the Army. General Knox and the Artillery did themselves great Credit. Lord Sterling and many officers were very active. The Enemy had so much the Start of us, the [night?] was stormy and our Men so much fatigued with the Exercise of the preceding Day that it were impossible to persue. The Heat of the Day was excessive. Many Men fell dead by the Violence of the Exercise and the intense Heat.

The commander in Chief was every where, his Presence gave Spirit and Confidence and his command and authority soon brought every thing into Order and Regularity.

The Enemies Loss upon their March through the Jerseys by Desertion, in Skirmishing, by Sickness and Heat, and in the last Action is estimated at upwards of 3000 Men. We have suffered considerably by the Heat. We marchd through a Country from Monmouth to Brunswick not unlike the Deserts of Arabia for Soil and Climate. The Enemy embarked their Troops at Hows Harbor [at Sandy Hook] opposite Staten Island. It is the opinion of Many that the Enemy will give us but Little more Trouble this Summer.

General Lee's conduct was so dissatisfactory to the officers and Men that were out with him in the Morning that General Scott and General Wayne, Two of the officers commanding Detachments, entered a formal Complaint against him which compelled his Excellency to put him under Arrest. He is upon Trial today which I expect will terminate with a Slight censure. I am really Sorry for the Affair as I fear it will create many Divisions in the Army.

I had like to have forgot to mention that the Rhode Island Troops were in Action and behavd very well. Capt [Thomas] Arnold is wounded in the Leg.[1]

I hope you and your Family are well. Long before this I suppose

Mrs Greene has got home. I wish to know where she has taken her Residence. Bill Littlefield writes that the children are well and the Little Girl is getting better of the Rickets.

My kind Love to all our Family, Brothers and Sisters, and to Mother Greene, Cousin Griffin and Sally. Remember me kindly to Sister Peggy and the Children. I would write Cousin Griffin but I have not Time. I am with affectionate Regard your [brother?]

N. GREENE

Tr (Theodore Foster transcript: RHi). In 1812, a few years after Jacob Greene's death, Theodore Foster transcribed a dozen letters addressed to Jacob, whose daughter married Foster's nephew, with a view to using them in a projected history of Rhode Island. Portions of the transcripts are almost indecipherable.

1. NG's role in the battle of Monmouth, although not a key one, was considerably more important than suggested by his brief reference to having had "the Honor to command the Right Wing of the Army."

Monmouth was a memorable battle in several respects. Although it was fought to a draw, each side could take pride in the outcome. For Gen. Henry Clinton, who had never before commanded in battle, it climaxed a bold and well-directed venture in which he succeeded in getting most of his army and all of his 1,500 wagons through some seventy miles of enemy territory. For Washington it was a triumph that an army that only a few months before had been reduced to a few thousand half-naked and ill-disciplined troops could now stand up to the pride of the British army. This, in turn, was a tribute to many people: to the hardy men who had stuck with the army all winter, to the recruits that had poured in during May, to Gen. Steuben's tireless drill work, to Commissary Wadsworth and Quartermaster Greene, to the militia of Pennsylvania and New Jersey, and to the French Alliance, which lifted the spirits of the soldiers as it did of all Americans. Gen. Clinton, who was to remain in command of the British army for the rest of the war, gained a respect for the American army that day that he was never to lose.

Monmouth was memorable in other ways. It was, for example, the last major engagement fought in the north; it was the longest battle of the war; and it was fought, as no other major engagement, in stifling heat. None who survived the day would ever forget the heat. With more than fifteen hours of sunshine, 28 June was the fifth day of a heat wave, which on the day of the battle saw temperatures close to 100° Fahrenheit. The sun beat down mercilessly on the men who fought back and forth through sandy fields and around steaming morasses with nothing but scrubby pines for shade. The British and Germans, with woolen uniforms and heavy packs, suffered especially; but on both sides dozens died of heat stroke, and those who survived were half-crazed with thirst and limp with heat exhaustion.

Finally Monmouth was memorable as marking the end of Gen. Charles Lee's military career, which ended in disgrace. As NG writes to Jacob, a formal complaint was entered against him by Gens. Wayne and Scott, and a month later a courtmartial found him guilty of disobeying orders, making a shameful retreat, and showing disrespect for the commander in chief in subsequent letters. In December, Congress upheld the findings. It is difficult to be dispassionate about this brilliant, eccentric, opinionated, ambitious, and sometimes irascible man. Even some nineteenth-century partisans of Washington considered that he was dealt with too harshly. Twentieth-century writers have gone much further in his defense. John Alden, in a scholarly and sympathetic biography published in 1951, saw Lee's conviction as a complete miscarriage of justice, a partisan decision that would have made Lee's exoneration tantamount to a condemnation of Washington. His conclusions are reinforced by Theodore Thayer's detailed study of the battle with the revealing title of *Washington and Lee at Monmouth: The Making of a Scapegoat.*

It was Lee's advance regiments that first engaged the British at Monmouth. As senior officer to Washington, Lee had been offered and had turned down the command of the detachment recommended by the council on 24 June (above) to strike at the British rear. He considered the small unit beneath his rank and agreed that Lafayette should be put in charge. When he learned, however, that there would be four thousand men involved, he changed his mind and exercised his seniority to get the command. Since he had opposed any attack on Clinton's army and had not hidden his disparagement of the new American army, Washington was far from enthusiastic in handing over the command to him. It must also have given Washington pause that Lee, who had been absent for sixteen months, was unacquainted, as he admitted, with the brigade and regimental commanders. He had also shown himself far from perspicacious in anticipating Clinton's drive across Jersey.

Despite these handicaps, Lee was a bold, competent, and experienced field commander; and most historians would agree with Thayer's assessment that Washington's selection of the twenty-year-old Lafayette had been far more dubious. (*Monmouth*, pp. 29–33) Lafayette was inexperienced as a field commander and ambitious to the point of rashness. He had gone forward in such haste and was so ill prepared that Washington felt compelled next morning to warn him that "Tho giving the Enemy a stroke is a very desireable event, yet I would not wish you to be too precipitate in the measure." (Fitzpatrick, *GW*, 12: 121)

By the time Lee took over from Lafayette on Saturday, 27 June, there was little time left if an attack were to be made on Clinton's army. Clinton had arrived near Freehold on the twenty-sixth, encamping his main army of some six thousand men under Cornwallis west of Freehold Court House and Knyphausen's four thousand troops (with most of the British baggage wagons) just east of the courthouse. A day's march would put them safely at Middletown, unsuitably high ground for an American attack. But Clinton chose not to advance immediately. By staying over the twenty-seventh to rest his men and horses, he virtually invited an attack by Washington, hoping perhaps to wipe out the humiliation of their retreat. On 27 June, Lee arrived at Englishtown, five miles northwest of Clinton. The same day Washington advanced the main army to Ponolopon Bridge, two and a half miles from Englishtown. Although Clinton may have invited an attack, at the same time, he made plans to move on toward Sandy Hook. He ordered Knyphausen to march at 3:00 A.M. on Sunday, 28 June, Cornwallis to follow two hours later.

Also on Saturday, the twenty-seventh, Washington asked Lee to call a council of his generals to plan an attack for the next morning. Lafayette, Wayne, and Maxwell were present, but Scott did not arrive until later. Morgan, somewhere to the south of Clinton, could not be reached. Since the council was ignorant of the area and of British dispositions, Lee told them in essence that they would have to play it by ear. At Washington's direction in a night message, Lee ordered Gen. Philemon Dickinson's New Jersey militia and Gen. Daniel Morgan's riflemen to open an attack on the enemy's flanks early in the morning and directed Col. William Grayson's Virginia regiment to support them. Unfortunately, the message that Morgan received was so confused as to date and time that Morgan sat out the entire battle waiting for his cue. Lee ordered Lafayette to command a division composed of Wayne's and Scott's brigades.

At 4:00 A.M. on Sunday, Knyphausen marched off for Middletown. Clinton was far more worried about an American attack on his long wagon train than he was about an attack on the main army under Cornwallis, whose six thousand troops were the cream of the British army. At 6:00 A.M. Dickinson had moved out to Tennent Meeting House, two miles east of Englishtown. By the time Lee's army of some 4,100 men and 8 cannon left their Englishtown camp, Knyphausen had progressed several miles along the Freehold–Middletown Road—a road that ran on high ground. Lee's road ahead was roughly parallel to Knyphausen's route and a few miles to the north, but it traversed an area cut through by ravines and swamp-bordered creeks. Knyphausen was far enough advanced that Clinton could turn his attention to Lee.

When Lee's segment reached the bridge across the first creek (at a place ominously called "West Morass"), Cornwallis was already through Freehold on the road to Middletown. Lee's army, with Wayne's and Scott's brigades under Lafayette in the lead, followed by Maxwell and Jackson's small detachment, made its way across the first and second ravines before they saw and were seen by Cornwallis's rear guard. Simcoe's hussars and dragoons attacked Wayne's vanguard, but were repulsed by a musket volley. Lafayette, while reconnoitering across the third morass, espied a large body of dragoons to the east on Briar's Hill, which Cornwallis had already passed. After Lee got his main army across the ravine, a short artillery duel ensued. At mid-morning Lee learned of a road leading off to the left toward Formans Mill which was free of the enemy. He decided on a broad encirclement move to the left against Cornwallis's rear while Wayne with a small detachment would "amuse" the enemy in the center.

Lee had barely started the maneuver, with Scott in the lead, when it appeared that Wayne's unit of some six hundred men were insufficient to cope with what the Americans had believed to be the rear guard but which turned out to be much larger. Clinton, still fearing a possible attempt on his baggage train, ordered Cornwallis and a force of two thousand dragoons, grenadiers, and light infantry to strike at Lee's center. It was this force that Wayne was in the process of "amusing." Lee reinforced Wayne with a few hundred men, with which Wayne was more than willing to attack. Lee, however, ordered him not to engage the enemy but to distract him while Lee could make his encirclement. The heat by this time had grown intense. Also, Clinton was bringing his full force to bear on Lee.

One of Lee's difficulties—perhaps no fault of his—was communicating with his regimental commanders. He sent an aide to confer with Scott, but the aide returned to report that Scott was no longer on the left where Lee had positioned him. Lee was flabbergasted. Having waited for some time, without further orders from Lee, Scott and Maxwell had decided to withdraw when they saw troops in the center retreating— probably Col. Eleazer Oswald's artillerymen, who had run out of ammunition. Lee thought of going after Scott to make him return, but becoming aware now that Clinton's entire force was pushing toward his army, he decided that, even though he had not ordered a retreat, he now had no choice but to do so. Lafayette, pressed by Cornwallis and learning of Scott's retreat, withdrew the rest of his men. This entire action had lasted but half an hour. It was now 1:30 P.M. Scott's brigade had withdrawn on their own, but Lee kept the rest of his troops more or less intact, offering effective resistance all the way. They fell back over the morass, then assembled near Freehold. During the entire retreat, Wayne showed his displeasure with Lee by refusing to speak to him. Scott eventually arrived back at Tennent Meeting House, where he met with Washington's advance under Lord Stirling. Lee, in the meantime, had retreated to a line selected by du Portail about a mile west of Freehold at Carr's House, still three miles from Washington's approaching army. With Clinton's brigades approaching this line, Lee ordered his men to form on an elevation back of the first morass, although some regiments had already retreated beyond this point.

Washington's first word of Lee's retreat reached him by way of a young fifer. Washington refused to believe it. He sent Robert Harrison, an aide, to investigate; Harrison reported that Grayson and other regimental commanders with whom he had talked did not know why they were retreating and were indignant, which, writes Thayer, "is good evidence of the fighting quality of the regimental officers, if not of their military sagacity." (*Monmouth*, p. 52) Washington soon met Lee face to face. Reports of witnesses vary greatly as to Washington's explosive reactions to Lee's retreat. Whether, as some say, the air was blue with Washington's curses, there is no disagreement that he was beside himself at what he considered a shameful retreat from Clinton's rearguard. Lee tried to explain that he had run into Clinton's main army of six thousand men and that prudence dictated he save his men. Washington apparently did not listen to this explanation, but in a few minutes he cooled enough to ask Lee to command the front line while he went back to form the main army behind the bridge. "As was his habit at a critical time or in the thick of a fight," writes Thayer, "Washington again proved himself courageous and decisive." (*Monmouth*, p. 53) Almost every officer present would have agreed with NG's words to Jacob: "The commander in Chief was every where, his Presence gave Spirit and Confidence and his command and authority soon brought every thing into Order and Regularity."

Such praise of Washington, however, does not imply that Lee had acted against orders or had been unwise in ordering a retreat as Washington and others maintained. As for acting against orders, as he was convicted of doing, a careful reading of Washington's words seems to support Lee's contention that he had been authorized to use his discretion. At Lee's trial Richard K. Meade, a Washington aide, testified he was directed by Washington to tell Lee to attack the enemy as soon as possible "unless some very powerful circumstance forbid it." (*Lee Papers*, 3: 8) In a letter to Gates early that morning, Washington said of Clinton's army that he intended to "harass them as much as possible," and to Laurens he wrote a few hours later that he had ordered Lee to "attack their rear if possible." (Quoted by Thayer, *Monmouth*, p. 39)

As for Lee's wisdom in withdrawing his men, the preponderance of the evidence would support Lee. Clinton, with his three to two numerical advantage (not to mention his qualitative advantages—especially in the number and ability of his dragoons and grenadiers) had no doubts about annihilating Lee if he had not retreated. Said Clinton: "Had Washington been blockhead enough to sustain Lee, I should have catched him between two defiles; and it is easy to see what must have happened." Of the eastern-most ravine, Clinton said it was one "which I might have held against the world." (Willcox, *Clinton*, p. 235)

When Washington rode back to the main line, Lee had but a few minutes to form a line on the heights above Middle Spotswood Brook before waves of Clinton's dragoons, grenadiers, and light infantry, with Clinton brandishing his sword in their midst, attacked. The fighting was severe. Olney's Rhode Islanders first pushed the enemy back with bayonets, then fell back. Simeon Thayer, NG's friend, lost an eye; Hamilton was almost killed; and Clinton barely escaped with his life. Lee's men held out for almost an hour.

In the meantime Washington helped Lord Stirling extend his line along high ground above Spotswood Brook, with Knox's artillery emplaced below. Washington, seeing Lee's spent forces, ordered them back to Englishtown to rest. Students of the battle have since wondered why they were not held in closer reserve; when Lee returned to the line, the battle was over.

Until this time NG had been concerned with supply matters. Now, Washington ordered him to march to Freehold to head off an anticipated attempt by Clinton to attack Washington's right. After marching for three miles, within two miles of Freehold, NG heard of Lee's retreat, and without orders he headed back to help Washington. As his division retraced their steps along Combs Hill, NG decided to order his eight or ten cannon to the top of the hill, bringing up Gen. Woodford with some six hundred Virginians to protect the artillery. NG was now to the right of Stirling's long line. The artillery from Combs Hill began to hit the British left. Cornwallis led a detachment across the creek to silence it, but he was driven back in a virtual rout by the heavy fire of NG's cannon and small arms.

Clinton made one last attempt on the American line by trying to turn Stirling's left flank. Washington sent Col. Joseph Cilley of New Hampshire with one thousand men to the defense. In a ferocious charge, Cilley's men advanced with muskets and bayonets against grenadiers and the famous Black Watch Highlanders, pushing them back with considerable losses. Some historians have seen this as the final turning point. Anthony Wayne, who had been restive all day at his inability to get at the enemy, made one dramatic offensive move with Pennsylvania, Maryland, and Virginia troops. In the charge British Col. Henry Moncton lost his life; Col. John Laurens almost lost his. Soon Wayne retired back across the creek. It was by now almost 4:00 P.M. For the next two hours, artillery on both sides fired, but the battle was over.

This time the British withdrew. They left doctors to care for the wounded, of which Clinton counted 170, a figure too low. Clinton reported 124 dead, 59 of them of heat exhaustion; but the Americans buried over 200 British. American losses were listed as 60 killed, 150 wounded, but the figure was also too low.

Clinton waited for the moon to sink, and then put his army in motion. It was midnight. The Americans were aware of the British continuation toward Sandy Hook, but other than assigning Moylan's horse to follow them, Washington could do nothing further with his weary army to impede Clinton's progress. Five days later Clinton was fortunate in embarking his troops at Sandy Hook for New York.

Charles Lee's long ordeal was soon to begin. Washington's quarrel with him might well have ended with the battle if Lee had not written a long letter two days later in which he demanded reparation for the injustice done him by Washington on the field. Washington answered by defending his actions, saying he found the terms of Lee's letter "highly improper." In a fit of anger, Lee wrote of the "tinsel dignity" attending Washington's office. In a third letter, he demanded a courtmartial. (Thayer, *Monmouth*, pp. 70–73, quotes the letters.) As noted above, he was eventually convicted on charges of disobedience of orders, for making a shameful retreat, and disrespect to the commander in chief. Although Alden and Thayer are convincing in their defense of Lee against the first two charges, they agree it would be difficult for a court to find him innocent of being disrespectful to Washington. John W. Shy would agree with them. Writes Shy: "No one who carefully reads the record of trial, examines the ground, and considers the British side of the battle would find Lee guilty of the first two charges. But no one who reads his letters to Washington will believe him innocent of the third. Under the circumstances an acquittal on the first two charges would have been a vote of no-confidence in Washington." (John W. Shy, "Charles Lee: The Soldier as Radical," in George Athan Billias, ed., *George Washington's Generals* [New York: William Morrow and Co., 1964], p. 45.)

A modern study of Monmouth, which includes geographical details not found in Thayer, is Smith, *Monmouth*.

To George Washington

[Paramus, N.J.[1] 12–14 July 1778?][2]

I would propose writing to the french Admiral that there are two objects. One of the two may be improv'd as a blockade or an investiture as circumstances and the practibillity of entering the Harbour of New York should be found.

The french fleet to take their station at Sandy Hook and block up the Harbour.[3] This Army to take a position near the White Plains to cut off the Land communication and to all appearance seem to design some serious opperations against Newyork and the troops there.

General Sullivan to be wrote to desiring to know what force he has that may be considerd in the character of regular troops, what force is from the neighbouring States and expected in a few days, and what Militia can be brought together in Eight days time and how the Magazines are prepard for such a consumption and whether there is Boats to make a landing upon Rhode Island, to learn the Strength of the Enemy there and the number of their Ships and of what force.

In the mean time the Admiral to make himself acquainted with the depth of water into Newyork and the Ships and force there. On the return of the Express from General Sullivan, the admiral to determin from the enquiry he shall make and the information General Sullivan shall give which will be the most elligible object. But if it should be found [that] the fleet can come into the Harbour of Newyork this Army will be ready to coopperate with him as far as the nature of the Country and the situation of the Enemy will admit.

The fleet from Sandy Hook can run into Newport in three days time; that station will be favorable for either the one or the other of the measures as should be found hereafter to be the most certain of success.

I would inform the admiral of the difficulty of approaching New-york by Land, of the Enemies strength there, and send a verbal account of our own strength and intended position. I would also send him a Copy of the Letter to G Sullivan if it is not thought dangerous, as it is possible it may fall into the Enemies hands.

AL (Washington Papers: DLC). This letter, of which one or more initial pages are missing, was not signed.

1. Since the battle of Monmouth, NG had been constantly occupied with making arrangements for moving and encamping the army en route to the Hudson, although Pettit had now arrived to help him. When Clinton slipped away from Monmouth during the night of 28 June after the battle, Washington made no attempt to follow with his exhausted troops. After caring for the wounded and burying the dead, the American army moved out on 1 July in two divisions and headed toward the Hudson via Brunswick and Paramus, N.J., camping in each place for several days.

2. The earliest date is determined by the first word received on 12 July that d'Estaing's fleet had been sighted off Sandy Hook. By 15 July NG had gotten the information on Rhode Island from Gen. Varnum that in this letter he suggests be sent for. (See NG to Washington, 16 July, below.)

3. Charles Hector, Count d'Estaing (1729–94), had been a French general before becoming an admiral in the French navy, a shift greatly resented by the French naval officers under him. (See below, NG to d'Estaing, 21 August; see also, Balch, *French*, pp. 117–18.) In April 1778 Vergennes had put d'Estaing in command of the Toulon fleet, which he ordered to American waters as the first move in France's war with England. In mid-May, d'Estaing sailed past Gibraltar with twelve ships of the line, five frigates, and some four thousand soldiers. Aboard the flagship *Languedoc* with d'Estaing was France's first minister to the United States, Conrad-Alexander Gerard. On 9 June, Vice Adm. John Byron sailed from England in pursuit to support Lord Howe's American fleet, but storms delayed the arrival of most of his fleet until September, a voyage that was to give him the sobriquet of "foul weather Jack."

The French fleet, in the meantime, appeared off the Virginia coast on 5 July. When d'Estaing learned that the British had evacuated Philadelphia, he sailed up the coast, anchoring off Sandy Hook, N.J., only ten days after the embarkation of Clinton's army at Sandy Hook following the battle of Monmouth. It was a lucky break for the British that the French fleet had taken almost three months in coming from Toulon.

D'Estaing had no immediate objective in mind. Lord Howe's fleet was in New York harbor; and since the French ships of the line were superior in number, size, and firepower, Howe had no intention of sailing out to do battle. On the other hand, Howe felt reasonably safe where he was, for the channel into the harbor around Sandy Hook was very narrow and it was usable by the deep-draft French ships of the line only at high tide. Howe lined his ships up just inside the Hook so that, should d'Estaing choose to bring his fleet into the harbor, the ships would have to enter through the narrow channel single file, and each would be successively vulnerable to the combined broadsides of several British ships. D'Estaing chose not to run that risk.

For more than a week he remained at the anchorage, taking on the few supplies that could be brought out in small boats and communicating with Washington by letter and through visits of Washington's French-speaking aides, John Laurens and Alexander Hamilton. Washington had favored a joint attack on New York City, but when it became obvious that d'Estaing had no intention of taking on Howe in New York harbor, an attack on Newport, which NG had favored, appeared to both Washington and d'Estaing as a logical alternative. Still in need of water and food supplies, the French fleet weighed anchor on 22 July and headed for Newport, R.I.

The arrival of the French fleet and the decision to attack Newport is covered by Freeman, *GW*, 5: 45–51; Gruber, *Howe Brothers*, pp. 304–10; and Mackesy, *War*, pp.

215–18. A brief account of d'Estaing's mission is in Jonathan R. Dull, *The French Navy and American Independence* (Princeton: Princeton University Press, 1975), pp. 111–15 and 122–23. On d'Estaing's arrival in Rhode Island and the subsequent weeks before the battle of Rhode Island, see below, NG to d'Estaing, 21 August.

To George Washington

Capt Drakes 7 miles from the ferry [N.Y.][1]

Sir   July 16th 1778

General Varnum is at this place and has very lately returnd from Rhode Island; he says that there are 1500 State troops including the Artillery Regiment. There is the Continental Battallion commanded by Col [Christopher] Greene about 130 strong.[2] Besides these 2500 Militia are orderd from the Massachusets, Conecticut, and New Hampshire States, part of which are already arrivd, and the others dayly coming in. General Varnum thinks there cannot be less than 3000 men already embodied under the command of General Sullivan that can be depended upon.[3]

General Varnum thinks there is not above 3000 of the Enemy at Rhode Island and only Six frigates.[4]

I find no place for encamping the troops short of 9 miles from the ferry towards Crumpond. I am with great respect your Excell[encys] most obedient humble Servt

NATH GREENE

ALS (Washington Papers: DLC).
1. NG had apparently crossed the Hudson the previous day in search of a camp back down the river toward White Plains. (See NG to Washington, 21 July, below.) Three days later Washington crossed with the last of the army and spent the night at Capt. Drake's. By 21 July, Washington was at White Plains. (Fitzpatrick, *GW*, 12: 192, 194) At this point he still did not know whether d'Estaing would attack the British fleet in New York harbor or sail for Newport, R.I. See above, NG to Washington [12–14 July].
2. The reference is to the Black Regiment, the only continental troops under Sullivan at this time.
3. The figures Varnum gives for the troops under Sullivan are vastly different from Sullivan's. Varnum presumably received his estimates from Sullivan, whom he had left three days earlier; yet Sullivan reported to Count d'Estaing on 25 July that he had only "sixteen Hundred standing Forces" (Hammond, *Sullivan*, 3: 640). If, as Varnum reported, the militiamen were coming in daily, the three thousand he reported Sullivan as having on the thirteenth should have increased to something on the order of four thousand by the time Sullivan wrote d'Estaing on the twenty-fifth. Even had Sullivan understated the numbers to d'Estaing as an excuse for lack of preparedness, the discrepancy is difficult to reconcile.
4. Varnum's estimate of enemy numbers was much too low. The number was more likely 4,500, and during the time Varnum was en route to White Plains from Rhode Island, Gen. Prescott landed at Newport with another 2,000 men that Clinton had sent from New York. See note, NG to d'Estaing, 21 August, below.

To Colonel Ephraim Bowen

[West Chester, N.Y., 17 July 1778. Money is coming from treasury; should apply to NG's brother[1] for supplies. Tr (GWG transcript: CSmH) 1 p.]

1. Jacob.

To Catharine Greene

Camp Croton River Westchester County
N York State July 17, 1778
I receivd your agreeable Letter of the 8th of this instant yesterday in the morning.[1]

I am very sorry to find you unwell. Why did you ride in the Night? What was your hurry? Why did you expose yourself unnecessarily, and risque any disagreeable consequences that might follow?

Sensible of your anxiety, and desireous of giveing you the earliest information after the battle of Monmouth I sent of[f] an express to Fish Kill with a line to Col Hay desireing him to forward your Letter by the first opportunity; which I hope you have receivd long before this.

You express a strong desire to get the Army on the East side of the North River and urge you have political as well as private reasons for it. Your private reasons I can interpret; but your Political ones I cannot devine. You may rest assured that there must be something very uncommon to prevent my coming home; you cannot have a greater desire to see me than I have you and the Children. I long to hear the little rogues prattle. Besides which there are many other matters that I want to settle.

You write you are politely treated at Boston. I am exceeding happy to hear it. They cannot flatter me more agreeably than by their respect to you.[2] What we love we wish to be regarded, and our partiality leads us to wish that others should feel the same attachment with ourselves. And where ever we find it, it produces an agreeable train of sensation.

You are envious then I find. Why so Caty are there others more happy than you? Are there not others less so? Look around you my dear and see where there are not many whose condition and prospects are far less ellgible than yours. It has ever been my study and ever shall be to render you as happy as possible. But I have been obligd in many instances to sacrafice the present pleasures to our future hopes. This I am sensible has done violence to your feelings at the time; but I trust the motives were so laudable and the consequences will be so salutary, that I shall meet with no difficulty in obtaining your forgiveness hereafter. Altho I have been absent from you I have not been inconstant in love, unfaithful to my vows, or unjust to your bed. Considering myself equally secure in your affection and fidelity I have presumed upon greater indulgences than [*several words illegible*] your own heart can witness for me.

At the close of the war I flatter myself I shall be able to return to your Arms with the same unspoted love and affection as I took [to] the field. Surfeited with the Pomp and parade of Public Life, I shall doubly relish domestic pleasures. To please my Love and educate my Children will be a most happy employment. My fortune will be small but I trust by good oeconomy we may live respectably.

[*signature obliterated*]

AL[S] MiU-C; photostat of original from the collection of Dr. Otto O. Fisher.
1. Her letter and his on Monmouth mentioned below not found.
2. He is probably referring to the Boston merchants, Samuel A. Otis and Benjamin Andrews, suppliers of the army.

To Governor Jonathan Trumbull of Connecticut

Sir   Camp, Crumb Pond[1] [N.Y.] 17 July 1778
Having been informed by the Dep'y Quarter Master General at Fish Kill that there is a Quantity of Cannon at Salisbury Works[2] which are wanted for the Publick Service, and that they are to be disposed of only by Orders from the Governor and Council of Safety: I am therefore to request that you will be pleased to cause the proper Orders to be lodged with the Managers of the said Works for the Delivery of such of the said Cannon as may be wanted for the Publick Service. I have the Honour to be with great Respect, Sir, Your most obedient humble Servant

NATH'L GREENE

LS (Ct).
1. Crum Pond was north of White Plains.
2. The Salisbury Works were in the northwest corner of Connecticut.

From Colonel James Abeel

[Reading, Pa., 20 July 1778. Is moving to Morristown soon to be nearer the army. NG will get very few tents since Col. Cox ordered tent makers and canvas to Philadelphia. Abeel could have saved money and remedied defects in Philadelphia but "Mr Mitchel is so great a Man that he told me he would not take any Advice or directions from me, or even receive any Orders."[1] Will send knapsacks and six thousand sets of horseshoes soon. LB (Abeel Papers: DLC) 3 pp.]

1. Mitchell was deputy quartermaster for Philadelphia. Abeel was not the only person critical of him as noted at Abeel to NG, 10 May, above.

From Colonel Ephraim Bowen

[Providence, R.I., 20 July 1778. $60,000 received; The General (Sullivan) has directed him to build "Fifty Flatt Bottomd Boats," which with other requests will take most of the money.[1] He will make it his "Particular Study" to give "utmost Satisfaction." ALS (RHi). 1 p.]

1. In anticipation of a possible move against Newport, Washington had advised Sullivan in a letter of 17 July to "make a collection of Boats proper for a descent," but Sullivan did not receive the letter until 23 July. Sullivan, therefore, had taken it upon himself to order the boats built to replace those the British had destroyed in a May raid. (See Washington to Sullivan, 17 July, and Sullivan to Washington, 24 July, Hammond, *Sullivan*, 2: 88–90 and 108–10; and Sullivan to d'Estaing, 25 July, ibid., 3: 640–44.)

To George Washington

Camp at the Plains [N.Y.]
July 21, 1778

Sir

Your Excellency has made me very unhappy. I can submit very patiently to deserved censure; but it wounds my feelings exceedingly to meet with a rebuke for doing what I conceivd to be a proper part of my duty, and in the order of things.[1]

When I left your Excellency at Haverstraw you desird me to go forward and reconnoiter the Country and fix upon some proper position to draw the troops together at. I was a stranger to all this part of the Country and could form no judgment of a proper place until I had thoroughly examined the ground.

Croton River was the only place that I could find suitable for the purpose, all circumstances being taken into consideration. I wrote your Excellency what I had done and where I was, that if you had any thing in charge I might receive your orders. I wrote you the reasons for my not waiting upon you in person were [that] I had many Letters to answer, and many matters to regulate in my department which prevented me from returning. Besides which it was almost half a days ride, the Weather exceeding hot and myself not a little fatigued. And here I must observe that neither my constitution or strength are equal to constant exercise.

As I was a stranger to all the lower Country, I thought it absolutely necessary for me to come forward. A thorough knowledge of a country is not easily obtaind; such a one at least as is necessary to fix upon the most elligible position for forming a camp.

The security of the Army, the ease and convenience of the troops as well as a desire to perform the duties of my office with a degree of reputation, all conspird to make me wish to fix upon the properest ground for the purpose. This it was impossible for me to do unless I came out before the Troops. And I must confess I saw no objection as your Excellency had wrote me nothing to the contrary, and what I wrote naturally led to such a measure.

I expected you on every hour and was impatient to get forward that I might be able to give some account of the Country when you came up. Before I left Crumpond I desird Mr Pettit to wait upon you at your arrival and take your orders; and if there was any thing special, to forward it by express.

If I had neglected my duty in pursuit of pleasure, or if I had been wanting in respect to your Excellency I would have put my hand upon my mouth and been silent upon the ocasion; but as I am not conscious of being chargeable with either the one or the other I cannot help thinking I have been treated with a degree of severity that I am in no respect deserveing of. And I would just observe here that it is impossible for me to do my duty if I am always at Head quarters. I have ever given my attendance there as much as possible both from a sense of duty and from inclination; but constant attendance is out of my power unless I neglect all other matters. The propriety of which, and the consequences that will follow, I submit to your Excellencys consideration.

Your Excellency well knows how I came into this department. It was by your special request, and you must be sensible there is no other man upon Earth could have brought me into the business but you. The distress the department was in, the disgrace that must accompany your operations without a change, and the difficulty of engageing a person capable of conducting the business, together with the hopes of meeting your approbation and haveing your full aid and assistance reconcild me to the undertaking.[2]

I flatter myself when your Excellency takes a view of the state things were in when I first engagd, and consider the short time we had to make the preparations for the opening Campaign and reflect with what ease and facility you began your march from Valley Forge and continued it all through the Country notwithstanding we were great part of the way entirely out of the line of preparations, you will do me the justice to say I have not been negligent or inattentive to my duty.

I have in every respect since I had my appointment strove to accommodate the business of the department to the plan of your Excel lency's opperations. And I can say with great truth that ever since I had the honour to serve under you, I have been more attentive to the public interest and more engagd in the support of your Excellencys charactor than ever I was to my own ease interest or Reputation.

I have never solicited you for a furlough to go home to indulge in pleasure or to improve my interest which, by the by, I have neglected going on four years. I have never confind myself to my particular line of Duty only. Neither Have I ever spard myself either by night or Day where it has been necessary to promote the public service under your direction. I have never been troublesome to your Excellency to publish any thing to my advantage altho I think myself as justly entitled as some others who have been much more fortunate. Particularly in the action of Brandywine.[3]

I have never sufferd my pleasures to interfere with my duty and I am perswaded I have given too many unequivocal proofs of my attachment to your person and interest to leave a doubt upon your mind to the contrary. I have always given you my opinion with great candour and executed your orders with equal fidelity. I do not mean to arrogate to myself more merit than I deserve or wish to exculpate myself from being chargeable with error and in some instances negligence. However I can speak with a becoming pride, that I have always endeavord to deserve the public esteem and your Excellencys approbation.

As I came into the quarter masters department with reluctance so I shall leave it with pleasure. Your influence brought me in and the want of your approbation will induce me to go out.

I am very sensible of many deficiencies, but this is not so justly chargeable to my intentions as to the difficult circumstances attending the business. It is almost impossible to get good men for the conducting all parts of so complex a business. It may therefore naturally be expected that many things will wear an unfavorable complexion; but let who will undertake the business they will find it very difficult not to say impossible to regulate it in such a manner as not to leave a door open for censure and furnish a handle for reproach. I am with all due respect your Excellencys most obedient humble Servt

NATH GREENE

ALS (Washington Papers: DLC).
1. Although this lengthy apologia was triggered by Washington's criticism (the nature of which is barely touched on in Washington's answer below), it obviously flowed out of the pent-up slights that NG felt from the failure of the commander in chief to commend him on various occasions. It had especially hurt him that his role at Brandywine the previous September had been overlooked, even though he might excuse it, as he did to Marchant four days later below, saying that Washington was prevented from "ever mentioning a single circumstance of the affair" because NG was "thought to be one of his favorites." Washington's more recent failure to compliment

him privately on his achievements as quartermaster general was due not to any lack of appreciation but rather to Washington's personality and mode of working with those close to him. See Washington's reply, below, on the same day.

Although NG's letter by its nature was self-serving, he did not, in fact, exaggerate either the efforts or the contributions he had made as quartermaster. It was unfortunate that someone else could not have pointed this out instead.

2. On his appointment, see above, NG to Reed, 9 March 1778.

3. On the subject of Brandywine, see below, NG to Henry Marchant, 25 July.

From George Washington

Dear Sir   [White Plains, N.Y. July 21, 1778][1]

I cannot at this time (having many People round me, and Letters by the Southern Post to read) go fully into the contents of yours of this date, but with the same truth I have ever done, I still assure you, that you retain the same hold of my affections that I have professed to allow you. With equal truth I can, and do assure you, that I have ever been happy in your friendship, and have no scruples in declaring, that I think myself indebted to your Abilities, honour and candour, to your attachment to me, and your faithful Services to the Public, in every capacity you have served it since we have been together in the Army. But my dear Sir, these must not debar me the priviledges of a friend (for it was the voice of friendship that spoke to you) when I complained of Neglect; I was four or five days without seeing a single person in your department, and at a time when I wished for you in two capacities, having business of the utmost importance to settle with the Count de Estaign (which made it necessary for me to see you as Qr. Mr. Genl. and) wch kept me closely engaged at Havestraw till the moment I crossed the No. R. But let me beseech you my dear Sir not to harbor any distrusts of my friendship, or conceive that I mean to wound the feelings of a Person whom I greatly esteem and regard I speak to you freely. I speak the language of sincerity, and should be sorry if any jealousy should be entertained, as I shall ever say more (in matters of this kind) to you, than to others of you, being very truly, Yr. Obedt. and Affecte.[2]

GO: WASHINGTON

ALS (NjP). Document is badly deteriorated; transcription has been aided by the printed copy in Fitzpatrick (*GW*, 12: 199–200). Fitzpatrick worked from photostat of the original a half century ago—then in the possession of Judge E. A. Armstrong of Princeton, N.J.

1. The date is determined by the reference to "yours of this date."

2. In a letter to Congress on 3 August, Washington praised NG's "judicious management and active exertions" in the quartermaster department, which Greene had found in a confused, distracted, and destitute state, adding that "by his conduct and industry" it had undergone a very happy change, enabling the army to make sudden move from Valley Forge to White Plains. (Fitzpatrick, *GW*, 12: 277)

To Colonel Ephraim Bowen

Sir

Camp White Plains [N.Y.] July 23, 1778

There is an expedition going on against Newport.[1] The forces that will be collected for this purpose will be considerable. Great exertions, therefore, will be necessary in our department. You must get the most active men to assist you that you possibly can.

A great number of Teams and Boats will be wanted upon the occasion. Pray do not let the expedition suffer for want of any thing in our line. If tents are likely to be wanted get all that Mr Chace, Mr Andrews and Mr Greene have.[2] I think you had better write them to send you all they have on hand.

I am in hopes to come and assist you myself and join the expedition: but am afraid I cannot obtain the General's assent.[3]

There is a line of Expresses established at the following places, to form an easy communication of Intelligence from Providence to this Camp. You must fix one at Mr John Greene's in Coventry to complete the communication. It must be done immediately. I am, Sir, your humble servant

NATH. GREENE

Tr (GWG transcript: CSmH).

1. Washington had sent word to Sullivan the day before by John Laurens that d'Estaing was sailing from New York to Newport and that he (Washington) was sending two brigades to join Sullivan. The brigades—Varnum's and Glover's—with Col. Henry Jackson's regiment were put under Lafayette the same day. (Fitzpatrick, GW, 12: 201–203)

2. Col. Thomas Chase, the deputy quartermaster in Boston; Benjamin Andrews, partner in Otis and Andrews; and NG's brother Jacob.

3. See NG to Marchant, 25 July, below.

Colonel Clement Biddle to Moore Furman

[White Plains, N.Y., 23 July 1778. Concerns NG's orders for forage for White Plains from New Jersey. ALS (MB) 1 p.]

To Nehemiah Hubbard

Camp at the White Plains [N.Y.]

Sir

July 23d 1778[1]

We want a chain of Expresses from Camp to Providence. You will please to fix one at New Haven, one at Durham, one at Colchester and one at Scotland.[2] The Expresses must be good trusty Men and well mounted. They must be fixt in twenty four Hours after the Receipt of this, and charged at their peril not to leave their post, on any pretence whatever; except to carry on the Public Letters. The Expresses must notify each other where they lodge, and notify all the

Neighbours at their first taking their Post for some Miles each way from their Quarters, that they may direct the Expresses, coming either from the Eastward or Westward, where to find their place of residence.

I shall depend upon you to execute this business as soon as possible, as it is a matter of great consequence. I am Sir your humble Servt

AL (Furnished by Richard Maass, White Plains, N.Y., 1973). NG did not sign the letter.
1. Hubbard received the letter in Hartford on 25 July.
2. Washington wanted the expresses because of the impending attack on Newport, R.I. His letter of 17 July to Sullivan did not reach Providence until 22 or 23 July. (In a letter to Washington on 24 July, Sullivan said he received it "Last Evening," but in a letter to d'Estaing the next day, he said he got Washington's letter on "the 22d Just after Noon." (Hammond, *Sullivan*, 2: 108 and 3: 640)

To General John Sullivan

Camp at the White Plains [N.Y.]
Dear General   July 23d 1778

I receivd your favor in answer to mine respecting Mr Bowen and am happy to find his appointment meets your approbation.[1]

You are the most happy man in the World. What a child of fortune. The expedition going on against Newport I think cannot fail of success. You are the first General that has ever had an opportunity of coopperating with the french forces belonging to the United States. The character of the American Soldiers as well as that of their officers will be formd from the conduct of the Troops and the sucess of this expedition. I wish you success with all my Soul and intend if possible to come home to put things in a proper train in my department and to take a command of part of the Troops under you. I wish most ardently to be with you.[2]

The battle of Monmouth and its consequences I suppose you have heard and seen the particulars of. General Lee is on tryal; the event uncertain as to the determination of the Court.[3]

A certain Northern heroe gave His Excellency several broad hints that if he was sent upon the Newport expedition great things would be done.[4] But the General [Washington] did not think proper to supercede *an* officer of distinguished merit to gratify unjustly a doubtful friend. Had it been necessary my little influence would not have been wanting to have prevented such a pice of injustice from being done you.

The good agreement that has ever subsisted between us and the prospect of a noble opportunity of acquireing reputation together with the certainty of your doing justice to every man who distinguishes himself in any manner whatever induces me to wish to join you upon this ocasion. Not as a Northern Heroe to rob you of your Laurels, but to share them under you.

I was an advisear to this expedition and therefore am deeply interested in the event. I wish a little more force had been sent. Count de Estaigne [d'Estaing] will block up the Harbour and you may wait until your plan is ripe for execution. I hope you wont precipitate matters until your force gets together. Every thing depends almost upon the success of this expedition. Your friends are anxious, your Enemies are watching. *I charge you to be Victorious*. The Marquis de la Fyette is coming to join you. Trust to your own judgement for forming the plan as you have every thing at Stake; and pray give your orders positive for the execution. The late transactions at the battle of Monmouth makes me drop these hints. Youl excuse the freedom I take and believe me to be with great respect your most obedient humble Servt

NATH GREENE

ALS (NhHi).

1. Neither letter found.

2. Washington had probably already determined to send NG to Rhode Island, but he did not so inform him until the next day. Washington justified his action to Congress by saying that since there was no prospect of the army's suddenly moving from White Plains, he "judged it advisable to send Genl. Greene to the Eastward . . . being fully persuaded his services, as well in the Quartermaster line as in the field, would be of material importance in the expedition against the Enemy in that Quarter. He is intimately acquainted with the whole of the Country, and besides he has extensive interest and influence in it." One can only wonder why he had not selected NG in the first place instead of the youthful Lafayette, since by that time (22 July) he had agreed with d'Estaing on not attacking New York City. On the division of the detachment between NG and Lafayette, see note, NG to Sullivan, 31 July, below.

During NG's absence the quartermaster's department was left in the capable hands of Charles Pettit, his assistant, although no surviving order or letter confirms this. It was mid-October before NG returned to White Plains to take back the reins. In the meantime, Pettit communicated with NG from time to time, but much of the correspondence has been lost. It would appear, however, that Pettit, whom NG trusted completely, made most of the decisions during this period and that NG approved them.

3. On Monmouth and Lee's trial, see NG to Jacob, 2 July, above.

4. Gen. Horatio Gates.

From Colonel James Abeel

[Reading, Pa., 23 July 1778. Has sent or is sending knapsacks, horse-shoes, and harness. LB (Abeel Papers: DLC) 1 p.]

Council of War

At a Board of General Officers, assembled at Head-Quarters at Reuben Wrights in the neighbourhood of White Plains, on Saturday the 25 day of July 1778.

Present
His Excellency, the Commander in Chief

Major Genls	Brigad'rs	
Putnam	Nixon	Wayne
Gates	Parsons	Woodford
Greene	James Clinton	Muhlenberg
Lord Stirling	Smallwood	Scott
Kalb	Knox	Huntington
McDougal	Poor	Portail
Steuben	Glover	Lewis Morris
	Patterson	

The Commander in Chief stated to the Board, that the Two Armies, which had heretofore acted in different Quarters, had formed a junction. That the whole was composed of Troops from the several States from New Hampshire to North Carolina inclusive. That the Army was about to take a Camp, which might possibly be of some perma[na]ncy: That for it's regularity and more effectual operation, as well as to prevent every possible ground of jealousy, and to preserve harmony through all its parts, it was necessary to adopt some mode of arrangement and a certain disposition.

Having stated those several matters to the Board the Commander in chief requested them to take them into consideration, and propounded the following Questions for their advice.

1st   Will it be best for the Troops of each State to encamp together?

Ans'r   It will be best that they should encamp together.

2d   What will be the best mode of arranging and disposing of the Troops throughout the line upon the present or a future occasion?

Answ'r   It will be best, that they should be arranged Geographically as far as circumstances will permit for the present Campaign agreable to the position of their respective States and their relative front to the Ocean and that they do parade all accordingly; and that this disposition and arrangement shall not fix or give any post of Honor between them.

The Board having given their advice upon the foregoing points, the Commander in Chief proceeded to state

That the proposed Camp at White Plains was about 15 miles from York Island. That the Enemy from the information he had received were in possession of Fort Independance &c on the Heights this side King's Bridge and also of Fort Washington and the strong grounds at the North entrance of York Island. That from the advices he had been able to obtain, they had Two Camps on Long and Staten Islands; but as to the precise number of men in each or either he was uninformed. That he could not ascertain the Enemy's present force on York Island and the Heights this side Kings Bridge, nor what their whole strength would be, if the Troops were drawn from Long and Staten Islands; However, that he should suppose it would amount to about 14,000, rank and file, fit for duty; and that from his latest and best accounts, they had Several ships of War between New York and Sandy Hook.

That by the last return we had 16782 rank and file fit for duty.[1] That out of this number a detachment of about 2000 had marched to the Eastward. That another detachment of about 400 had moved towards the Western frontiers of this State. That Maxwells Brigade consisting of 1100 were at Elizabeth Town in Jersey. That Vanschaicks Regiment of about 400 was in the Neighbourhood of Hackensack. That about 900 fit for duty were at the Posts in the Highlands and at Kings Ferry, besides the new levies which are ordered down. That the remainder of the Army amounting to between 11 and 12,000 were at White Plains and in their vicinity. That the French Squadron, under Admiral Count D'Estaing had left Sandy Hook and put to Sea.

The Several matters above, having been before the Board, the Commander in Chief requested, that after their consideration of the same, they would deliver their opinions, upon the following questions.

1st   Whether we can make an attack upon the Enemy's Posts, either on the Heights on this side King's Bridge, or on those on York Island with a probability of success?

Answer We cannot make an attack with any probability of success.

2d   If an Attack cannot be made, in the opinion of the Board, with a probability of success, should the Army advance and take Post nearer the Enemy, or continue on the Grounds it now occupies, at or about the White Plains?

Answer The army should not advance.

ISRAEL PUTNAM	W SMALLWOOD
HORATIO GATES	H KNOX
NATHANAEL GREENE	ENOCH POOR
STIRLING	JNO PATERSON

THE B'ON DE KALB   ANT'Y WAYNE
ALEX'R MC DOUGALL   WM WOODFORD
STEUBEN   P MUHLENBERG
JNO NIXON   CH'S SCOTT
SAM'L H PARSONS   J HUNTINGTON
JAMES CLINTON   DUPORTAIL

DS (Washington Papers: DLC).
1. Washington's estimates are considerably lower than his official returns only one week later. On 1 August he reported 15,508 in the White Plains area, not counting 1,260 in the cavalry and artillery. On the same date, the total number in his army was given as 19,460, exclusive of Varnum's brigade (then en route to Rhode Island). The difference in the figures was partially accounted for by recruits during the week. The official returns dated 1 August are printed in Lesser, *Sinews*, pp. 76–77.

To Henry Marchant

Camp White Plains [N.Y.]
Dear Sir   July [25?] 1778
I am informed the congress have the appointment of all the agents to be employed for the disposal of British property captured by the French navy. If the information is true, and there is one to be appointed for the State of Rhode Island, I would beg leave to nominate my brother Jacob. You know he has made no small sacrifices and devoted great part of his time to the public service for several years past. If you can procure him this appointment you will lay both him and me under equal obligations. However, you will judge of the justice and propriety of the application and take your measures accordingly.[1]

The expedition against Newport will be attempted. The French fleet is to block up the harbor, while General Sullivan raises a land force to take off the garrison. I believe and hope I shall have an opportunity to go upon the expedition, first to put the business of my department in a proper train and then to join in the execution of the plan.

I am told you are making great preparations for the reception of the French ambassador. The public audience will be a grand exhibition, the dignity and splendor will be new and singular in America, and excites a curiosity in me to see the audience, as I never saw the like.[2]

I hear General Arnold has rendered himself not a little unpopular with the officers of the army in Philadelphia, by not giving them an invitation to a ball he gave the citizens. I am very sorry for this circumstance, as it will render his situation disagreeable, owing to the clamor and cabal of those who conceive themselves injured.[3]

The great exertions that have been made in the Q.M.G. department contributes greatly to the success of the army in the operations through New Jersey. It has been and will be very expensive; but it is unavoidable; and altho it is not possible to correct every imposition and stop all abuses in so complex a business, I am persuaded there has been as much economy as the circumstances of the department and the state of the times would admit.

I hope his excellency will do me the justice to say I have done my duty.[4] The army must have remained until this hour at the Valley Forge, had not some person undertaken the business with more spirit and activity than those formerly in it. However, his Excellency, for fear of being chargeable with partiality, never says anything to the advantage of his friends. In the action of Brandywine last campaign, where I think both the general and the public were as much indebted to me for saving the army from ruin as they have ever been to any one officer in the course of the war; but I was never mentioned upon the occasion.

I marched one brigade of my division, being upon the left wing, between three and four miles in forty-five minutes. When I came upon the ground I found the whole of the troops routed and retreating precipitately, and in the most broken and confused manner. I was ordered to cover the retreat, which I effected in such a manner as to save hundreds of our people from falling into the enemy's hands. Almost all of the park of artillery had an opportunity to get off, which must have fallen into their hands; and the left wing posted at Chadsford, got off by the seasonable check I gave the enemy. We were engaged an hour and a quarter, and lost upwards of an hundred men killed and wounded. I maintained the ground until dark, and then drew off the troops in good order. We had the whole British force to contend with, that had just before routed our whole right wing. This brigade was commanded by General Weedon, and, unfortunately for their own interests, happened to be all Virginians. They being the general's countrymen, and I thought to be one of his favorites, prevented his ever mentioning a single circumstance of the affair.

The battle of Germantown has been as little understood as the other by the public at large, especially the conduct of the left wing of the army. Great pains has been taken to misrepresent the transactions of that day. I trust history will do justice to the reputations of individuals. I have the satisfaction of an approving conscience, and the confirming voice of as able a general as any we have in the service, namely Gen. McDougall, who knows the report that the troops were delayed unnecessarily to be as infamous a falsehood as ever was reported; the troops were carried on to action as soon as it was possible, and in good order.

However, as I said before, I trust history will do justice to the reputation of those who have made every sacrifice for the public service. It is going on four years since I have spent an hour at home, save one that I stopt on my march from Boston to New York. There is no man gone through more fatigue or been more attentive to duty than I have since I belonged to the army. But men and actions have been so miscolored that little benefit is to be expected from a series of good actions. Refined policy is too prevalent for merit to be in much estimation. I expected when we were first formed into an army, that we were going upon a truly republican principle, that merit only was the criterion; but I find a few friends at court is of much greater consequence than all the services a man can perform in the field.

Being in haste, I can only add, that I am with great respect your most Obedient, humble servt,

NATH. GREENE

Reprinted from an unidentified mid-nineteenth-century newspaper article filed with GWG transcripts, CSmH. The letter was reprinted with some changes and omissions in Greene, *Greene*, 2: 102–5.
1. No record of such an appointment by Congress has been found.
2. Because M. Gerard was the first ambassador to present himself to the new United States, the members of Congress were acutely conscious that they were establishing a precedent for years to come. It was 6 August before they could agree on the proper protocol and get the statehouse cleaned after its occupation by the British. After the congressional formalities, there followed a public reception replete with band music and firing of a cannon. (Burnett, *Letters*, 3: xix–xxii and 363)
3. Benedict Arnold, still recovering from a leg wound sustained at Saratoga in October 1777, had been put in command of Philadelphia after the British evacuation.
4. See note, Washington to NG, 21 July above, on Washington's letter to Congress.

To General George Weedon[1]

Camp at the White Plains [N.Y.]
My dear General   July 25th 1778
    I this moment heard you was at or near Philadelphia, had I known it before you should have heard from me. If you have been there for sometime why have you been silent?
    The prodigeous quantity of business I had upon my hands and the great hurry in which we left the Valley Forge, deprivd me of the opportunity of takeing a formal leave of you. However I dare say when you consider I had the whole machinary of the Army to put in motion, Supplies of all kinds to attend to; Camps to look out; Routes to fi[nd] orders of march to furnish to the General officers. Orders to give to those going into Philadelphia as well as to those to remain on the ground. Your friendship will readily excuse me.
    You know I esteem and regard you as an officer and a Gentleman

nd that is sufficent without being formally attentive to all the rules
f politeness.

I had a most terrible time of it through the Jerseys not a soul
) assist me except the Brigade Q Masters until after the Battle of
Monmouth. Then Mr Pettit and Major Forsyth joind us.

Pray what are the Peoples oppinions of the transactions of that
ay? General Lee was rather unfortunate.[2] I wish you would write
ne a good long letter with all the remarks and observations you hear.
he Express is waiting. I can add no more only that I am with sincere
egard your humble Sert

N GREENE

LS (MnHi).
1. On Weedon's retirement from the army, see NG's letter to him of 27 April,
pove, and Weedon to NG, 5 October, below.
2. On Monmouth and Charles Lee's trial, see above, NG to Jacob, 2 July.

From General Benedict Arnold

Philadelphia, Pa., 25 July 1778. Ill health and business has prevented
nforming NG more about "Affair we had in Contemplation."[1] French
eet has gone to Rhode Island. Has sent "his Excell'cy" a box of oil,
ome of it for NG. Tr (GWG transcript: CSmH) 1 p.]

1. It is not known what "Affair" they had in mind.

From Colonel James Abeel

Reading, Pa., 26 July 1778. Has sent 12,067 pairs of horseshoes; is
ending 1,827 more pairs and 1,217 haversacks; has all the smiths at
York making them. Also sent harness and traces. Soon moving to
Morristown. LB (Abeel Papers: DLC) 1 p.]

To Henry Laurens, President of the Continental Congress

ir   Camp White Plains [N.Y.] 27 July 1778

His Excellency General Washington having been pleased to fa-
our me with a Sight of two Papers which had been delivered to
im by General Gates, one of which contains a List of the Persons
mployed in the Northern Department under the Direction of the
Deputy Quarter Master General, a Copy of which I am informed has
een transmitted to Congress by General Gates; the other, a Resolu-
on of Congress thereon of the 23d of June, which seems to imply a
ensure on the conduct of the Quarter Master General or his Deputy
n that Department, I think it necessary to trouble Congress with the

Mention of a few Facts which I doubt not will satisfy them that no Par of that Censure can justly fall on me.[1]

In the Month of May last, when General Gates was about to tak the Command on Hudson's River, I made a Journey to Fishkill in or der to examine into and regulate the Business of the Quarter-Master General's Department. In a Conversation with General Gates h proposed that this Business, in the Northern District, should be pu under his Direction, and offered to take the Trouble of making th necessary Arrangements, to which I readily consented, and though myself happy in having committed it to a Person I supposed in a Respects so well qualified to direct the Management of it. On m leaving Fishkill I left a Letter for General Gates informing him wha I had done in that District, and referring that of Albany entirely t him; and I never doubted that if any Errors or Abuses were found especially in the Latter, they would have been immediately corrected and that I should in due Time have been favoured with a State c the Department. A Copy of this Letter I shall take the Liberty t inclose herewith.

Sometime afterwards I was honoured with a Letter from Genera Gates which contains all the official Information I have been favoure with on the Subject, a Copy of which will also be inclosed. By thi Letter you will observe there is not the most distant Hint of an supernumerary Officers being employed, or other Abuses or irregu larities committed in the Albany District, and I rested satisfied tha everything there was properly regulated and going on well. It there fore appeared to me not a little strange that the first Intimation received of an undue Number of Officers being kept in pay in tha Quarter should arise from a Resolution of Congress for correcting th Abuse, and that too, founded on a Complaint or Report transmitte by the very Person on whom I relied, at his own Request, to remov all Causes of Complaint. A written State of Facts delivered me by Co Lewis the Deputy Quarter Master Genl at Albany, of which a Copy i inclosed, will make it appear the more extraordinary that such Complaint should be transmitted by General Gates.

The Nature of the Business requires that almost every Deput Quarter Master Genl should employ a Number of Assistants, Clerk and other subordinate Officers; and as, from the Movements of th Army and other Circumstances, the Business, at many Posts an Districts, is fluctuating, and requires, in order to avoid unnecessar Expence, that these subordinate officers should have but temporar Appointments, I have invariably given it in Charge to every Deputy have appointed to take especial Care to keep no such Officer on Pa within his District longer than the publick Service should require i Colonel Lewis having, as I had understood, been appointed imme

Hudson Valley and Southern
NEW ENGLAND

Phil Booth

iatly by Congress, and being under the Eye of the Commanding
ifficer of the Northern Department, I did not think it requisite,
specially as I heard no Complaints concerning him, and much other
usiness claimed my Attention, to send him any particular Instruc-
ons; and, indeed, as there was but little Business expected in his
istrict, and from his Character and Standing in Office, as well as for
ie Reasons before mentioned, I did not conceive it at all necessary. I
ave the Honour to be with great Respect Sir Your most obedient
umble Servant

NATHANAEL GREEN E

5 (PCC, Item 155: DNA).
1. For background, see above, NG to Gates, 15 May; Gates to NG, 31 May; and
organ Lewis, the deputy quartermaster at Albany, to NG (June 1778). One resolution
thorized Gates "to dismiss all the supernumerary staff officers" in his district; the
her ordered that Gates's letter of 17 June be referred to the committee of arrangement,
here it appears to have died. (*JCC*, 11: 633)

To General John Sullivan

Dear General   Coventry [R.I.] Iron Works July 31, 177⟨
I arrivd at this place last Evening about 9 oClock and being a littl
fatigued, haveing rode from Camp in three days,[1] I propose to refres⟨
myself today and wait upon you tomorrow, unless there should b⟨
something special that renders my attendance necessary immediately
in which case I will set out without delay. Youl please to inf[orm] m⟨
by the return of the Express.

Inclosd is a Letter from His Excellency General Washington.[2]

I have forty Ship Carpenters and Boat builders coming on to pu⟨
things in readiness in the Water department for the expedition an⟨
there is a most excellent fellow at the head of them, Major Eyres.[3]
am Sir your humble Servt

NATH GREEN⟨

ALS (NhHi).

1. It was a trip of some 170 miles, the first time he had been home since earl⟨
April 1776.

2. Washington's letter of 27 July directed Sullivan to "dispose" his continent⟨
troops among the militia, placing one half under NG and the other half under Laf⟨
yette. "Besides the service," he said, "which General Greene will be of, both in Counc⟨
and in the Field, upon this very interesting and important occasion, his presence wi⟨
contribute greatly to expedite your Operations by an earlier provision, it is probable, ⟨
many matters in the line of his Department." (Fitzpatrick, GW, 12: 238)

In a letter that NG also carried to Lafayette, Washington emphasized, as h⟨
undoubtedly had done with NG in person, that this was a special assignment for th⟨
quartermaster general since he "could not with propriety act, nor be equally usef⟨
merely in his official capacity of Quarter Master General." (Ibid., 237)

3. Benjamin G. Eyre was superintendent of the boat department.

To Governor William Greene of Rhode Island

Sir   East Greenwich [R.I.] Aug 2d 177⟨
Upon enquiry I find there is an order from the Council board fc⟨
drafting one half the whole Militia in the State. I presume the inten⟨
tion of the board was to have one half of all those actually fit for dut⟨
drafted and no others for the intended expedition.[1]

If this was the intention of the board I am afraid both they an⟨
the General [Sullivan] will be disappointed in their expectation⟨
There being many drafted that are unfit for duty and are now getin⟨
clearances.

It will be necessary for the board to issue their orders that on⟨
half of the Militia fit for actual service be drafted and none others ⟨
that those that are unfit for duty provide others to serve in the⟨
places. If something of this sort dont take place there will be a gre⟨
diminution of the expected force.

You will pardon the freedom I take in hinting these matters ⟨

our Excellency and believe me to be with great respect Your most
bedient humble Servt

NATH GREENE

LS (R-Ar).
1. The efforts of the R.I. Council of War to raise a militia unit were only partially
uccessful. In the words of a resolution of the Assembly on 2 September, many citizens
were so destitute of public spirit" that they would neither serve nor hire a substitute.
Bartlett, *Records*, 8: 452.)

To Count d'Estaing

ir   East Greenwich [R.I.] August 4th 1778
    I received your Excellency's polite Note by Major Franks on my
vay to the fleet: and intended to have done myself the honor of
vaiting upon you without the least previous ceremony; but the acci-
lents of the day prevented my being in season, and as the day was
ar spent and the wind failing I was obliged to put back again and
vait some future time more favourable to my wishes.[1]
    I sent you a couple of Letters which I intended to have had the
tonor of delivering with my own hand, but being under the necessity
of returning last night and not knowing but they might contain some
nteresting matters of business, I thought it most advisable to forward
hem by Major Franks.[2]
    I shall ever esteem myself happy in an opportunity to form an
cquaintance with a Gentleman whose character is so illustrious as
hat of your Excellency's, but I feel myself too deeply interested in the
uccess of the intended expedition, to delay any necessary prepara-
ions, or to gratify my ambition, at the expence of time so precious to
our Excellency, and so necessary to me.
    I hope for the honor of soon meeting you in Newport and testi-
ying my great regard and profound respect. I am your Excellency's
nost Obedient humble Servant

NATH GREENE

LS (Photostat in DLC from the original in the Archives de la Marine,
Archives Nationales, Paris; subseries B4, vol. 146, f. 133).
1. The *Languedoc*, d'Estaing's flagship, was anchored in Narragansett Bay off
Conanicut Island. The note from d'Estaing has not been found.
2. One of the letters NG delivered was from Washington, dated 26 July. D'Estaing,
vho had written Washington on 3 August, added a postscript to acknowledge Wash-
ngton's letter and to say he was going to look for NG on shore. "The reputation of this
General Officer," d'Estaing added, "made his arrival to be wished. His influence on his
ountrymen and his knowledge of the country will render him formidable to our
ommon enemy." D'Estaing's letter in French is in the Washington Papers, DLC,
ccompanied by a translation, from which the quote is taken.

To Colonel Jeremiah Wadsworth

Dear Sir   Providence [R.I.] August 4th 177'
    I am here and as busy as a Bee in a tar barrel, to speak in th'
sailors stile.
    I am happy to inform you that every thing in your departmer'
seems to equal our wishes, it was the first enquiry I made and receiv'
the most flattering answers.[1]
    Will you want a quantity of Rum? If you should, please to giv'
the price to be deliverd at Norfolk. My brothers has some; an'
services you can render them consistent with your trust will be dul'
acknowledged. Please to write an immediate answer.
    We intend to give the Enemy a cursed floging. We are almost i'
readiness. Yours

N GREEN'

ALS (CtHi).
1. Commissary Wadsworth was with Washington's army at White Plains.

From George Washington

                                    Head Quarters White Plains [N.Y'
Sir   8th Augt 177'
    I received your favor dated the 4th Inst. informing me of you'
arrival at Providence, and the flattering disposition of things in th'
quarter.[1]
    We have just received an account from Genl Maxwell of Lor'
Howes sailing from the Hook with his fleet of armed vessels early o'
Thursday morning last. Whether it is to make demonstrations c'
fighting the Count d'Estaign in order to favor the withdrawing c'
reinforceing of the troops on Rhode Island is not easy to determine.'
would hope however that it is not to join a squadron from Englanc'
or if it is that your operations will be determined before they can act.'
Wishing you all manner of success and glory, I am Sir your obt an'
very hbl servt

    P. S. You have referred me for particulars to a letter from Ger'
Sullivan. No such letter came to hand.

Df (Washington Papers: DLC).
    1. Letter not found.
    2. See below, NG to d'Estaing, 21 August.

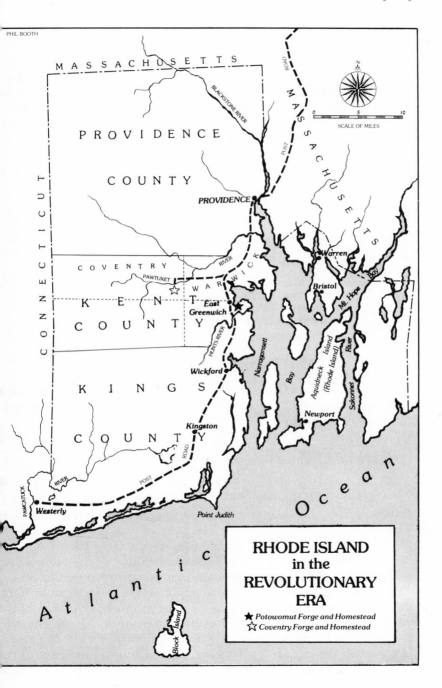

PHIL BOOTH

RHODE ISLAND
in the
REVOLUTIONARY
ERA

★ Potowomut Forge and Homestead
☆ Coventry Forge and Homestead

To Catharine Greene

[Camp near Newport, 16 August 1778. Sorry she is unwell and anxious about him. Providence protects "in the most perilous situation," but he also acknowledges his safety is "in the book of fate." Wishes he was at liberty to cultivate the "growing genius" of his children. Thanks Nancy Vernon for pies and puddings. "The French fleet has not returned. We are within two miles of Newport, and are to begin our approaches to-night."[1] AL (NjP) 4 pp.]

1. On the French fleet and attack on Newport, see below, NG to d'Estaing 21 August.

From Martin Hunter[1]

[Warwick, N.Y., 20 August 1778. Concerns three horses NG had ordered in May. ALS (PPAmP) 1 p.]

1. Hunter was an assistant deputy quartermaster under Udny Hay.

Nathanael Greene to General John Sullivan on behalf of General Officers

[Camp before Newport, R.I., 21 August 1778. Board of officers who were asked their opinion, reply that Col. Henry B. Livingston was entitled to have been made commander of the "light Corps," although with operations reduced to a siege, such troops will be returning to their respective corps. DS (NhHi) 2 pp.]

General Greene's Remonstrance to Count d'Estaing[1]

[Aboard the *Languedoc*][2] Aug't 21st 1778

I have several matters to recommend to your Excellencys consideration before you take your final Resolution for quiting this Harbour.[3]

The expedition against Rhode [i.e., Aquidneck] Island was undertaken upon no other condsideration than that of the French fleet and troops acting in conjunction with the American Troops.

There has been great expence and much distress brought upon the Country in calling the Militia together at this busy season of the year. A force nearly sufficient for the reduction of the place is now collected and all the necessary apparatus provided for subdueing the Garrison. If the expedition fails for want of the countenance of the Fleet and Troops on board, It will produce great discontent and murmuring among the people.

The Garrison is important, the reduction almost certain. The influence it would have upon the British Politicks will be very considerable. I think it therefore highly worth runing some risque to accomplish.

The distress of the French Fleet is an objection against prosecuting the expedition, and furnishes an argument for going round to Boston. I would beg leave to observe to your Excellency that it is the general opinion of those best acquainted with the Coast, that the Fleet runs a much greater risque in attempting to go round to Boston, in the present shattered state they are in, than they possibly can by staying here. Masts, Spars, Provisions and every kind of assistance that can be had in Boston, can with equal ease and in as short a time be provided here, that is necessary either to refit or accomodate the Fleet.

If there should appear a superior force upon the Coast there is a safe asylum up in Providence River above Conanicut Point where not more than two Ships can go abreast and where any number of Land Batteries can be erected for the protection of the Fleet.

I would just remark further to your Excellency that the Harbour of Boston is much easier blocked up than this—much more difficult to get in and out at, and is not by any means so well situated to distress the British trade and communication as the Harbour of Rhode Island.

I would not wish to urge your Excellency to a measure that has not the common interest of the two Nations for its object; but I cannot help thinking the interest of the two Nations is highly concernd in the success of the present expedition. The Reputation of their Arms is at Stake. It also being the first instance of cooperation of forces the failure will produce a disagreeable impression respecting the Alliance, and leave a door open for our Internal enemies as the common enemy to annimadvert upon the conduct of our allies in leaving us at such a critical period.

I had not the honor to be personally known to your Excellency untill this morning. Neither can I presume you to be much acquainted with my charactor or conduct. The Marquis de la Fyette is well acquainted with both, who I flatter myself will inform you how far you may rely upon my opinion, information and Integrity.

I wish the most cordial harmony may subsist between the French Nation and the Americans; and in a particular manner among the officers. I hope therefore if there has appeared any little indiscretions on our part as to personal attention in the conducting of the business of the present expedition, that the greatness of your Excellencys mind will pass them over as too trifleing to be brought in competition with our great and natural Interest.

I think I may venture to promise in behalf of my Countrymen,

that they will render your Excellency every assistance in repairing
your Fleet you can wish or desire, as far as the Resources of the
Country will admit. I have the honor to be Yr Excellencys most
humble Servt

N G

N B Should it be necessary to have the Ships piloted up Providence
River Mr Brown and Mr Wall will undertake it at the risque of their
Lives.
It is already my opinion that with the assistance of the French
Fleet and French forces, we can get possession of Newport in two
Days.

ACyS (Washington Papers: DLC).
    1. NG's copy has no heading. On the last page it is docketed both as "Genl
Greene's remonstrance to Count De Estaing" and "Remonstrance: Maj. Genl Greens
to Count D'Estaing." On the writing of the document, see last paragraphs of note 3,
below.
    2. In a letter to Washington on 23 August, Sullivan speaks of "General Greens
written Remonstrance Drawn up on Board the Languedoc." (Washington Papers, DLC)
    3. A month had elapsed since d'Estaing had sailed from Sandy Hook to join
the Americans in attacking Newport. Much had happened in the month. Hopes had
run high for the success of this first collaborative effort of the new allies—possibly
thereby even ending the war. But delays, a destructive storm, misunderstandings, and
recriminations had put those hopes in jeopardy.
    (For background, see NG to Washington, [12–14 July]; Bowen to NG, 20 July;
NG's letters to Bowen, Hubbard, and Sullivan, 23 July; NG to William Greene,
2 August; and Washington to NG, 8 August and 21 August.)
    When d'Estaing anchored off Pt. Judith, R.I., on 29 July, he was disappointed to
find the Americans far from ready to join in an attack. Gen. Sullivan had learned from
Washington only five days earlier that such an offensive was planned. By this time his
army consisted of Col. Christopher Greene's Black Regiment of 130 men, none of them
with battle experience, and perhaps 2,000 New England militiamen, many of them
seasoned soldiers, but many also fresh from farms or shops. (As noted, NG to
Washington, 16 July, above, there were discrepancies in numbers of militia reported.)
En route to Providence under the command of the twenty-year old Lafayette were
some 2,000 continentals, consisting of Varnum's and Glover's brigades and Col. Henry
Jackson's regiment, which Washington had dispatched from White Plains the day
d'Estaing sailed; but it would be another week before they covered the 170 miles
to Providence.
    Although the French admiral chafed at American unpreparedness, Sullivan had
actually acted with vigor and speed. He had dispatched urgent letters to various New
England officials for men and supplies, and after 1 August he had the help of Nathanael
Greene in rounding up supplies and getting boats built (the men even working at night
by lanternlight). But neither Sullivan nor Greene could hurry up the militia or Lafayette's continentals. The militia that were in camp, moreover, were sorely in need of
unit training.
    The British had acted with greater alacrity. Only two days after Gen. Clinton got
word in New York of d'Estaing's arrival off Sandy Hook, he sent some 2,000 troops
under Gen. Prescott through Long Island Sound to reinforce Gen. Pigot's garrison at
Newport. Their arrival on 15 July brought the number of British defenders to 6,700, at
least double the number of Sullivan's forces. Each day that the Americans delayed was
used by Gen. Pigot to strengthen his defenses. Rhode Island—henceforth in this
account called by its Indian name of Aquidneck Island—extended some fifteen miles

north and south and was three miles at its widest. At its southwest corner, its harbor opening to the so-called middle passage, was Newport, once a thriving seaport but now largely reduced to the business of supporting the British garrison. Those Americans still in residence were considered by Sullivan's army as neutralists at best and Tories at worst. Although the British commanded the entire island, their activities were centered in Newport.

Pigot's first line of defense had been established on the high hills at the north end of the island, his artillery covering Bristol Ferry, the connecting link in the land route from Providence. He had used the time principally, however, in strengthening the inner and outer lines of defense that ran roughly parallel to each other just to the north and east of Newport. As a precaution against attack, he had disarmed the civilians on the island outside the lines, had filled wells and felled trees, and had brought livestock within the Newport lines.

Lord Howe had also used the time effectively. By 30 July his fleet in New York had been strengthened with several ships of the line, including the 74-gun *Cornwall*, one of Byron's ships that had become separated from his fleet and preceded it across the Atlantic by several weeks. Although d'Estaing's ships still carried more and larger guns, Howe was close enough to being on an equal footing with the French fleet to lure d'Estaing from Rhode Island waters. He determined to sail from New York on 2 August, but had to wait until the sixth for favorable winds. By the time Washington sent off a warning to Sullivan, Howe was two-thirds of the way to Newport.

In the meantime d'Estaing had not been completely idle. He and Sullivan, after some disagreement, had finally worked out a plan of action, communicating chiefly through Washington's French-speaking aide, John Laurens. As part of the plan, d'Estaing had cleared the eastern (Sekonnet) passage of British vessels and had forced the British to evacuate Conanicut Island. As soon as the Americans were ready, the next step would be for d'Estaing to force the middle passage past British shore batteries at Newport and then put his four thousand troops ashore on the western side of Aquidneck Island to the south of Pigot's northern-most redoubts. At the same time, Sullivan would land his troops from Tiverton to the eastern side of the island under cover of the French frigates in the eastern passage. It was assumed that their combined forces would be sufficient to storm the British lines near Newport while d'Estaing would help reduce British defenses with his ships' guns and would guard against any kind of reinforcement of the British garrison. (Only later did Sullivan and NG see d'Estaing's most vital role as landing men behind the enemy lines. See below, NG to Washington, 28/31 August.)

Sullivan had no exact count of his militia, but by 4 August, when Lafayette's two thousand continentals arrived in Providence, Sullivan may have had a grand total of over six thousand men, with more coming in hourly. He was still not ready. He had to get the troops from Providence around the north end of Mt. Hope Bay and down to Tiverton, had to give minimal training in embarking and disembarking to what he called his "Motley and dissarranged Chaos of Militia," many of whom had never been in a boat. (The quote is from Hammond, *Sullivan*, 2: 197.) With the advice of NG, he set Saturday, 8 August, for the landing. It was none too soon for d'Estaing, who had done his best to hide his impatience with Gallic politeness. He not only badly needed supplies (especially fresh water) and to get his men ashore after four months, but he was acutely aware that every day Byron's and Howe's fleets were nearer Newport. Relations between Sullivan and d'Estaing were not helped, as they might have been, by the youthful Lafayette. At Washington's direction, Sullivan had assigned half of Lafayette's continentals to NG, the militia units to be spread amongst the continentals. Lafayette was to command the left wing, NG the right. Lafayette, however, was insistent that he should command a mixed French-American force, and when Sullivan resisted his importunities, the young Frenchman used d'Estaing to pressure Sullivan. Despite NG's and John Laurens's affection for the young marquis, NG thought him now driven by his "great thirst for glory and national attachment," and Laurens considered that Lafayette's "private views withdrew his attention wholly from the general interest." (NG to Washington, 28/31 August, below, and Laurens, *Letters*, p. 218). Lafayette's attitude undoubtedly contributed to Sullivan's later impatience with the French allies. Sullivan finally gave in, agreeing that Lafayette should have Jackson's continentals and enough militiamen to give him a thousand Americans to join with a French contingent.

When more militia were still drifting in on Friday, 7 August, Sullivan postponed the invasion from Saturday until Sunday 9 August, but d'Estaing stuck to his plan of running the middle passage with his main fleet on Saturday, the eighth. Pigot had sunk most of the British transports to block Newport harbor, but d'Estaing had no intention of attacking the city. He ran past the British batteries with little damage to his ships, and by mid-afternoon of 8 August, he had reached Dyer's Island north of Newport, prepared to land his four thousand troops as well as many of his sailors. At this point Pigot withdrew his forces from the redoubts at the north end of the island. As new American militia units came in, Sullivan had decided to delay his landing once more—this time until Monday, the tenth—and had just notified d'Estaing accordingly when he learned of Pigot's withdrawal. A hasty meeting with NG and the other general officers induced him to send a force immediately under Col. Topham to take over the British redoubts at the north end of the island. The rest of the army soon followed in flat-bottomed boats. D'Estaing learned of the landings only an hour after receiving Sullivan's first message delaying the invasion. The French were hurt that the Americans had landed first. Laurens reported them as talking "like women disputing precedence in a country dance," although d'Estaing later admitted Sullivan was right. (Laurens, *Letters*, p. 220) As the French troops were disembarking on Monday morning, d'Estaing went ashore to confer with Sullivan. At this point a French sailor aloft sighted a white sail to the southwest, then another, and another, until more than thirty sails came into view. Despite Sullivan's disbelief it was Lord Howe's fleet. "If the Admiral had been David Garrick himself," William Willcox has written, "he could not have timed his entrance better." (Willcox, *Clinton*, p. 245) Howe anchored off Point Judith to keep watch on the French fleet.

D'Estaing, annoyed that American intelligence had not warned him, immediately began to reembark his men. Although Sullivan pleaded with him to stay and complete the assault, d'Estaing would not run the risk of being attacked by Howe within Narragansett Bay. With Howe's fleet in the offing, the French admiral did not share the confidence of Sullivan and his officers that they could complete the assault of Newport without being molested by Howe. Taking advantage of a northeast wind early next morning (10 August), the French fleet sailed out of the bay; but Howe, whose purpose for the time being, at least, was to lure the French away from Newport, was not about to give battle. All day on the tenth, with Howe well in the lead, the two fleets ran before the brisk northeast wind. By evening, d'Estaing was still six miles from closing with Howe; morning found them eighty miles south of Newport. However disinclined Lord Howe was to take on d'Estaing without the aid of Byron (who was still more than three weeks away), he was goaded to do so by his own self-respect and the expectations of his captains, who envisioned a glorious victory under the celebrated admiral, a man justly regarded as one of the ablest seamen of his age.

Knowing he could not attack against the wind, Howe began a long drawn-out maneuver to get to the windward—i.e., to get the "weather gage" of the French. D'Estaing, whose training had been as a soldier, seems to have been unaware of the object of Howe's maneuver. By mid-afternoon Howe had almost succeeded in completing it. It was a brilliant maneuver, but fate decreed it would never be determined whether Howe could have dealt the French a crippling blow, for at this point the northeast wind increased to gale proportions and soon thereafter to hurricane force. For two and a half days, the storm raged unabated, scattering ships, ripping sails and shrouds, and snapping spars and masts. Howe's flagship lost its top masts, and d'Estaing's (the *Languedoc*) lost her masts and bowsprit. When the storm was over, a few single engagements ensued. The *Languedoc* barely escaped destruction by the British *Renown*. Other single engagements did damage and killed men on both sides, but neither side was victorious. Howe's ships limped back to New York while d'Estaing's captains voted to head directly for Boston, as their original orders had instructed them to do in case of trouble. But d'Estaing, having promised Sullivan he would return, decided the fleet must at least stop at Rhode Island on the way to Boston.

In the meantime, the Americans, who had encamped at the north end of Aquidneck Island, suffered almost as much as the two fleets. The celebrated John Hancock, at the head of a Massachusetts militia unit, had arrived just as the fleets sailed off. His unit brought Sullivan's strength to nearly ten thousand—enough, in the estimation of Sullivan and his officers, to strike without the aid of the French. Sullivan, therefore, ordered the army to march early on 12 August, but that night the storm hit them with full fury. It tore up tents and levelled the camp, filling trenches, destroying stores, and soaking powder and cartridges to uselessness. Without protection from the wind and rain, the men found sleep impossible. Lacking dry ammunition, the Americans' situation was desperate. The east passage was too rough for retreating, and if Pigot attacked, the Americans had only their bayonets with which to resist—a notoriously poor weapon in the hands of the militia. Pigot, in fact, did consider attacking, but fortunately for Sullivan, the British had also fared badly in the storm.

When the storm subsided on 14 August and much of their powder had been replaced by Gov. William Greene, Sullivan and his council decided to begin the attack the next day. They made this decision even though the storm had caused many of the militia to desert. At 6:00 A.M. on 15 August, the army moved south, with Varnum's brigade under NG on the right, marching down the west road and flanked by Gen. Whipple's New Hampshire militia; while Glover's brigade under Lafayette on the left marched down the east road, flanked by Gen. Tyler's Connecticut militia. (Lafayette, of course, had had to give up commanding any of his countrymen.) Between the two columns were Ezekiel Cornell's regiment and Col. Christopher Greene's Black Regiment. A mile in advance were Col. Henry Livingston's light infantry with John Laurens and the redoubtable Silas Talbot in command of units. And at the head of the army, surrounded by some two hundred horsemen, rode Gen. Sullivan. It was a brave attempt on Sullivan's part, since it had been the prospect of French collaboration that had induced him to make the attack. By 2:00 P.M. the army was within two miles of the outer British line.

As early as 25 July (before NG arrived), Sullivan's council of war had decided their main thrust against the outer line would be directed at Honeyman's Hill from the east. Since the British had flooded the marsh at the bottom of the hill and the attackers would be under direct British artillery fire as they made their way across the swamp and up the steep hill, casualties threatened to be very high. Those who have since studied the topography consider that an attack from the north, nearer the Bay, against Tominy Hill would have been less costly. However disadvantageous the point of attack selected by the Americans, Gen. Pigot was not overly confident that the British could hold out against it. On 16 August he sent word to Clinton in New York for help or for transports to evacuate the garrison, mentioning for the first time the possibility of surrender.

Despite continued desertions of the American militia (most of them unseasoned), the American camp was confident of victory. The night of 18 August, they began to raise a five-gun battery on the left. By the morning of the nineteenth, the battery began to fire four eighteen-pounders. As they were digging their approach trenches closer to the British lines, shortly after midday on the twentieth, d'Estaing's fleet was sighted on the horizon. By 5:00 P.M. it had dropped anchor off Brenton's Point. D'Estaing had kept his word; he had returned. Spirits rose in the American camp—but not for long. Instead of staying to aid in the assault, d'Estaing sent word early on 21 August that he intended to proceed to Boston for repairs (Hammond, Sullivan, 2: 240–42). Sullivan and his fellow officers were aghast. Only hours earlier they had been confident of defeating the British without the aid of a single Frenchman or French ship. Now they were suddenly emphatic, almost distraught, in declaring their need for the French. Nothing had changed outwardly, but the sudden uplift of spirits at the sight of the French fleet, followed by the equally sudden disappointment over its leaving, seems to have undermined their confidence. In any case, from Sullivan downward the most urgent objective was to keep the French fleet from leaving.

It was at this juncture that Sullivan sent Greene and Lafayette to confer with d'Estaing aboard the badly damaged *Languedoc* in the hopes they might dissuade him from sailing for Boston—at least for forty-eight hours, until a joint operation could be undertaken. Shortly after the receipt of D'Estaing's letter on Friday morning 21 August, Greene and Lafayette set sail for the French fleet. With them Sullivan sent his old friend, Col. John Langdon, former member of Congress and New Hampshire ship agent who had brought a militia unit to Rhode Island. (Sullivan to Washington, 21 August 1778, PCC, Item 160). Apparently they were taken to the French fleet by John Brown, the Providence merchant shipowner who had shared his intimate knowledge of Rhode Island waters with d'Estaing before the storm. (D'Estaing's reliance on Brown is revealed in two letters to Sullivan earlier in August [Hammond, *Sullivan*, 2:172, 183]; the fact that Brown accompanied them is confirmed in NG to Brown, 6 September, below, where NG recalled a conversation with Brown "the night we returned from the fleet." Lafayette mentioned only NG and himself as having gone aboard in his letter of 25 August to Washington. [Gottschalk, *Lafayette Letters*, pp. 56–61]).

Later that morning Greene and Lafayette were piped aboard the *Languedoc* and shown to the admiral's quarters. With Lafayette interpreting, NG put forth the arguments he subsequently embodied in the remonstrance printed above. From NG's later report of the meeting, Gen. Sullivan was convinced that the French admiral was swayed by NG's arguments, that, in Sullivan's words, "the Count himself wished to Come in but his Captains were to a man for Leaving us" because they were "Determined to prevent his Doing any thing that may Redound to his Credit or our advantage." John Laurens, Washington's aide, received a similar impression that d'Estaing was being pressured by "a Cabal of Marine officers who wish his destruction because he was introduced from the land Service into their Corps." (Sullivan's and Laurens's letters of 23 August in the Washington Papers, DLC, do not cite NG as their source, but their only contact with d'Estaing after his letter of that morning was through Greene and Lafayette.)

It will never be known whether d'Estaing deliberately misled NG by leaving the impression that he was willing to stay if he could only convince his captains. It was certainly with d'Estaing's approval, and possibly even at his suggestion, that NG stayed aboard the *Languedoc* that afternoon in order to write out his arguments in the formal remonstrance. Presumably d'Estaing would use it in an effort to win over his captains. NG also made a copy to take back to Sullivan. It was evening when he and Lafayette returned to camp. They had no indication that the captains had responded favorably to the remonstrance (or, for that matter, whether they had even seen it). By morning, however, as the French fleet was reported as putting out to sea, it was apparent that Greene's and Lafayette's mission had failed. At this point the disappointed Sullivan sat down to pen the protest of 22 August printed below.

Dearden, "R.I. Campaign," covers this first Franco-American joint operation, but there is no modern published account. Gruber, *Howe Brothers*, pp. 310–19, has a good account of Lord Howe's maneuvering with d'Estaing's fleet before the storm; Willcox, *Clinton*, pp. 242–48, has a brief account; see also Freeman, *GW*, 5: 47–69; Whittemore, *Sullivan*, pp. 83–102; and Gottschalk, *Lafayette*, pp. 240–53. On the French fleet, see Doniol, *France*, 3: 233–56, 321–94, 447–64.

From George Washington

Dear Sir   Whiteplains [N.Y.] Aug 21, 1778

On Wednesday afternoon I received your favor of the 12th and 13th Inst.[1] by Mr Hulet the Pilot, who did not arrive in Camp till then. I am much obliged by your particular relation of matters, and request that you will continue it from time to time whenever oppertunity will permit.

There was one circumstance in your relation, of which I was exceedingly sorry to hear. You will readily know which it is.[2] I wish the utmost harmony to prevail, as it is essential to success, and that no occasions be omitted on our part to cultivate it.

Your operations have been greatly retarded by the late violent storm, but as it is now over, I trust things will go on prosperously, and that you will be rejoined by Count D'Estaign who has been kept out so long by it. Indeed, from General Sullivans Letter of the 17th, I flatter myself you will have made a compleat reduction of the Enemy's force before this reaches you, and that the next advices I receive will announce it.[3] If the fact is otherwise, let me beseech you to guard against Sortees and surprizes. The Enemy, depend will fall like a strong man, will make many sallies, and endeavour to possess themselves of, or destroy your Artillery and in one of these, should they put the Militia into confusion, the consequence may be fatal.

By a Letter which I received yesterday from Genl Maxwell inclosing one from Major Howell (whom I have stationed at Black Point[4] for the purpose of observation) it appears certain that Sixteen of Lord Howes fleet entered the Hook on the 17th. That on that, and the preceeding day, there had been heard severe Canonades at Sea, and that it was reported in New York that a 64 Gun Ship and several Transports had been taken by the French Squadron.[5] I wish the facts may be so as to the capture and that the Count may be with you to give a narrative of it himself.

I cannot learn that Admiral Byron is arrived, nor do I believe that he is.[6] It is said that one ship only of the Corke Fleet is yet arrived. I have not time to add more, as Majr Blodget is in a hurry to proceed, than to assure you that I am, with the most perfect esteem and regard Dr Sir yr obliged and affect. Friend

GO: WASHINGTON

ALS (Washington Papers: DLC).
1. Letter not found.
2. NG had undoubtedly written Washington about Sullivan's protest to d'Estaing on his pursuing Howe's fleet on 10 August.
3. Sullivan's optimistic letter of 17 August to Washington not found.
4. Near Sandy Hook, N.J.
5. The only British vessels the French had captured were the bomb ketch *Thunderer* and the sloop of war *Senegal*. (Dearden, "R.I. Campaign," p. 129)
6. Admiral Byron did not arrive until mid-September. (Gruber, *Howe Brothers*, p. 323)

A Protest of the General Officers on Rhode Island to Count d'Estaing

Camp before Newport [R.I.] Augt 22d 1778

The General officers of the american Army now on Rhode Island having through their present Commander in Chief in this department

represented to his Excellency Count d'Estaing the ruinous consequence which must result to this army From the abandoning the
harbour of Newport at this time and proceeding with his fleet to
Boston, which representation with many weighty reasons to induce
him to remain at this Port, he has been requested to Lay before his
officers who Seem in general to be of opinion that his Fleet Should
immediately proceed to Boston, Esteem it their Duty as officers in the
american army, as Allies to his most Christian Majesty, as officers
concerned For the interest and honor of the french nation and interested in the welfare of the United States to Enter their protest
against the measures which his Excellency the Count d'Estaing is
about to pursue.

1st Because the Expedition against Rhode Island was undertaker
by agreement with the Count d'Estaing an Army has been collected
and immense Stores brought together For the reduction of the Island
All of which will be Liable to be lost Should he depart with his fleet,
Leave open the harbour to receive reinforcements from New York
and Ships of war to cut off the Communication with the main and
totally prevent the retreat of our Army.

2dly Because the proceeding of the fleet to Boston can answer no
valuable purpose, as the injury it has received can be repaired much
Sooner here than at Boston and the vessels Secured against a Superior
naval force much better here than there.

3dly Because there is the most apparent hazard in attempting to
Carry round Nantucket Shoals those Ships which are disabled and
will in all probability end in the total loss of two of his most Christian
Majesty's Ships of war.

4thly Because the taking of dismasted Ships out of port to carry
them to another port to receive their masts instead of having their
masts brought to them is unwarranted by precedent and unsupported
by reason.

5thly Because the honor of the french nation must be injur'd by
their fleet abandoning their allies upon an Island in the midst of an
Expedition agreed to by the Count himself. This must make Such
unfavorable impression on the minds of Americans at Large and
create Such Jalousies between them and their *hitherto Esteemed* Allies
as will in great measure frustrate the good intentions of his Most
Christian Majesty and the american Congress who have mutually Endeavoured to promote the greater harmony and Confidence between
the french people and the Americans.

6thly Because the apprehension of Admiral Byrons being upon the Coast with a Superior fleet is not well founded as it wholely arises from the master of a British merchantman who Says he was told by the Greyhound frigate that Admiral Byron was Spoke with on the 24th of June off the Western Islands and accounts from England up to the 24th of June mention nothing of his having Sail'd and more than Eight weeks having Elapsed Since the fleet was Said to be near the Western Islands and no accounts having been had of their arrival in any part of America, it is Evident that this relation [i.e., account] must be false. As to the Captains of two of the french Ships, Supposing that they had discovered a three Decker, it is possible that in the thick weather they may have been deceived but Even if they are not it is by no means evident this Ship belong'd to Byron's fleet and even if it did, it only proves that this Fleet has been Seperated and must rendezvous in Some place before they can act, of which the french fleet cannot fail to have a timely notice, and before it is probable they can act the Garrison may be easily reduced.

7thly Even if a Superior fleet Should arrive the french fleet can be in no greater Safety at Boston than at Rhode Island. It can as easily be blockd up in the former as the latter place and can be much Easier defended in the Latter than the former.

8thly The order received from the King of France for his fleet to retire to Boston in case of misfortune cannot without doing injustice to that wise and good Monarch be Supposed to Extend to the removal of the whole fleet in the midst of an Expedition on account of an Injury happened to two or three of his ships.

9thly Because Even though the facts pretended were fully prov'd and it became necessary for the fleet to proceed to Boston yet no possible reason can be assigned for the Count d'Estaing's taking with him the Land forces he has on board and which might be of great advantage in the Expedition and of no possible use to him in Boston.

We therefore for the reasons above assigned do in the most Solemn manner protest against the measure as derogatory to the honor of France, contrary to the Intention of his most Christian Majesty and the Interest of his nation and destruction in the highest degree to the welfare of the United States of America, and highly injurious to the alliance formed between the two nations.[1] Signé

JNO SULLIVAN	WM WHIPPLE
NATHANAEL GREEN	JOHN TYLER
JOHN HANCOCK	SALOMON LOVELL

J. GLOVER   JON'N SITCOMB [TITCOMB]
EZEK CORNELL
Fair copy which conforms to the original.[2]

ESTAING

DS (Washington Papers: DLC).
1. This protest, which NG signed with great reluctance, differed greatly from his moderately worded remonstrance above. That document, as noted, was written on board the French flagship (with d'Estaing's explicit approval), in the hopes that it would persuade his captains to reconsider their decision to sail for Boston.
This document was written after it was known that the fleet had sailed; and although John Laurens was dispatched in a fast privateer in hopes of overtaking it, there was not the slightest prospect that the protest would induce d'Estaing to turn around and sail back to Rhode Island. As it happened, Laurens was unable to catch the French, and the letter was sent overland by express to Gen. Heath in Boston, who delivered it to d'Estaing on his arrival in Boston harbor. Since the protest could not bring back the French fleet in the immediate future, what, then, was its purpose?
Whatever the effect of the document on the French, its purpose was certainly not to alienate America's only ally, an ally that had already done much to sustain it. Insofar as John Sullivan, the author, thought about it at all, he probably saw it as no more than a bit of New England wrist-slapping: if a friend has done wrong let him know it; even punish him a little. It is doubtful if Sullivan gave it much thought; he wrote impulsively from profound disappointment, frustration, and fear of failure (which had plagued his military career), and it welled up in him, perhaps uncontrollably. At the same time, he also expressed the feelings of many of the frustrated officers and soldiers under him. (Dearden, "R.I. Campaign" quotes a number of private comments of subordinate officers that show even less understanding and tolerance of the French position, pp. 153–55.)
Lafayette, not surprisingly, refused to sign the document. He describes his reaction in a letter to d'Estaing the same day. He was furious, he wrote, that the American generals would expect him to take part in such a protest, and he made it clear to them that France was dearer to him than America. (Lafayette's letter, in French, is printed in Doniol, France, 3: 349.) When the protest caught up with d'Estaing in Boston, he too, not unnaturally, took umbrage at the reflections on himself and France. John Laurens said that d'Estaing declared the protest "imposed on the Commander of the King's Squadron the painful but necessary law of profound silence." (Laurens to Washington, 2 September 1778, Washington Papers, DLC)
The American soldiers besieging Newport did not see the protest, but news of the French withdrawal had already spread rapidly through camp. As a result, many of the unseasoned militia took off for home. It was this loss of men (on top of his initial disappointment) that reawakened Sullivan's ire and led him on the morning of 24 August to issue an order that ended on an intemperate and insulting note. After assuring his men at some length that they were not "in the least endangered" by the move, he yet hoped, he said, "the Event will prove America able to procure that by our Arms which her Allies refuse to assist in Obtaining." (Washington Papers, DLC; Hammond, Sullivan, 3: 645, who cites the same source, transcribes "her Allies" as "his Allies.")
The next morning Lafayette angrily confronted Sullivan with the order. Sullivan admitted that without knowing the precise nature of d'Estaing's orders, he had been too severe, and he placated Lafayette by agreeing to correct his inflammatory statement in orders the following day—which he did. (Gottschalk, Lafayette, p. 258) In those apologetic orders of 26 August, he had not intended, he said, "to Censure an act which the Admirals orders might render absolutely Necessary." Although hoping for a speedy return of the French fleet, he pointed out to his men that "however mortifying the Departure . . . we ought not to suddenly to Censure the movement, or for an act of any kind to forget the aid and protection which had been offer'd to us by the French since the Commencement of the present Contest." (Carlisle Orderly Book, 26 August, 1778, pp. 49–50, RHi). Lafayette sent both orders to d'Estaing, who was mollified by

the second, even going so far in a letter to Sullivan of 30 August to say he would personally lead a detachment of Frenchmen under the American commander, only one of the means by which Sullivan should know that "the French delicacy cannot have been wounded by an impulsive moment followed by mutual regrets." (Hammond, *Sullivan*, 2: 277–78)

On 23 August, Sullivan forwarded the officers' protest, along with NG's remonstrance and other letters, to Washington, who, in turn, sent them on to Congress without comment. Congress, concerned over giving solace to the enemy and to domestic Tories by exposing differences with America's ally, resolved that the documents "be kept secret" except from the French minister (Gerard) and that Washington "take every measure in his power that the protest of the officers . . . be not made public." (*JCC*, 11: 848–49).

Through this period of rough sailing for the alliance, NG's temperment tended to place him in the role of pouring oil on the troubled waters. After signing the officers' protest with great misgivings, he wrote a letter to Lafayette that unfortunately has not reappeared. The letter, Lafayette told Washington, was "very different from the expressions I have right to complain of." Gen. Greene, he said, seems "very sensible of what I feel. I am very happy when in situation of doing justice to any body." (Lafayette to Washington, 25 August 1778, Gottschalk, *Lafayette Letters*, p. 61) NG's letter seems to have been Lafayette's one solace, for in the same letter he told Washington he was "more upon a war-like footing in the American lines, than when I come near the British lines at Newport." (Ibid., p. 59)

Washington wrote NG a few days later (1 September, below) that he depended much upon his temper and influence to conciliate the animosity he plainly perceived. Despite Washington's firm recommendation to Sullivan to cultivate "harmony and good agreement" with the French, Sullivan wrote another insulting letter to d'Estaing in September that again strained relations. (Washington's letter of 1 September is in Fitzpatrick, *GW*, 12: 385–86) Again, NG stepped in to smooth matters over. (See below, NG to d'Estaing, 23 September, and d'Estaing to NG, 1 October.)

2. D'Estaing's note is in French.

To William Knox

[Camp near Newport, R.I., 22 August 1778. Orders copy of Boyer's *Pocket Dictionary* by "Post Rider."[1] Fears French fleet are leaving. ALS (NjMoW) 1 p.]

1. William was running his brother Henry's bookshop in Boston. (Callahan, *Knox*, p. 101)

To Charles Pettit

Dear Charles[1]   Camp [near Newport, R.I.] Aug 22d 1778
    Your two long Letters came to hand last night.[2] I was on board the French fleet. I have only time to tell you the Devil has got into the fleet. They are about to desert us, and go round to Boston. The Garrison would be all our own in a few days if the fleet and French forces would but only cooperate with us, but alas they will not. They have got a little shatterd in the late storm and apprehensive of a junction of Byrons and Hows fleets may prove their ruin. They are therefore determin to quit us immediately. I am afraid our expedition

is now at an end; like all the former attempts it will terminate with disgrace, because unsuccessful. Never was I in a more perplexing situation. To evacuate the Island is death, to stay may be ruin.[3]

The express is waiting at the Door. I am oblig'd therefore to defer giveing you the particulars until a more favorable opportunity; and to renew my promise of writing you more fully in my next.

My best respects to General Read if at Camp and to Col Cox in your next Letter. Where is poor Blodget?[4] Yours affect

N GREENE

ALS (NHi).
1. NG allowed himself a rare touch of intimacy in addressing his friend and assistant by his first name. As was customary in letters at this time, he almost always addressed his close friends, and even his brothers, as "Sir" or "Dear Sir." As noted above, NG to Sullivan, 23 July, Pettit was carrying on in the place of NG as quartermaster general.
2. Letters not found.
3. His spirits had risen by the next day when he wrote Sullivan. See below.
4. NG's aide, William Blodget, was en route from White Plains. See Washington to NG, 21 August, above.

General John Sullivan to General Greene et al[1]

Sir   Camp Before Newport [R.I.] August 23d 1778

The Count De Estang having abandoned us, in the Present Enterprize, And opened the Harbour for the Reception of Reinforsements from New York, It becomes my part, to inform the General Officers, and officers commanding Brigades of my present force, and that of the Enemy, as nearly as can be collected, and at the same time to request Their oppinion upon Several Questions. The Number of Our army amounts to Eight Thous'd one hundred and 74 rank and file Exclusive of Eight Hundred Artillery men, The whole exceedingly well officer'd, And a Reinforsement of three thousand men will probably be here in a few days. The Number of the Enemy from the best Calculations amounts to about Six thousand Including Artillery men, Sea men &c. In Our present Situation, One of three things only can remain to be done, Viz: To Continue the Seige by Regular approaches and Hazard the arrival of a Reinforsement. To make an immeadiate attack on their Lines, Or to Retreat from the Island, with the Stores &c. which have been collected. Your oppinion upon which of these three is most advisiable in our present Situation is Requested. Should you be for continuing the Siege you will mention your oppinion Respecting the Securing a Retreat, in case a British Fleet should arrive with a Reinforsement. Should you be of oppinion that an attack Should be made, you will please to point out the manner in which you would wish it to be carried into Execution. Should your oppinion be in favour of a Retreat you will please to Signify whether you think it Should take place immeadiately and your Reasons for its taking place at all. Your oppinion in writing upon these Questions is expected without Loss of Time. I am Dear Sir with much Esteem Your most Obt Servant

JNO SULLIVAN

LS (Washington Papers: DLC).
1. This only known copy of Sullivan's letter is unaddressed. From the replies to it printed in Hammond, *Sullivan* (2: 248–63), we know that copies went to Gens. John Tyler, Ezekiel Cornell, William Whipple, James M. Varnum, and John Glover; and to Cols. William West, William Shepard, and James Livingston. Other colonels, especially Christopher Greene, probably received copies, but their answers have not come to light. NG's response follows.

To General John Sullivan

Sir   Camp before Newport [R.I.] August 23d 1778
    You inform me that the French fleet have deserted us and left the Harbour open to receive reinforcements, and that there is but one of three measures to pursue: To continue the Seige by regular approaches, attempt the Garrison by storm, or affect an immediate retreat and secure our stores. You further inform me that the Enemy's collective strength is about 6,000 and that your own force is 8,174, Infantry Rank and file, besides a well appointed Artillery, and that you expected a reinforcement in two or three days of 3,000 men.
    In this situation and under these circumstances you demand my Opinion which of the three measures it is your duty and Interest to pursue.
    It will be a folly to continue the seige by regular approaches. We are so contiguous to New York and their strength and security there enables them to detach such a force that upon joining the Troops here they would be too formidable for your Army to contend with, besides which the Island will soon be inviron'd on all sides by shiping [i.e., British navy], that it will render it difficult for us to support an Army or effect a retreat from this place. I therefore think that a continuation of the siege will not answer any valuable purpose, especially as the operations are too slow for the patience, or length of time the Militia are engaged for.
    A storm and a retreat will require nearly the same previous preparations and dispositions to be made for the one as the other. If we storm, all our stores of every kind must be removed to the upper end of the Island for fear of a repulse, in which case we could not collect ourselves untill we got up to the fortifications at the North end. Those works should be well garrisoned and furnished with a

detachment of Artillery. The forts upon Tiverton should also be garrisoned and some good heavy pieces of Artillery sent there. All this should be done without loss of time. This disposition I think will be necessary whether we continue the Seige, attempt the place by Storm or effect a speedy retreat.

The reasons for a retreat are strong and many; you have the flower of all New England in your Army, your regular force is small, and your whole strength not very great; should you meet with a misfortune the blow will be terrible to these States. You have a prodigious quantity of valuable stores here, the loss of which by a precipitate retreat would greatly distress us. The face of the expedition is now totally changed by the desertion of the fleet. This expedition was planed upon the single condition that the French fleet and forces should cooperate with ours, and our strength was calculated accordingly. The only place where we could attack the enemy to advantage we are now deprived of the Opportunity of improving by the fleets leaving us. The Enemy can soon recieve reinforcements to make them superior to us in strength which would oblige us to a precipitate retreat that might be attended with the loss of many men and a great part of our stores.

The time for which the Rhode Island Militia were engaged is now near expiring. It will be difficult to detain them any longer, and if you should, they will be mutinous, difficult to govern and of little service in our future Operations. There are many other reasons that urge a retreat, but these may suffice and would be sufficient in my humble opinion to justify you in affecting one immediately.

However, as our forces are all collected and in pretty good health, and as there will be no additional expences to the public to attempt to possess ourselves of the Town by surprise, I shall take the liberty to suggest a plan for your consideration. I am sensible that neither the number nor quality of our Troops would justify an attack upon the Enemy's lines by open storm; but as many advantages are lost for want of being attempted, it may be well for you to consider how far you can be justifyed in risqueing the consequences that may follow the attempt.

The Garrison is said to be 6,000 strong. They are well fortified with Lines, Redoubts and Abattis. Your strength is but little above 8,000. To attack 6,000 regular troops in Redoubts, with an expectation of carrying them would require 15,000 Troops of equal or superior quality. You have but about 3,000 Regular troops and 5,000 Militia. Therefore it is a folly to think of effecting any thing by open storm. If any thing can be effected it must be by stratagem.

Upon reconnoitering the works I observe a Redoubt round a house at the head of Eastons Beach which commands that pass. If we could possess ourselves of this redoubt we might possibly open a passage within their lines by the way of the beach. I would pick out 300 Men of the best troops in the Army and give the command to a good *officer* who would be provided with Boats at Satchusest Beach all compleatly man'd with good Oars Men to land the party some distance South of the Redoubt; which they should attempt to possess themselves of by fixed Bayonets. I would have a body of troops ready at the entrance of the Beach to push over for their support; if they should succeed and the whole Army to follow in order and file off to the left and get upon the high ground on the back of the Town, and there form in good order.

If the enemy should attack the Column as it moves forward there must be detachments to check their advances and keep them in play while the Troops are passing. In order to get a good and sufficient body of troops for the purpose, I would recommend a draught from the Militia of all such Soldiers as have been in service before and have them incorporated with the Continental and State Troops, or else to form them into separate Corps and pick a corps of Officers to command them from Among the Militia, State or Continental Troops as it shall be found they can be spared and as they appear suitable to the command.

With the rest of the Militia I would make sham attacks along their Lines from Tamminy [Tominy] Hill to our Batteries in order to hold as much of the Enemy's force upon the out Lines as possible while we get footing within. The Militia not to begin their attack untill we give them a signal by a Rocket and the Column not to begin to move across the Beach untill the advance party fire a Rocket, which will answer two valuable purposes: it will serve to direct our own motions and make the Enemy think there are other principal attacks to commence, which will leave them in doubt how to direct their force.

The troops posted along in front of the Enemy's lines will answer another valuable purpose. It will prevent the Enemy from sallying (if we should meet with a repulse) and of attempting to cut off our Retreat.

The Quarter Master should have as many Teams provided as will take up all our Baggage, Stores, Cannon and Mortars at once, which should move off for the upper end of the Island the moment we begin our motions for the Storm. I would recommend the fore part of the night for the attempt as the Enemy will be less upon their guard. If we should get footing it will give us time to make the necessary dispositions before they can attack us; and if we meet with a repulse it will afford us an opportunity to draw off our men with more safety as our disposition cannot be known in the night.

If we were not situated as we are I could not recommend this attempt because the chance is not equal; but our particular situation demands every attempt that reason or common sense can justify. I think it therefore worthy your attention. I can only assure you if you should think the measure eligible, I will chearfully undertake any part of the execution and will give you every possible aid in my power to render it effectual.[1] I have the honor to be with great respect Your most Obedient humble Servant

NATH GREENE

ALS (NhHi).
1. NG must have discussed his proposed stratagem with Gens. Tyler, Varnum, and Glover, for their replies to Sullivan, although much less detailed, make the same proposal, even down to suggesting the identical number of men (300) in the landing party at Easton's Beach. In the draft of a letter to John Brown on 6 September (below), NG first acknowledged that he had made the proposal, then changed the wording to read that "it was proposed." Gen. Ezekiel Cornell and Cols. Shepard and Livingston favored retreating at once. (See Hammond, *Sullivan*, 2: 248–63.)
As NG pointed out to Washington (28 August, below) and to John Brown (6 September), the plan was given up because too few seasoned troops were available.

To Catharine Greene

[Camp near Newport, R.I.] 26 Aug. 1778

Judge Potter is polite enough to call at my quarters and offer his services to bring you a letter. I wrote you this morning by the way of Providence, but for fear that should not come to hand I embrace this opportunity.[1] I am not very well in health. I have been a little troubled with the asthma but have got over it.

I hope you and the children are well. Patty, you say, is getting on finely. I am sorry you wear such melancholy countenances at Coventry, but it is natural to the family. Jacob is one of Doctor Young's disciples; he is always looking over the black page of human life; never content with fortune's decrees.

Miss Nancy [Vernon] don't like the note I sent her; she says she won't correspond any more with me. She don't like the insinuation of being an old maid. Poor girl! I am afraid her romantic conceptions of human nature will lead her to pass the flower of life, and then her pride won't permit her to marry. How wretched this state, to be always at war with one's inclinations. I am in hopes to see you in a week or fortnight.

Excerpt reprinted from Greene, *Greene*, 2: 123–24.
1. Earlier letter not found.

To General William Heath

Sir

Camp near Newport [R.I.]
August 27th 1778

I received your favour of the 18th Inst. this evening.[1]

I have endeavoured to keep Colo Chace fully supplied with cash to satisfy all the demands against the department, but it has not been fully in my power owing to the difficulty of getting the money from the Treasury. The drafts upon the Office are so great that it is almost impossible to answer the demands seasonably.

The monies you have advanced to Colo Chace since my appointment I presume was to discharge the old arrearages,[2] as I am persuaded his disbursements under me cannot much exceed the sums I have advanced him, and what he writes me he is now in debt.

I shall transmit Colo Chace in a few days an order on the Loan Office at Boston for 150,000 Dollars, which I hope will be equal to all his wants.

I thank you for your good wishes for the success of the expedition against Newport, but our hopes are all vanished since the French fleet has left us. The storm has proved a cruel misfortune; it has deprived us of the very foundation of the expedition, which would never have been undertaken but from the assurances of the French fleet and forces cooperating with us. However the shattered state of the Fleet and the Admiral's particular instructions from the Court of France obliged him to abandon the enterprize, altho he had the fullest evidence of its being crowned with success in a few day's.

Several [British] ships have come in to the harbour of Newport yesterday and today. A reinforcement is hourly expected. Our force is melting away very fast. We shall be obliged to depart if there comes in any considerable reinforcements.

The Enemy are very strongly fortified with Redoubts; Lines of Abatties.[3] They are almost encircled by water. There is but one narrow side where they can be approached, and that very difficult of access, from the make of the ground and a pond they have formed almost across their front. On the back of these are all their fortifications. That it is impossible to storm the Garrison especially as they have more regular troops than we have.

If we could have got into their rear which we might have done with the assistance of the shipping, we might have succeeded with great ease. However providence has thought proper to order it otherwise, perhaps for our good, altho' difficult to concieve of.

The disappointment is very great and our mortification not less so. To loose such a prize that seemed so much in our power is truly vexatious. I am with great regard Your humble servant

NATHANAEL GREENE

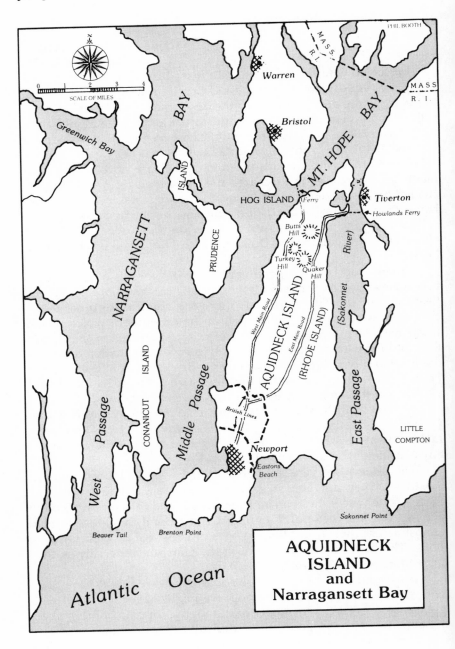

LS (MHi).
1. Letter not found.
2. Thomas Chase was deputy quartermaster in Boston.
3. On the battle of Rhode Island, see below, NG to Washington, 28/31 August.

To George Washington

Sir

Camp near Newport [R.I.]
August 28/31, 1778

Your Excellencys favor of the 21st came to hand the evening of the 25th.

In my last I communicated to your Excellency the departure of the Count de Estaing with his fleet for Boston. This disagreeable event has, as I apprehended, ruined all our operations. It struck such a panic among the Militia and Volunteers that they began to desert by shoals. The fleet no sooner set sail than they began to be alarm'd for their safety. This misfortune damp'd the hopes of our Army and gave new Spirits to that of the Enemy.

We had a very respectable force as to numbers between Eight and nine thousand rank and file upon the ground. Out of these we attempted to select a particular Corps to possess ourselves of the Enemies Lines partly by force and partly by stratagem; but we could not make up the necessary number that was thought sufficient to warrant the attempt which was 5000 including the Continental and State Troops. This body was to consist of men that had been in actual service before, not less than nine months. However, the men were not to be had and if they could have been found there was more against it than for it. Col Laurens was to have opend the passage by landing within the Enemies Lines and getting possession of a Redoubt at the head of Eastons Beach.[1] If we had faild in the attempt, the whole party must have fallen a sacrafice, for their situation would have been such that there was no possibility of geting off.

I shall inclose your Excellency a plan of the Enemies works and of their strength from the best accounts we are able to get. They have never been out of their Lines since the siege began till night before last. Col Bruce came out with 150 men to take off a small Piquet of ours Posted at the neck of Eastons Beach. He partly succeeded in the attempt by the carelessness of the old guard. He came over after dark and lay in Ambush, that when the new guard went down to take their post the enemy came upon their backs before they discovered them, it being very dark. We lost 24 privates and two Subalterns. Ten of the Piquet got off.

Our strength is now reduced from 9000 to between 4 and 5000.[2] All our heavy cannon on garrison Carriages, heavy and superfluous Stores of every kind are removd to the main [i.e., mainland] and to the North end of the Island where we intend to intrench and attempt to hold it and wait the chance of events. General Hancock is gone to Boston to forward the repairs of the fleet and to prepare the mind of the Count for a speedy return. How far he will succeed I cannot pretend to say. I think it a matter of some doubt yet whether the enemy will reenforce, or take off this Garrison. If they expect a superior fleet from Europe they will reenforce; but if not they will remove the garrison.

Your Excellency may rest assurd that I have done every thing in my power to cultivate and promote a good understanding both with the Count [d'Estaing] and the Marquis [de Lafayette] and flatter myself that I am upon very good terms with them both.³ The Marquises great thirst for glory and national attachment often runs him into errors. However he did every thing to prevail on the Admiral to cooperate with us that man could do. People censure the Admiral with great freedom and many are imprudent enough to reproach the Nation through the Admiral. General Sullivan very imprudently issueed something like a censure in General orders. Indeed it was an absolute censure. It opend the mouths of the Army in very clamorous strains. The Genl was obligeed to explain it away in a few Days. The fermentation seems to be now subsiding and all things appear as if they would go smoothly on. The Marquis is going to Boston also to hasten the Counts return and if possible to get the French Troops to join the Land forces here, which will more effectually interest the Count in the success of the expedition.

Five sail of British Ships has got into Newport within two Days past. We have heard nor seen nothing of the Fleet of Transports your Excellency mentioned in your Letter to General Sullivan of the 23d.⁴ If they arrive with a large reenforcement our Expedition is at an end. Unless it is by way of blocade and that will depend upon the French fleets being superior to that of the British.

General Sullivan has done every thing that could be expected and had the fleet cooperated with us as was at first intended and agreeable to the original plan of the expedition we must have been successful. I wish it was in my power to confirm General Sullivans prediction of the 17th but I cannot flatter myself with such an agreeable issue. I am sensible he is in common very sanguine but his expectations were not ill founded in the present case. We had every reason to hope for success from our numbers and from the enemies fears. Indeed General Pigot was heard to say the Garrison must fall unless they were speedily relievd by a British fleet. If we could have made a landing upon the South part of the Town two Days would have put us in compleat possession of it. Nothing was wanting to effect this but the cooperation of the fleet and french forces. The disappointment is vexatious and truly mortifying. The Garrison was so important and the reduction so certain that I cannot with patience think of the event. The French Ship that was missing has got into Boston. The rest of the Fleet have not got there yet, or at least we have no accounts of their Arrival.[5]

We are very anxious to learn the condition of Lord Hows Fleet. The French 74 [gun vessel] that has got into Boston had an Engagement with a British 64. The Capt and Lieut of the former were both wounded; one lost a Leg, the other, an Arm.

Our Troops are in pretty good health and well furnished with Provisions and every thing necessary for carrying on the Expedition.

Our approaches were pushed on with great spirit while we had any hopes of the fleet cooperating with us; but the People[6] lost all relish for diging after that.

People are very anxious to hear the issue of General Lees tryal. Various are the conjectures; but everybody agrees he is not acquitted.

                                        Augt 31 Camp Tiverton
I wrote the foregoing and intended to have sent it by express that went off in the morning but while I was writing I was inform'd the Express was gone and the change of situation and round of events that have since taken place has prevented my forwarding what I had wrote, as matters seemd to be coming to a crisis.

On the evening [eve] of the 29th the Army fell back to the north end of the Island. The next morning the enemy advanced upon us in two Columns upon the East and West road. Our Light Troops commanded by Col Livingston and Col Laurens attacked the head of the Columns about seven oClock in the morning but were beat back. They were reenforced with a Regiment upon each road. The Enemy still provd too strong. General Sullivan form'd the army in order of battle and resolved to wait their approach upon the ground we were encamped on, and sent orders to the Light troops to fall back. The Enemy came up and formd upon Quaker Hill, a very strong piece of ground within about one mile and a 1/4 of our Line. We were well Posted with strong works in our rear and a strong redoubt in front partly upon the right of the Line.

In this position a warm Cannonade commenced and lasted for several hours with continual Skirmishes in front of both Lines. About two oClock the Enemy began to advance in force upon our right as if they intended to dislodge us from the advance Redoubt. I had the command of the Right Wing. After advancing four Regts and finding the enimy still gaining ground I advanced with two more Regiments of regular Troops and a Brigade of Militia and at the same time Gen Sullivan orderd Col Livingston with the Light Troops under his command to advance. We soon put the Enemy to the rout and I had the pleasure to see them run in worse disorder than they did at the battle of Monmouth. Our Troops behavd with great spirit and the brigade of militia, under the command of General Lovel advanceed with great resolution and in good order and stood the fire of the Enemy with great firmness. Lieut Col [Henry Brockholst] Livingston, Col Jackson, and Col Henry B[eekman] Livingston did themselves great honor in the transactions of the day. But its not in my power to do justice to Col Laurens who acted both the General and the Partizan. His command of regular Troops was small but he did every thing possible to be done by their numbers. He had two most Excellent officers with him, Lieut Col Flaury [Fleury] and Major Talbott.

The enemy fell back to their strong ground and the Day terminated with a Cannonade and skirmishes. Both armies continued in their position all Day yesterday, Cannonading each other every now and then. Last night we effected a very good retreat without the loss of men or Stores.

We have not collected an account of the kild and wounded, but we judge our loss amounts to between two and three hundred and that of the Enemies to much more.

We are going to be posted all round the Shores as a guard upon them and in that state to wait for the return of the Fleet which, by the by, I think will not be in a hurry.

It is asserted that Lord How arrivd last night with his fleet and the reenforcement mentioned in your Excellencys Letter to General Sullivan. If the report is true, we got off the Island in very good season.

The Marquis went to Boston the Day before the action and did not return until last night just as we were leaving the Island. He went to wait upon the Admiral, to learn his further intentions and to get him to return again and compleat the expedition if possible.

I observe your Excellency thinks the enemy design to evacuate Newyork. If they should, I think they will Newport, also; but I am perswaded they will not neither for the present.

I would write your Excellency a more particular account of the battle and retreat but I immagin General Sullivan and Col Laurens has done it already and I am myself very much unwell, have had no sleep for three Nights and Days, being severely afflicted with the asthma.[7] I am with great respect Your Excellencys most obedient humble Servt

NATH GREENE

LS (Washington Papers: DLC).
1. On NG's plan for landing at Easton's Beach, see his letter to Sullivan of 23 August, above.

2. As seen in note 7, Sullivan probably had between five and six thousand men by the twenty-eighth.

3. On NG's role in mollifying the French, see Washington's letter of 1 September, below.

4. The vessels that had arrived in Newport were part of Lord Howe's fleet en route to Boston. The fleet that Washington had mentioned in his letter of the twenty-third to Sullivan was Clinton's, which arrived off the Rhode Island coast two days after NG started this letter. See note 7 below.

5. See note, NG's Remonstrance to Count d'Estaing, 21 August, above.

6. NG often spoke of the troops as "the people."

7. As far as it goes, NG's brief summary of the battle is accurate, although, as he expected, it is far less complete than Sullivan's account. More objective than Sullivan's, however, and by far the most thorough of modern accounts, is Dearden's "R.I. Campaign," which not only makes careful use of every known source but is a well-balanced narrative. The following account is taken largely from his chapter on the battle, pp. 157–79.

When on 24 August, Gen. Sullivan learned from Washington of the hundred British vessels that were headed toward Newport, his council of war decided the army should withdraw to the fortifications near Butts Hill at the north end of Aquidneck Island and wait there until they learned whether or not d'Estaing would return. Two days later they hurried Lafayette off to Boston by horse to sound out d'Estaing. (He rode the seventy miles in seven hours.) At 9:00 P.M. on 28 August, NG led off from the trenches outside Newport with the first contingent up West Road. By midnight the last of the troops had withdrawn, and by 3:00 A.M. they were pitching their tents near Butts Hill, without having been detected by the enemy. While the men snatched a little sleep, Sullivan and his officers planned their defense against what they were forced to assume would be a British attack.

Somewhat south of Butts Hill, Sullivan deployed his army of five to six thousand men along a fortified line almost two miles long which stretched across Aquidneck Island from East Passage on the east to Narragansett Bay on the west. Gen. John Glover's brigade was stationed on the left, near East Road and facing Quaker Hill, his left flank protected by Gen. John Tyler's Connecticut militia. To Glover's right, in the center, was a brigade temporarily under Col. Christopher Greene, NG's kinsman and hero of Red Bank, who had been shifted from his usual command of the Black Regiment. Butts Hill stood to their rear. To Col. Greene's right, the line was extended to West Road by Col. Ezekiel Cornell's R.I. Brigade. Across West Road from Cornell, facing Turkey Hill to the south, was Gen. James M. Varnum's brigade, flanked on the far right by Col. Henry Brockholst Livingston's regiment. Holding a redoubt on the far right was Christopher Greene's Black Regiment, now under NG's longtime friend, Maj. Samuel Ward, Jr. NG was in command of the entire right wing. Three miles in front of the line, Sullivan posted the light infantry unit of Col. John Laurens on West Road and that of Col. Henry Beekman Livingston on East Road.

It was daybreak before the British commander, Gen. Robert Pigot, learned that the Americans were gone. He immediately sent Gen. Francis Smith with several regiments up East Road in pursuit and Gen. Friedrich Wilhelm von Lossberg with Hessian and Anspacher battalions up West Road. Gen. Prescott was assigned to take over Honeyman's Hill.

In the early morning hours of 29 August, there was brisk fighting between these two advancing columns and Sullivan's advance units. For a while Col. Henry Beekman Livingston and his men on East Road brought Gen. Francis Smith's regiments to a virtual standstill by firing from behind walls and trees then falling back. When Smith was reinforced, Livingston was forced to fall back. Along West Road, Col. Laurens, using similar tactics, struck savagely at von Lossberg's Germans. Before their superior firepower, Laurens slowly retreated to Turkey Hill, then finally back to NG's sector. Progressing northward on East Road, Gen. Smith took Quaker Hill to the south of American lines, then began assaulting Glover's sector. Smith met with such sustained fire from Glover's artillery and small arms that the British were forced to withdraw with considerable losses. Smith's subsequent artillery bombardment from Quaker Hill failed to dislodge Glover.

A lull in the British attacks at mid-morning led NG to propose that Sullivan launch an all-out attack against the enemy. Sullivan vetoed the proposal, and, as NG later admitted in a letter to John Brown (6 September, below), he "believd the General had taken the more prudent measure." Soon, three British frigates and a brig started bombarding American lines from Narragansett Bay but sailed back when NG managed to train two 18-pounders and two 24-pounders against them. In the meantime, von Lossberg had attempted to outflank Samuel Ward's redoubt near the west end of the island; in fierce hand to hand fighting, the Black troops twice repulsed von Lossberg.

At about 2:00 P.M., von Lossberg, now reinforced, made an all-out attempt on NG's wing. Advancing past Ward's redoubt, he made some inroads against NG's regiments. But NG counterattacked with the aid of two additional continental regiments (one, the Second Rhode Island, under his old friend, Israel Angell), Solomon Lovell's Massachusetts Militia, and Col. Henry Beekman Livingston's light corps. With muskets and bayonets, NG's 1,500 troops sent von Lossberg back in confusion. As NG wrote to Washington above: "We soon put the Enemy to the rout and I had the pleasure to see them run in worse disorder than they did at the battle of Monmouth." Sullivan considered an assault on Turkey and Quaker Hills but gave it up because his men had been too long without sleep or food, and they would have been exposed to a heavy artillery barrage before they reached the slopes of the hills. Toward evening there was a final unsuccessful American attempt to surround the Hessian Chasseurs; then the day petered out with an exchange of artillery. The battle of Rhode Island was over.

The Americans, including the militia, had done themselves proud that day, but it had been a bloody fight. Dearden gives American casualties as 30 dead, 137 wounded, and 44 missing; and British casualties as 38 killed, 210 wounded, and 44 missing—128 of these being German. ("R.I. Campaign," pp. 175–76)

The next day, August thirtieth, the fighting was limited to occasional exchanges of artillery. When Sullivan got word that Clinton's fleet was off Block Island and that d'Estaing was not returning, a council voted to retreat to Tiverton across Mt. Hope Bay. From American preparations and an American deserter, the British anticipated the retreat, but fortunately for the Americans, Pigot had become ill, and Prescott, in his absence and without specific orders, did not care to risk an attack. At 8:00 P.M. the Americans began to march for Howland's Ferry; by 3:00 A.M. the last of them had left the island. Once again Glover's Salem Volunteers manned the boats that carried the army to safety. Midway through the evacuation, the weary Lafayette returned from Boston to help. The brave young Frenchman could not hide his bitter disappointment that he had not been in the fight.

Clinton arrived in Newport on 1 September, annoyed that Pigot had not waited for his reinforcements before attacking. He was right to be annoyed. With their combined forces, it could have spelled complete disaster for the Americans. As NG admitted in his letter above, if the report of Clinton's arrival was true, "we got off the Island in very good season."

To Catharine Greene

Camp near Bristol Ferry [R.I.] August 29, 1778

. . . For fear you should hear any vulgar reports circulating about the country, I have sent George to inform you that we have had a considerable action to-day; we have beat the enemy off the ground where they advanced upon us; the killed and wounded on both sides unknown, but they were considerable for the numbers of troops we had engaged.

We retreated back here last night, with an intention to hold this part of the Island. The enemy advanced upon us early this morning, and a pretty smart engagement ensued between our light troops and their advance party, and a severe action ensued with nearly the whole right wing. I write upon my horse and have not slept any for two nights, therefore you'll excuse my not writing very legible, as I write upon the field. Colonel Will. Livingston is slightly wounded.[1] My aids all behaved with great gallantry.

Excerpt reprinted from Greene, *Greene*, 2: 129.
    1. Col. William Smith Livingston had been NG's aide in 1776 and resigned from the army in October. (See below, Livingston to NG, 23 October.)

From George Washington

Head Quarters White Plains [N.Y.]
Dear Sir   1st Septr 1778
    I have had the pleasure of receiving your several letters, the last of which was of the 22d August.[1] I have not now time to take notice of the several arguments that were made use of for and against the Counts quitting the Harbour of Newport and sailing for Boston. Right or wrong, it will probably disappoint our sanguine expectations of success, and what I esteem a still worse consequence, I fear it will sow the seeds of dissention and distrust between us and our new allies, except the most prudent measures are taken to suppress the feuds and jealousies that have already arisen. I depend much upon your temper and influence to conciliate that animosity, which I plainly perceive by a letter from the Marquis, subsists between the American Officers and the French in our service.[2] This you may depend will extend itself to the Count and the officers and men of his whole Fleet, should they return to Rhode Island, except upon their arrival there, they find a reconciliation has taken place. The Marquis speaks kindly of a letter from you to him upon this subject.[3] He will therefore take any advice coming from you, in a friendly light, and if he can be pacified, the other French Gentlemen will of course be satisfied, as they look up to him as their Head. The Marquis grounds his complaint upon a general order of the 24 Augt the latter part of which is certainly very impolitic, and upon the universal clamor that prevailed against the french nation.
    I beg you will take every measure to keep the protest entered into by the General Officers, from being made public. The Congress, sensible of the ill consequences that will flow from the world's knowing of our differences, have passed a resolve to that purpose. Upon the whole, my dear Sir, you can conceive my meaning better than I

can express it, and I therefore fully depend upon your exerting yourself to heal all private animosities between our principal officers and the french, and to prevent all illiberal expressions and reflections that may fall from the Army at large.

I have this moment recd a letter from Genl Sullivan of the 29th Augt in which he barely informs me of an Action upon that day, in which he says we had the better, but does not mention particulars. I am &ca

Df (Washington Papers: DLC).
 1. Of the letters NG wrote Washington from Rhode Island in August, the only one that has been found is that of 28/31 August, above, which Washington had not yet received. His letter of 22 August undoubtedly contained news of the French fleet's sailing to Boston and of the officers' protest of 22 August, above.
 2. Lafayette's letter of 25 August is reprinted in Gottschalk, *Lafayette's Letters*, pp. 56–61 (from the American edition of Lafayette's *Memoirs*).
 3. Letter not found, but its effect is noted, General Officers to d'Estaing, 22 August, above. Also discussed there are Sullivan's general order of 24 August (that Washington mentions) and the roles that NG and Lafayette played in helping to prevent the alliance from falling apart.

To the Rev. John Murray

[Coventry, R.I. after 1 Sept. 1778]
You may remember, I promised you a letter at the close of every campaign. Had I the tongue of a Murray to proclaim, or the pen of a Robertson to record, the occurrences of this campaign should be delineated to the honor of America.[1] The Monmouth battle, and the action upon Rhode-Island, were no small triumphs to us who had so often been necessitated to turn our backs. To behold our fellows, chasing the British off the field of battle, afforded a pleasure which you can better conceive than I describe. If, my dear Murray, I had before been an unbeliever, I have had sufficient evidence of the intervention of Divine Providence to reclaim me from infidelity: my heart, I do assure you, overflows with gratitude to Him whose arm is mightier than all the Princes of the earth.[2] In the midst of difficulties, and I have encountered many, my heart reverts to you; were you addressing me from the pulpit, you could convince me that considering the world to which I am hastening, I have not the least cause of complaint. I sigh for an opportunity of listening to the music of your voice.

Are you and the priests upon any better terms? Or are they as mad with you as ever? Well, go on and prosper, and God bless you to the end of the chapter.[3]

Reprinted from John Murray, *The Life of the Rev. John Murray* (with notes by L. S. Everett), 7th ed. (1840), pp. 254–55.

1. William Robertson (1721–93), the Scottish churchman and historian, noted for his three-volume history of the reign of Charles V.
2. An unusual religious expression for NG.
3. He refers to the problem Murray was encountering in Gloucester, Mass. See above, To Whom it may Concern, 27 May 1777.

To John Brown

Sir   Coventry [R.I.] Sept 6th 1778
  In all Republican Governments every person that acts in a public capacity must naturally expect to have observations and Strictures made upon his conduct. This is a tax generally laid by all free Governments upon their Officers either Civil or Military, however meritorious. I am not surprisd therefore to hear the late unsuccessful expedition against Newport fall under some degree of censure; but I must confess I am not a little astonished to hear such a principal charactor in Society as you throw out such illiberal reflections against a Gentlemans conduct merely because he took his measures different from your Opinion.[1]
  This Expedition was pland upon no other consideration than that of the French fleets cooperating with the American Troops. The Strength of the Garrison was consider'd and a force orderd to be leveed accordingly, that might be sufficient to compleat its reduction. In forming the estimate there was the aid of the fleet and the assistance of 3500 French forces that were on board the fleet taken into consideration. The loss of this force with that of the Aid of the French fleet was a sufficient reason for abandoning the Expedition.
  You say you think the expedition was ill pland and worse conducted.[2] In the first place that the forces were drawn together at an improper place. I must beg leave to dissent from you in opinion. Was there any time lost by the Continental Troops coming to Providence? There was not, for they all got together some Days before the Militia. Would it not have been extreme difficult, if not impossible, to have brought the forces to have acted in concert with each other? One body at Tiverton and the other at Boston Neck; and divided as they were both parties would have been unequal to the descent. If either party was sufficient of its self then the other part was superfluous. Besides the objections of a division of forces and the distance apart, There are two other objections against the measure; one is the difficulty of embarking a body of Troops from that ruged Shore, the delays that Storms and high Winds might produce, The Accidents that might happen in crossing where there is such a large swell agoing; and the Langour that a sea sickness might produce among the men Is one objection. The other is there was no Stores or magezines of any kind at South Kingston to equip and furnish the Troops

for the attempt, besides which it was necessary for the General to have all his Troops together that he might select only such men and officers as were most suitable for the enterprize. If the Troops had been collected at South Kingston it would have too fully explaind our intention and put the Enemy upon their Guard. Whereas landing upon the Northend of the Island led the enemy into a belief that we intended to carry the Garrison by regular approaches, Which would have given us an opportunity of reembarking the Troops and landing upon the South part of the Island without being mistrusted. This was the plan of attack and it must have succeded had our strength been sufficient and the disembarkation countenanced by the Fleet.

You cannot suppose that General Sullivan wants spirit or ambition to attempt any thing that reason or common sense can justify. It is the business of every General Officer that is desireous of distinguishing himself to court all opportunities to engage with the Enemy where the situation and condition of his own forces and that of theirs will admit of it. But the safety of our Country is a greater object with every man of principle than personal glory.

Before a General Officer engages in any hazardous enterprize, he should well consider the consequences of success and failure, whether the circumstances of the community will not render one infinitely more prejudicial than the other can be beneficial. The strength and quallity of the Troops should be considerd that you are about to attack. How they can be approached and by what means you can secure a retreat. Then you have to take into consideration the number and quallity of your own Troops, how they are found, what temper they are of, whether they are regular or irregular and how they are Officerd. Even the Wind and weather are sometimes necessary considerations and not [to] be neglected.

I have heard many people foolish enough to suppose that it was only necessary for a General to lead on his forces to ensure success without regard to the strength or situation of the Enemy or the number or goodness of his own troops. Those that have often been in action can only judge what is to be expected of good, bad and indifferent Troops. Men are often struck with Pannicks and they are generally subject to that passion in a greater or lesser degree according as the force of dicipline has formd the mind by habit to meet danger and death. I dare say many a man has gone from home with a determined resolution to meet the enemy, that has shamefully quited the field for want of a habitual fortitude. Men often feel courageous at a distance from danger that faint through fear when they come to be exposd. Pride and Sentiment supports the Officer, Habit and Enthusiasm the Soldier; without these there is no safe reliance upon men.

I remember you recommended an attempt to effect a landing upon the South part of the Island the night we returnd from the fleet.[3] But I could not possibly suppose you to be serious because it was impossible for us to get the Boats round seasonably, draw out the Men and Officers proper for the descent, and effect a landing before Day. It was therefore impracticable if it had been ever so eligible. But I am far from thinking under our circumstances the measure would have been justifiable by reason or common sense in a common view much less by Military Maxims. The Day after the Fleet saild there was such a great change took place in the two Armies; but particularly in ours, whose spirits all sunk upon the departure of the fleet except the few Regular troops, and it had its effect upon them, That nothing could be attempted with the hopes of success. The Garrison in Newport that before gave themselves up for lost now collected new courage and would have defended themselves with double obstinacy.

Suppose General Sullivan had attempted a landing and actually effected it and the Garrison had defeated his Troops, what would have been the consequence? The whole would have been made prisoners and not only the party that Landed; but all those that remaind in Camp with all our Stores of every kind. Was the object important enough for such a risque? Was the chance equal of our succeeding? Every one that will suffer himself to reflect a moment will readily agree that neither the importance of the object nor the chance of succeeding would have warranted the attempt. It must be confest the loss of such a Garrison would have given the British Army a deadly wound. But the loss of our Army would have put our cause in jeopardy. Remember the effect of the Garrison of Fort Washington. There was men enough there to have defended themselves against all the British Army had they not have been struck with a Panic; but being most of them irregular Troops, they lost all their confidence when the danger began to grow pressing and so fell a prey to their own fears.[4]

But when you take into consideration the little prospect of our effecting a landing where there was Batteries almost all round the Shores and where the Enimy had Cutters to intercept any attempt, and Guard Boats to make discoveries, The measure would look more like madness than rational conduct.

There was another objection to the measure, that was our force was unequal to the attempt. The party detach'd to make the landing should have been superior to the whole Garrison. The remaining part left in Camp to cover the Stores and cooperate occasionally with the detachment after they had effected a landing, should have been equally strong for both being so circumstanced as to render it necessary to be able, independant of each other to resist the whole British Garrison, if either had been deficient it might have provd the ruin [of] all.

If the party that was landed had not been superior to the Garrison they [might] have been defeated and not haveing any Ships to cover their retreat all would have been lost. Or if during the embarkation the Garrison had sallied, the Troops left in Camp would have been put to the route [rout], and nearly the whole have been made prisoners and all our Cannon and Stores fallen into their hands.

These are common and probable events in War and to be guarded against accordingly. The Garrison at Newport was generally thought to be 6000 strong including Sailors. Our force amounted to 9000 at most, indeed the Field returns made it but 8174 and the much greater part of these Militia; but I would swell it to the utmost extent and still you see it will fall far short of the necessary number to warrant the measure even supposing ours to have been all regular Troops. Here I cannot help remarking that some People seem desireous of deceiveing themselves with regard to our strength. They [are] rather inclind to credit The Votes of Assembly, and the resolves of Councils of War with regard to numbers than returns actually taken upon the ground. Would not a General Officer be a fool to take a measure from numbers voted him for an expedition without examining them to see how they agreed? Some I hear assert that our strength must have been much greater than appears by our returns from the number of Rations that were drawn. I remember very well last Winter at Valley Forge our Army drew 32000 Rations, when the most we could muster fit for duty was but 7500. And In all irregular Armies there will be generally a third more Rations drawn than is in a well appointed one to have the same strength upon the ground. Therefore there can be no safe conclusion drawn from the circumstance of the Rations, their being either greater or less is no certain evidence of the real strength of an Army.

I am further informd you think this expedition has been the worst concerted and the most disgracefully executed of any one during the War. I must confess I differ widely from you in opinion. I think it prudently concerted and honorably and faithfully executed. If the General had attempted to have stormd the Lines in common form he would have met with a disgraceful defeat. Some people are foolish enough to think that because the Northern Army carried Burgoynes Lines that these might have been attempted with equal success, not adverting to the difference of circumstances. These Lines were ten times as strong as those of Burgoynes; besides which the enemy came out of their works there and our people drove them back again and entered pell mell with them. Burgoynes force was much less than this

Garrison, His Troops much dispirited, the Army that surrounded them in regular Troops more than as strong again as ours.

Remember the loss of the British Army before Ticonderoga last [French and Indian] War in attempting to Storm Lines inconsiderable compared with the fortifications at Newport and defended with a less number of men in the Works than were here. Recollect the fate of the British Army at Bunkers Hill in attacking slight Works defended by new levied Troops. Consider the disgrace and defeat that happend to the Hessians in the Attack upon the inconsiderable Redoubt at Red Bank.[5] And then form a judgement what prospect General Sullivan had of success in makeing an Attack with an Army composd principally of raw Militia upon a Garrison as strong as that at Newport consisting almost wholely of regular Troops and fortified so securely as they were.

There was but one possible mode of attack by storm which was proposd[6] to the General, but the men necessary for the attempt could not be found and consequently the attack could not be made.

I am told you censure General Sullivan for not bringing on a general action and urge my opinion as a proof of the propriety. I remember you asked me why there had not been a general action when you was at the Island the even'g of the day of the battle. I told you that I had advisd to one in the morning; but that I believd the General had taken the more prudent measure. He had fought them by detachment, defeated and disgracd them without runing any great risque.

Our numbers at the time we left the enemies Lines were not much superior to the Garrison; we knew they expected a reinforcement hourly. Had any considerable force arrivd the Night we retreated, landed, and marched out with the old Garrison, we should have met with a defeat. The smallness of our Numbers, the dispirited state that all Troops are in on retreat together with the probabillity of the Enemies have'g receivd a reinforcement, determind the General not to risque a General Action when he was sure of an advantage in a partial one, and by risqueing a general one He exposed the whole of the Troops to certain ruin upon a defeat, [He] thought the other measure most advisable and I think so too upon cool reflection altho I thought otherwise at the time.

I have seen as much service almost as any man in the American Army and have been in as many or more Actions than any one. I know the Charactor of all our General Officers as well as any one; and if I am any judge the expedition has been prudently and well conducted and I am confident there is not a General Officer from the commander in chief to the youngest in the Field that would have gone greater lengths to have given success to the Expedition than

General Sullivan. He is Sensible, Active, Ambitious, brave and persevereing in his temper; and the object was sufficently important to make him despise every difficulty opposd to his success as far as he was at liberty to consult his own Reputation; but the public good is of higher importance than personal glory and the one is not to be gratified at the risque and expence of the other.

I recollect your observations to me on board the fleet, that the reputation of the principal Officers depended upon the success of the expedition. I have long since learnt to despise vulgar prejudices and to regulate my conduct by maxims more noble than popular Sentiment. I have an honest Ambition of meriting the approbation of the public; but I will never go contrary to my judgment or violate my honor or conscience for a temporary salute.

If the Congress or any particular State who entrusts their Troops under my command thinks proper to give orders to run all risques and hazzards to carry a point I would chearfully lead on the men; but where it is left discretionary I must act agreeable to the dictates of my own judgment.

People from consulting their wishes rather than their reason and by forming a charactor of the spirit and firmness of irregular Troops more from general orders sounding their praise than from any particular knowledge of their conduct, are led to expect more from such Troops, than is in the power of any person to effect with them.

I would just remark one thing further to you: that an attack with Militia in an open Country where they could get off upon a defeat, might be very prudent which would be very rash and unwarrantable upon an Island.

I have wrote this much in justification of a Persons charactor whom I esteem a good Officer and who I think is much more deserving your thanks and that of the public also than reproach. With regard to myself it was unnecessary for me to say any thing in justification of the measure of calling the Troops together at Providence; because I had no voice in it; neither was I opposd to a storm, providing a proper number of men of suitable quallity could be found fit for the attempt. My advice for a general Action I think was wrong, and the retreat that followed every body must allow was necessary and that it was well conducted.[7]

I have been told that your brother Nicholas let fall some very ungenerous insinuations with regard to me a few Days before the Action upon the Island.[8] These are the rewards and gracious returns I am to expect for years of hard and dangerous service, where every sacrifice of Interest, ease, and domestic pleasure has been given up to the service of my Country. But I flatter myself I am not dependant upon the State of Rhode Island for either my charactor or consequence in life. However, I cannot help feeling mortified that those that have been at home making their fortunes, and living in the lap of luxury and enjoying all the pleasures of domestic life, should be the first to sport with the feelings of Officers who have stood as a barrier between them and ruin. I am Sir Your most Obedient and very humble Servt

N GREENE

ADf (CtY). Portions checked with a copy in the Sullivan Papers, MHi.
    1. Brown admitted in a letter to Sullivan on 11 September that he may have called it an "Inglorious Campaign & perhaps wors in its Consequences." He justified such comments by saying, "Disappointed persons will allways Espetially at the moment of missfortin Say harder things than they would at any other hour," acknowledged that he was one of those especially disappointed but added that he had never said anything critical of Sullivan. (Hammond, *Sullivan*, 2: 330) If Brown had been critical of Sullivan, he more than made up for it by serving on a committee of the Assembly as well as one named by the Town Meeting of Providence to thank Sullivan in person for his efforts. (Ibid., 2: 523, 539)
    2. On the Rhode Island expedition and the battle, see above, NG to d'Estaing 21 August, and NG to Washington, 28/31 August.
    3. Brown had accompanied NG when he went aboard the French flagship, the *Languedoc*, in an attempt to persuade d'Estaing to stay in Rhode Island waters on 21 August.
    4. Certainly an overstatement on NG's part. For information on the fall of Ft. Washington, see above, vol. 1: 352–59n.
    5. See above, NG to Colonel Greene, 26 October 1777.
    6. NG had first written in the draft "I proposed."
    7. A most generous admission by NG and also an accurate one. See above, NG to Sullivan, 23 August.
    8. See below, Nicholas Brown to NG, 14 September.

To General John Sullivan

Dear Sir   Coventry [R.I.] Sept 7th [1778]
    By a Letter this moment receivd from Major Courtland I find I am not to expect the pleasure of your company to dine with us to Day. Should be glad to know when you can make it convenient.
    Am sorry to hear of the destruction of Bedford. General Clinton deserves to be immortallisd for this memorable action. It is highly worthy so great a commander.[1] He has forgot how he run the other Day in the Jerseys at the head of all his Troops. If he wanted to fight he had then an opportunity. But there is something so low, dirty and unworthy in this Action that I am surprizd he would be concernd in it, and more especially as he reprobated General Vaughns conduct up the North River last fall for a similar conduct.[2]
    I am clear in opinion it is the intention of Clinton if possible to burn Providence and he is makeing these manouevers at New London and at Bedford to divide and draw off our force.
    Tylers brigade is gone and I suppose more force will be demanded to the Eastward.[3]

In attempting to cover too much we shall expose every thing. Some principal objects should be adverted to and the others must take their chance.

Warwick is now left open; will you have part of the Troops at Patuxit orderd there or not. I wish to know your mind upon the matter.[4]

Should be glad to know the particulars of Bedford affair and any other intelligence that may come to hand.

The Artillery is wanted at [East] Greenwich. Please to order it forward for fear Mr Clinton should try his success this way. I am with great respect and esteem your most obedient humble Servt

NATH GREENE

ALS(NhHi).

1. As noted above, NG to Washington, 28/31 August, Gen. Henry Clinton arrived at Newport only hours after the last of Sullivan's troops had escaped from the island. Three days later Clinton returned to New York, but he transferred the transports and troops he had brought from New York to the command of Gen. Charles Grey, with orders to raid New Bedford and Martha's Vineyard, in the hope, said Clinton, "It will serve to convince these poor deluded people that that sort of war . . . will sooner or later reduce them." During 4–6 September, Grey attacked New Bedford and Fair Haven in Buzzard's Bay, destroying almost $325,000 in property, including seventy vessels, many of them privateers. (Willcox, *Clinton*, p. 251, from which Clinton's quote is taken; Mackenzie, *Diary*, 2: 392–94; Gordon, *History*, 3: 169)

2. During Clinton's expedition to the Highlands in October 1777, John Vaughan had led the column that captured Ft. Montgomery. NG refers to his burning the village of Esopus, near Kingston, N.Y. (*DNB*; Willcox, *Clinton*, p. 188)

3. Gen. John Tyler's Connecticut militia had participated in the battle of Rhode Island.

4. Warwick is the town where NG had spent most of his life.

To Governor William Greene of Rhode Island

Sir   Coventry, [R.I.] Sept. 11th, 1778.

The growing extravagance of the people, and the increasing demand for the article of forage for the use of the public, require the immediate interposition of legislative authority to fix some limits to the price of articles taken for the use of the army; for without, it will be impossible to furnish money to answer their demands, or to procure forage sufficient to subsist the cattle of the army.[1] This evil, if it is permitted to rage, will soon become intolerable if the forage is to be furnished by contract, because the people enlarge their prices as our wants grow more pressing. Two evils will result from the present state of things: our funds will be found unequal to the expense, and consequently it will sap the very foundation of all opposition. The people in hopes of greater gain will withhold their forage until they starve our cattle. It has been proved to be impracticable to regulate trade and commerce in general; and perhaps if it could be effected it might not be found to answer the great purposes of society, so well as that medium which is formed by the mutual wants of the buyers and sellers.[2] But a partial regulation, so far as respects the supplies of the public, I conceive to be absolutely necessary, and at the same time perfectly consistent with private right and the public welfare.

I submit the matter to your Excellency's consideration and that of your council, and should be glad of your advice and direction as to the modes and means of supplying the army with forage.[3] I am, with the most perfect esteem, Your Excellency's obedient, humble servant,

NATHANAEL GREENE

N. B. The prices of hay, grain, and carriage hire by the day, was regulated in Pennsylvania, so far as respected the supplying the public [i.e., the government], and it had a happy effect. I believe the same policy took place in New Jersey, where hay was regulated at twenty dollars per ton, and grain in proportion.

Reprinted from RIHS, *Coll.*, 6: 217–18.
1. For more on this pressing problem, see his letters to Gov. Trumbull of Connecticut, 14 September, and to Washington, 16 September, below.
2. On the New England Convention's recommendation for regulating all prices, and for NG's and Gov. Greene's reluctance to do so, see above, Greene to NG, 6 March 1778.
3. The governor's response has not been found. If he favored NG's proposal, he did not persuade the legislature, nor did a circular letter from Washington to the governors. (This letter, printed in Fitzpatrick, *GW*, 12: 478, is mentioned in Washington to NG, 22 September, below, as being written to the legislatures.) Only after a plea from Congress on 30 November did Rhode Island enact legislation to regulate the price or authorize the impressment of forage, horses, etc. The legislation, however, was soon rescinded. (See below, Governor Greene to NG, 15 January 1779.)

To General John Sullivan

[Coventry, R.I., 11 September 1778. Encloses an address to Congress written in behalf of Sullivan's brother, Ebenezer. Hopes the short address will suffice.[1] Excerpt reprinted from Hammond, *Sullivan*, 2: 331. Enclosure missing. 1 p.]

1. See below, Ebenezer Sullivan to NG, 16 October.

To Major Richard Claiborne[1]

[Coventry, R.I., 12 September 1778. Printed commission as deputy quartermaster general for an unspecified area.[2] DS (PCC, Item 41: DNA) 1 p.]

1. Claiborne, a Virginian, had formerly been a lieutenant of the First Continental Artillery and brigade major of Weedon's brigade. (Heitman, *Register*) He served throughout NG's tenure as a deputy in various locations. Claiborne played a major role

in the preparations for Sullivan's Western Expedition in the spring and summer of 1779, as his letters to NG in May 1779, below, indicate. During NG's Southern Campaign he was helpful as Virginia state quartermaster.

2. This is the only printed commission for a deputy that has come to light.

From Henry Laurens, President of the Continental Congress

[Philadelphia] 13th Sept. [1778]

Delivered Colo John Mitchell, Deputy Quarter Master General an Act of Congress of the 12th Instant forbidding the purchase of Wheat for forage, unless in the vicinity of the Camp and in cases of absolute necessity: also directing the Quarter Master General to consult with the Commander in Chief upon the propriety of reducing the stationary teams of the Army &c.[1]

LB (PCC, Item 13: DNA).
1. Act can be found in *JCC*, 12: 906.

To Governor George Clinton of New York

Dear Sir   Providence [R.I.] Sepr 14th 1778

The great scarcity of grain in this state, the distress of the Inhabitants and the number of men that my brothers have to feed in the common order of their business, together with the encreased numbers they now employ in manufactureing a large quantity of tools for the Qr Mr Generals department Have put them upon the measure of attempting to import a quantity of Flour from the State of New York.

This will be handed you by Mr Christopher Greene a brother of mine who has the direction of the business. He will apply to your Excellency for a permit, which I must beg you to grant him; both from a regard to the distress of the People, and to promote the business of the Quarter Master Generals department under their direction.[1] I have the honor to be with the greatest respect Your Excellency's most Obedt humble servant

NATH GREENE

ALS (ICU).
1. The New York Committee of Safety, alarmed by the drain of foodstuffs to New England, imposed an embargo on grain and flour in 1776, as Connecticut had done the previous year. (For a discussion of embargoes and NG's opposition to them as retaliatory measures leading to disunity, see above, NG to Unknown Person, 20 May 1777, and NG to Gov. Cooke, 10/11 July 1777.) Although New York waived the embargo for civil shipments under special circumstances, Clinton refused to end it even when Massachusetts threatened to cut off shipments of salt to New York. Whether the governor granted such an exemption to Christopher Greene is not known. The embargo was not repealed until June 1781. (See John A. Krout, "Finance and Army Supplies," in Alexander C. Flick, ed., *History of the State of New York*, vol. 4, *The New State* [New York: Columbia University Press, 1923]: 144–45.)

To Governor Jonathan Trumbull of Connecticut

[Coventry, R.I., 14 September 1778. Increasing public demand for forage necessitates regulation of prices—especially of forage—to the army, although regulation in general has "pretty fully proved to be impracticable." One of the evils of the present system is "while the People withhold their Forrage, in hopes of a larger price, our Cattle must inevitably starve."[1] Cy (Ct) 2 pp.]

1. See also his letters on the same subject above to Gov. William Greene of Rhode Island, 11 September; below to Washington, 16 September, and to Jeremiah Powell, 17 September.

From Nicholas Brown

Sr   Provid. [R.I.] Sep. 14. 1778

To my very graetist surprize Brother Jno B Shew'd me a paragraff in Letr to him, wherein you say you had ben told that I had "let fall some Ungenerous insinuations with regard to" You.[1] This you may rely upon is Intirely without the least foundation, for I am sure that I allways Revered the Charractor of Genl Green both in thought [and] word. That I am Abssolutly sure nothing of the Kind Could come from me But think myself very unhappy in livg [living] in a Day when mankind use such freedom with Gentlemens Charractor or for mischief Should undertake to Tell of things they *never heard or misunderstood* to Create Anemosety amonst the Graetest [and] best friend. I must sr request the favr of Know'g your Author That I may see the person face to face for I am sure it must be a mistake.

I Know the times are such that If Gentl of your Station Should listen to what may be said to be said they would have nothing else to Do but to here and never here the Truth. I am in Truth your most respectfully Esteemd obd and very Humbl servt[2]

ADf (RPJCB).
1. The paragraph is quoted at the end of NG to John Brown, 6 September, above.
2. NG responds to this letter on 4 October, below.

From Colonel John Davis

[Carlisle, Pa., 14 September 1778. Has sent military stores to Philadelphia and returns to Col. Cox. Twenty wagons still on hand. Cy (Davis Papers: DLC) 1 p.]

From George Washington

Head Quarters White Plains [N.Y.]
Dear Sir   Sepr 14th 1778
The Board of War have advised me of a large quantity of ready
made cloathing for the use of the army in the possession of Mr Samuel
Fletcher of Boston which they have ordered to be immediately sent
on to Springfield and Hartford in the first instance and afterwards to
the army.[1] You are aware of the mismanagement there has been in the
manner of transporting cloathing which has commonly been brought
forward in small parcels, without guards or conductors; a mode
always productive of delay, frequently of loss. An apprehension of
similar mismanagement in the present case and an anxiety to have
the necessities of the troops at this advanced season supplied as
speedily as possible, have induced me to call the attention of General
Heath to the matter. I have directed him in conjunction with your
assistants to employ every resource for hastening the transportation.
Agreeable to this idea, I would wish you to make every arrangement
you can in your department for that purpose. Good use should be
made of the return waggons on the occasion, but in an affair of such
consequence every additional resource that may promote dispatch
should be improved.

The wants of the army and the season of the year are sufficient
motives for every exertion to bring on so valuable a supply of cloathing, but there is at this juncture a further reason for it, of the greatest
weight. Congress have come to a resolution to inlist all the drafts in
service for the Continental bounty to serve during the war. It is the
opinion of the officers, that if the cloathing was on the spot, so that
every reinlisted man could be furnished on hand with a good suit of
cloaths it would have a most powerful influence in promoting the success of that resolution. So many promises have been made to the men
which have never been fulfilled that they will now trust to nothing
but actual performance. If you think your going to Boston will be
serviceable it will be perfectly agreeable to me.[2] With the greatest
regard and esteem I am Dear Sir Yr Most Obedt serv

Df (Washington Papers: DLC).
1. The Board of War, having virtually taken over the functions of the clothier
general, had enlisted Washington's aid in getting clothing (mostly French) from the
Boston merchants, Otis and Andrews, and the clothier agent, Samuel Fletcher. NG's
only responsibility as quartermaster was to transport the clothing.
Washington, interested in more than covering the men's nakedness and providing
warmth, stressed to Otis and Andrews the need to provide sergeants with clothing
that differed from that of privates "both as to fineness of Cloth and mode of finishing,"
as nothing, he said, "contributes more to keep up that distinction which ought to
subsist" between them. Commissioned officers, of course, should receive clothing of

higher quality. (Fitzpatrick, *GW*, 12: 451–52; see also his letters to Heath, 14 September, and to Samuel Fletcher, of the same date, pp. 445–46 and p. 453.)

2. NG had decided to go to Boston before receiving Washington's letter, possibly to confer with d'Estaing. (Nicholas Brown's letter of this date, above, was addressed to him at Boston.)

To George Washington

Sir   Boston Sept 16th 1778

The growing extravagance of the people and the increasing demand for the article of forage in this quarter has become a very alarming affair. Hay is from 60 to 80 Dollars per tun and upon the rise. Corn is 10 Dollars a bushel and oats 4 and every thing else that will answer for forage in that propotion. Carting is 9/ per mile by the tun and People much dissatisfied with the price. I have represented to the State of Rhode Island and Conecticut the absolute necessity of Legislative interposition to settle the prices of things upon some reasonable footing of all such articles and services as are necessary for the use of the Public in my department.[1] I am going to do the same to the Councel of this State. What effect it will have I cannot say; but if there is not some thing done to check the extravagance of the People there is no funds in the Universe that will equal the expence.

The late affray that happend in this place between the People of the Town and those of the Fleet has been found to originate from a parcel of soldiers belonging to the Convention Troops [i.e., Saratoga prisoners] and a party of british sailors which were engaged on board a Privateer.[2] The secret enemies to our cause and the British officers in the neighbourhood of this place are endeav[or]ing to sow the seeds of discord as much as possible between the Inhabitants of the place and the French belonging to the Fleet. The French officers are well satisfied this is the state of the case and it fills them with double resentment against the British. The Admiral [d'Estaing] and all the French officers are now upon an exceeding good footing with the Gentlemen of the Town. General Hancock takes unwearied pains to promote a good understanding with the French officers. His House is full from morning till Night.

I had a Letter from the Marquis day before yesterday. He writes me he is endeavoring to represent every thing in the most favorable colours to the Court of France in order to wipe away the prejudices that the Letters of some of the more indiscreet may make upon that Court.[3] All the French Officers are extravagantly fond of your Excellency; but the Admiral more so than any of the rest. They all speak of you with the highest reverence and respect.

General Hancock made the Admiral a present of your Picture.

He was going to receive it on board the Fleet by the firing a Royal salute. But General Hancock thought it might furnish a handle for some of the speculative Politicians to remark the danger of charactors becoming too important. He therefore dissuaded the Admiral from carrying the matter into execution.

I find by your Excellencys Letter to General Sullivan that you expect the Enemy are going to evacuate Newyork; and that its probable they are coming Eastward. I can hardly think they mean to make an attempt upon Boston notwithstanding the object is important and Unless they attack Boston there is no other object worthy their attention in New England.[4] I am rather inclind to think they mean to leave the United States altogether. What they hold here now they hold at a great risque and expence. But suppose they actually intend to quit the Continent, they will endeavor to mislead our attention and that of our Allies until they can get clear of the Coast. The Admiral is fortifying for the security of his fleet, but I am told his batteries are all open in the rear which will be but a poor security against a Land force. General Heath thinks there ought to be some Continental Troops sent here; but the Councel wont turn out the Militia, they are so confident the Enemy are not coming here.

If your Excellency thinks the Enemy really designs an attack upon Boston it may not be amiss for you to write your opinion to the Councel board, for I suspect they think the General here has taken the alarm without sufficient reasons. The fortifications round this place are very incompleat and little or nothing doing upon them. I have given General Heath my opinion what Posts to take possession off if the enemy should attempt the place before the Continental Army gets up. From 4 to 5000 Troops have arrivd at Hallifax. Their collective strength will make a formidable army.

I wish to know your Excellencys pleasure about my returning to Camp. I expect Mrs Greene will be put to bed every day. She is very desirous of my stay until that event, and as she has set her Heart so much upon it I could wish to gratify her for fear of some disagreeable consequence as women sometimes under such circumstances receive great injury by being disappointed.[5]

General Sullivan granted me leave to come here upon the business of my department. I expect to return in a few Days. Major Gibbs is with me and is going to Portsmouth.

This is the third Letter I have wrote since I have had a line from your Excellency.[6] Should be glad to hear from you when at liesure. I am your Excellency[s] obd Servt

N GREENE

ALS (Washington Papers: DLC).

1. See above, NG's letters of 11 September to Gov. Greene and 14 September

to Gov. Trumbull. He wrote to Jeremiah Powell of Massachusetts on 17 September, below. Washington responded by writing to several states also. See his letter to NG of 22 September, below.

2. He refers to an incident of 5 September, when a group of French officers were attacked and severely beaten (one being killed) by a Boston mob when the officers tried to break up an altercation at a French bakery. (Fitzpatrick, *GW*, 12 : 476–77n; Freeman, *GW*, 5: 76n)

3. Letter not found. Lafayette had indeed been working diligently behind the scenes to repair the damage done to American feelings by the departure of the French fleet from Rhode Island, as well as presenting the American position to the French Court. He sent several letters to France via pouches that d'Estaing carried on board the fleet. (Gottschalk, *Lafayette*, pp. 270–73)

4. Washington's letter to Sullivan was written on 12 September and is in Fitz-patrick, *GW*, 12: 432–44. His fears were unwarranted since Howe's fleet had already left Rhode Island waters on 9 September and arrived in New York on the evening of 11 September. (Gruber, *Howe Brothers*, pp. 321–22)

Having received this intelligence, Washington wrote Sullivan on 13 September that the "facts with which I have been hitherto furnished" were not sufficient to determine whether there would be (1) an attack upon this army, (2) an enterprise against the French squadron, or (3) a simple evacuation of New York unconnected with any offensive operation in the territories of the United States. He cautioned Sullivan, however, to remain on his guard against a British "eastward" expedition. (Fitzpatrick, *GW*, 12: 444)

5. Catharine was then expecting her third child, Cornelia, who was born 23 September.

6. Letters not found.

To Jeremiah Powell, President of the Massachusetts Executive Council

Sir   Boston Septr 17th 1778

The growing extravagance of the people, and the increasing demand for forage for the use of the public, render Legislative inter-position absolutely necessary to fix some limits to the price of articles wanted for the United States. Without this, it will be impossible to furnish money to answer the People's demands, or procure forage sufficient to subsist the public Cattle. If this evil is permitted to rage, it will soon become intolerable. The hire of teams for transportation, houses for the Convention Officers and purchasing forage for the States, will become impracticable, if it is to be done by the simple mode of contract. People will increase their demands in proportion as our wants grow more pressing. Two public injuries will result from the present state of things, one is the public funds will be found unequal to the expence and consequently it will sap the very founda-tion of national defence; the other is, the people will withhold their teams, forage &c in hopes that a higher price will be given, during which time, our Army may suffer, and our Cattle must inevitably perish.

The regulating trade and commerce in general has been already proved to be impracticable,[1] and perhaps if it could be effected it might not be found to answer the great purposes of Society so well as that medium which is formed by the mutual wants of the buyer and seller. But a partial regulation so far as respects the supply of the public, I concieve to be absolutely necessary; and at the same time perfectly consistant with private right & the public welfare.

Hay is now from 60. to 80. dollars pr ton, Corn 10. dollars pr Bushel, and every other species of Forage in that proportion. Carting by the Ton is nine shillings a mile, house rent for the Convention Officers, eight dollars a room by the week, and as extravagant as these prices may appear the people are not satisfied. It is not difficult to foresee the consequences that will arise from the present state of things.

The public officers have no power to procure forage or teams for transportation; but by the common modes of contract. The delays and disappointments that origionate from this long, tedious and uncertain mode, often prove very injurious to the public service. Besides which the people rise in their demands in proportion as the business is pressing, and often forsake the public service, for private employment where they can get larger profits. And in some instances where they have been compeled to fulfill their contracts contrary to their wishes, they have brought actions against the public Officers for large damages, and recovered them. This is a public greviance, and only serves to saddle them with an unnecessary and additional expence. I concieve it therefore not only necessary to state the value of such articles, and fix the wages of such services, as may be wanted for the public purposes; but also to give proper powers to some person or persons for supplying the public on those conditions, and in as expeditious a manner as the nature of the business will admit, or the public welfare may require.

Pensylvania and I think New Jersey adopted a similar policy. The same is now recommended to the State of Rhode Island and that of Connecticut, which I make no doubt they will also adopt.[2]

I submit the matter to the honorable Board, and beg their interposition to put a stop to the present prevailing public impositions.[3] I have the honor to be with the greatest respect Your most Obedt humble servant

NATHANAEL GREENE

LS (M-Ar).

1. On the failure to regulate the price of articles in general trade, see note, William Greene to NG, 6 March 1778, above.

2. See NG's letters to Gov. Greene of Rhode Island and Gov. Trumbull of Connecticut of 11 and 14 September, above.

3. On 19 September the Council and House of Representatives of Massachusetts appointed a joint committee to "consider Genl Greene's Letter & the papers accompanying same." A few days later, both houses accepted the commitee's report that

it was "impracticable to pass a partial Regelating bill and carry it into Execution—Especially when we consider the attempts that have allready bin made to Regelate the prise of Articals in General." (Document filed with NG's letter to Powell, M-Ar)

To George Washington

Sir   Boston Sept 19th 1778

Your Excellency's Letter of the 15th came to hand last night.[1] I have waited upon General Heath and have got the state of the cloathing department. Mr Fletcher has forwarded for Springfield from this place between 10 and 12000 Blankets, 7669 pair of Shoes, 8000 Suits of Uniforms and 2000 Shirts. He is forwarding from Portsmouth about 15,000 Pair of Hose and 11,000 Suits of Uniforms.[2] Messrs Otis and Andrews have 5000 Suits of Uniforms in the Hands of the Taylors. They thing [think] they will be compleated in a month at the farthest. General Heath has order'd all the cloths out of Town except about 10 or 12 Days work for the Taylors which may delay the business some.

I shall send a man from hence to Springfield to see whether the cloathing forwarded from this place has arrivd all safe there and if not to take the necessary steps to get it forward.

All the cloathing that has been sent on for some months past has gone under the care of proper conductors. But I have now desir'd General Heath to add a small guard to each brigade of Teams. The cloathing shall be forwarded as fast as it is possible to get Teams; but there being no powers given the quarter master to impress, and the demand for private commerce, renders it difficult to procure a full supply. Merchants are giving 12/ a mile per Ton for transportation.[3]

It is reported here that General Gates has advanced as far as Danbury on his way for this place. General Heath is greatly alarmd at it. He thinks it will be a most degrading circumstance to him as he has had the command here to be supperceded at the approach of the Enemy. Your Excellencys coming would give him pleasure but any body else will hurt him exceedingly. I hear General Sullivan declares by all that is sacred that he never will submit to an order of General Gates. I think General Sullivan is wrong, but I wish he may not be sent if there is any possibillity of avoiding it without involving your Excellency in any new difficulties with General Gates. It is my opinion that none of the Major Generals that took commissions after General Gateses appointment can with any propriety dispute his rank unless they made that reserve condition at the Time of accepting their commissions.

Was not General Gates by resolve of Congress stationed at the Post of the North River for the security of the High Lands and will not there be a propriety in his remaining there, provided the grand Army comes to the Eastward.[4]

I thought it my duty to mention these matters with regard to Generals Heath and Sullivan that your Excellency might be seasonably advertisd.

In my last I wrote your Excellency that the affray that had happend in this Town between the French and the Inhabitants, had not made any bad impressions upon the minds of the former; but I am afraid from several little incidents the French officers are not altogether satisfied. However they mix with the Inhabitants very freely, all except the Count [d'Estaing] who remains on board the Fleet the much greater part of the Time.[5]

The great and General Court of this State are now siting here. They have orderd in 3000 militia to guard the Town of Boston until the Continental army can come to its releif, Should the Enemy think proper to make a dessent here. However I cannot perswade myself they are coming this way. I think their destination might be to the West Indies. There is a report in Town by some of the late arrivals that a Spannish fleet with a considerable land force has arrivd in the West Indies.[6] If that should prove true it may serve as a clue to explain the Enemies movements by. I am with the greatest regard your Excellencys most obedient humble Servant

NATH GREENE

ALS (Washington Papers: DLC).
    1. The draft, dated 14 September, is printed above.
    2. See below, Fletcher to NG, 22 September.
    3. Unlike some other states, Massachusetts had not authorized the quartermaster to impress the means of transportation.
    4. Washington's reasons for sending Gates to Danbury are discussed in his first letter of 22 September, below.
    5. See above, NG to Washington, 16 September.
    6. The report was an unfounded rumor.

From Samuel Fletcher

[Boston, 22 September 1778. Has sent to Springfield 10,000 blankets, 7,669 pairs of shoes, 8,000 suits, and 2,000 shirts. Next week he will have remaining 5,000 pairs of hose and 10,000 suits.[1] Cy (Washington Papers: DLC) 2 pp.]

    1. See above, Washington to NG, 14 September, and NG to Washington, 19 September.

From George Washington

Head Quarters Fredericksburg[1] [N.Y.]
Dear Sir
22d Sepr 1778
I was yesterday fav'd with yours of the 16th. The exorbitancy of the price of forage to the Eastward exceeds what I had any conception of, and should the seat of War be transferred to that quarter, the prices, high as they are, would no doubt rise with the demand. Mr Pettit and Colo Biddle, alarmed at the prices of that article in this quarter, and finding the people every day more unwilling to part with it from a hope that withholding it will still enhance the value, have drawn up a representation of the matter to me, which I am forwarding to the Legislatures of Pennsylvania, New Jersey, New York, Connecticut, Rhode Island and Massachusetts, with a desire that they will interfere, and endeavour to fall upon ways and means to regulate the prices and oblige the farmers to part with their Grain and Hay.[2] Whether they will take up this matter or if they do, whether the end will be answered I cannot determine. I am afraid that the depreciation of our money is the Root of the evil, and that, untill it can be remedied, all our endeavours will be in vain.

I am exceedingly pleased to hear that the unhappy affray at Boston has been traced to its true source, and that the French Gentlemen are convinced that it did not originate with the inhabitants of the Town.[3]

I cannot determine what the next move of the Enemy will be. By withdrawing their fleet and the troops under Genl Gray from the Eastward, our apprehensions on account of Boston are relieved for the present.[4] A little time must determine whether they mean to winter in New York, remove from thence to some other part of the Continent, or quit the States intirely.

To be prepared to march Eastward should circumstances require, or to support the Posts in the Highlands should the enemy turn their views that way, I have advanced Genl Gates to Danbury with five Brigades. Lord Stirling with the second line will lay hereabouts and Baron [de] Kalb with his division, between this and West Point. Genl Putnam, with three Brigades in addition to the former Garrison, is at West Point. Genl Scott, with the light Corps and all the Horse, is advanced in front near our old position at the White Plains.

The particular situation of Mrs Greene is a sufficient apology for your remaining at home at present. You may at the same time be making any necessary arrangements in your department, especially those for forwarding the Cloathing from Boston to Springfield and Hartford. Major Nicholas is appointed by the Board of War to superintend that Business, and I therefore wish you to give him every kind of assistance and advice.[5] I am &c

Df (Washington Papers: DLC).
    1. When Washington shifted the army from White Plains on 15 September to meet any of several possible British threats, Lord Stirling's division was ordered to Fredericksburg, N.Y., where Washington set up his headquarters on 20 September. (Fitzpatrick, GW, 12: 463, 472) Fredericksburg remained his headquarters until the end of November.
    2. The circular he sent the same day to the chief executives of those states is reprinted in Fitzpatrick, GW, 12: 478, but his letters had little effect.
    3. See above, NG to Washington, 16 September.
    4. Gen. Charles Grey (1729–1807) had commanded the New Bedford–Fairhaven raid in early September (NG to Sullivan, 7 September, above). He was the same "No-flint" Grey who surprised Anthony Wayne's brigade at Paoli a year earlier. (See note at Council of War, 28 September 1777, above; DNB.) As noted in Pettit to NG, 1 October, below, Grey repeated the tactic at Tappan on 28 September 1778.
    5. Samuel Nicholas of the continental marines.

From George Washington

[Fredericksburg, N. Y., 22 September 1778. Most important that supplies be forwarded to the French fleet. Df (Washington Papers: DLC) 1 p.]

To Count d'Estaing

Sir   Boston Sept. 23d. 1778
    I am Exceedingly hurt at the contents and Stile of General Sullivan's letter and the more I think of it the more I am astonished.[1] I am persuaded it is not the sentiments of his heart. I have often heard him speak of your Excellency in the most respectfull terms, not only with regard to your abilities, but politeness and Exact attention to duty. This Letter is so different from the general tennor of his conversation that I am at a loss to account for it. I cannot help thinking but that he labours under the same delusion, that he seems to suspect your Excellency to be influenced by. However, whatever may be the sentiments of General Sullivan, I beg your Excellency not to form an opinion of the other American general officers from the complexion of that Letter. I can assure you with great sincerity and truth, that they entertain the highest respect and veneration for your person and character, and give me leave to add that no one feels a warmer regard and greater respect than my self.
    We consider ourselves under great obligations to France for their generous and seasonable interposition, and I should be very sorry to be thought ungreatfull or to be wanting in respect to your Excellency who came for the sole purpose of befriending us.
    I am just setting out from this place for Rhode Island and from thence going to join the army under the Command of his Excellency General Washington, where I shall not fail to acknowledge the great

politeness and respect your Excellency has shewn me since I came to Boston. I shall be allways happy in an opport[unity] to serve your Excellency, that I may have it in my power to testify my regard and respect for your person and character. I have the honor to be with the greatest respect, your Excellency's most obedient and humble servant[2]

NATH GREENE

Cy (Paris, Archives Nationales, Archives de la Marine, Subseries B⁴, vol. 146, f. 223; from photostats at the Library of Congress).

1. Sullivan's letter, which d'Estaing had probably handed to NG aboard the *Languedoc* in Boston harbor, has not been found. As noted above, the General Officers to d'Estaing, 22 August, Sullivan had apologized for his insulting general order of 24 August; and through the intercession of Lafayette and NG, he had worked his way back into the good graces of d'Estaing. What aroused him to open up the old wounds now is not known.

2. The fact that NG's letter mollified d'Estaing is obvious from his answer of 1 October, below.

To Colonel Henry Jackson[1]

Dear Sir   Providence [R.I.] Sept 25th 1778

Lt Col [Ephraim] Bowen the Deputy quarter master General of this State informs me that a party of your detachment broke open a Store where there was deposited a quantity of quarter masters Stores and took out a number of articles. A proceeding like this is highly criminal and dangerous, and will reflect great dishonor upon you unless you take all the pains in your power to bring to justice the delinquents. I beg you therefore for your own reputations sake, as well as that of preventing future attempts of the kind, that you would make dilegent search into the matter, and if you can find any of the articles confine the persons that have them in possession. Col Bowen will send you a return of the articles missing.[2] My compliments to the Gentlemen of your detachment. I am with great regard your Most Obedt humble Sert

NATH GREENE

ALS (PHC).

1. Col. Jackson, commander of a Massachusetts continental regiment, had been especially commended by NG for his part in the battle of Rhode Island. (See above, NG to Washington, 28/31 August.) His regiment remained in Rhode Island to defend against British raids until the regiment was ordered to Boston in August 1779 to join the ill-fated Penobscot expedition. (Arnold, *R.I.*, 2: 440–43) Jackson was brevetted a brigadier general in 1783. (Heitman, *Register*)

2. See below, Bowen to Jackson, 25 September.

Ephraim Bowen to Colonel Henry Jackson

[Providence, R.I., 25 September 1778. Directed by NG to enclose a return of stores taken by his troops.[1] ALS (WHi) 1 p.]

1. See above, NG to Jackson, 25 September.

To Colonel Ephraim Bowen

[Coventry, R.I., 29 September 1778. Returns needed soon. Pettit needs tents and NG a good wagon "to carry on to camp 4 or 500 Boxes." Tr (GWG Transcripts: CSmH) 1 p.]

To James Calhoun

Coventry Rhode Island
Sir   Sept 30th 1778
     This will be handed you by Mr Griffin Greene a relation of mine. He is upon a plan of business to the Westward. I take the Liberty to recommend him to your particular notice. If you can give him any advice or render him any services in the execution of his business you will oblige me as he is connected in business with a brother of mine. If he should have ocasion for more cash than he brings with him or should want Letters of credit Please to furnish him and I will be responsible for his engagements.[1] I am Sir with great regard Your Most Obedient humble Servt

NATH GREENE

ALS (CtHi).
     1. This was purely a personal request by NG to help his cousin conduct his business in Maryland. NG emphasized this in his letter to Calhoun, 13 October, below. Calhoun was the deputy quartermaster in Baltimore.

To General John Hancock

Dear Sir   Coventry [R.I.] Sept 30th, 1778
     On my return Home I met a Servant coming for me. Mrs Greene was very ill. She had been in travail two Days. I got Home about nine at night the evening of the Day I left your House. I found Mrs Greene in bed very ill.[1] The Storm was very severe and I as Wet as if I had been towed the whole distance in Water.
     I hope you had a very splendid and social entertainment with the Admiral and the officers of his Fleet. I am anxious to see the account of it.[2]
     Your politeness and hospitallity shewn me while I was in Boston

leserves my warmest acknowledgments. The reception I met in Boston in general but more particularly from you was doubly agreeable as it was a kind of evidence that my public Charactor did not stand in an unfavorable point of Light there.[3] I shall be always happy in your good opinion and shall make it my study to deserve it. There are few men if any to whom the Public are equally indebted as they are to you. I am an admireer of your Virtues. You will therefore allow me to speak what I feel.

Please to make my and Mrs Greene[s] compliments agreeable to Mrs Hancock. My compliments to Col Brimmer and Col Babcock. I am with the most perfect esteem and regard, Your Most obedient humble Servt

NATH GREENE

ALS (CtY).
1. On 23 September, Catharine gave birth to Cornelia Lott Greene, named after a daughter of their friends, the Abraham Lotts of Beverwyck, N.J. See note, NG to Catharine, 20 May 1777, #2, above.
2. John Hancock, one of the wealthiest of Bostonians, was also one of the most hospitable. The Hancocks had entertained d'Estaing and his officers in their elegant Beacon Hill house before NG went to Boston and again, apparently, after he left. (Gottschalk, Lafayette, pp. 257, 264) Like NG, Hancock did much to erase any hard feelings the French were harboring. The French admiral, Freeman has pointed out, formed an exalted opinion of Hancock, calling him, with some exaggeration, "a great statesman and an able General." (Freeman, GW, 5: 70n)
3. See below, 1 October, from d'Estaing.

To Governor William Greene of Rhode Island

[Coventry, R.I., late Sept., 1778][1]
. . . authorises you to demand it of right from the most solemn engagement. Is this a generous return for the spirited exertions of the State after the battle of Lexington? Who has done or sufferd as much as you from first to last? But alas all stands for nothing.

His Excellency has just inform'd me that he has determind in consideration of your distressed situation to leave General Glovers brigade and call off Jacksons, [Henry Beekman] Livingstons, and Webbs Regime[nts]. I wish it was in his power to do more but believe it is not.

I shall always be happy to render either your Excellency or the State any services in my power; and beg youl please to command me upon all occasions where[i]n I can be useful.

I am engagd in a most troublesome and disagreeable department. I found it in the greatest distress and all in confusion. By industry and address I have got it in a tolerable way. And I think I can claim a great share in the honor and advantages of the battle of Monmouth. For it is confest by every body that the army could not have got from Valley Forge at the time they did had it not been for the extraordinary exertions we made to put the Army in a condition to move.

The appointment is flattering to my fortune, but humiliating to my Military pride. I am perswaded I save the public Millions of dollars. Yet I am told some thinks my merit less than my reward. I have some expectations of being sent to the Southward which will free me from the disagreeable department I am in.

I write to you in confidence.

My respects to Mrs Greene and all the family. I am Your Excellencys obedt Sert

N GREENE

ALS (MiU-C). Incomplete.
1. The context dates this approximately.

From Count d'Estaing

Sir   Boston Road, [in the harbor] October 1, 1778

The letter which your Excellency did me the honor of writing to me when you were leaving Boston, was of a nature to console me for the little irregularities which you perceived in General Sullivan's letter, which I took the liberty of communicating to you upon receiving it.[1] It is from you and what you are, that it is doubtless suitable and flattering to judge of the respectable and amiable qualities of the American general officers whom I have not the honor of knowing by correspondence or personally; it is with cordial warmth that I render homage to truth in assuring you that on every occasion I have had reason to admire their zeal and talents, and to feel personal satisfaction for their behavior with regard to me; and to add to the motives of duty those of inclination and attachment which I shall always profess to have for them. I shall be enchanted if the assurance and the homage of these sentiments appear to you of any value. With respect to the conduct, more or less moderate, that General Sullivan seems to have adopted in his literary commerce with me, as a zeal and devotion for the common cause, which I glory in, had engaged me to style him my General, he avails himself of the privileges which this title gives, beginning as you saw in his letter, by scolding me unjustly, and finishing by telling me in confidence that he has rivals whom he supposes his enemies. This mixture of chagrin and confidence being confined personally to me, did not offend me. There is another more important article, and which I am not at liberty to pass in silence. I mean the obstinacy which General Sullivan exhibits in national imputations; and the abuse of his place in filling incessantly the public papers which are under his direction with things which might at length create ill blood between the individuals of two nations who are and ought to be united. It is wounding their interests in a capital manner to dare by indiscretion or passion to foment what ought to be extinguished if it exists. I have been obliged lately to entreat General Sullivan to reflect on this subject. In doing it I observed all the deference that was due to him; but my quality as a public person and that of his well wisher, equally imposed this law on me.

I hope that your Excellency and your respectable colleagues will not disapprove my conduct. To merit that it should please them will ever be one of my desires, as well as to prove to you particularly all the consideration which I have for you and them, and the respect with which I have the honor of being, Sir, Your Excellency's Most humble and most obedient servant.[2]

Reprinted from Greene, Greene, pp. 148–49. The copy from which G. W. Greene made his transcription appears to have been an English translation that d'Estaing sent to NG, knowing that he did not read French. A copy in French is at MiU-C.
  1. This is in response to NG's letter of 23 September, above.
  2. Original was signed "Estaing" (MiU-C).

From Colonel Charles Pettit

Fredericksburg [N.Y.]
Dear Sir   1st October 1778
    Since I had the Pleasure of receiving your favour of the 12th of September I have not had Leisure enough to set about giving you anything like a Reply to it; indeed I had given you so long a Letter written mostly before yours came to hand that I felt the less Concern about writing to you again immediatly.[1] The Army being thrown into different Columns made so many different Armies, each having its Wants and requiring Attention; and Col. Hay's being in a Manner drawn from me by his ill Health, left me under some Difficulties. The reduced State of our Horses and the Prodigious Demand for Teams to transport Provisions to Boston added not a little to my Embarrassment. However we got the Army to the respective Stations tolerably well and are recruiting our Horses as fast as we can on Grass, for which our scattered Situation gives us some Advantages.[2]
    I have done all I could under so many Entanglements to give Satisfaction at Head Quarters; but for want of proper officers at the Heads of some of our Departments I have constantly found myself obliged to attend too much to the Detail of some Branches to be able to give the Attention I wish to the grand Machine which ought always to be almost the only Business of the Man at Helm. I believe I have

had tolerable Success in my Endeavours to please; at least I have met with no sour Looks nor heard any serious Complaints, tho' I have Reasons to believe a certain M. G., as I hinted to you before, has not been sparing in detractive Innuendoes.[3] In other Companies I know he has not, whatever he may have said at Head Quarters where I believe he is on no better than *civil* Terms. Neither do I know that I have any Differences to heal with any of the Officers of the Army. I have not thought myself at Liberty to grant all the Favours they have asked (and perhaps been accustomed to receive) at the publick Expence; but I have endeavoured to make my Refusals as smooth as possible, and with the Considerate I believe they have not given offence. In this I have been governed by a Sense of Duty to the Publick rather than a View to gaining Friends at it's Expence.

As to Major Painter, on perusing the Proceedings of the Court of Enquiry, I find they place him in a Light that hardly subjects him to Censure, and I did not think it prudent, all circumstances considered to displace him. I have a poor opinion of the Man and had I not expected you would be here to take the Matter up, I should have gone farther into his Affairs, but I have been the more sparing in taking any capital Steps or making any general regulations from the Consideration that you would soon be at the Head of Affairs yourself and I wished all such Things to be adapted to your views rather than to mine, as I shall probably be much less with the Army than you will. I should, however, have done more in this way than I have ventured upon had I not constantly expected you were within a week or two of Returning. The Coblers of Painters Corps have been turned to other employments and I believe there are none retained as Artificers but such as are usefully employed.[4]

The Forage Department is still a painful Morsel. Whenever I find myself in a Situation to trace our Prospects with some Pleasure, the coming across that [i.e., the forage problem] obstructs my View and turns me back rather mortified. I mentioned to you my Application to the General on that Subject. He has wrote to 5 or 6 Governors and transmitted Copies of my Letter to him and Col. Biddle's to me. What will be the Effect Time will discover.[5]

The Want of Money is another Subject not a little distressing. The fine Promises we were flattered with of the most ample Supplies after the first Month have not been performed, and in that Respect I am now in a paltry Situation. I have enough left to keep up our little Expenditures in the office for a Week or two and that is all; but every Deputy eastward of [the] Delaware is little better than a Bankrupt Furman, Lewis, Hay, and Hubbard are all calling upon me and have been for some Time past. Smith sent a Man on purpose for Cash last week. I sent him 18,000 Dollars which was all I could spare, and with t sent him an order to build Barracks for 100 Men, which order Genl Knox obtained from Head Quarters. Money is also wanted at Boston, and by what Col. Cox writes to me they are not better off on the West side of [the] Delaware.

As to an account of our Disbursements and an Estimate of Expenditures, I cannot, till I can shift the Burden of other Business off my Shoulders, attempt it. I want much to get a complete Invoice of all the Stores which have been sent from the eastward that I may from thence find out what is become of them and what Part has reached the Army; I fear our bustling Friend Abeel will have so jumbled them with other Things that we shall not be able to check them in the Manner I could wish. Johnston Smith has been to Philadelphia and has lodged his Accounts there. I thought it unnecessary to have them here as I could not give them the Time which I am confident they will require to understand them. They remain I suppose among the choice pieces of Entertainment reserved for me in Philadelphia.

The Plan of the Western Expedition I hear has been much curtailed. Let the Board of War answer for that Business.[6]

You express some Surprize that our Horses should have fallen away [i.e., grown thin] in a stationary Camp at White Plains. Do you consider how soon the Pasturage within our Reach must have been destroyed, and how little Forage we could draw from the Country round it? Do you consider also that besides foraging in the Country, and the Camp Duty of various Kinds, 100 Teams per Day were employed in going over the abominable Hills to and from Tarry Town? Of these you can have some Idea. But the grand Cause of Destruction was the innumerable Swarms of Flies created and collected by the Filth of the Camp and the Number of Horses which tore down the Park, and other Horses preserved from Labour, vastly more than those which were constantly employed with good Usage out of Camp. I have said before, that the Horses are now recruiting; some fresh ones are come and coming in, and I have got some 30 Teams come and more coming from Connecticut, so that altogether I hope to move the Army with Tolerable Facility whithersoever it shall be ordered, especially as it does not seem likely to be called to any violent push. As to the Notion of its going Eastward, it always appeared to me improbable. I did not mention it to you as my Opinion, but as a matter that the Genl choses to prepare for in Case it should become necessary. The being prepared sometimes prevents the necessity. Though, by the Bye, I do not know in what Manner the Enemy could distress us so much as by drawing our Army that Way, for Reasons that I am sure need not be mentioned to you.[7]

Lengthy as my Letter is already, I find on revising it since Supper, if I was to write it over at Leisure I could say much more under each

Head; and some Things I could wish to add; but I have another Letter
yet to write to you tonight, and you are so soon coming this Way
that I am not so anxious to inform you minutely of our Doings and
Situation as I should otherwise be.

Since we moved at a Distance from N. York the Enemy have been
prowling about as high as the [White] Plains; indeed a small Party of
Horse in pursuit of one of ours came as far as the Meeting House, the
Hospital, in Purchase Street, 3 or 4 miles above the Plains. They have
also been over in Bergen County in some Force, and last Sunday
night, or rather Monday morning, surprized Col Baylor in Bed at
Hackensack. The Col. and his Major, Clough, are both too badly
wounded to be moved and were left Prisoners on Parole; near 30 Men
are killed and taken. I am told it was a kind of Massacre as little or
no Resistance could be made.[8] Woodford's Brigade was immediately
ordered down from the Highlands and Lord Stirling went over to take
the Command in Jersey. Yesterday His Excely went over to Fishkill to
be at Hand to direct as Occasion should require. This morning the
two Pensa [Pennsylvania] Brigades marched from hence but soon
returned to their Ground, from whence I suppose the Enemy are
gone in.

Yesterday I was told by an officer from the line that the Intelligence by Women and Deserters was that 10 Regts were embarked
and sailed for Jamaica. Today I am told as a serious Truth that Genl
Clinton has advertised such of the Inhabitants of New York as choose
to go off to be ready by the 8th of Octr.

How does your Horse turn out which was sent you by Mr Guyer?
McCully is in good order. He has not been used till since we came to
this Place, and now I, or rather old John, suffer no one to mount him
but myself. I have rid him two or three Times and admire him more
each Time. The Roan is also preserved for Major Burnet, but he does
not choose to get very fat.

My Paper is so near full that I shall leave what remains to be said
to some farther opportunity. I am, with the sincerest Regard, Dr Sir
Your most obedient Servant

CHA PETTIT

ALS (MiU-C).
1. Letters not found.
2. On the movement of the army, see above, note, Washington to NG, 22 Sep
tember #1.
3. Gen. Gates. See above, NG to Laurens, 27 July.
4. Elisha Painter of Connecticut, a major of artificers, had been found guilty by a
courtmartial on 28 September of being absent from his post at West Point and of
neglecting his duty. He was sentenced to be cashiered from the army. On appeal he
was granted a new trial on 28 October, but died while the case was still pending
(Fitzpatrick, GW, 13: 73n)

coming this Way that I am not so anxious to inform you
minutely of our Doings and Situation as I should otherwise be.

Since we moved at a Distance from N. York the Enemy
have been prowling about as high as the Plains: indeed a
small Party of Horse in pursuit of one of ours came as far
as the Meeting House, the Hospital, in Purchase Street, 3 or 4
Miles above the Plains. They have also been over in Bergen
County in some Force, and last Sunday night, or rather Monday
Morning surprized Col. Baylor in Bed at Herringhook. The
Col. & his Major, Clough, are both too badly wounded to be moved
& were left Prisoners on Parole; near 50 Men are killed and
taken. I am told it was a kind of Massacre as little or no
Resistance could be made. Woodford's Brigade was immediately
ordered down from the Highlands & Lord Stirling went over to
take the Command in Jersey. Yesterday His Excel.t went over to
Fishkill to be at Hand to direct as Occasion should require. This
Morning the two Pens.a Brigades marched from hence, but
soon returned to their Ground, from whence I suppose the
Enemy are gone in.

Yesterday I was told by an Officer from the Lines that the
Intelligence by Women and Deserters was, that 10 Reg.ts were
embarked and sailed for Jamaica — today I am told as a serious
Truth that Gen.l Clinton has advertised such of the Inhabitants
of New York as choose to go off, to be ready by the 8.th of Oct.r

How does your Horse turn out which was sent you by
Mr. Guyer? M.c Cully is in good order — he has not been used
till since we came to this Place, and now I suffer no one to
mount him but myself. I have rid him two or three Times
and admire him more each Time. The Roan is also preserved
for Major Burnet, but he does not choose to get very fat.

My Paper is so near full that I shall leave what remains
to be said to some farther Opportunity.

I am, with the sincerest Regard, D.r Sir
Your most obedient Servant

Cha. Pettit

Hon.d Major Gen.l Greene

Letter from Charles Pettit, 1 October 1778
(Courtesy of William L. Clements Library at the University of Michigan)

5. See note, Washington to NG, 22 September #1, above.

6. Congress, in view of the continuing Indian threat on the frontier, decided on 11 June to send an expedition against the Senecas, with Gates in command. (*JCC*, 11: 589–90) No preparations were begun for the expedition, however, even after the Wyoming Valley "Massacre" of early July. In a letter to the Board of War on 3 August, Washington explained that he could not spare any men for an expedition for the time being. (Fitzpatrick, *GW*, 12: 261–66) The board accepted his reasons and on 3 September, Congress decided to put off any expedition. (*JCC*, 12: 868)

Without authorization, William Butler launched an expedition against the Indians in the Mohawk Valley in October 1778 that provoked the massacre of thirty whites at Cherry Valley, N.Y., on 11 November. These events helped to set the stage for Sullivan's Wyoming expedition of 1779. (Sosin, *Frontier*, pp. 115–16)

7. He refers to a possible British attack on Boston.

8. The action occurred at Old Tappan, N. Y., on 28 September when British Gen. Charles Grey surprised a force of one hundred sleeping Americans. American losses in the bayonet attack, according to Peckham, *Toll*, p. 55, amounted to sixteen killed, sixteen wounded, and thirty-eight captured.

George Baylor (1752–84) of Virginia, a former aide to Washington, had carried the news of the American success at Trenton to Congress. He recovered from his wounds to become commander of the First Continental Dragoons. He was brevetted a brigadier general in 1783. (*DAB*)

Alexander Clough of New Jersey died of the wounds he sustained in the attack.

9. Possibly Jacob Cuyler, the deputy commissary of purchases in the Northern Army.

From Colonel William Smith

Sir   Springfield [Mass.] 1 Octor 1778

Your favour of yesterday I recd the same evening.[1] I have forwarded to Boston every Barril of Provisions that has arrived. I have also sent into camp every kind of Stores that has been called for. No provision has been detained in my Department that was directed to Boston, and if twice the Quantity had been here could have forwarded it. There is arrived here seventy Loads of French Cloathing. There's no orders yet for any of it to be sent on. It is safely lodged in the new store which is finished this day, and is sufficient to contain all the French Cloathing for which purpose the Agent has requested to have it reserved.

I have lately recd a Letter from Jacob Cuyler DCP [Deputy Commissary of Purchases] requesting me to forward to Kinderhook as soon as Possible upwards of 3000 Bushels Salt that is stored Six Miles from this place. Have sent him near thirty Loads and will exert my self to send the remainder. The teams load back with Flour.

Expecting a great call for teams. Have engaged near thirty for three and Six Months at 20/ per Day. They are to begin service in a Week.

The Condition of Military Stores are very bad. We are under the necesity of dividing them into Barns and Sheds, and are continually removeing them at the pleasure of the owners of those buildings.

The place improved for an Elaborotary is a Barn, and not very convenant. Part of the men employed therein are obliged to Quarter on the other side the river for want of a Barrack. Col Mason has applyed to me for to build a Barrack and Eloborotary.² Please to inform me if it's agrable to you that they should be built.

I have three scowes, eight men and an overseer employed at the Ferry.

The Forage purchased and collected is 140 Tons of the Best Hay within the distance of ten miles from Springfield. I have not any Quantity of Grain purchased, the Farmers not haveing yet thrashed. As soon as possible will send Mr Pettit my account of Expenditures with the probable expence to compleate the year. Col Chase [in Boston] having rasied the Price of carting expect to be under the necessity of doing the same here. I am Sir yr hble Servt.³

W. SMITH

ALS (MiU-C).
   1. Letter not found.
   2. David Mason, an officer in Knox's continental artillery, at this time was deputy commissary general of military stores at Springfield. (Heitman, *Register*) For background on the location of the elaboratory see above, NG to John Adams, 5 April 1777.
   3. Smith enclosed a price list of forage and lumber.

From George Washington

[Fishkill, N.Y., 1 October 1778. Notes attack on Baylor's regiment. Intelligence hints at a British evacuation of New York City. Partial retaliation by Col. Richard Butler and Maj. Henry "Light Horse Harry" Lee for the Tappan attack.¹ LS (MiU-C) 2 pp.]

   1. For details on the battle at Old Tappan or Harrington, N.Y., see above, Pettit to NG, 1 October.

From Captain John Gooch

Dear General   Boston Oct 2d 1778
   I have just Recd a Letter from Colo Biddle with six thousand Dollars and an asurance of twenty four thousand more in a few Days. Had I been fully supply'd with money at my first coming into this Department could have saved the Publick at least 7000 £ as Hay was then from 12 £ to 15 and now is from 24 to 26 per Ton. I intreat I may not be so necessitated again.

   Colo Chase thinks the Forage Departmt is under his Direction. As I have the appointment of all my officers and paying them, I dont see with what propriety he can interfere.¹ I know of no futher Business he has in it than giveing orders which I am to recive according to my Instructions Recived from Colo Biddle. There is a Resolve of Congress[2] that the members shall have their Horses kept in the Continental Stable and pay for their keeping. Colo Chase settles those accounts; if the accounts are to be settled, some by the officer of one Depart and some by another, how will it be possible for me to settle my Accts. The Colo and myself have no dispute about it, but beg you would settle the affair, that each may know his Department and the sooner it is done the less Confusion will happen, for as it is carried at present it must necessaryly produce great confusion in the settlement of accounts.

Mrs Gooch begs to be respectfully remembered to you and Lady, thinks at the same time it was very unkind when you was in Town you never called to see her. My Respectfull Compliments to Mrs Greene, Mr Jacob and Family. I am with greatest Respect your most obedt and most hble Servant

JOHN GOOCH

N B Would be glad to know if all orders to Recive Horses should not be in writeing as it [is] here much disputed.

ALS (MiU-C).
1. For previous and subsequent problems with Chase, see above, Griffin Greene to NG, 24 May, and below, John Gooch to NG 24 and 25 October.
2. That is, the Massachusetts legislature.

From General James M. Varnum

Sir   Warren [R.I.][1] Octr 3d 1778
Your favor of this date I have recd.[2] Mr Littlefield will attend you. Am much obliged to you for your Intelligence of the Enemy's Movements. Their Positions at Hackensack and the English Neighborhood are well adapted to cross North River and Attack the Rear of Genl Washington should he attempt New York in their divided State. At any Rate, they may be securing Winter Quarters for part of their Army on the West Side Hudson's River. This will prove favorable to Descents upon Long Island.[3] What their final and ultimate Determinations are, the Devil, I believe, only knows, as they are under the compleat Influence of Toryism. I am happy in hearing Mrs Greene is safely in Bed. Be pleased to make my best Compliments to her. Mrs Varnum is at Governor Bradford's.[4] She is well, and I am certain would be much pleased in visiting Mrs Greene, but has not been able to procure Work women to put her in decent Attire. Be so kind as to mention me, with Respect, to the Gentlemen of the Army. I am Sir, with perfect Esteem, your very obdt humble Servt

J. M VARNUM

ALS (PHi).
1. Since the battle of Rhode Island, Varnum's brigade was once again under Lafayette and encamped at Warren, R.I., on the mainland north of Aquidneck Island.
2. Letter not found.
3. Favorable, that is, for American raids.
4. Former Lt. Gov. William Bradford.

To Nicholas Brown

Sir
Coventry [R.I.] Octo 4, 1778
Your favor of the 14th of Sept was handed me by your Brother John in Boston sometime since. I should have answered it before, but your denial of the charge alluded to in your Letter, together with the warm assurances of your friendship and esteem left me nothing to say but who was the Author.

Your observation is very just. This is a molevolent age. A season wherein envy, malice, and detraction are very predominant. The greater circumspection is necessary. The Sentiments, Opinions and observations of the first Charactors are carefully watched by the Vulgar and disaffacted. The People at large take their Tone from a few and where those few give an improper bias to the People at large, they do great injustice to the charactors and feelings of Individuals and to the community in general. How grateing is the consideration to those Officers that have taken their lives in their Hands in the infancy of this dispute, to lend their feeble Aid in Shielding their Country from the Storm of approaching Tyranny; To find themselves wounded by the Shafts of reproach, thrown from the hand of those from whom they had the greatest reason to expect the warmest thanks. I say how grateing this consideration and how discourageing to future exertions.

I am fully sensible of the propriety of your remarks that it is a folly to pursue the vulgarities that leads to the source of public detraction. I readily grant it is an endless task, and a fruitless employ. There are few Persons that has a more thorough contempt for vulgar opinions than I have; and none whose Ears is more shut against secret whisperers and artful insinuations. But when I find myself attacked by certain charactors whose good opinion I have an honest ambition of meriting I cannot help feeling myself sensibly hurt.

Public gratitude I know is a monster in politicks and he that expects an adequate compensation for the Time and sacrificees made in their employ, will find himself greatly disappointed. But for the honor of human Nature I would wish to think differently of private Friendship. Your family is one of the first in this State and one whose good opinion and freindship I have always indeavord to cultivate. Therefore the least reproach would be the more sensibly felt. I have not time to add more only that I am with great truth and sincerity your freind and most obedient humble Sert

NATH GREENE

ALS (RPJCB).

To General John Sullivan

[Coventry, R.I., 5 October 1778. Hopes in the future that officers of the quartermaster department can have access to the public stores as do others of the line.[1] ALS (NhHi) 1 p.]

1. Sullivan's response has not been found.

To George Washington

Sir   Coventry [R.I.] Octo 5th 1778
     Your Excellencys favor of the 22d of Sept and the 1st of October came to hand last Evening.
     I am exceeding sorry for Col Baylors misfortune. The surprise is the worst part of the affair; and no Man will more sensibly feel upon the occasion than the Col should he recover.[1]
     Col Butlers and Major Lees surprise made upon the Chasseurs was a compleat one. These two events serves to shew how much in War depends upon attempts.[2]
     I fancy the Enimy are forageing for the use of the Garrison at Newyork, and will withdraw themselves as soon as they have compleated their work. Their future operations is merely conjectural. However as France is not prepard to carry on any offensive operations in the West Indies against any considerable force, A part of the British Army will be detachd there to secure the Islands against any little attempt. The remainder will continue at New York and Newport in order to keep us in Awe and to make some further tryal to negotiate a peace not only with us but through us with France.[3]
     The depreciation of our Money is an alarming circumstance and the remedy difficult to be found. Nothing but taxation and a high Interest can work an effectual change. Legislative interposition may produce some temporary advantages; but not a radical cure for the Evil.[4]
     I shall set out for Camp to morrow or next Day at furthest; the State of the clothing business I shall give your Excellency particular information about at my arrival in Camp, but I beleive every necessary measure is taken to get it forward so far as it depends upon my department.

I was told yesterday that General Sullivan had wrote to your Excellency to have me stationd here this Winter.[5] However agreeable it is to be near my family, and among my Friends, I cannot wish it to take place, as it would be very unfriendly to the business of my department. I wrote yesterday to General Sullivan for leave to join the grand Army, and expect his answer to Day. I have the honor to be with the greatest respect and regard Your Excellencys most obedient humble Sert

NATH GREENE

ALS (Washington Papers: DLC).
1. See above, Charles Pettit to NG, 1 October.
2. See above, Washington to NG, 1 October.
3. A very accurate account of the strategy the British employed. On 3 November, the day before d'Estaing escaped from Boston, Maj. Gen. Grant sailed from New York with five thousand men, escorted by a minimal naval force under Commodore Hotham. For the next five weeks, the transports sailed on a parallel course with the French. Luckily for the British, d'Estaing was not aware of this. As it was, Grant safely joined the British West Indies fleet on 10 December, and they took the island of St. Lucia before d'Estaing could relieve it. (Willcox, *Clinton*, pp. 253–54)
4. See Appendix I on depreciation.
5. Sullivan had written Washington on 15 September that NG's "absence would be most sensibly felt by me." (Hammond, *Sullivan*, 2, 341–44; see also Sullivan to NG, 5 October, below.)

From Doctor John Morgan

[Philadelphia, 5 October 1778. Recounts at great length his dispute with Congress over the Hospital Department. Also reminds NG of his illness in New York and what great pains Morgan took to bring him back to health. "The purport and meaning of this Letter is to inform you that Congress hath, at last, appointed a Committee to hear me, as you may see by the inclosed Address, and to request you will be so obliging as to send me such a certificate of what you know of my Conduct, as Truth and Candour may authorize, for the manifestation of my Guilt or Innocence, which I may produce before the Committee at my approaching Trial."[1] ALS (PU) 3 pp.]

1. The subject of the letter is treated fully above, vol. 1: 251n, 283–84n, 312–13n. See also NG's response to Morgan of 10 January 1779, below.

From General John Sullivan

Dear Sir   Providence [R.I.] October 5th 1778
Nothing but a Singular Regard for your Reputation and a Desire to promote the General Interest of America could bring me (Cordially)

Letter from John Sullivan, 5 October 1778
(Courtesy of the Newport Historical Society, Newport, R.I.)

to Consent to your Departure for the main Army. The Reasons in your Letter of yesterday are too Cogent for me to Refuse my assent to a Departure which Though it must Serve The General Interest of America must Leave me too great a Share of anxiety and Regret.[1] You have been too long acquainted with me to Suppose me Skilled in flattery and will therefore believe me when I Say that I feel myself too soon[?] deprived of the Sharer of my Confidences, The assistant of my Councills and partner in Supporting the Burthens of the war. I can assure you Sir that while you have my best wishes for your safe arrival at the main Army and Success in your Department while there, my grateful Acknowledgments Shall follow your good services to me while acting in this Department Accompanied by my most Earnest wishes for your Return. The Repeated Instances of your Friendship to me and the high Confidence which I have Justly placed in you will be an Eternal Bar to the effect[?] of those malicious whispers you have been pleased to mention in your Letters. I feel myself exceeding happy That you appear to be Satisfied with the Justice Done to your Character in this Department and that you have no Reason to Repent the friendly offer of your assistance where it was So much wanted and where it did Such Essential Service.[2] I beg my Compliments to your Lady and that you will Ever believe me to be with the highest Sentiments of friendship, Esteem and Respect Dear Sir your most obedt Servt

JNO SULLIVAN

ALS (RNHi).

1. Letter not found, but NG's reasons for not staying are given in his letter to Washington, above, 5 October.

2. Sullivan had numerous proofs of NG's respect and support during and after the Rhode Island campaign, not the least of which was NG's unsolicited and spirited defense of Sullivan in his letter to John Brown, 6 September, above.

From General George Weedon

Fredericksburg [Va.]
My dear General   Octobr the 5th 1778
    I embrace the earliest opportunity of writing you after my return home, which was not till the 3d Inst owing to sickness. I wrote you a long letter from Phila some few days before I left it and committed to the care of Colo Cox for a safe conveyance.[1] No doubt you recd it. I must (tho' late) congratulate you on the Rhode Island expedition, which I think stands high, very high, in the list of American Operations and reflects great honor on those that Conducted it. It affords me no small Satisfaction and happiness at seeing you Active in this,

as well as in all other places where laurels were to be purchased, and in finding it publickly Acknowledged that you won and wore them.[2]

My own private opinion wanted nothing to establish your fame and worth with me but I've not been a little Supprized at hearing some people say, since the Rhode Island affair, that Green at [had?] retrieved his Charactor! I have Asked when he had lost it, or what rascal had ever d[e]famed it, and have been answered that they had heard so and so. Such calumny can never hurt real merit which will in the end shew itself under every Disadvantage and finally burst on the heads of the Cencorious to there eternal shame and Disgrace. Those opinions, however unjust and beneath notice, are effectually eradicated. I am happy it is so, as I know the Delicate feelings of my friend, and how justly and deservingly he merits the rewards due to the brave, the prudent, and diligent Soldier.

Congress and myself run another heat before I left them. They got the start of me formerly, and by Jockeyship keep it. I am not however distanced, and Bottom may still save me. They not determining on my first letter which I wrote them at York, and which I shewed you a copy of at Valley Forge, drew another from me of a more explicated and positive nature, in which I stated facts, recited there own resolutions, and requested of them either to revise there Resolution of the 19th of March, that an opportunity might be given of fixing the rank of the officers thereby determined on, according to the usual practices of Armies, and those established rules which promote the military Service, Or, if they choose to continue me in the Line as it was then arranged, to give me separate Service or leave to retire till I could take an Active part with propriety. They resolved on the latter, but wisely added that If I did not serve again I should receive no pay, So that it remains in my opsion [option?], when they think proper to offer, whether I will Accept. The Service shall be honorable, I promise them, that draws me out again, tho' my heart and Soul is with you. G[ouverneur]: Morris was my particular friend in debate as was many other able Speakers, who condemned the measures that brought on the dispute, and justified the conduct I had pursued in Consequence.[3]

I have not had time since my geting home to cast about the political Circle in this part of the world, so that I can give you no news in this latter, but as I hope our Corespondence will be permenant shall scrape together something for you against I write you again, which shall be the moment I am advised of your notifying the proposial by letter under your Signature. Kitty has [sent?] her love to you and lady, and if you will please present mine at the same time, you will very much oblige your affectionate friend and most obt Servt

G WEEDON

ALS (MiU-C).

1. Letter not found.

2. Weedon had been somewhat misinformed about the action at Rhode Island. By the time he wrote NG on 9 November, below, he had learned more about it.

3. For details on his problem with Congress, see above, NG to Weedon, 27 April.

From Henry Laurens, President of the Continental Congress

[Philadelphia, 10 October 1778. Delivering via John Mitchell an Act of Congress of 2 October continuing the embargo until the end of January 1779.[1] LB (PCC, Item 13: DNA) 1 p.]

1. Concerned that the export of certain items not only hurt the army but often, when ships were captured, aided the enemy, Congress on 8 June 1778 had laid an embargo against the exportation of "wheat, flour, rye, Indian corn, rice, bread, beef, pork, bacon, live stock, and other provisions" from 10 June until 15 November, and it "earnestly recommended to the respective states to take the most effectual measures for carrying the . . . resolution into immediate execution." Most states complied.

Congress undoubtedly intended the act primarily to prevent goods from leaving the country, but as the resolution was worded, the only listed items it allowed to be carried between states were "such provision as shall be necessary for the stores" of the vessels trading "to and from these states." (JCC, 11: 578–79) Congress amended the embargo on 2 September 1778 to accomodate Washington's need to feed the Convention troops in and around Boston. (JCC, 12: 861) The extension of the act is in JCC, 12: 976.

On the independent embargoes that had already been levied by some of the states, see above, NG to Unknown Person, 20 May 1777.

To James Calhoun

Dear Sir   Camp [Fredericksburg, N.Y.] Octob 13th 1778

I wrote to you some little time past by a Relation of mine Mr Griffin Greene from the State of Rhode Island In which I requested you to give Mr Greene such Letters of recommendation and credit as he might stand in need of to execute his business to the best advantage.[1] I also desird you to give him all the assistance in your power and to lend him such sums of money as he might want and that I would be responsible.

For fear you should mistake my intentions, I have thought proper to write you this Letter to acquaint you that it was not, nor is not my intention, that you should give Mr Greene any Aid or assistance in business that he may undertake which will interfere in the least degree with the duties of your Office or effect its Reputation. Neither must you lend Mr Greene any Public monies. If he should want cash and you cannot supply him without makeing use of the Public monies his demand must not be complyed with.

I make it a standing rule never to make use of the Public money for any private purposes whatever.

But if you can oblige Mr Green in your private capacity or furnish him with money out of your own private Stocks without injury to yourself, I shall be much oblige to you to do it. I am with great respect and regard Your most Obedient humble Sert

NATH GREENE

ALS (NcD).
   1. See above, 30 September.

To Henry Marchant

Camp at Fredericksburg, [N.Y.]
Dear Sir,   October 15, 1788[1778]
   Your favor of the 16th of September came to hand a few days since. I am very happy to hear you express yourself so favorably upon the subject of the Rhode Island expedition. I think the army did everything that could be rationally expected of them. But the issue was so different from the prospect that gave rise to the plan, and success so necessary to guard against reproach, that I did not expect to escape some degree of censure.[1]
   You mistake me, my dear sir, if you think I meant to complain of Congress to my friends in it, for not taking more particular notice of me. I freely confess I have ever had an honest ambition of meriting my country's approbation; but I flatter myself I have not been more solicitous to obtain it than studious of deserving it. However, people are very apt to be partial to themselves; but I have sometimes thought my services has deserved more honorable notice than they have met with, not from Congress, but the army.[2]
   I thank you kindly for your friendly hints upon the state of the Quartermaster's department. I am sensible of the difficulty of conducting such an extensive business without leaving some cause for complaints. But I cannot help think the agents employed are nearly in the same predicament that Lord Chesterfield says ministers of state are. They are not so good as they should be, and by no means as bad as they are thought to be. A charge against a quartermaster-general is most like the cry of a mad dog in England. Every one joins in the cry, and lends their assistance to pelt him to death. I foresee the amazing expenditure in our department will give rise to many suspicions; and I make no doubt there will be some impositions and many neglects; but the great evil does not originate either in the want of honesty or economy in the management of the business, but in the depreciation of the money and the growing extravagance of the people. I have taken all the pains in my power to fix upon the most deserving characters as agents to act under me, and always gave the most positive instructions to retrench every unnecessary expense.

It was with great reluctance that I engaged in this business. The committee of Congress and the Commander-in-chief urged it upon me contrary to my wishes. They painted the distress of the army and the ruin that must follow unless that I engaged in the business, as there was no other to be found who could remove the prejudices of the army and supply its wants. Before I would undertake it, both the committee and the General promised to give me all the aid and assistance in their power.

How far the business has been conducted to the public satisfaction I cannot pretend to say, but I am persuaded the successes of the campaign are owing to the extraordinary exertions made in this department to accelerate the motions of the army.

I readily agree with you that, so far as the commission allowed for doing the public business increases the expense, so far it is injurious (to) its interest; but I cannot suppose that I have given an appointment to one person who would wish to increase the public charge for the sake of enlarging his commission. However, I may be deceived. I wish it was possible for the public to get their business done without a commission; but I am persuaded it is not.[3] Be that as it may, the evil, if it be one, did not originate with me. The commission given to most of the deputies in the western States under the former Quartermaster-general [Mifflin] was much higher than is now given. The Board of War gave larger commissions for such persons as they employed in the department before I came in than I would give to the same persons afterwards.[4] I have got people upon the best terms I could, and I hope there is few, if any, but what are men of principle, honor, and honesty. To the eastward [New England] I am confident there is no abuse of the public trust worthy notice. You may depend upon my keeping a watchful eye over all the branches of the department, and no impositions shall pass unnoticed. But as I am at so great a distance from many parts of the business, abuses may prevail for some time, unless my friends will be kind enough to give me seasonable information.

Reprinted from Greene, *Greene*, 2: 395–97.

1. Letter not found, but Marchant's sentiments must have been similar to those he expressed to Gov. William Greene in a letter of 6 September. "I somewhat console myself upon such occasions with the consideration of the honor we procure to ourselves, as well as a consciousness of having well discharged our duty to ourselves and posterity." Marchant then noted, "Our conduct will raise our character abroad, as well as at home, under this disappointment; for to conduct well and bravely under unforeseen events and misfortunes is great heroism." (Staples, *R.I.*, pp. 198–99)

2. For similar sentiments with additional detail, see above, NG to Marchant, 25 July.

3. See above, note, NG to Joseph Reed, 9 March.

4. Mifflin had received a commission at one time of 5 percent on his purchases—five times the combined commissions of Greene, Pettit and Cox. It is not known what

commissions were paid to Mifflin's deputies in the "western states" (NG refers especially to Pennsylvania), but some of those to the east had received no commission under Mifflin. (For example, see Hugh Hughes to NG, 23 April, above.) NG paid his deputies commissions of only 1.5 to 2 percent, although most of them also made commissions as forage masters.

Council of War

At a Council of War held at Fredericksburgh [N.Y.]
October 16th 1778

Present

Major Generals	Brigadier Generals
Gates	Nixon
Greene	Parsons
DeKalb	Smallwood
McDougall	Knox
Steuben	Patterson
	Wayne
	Hand

The Commander in Chief informs the Council, that the enemy's whole force in these States still continue in two principal divisions one at New York and its dependencies consisting of about thirteen thousand; the other on Rhode Island consisting of about five thousand. That a considerable detachment from the former sent three or four weeks since into Bergen county, in the Jerseys, have hitherto been employed in a forage, part are said to have lately returned and the remainder it is given out, intend to cut a quantity of wood before they leave the Jerseys.

That their fleet was still in the harbour of New York the 9th instant rumoured to intend sailing shortly for Boston.[1]

That the general current of intelligence from New York indicates preparations *to be in readiness* to leave that post, and more particularly a design of making a considerable detachment, generally supposed for the West Indies, the number mentioned from ten to fifteen regiments which are reported to have been fitted up by the reduction of some other regiments. That an officer of ours, prisoner with the enemy, just exchanged, brings an account of the actual imbarkation of a large body of troops, on Saturday night and Sunday last, said to be destined for the Southward, of which however, no confirmation has been received from any other quarter.

That our whole force in this quarter is about fifteen thousand rank and file, fit for duty, including the two brigades in the Jerseys, and the garrison at West Point, a considerable part of which have completed and will soon complete the term of service, for which they are engaged.

That General Sullivan has under his Command at Providence and its dependencies about 3500 Continental and State troops.

From this State of facts and under these circumstances, The Commander in Chief requests the opinion of the Council, whether it will be prudent and advisable to make a detachment from the main army towards Boston, and of what force.[2]

He further informs the Council, that he has been impatiently waiting for the movements of the enemy to ascertain their intentions for the Winter, in order to enable him the better to judge of a proper general disposition of the army in Winter quarters; but the uncertainty, in which their designs still continue involved and the advanced season of the year, will no longer admit of delay, in fixing upon a plan for this important purpose. He therefore requests the advice of the council on the following points; whether the army shall be held in a collected state during the Winter and where? whether it shall be distributed into contonments and in what particular manner? what precautions shall be adopted in either case to shelter the troops and procure subsistence both of provisions and forage?

He observes, That in determining these questions, the considerations principally to be attended to are, the actual Strength and situation and the probable designs of the enemy; the Security, good government and discipline of the army, the difficulties of subsistence and accommodation, the protection of the country, the support of our important posts, the relation proper to be preserved with the French, considering the degree of probability of its remaining where it now is, and of a winter operation against it, and the occasional succour it may derive from the troops under General Sullivan and from the Militia of the Country.[3]

He finally informs the Council that some time since, he directed the Qutr Master General to endeavour to provide materials for barracks. The result of his measures will appear in a letter from Mr. Pettit hereunto annexed.[4]

FC (Washington Papers: DLC).

1. In the months after the battle of Rhode Island, the Americans were as baffled by Gen. Clinton's intentions as they had been by Gen. Howe's the previous year. Their bafflement was due not only to baseless rumors—some deliberately dropped by the British, some founded on faulty intelligence—but to the British commander's indecisiveness. Clinton was certain of only one thing: he had no intention of evacuating New York City or even stripping it down to a small garrison.

Following his unsuccessful attempt to capture Sullivan's force in Rhode Island (NG to Washington, 28/31 August, above), Clinton returned to New York on 2 September, but not before ordering Gen. Charles Grey to conduct raids along the Massachusetts coast at Fairhaven, New Bedford, and Martha's Vineyard. (See above, NG to Sullivan, 7 September.)

Lord Howe's fleet, its commander more interested in resigning his command to the tardy Adml. Byron than engaging the French fleet, pursued d'Estaing and arrived off Boston on 30 August. Finding that the French fleet was much too well protected by shore batteries to risk an action, Howe ended his unproductive chase on 2 September. Two days later he encountered Gen. Grey and agreed to wait off Block Island until the outcome of Grey's raids was known. After hearing from Adml. Byron on 8 September that the new commander of the fleet would be sailing from Halifax to New York as soon as possible, Howe reversed his plans and hastily sent word for Grey to return to New York. Howe, himself, left Block Island on 9 September and arrived in New York on the eleventh, promptly resigning his command (on a temporary basis) to the incompetent Rear Adml. James Gambier until Byron, a more senior officer, arrived.

Clinton was disturbed at Howe's hasty resignation, since he had the greatest admiration for the admiral's abilities. In an attempt to prevent Howe from making his resignation effective, Clinton offered six thousand troops for a combined attack on Boston, but the offer was declined. Thus, on 24 September, the frustrated and disenchanted Howe sailed for Rhode Island where he conferred with Byron concerning the command of the fleet and then, on 26 September, sailed for his beloved England.

Howe's departure did not terminate Clinton's hopes for an attack on Boston, but it now depended on Byron, Howe's unfortunate successor. Having been forced back to Rhode Island by high winds after reaching Sandy Hook, "Foul Weather Jack" Byron finally reached New York in early October, nearly a month after the bulk of his fleet had arrived and four months after his departure from England. Despite Byron's willingness to commit his fleet in a joint operation against Boston, Clinton subsequently demurred, first because he had much more confidence in Howe than in Byron, who knew very little about Boston, and second because Clinton now feared another American advance upon Rhode (Aquidneck) Island.

In the face of Clinton's loss of resolve in attacking Boston, Byron proceeded to refit his somewhat battered fleet in order to blockade the French in Boston Harbor. He set sail from New York on 19 October but did not reach Boston until 1 November. On the next day, as was his luck, his fleet was scattered by a severe storm. D'Estaing's fleet was able to evade the British on 4 November in the midst of a gale, which left Byron little choice but to proceed to Rhode Island where he regrouped and repaired his ships.

Byron did correctly surmise that d'Estaing's objective was the West Indies, and he sent a warning to Clinton that with a French squadron in the Atlantic, the planned expedition to St. Lucia should be postponed until the location of the French was determined. Clinton did not receive the message in time, and on 3 November the British expedition set sail under Maj. Gen. Grant. (See above, NG to Washington, 5 October, for details on this British expedition.) Byron's fleet subsequently sailed to the West Indies on 14 December, effectually ending British operations for the season. (Mackenzie, *Diary*, 2: 390–91, 398, 414, 419, 432; Gruber, *Howe Brothers*, pp. 320–24; Willcox, *Clinton*, pp. 250–54)

2. Troops would soon be sent toward Boston. See below, NG to William Smith and NG to Varnum, 24 October.

3. For NG's responses to Washington's queries see below, NG to Washington, 18 October.

4. Pettit's letter describing the preparation for building barracks along the Hudson River can be found in the Washington Papers, DLC.

From Henry Laurens, President of the Continental Congress

[Philadelphia, 16 October 1778. Encloses resolution of 13 October, directing the paymaster general of Georgia to give such sums as necessary to the deputy quartermaster in the area.[1] LB (PCC, Item 13: DNA) 1 p.]

1. See *JCC*, 12: 1009.

From Captain Ebenezer Sullivan

[Boston, 16 October 1778. Effusively thanks NG for his note to Congress on Sullivan's behalf.[1] ALS (MHi) 1 p.]

1. See above, NG to John Sullivan, 11 September. John's brother, Ebenezer, a captain in a Massachusetts regiment, had received no pay while a British prisoner from May 1776 to early 1778 because he was left out of the new arrangement of the army in 1777. Despite the protests of his brother, of NG, and of Washington, it was 1780 before Congress paid him. (Fitzpatrick, *GW*, 11: 92–94; Whittemore, *Sullivan*, pp. 80–81; *JCC*, 12: 970, 18: 991)

APPENDIX I

(Table from Anne Bezanson, *Prices and Inflation during the American Revolution*, p. 65 is illustration #17)

SPECIE EQUIVALENTS

THE RELATION OF CONTINENTAL MONEY TO SPECIE
December 1775–April 1781

Year & Month	Ratios			Median corrected by three-months moving average			Ratios			Median corrected by three-months moving average		
	Webster Merchants	Specie	Commodity	Webster Merchants	Specie	Commodity	Webster Merchants	Specie	Commodity	Webster Merchants	Specie	Commodity
1775							1779					
Dec.		1.04										
1776												
Jan.							8.0	8.00	7.99	141.0	136.7	138.5
Feb.							10.0	9.91	9.95	138.9	143.0	134.5
Mar.							10.5	9.77	11.50	130.9	150.4	127.2
Apr.						110.4	16.1	12.17	16.21	106.5	137.5	117.8
May						120.6	23.0	16.46	17.12	108.9	139.0	120.5
June						135.5	20.0	17.67	20.07	111.8	128.9	111.2
July		1.08				136.1	19.0	19.62	25.12	112.9	112.9	94.8
Aug.						133.4	20.0	21.72	25.10	117.2	116.1	95.8
Sept.		1.14	1.75			136.0	24.0	22.24	26.82	144.7	144.8	132.8
Oct.		1.25	1.75			126.0	30.0	30.00	28.68	154.4	161.9	158.0
Nov.		1.25				126.0	38.5	36.00	34.88	176.8	179.7	178.1
Dec.		1.50	1.50			151.8	41.5	42.22	45.60	193.9	200.9	191.9
1777							1780					
Jan.	1.25		1.44	171.4	154.0	142.4	42.5	40.00	43.30	169.9	178.6	166.7
Feb.	1.5	1.50	1.85	157.2	150.5	139.5	50.0	45.25	47.73	174.1	183.9	181.7
Mar.	2.0	2.00	2.06	139.7	127.8	124.1	62.5	61.50	57.51	167.0	171.5	176.5
Apr.	2.0	2.50	2.26	137.1	134.0	137.7	60.0	61.21	57.98	170.4	170.5	176.0
May	2.5		2.16	128.4	107.2	144.5	60.0	59.67	61.20	178.9	181.8	180.6
June	2.5	3.72	1.80	125.8	112.7	159.2	60.0	56.30	59.10	167.1	171.9	163.6
July	3.0	3.06	2.36	123.0	97.0	136.5	62.5	61.38	66.08	161.5	165.7	157.0
Aug.	3.0		3.50	138.0	123.6	148.4	70.0	70.00	72.87	154.9	157.8	151.6
Sept.	3.0	3.00	2.50	154.7	139.4	151.2	75.0	72.33	73.08	149.4	156.5	149.1
Oct.	3.0	3.00	3.22	148.3	151.3	155.0	77.5	70.00	76.98	145.6	154.0	148.5
Nov.	3.0		2.90	174.2	186.0	175.8	90.0	86.87	87.68	141.2	147.3	146.1
Dec.	4.0		3.78	158.1	204.3	178.5	100.0	99.54	93.74	137.9	138.0	142.8
1778							1781					
Jan.	4.0		3.08	138.4	213.2	191.4	100.0	103.33	98.54	122.7	124.5	128.5
Feb.	5.0	2.71	2.54	141.6	212.0	196.3	110.0	102.50	103.72	132.0	134.7	137.0
Mar.	5.0		4.50	144.4	243.6	198.4	127.5	125.00	123.02	113.7	123.1	125.7
Apr.	6.0	2.28	4.60	142.8	221.2	153.8	167.5	146.67	139.74		118.3	
May	5.0	3.53	5.74	153.3	234.5	152.7						
June	4.0	4.00	4.72	178.3	201.1	158.5						
July	4.0		4.16	182.9	195.0	171.0						
Aug.	5.0	4.17	5.00	174.3	185.4	172.4						
Sept.	5.0		5.00	171.6	195.5	167.3						
Oct.	5.0	4.00	5.40	152.7	165.8	145.9						
Nov.	6.0	5.72	6.34	155.2	159.4	145.0						
Dec.	5.0	6.84	6.47	157.4	153.3	151.5						

APPENDIX II

Items Handled by Quartermaster Department

This list was gleaned from letters of NG and from his assistants and deputies during 1778–80. It is not exhaustive; a complete list would probably be twice the length.

CAMP EQUIPAGE
Bags
Barrels
Door Locks
Iron Box
Iron Pots
Iron Spoons
Kegs
Kettles
  Brass
  Iron
Pails (wooden)
Ropes
Stew Pans
Stools
Tar Pots
Tent Lines
Tent Pins
Tent Poles
Tents
  Common
  Horseman's
  Marquees
  Walled
Trenchers
Water Buckets
Wooden Bowls

GUNNER'S STORES
Gun Carriage and Gun
Howitzers
Junk for Wads
Ladles

Linstocks
Match Rope
Pins for Gunshot
Prickers
Rammers
Sheep Skins
Sheetlead for Aprons
Shot
  Double headed
  Grape
  Langrage
  Round
Sponges
Stools for Gunshot
Swivels
Pump Nails
Tomkins
Worms

SOLDIER'S ACCOUTREMENTS
Breeches
  Leather
  Worsted
Canteens
Cartridge Boxes
Compasses
Haversacks
Hose
Iron Cups
Knapsacks
Leather Soles
Mess Bowls
Petticoats

Portmanteaus (leather)   Trousers
Powder Horns   Valises
Regimental Coats   Canvas
Shoes   Leather
Shot Pouches   Waistcoats

(The quartermaster department provided clothing only in emergencies, although it was normally responsible for its transportation.)

STATIONERY SUPPLIES   Gauges
Glue   Gimlets
Ink Powder   Gouges
Ink Stands   Grindstones
Military Books   Hammers
Paper   Handbarrows
Pen Knives   Hasps
Quills   Hatchets
Sealing Wax   Intrenching Tools
                               Iron Squares
TOOLS AND HARDWARE   Iron Stands
Adzes   Iron Wedges
  Carpenter's   Mauls
  Cooper's   Maul Rings
Augers   Nails
Axes   Nail Rods
  Narrow   Paring Knives
  Broad   Pickaxes
  Mortising   Picks
Bellows   Pincers
Bill Hooks   Planes
Bolts   Plugs
Buttresses   Rules
Caulking Tools   Saws
Chalk Lines   Cross-cut
Chisels   Half-round
Compasses   Hand
Crowbars   Pit
Cutting Boxes   Saw Files
Cutting Knives   Saw Sets
Drawknives   Scalping Knives (for skinning)
Drilling Tools   Screw Drivers
Fascine Hatchets   Screws
Fascine Knives   Scythes
Frows   Scythe Stones

Shingling Hatchets
Shovels
Sledges
Spades
Spikes
Staples
Tennon Saw Files
Tentmakers Equipment
  Bodkins
  Geese
  Leather Palms
  Needles
  Scissors
  Thimbles
  Thread
  Wax
Tomahawks
Vices
Wedges
Wheelbarrows
Whetstones
Wood Squares

TRANSPORTATION ITEMS
(LAND)
Belly Bands
Branding Irons
Breech Bands
Bridles
Carts
Cart Saddles
Cart Wheels
Chains
  Artillery
  Breast
  Lock
  Surveying
  Tongue
Chain Traces
Collars
Cruppers
Doubletrees
Dung Forks
Feed Bags

Forage Bags
Girths
Halters
Hames
Harness ("horse furniture")
Hay Forks
Horses
  Riding
  Wagon
Horse Shoes and Nails
Iron Traces
Leather Lines
Nose Bags
Ox Carts
Ox Yokes
Saddles
Saddlebags
Scale Beams and Weights
Singletrees
Sledges
Wagons
  Close Bodied
  Covered
  Open
Wagon Clouts
Wagon Covers
Wagon Harness
Wagon Whips
Wheels
  Cart
  Wagon
Wheel Rims
Wheel Spokes

TRANSPORTATION ITEMS
(WATER)
Anchors
Blocks
Canvas
Chains
Gimbals
Main Yard
Marline
Masts

Oakum
Oarlocks
Oars
Pitch Kettles
Rope
Sails
Spunyarn
Suit of Colours
Tar
Thrums for Mops
Vessels
  Barges
  Batteaus
  Durham Boats
  Row Galleys
  Scows
  Skiffs
  Wagon Boats

Xebeques
Winches

UNFINISHED PRODUCTS

Calf Skins
Canvas
Hides
Homemade Cloth
Iron Bars
Linseed Oil
Neats Leather
Sheep Skins
Sheet Iron
Steel (pieces)
Tar
Tin (sheets of)
Tow and Hemp Cloth
Twine

INDEX

Continental Congress (*cont.*)
officers, 278n; responsibility for army
problems, 278n; and Board of War,
279n, 293, 415n; Weedon's dispute
with, 297, 305–6 and n, 362–64 and n,
544; and rank of officers, 297, 305–6 and
n, 353n, 362–64 and n, 372n, 544; and
price regulation, 299, 300n, 342, 515n,
545 and n; appointment of NG as QM
general, 315, 316, 372n; on privateering, 317n; on disbursement of *Symetry*
prize, 317n; and certificates, 325n; and
plan for 1778 campaign, 348n, 378; and
military secrets, 348n; authorizes sei-
zure of horses, 365n; and Udny Hay,
372n, 419, 437; and loyalty oaths, 398n;
and horses for Steuben, 417; and Morgan Lewis's appointment, 418; and
compensation for damages to civilian
property, 419–20n; and portmanteaus
and valises for officers, 420–22, 443;
and horses, saddles, and bridles for
officers, 421–22; and British peace proposals, 423, 424n; accepts Conway's
resignation, 424n; and money for QM
department, 426, 432; authorizes
bounty for maréchausée, 427n; and
Charles Lee's trial, 452n; NG praised to
by Washington, 464n; and agents for
captured British property, 470, 472n;
and Gerard reception, 472n; and
officers protest to d'Estaing, 491n, 505;
and military commands, 512; and claim
of Ebenezer Sullivan, 515, 551; act forbidding purchase of wheat for forage,
516; and enlistments, 518; and the
western expedition, 536n; resolution
concerning stabling horses, 538; John
Morgan's dispute with, 541. *See also*
Board of War; Committee at Camp;
Hancock, John; Laurens, Henry; Treasury Board
Continentalism: NG on, 10, 13n, 51–52,
60, 70, 88, 89n, 104, 118; not practiced
by states, 89n, 117, 300n. *See also* Articles of Confederation; Embargoes;
Prices, regulation of
Convicts, 289
Convention army: in Boston, 519, 545n;
housing for officers of, 521–22
"Conway Cabal," 179n, 243–44, 250,
252–53 and n, 260, 277–79n, 293–94,
343, 366, 406; NG on, 275, 303, 316, 317,
326; historiographical interpretations,
277–78n; role of Horatio Gates in,
277–79n; role of Thomas Conway in,
277–79n; McDougall on, 295; and
Canadian expedition, 295; William

Greene on, 298–99; George Lux on,
367, 409–10
Conway, Thomas, 106, 114, 145, 160n,
168, 184, 188, 192, 410, 412; *biog.*, 103n;
and battle of Brandywine, 160n; and
attacking British at Germantown, 169;
and battle of Germantown, 173–75n;
and rations issue, 194; troops of, 239;
NG on, 243–44, 248, 252–53 and n, 260,
275, 303, 423; Lafayette on, 243; promotion of to major general, 243, 249–50,
253n, 279n; Laurens and, 250; and
Canadian expedition, 275–76 and n,
279n, 293–94, role in "Conway Cabal,"
277–79n; letter to Horatio Gates, 278–
79n; and Washington, 278–79n, 293;
resignation from Board of War, 279n;
inspector general of the army, 279n;
resignation from army, 279n, 423, 424n;
duel with Cadwalader, 279n; returns to
France, 279n; George Lux on, 367, 411
Cooch's Bridge, Del., 153n
Cook, James, 252n
Cooke, Nicholas, 244, 277; *letters to*, 4, 10,
14, 16, 34, 117, 128, 254, 259, 274; *letters
from*, 19, 56, 256, 345; appeals for Continental troops for R.I., 14n; and R.I.
recruiting, 19–21 and n, 249n; orders
R.I. militia collected, 42; NG on lost
letter to, 117; and the Black Regiment,
249n; succeeded by William Greene,
408n
Coopers Ferry, N.J./Pa., 214, 215n, 358,
450
Copper, 344
Cordage, 374
Cork, Ireland, 487
Corn, 327; near Head of Elk, 151, 152n;
price of, 519, 522; embargo on export
of, 545n
Cornell, Ezekiel: and expedition against
Aquidneck Island, 485n; signs protest
to d'Estaing, 490; Sullivan's queries to,
493n; favors retreat from Aquidneck
Island, 496n; and Battle of R.I., 503n
Cornwall, HMS, 483n
Cornwallis, Charles (Earl), 218; and
Washington's forces after Trenton, 3n;
and action at Boundbrook, 56n, 59;
troops of, 107n, 153n, 205, 210n, 212,
220, 223; in battle of Brandywine, 158–
61n; and Philadelphia, 169n, 172n, 217,
219–20n; and battle of Germantown,
176n; and assault on Red Bank, 200,
201n; crosses Schuylkill, 205; in N.J.,
212n; at Ellis home, 214; chooses
Gloucester crossing of the Delaware,
215n; and action at Whitemarsh, 237n;

Richard K. Showman has been associated with the Rhode Island Historical Society as editor of these volumes since 1972. He is assistant editor of *The Harvard Guide to American History*.

Robert E. McCarthy is special lecturer in history at Providence College and assisted in organizing bibliographies for *The Harvard Guide to American History*.

Margaret Cobb assisted in the publication of *The Susquehannah Company Papers*.